TWENTIETH-CENTURY
BRITISH HISTORY
Made Simple

The Made Simple series
has been created
primarily for self-education

In the same series

Accounting
Acting and Stagecraft
Additional Mathematics
Advertising
Anthropology
Applied Economics
Applied Mathematics
Applied Mechanics
Art Appreciation
Art of Speaking
Art of Writing
Biology
Book-keeping
British Constitution
Business and Administrative
  Organisation
Business Statistics
  and Accounting
Calculus
Chemistry
Childcare
Commerce
Company Administration
Company Law
Computer Programming
Cookery
Cost and Management
  Accounting
Data Processing
Dressmaking
Economic History
Economic and Social Geography
Economics
Effective Communication
Electricity
Electronic Computers
Electronics
English
English Literature

Export
Financial Management
French
Geology
German
Human Anatomy
Italian
Journalism
Latin
Law
Management
Marketing
Mathematics
Modern Biology
Modern Electronics
Modern European History
New Mathematics
Office Practice
Organic Chemistry
Philosophy
Photography
Physical Geography
Physics
Pottery
Psychology
Rapid Reading
Retailing
Russian
Salesmanship
Secretarial Practice
Social Services
Soft Furnishing
Spanish
Statistics
Transport and Distribution
Twentieth-Century British
  History
Typing
Woodwork

TWENTIETH-CENTURY BRITISH HISTORY
Made Simple

Peter King, BA, MLitt

Made Simple Books

W. H. ALLEN   London

A Howard & Wyndham Company

Printed and bound in Great Britain
by Richard Clay (The Chaucer Press) Ltd, Bungay, Suffolk
for the publishers, W. H. Allen & Company Ltd,
44 Hill Street, London, W1X 8LB

ISBN 0 491 02389 8 casebound
ISBN 0 491 02399 5 paperbound

Preface

The main aim of this book is to give an account of British history from the turn of the century to the present day. During the twentieth century Britain has changed from the world's greatest imperial and economic power into a relatively poor member of the Common Market with scarcely any overseas responsibilities. At the same time the Empire has changed into a Commonwealth which, if it practises and sometimes acknowledges common bonds and interests, has little common ground politically. Yet during this period of decline the country has taken a decisive part in two world wars, and linked itself in stronger military alliances and more closely to Europe than ever before. During a century when every major European country has fallen under dictatorship it has preserved parliamentary democracy, fundamental liberties and a popular monarchy. It has recovered from the worst crises to face capitalism so far in the 1930s, and it has set examples in such fields as science, culture and social welfare remarkable in a world that has been increasingly dominated by superpowers.

These themes are of interest to people who want to understand modern Britain with its present problems, and also the changes that have taken place in the last few generations at an unprecedented rate. They are themes increasingly taken up by examining boards as questions appear requiring knowledge of the post-1945 period, and even into the early 1970s. Current affairs often play a part in social science and general studies courses, and are relevant to those studying such matters as legal changes, class structure or economic policy. It is to meet the need for a book covering the whole century in a uniform way and brought up to date that *Twentieth-Century British History* has been written. It can be used by a wide range of students although it is primarily aimed at A Level GCE, professional and first-year degree examination candidates. The chapters have detailed subheadings for easy reference, and, as usual in the Made Simple series, reading lists and essay questions provide for further study and help revision.

Many people have helped with the preparation of this book, and I should particularly like to thank the typist, Mrs M. Scotland, and Mr R. Postema of W. H. Allen Ltd.

P. KING
April 1979

v

Contents

x *Contents*

1

EDWARDIAN ENGLAND: 1900–14

Harold Macmillan wrote that August 1914, when Great Britain entered the First World War, was

'the beginning of the end of Europe's supremacy, and of the predominance of the white man in the world. From this date began the end of the old British Empire, and the capture of the greatest Euro-Asian country, Russia, by the strange doctrines of a German Jew internationalist—Karl Marx.'

Some historians like Barraclough have suggested that decline in political and economic power had already started by the turn of the century, and would have advanced anyway with the logic of population growth, and the transmission to the rest of the world of nationalism, capitalism and industrial society. Even if this is so, 1914 and what followed is clearly the major catalyst in this change; the world before that date of 'Upstairs, Downstairs' is remote whereas we would have some sympathy for the people and problems of the 1920s. Choosing a time to start modern history is a dubious process, but the onset of the Great War with its antecedents and consequences constitutes an undoubted turning point. In Europe the war weakened political and economic structures and provided the excuse for fascism and communism, which were to dominate history thereafter. The war brought America into the ring of the great powers although she retired for the next few rounds, and by helping the Revolution of 1917 paved the way for the rise of Communist Russia to great power status by 1945. The war undermined class distinction, capitalism and the Christian religion, and it strengthened internationalism, socialism and humanism.

These trends were largely concealed at the time, and were not finally brought home to British governments until the 1960s. Macmillan himself was regarded as the last of the Edwardians, speaking the language of vanished great power status and an extinct social world. When Dean Acheson said in 1962 that Britain had lost an empire and not found a new rôle there was an outcry and Macmillan reproved him, but truth will out in the end, even in politics. Seaman called his work on the period 1902 to 1951 *Post-Victorian Britain*, and the student of history discerns far more quickly than those who lived through the period the trends of change and decline that were in movement at the turn of the century. It was not until 1945 that economic decline, and perhaps even later that political decline became apparent to the informed. It was later still before the man in the street came to realise that if he was nearing retiring age his life had spanned the decline of the world's greatest empire.

A. The Government, the Parties and their Policies

A1. Liberal Governments: 1906–14
In 1906 the Liberals entered office after 11 years' Conservative rule, with Henry Campbell Bannerman as their Prime Minister, after a landslide

election which returned 377 Liberals with an overall majority of 84. The Conservatives were reduced to 157 while the other two main parties, the Irish Home Rulers and the Labour Representative Committee, had 83 and 29 respectively. Following an agreement made in 1903, 24 MPs were returned as Lib-Labs so the election is important also for the appearance in British politics of organised labour. The two Liberal ministries that followed are often regarded as major reforming governments, but it is important to realise four facts about British politics in the early years of the century. Each of them limited the likelihood of any government being dedicated to sweeping reforms. They were:

(a) After the Reform Acts the vote had been given to 8½ million adults. Many businessmen had two votes—one for their home and one for their office—and one man, one vote did not yet prevail.

(b) Although landed property was slowly yielding power (Justices of the Peace were freed from a property qualification in 1906), there was still a property qualification in local government, and the greater part of the Commons consisted of men of independent means closely related to the landed classes.

(c) There was not yet a two-party system and indeed from 1915 to 1922 and 1931 to 1945 Britain was ruled by coalitions.

(d) In the two elections of 1910 held over the Lords' dispute, the Liberals lost their massive majority, and subsequently most by-elections. In 1914 the parties stood at Liberals 260, Conservatives 288, Labour 40, and Home Rulers 83.

These facts go some way to explain why the government became increasingly less prone to reforming measures, and why there was so much delay and lack of purpose in foreign policy in June–August 1914.

The Liberals were pledged to social reform at home, and conciliation abroad; both issues which Campbell Bannerman had taken up during the Boer War. He had healed Liberal divisions over Irish Home Rule and Imperialism by concentrating on evidence for widespread poverty that social investigators and the condition of recruits for the war had highlighted after a period of comparative Tory neglect. This commitment to social reform was, however, partly in the interest of killing the socialist challenge. The commitment was limited by Liberal belief in free trade and 'laissez faire', which prevented the raising of enough taxes to make possible anything like a welfare state. Nearly all their social reforms were limited and the Victorian Poor Law remained unreformed. Some of their reforms were clearly the product of political bargaining. Trade union laws in 1906 and 1913, special acts for the miners in 1908, 1911 and 1912, and the payment of £400 a year to members of parliament were concessions to Labour. The introduction of the third Home Rule Bill in 1912 followed Irish support the previous year for reform of the Lords.

In April 1908, Herbert Asquith succeeded Campbell Bannerman, and he was to remain Prime Minister until December 1916. He had served his political apprenticeship under Gladstone as Home Secretary. He had been something of a reformist behind the scenes at the Home Office, and when he was Chancellor of the Exchequer (1906–08) introduced the distinction between earned and unearned income. In foreign affairs Asquith supported the Liberal Imperialist wing of the party led by Lord Rosebery and in 1894, after a society marriage, he became more of a Whig than a radical as his later backtracking on women's suffrage and failure to carry out radical measures in the early years of the war were to show. For many years, however, he was a superb leader of cabinet and Commons, although capable of aristocratic disdain and more commonplace inebriation. Spender and Jenkins give favourable pictures of Asquith, although much that was done was achieved by the cabinet's galaxy of talent.

David Lloyd George entered politics in 1890, and with skill in publicity and making money had risen to high office as Chancellor in 1908. The budget of 1909 made his reputation, although it was largely unfounded since the budget contained little that was radical, and was not followed, even under war-time stress, by any spectacular changes. Sir Edward Grey, the Foreign Secretary, and Lord Haldane at the War Office represented the Whig element in the party while Fisher at the Admiralty, and Churchill at the Board of Trade, Home Office and Admiralty (1911) represented the more radical element. The government contained numerous able men like Birrell at the Irish Office, and continued to recruit new talent such as Herbert Samuel at the Local Government Board in February 1914. It was a strong team, and there were only two appointments that aroused criticism. One was the Labour man, John Burns, at Local Government where he achieved little before being moved to the Board of Trade. The other was the involvement of Sir Rufus Isaacs, the Attorney General, in the Marconi scandal soon after he was appointed as the first law officer to enter the cabinet (1912).

A2. Conservative or Unionist Opposition

Under Lord Salisbury (Prime Minister, 1895–1902) and his nephew A. J. Balfour (Prime Minister, 1902–05), Imperialism had been the keynote of Conservative policies, particularly since Joseph Chamberlain had taken the Colonial Office in 1895, and was leader of the Liberal Unionists. The Conservatives had been forced to abandon what was known as 'Splendid Isolation' in foreign policy, and had concluded an *entente* with France after a period in which Britain had been in conflict with both France and Germany on colonial matters. They had reconquered the Sudan (1896–98) and the Boer Republics (1899–1902), and as a result of these wars had started army reforms. Rivalry with Germany had led to a naval scare and when the *Dreadnought* was laid down in 1905 a naval race started.

Chamberlain had been involved in sharp practice over the Jameson Raid, and his injury in a cab accident enabled Salisbury to transfer power smoothly to his nephew. Balfour had been a great Commons man and an excellent Irish Secretary, but he was too much of a philosopher to make a successful prime minister, particularly at a time when Conservatives needed to repair damage done to the economy by war, and carry out social reforms. Chamberlain launched a plan for tariff reform (1903) which involved a tariff against foreign manufactures and a preference for imperial markets, which would put up the price of foodstuffs. The Conservatives were won over to this policy, and in 1906 only 11 free-trading Tories were returned. But Balfour was unable to make up his mind, avoided votes by walking out, and put his policy on half a sheet of notepaper. Above all he failed to embark on reforms, and when unemployment rose to 12 per cent in the winter of 1905 he allowed Tories to oppose the Unemployed Workmen's Act introduced by a private member. He then resigned in December hoping that Campbell Bannerman would be unable to form a government, only to be defeated at the election in January 1906.

The Conservatives retained Balfour as leader, and he declared in 1906: 'The great Unionist party should still control, whether in power or in opposition, the destinies of this great Empire.' He proceeded to do this by using the Conservative majority in the Lords, where only 83 described themselves as Liberals. Young has sought to defend his action by stressing that society then gave preponderant power to property, and that it would be unthinkable for Tories to stand aside and allow radicalism to triumph. Moreover, the landed interest were actually strengthened at this time by agricultural revival and prepared to back him. The Lords became 'Mr Balfour's poodle', and there can be little doubt that this was a political error. The elections of 1910 showed there was a shift in public opinion, and the Tories unwisely tried to wreck the government too soon. After the Parliament Act Balfour stepped down, and as Walter Long and Austen Chamberlain were rivals the party compromised with Andrew Bonar Law. His choice in 1911 is interesting since not long before the Tories had looked down on Chamberlain being in trade, and they now accepted a Scots Presbyterian iron merchant. Described as a 'natural second fiddle', his choice was probably a mistake since he was easily led by stronger characters and fell under the influence of two fellow nonconformists, Carson and Lloyd George. His Ulster policies were to lead to constitutional crisis again in 1914.

A3. Crisis for the Liberal Party

In 1936 Dangerfield argued that Asquith's ministry was heading for catastrophe by 1914 because of the insoluble problem of Ireland and the mounting violence in British politics by unions and suffragettes. He claimed the government was bankrupt of ideas, and faced with Tory opposition that was contemplating armed conflict. Ever since historians have examined the question of the decline of the Liberal Party from such power in 1906 to permanent disarray by 1916. In 1966, Wilson added new fuel to the controversy by arguing that the party declined after 1914. Looking at pre-1914 events he said, 'Did these add up to a pattern of violence rather than accidental convergence of unrelated events? Some of the problems were passing: the Upper House had been put in its place, and the strike wave appeared to be receding. The other problems were not manifestly insoluble.'

Three different arguments have become confused. They are:

(a) *The decline of European Liberalism*, personified by the German National Liberals declining before the Social Democrats, and by the rise of organised labour and left-wing parties. Historians such as Cole and Postgate see Labour taking over the working man from the Liberals while the Whig elements finally went Tory. In this case it was Lloyd George and not Asquith who destroyed the Liberals because in 1918 he gave one man, one vote, and altered the balance of seats which had previously favoured county as against town (by 378 to 292 in 1914).

(b) *The decline of English Liberalism*, and therefore of the Victorian Liberal Party. This started with the split of 1886 over Home Rule caused by Gladstone and Chamberlain, and grew with the split between Liberal Imperialists under Rosebery and Little Englanders under Harcourt. Glaser has argued that the moral basis of liberalism—nonconformity and the individual conscience—also ceased to be a potent factor, and issues like Welsh Disestablishment and the licensing laws favoured by Asquith and Lloyd George were not seen as radical or reformist. The economic bases of liberalism—low taxes, no tariffs and minimal government interference—were under threat by 1909, and were sapped after 1914.

(c) *The decline of Asquith's government.* By 1911 the party was becoming stale on issues like women's votes, although in 1914 Lloyd George was preparing further insurance and education reforms. In foreign policy they stood on their heads with Lloyd George's Mansion House speech in 1911. They helped labour, but they fired on strikers. State control was extended to the Port of London and the telephones, and the Official Secrets Act (1911) struck a blow at freedom of expression.

B. The Main Issues Facing the Liberal Governments

B1. The Irish Question

The nineteenth century Irish question had been several questions: religion, land and politics, underpinned by racial differences and grinding poverty. Parnell had formed Irish members into the Home Rule Party, and in 1886 Gladstone had accepted this as Liberal policy causing Chamberlain to leave with the Liberal Unionists and join the Conservatives. The first Home Rule Bill failed in the Commons, but not before a section of Tories led by Lord Randolph Churchill had raised the rights of Protestant Ulster into a political issue with slogans such as 'Home Rule means Rome Rule'. In 1893 Gladstone produced a second bill, but the Lords defeated it because they feared loss of their power as landlords and out of imperialist sentiment. This had raised the issue of Lords' reform. After the Parnell divorce case the Home Rulers had split, but by 1901 they were united under John Redmond. For a time the Liberals had moved to a 'home rule by stages' policy because of divisions in their party, but once the Parliament Act had passed the power of the Lords was limited, and in April 1912 the third Home Rule Bill was introduced.

By this time many of the grievances that led to Home Rule demands had been dealt with by the Tories:

(a) Ashbourne's Act of 1885, added to in 1891 and 1903, had provided money for land purchase by the Irish. By 1909, 270,000 purchases had been made, and 46,000 were being negotiated.

(b) Basic agricultural conditions were helped by the Congested Districts Acts (1891, 1903, 1909), which enabled improvement to occur. Government grants were given, and the Irish Agricultural Organization Society supported co-operative farming. By 1914 there were 900 societies.

However, the long history of English oppression and failure to grant Home Rule had led to a demand for total independence fuelled by funds from American and Australian Irish, and cultural groups seeking to revive Gaelic customs and language (Gaelic League, 1893). In 1905 Arthur Griffiths founded Sinn Fein, and the same year Sir Edward Carson set up the Ulster Defence Council to oppose this change. The new Home Rule Bill was thus soon outflanked by two nationalist groups.

(*a*) An Ulster Covenant was signed by 200,000 and the Ulster Volunteers numbered 80,000. Plans for a provisional government were drawn up, and in July 1912, Bonar Law announced his support for Ulster.

(*b*) While the bill was passed and rejected twice by the Lords under the terms of the 1911 act, the Tories gave full backing to the actions of Carson, and in November 1913 came out in favour of partition. This led to the formation by Macneill and Pearse of the Irish Volunteers.

Matters were not improved by the connection between Irish discontent and labour troubles in England. The Irish Transport Workers' Union, founded in 1908 by Connolly and Larkin, produced unrest culminating in the Dublin tramworkers' strike (August 1913–January 1914). In March 1914 Connolly formed a Citizens' Army.

Liberal reaction to these moves was a mixture of bold statements and weak compromises, which gave Tories hope that they would cave in under pressure :

(*a*) Bonar Law suggested the King should dissolve parliament in September 1913, and early in 1914 Tories were advocating that the Mutiny Act should not be passed.

(*b*) Lord Roberts and the director of military operations, Sir Henry Wilson, were both Anglo-Irish. Within the army Sir John French, Chief of Staff, and Sir Arthur Paget, C. in C. Ireland, were against coercing Ulster.

This led to the Curragh 'Mutiny'. In March 1914 the government seemed to be contemplating firm action. Churchill moved fleet units to the Isle of Arran, and Seely reinforced Ulster garrisons. Paget obtained from Seely a concession that officers who objected to such duties need not serve, but could disappear or resign : 58 out of 70 officers led by Gough said they would rather be dismissed. Asquith dismissed Gough, French and Seely, but did not touch Wilson and had to take over the War Office himself. Further displays of weakness followed. Protestants were allowed to smuggle in 30,000 rifles at Larne in April without hindrance while Irish volunteers were fired on doing the same thing at Hill of Howth in July. In the end the Great War overtook events. The Liberals passed the act in September, and suspended it for the war.

B2. Votes for Women

During the nineteenth century women's emancipation had begun in legal and educational matters. The Divorce Act (1857) and the Married Woman's Property Act (1882) had been examples of the first, and the start of university education at Girton (1873) and Lady Margaret Hall (1879) of the second. Women had begun to enter the professions. Most women in employment were domestic servants, but here also there had been a change. In 1851 there were 19 female clerks in Britain and by 1911, 146,000.

Under these circumstances political rights could not be indefinitely delayed. The first bill appeared in 1870, and a Society for Obtaining Political Rights was established. During the Victorian period steady progress was made :

(*a*) Women obtained the vote in municipal (1869) and local elections (1888).

(*b*) They obtained the right to sit on school boards (1870), and as poor law guardians (1875).

(c) The Qualification of Women Act (1907) allowed them to take office on local councils.

By the 1900s there were two groups in being: the moderates, called the NUWSS, led by Mrs Fawcett, and the radicals, called the WSPU (1903), led by Mrs Pankhurst. It seemed illogical to deny the national vote while conceding the local vote, but opponents argued women did not own property and were a majority of the voters. Many Liberal MPs pledged themselves to the cause in 1906, and it was disappointment with failure to honour the pledge that led to trouble. In 1912, after supporting change, Asquith declared: 'The grant of parliamentary suffrage to women would be a political mistake of a very disastrous kind.' Government action was confined to two bills in 1912 and 1913 which were lost in parliamentary manoeuvres.

A women's campaign started in 1909, and the government reacted by imprisonment, and when they refused to eat, with forcible feeding. In 1913 the Prisoners (Temporary Discharge) Act allowed for release and re-arrest and led to a secret 'underground railroad' among the houses of rich supporters. There were few working women involved, although Sylvia Pankhurst did settle in the East End. Attacks on the House of Commons were followed by a campaign of violence which began in March 1912, and did little to help their cause. On 4 June 1913 Emily Davidson threw herself in front of the Derby horses and was killed. Mrs Pankhurst was arrested at her funeral procession, and public sympathy seemed to be waning.

B3. Labour and the Unions

When the first TUC met in 1868 the majority of its 34 delegates represented skilled craftsmen or artisans of the mid-Victorian trade union movement. It was during the last quarter of the century that modern unionism with unskilled workers in large unions spread after successful struggles by gas workers and dockers in 1888–89. Membership rose from 750,000 in 1888 to two million in 1900, and had reached 4,145,000 by 1914. The largest union was the Miners' Federation with nearly 900,000 members, and during the Edwardian period other big unions appeared, including the National Transport Workers' Federation (1910) and the National Union of Railwaymen (1913). By January 1914 these three unions had come together in a loose 'triple alliance' to further their aims.

The growth of unions was caused by the spread of education and socialist ideas to the better off working class, and by the adverse economic conditions with unemployment high, and after 1910 real wages falling. The employers reacted strongly to this growth because it involved restrictive practices and higher wages at a time of fierce competition with Germany and America. Strikes were broken by lock-outs, and local unions preferred to national ones so that blacklegging could be used. The unions were attacked particularly through the courts in two famous cases:

(a) *The Taff Vale Case.* The Taff Vale Railway Co. sued the Amalgamated Society of Railway Servants for damages and costs of £32,000 and won their case (1901).

(b) *The Osborne Case.* W. W. Osborne, secretary of the Walthamstow branch of the same union, sued for an injunction to stop the union taking the new political levy of 1*d* a week for the Labour Party, and won (1909).

Nor were these isolated attacks. In Lyons *v.* Wilkins (1898) and Quinn *v.* Leathem (1901) the right to picket was seriously brought in question.

These moves encouraged the new Labour party, and persuaded the Liberals to support union reform which they had opposed in Gladstone's day. As a result two important acts were passed:

(a) *The Trades Disputes Act* (1906). This forbade the suing of unions for any tort while they were acting in their corporate capacity. It clearly defined the right to picket, and intimidation as a criminal act, not just taking part in picket activities.

(b) *The Trade Union Act* (1913) allowed unions to collect the political levy provided a majority of members agreed in a ballot, and contracting out of paying was permitted.

Although acts set up an eight-hour day in the mines, reformed the Mines Acts, and introduced minimum wages in the mines, there was no general factory legislation, leaving the Tory act of 1901 as the main measure.

By the mid-1880s it was clear that continental socialism on the marxist pattern, started here by Henry Hyndman in the Social Democratic Federation (1881), was unlikely to succeed. The government broke up demonstrations in 1886–87, and the growth of anarchism in France damaged the movement in the early 1890s. The TUC first supported parliamentary candidates in 1871, and a Lib-Lab MP had been elected in 1874, but what was needed was a working-class party. This came from the trade unions with Keir Hardie's Scottish Labour Party in 1888, and in 1892 three Labour independents were returned to parliament. The next year the Independent Labour Party (ILP) was founded, consisting of Scots and English trade unionists, trades councils, the Social Democrats and the Fabian Society. In 1899 the TUC demanded a new body since the ILP had achieved little, and in 1900 the Labour Representative Committee was formed. Two members were returned in 1900, but attack on the unions increased membership, and the secretary, Ramsay MacDonald developed the party so that it secured 29 seats in 1906. The SDF left in 1901 so at the start the Labour Party was essentially a trade union rather than a socialist party. The Fabian Society (1884), worked out policies for securing socialism in Britain through evolution and not revolution. Many of the early members were chapel speakers and the party drew radicals from the Liberals by its moderate stance.

The moderation of labour unions and party alike led to the growth of a new and short-lived movement during the 1900s called syndicalism. This sprang from International Workers of the World (1905) and the ideas of George Sorel. He advocated using industrial weapons like sabotage and the general strike to secure political ends. Outbreaks were widespread in Europe including *Semana Tragica* in Spain (1909) and the Belgian general strike (1913). In Britain Tom Mann, Arthur Cook and James Connolly backed the movement, and in 1905 the Socialist Labour Party started on 'Red Clydeside' to support these views. The influence of the movement was limited, and the government over-reacted, but this was sufficient to guarantee a period of bad labour relations between 1910 and 1912, particularly among railwaymen, dockers and miners. Strikers were shot by troops for looting in Liverpool and Llanelli.

The government was unclear how to handle the situation, but it did make efforts to arbitrate. The Rollit award, for example, settled a London dock dispute, and Lloyd George was directly involved in ending the railway strike of 1912. The response of recruits in 1914 showed how little the men had been influenced by revolutionary motives, but the episode left a legacy of bitterness.

B4. The House of Lords

Reform of the Lords had long been debated in the Liberal party. From the mid-1880s the Lords became a permanent Tory preserve in contrast to the eighteenth century, when it was permanently Whig. Gladstone's Irish policies affected many of the aristocracy, and the radicalism of Dilke and Labouchere produced a divide between the Liberals and most of the Lords, although this must not be exaggerated in view of the government ministers who sat there, including half of Asquith's cabinet. Chamberlain had launched a campaign against them, and after they rejected Home Rule in 1893 Morley had coined the slogan 'mend them or end them'. But in 1906 Lords reform was not an election issue, and it was Balfour's action that created the new controversy. (See Section A2.)

The Lords tried to become a blocking chamber instead of merely revising bills, and rejected measures on arbitrary grounds, passing the Trades Disputes and Workmens' Compensation Acts, but rejecting between 1906 and 1908 the Plural Voting, Education and Licensing Bills. By June 1907 the Commons had passed resolutions, but it was not until the budget of 1909 that the issue was forced. The budget was neither radical nor seriously damaging to the landed classes (see Section D3), but the Lords rejected it in November 1909. This flouted a convention of the constitution, and was done in spite of attempts to restrain them. It seems that Lloyd George deliberately chose to aggravate the Lords by emphasising that it was a 'war budget' against privilege rather than one designed to pay for Dreadnoughts. He made a series of speeches at Limehouse and Newcastle designed to infuriate. At the latter he said: 'The question will be asked—whether five hundred men, ordinary men, chosen accidentally from among the unemployed, shall override the judgement—the deliberate judgement—of millions of people who are engaged in the industry which makes the wealth of the country?'

There followed a constitutional crisis. Asquith dissolved, and the election of January 1910 produced a decline in Liberal fortunes, partly accounted for by the non-Liberal spirit of the budget itself. The figures were Liberals 275, Conservatives 273, Irish 82, and Labour 40, so that although they had a majority of 124 this was dependent on other parties. The Irish bargained with the government for Home Rule because they did not like the whiskey tax in the budget. The budget passed the Commons in April 1910 with a majority of 93, and the Lords without a division. Radical Liberals demanded a major reform, and moderate Conservatives accepted that the Lords should be reconstituted. Edward VII refused to create peers to swamp the Lords and get the bill through without a second election, and when he died in May no solution had been arrived at; 21 meetings were held between the party leaders to reach a compromise, but a large element in the Tory party backed by Salisbury, Chamberlain from his sick bed, and Carson, urged resistance, and Balfour gave way. Asquith then demanded the second election, and after hesitating for five days the King accepted. The election of December 1910 did not help matters since the results were Conservatives and Liberals 272 each, Irish 84, and Labour 42.

The Parliament Bill was introduced in February 1911, and subjected to 900 amendments before it passed to the Lords. By then a substantial party led by Lord Halsbury was determined to reject it, and this did not consist merely of hunting personalities. Last-ditchers rallied and it looked as if defeat would ensue. On 20 July Asquith announced he had secured the King's consent to create 249 new peers, and four days later he was howled down in the Commons. However, Morley was adamant in the Lords about the government's intention, and the Archbishop of Canterbury said if they did not vote for the bill they would be 'the laughing stock of the British dominions beyond the seas'. The bill passed by 131–114, with 37 Unionists and 13 bishops voting for the government. The provisions were:

(*a*) No money bill was to be subject to any delay or amendment by the Lords, and the Speaker would decide what constituted a money bill.

(*b*) The Lords' veto would not apply if a bill was passed in three successive sessions covering two years.

(*c*) The maximum length of parliament was reduced to five years.

Although seen as a revolution, the end-product was not radical. In the short term it enhanced Asquith's standing, and lowered that of Balfour. It made Lloyd George's political reputation, and ensured that Home Rule would pass. The Lords retained considerable power in the last two years of a government's life, and still retain more power than any hereditary chamber.

C. Great Britain as a World Power

C1. The British Empire

The focus of British foreign policy was the preservation of the Empire. In Edwardian times this had still to reach its full extent. At the start of the period the Transvaal and the Orange Free State were annexed, and at the end, Cyprus and Egypt, while during the decade expansion went on in the Malay and Arab Gulf States. Comprehensive agreements were made with France and Russia to settle a number of difficulties and define Britain's sphere of influence in Egypt, Persia, Afghanistan and Tibet. The Empire covered a quarter of the world's land surface, and contained roughly a third of the world's population. After post-war annexations it covered 14 million square miles and was thus the greatest empire the world had ever seen. In Edwardian times few doubted that the words of the Coronation Ode (1902) 'Wider still and wider may thy bounds be set' were true, and the imperial idea was a major political influence. It was made up of diverse strands—nationalism, economic ambition, moral concepts, religious fervour and political reality. Sometimes it came close to racialism, as in Pearson's *National Life and Character* (1893), but it was also taking up the white man's burden. There were already critics. In 1902 J. A. Hobson wrote *Imperialism*, in which he denounced its economic motives, and in 1905 R. Jebb wrote *Studies in Colonial Nationalism*, warning that the

Empire exported its own political principles. Apart from murmurs in India, Ireland and Egypt there was little to worry the government.

The Empire consisted of three main divisions:

(a) *The dominions*. Canada was the first in 1867, but in the Edwardian period three more were added—Australia in 1900, New Zealand in 1907 and South Africa in 1910. These were the 'white dominions', colonies of settlement embarking on industrialisation and with nascent nationalism. However, their foreign and defence policy was dictated from London and in 1914 they automatically entered the war. They were still loyal to kith and kin, and sent contingents to the Boer War in 1899.

(b) *India*. Since 1876 the sovereign had been emperor, represented by a viceroy, and with its large army and Britain's massive stake in the economy, India was valued more than any other part of the Empire. Lord Curzon, the first Edwardian Viceroy, had pursued a forward policy in Tibet and the Persian Gulf, and Lord Kitchener had been sent out as Commander in Chief to reorganise defence in the North-West Frontier Province (set up in 1901). The Viceroy, Lord Hardinge, travelled through the country attended by 700 servants in an imperial train, with soldiers stationed every 200 yards along the line. Behind him lay a vast bureaucracy masterminded by 5,000 civil servants, and administered at grass roots level by 246 district officers. A British army of 50,000 and a native army defended the subcontinent. A Congress Party had been founded but only a small percentage of educated Indians doubted the power of the Raj. In 1909 the Morley-Minto Reforms began the process of creating representative institutions.

(c) *The colonies*. These were ruled by the Colonial, Foreign and India Offices and were some sixty in number. They were diverse, some being protected states where Britain practised indirect rule (Malaya), and some Crown colonies. Some were run by the military. Chamberlain had seen these tropical possessions as 'being in the condition of undeveloped estates, and estates which can never be developed without imperial assistance'.

Chamberlain had done much to focus attention on the Empire with the Diamond Jubilee, and the Colonial Conference of 1897. He was eager to see it more closely united in a federation, and at each of the Colonial Conferences held during this period (1902, 1907, 1909) schemes were put forward. It seemed as if economically the Empire was drawing closer together. By 1914, 47 per cent of Britain's overseas investment and 37 per cent of her exports went there. Emigration had doubled to 470,000 a year during the decade, with 78 per cent in 1913 bound for the colonies. Three different ways of consolidating the Empire were put forward:

(a) *Economic cooperation*. Chamberlain created the Imperial Department of Agriculture and the School of Tropical Medicine. A Colonial Loans Act gave money for transport, and the Gold Coast railway was completed. The old companies were bought out in places like Nigeria (1900). But apart from a Penny Post, and discussions on cables, little was achieved.

(b) *Imperial preference* was launched by Chamberlain in 1903 to bind the Empire together and defeat foreign competition. The dominions and the British electorate rejected it until 1931–32.

(c) *Defence cooperation*. As the dominions drew away Britain argued they should pay a share of the defence burden. Canada refused to create a navy, but after the 1909 meeting New Zealand and Malaya each agreed to provide a cruiser, and in 1911 the Royal Australian Navy was created.

The Edwardian Period was thus a period of unrestrained jingoism. The poetry of Kipling and the music of Elgar were the outward expression of this pride in an Empire 'on which the sun never set'.

C2. British Foreign Policy

For 20 years Salisbury dominated foreign policy, keeping the country out of entangling alliances and expanding the Empire by cautious diplomacy and the occasional use of gunboats at Fashoda or Wei-hai-Wei (1898). In the Near East he had swung Britain away from traditional support for Turkey towards Balkan nationalism, and he had staked out British power in Africa, South-East Asia, the Far East and the Pacific. Although he never used the phrase, his policy is often referred to as 'splendid isolation'. In fact, it suited Britain to be isolated, with its small army and large navy. What made it more practicable was that Salisbury and Bismarck were close since both regarded France as dangerous, and provided Britain kept out of European affairs Bismarck was prepared to back her in Egypt after 1882. In 1890 Bismarck fell from power, and it was the policy of the Kaiser, William II, that forced Britain to abandon her aloof role. When in the Boer War every country in Europe opposed her the time for change had come. Salisbury stepped down, and Lansdowne began to seek for allies. There were five main strands to the growing rivalry of Britain and Germany:

(a) *Economic rivalry*. Germany, was Britain's main industrial competitor, sheltered behind tariffs, protected with cartels and government aid. She overtook Britain in iron and steel, and challenged her in coal and shipbuilding. She was ahead in chemicals and electrical engineering.

(b) *Naval rivalry*. In 1898 German naval policy altered, and a naval race began. The creation of a German Pacific Fleet and the Kiel Canal from 1895 were both directed at Britain. It was clear when the gunboat *Panther* arrived in Morocco in 1911 how this navy was to be used.

(c) *Colonial competition*. The Kaiser believed in 'a place in the sun' for Germany. He backed the Boers with arms and public support (The Kaiser's Telegram, 1896) and seized Pacific bases and islands.

(d) *Drang nach Osten*. William abandoned Bismarck's alliance system for a policy of supporting Austria, penetrating the Balkans and overawing Turkey, thus defeating Russia and Britain at one stroke. In 1898 the Kaiser proclaimed himself protector of Mohammedans. The German ambassador persuaded the Sultan to grant railway concessions (1902 and 1905) to the Gulf and Mecca which threatened the Indian route. In 1913 Von Sanders went to reform the Turkish army.

(e) *Diplomatic confusion*. William had respected Victoria but disliked Edward, who he believed tried to encircle him by friendship with France and with his cousin, Nicholas II of Russia. Attempts at an Anglo-German alliance broke down in 1901 and thereafter the Kaiser believed in British perfidy.

Foreign policy by the time Sir Edward Grey took over in 1906 was thus conducted in strident nationalist tones. Two armed camps had built up in Europe based on alliances between Germany and Austria (1879), and France and Russia (1893), and there were diplomatic crises over questions of national prestige. The atmosphere of mutual dislike is shown in the spy story about the Germans, *The Riddle of the Sands* by Erskine Childers (1903), and by Du Maurier's play *An Englishman's Home* (1909). Lord

Roberts led a campaign for conscription, and Baden-Powell's scouts (1907) were part of a policy designed to rouse the country to the threat. Grey was urbane and sensitive, and did his best to calm the situation. On the other hand, the Liberals accepted much of what Balfour's government had done, and continued a policy of rearmament and staff conversations.

In defence policy, although expenditure on the army fell, a major reform was carried out, and an army of six divisions was ready to take its place on the left wing of the French. Staff conversations were started in 1905, and Sir Henry Wilson cycled round Belgium to prepare war plans. The Navy was greatly strengthened and in 1912 the Royal Flying Corps was started, with 272 craft ready by 1914. Naval strategy was reformed, and joint conversations held so that by 1913 it was clear that in a future war the British would concentrate in the North Sea, and leave the Mediterranean to France. On the other hand, Haldane was sent to Berlin to obtain a 'naval holiday' in 1912 and 1913, although he failed. In the Near East a number of steps were taken to counteract German influence. Treaties were signed with sultans, as in Kuwait (1903), and agreement reached with Russia over Persia. In 1911 Britain intervened to ensure the carrying out of this agreement, and the government bought 50 per cent of the shares in the Anglo-Persian Oil Company, halting German expansion. Grey and Lichnowsky, the German ambassador, tried to negotiate a wide agreement on the area, which was completed by June 1914 and not ratified. At the same time the Anglo-Russian agreement (1907) was strengthened by naval conversations.

The main criticism of Grey rests on his failure to align Britain now she had left isolation. The Anglo-Japanese Alliance of 1902 was strengthened in 1905 and 1911. In 1904 the Anglo-French Entente concluded many years of colonial disputes in places as varied as Siam, the New Hebrides, Madagascar and Newfoundland, and in 1907 the Anglo-Russian Entente brought stability to the frontiers of India. The implication of these agreements was obvious—Britain was setting her world house in order to prepare for a German threat. The staff conversations with France made it clear on which side of the alliance system Britain was to be found, but Britain entered no specific alliance and in 1914 all Grey would do was appeal for a conference. But this underestimates Austrian and German determination to fight; the German war plan envisaged defeating Britain and France, and the Germans did not regard her 'contemptible little army' as carrying much weight. Moreover, on two occasions Grey had made it plain on which side Britain stood during the Moroccan crises, when the Germans tried to humiliate France in 1905 and 1911. In the first crisis it was British support that forced Germany to climb down and agree to the Algeciras Conference, and in the second Lloyd George made the government's position plain in a strong pro-French speech. A Franco-German agreement followed in November. Moreover, British neutrality also enabled Grey to intervene to prevent war spreading in 1912–13, when the Balkans were in ferment, and he arranged the Conference of St James'.

In 1914 Grey was in an awkward position. His party contained many who were not in favour of war, and at first the significance of the murder of Franz Ferdinand at Sarajevo (28 June) was unclear. On 23 July, Lloyd George said our relations with Germany were better than they had been for years, and the same day Austria despatched her ultimatum to Serbia. Russia (24 July) and France (30 July) begged Grey to declare he adhered to their side, but this would not have stopped the war. Germany deliberately rejected Grey's offer of a conference on 27 July, Austria declared war on Serbia with German support on 28 July, and only then did the Kaiser send a telegram to the Czar, and on the next day one to Austria, urging them to talk to Russia. Lloyd George said he knew of no member of the cabinet who would have supported taking sides, and even on 30 July, when the question of Belgian neutrality was first raised in the cabinet, no one favoured a firm stand. As Ensor rightly said, 'It has been suggested that Grey might have averted war by announcing earlier that Britain would take arms against a violator [of Belgium]. But he could not have announced such a policy down to August 2nd because something like half the cabinet opposed it.'

By then 'war to time-table' had begun since the eastern part of the German plan had to be followed by a swift declaration of war on France, which meant violating Belgium. In 1914 no other plan was available, and on 3 August Germany declared war on France and invaded Belgium. The waverers strengthened. Bonar Law agreed to support intervention. Asquith and Grey were still faced with about ten opponents, but Grey argued that a victory over France obtained by smashing Belgium left Britain in a position where we would have to accept German dictation. Burns resigned, and the other opponents, including Morley, Simon and Samuel, tried to hold the ring. Germany then invaded Luxemburg, and the cabinet hardened its resolve to send an ultimatum on the lines of Gladstone's 1870 request. Morley was right in seeing Belgium as an excuse for supporting France but our interests were also at stake. As Spender said: 'Immense importance was attributed at the time to the diplomacy of the twelve days before the war, but in historical perspective it seems little more than the registering of a foregone conclusion.'

Grey did not see war with Germany as inevitable in 1914, but it was inevitable at some time since German victory would have left the two world powers face to face. Britain went to war with Japan, France and Russia as allies, and her stake was nothing less than the preservation of her hegemony. Asquith, Grey and Haldane were sitting smoking when the end came, and Grey said 'the lamps are going out' all over Europe. It was ironical that the Liberals entered the most devastating of wars, and the Whig element of their party brought to an end the Edwardian era.

C3. Defence Policy

In the early 1870s Cardwell had carried out major reforms, but since then little progress had been made. The army usually encountered foes with inferior fire power, and even sustained bad defeats at their hands. It was a professional body, unlike conscript continental armies. There was no general staff, and manoeuvres were scarcely ever held. In 1890 the Hartington Commission had recommended changes, but the Duke of Cambridge as C. in C. stood in the way until 1895. His successors were no more willing to learn from European example, and the Boer War revealed deficiencies at every level as bad as those in the Crimea, including faulty medical services, inadequate supplies, lack of tactical and strategic planning, poor intelligence and lack of organisation above the regimental level.

A Commission reported in 1904 under Lord Esher, and it was he, Lord Knollys and the King who vigorously backed new policies. Balfour supported them, and Haldane was brought in early to ensure continuity under the Liberals when he was War Minister. Thus, the opponents of expenditure like Churchill and Harcourt were outwitted by reducing costs while the purpose of the army was completely changed. The main reforms were:

(*a*) Conservative changes concerned with organisation. A Committee of Imperial Defence was set up (1904), with the prime minister in the chair to plan overall strategy. Following the Esher Report the C. in C. was abolished and an Army Council set up to run supply and administration.

(*b*) Liberal reforms of Haldane assisted by Wilson and Esher. In 1907 plans were laid to produce a BEF of six divisions, and to back this with 14 territorial divisions which replaced the militia, yeomanry and volunteers in 1908. Efficiency was improved with the OTC system at schools, reform of regimental administration, new Field Service Regulations, and a War Book to facilitate mobilisation.

Britain was thus able to enter a continental war with distinction for once in 1914.

Throughout the period the navy was the focus of attention. In 1889 the Naval Defence Act provided that Britain should have a fleet equal in size to her two largest rivals (France and Russia), and a massive fleet was maintained which numbered 153 ships in 1897. Unfortunately, it had not been involved in a modern action; it relied on bluff, its traditions were those of Nelson's day, and many of the ships were out of date. The appearance of German and Russian Pacific fleets, the building of a German navy and the Japanese victories in 1904–05 forced Britain to realise that her naval supremacy was being challenged. The reforms were carried out under four First Lords of the Admiralty—Cawdor, Tweedmouth, McKenna and Churchill—and two First Sea Lords—Sir John Fisher (1904–10) and Prince Louis of Battenberg. Unlike the army reforms, there was not complete success. The Naval War Staff of 1912 was not effective and, in tactical terms, according to Ensor, the navy was defective in gunnery, shells and mines.

Given these limitations the achievements were remarkable:

(*a*) Conditions. Below-deck conditions were improved with ships' bakeries and cutlery. Training hulks were scrapped and ships' barracks built at Chatham and Devonport.

(*b*) Officer training. In 1903 RNC Dartmouth and Osborne were established to give officer training to cadets, including engineering.

(*c*) New bases were established at Rosyth and Scapa Flow, and Dover made into a naval port. The disposition of the fleets was altered, bringing them back to home waters, cooperating with the French, and holding combined manoeuvres in 1914.

(*d*) Cuniberti's design for the *Dreadnought* was accepted, and in 1906 the first was launched. The aim was to improve speed, mobility, engine power, gunnery and general armament. The ship had 12-inch guns, and a speed of $17\frac{1}{2}$ knots. In 1912 the Queen Elizabeth class with 15-inch guns and a speed of 21 knots were introduced.

(*e*) Cruisers started with the Inflexible Class in 1909, and there were nine by 1914. In 1912 the E5 class of submarine was introduced, but Britain was behind Germany, whose vessel had four times the range.

In 1914 Battenberg and Churchill decided to keep the fleet in being in July, and Britain was ready for war with some 29 battleships to Germany's 17. While expenditure on the army fell between 1905 and 1914 from £29.8m to £28.84m, that on the navy rose from £33.38m to £51.55m.

D. The British Economy and the Structure of Society

The take-off into an industrially based society had started in Britain in the 1780s, and by 1850 the country was the workshop of the world. By the 1870s there were signs that the economy was starting to lose its initial advantages, and by 1900 America and Germany had emerged as major competitors. Asa Briggs has pointed out that free trade was adopted when it suited Britain because there were no effective competitors. It was adhered to when other countries were adopting high tariff policies. The Fair Trade League of the 1880s and the Tariff Reform campaign of 1903–06 failed, while America and Germany increased their tariffs. Moreover, Britain exported her own competition. British experts helped to create Russian and Japanese industries, and to spread industrialisation to countries like India and Canada. British railways and banks provided the sinews for new industrial nations, thus making it harder to sell the traditional exports. In 1914 two thirds of these were still coal, iron and steel, textiles, ships and heavy engineering.

It was hard to diversify or adapt, and the depression in trade was said to be due to 'unfair' competition or temporary factors. Falling world prices encountered expensive methods, spreading restrictive practices, and a second generation of industrialists prepared to live off the previous one. They could do this because, protected and controlled by the Gold Standard, British banking and insurance were yielding a favourable balance of payments. In 1914 there was a healthy surplus of £181m covering a deficit on visible trade. The Tariff Commission of 1904–07 argued that depression was temporary and largely the result of the Boer War. Had they examined the first production census in 1907 they would have seen more cogent reasons for decline. Outdated methods, overmanning, failure to use new power sources or even compete in light engineering products meant that output per man was relatively low, and costs correspondingly high. Three sets of figures illustrate the overall picture:

(*a*) In population Britain was overtaken as a great power in terms of a large home market and a growing work force:

	Great Britain	Germany	United States
1870/71	31.8	41.0	38.5
1890/91	41.9	56.3	75.9
1910/11	45.3	64.9	91.7

(*b*) Although Britain produced more, with an elevenfold increase in absolute terms, the country was being overtaken relatively:

Coal (million tons)

1870	112	34	10
1900	228	149	244
1913	292	277	455

Steel (million tons)

1870	0.7	0.3	No figure
1900	5.0	6.7	10.0
1913	6.5	14.0	32.0

(c) Although Britain's volume of trade rose by 49 per cent between 1903 and 1913, her total percentage of world trade fell:

1900	20	17	30
1914	14	16	36

D1. Edwardian Industry

The coal industry was the largest occupier of labour and the main base industry besides a major exporter, and it was growing fast. New coalfields were opened in Kent in 1907, for example, and maximum production was reached in 1913. But efficiency was declining seriously. There was little attempt to mechanise, and in 1913 only 8 per cent was so mined. Production per man-year fell from 301 tons (1897/99) to 289 tons (1905/07) while in America the reverse occurred. Britain's main export was textiles, which accounted for 51.2 per cent: but her share of the world market fell from 54 per cent to 40 per cent between 1880 and 1914 with Indian and Japanese competition. Britain retained her lead in quality cloths but in cheaper cloths, American mechanisation went ahead of Lancashire. The Northrop Loom meant that the ratio of workers to looms in America was 1 to 20, while in Britain it was 1 to 4. In iron and steel Britain paid the penalty for inventing and using the earlier processes that others had improved. In heavy steel the Bessemer and Siemens processes were more widespread than the Gilchrist-Thomas, which was widely used in Germany. In shipping, although Britain retained her lead, there was strong resistance by the craft unions to using electrical machinery. Turbine engines had been developed by Sir Charles Parsons (1897), but there was little interest, and the first two turbine ships for the navy sank in 1901.

There were organisational defects also. Small family firms still predominated in industry with a strong dislike of monopoly, but this meant that it was harder to raise capital and caution replaced enterprise. Half the companies floated on the Stock Exchange between 1890 and 1914 were not joint stock although the Companies Act (1907) improved matters. People with money to invest took it overseas, and lived off the capital. The idle rich were no myth; nor were their small undercapitalised firms. There were 20 major banks, 120 railway companies, and 1,000 coal owners. New industries were similarly fragmented so that there were 90 producers of motorcars. These firms had to compete with giant American trusts with their benefits of economy of scale. Of course, there were amalgamations like the Imperial Tobacco Company (1901–02), but they were few.

An examination of new developments in industry illustrates these points:

(a) Britain lagged behind in the chemical industry, and chemically based ones like aluminium (1888) and rayon (1892). Germany protected hers with a tariff and government aid.

(b) Electricity as a source of power for industry developed only on the Tyne, and in 1907 only 16 per cent of engineering was electrical. The Electricity Supply Act of 1882 restricted its use until 1898.

(c) The Tramways Act of 1870 held up this major form of transport. Some-

thing was done with the Light Railways Act (1896) but progress was slow—
London only changed over to electric trams after 1901.

(*d*) Electrifying the railways went slowly. The London 'Tube' was opened
in 1900, and the Underground electrified after 1903. Surface electrification began
on the LBSCR in 1909.

(*e*) Motorcars were restricted by law from 1865 to 1896. In 1903 came the
first speed limit and motor tax, and this was increased in 1909. The car industry
grew from the bicycle boom of the 1880s, but in 1913 only 38,000 were produced.

The failure to modernise or innovate was related to education. The
public schools which dominated government and where manufacturers
sent their children regarded science as 'stinks', and taught an almost exclusively classical curriculum. For those leaving elementary school there
were few opportunities of acquiring skills except through crusted apprenticeship methods. The Technical Education Act (1889) made a start but it
was pitiful compared with the German technical high schools. There were,
however, some signs that the relationship between education and economic
growth was understood. The Manchester School of Technology was
founded in 1877, and the London School of Economics in 1895. In 1907
the Imperial College of Science and Technology began, and many of the
new civic universities emphasised science and economics. These included
Birmingham (1900) and Bristol (1909). The government started to show
an interest. The National Physical Laboratory (1902) and the Medical
Research Council (1913) were examples. In spite of these changes, Britain
was 'a working museum of industrial archaeology'. This was something
of an exaggeration for during the war British industry underwent vast
changes, but the situation was unsatisfactory.

D2. Agricultural Renaissance

In late Victorian England farming had a depression in prices which led
to a fall in profits, rents, and output of wheat and meat faced with cheaper
foreign products. But by 1896, agriculture was reviving with prices of all
products except wool recovering. Rents increased and agriculture retained
its place in the economy, providing 6 per cent of the National Income. The
labour force was steady at 970,000 and in the case of farm-hands actually
rose by 23,000. Keen applied the term 'renaissance' to the Edwardian
period, and Ernle said that farming in 1914 was 'sound and prosperous'.
This should not be taken too far. Britain imported four fifths of her
cereals, two fifths of her meat and a high proportion of other cash crops.
Agriculture remained labour intensive and resistant to mechanisation.
Conditions for the labourers were bad, and a Royal Commission (1906)
investigated them. In 1912 George Edwards organised some labourers in
a union.

Since parliament was composed of the landed classes it took more
interest in agriculture than industry. Two commissions (Richmond, 1879–82,
Eversley, 1893–97) investigated the reasons for decline. A Board of Agriculture was set up in 1889 and legislation developed to reduce the power of
landlords and to provide security for small tenants. The government helped
with an Agriculture Rates Act (1896) which reduced rates by half, and by
giving grants (starting with £5,000 in 1888) for rural education. These

measures helped farmers who responded to the depression in four ways:

(*a*) By developing scientific agriculture. At Cambridge, Biffen researched in wheat and animal nutrition. At Oxford, an Institute of Agriculture was started. In 1913 government-subsidised Farm Institutes began winter courses.

(*b*) By adopting scientific methods. Dairy farming came to provide a fifth of the agricultural product. Milking machines had been developed by 1890. Fertiliser was extensively used and basic slag developed by Munro and Wrightson was in use after 1885. Pirie's plough (1863) at last became general although oxen were still in use in Sussex.

(*c*) Farms diversified to mixed farming. Chickens, dairy produce, fruit and vegetables spread in spite of European competition. Tudor methods of hop production were revolutionised. Swedes and sprouts were developed, and tomatoes and asparagus became commercial products.

(*d*) The traditional wheat areas declined, but pastoral diversified into the dairy side—only sheep flocks fell in size. Breeding societies were set up to provide herd (Guernsey, 1885) and flock books (Romney Marsh, 1895) to improve strains.

D3. National Finance

The City of London was the financial centre of the world; a position built up since the Napoleonic wars as a result of the profits made from the Industrial Revolution. A series of institutions for running central and branch banking, investment and insurance had been developed 'as safe as the Bank of England'. There was confidence in the integrity of the City and a social code destroyed those who broke the rules. The rules themselves worked well, and although, as in 1890 or 1907, there were momentary panics, the stability of London was the keystone of an arch of credit resting on the Gold Standard and the banks. The Gold Standard was all but universal and provided a self-regulating mechanism for prices based on the world gold supply. After the lean years of the 1880s, gold discoveries in South Africa and the Klondyke enabled prices to recover. Exchange rates were fixed in terms of gold and this benefited Britain in the terms of trade. After 1844 Britain had developed a central bank, which other nations did not possess. This controlled credit and protected the banking system from collapse. The main field for investment was the Empire, which was yielding £400m in interest by 1914.

This astonishing achievement created what Briggs called an 'Invisible Empire' of credit and financial control which meant that Argentina or Persia was largely in British hands. It grew up in the era of free trade when low taxation and low wages meant that profits were available to invest, and government exerted no controls. Liberal Manchester School economists like Jevons and Marshall supported free trade as strongly as ever, and government took only a small share. Pre-war the national income was estimated at £1988m, and only 5.5 per cent was devoted to social expenditure. There were only 1¼ million income-tax payers, and they paid 9*d* in the pound. For years governments struggled to keep the budget below £100m, but by 1901 it had reached £132m. The Boer War cost £222m, and this raised taxes. By 1914 the total had reached £209m.

Although outwardly everyone was as orthodox financially in 1910 as in 1850 a change was in fact taking place, and Hicks has shown that government was beginning to take on new rôles using money for social ends. Loans and grants for specific purposes such as education started as early as 1833, and both parties made them to agriculture or shipping. Control over local government finance was strengthened by substituting elected councils for landlords' power and then controlling them through the grant in aid. In some cases the state was even spending directly, as it has on fever hospitals since 1866, and in 1905 the Tories were unable to prevent an act authorising a local rate to help the unemployed. The actuarial principle was broken in education by 1891 when it was made free at primary level and the Poor Law Board accepted that for children and the old deterrence was not the only consideration. Gradually therefore taxation began to assume new forms. It became redistributive with the start of death duties in 1894, which were increased in 1909, and it became progressive by distinguishing earned and unearned income in 1907 and starting a super-tax in 1909. It is in the context of those changes that Lloyd George's budget of 1909 should be considered. Its main provisions were:

(a) Below £3,000 income tax was to stay at 9*d*, but above it rose to 1/2*d*. In addition there was to be a super-tax of 6*d* in the £ on all incomes over £5,000.

(b) Death duties were raised on estates between £5,000 and £1m to bring in £4.4m in a full year.

(c) Tobacco, spirits, liquor licences and stamp duties, together with £3m from the Sinking Fund, represented the usual methods of raising tax.

(d) Three taxes on land were introduced. There was a 20 per cent tax on the increase in value of a site when it changed hands, a duty of ½*d* in the pound on the annual capital value, and a tax of 1*s* in the pound on the annual value of land leased to mining companies.

(e) Child allowances were introduced with £10 for every child under 16, provided parental income was less than £500 a year.

With this money Lloyd George proposed to cover a deficit of nearly £16m, pay old age pensions and for naval rearmament, and provide for expanding social demands. In addition, he proposed to introduce a Road Fund with £600,000 provided by taxes on petrol and licences, and a Development Commission with funds of £200,000 to investigate country life and natural resources and carry out a complete land valuation. It was not revolutionary. The extra revenue amounted to one half of one farthing in the pound of the national income. It was an attempt to stave off tariffs, but it also violated liberal principles by increasing taxes and providing social expenditure. Sectional interests such as brewers and motorists were outraged, and above all the landed classes. They saw the steps as derisory, and therefor punitive, and they were not blind to the implications. The Budget Protest League was formed and the Tories lost their head. Lansdowne, who had not intended to oppose the budget, said it was 'a monument of reckless and improvident finance'. After five days' bitter discussion the Lords rejected it by 350 to 75, thus starting a crisis (Section B4).

E. The Rich and the Poor

E1. The Differences in Society

Historians of Edwardian Britain tend to be divided by the class which they study. Priestley observed, 'The Edwardian Age was never a golden age, but seen across the dark years afterwards it could easily be mistaken for one.' If you were rich you could hardly avoid mistaking it: 0.5 per cent of the people owned 65.5 per cent of the capital and 2.5 per cent owned two thirds of the National Income. On this they paid little tax and small wages, enabling them to live a life of luxury. In 1911 there were 60,000 people of independent means. 1,658,000 domestic servants toiled for the benefit of the upper and middle classes. At the other extreme the great mass of people possessed less than £10 in savings, worked a 52-hour week, earned less than £160 a year and saw the real value of their meagre wages fall by 5 per cent between 1908 and 1914. Thirty per cent of the nation lived at or below a meanly drawn poverty line, and 16 per cent in such poverty that they were actually starving. Unemployment was the lot of millions of workers in docks and farms employed on a seasonal basis, and the average rate ran as high as 6 per cent, or in poor years double that, without any relief or savings to live on except what charity provided. In 1902 Jack London wrote *The People of the Abyss*, in which he contrasted the festivities for the Coronation in London's West End with the squalor of the East End. The report of a committee in 1904 on recruits for the Boer War showed that 34.6 per cent were rejected after inspection, but the numbers rejected before nearly doubled that figure. In 1917 the figure was still 31.5 per cent with marked disabilities and 10 per cent totally unfit. Two million families lived on less than £1 per week and they all suffered from bad housing, poverty, insanitary workplaces, poor diet, inadequate medical facilities and poor clothing.

E2. Demands for Reform

From the 1870s the collectivist state began to develop; Dicey placed its start in 1865. This meant that government began to recognise it had other responsibilities beyond internal order and external security. It began to intervene in the economy and the social problems of the country as a matter of principle, and by the 1890s this trend was readily apparent, and was made explicit in Gladstone's Newcastle Programme (1891). Victoria said this was 'almost communistic' in places and a number of contemporaries began to acknowledge the new rôle of the state. Harcourt commented in 1889, 'We are all socialists now', and in 1895 the *Economist* spoke of the new functions of the state building up like a coral island piece by piece. This trend is of vital importance since it ran parallel to the growth of socialism itself, and laid the basis of much political activity in the twentieth century. Several historians have drawn attention to this trend. J. M. Roberts has analysed the Victorian origins of the Welfare State. M. Bruce has argued that the Unemployed Workmen's Act (1905), by giving a Treasury grant of £200,000, initiated the principle of welfare spending from general taxation. Tory Democracy rather than Gladstonian Liberalism was at the root of the political moves in this direction, and it was not until Campbell Bannerman converted the Liberals to social reform that they fell into line. In a speech at Perth in June 1903, he referred to 12 millions 'underfed and on the verge of hunger'. There were five main reasons for the trend:

(a) *The growth of democracy and education.* The electorate was growing, and at local government level the acts of 1888 and 1894 created an opportunity for Socialist councillors. The establishment of free primary education in 1891 was followed by movements like the WEA (1903) which provided information on social problems. Toynbee Hall in the East End of London was one such centre.

(*b*) *Gas and water Socialism.* The municipalities were rivals in providing new services. By 1900, 299 out of 317 corporations were carrying out productive undertakings such as gasworks, tramways or electricity. After 1880, when Liverpool issued municipal stock, others followed and by 1910 they had invested £600m.

(*c*) *Social pity.* The foundation of public school missions, 'slumming' by the rich, the influence of evangelical and High Church clergy, the work of the Salvation Army, Dr Barnardo's and other charitable organisations brought much to light that could not be ignored.

(*d*) *Scientific interest.* Sociology was developing (Sociological Society, 1903, British Institute of Social Service, 1904) and statistics and sampling methods were applied to human problems. Charles Booth's *London Life and Labour* was completed in 1903. Seebohm Rowntree's survey of York with its definition of poverty appeared in 1901.

(*e*) *The growth of Socialism.* The unions, the Labour parties and the fringe organisations focused attention on social rather than political problems. The works of Henry George or Graham Wallace, the plays of Bernard Shaw and John Galsworthy, the writings of Reeves and Masterman and the work of the Fabians such as *Essays in Socialism* (1908) drew attention to the problems and proposed solutions.

Although it would be wrong to overemphasise the lack of social provision in Victorian England with a network of private charity and church activity, the gaps were apparent and getting worse. Reforms such as old-age pensions, proposed unofficially in the 1870s and officially in 1895, were neglected. Liberals were convinced that reform was vital as Churchill pointed out in an article called 'The Untrodden Field in Politics' (1908). Apart from the Poor Law (where a commission from 1905 to 1909 remained divided and little was achieved), reform affected nearly every aspect of the social scene in the 1900s. It must be stressed, however, that much of the law-making was limited in scope or long overdue. In an important year such as 1911 the government produced only 450 pages of laws. There was no intention to create a welfare state as we know it. Actuarial principles were applied if at all possible, some laws were only permissive, and nearly all applied to restricted categories. In spite of these limitations it is true that the reforms of this period rank it with the 1870s and the 1940s as a major reforming decade.

E3. Beginnings of a Welfare State

Ministers such as Lloyd George, Churchill, Samuel and Buxton carried welfare measures and were backed by committed civil servants. It was Churchill who introduced Beveridge to the Board of Trade in 1909. In insurance, Llewellyn Smith, Braithwaite and Masterman were involved. In criminal reform Sir Evelyn Ruggles-Brise and Sir Herbert Samuel were influential. In educational matters Sir George Newman and Sir Arthur Newsholme played key rôles. The reforms were thus a collective effort by an increasingly expert and growing Civil Service and Liberal ministers who were also influenced by personal factors. Lloyd George's father died of tuberculosis and he had visited Germany to see the reforms that Bismarck had introduced. Churchill was influenced on prisons by his father's old friend Wilfred Blunt. The main reforms were:

(a) *Old Age Pensions Act, 1908.* The act provided for all those with incomes under £31 a year over 70 to have 5s a week up to £21, but less over that line. Anyone who had been on poor relief in the previous year, in prison in the previous ten (later two) years, or had failed to work habitually, would not receive a pension. By 1914 the number receiving one was 970,000 and the cost, estimated at £6m, had doubled.

(b) *The National Insurance Act, 1911*, divided into two distinct parts:

(i) Health Insurance, which came into operation in January 1913. All workers earning less than £160 a year between 16 and 60 were included—this covered 15 million. Contributions of 4d (worker), 3d (employer) and 2d (state) entitled you to free medical treatment at a panel doctor's, sickness benefit of 10s a week for 13 weeks, and 5s a week for 13 more weeks, 5s a week disability benefit, and 30s maternity grant. It did not cover hospital treatment, or wives and children.

(ii) Unemployment Insurance. Employer, worker and government each paid $2\frac{1}{2}d$ in return for which the workers obtained 7s a week, qualifying for one week of benefit for every five contributions up to 15 weeks a year. It covered building, shipbuilding, mechanical engineering, iron-founding, vehicle building and sawmilling—some $2\frac{1}{4}$ million people. The fund had a surplus of £3$\frac{1}{4}$m in 1914.

(c) *Unemployment.* At first the Liberals strengthened the 1905 Act in 1906 with Distress Committees seeking to place men in work, but the Act lapsed. In its place Churchill was determined to have labour exchanges and after fighting Labour and Civil Service opposition he secured an Act in 1909. In February 1910 the first of 83 exchanges opened, and by 1914, 430 were providing 3,000 jobs a day and filling one third of the available vacancies.

(d) *Infant welfare.* The infant mortality rate was high, and even rising among poorer people while the general death rate was falling. In 1899, at 163 per 1,000, it was the highest ever recorded. A whole range of measures was taken—milk dispensaries (1899), health visitors, compulsory notification of births (1907, 1915), reform of midwives (1902, 1910), maternity clinics (St Pancras, 1907) and maternity benefits. Small grants were received from the LGB and made official in 1914. The fall in mortality was spectacular—from the 1899 figure of 163 to 95 per 1,000 in 1912.

(e) *Children's welfare.* Reform was brought about by reports of school attendance officers, and by strategic fears about the quality of the nation's children. The Children's Act (1908) codified no less than 39 previous measures dealing with negligence and cruelty, set up juvenile courts, and remand homes instead of prison. In 1906 the Provision of Meals Act provided a $\frac{1}{2}d$ rate and by 1910 some 96 authorities provided 9 million meals. In 1914 the Treasury agreed to pay half the cost, and Children's Care Committees were set up. In 1907 school medical inspection began and in 1912 grants for essential hospital treatment started.

These were the main welfare measures, but the government's activities affected a wider field. Among other measures passed were:

(a) *Conditions of work.* The Workmen's Compensation Act of 1906 extended the 1897 measure to some 6 million workers. The Trades Boards Act (1909) applied to four industries (tailoring, chain and paper-box making, and lace and net finishing) and established wages' councils affecting 200,000 workers. The Mines Act (1911) laid down regulations for training, safety measures and accident procedures. The Shops Act (1910), in which the government failed to carry a 60 hours' limitation, secured a half holiday.

(b) *Criminal law.* Reform of prison conditions was carried forward under the Prisons Act of 1898 by such measures as those of March and July, 1910, reducing solitary confinement. The Probation of Offenders Act (1907) introduced the probation system, and the juvenile reformatory or Borstal instead of prison.

Plenty was left undone, as any survey of the 1920s will show. Major areas such as the Poor Law and housing were left largely untouched, but in view of the pressure of other events this remains an impressive programme. As Gilbert says, 'Although by no means solving the problems of the condition of the people, it settled the lines upon which the eventual solution would be found.'

Further Reading

Aikin. K. W. W., *The Last Years of Liberal England, 1900–1914*, Collins, London, 1972

Bruce, M., *The Coming of the Welfare State*, Batsford, London, 1965.

Ensor, R. C. K., *England 1870–1914*, Oxford University Press, London, 1936.

Fulford, R., *Votes for Women*, Faber and Faber, London, 1957.

Jenkins, R., *Asquith*, Collins, 1964, and new edition, 1978.

Lyons, F. S. L., *Ireland Since the Famine*, Weidenfeld and Nicolson, London, 1971.

Magnus, P., *Edward VII*, John Murray, London, 1964, and available in Penguin Paperbacks, 1967.

Pelling, H., *A History of British Trade Unionism*, Macmillan, London, 1977, and available in earlier edition in Penguin Paperbacks, 1963.

Priestley, J. B., *The Edwardians*, Heinemann, London, 1970, and available in Sphere Books as a paperback, 1972.

Steiner, Z. E., *Britain and the Origins of the First World War*, Macmillan, London, 1977

Questions

1. What is modern about the period leading up to the First World War?
2. What do you understand by the phrase 'the Edwardian Age'?
3. Was the Liberal Party 'heading for catastrophe' by 1914?
4. What issues were raised by the struggle of Lords and Commons between 1909 and 1911?
5. How far reaching were the social reforms carried out by the Liberal governments of 1906–14?
6. Why were labour relations increasingly a political issue after 1900?
7. To what extent was Britain's position as a world power under attack by 1914?
8. Why did Great Britain enter the war in August 1914?

2

THE GREAT WAR: THE COURSE OF EVENTS

The Great War was not the first world war. It was essentially a European war, and its primary objective was to defeat the Central Powers, particularly Germany. Starting with a traditional war of movement, it developed into a war of attrition varied by a knock-out blow to break through the entrenched lines, and then by dispersed attacks at various points. In the end Germany surrendered and the Allies won because of what happened on the Western Front, where the conflict was one of the decisive battles of history. When criticising either generals or politicians, tactics or strategy this is the central fact to bear in mind, for defeat on the Western Front would have been followed by a German victory throughout Europe. On the other fronts Russia was knocked out, and brought to the brink of revolution, and Italy reduced to near chaos. Serbia was conquered and Rumania defeated. The victory was an Anglo-French one, justifying the arguments of Westerners like Haig.

In the end the war became a duel between the two empires of Germany and Britain. Until 1918 German intakes into the forces reflected their rapid birth rate in earlier years while the French continued to decline because of their sluggish birth rate. France's losses in men and industrial power meant that by 1918 she was increasingly dependent on Britain.

The war ended with Britain 'the strongest power in the alliance' with 66 divisions, 22,000 military aircraft and 61 battleships. During the last year of the war Britain entered a new campaign of intervention in Russia while pressure was at its height on the Western Front.

Naval warfare had as its ultimate aim the defeat of mainland Germany by blockade, and the fleet was kept in being as far as possible to prevent a German breakout. In spite of much talk it was not used offensively to attack the coasts of Germany. Naval actions across the globe were brought about by the need to cut off German supplies and preserve our own. By clearing the high seas, Britain was able to prevent Germany securing fresh allies and to mop up German colonies with the aid of her Empire and Japan. One main thrust of German pre-war policy had been to undermine British world influence, and had she won large colonial demands would have been presented. Even in December 1916 the moderate Bethmann Hollweg demanded colonial compensation. The sideshows in the Middle East and the colonies were wasteful of men and resources, but they attained their object—the addition to the Empire of 13 million subjects. Together with the capture of the navy, the destruction of trading connections and the expulsion of the Germans from the Middle East, this represented the defeat of each of the main pre-war German threats (Chapter 1, C2). Thus if the strategy of 'knocking away the props' had little direct military impact it was far from 'cigar butt strategy', as Taylor called it. Mistakes arose because the allies never created an overall strategy—the politicians remained at the mercy of the generals, and apart from such gestures as the sending by Russia to Britain of the captured German navy codes, or the attempt to force the Dardanelles, coordination never occurred. On the Western Front the allied generals met only once in 1918; it remained a European war waged on nationalist lines.

A. Strategy of the War

A1. Kitchener's War

The BEF was committed to the French left wing under its commander, Sir John French. Since the German Schlieffen Plan involved the invasion of Belgium this meant that a small, inexperienced army was placed in the direct line of Europe's finest force. Although Britain went to war to defend Belgium there was no possibility of altering the plans, and such was the onrush of the Germans, and their victories further south, that French wanted to withdraw altogether. Kitchener hastened to France to persuade him to stand firm, making a decisive contribution to the holding operation of the Marne. Kitchener retained office until he was drowned in June 1916, but by then he had been largely superseded by Sir William Robertson, the CIGS, and undermined by increasing political interference. Thus, Lloyd George, who was Minister of Munitions, insisted on the importance of machine guns while Kitchener disagreed. There was no central direction of the war—merely an enlargement of the Army Council into a War Council, and later into a War Committee. Asquith stood aside, and during 1915 the generals had it their own way. This was unfortunate since the position on the Western Front did not allow for offensive warfare, and they determined on it. As a result there were costly defeats, and although French tried to blame the government for not supplying shells this rang false by the end of the year with Lloyd George in charge of munitions. As a result he was replaced by Sir Douglas Haig in December 1915. By this time Kitchener's long-term policies had matured with an army of 21 divisions ready to try a new approach to breakthrough.

A2. Westerners and Easterners

By November 1914 the Schlieffen Plan had failed, and stalemate was created since neither side had planned a static war. Each believed it could break out, and during 1915, 1916 and 1917 it was the allies who tried. In 1918 it was the Germans, but each failed because the weight of armament was sufficient to deter advance much beyond costly salients. Railways enabled reserves to be brought up quickly while supplies took longer to arrive so when breakthroughs were achieved they were not followed up. The weight of artillery increased, but this made conditions worse for the infantry and even tank advances could not be sustained. It is very easy to be an armchair critic of this situation, but it is difficult to see what the generals could have done. They persisted too long in offensives in the hope that cavalry could be used, but the basic planning of the offensives was often correct. What went wrong was that there were delays, and the Germans then acted, throwing the plans into disarray. Difficult though it was with such vast numbers, greater flexibility was needed and not achieved until 1918.

Opinion was soon divided over whether victory could be won under such circumstances. The Westerners argued that it must come in France and

Belgium because the Germans were unwilling to give up these areas, and would only be defeated by invasion of the homeland. This theory was buttressed by the view that continual attack would bleed the enemy white. In the end these theories proved right. Ludendorff gave up because his army was full of raw recruits who were deserting and the German homeland was threatened. What went wrong was that the allies had to coordinate nations, but the Germans only corps, so they were more flexible, and as they operated on internal lines could move troops rapidly. The Westerners argued that diversionary wars elsewhere sapped their strength, but this was only true in the early part of 1918. At other times in order to win cooperation for sideshows the main weight on the Western Front was actually increased.

The Easterners were strongly criticised for little wars. The India Office launched the Mesopotamian campaign, while the War Office insisted on protecting the Canal, and knocking out Turkey. The Foreign Office demanded advances north to help relieve the pressures on Russia. Troops were sent to Salonika to help Serbia when it was too late, and thereafter deployed to little use until July 1918. Attempts were made to bribe Bulgaria and Rumania to be allies, but the defeat of the latter forced Britain to sabotage the oil wells there. The Dardanelles operation was well conceived, but so clumsily executed that it proved a mortal blow to the Easterners. All the aid that was given to Russia did not keep her in the war. The Turkish war absorbed a million men, death rates in 'Mespot' were appalling and Britain sustained her biggest defeat.

Some said the sideshows delayed victory on the Western Front. To this the Easterners replied that they cut losses (which was not true) and that they contributed to ultimate victory (which was). The fall of Turkey, Bulgaria and Austria left Germany without an ally, and with no means of reaching world supplies. Even if Britain had not won in 1918 this would have made victory in 1919 certain. By weakening Austria, pressure was relieved on Italy and Russia which enabled them to hold out a little longer, and Germany had to send help to the Austrians. If the sideshows prevented Britain taking advantage of breakthroughs they prevented the Germans from seizing on these mistakes since throughout the war they deployed troops elsewhere than on the Western Front. Above all it was argued that Britain's interest in humbling Germany arose from her world position, and that her gains should be overseas, not at the expense of Germany. With British troops in Baghdad, Jerusalem and Constantinople this object was achieved. There were no French troops in Berlin.

A3. Anglo-French Cooperation

Since the main theatre of war was France, ultimate victory depended on the degree of cooperation between the allies; this was at first non-existent, and then took place with bitter rivalry never far below the surface. Moreover generals had to heed the politicians who supplied them, and they in turn responded to the electorate. A vicious circle developed of offensives to make defeats palatable, leading to more sacrifices, and quite often all concerned, including Haig and Lloyd George, were deflected from their original plans.

The main difficulty was that the French contribution was the largest until 1918—at the end of 1915 it was 95 to Britain's 57 divisions, and therefore Joffre was in reality the supreme commander, but neither French nor Haig wished to accept this. Since Joffre and Nivelle were addicts of the offensive this stubbornness made sense, but in the end Britain was forced to cooperate with the larger bulk of the French army. Thus, in June 1915 when the first allied conference took place at Calais to discuss the Dardanelles, Joffre allowed it to go ahead, but only in exchange for agreement to the Loos offensive. Neither Kitchener nor French thought much of the proposal, but in Taylor's words 'British soldiers died so that France could be kept in the war'. In December 1915 a military conference was held, and plans laid for an offensive on all three fronts against Germany. Haig replaced French later that month and, provided with 57 divisions, felt able to accept. Numerically the allies had 139 divisions to Germany's 117, but unfortunately the latter planned to bleed France white by attacking Verdun, and although Joffre knew it was militarily useless to defend Verdun, he left the plan for a joint offensive intact. The French contribution to the British thrust on the Somme was reduced by Verdun from 40 to 5 divisions. Haig wanted to roll up the Germans in Flanders, but Joffre wanted Britain on the Somme to back him. Kitchener insisted that Haig follow this line. Then Joffre asked for the attack to be moved forward by one month, and this was accepted. The result was the heaviest loss of any army on a single day in the war.

It was not true that the British army 'lost faith in their cause, in its leaders, in everything except loyalty to their fighting comrades. The war had ceased to have a purpose'. Had this occurred, 1917 and 1918 would have seen complete collapse. It was Joffre who fell in December, not Haig. It was Germany who put forward peace proposals and replaced Falkenhayn with Ludendorff and Hindenburg. In Britain, Lloyd George came in to wage war more resolutely, and in January 1917 an allied meeting at Rome discussed the future. Lloyd George pleaded for an offensive in Italy, but was overruled. Nivelle, Joffre's successor, had already devised a plan for a Western Front offensive, and Lloyd George's hostility to Haig combined with his known preference for sideshows to force the generals to agree in February 1917. The war cabinet accepted the plan without consulting Robertson. The Aisne offensive failed although the British backing was successful. In April, Nivelle was replaced by Pétain, who had to contain the French army revolt which affected 54 divisions, and by May Haig was convinced that a new British offensive nearer to Ypres would bring success. Vimy Ridge and Messines encouraged him to think a breakthrough was possible, although Robertson was sceptical, and the Intelligence staff rejected the plan. Even Foch said Germans and mud were an impossible combination.

Haig came to London to argue the case before the small War Policy Committee Lloyd George had established. Since Haig had been right earlier in the year it would have been a bold man who would question him now. Except Milner, all accepted his arguments. He said an advance of 30 miles could reach the submarine bases, and claimed the French were asking him to relieve the pressure, although Pétain had only asked for diversionary attacks. Lloyd George did not give full attention to the arguments, and on July 25 the cabinet agreed. By then the element of surprise had been lost and a delay of 53 days brought the offensive perilously close to winter. After further delay in mid-August the offensive continued until November when it failed at the same time as disaster struck in Italy and Russia left the war. In Taylor's words, 'it was the Germans on whom success seemed to smile in the autumn of 1917'.

A4. Unified Command and Final Victory

In November 1917 a conference decided to create a Supreme War Council with Foch as chairman. It was to be attended by the prime ministers and to have a permanent secretariat so that Lloyd George could at last get a second opinion to set against Robertson and Haig. The committee was to prepare a general reserve of 30 divisions, but that scheme was scuppered by the generals. Lloyd George removed Robertson, but his successor Wilson was equally pro-offensive. The first meeting of the SWC failed to keep Russia in the war, American entry stirred up divisions among the allies, submarine warfare had bitten deeply, and the Germans still believed victory to be possible in 1918. But Lloyd George now had the backing of a strong French government under Clemenceau, who took office in November 1917. Ludendorff started to plan but found he lacked the resources for the series of knockout blows he proposed. Even with 52 divisions from the East the opposing forces were about equal, and the blockade was lowering morale and reducing supplies. However, the Germans had the element of surprise, and did well in March. On 26 March at Doullens, Milner handed over to Foch the coordination of efforts, and in April 1918 he became Commander in Chief, able to hold reserves and allow retreats, drawing the Germans on rather than standing to fight. During this period Haig fought the battle of his life in the north, outnumbered two to one by the Germans and culminating with the battles of 12 April. The line held next day, and by 29 April the advance was contained. The other German offensives were held, and a fourth abandoned on 20 July. Four days later the decision for a general offensive was reached, and launched on 8 August to be followed by battles that were 'classic examples of the military art'.

B. The Western Front

Both sides expected a war of movement with the Schlieffen Plan aiming to capture Paris, and the French Plan 17 for offensives into Germany. Indeed, the size and fire power of the armies was held to indicate that the war could not last long.

B1. 1914: War of Movement

(*a*) The German attack entered Belgium and swept into Brussels on 20 August.

(*b*) The French launched two offensives in the south, which were costly failures, before transferring troops too late to meet the German threat. They were defeated, and Namur fell on 23 August.

The delay afforded by the Belgians enabled the BEF to cross and take up its position.

(*c*) The British repelled superior German forces at Mons, but French defeat forced them to retire. French beat off attacks as the BEF retreated 170 miles by 3 September

(d) Since the German lines were extended the Belgians tried sabotage, and the Germans carried out reprisals. A total of 119,000 Belgian refugees came to Britain.

The onrush of the Germans caused panic in Paris, and the government fled, but it was decided to hold the city. At this point the Germans made a fatal error since they did not realise how far the left of the allied line extended, and, fearing that Paris would separate him from Bulow, Von Kluck turned inwards, crossing the allied front.

(e) The allies then advanced in the Battle of the Marne (6–13 September), driving the Germans back. The German commander had a breakdown and was replaced by Falkenhayn. He obtained an orderly withdrawal beyond the Aisne, where the line stabilised.

The Germans pressed their attack on Antwerp, where the Belgian army had retreated. An ill-equipped British naval division of 8,000 was sent, but could give little help. Antwerp fell on 10 October, and the British were interned. The Germans in turn tried to bend the British left flank back.

(f) 20 October to 14 November saw the race to the sea, with four German attacks on a wide front which were defeated.

(g) From 21 October to 11 November the BEF was destroyed at Ypres with 1 in 10 killed, but eventually the Germans were held in a salient.

As winter closed in a system of trenches was started, and shallow dug-outs were replaced by lines three and four deep, and sometimes 40 feet down. The Germans built in concrete in some places from the start, and it was clear that defensive fire power from machine-gun nests was likely to make attack difficult. The allies were determined to break the stalemate even if only to prevent the total defeat of Russia, but they failed to appreciate the difficulties of penetration in depth. Advance was made difficult by barbed wire, mine fields and the artillery barrages which created serious obstacles. Trench war began, and neither terrain nor weather helped matters.

B2. 1915: War of Offensives

(a) It was decided to advance at Neuve Chapelle (10–12 March) with a monster barrage, but the allies ran out of ammunition, telephone wires were cut, and reserves were not ready. When the Germans counter-attacked the front stabilised one mile forward, but since German losses were greater it was decided to try again.

(b) The Germans attacked at Ypres (22 April–13 May) using poison gas. It was effective for a thousand yards, but subject to wind, and the salient contracted by about five miles.

Need to help the Russians, back up the Italians and cover French failure in Artois led to fresh offensives.

(c) From 9 to 25 May the British offensive at Festubert (Aubers) penetrated the first trench line, but ran into machine guns and was outnumbered 5 to 2. The barrage ran out of ammunition after two days

During the summer munitions reform and new troops encouraged French to a further offensive. By this time the Germans had reinforced their lines, and were using new weapons like liquid fire.

(*d*) An attack was launched at Loos (28 September–13 October) relying on gas to capture the town, but there were not enough guns, the wire was not cut, and exhausted reserves raised casualty figures to 47,000 in the first three days. There was 'colossal blundering' in staff work and communications. French fell as a result.

B3. 1916: Verdun and the Somme

Falkenhayn was under pressure to secure a victory and decided to attack Verdun, relying on French determination not to surrender the fortress even though they had removed many guns, making it difficult to hold.

(*a*) The battle lasted from 21 February to 11 July, beginning with a bombardment and a German advance which captured Douaumont and Vaux. Then the Germans made the mistake of putting in too many men in a narrow front, and both sides slogged away until 377,231 French and 337,000 German casualties had occurred. After the Somme offensive the French recaptured the forts. Undoubtedly the battle weakened the French, but it also damaged the Germans who did not capture it.

These events cut across the joint British-French plans for an offensive. Haig had wished to fight in Artois, but agreed to Picardy simply to keep the armies close together. As pressure mounted at Verdun the French divisions fell in number, and the date for attack was advanced one month. It was made against a heavily fortified section of the line, and after a preliminary bombardment which was too extended.

(*b*) The Battles of the Somme (1 July–19 November) were the testing ground for the new conscript army, and the grave of the mighty volunteer army. They were the first in which British commanders had to deal with a continental size army. Four phases can be discerned:

(i) 1–12 July. The British held up on the left in spite of heavy casualties, including 20,000 on the first day, and on the right captured Mametz.
(ii) 14 July–9 September. Attack was successful, and the cavalry were used with a breach in the German lines widening to seven miles.
(iii) 15 September–10 November. 24 tanks were used at Flers, but there was no back-up. The British captured Thiepval and the French were within three miles of Peronne. The last German line was reached.
(iv) 13–19 November saw the capture of Beaumont Hamel and Beaucourt, but a break in the weather caused the offensive to be called off.

The losses on the Somme have led to different views about the value of the battles, but what critics never make plain is how they would have acted faced with the world's chief military power. As Kitchener said, 'We have to make war as we must, and not as we should like to.'

B4. 1917: War of Attrition

When Joffre was dismissed the French appointed another exponent of the offensive, Nivelle. Haig had prepared an early British offensive, but Lloyd George was determined to subordinate him to the French and went along with Nivelle's plan for a knockout blow with one million men and 5,000 guns against the Hindenburg Line, turning it to the north and south.

(*a*) From 16 April to 21 May the French attacked on the Aisne, but failure to reach objectives led to revolt in the ranks. Nivelle was now sacrificed to Pétain to restore morale.

The result was that Haig's original supporting rôle became the major engagement, and he had to fight to relieve the French rather than for the objective of turning the German flank. The extension gave the Germans time to move reserves, with disastrous results.

(*b*) 9–11 April. After wire had been cut and aerial reconnaissance had pinpointed targets, a scientific bombardment was carried out, and an advance of 12 miles secured at Arras. Vimy was captured, Harp seized with the aid of tanks, and seven miles of Hindenburg Line captured.

(*c*) Before continuing it was necessary to secure the position in Ypres, and on 7 June massive explosions caused by mining and bombardment led to the capture of Messines.

These early successes had not convinced Lloyd George, and, as Taylor observes, 'some of the Flanders mud sticks' to him for causing delays while the pros and cons of further offensives were argued. German reinforcements of 40 divisions could be brought from before the silent French front, and the rainy season was appreciably nearer. Haig had equality of numbers, but suffered the disadvantage of being the attacker, and had no French support.

(*d*) The Third Battle of Ypres lasted from 31 July to 6 November, culminating in the capture of Passchendaele, which merely created an unwieldy salient, and led to fighting that was 'the last word in human misery'.

However, fearing total Italian collapse, and the arrival of divisions from Russia, Haig determined on one more attack.

(*e*) The Battle of Cambrai (20 November to 7 December). With 450 tanks the British advanced 7 miles, but reserves were not ready, and defeats forced the attack back.

There had been limited successes, and tactics were becoming more sophisticated, but overall it was 'strategically a British failure', and the casualties were the worst of the war in spite of attempts by the official historians to reduce them by 50,000. German losses were fewer. A total of 79 divisions remained on the Russian front in spite of withdrawals, the Italians were crushed at Caporetto, and the Hindenburg Line was intact.

B5. 1918: War of Movement Again

Time was running out for the Germans, with starvation, and the impending Americans, although it is wrong to see their eventual contribution of nine front-line divisions cancelling out the loss of Russia. Ludendorff massed 192 divisions for a German breakthrough, but these included raw recruits, 60,000 withdrawn from transport, and even an Austrian division. His aim was to split the French and British armies by a series of blows, crumbling rather than smashing the front and taking advantage of the salients created the previous year. But on the allied side, in Thomson's words, there was 'a new quality of generalship'. Haig understood how to resist to the last man, and how to attack, and both qualities were to be needed. He had in Rawlinson, Gough, Plumer and Byng effective subordinates. Munitions were reaching their peak, and there was still no shortage of men.

Ludendorff planned four great offensives:

(a) The Second Battle of the Somme (21 March to 4 April) started the struggle and swept forward to within 7 miles of the vital rail link at Amiens. The deployment of reserves by Foch halted them.

(b) The Battle of the Lys (9–29 April); aided by fog and using gas, the Germans attacked two Portuguese divisions, and broke through on a 30-mile front. The Germans were held with the aid of four French divisions

(c) The Third Battle of the Aisne (27 May–5 July) was the most rapid advance since 1914, and swept to within 40 miles of Paris.

(d) The Second Battle of the Marne (15 July–4 August) was launched to west and east of Rheims. Foch had reinforced at this point with 12 divisions taken from Haig, who ignored Lloyd George's request not to give them. On 18 July, using 346 tanks, the French advanced 4 miles in a day and took 40,000 prisoners. The offensive was called off, and on 24 July the allies prepared to advance.

By this time the German army was in difficulties. Ludendorff's tactics gave the impression of indecision and lines of communication were stretched just when the RAF came into action. Troops deserted on seeing how well fed the Allies were. No attempt was made to consolidate.

(e) The Battle of Amiens (8–15 August). Haig with 604 tanks cleared Amiens and gained 15 miles of front. Byng crossed the Ancre and reached Bapaume on 29 August and a series of punching attacks recaptured all lost ground.

(f) The Hindenburg Line was the next objective, and on 26 September it was attacked. In the north (fourth Ypres) the line was turned, in the centre the French entered St Quentin, but in the Argonne the inexperienced Americans lost 100,000 at St Mihiel.

Ludendorff decided on 29 September that the Germans must surrender, but he was determined this should not be unconditional since German armies still stood on allied soil, and after a fortnight of negotiations over the Fourteen Points he was all for carrying on a defensive war in 1919. He was dismissed on 26 October because such arguments were becoming absurd—the Germans had lost a third of their guns, their allies were being knocked out, the Allied Forces had 385,000 prisoners.

(g) In the north the fifth battle of Ypres (14–20 October) freed the coast, German resistance was broken at Cambrai and Le Cateau; Bruges and Lille were occupied. On 11 November Mons was entered.

(h) In the south Americans and French were slowing down, but after 5 November the pace quickened again, and became a rout. Only transport difficulties held up more rapid advance, and there was only one rested German division left.

C. European Sideshows

In any European history of the Great War the campaigns in the Balkans, Italy and Russia would be given greater space than is necessary in a British history, for although Britain gave aid in all three spheres her contribution was always a small one. Those like Lloyd George who wanted to enlarge it failed until the last year of the war, but there was always a plentiful supply of reasons for going to the aid of allies with troops or supplies.

C1. The Balkan Wars

Austrian incompetence meant that in December 1914 Belgrade was still in Serbian hands. This fact, and Russian requests for diversions, led Asquith and then Lloyd George to become involved in the Balkans. The only Balkan state which openly favoured Germany was Bulgaria which, in spite of tempting allied offers at the expense of Greece, signed an alliance with Germany in September which cleared the way for a double attack on Serbia in October 1915. By 23 November the Serbs were in retreat, and were evacuated by sea. This German southward thrust led the British to three interventions:

(*a*) In October 1915 a Franco-British force violated Greek neutrality and occupied Salonika with 50,000 troops. A series of northward offensives failed due to the terrain, and deaths from typhus and malaria.

(*b*) When King Carol of Rumania died a treaty with Germany lapsed, and by July 1916 an agreement with the allies was signed. Once again the Germans seized the country (August–December 1916) and the troops in Salonika were of no use.

(*c*) With the whole of the Balkans under German/Austrian control, Greece became vital. As early as October 1915 Britain had offered Constantine, the pro-German king, Cyprus for his support. The King scrapped the constitution and expelled Venizelos, the pro-Allied statesman. In December 1916 there were riots, so Venizelos was made leader of a rival government, and in June 1917 Constantine was deposed and Greece entered the war.

It was not until 1918 that Lloyd George got his way, partly because Clemenceau supported a more active French role.

(*d*) In September Bulgaria was invaded and, not used to flame throwers and aeroplanes, quickly surrendered. Sofia was entered on 30 September.

(*e*) The British under Milne turned south to occupy Constantinople, while the French advanced north, reaching the Danube on 10 November and forcing the Austrians to surrender on 3 November.

C2. The Italian Campaigns

Although Italy entered the war in May 1915 she was a reluctant ally, and did not make war on Germany until August 1916. The Italian army was in Lloyd George's view capable of great things, and in 1917 he urged it to take the brunt of the war. But Cadorna was incompetent as commander, and the officers were of little use. The Italians lacked war industries, and were a drain on Allied finance (Britain lent £370m). The terrain was worse than the Western Front, the troops were ill trained and badly looked after. On the Carso 200 a day died of frostbite, and there were frequent desertions since the war was near to the main cities. There were anti-war riots in Venice and Turin, and Italian losses were much greater in proportion to the other Allies.

(*a*) From June 1915 to August 1917 the Italians fought 11 battles of Isonzo in the Alps to force a way into Austria. Apart from a major success at Gorizia the Italians gained about seven miles, and a twelfth attack which would have broken the Austrians was called off.

(*b*) In February 1917 Austria reorganised, helped by the Germans. An offensive was launched when the Italians were in disarray. In October the Italians were defeated at Caporetto, and forced to retreat.

(*c*) British aid was sent, and an Austrian offensive in June 1918 was contained. On 23 October the battle of Vittorio Veneto began, and helped by British engineers the Italians advanced rapidly. An armistice was concluded at Villa Giusti on 4 November.

C3. The Russian Front

At the start of the war public confidence in Russia's 15 million troops was such that they were rumoured to have landed in Scotland, but the Russian front of 550 miles facing Germany and Austria meant that they were confined to one theatre of the war. The Germans undermined Russia directly by defeats and indirectly by encouraging subject nationalities and pro-Germans at court. They even supported the Bolsheviks, and brought Lenin to Russia in a secret service operation in April 1917. The war in the east consisted of offensives over vast tracts of territory, owing to the lack of defensive lines and poor communications.

(*a*) During 1914 the Russians mobilised quickly, and defeated the Germans. They invaded Austria, captured Lemberg and defeated the Austrians. The German counter-attack defeated the Russians at Tannenberg and two battles of the Masurian Lakes.

(*b*) At first in 1915 it looked as if Russian victories would continue. The Austrians were defeated at Prsemysl, but a counter-attack recaptured Prsemysl and Lemberg and entered Warsaw in August. A great German offensive cost the Russians 2 million losses, and drove them back 200 miles to Brest Litovsk. It was this situation that called forth the Dardanelles efforts.

(*c*) After economic and political changes the situation in Russia improved, and Brusilov was able to launch an offensive against the Austrians in June 1916. It petered out before Lemberg, but had cost the Central Powers in casualties.

By the end of 1916, with 30 per cent of her industry and 16 per cent of her territory in enemy hands, Russia was in a serious condition made worse by government muddle. The Czar dominated a series of weak ministers, there was corruption and incompetence and, above all, economic chaos. The allies were determined to keep Russia in the war; Kitchener was going there when he was drowned. In January 1917 Milner arrived, and after Kerensky took over in March aid was promised, and a port constructed at Murmansk to bring in supplies.

(*d*) This was followed by the last Russian offensive which ended in defeat at Tarnopol. The Bolshevik Revolution occurred in October and in November an armistice was signed. Peace negotiations opened, at Brest Litovsk, and a peace treaty was signed in March 1918.

This presented the allies with grave problems since vast areas of Russia fell into German hands. New states were set up on the German Baltic coast. Russian recognition of Poland was matched by Allied recognition of the Czechs, whose army fighting in Russia was cut off. British and Japanese troops landed at Vladivostock to help the Czechs in April, and in July 1918 intervened in northern Russia at Archangel and Murmansk to protect supplies. In August, British intervention in southern Russia began with a force to protect the oil supplies at Baku (Chapter 4, C2).

D. Conquest of the Ottoman Empire

After Turkey joined Germany in October 1914, Britain had an excuse
for eliminating German influence in the area. Cyprus and Egypt were annexed. With half an eye on the Moslems in India, Britain also supported
the Arabs as a counter to the Turks, and two campaigns were fought in
Palestine and Mesopotamia involving a million troops which constituted
her second largest war effort.

D1. The Dardanelles Expedition: 1915–16

Discussion of what rôle Britain would take against Turkey was given
added point by a Russian appeal in January 1915, and the War Council
under the promptings of Lloyd George, Churchill and Fisher accepted the
concept of forcing the Straits and taking Constantinople. At the time it was
feasible, and had it succeeded would have probably taken Turkey out of
the war. Failure came from tactics, not the strategy.

(a) The failure at sea. The preliminary bombardment was a success and two
forts were destroyed, but it was decided to use old ships (March); ammunition
ran out, and when the ships hit a minefield, it was decided to withdraw.

(b) Without a meeting of the War Council it was decided to substitute a
military landing to clear the guns. It was estimated that only 150,000 would be
needed, and a force under Sir Ian Hamilton was assembled, and found to be
so lacking in organisation that it retired to Egypt to organise, thus warning the
Turks.

The Turks, organised by Kemal Pasha, now had six divisions instead of
two ready to meet Britain's seven.

(c) The first landing took place in April with the loss of 6,000 men. Lack of
landing craft, delays and the absence of Hamilton on board ship meant no
attempt was made to leave the beaches where the troops were pinned down.

Kitchener resolved to strengthen the army to 12 divisions, augmenting the
Anzacs and adding fresh troops under Stopford. Hamilton's plan was to
capture the heights from Gabe Tepe to Maidos with a three-pronged attack
of ANZACS on Sari Bair, a British diversion at Achi Baba and a new
landing at Suvla Bay.

(d) Unhappily the three commanders did not cooperate. The Suvla Bay landings failed to capture Anafarta Heights, and a second attempt also failed.
Attacks on Achi Baba and Sari Bair were beaten off, and even Asquith was
driven to say the generals ought to be court-martialled.

Months of argument followed until Kitchener was sent out and decided on
evacuation. This was carried out in December and January without loss.
Total casualties were 200,000, of which half died of illnesses ranging from
dysentery to frostbite. At home Fisher's career was finished and Churchill's
interrupted.

D2. The March to Jerusalem

Germany stirred up Turks and tribesmen in Libya, and Britain's position in Egypt was threatened. After subduing the tribesmen, it was decided to advance against Turkey.

(*a*) The first advance was led by Sir Archibald Murray. A new railway and water pipeline were laid, and Murray then tried to advance up the coast only to be defeated at Gaza (March–April 1917).

(*b*) The Arab Alliance. On 5 June 1916 the Hashemite ruler, Hussein, revolted and captured Mecca. The pro-Arabists in Egypt sent Sir Ronald Storrs to investigate and with him Lawrence, who became friends with Feisal. Britain promised Hussein an Arab kingdom if he would launch a guerilla war.

(*c*) The war was successful, holding down 50,000 Turks. The railway line was sabotaged, and in July 1917 Aqaba captured. The British gave gold and armoured cars to this effective fifth column.

Murray was replaced by Sir Edmund Allenby who fought a slow but brilliant campaign.

(*d*) Victories at Beersheba (17 October), Gaza and Jaffa (7–16 November) cleared the way for desert advances with cavalry, and on 9 December Jerusalem was captured.

(*e*) Lawrence and Allenby did not trust each other, and after a victory at Tafila (January 1918) Lawrence wintered at Kerak. An attack on Ma'an failed. Consequently, although Allenby took Jericho (February 1918) he was held at Salt when he crossed the Jordan.

(*f*) On 19 September Allenby advanced, aided by a diversionary raid on Derna. 15,000 cavalry cut the Turks' lines and defeated them at Megiddo. Damascus fell on 1 October and Aleppo on 26 October.

In October, backed by Lawrence, Feisal proclaimed the Arab kingdom in Damascus and the Middle East problem had begun. The campaign had tied down 150,000 Turks, and secured British Mediterranean power. An armistice was concluded at Mudros (30 October) and on 13 November the Allied fleets anchored at Constantinople (Chapter 4, A5 and C5).

D3. 'Mespot' and the March to Baghdad

With oil increasing in importance, and German threats, it was decided to intervene in 'Mespot' 'to maintain the authority of our flag in the East' (Asquith). Unwisely there was divided authority until February 1916 and by then the makings of a great defeat.

(*a*) In November 1914 Sir John Nixon landed at Basra, and secured the oil wells. It was decided to advance, lacking numbers, transport or medical supplies for a desert war. Instead of three only one division set out under Sir Charles Townshend, and 500 miles from base was forced to fall back on Kut.

(*b*) The Siege of Kut (3 December–29 April 1915). The Turks could bring up reinforcements, but Britain could not. In the town medical supplies ran low, and men were forced to eat mules; 8,000 were taken, and nearly all perished in a desert march to Aleppo.

Sir Stanley Maude took over, some 300,000 troops were committed and major reforms carried out. Kut was recaptured on 24 February 1917, and Baghdad occupied on 11 March as a vital rail and road link. Troops were then despatched into Persia. Maude advanced, defeating the Turks at Ramadi, but he died of typhoid on 18 November, and was succeeded by Marshall, who continued north reaching Mosul on 3 November 1918.

E. War on the High Seas

The British Grand Fleet under Jellicoe and, after November 1917, Beatty, was the most important factor in Britain's war effort. Its commander 'was the only man on either side who could lose the war in an afternoon'. This was not because defeat would be followed by invasion. Such an enterprise was not discussed by the German General Staff. It was because of the other tasks the navy performed. Twenty million troop journeys were made across the Channel without loss, and supplies likewise had to pass unmolested across the narrow seas. A distant blockade of Germany was enforced which it has been estimated accounted for the death of 670,000 and helped to bring about a revolutionary situation by November 1918. Naval power gave freedom of manoeuvre to help allies, and protect our interests. It was only in submarine warfare that the Germans came close to success, and their rigour in that respect cancelled out neutral objections to Britain's blockading policy, and helped to bring America into the war. The value of naval power was demonstrated on the first day of the war, when Germany's submarine cables were cut.

E1. North Sea Clashes

The war started with an attempt to entice the Germans from their bases and a battle with Hipper's cruisers at Heligoland (28 August) in which the enemy lost four ships. This was balanced during the year by four British losses by submarine or mine which caused the fleet to take station off north-west Scotland for a time. In December the Germans bombarded Whitby, Scarborough and Hartlepool, and escaped in fog. When they made a second attempt on the Tyne in January 1915 they were intercepted on the Dogger Bank and one ship was sunk, but owing to a communications mix-up they managed to escape. Raids on the English coast continued. Lowestoft was attacked three times, and as late as January 1918 the Thanet resorts were attacked. Early in 1916 the Germans sent out five commerce raiders into the North Sea. Only two were caught although they were driven back to base by early 1918.

In May 1916 came what many thought would be the decisive encounter between the main fleets, with 145 British and 110 German ships involved in the Battle of Jutland, but the result was indecisive. Germany lost one battleship, one battle cruiser, four armoured cruisers and five destroyers and Britain lost three battle cruisers, three armed cruisers and eight destroyers, comparable tonnages of 61,000 and 112,000 respectively, but if the two German battleships permanently disabled were added, the German tonnage lost would be 119,000. The German Fleet made forays into the North Sea in August 1916 and April 1918, but its morale was seriously weakened, and it played no further part in the war. When it was ordered to make a last-ditch stand by Scheer in October 1918 mutiny broke out and on 3 November the Red Flag was raised at Kiel.

E2. Oceans of the World

The other German fleet was in the Far East under Von Spee, but when the Japanese laid siege to Kiao-Chow (2 September–7 November) it was forced to disperse:

(*a*) The *Emden* went into the Indian Ocean, where it sank 70,000 tons of shipping before it was destroyed off the Cocos Islands (9 November 1914) by the Australian Navy.

(*b*) Von Spee sailed across the Pacific defeating the British at Coronel (1 November). He pursued the survivors into the South Atlantic where he was defeated by Sturdee at the Falkland Islands (8 December) with the loss of four ships.

(*c*) The commerce raider *Dresden* escaped, but was forced to scuttle at Juan Fernandez in March 1915.

E3. Naval Blockade

In Napoleonic times Britain had adopted a close blockade of ports, but in the Great War relied on a distant blockade which interfered with neutral shipping. Britain also defined contraband in such a way as to offend neutral opinion. Blockade was regulated by agreements in 1856 and 1909 and although Britain had not ratified the latter Asquith stuck to it until July 1916. A full blockade started in March 1915 with the Reprisals Order after the Germans had announced that they would not pick up survivors, and in February 1916 the Ministry of Blockade was set up to wage economic war in spite of growing protests from America and the Scandinavian countries, since the effects there were serious. However, the blockade had the desired result. The Turnip Winters in Germany from 1916, and the starvation of Vienna by January 1918, made a contribution to victory.

E4. Submarine War

During the war 22,258 naval and 14,661 merchant service men were killed, and the majority perished in the submarine war. The Germans claimed rules of war did not apply to craft under the surface, and behaved accordingly. They abandoned survivors and attacked passenger and neutral ships, and this continued even while they pleaded for favourable treatment. On 12 October 1918 the passenger ship *Leinster* was sunk with 450 deaths. This sinking was one indication that the campaign against the U-boats, ingenious though it was, was not outstandingly successful: 178 were destroyed, but 142 remained to surrender in November 1918. The submarine was Germany's blockade of the Allies, and the sinking of 40 per cent of British merchant shipping and the start of rationing were evidence that it was successful. But by May 1918, after the Ministry of Shipping and the Admiralty had been reorganised, Britain was building ships faster than they were being sunk, and in that sense the U-boats were beaten. The struggle can be divided into three periods:

(*a*) Limited U-boat warfare from February to December 1915 started with random sinkings, and then systematic attacks including the *Lusitania*, with the loss of 128 American lives. The amount sunk rose from 241,201 tons in 1914 to 855,721 tons in 1915, but the Kaiser still urged restraint, and this was applied in September 1915.

(*b*) Intensified U-boat warfare from February to December 1916, when the Germans announced they would attack neutrals. Britain armed merchant ships and sent out Q-ships (disguised) which sank 11 U-boats. American protests over sinkings like the *Sussex* increased, and hospital ships like the *Britannic* (November) were sunk.

There was conflict in Germany between Bethmann Hollweg and the

General Staff about how ruthless war should be, but after peace proposals collapsed and Ludendorff came to power, the third phase began.

(c) Unrestricted submarine warfare was declared in February 1917 and continued to the end. Tonnage sunk increased rapidly, and then tailed off as countermeasures were taken from 1,237,634 tons in 1916 to 3,729,785 tons in 1917 and 1,694,749 tons in 1918.

At home Lloyd George cleared out Carson and Jellicoe and adopted firm measures to deal with the situation when he found Admiralty contentions that 2,500 ships leaving ports were too many to defend were false since the actual figure was 140; the rest being coastal shipping. The measures were:

(a) The laying of barrages. The Dover Barrage was started in April 1917. A North Sea Barrage was nearly completed from Scotland to Norway.

(b) The Harwich and Dover Patrols were formed. On 23 April 1918 they raided Zeebrugge and Ostend sinking ships in both harbours although not completely blocking them.

(c) On 26 April 1917 Lloyd George insisted on convoys, and on 10 May the first Atlantic one sailed. The Scandinavian in April and the Mediterranean in July completed the picture.

(d) By December 1917, 3,084 minesweepers and patrol boats were at work; 90 U-boats were attacked from the air. Camouflage and the hydrophone helped evasion, and depth charges and mines were improved.

Further Reading

Barker, A. J., *The Forgotten War* (Mesopotamia), Faber and Faber, London, 1967

Falls, C., *The First World War*, Longmans, London, 1960.

Gilbert, M. (ed.), *First World War Atlas*, Weidenfeld and Nicolson, London, 1970.

Liddell Hart, B. H., *T. E. Lawrence in Arabia and After*, Jonathan Cape, London, 1945.

Liddell Hart, B. H., *The First World War*, Cassell, London, 1970.

Marder, A., *From Dreadnought to Scapa Flow*, Oxford University Press, London, 1961–66, 3 vols.

Moorhead, A., *Gallipoli*, Hamish Hamilton, London, 1956, reprinted in illustrated edition, Macmillan, Australia, 1975.

Palmer, A., *The Gardeners of Salonika* (The Balkans), André Deutsch, London, 1965.

Taylor, A. J. P., *The First World War*, Hamish Hamilton, London, 1963, available in Penguin Paperback, 1966.

Terraine, J., *The Western Front 1914–1918*, Hutchinson, London, 1964.

Questions

1. What part did Great Britain play in the winning of the Great War?
2. What criticisms can be made of the 'sideshows' in the First World War, and how valid were they?
3. To what extent was the series of defeats on the Western Front inevitable?
4. Did the navy live up to expectations in the Great War?
5. Why is the Dardanelles Campaign so important in any critical assessment of the war?
6. What were the main difficulties in Anglo-French relations during the Great War?
7. Why was Britain involved in two campaigns in the Middle East during the First World War?

THE GREAT WAR: POLITICS, ECONOMICS AND SOCIETY
1914–18

The term 'Great War' used to describe the conflict reflects the impact it had on contemporary minds. It was spoken of as 'the war to end all wars', securing ultimate victory but costing dearly in lives and, to a lesser extent, resources. Since then the impact of the war has been widened to include the decline of the Empire, and even of Western civilisation as a whole. The war impressed because of the numbers involved; abroad it was the first war with a mass conscript army; at home, the first in which an important part of industrial life was kept going by women. It impressed because of the technical and social changes that it brought about, and the massive cost.

In recent years the word 'revolutionary' has increasingly been applied to its impact on Britain. Historians have argued for a degree of disillusionment among workers combined with augmented power and military experience which brought about a '1917 situation' in Britain in 1919. Marwick in *The Deluge* deals with the socio-economic impact of the war, and states that it is too strong to call the changes revolutionary. Some of them, like government intervention or women's political rights, were advancing under their own momentum, and were in some ways reversed after the war during a 'back to normal' period. Barnett in *The Decline of British Power* stressed the impact of technical and scientific change, and the revelation of imperial weakness leading to demands for dominion status. He spoke of an 'industrial revolution carried through at breakneck pace'. The change in the rôle and structure of the government after 1916 has been described by Taylor as a revolution British style, and commentators at the time spoke of the sudden eclipse of the old political and social world before war profiteers. Pollard has drawn attention to the increase in taxation, the spread of government into industry and trade, the regulation of matters like the housing market, and the direct involvement of organised labour in government. None of these moves was made by Liberals or Tories with much willingness, and certainly not to increase the trend towards democracy and socialism—but that was the effect as the coming of 'one man, one vote' and of Labour as the official Opposition in 1918 was to prove. Yet Mowat argued that in the 1920s much of the old order had 'changed little', and the interwar period was Conservative-dominated.

The Great War has in recent years been subjected to a barrage of criticism by historians, and one publication describes it as 'the foulest war in history' where 'while statesmen and generals blundered, the massed armies writhed in a festival of mud and blood'. Revisionism is bound to occur, and is happening in relation to the Second World War, but in the case of the Great War it has been particularly savage. Criticism has come from those who dislike all wars and therefore this one in particular, since it was won by the forces of reaction after a frightful conflict. Left-wing historians like to see it as capitalism gone mad with armament barons and colonial investors urging the masses to death on the barbed wire. Others confine

themselves to particular aspects such as war profiteering or military incompetence. This chapter looks at the impact of the war on society, and
then at the changes it produced.

A. The Impact of the Great War

A1. Total War

Watson states the war was 'the most bloody the world has ever experienced', whereas there have been numerous wars more bloody. Britain lost
a smaller proportion of its population than America during the Civil War.
The economic impact of the Second World War was far worse than that of
the Great War. Trench war was terrible, but the civilian population of
Britain was largely spared the horrors of the Second World War, and far
fewer women were killed. There were fewer deaths from atrocities and
starvation, and new weapons actually reduced the rate of slaughter rather
than increasing it, as in the Second World War. Excluding Empire casualties, Britain's dead numbered 702,410, of which 512,564 were killed on the
Western Front. One and a half million seriously wounded should be taken
into account. France lost twice as many in proportion to her population,
and Italy nearly three times as many in a shorter time. There was much
talk of the slaughter of a generation, but this argument cannot be sustained.
The percentage fall of males in the population was slight, and the loss of
population by death, due no doubt to improved standards of living, was
less in 1911–21 than in 1901–11.

A2. War Weariness

The Great War was not over by Christmas, but it did not last as long as
the Second World War. Arguing from incompetence, class bitterness and
the sheer horror of war, historians have tried to maintain that there was a
change in mood—that patriotism became discredited, and war weariness
apparent. There is little evidence to support this argument. The cheering
crowds were followed by two and a half million volunteers. The crowds
cheered in Washington in 1917 just as vigorously when America entered
the war. The politicians became more ruthless and the generals more determined. Lloyd George and Clemenceau reflected a hardening of determination, not a weakening of will, and Lloyd George won an election as the
maker of successful war. There were mutinies in the French and Russian
armies, but no such occurrences in the British army. Successful candidates
at elections were often officers, and Eden and Macmillan were two examples
of this trend which was the reverse of the class-conscious bitterness some
historians argue existed. There were 16,000 conscientious objectors but
only 1,500 refused to do anything for the war effort. Apart from the period
May 1915 to December 1916 there was sharp party warfare, but criticism
of the war effort declined, and in parliamentary divisions on a negotiated
peace in 1917 the numbers in favour fell from 32 to 18.

Of course, the government relied on the current political climate which
saw patriotism and war as justifiable. They matched the public mood which
showed itself in anti-German riots. At the end they called loudly for retri-
bution. Such public moods were encouraged by propaganda, censorship
and the strict enforcement of the Defence of the Realm Acts (1914, 1915).

But in the end, as Taylor admits, 'No doubt the people ought to have demanded an end to war. In fact, fiercer war was from first to last the popular cause.' In June 1917 the Commission on Working Class Distress was unable to find evidence of anti-war feeling. There were 'Stop the War' demonstrations in North London in January 1916, but the workers were annoyed about conditions in factories, high prices and alleged conscription anomalies, not about grand strategy or a desire to surrender.

A3. The Evil of War
If the war was less devastating than has been claimed, why is there evidence to the contrary? The reason is that a section of intelligent and literate opinion was shocked, and this group had a strong impact on the narrow government circles of the day. The views of Clifford Allen, Lionel Curtis and John Maynard Keynes, for example, had much weight in political circles. The League of Nations Society, set up in 1915, was evidence of this feeling, and of course the left were opposed to the war on theoretical as well as human grounds, hoping for the fall of the establishment. The governing classes were shaken because they gave proportionately more. Asquith lost a son and Bonar Law lost two; the lists of dead were long in the chapels of public schools. In May 1927 Baldwin could speak of a world 'still suffering from the shock of war', and the horrors of war were one of the strongest arguments for disarmament and later for appeasement. It can be argued, as Barnett does, that the will of the governing class was sapped by the war.

These feelings were given expression by poets and memoir writers, although it should be pointed out that there was a massive literature on the other side. Many of the writers were objecting to features of the war, and not to war as such—Owen, Sassoon and Graves were all brave soldiers; and the same writers had a far more vigorous dislike of German militarism and atrocities. Often the writers of so-called anti-war literature came from sophisticated backgrounds and found themselves plunged into living conditions which the workers had to put up with already in the slums. Ordinary soldiers' memoirs are far less hysterical, and quite often have wry humour in the midst of carnage. It is also true that many critics had officers' quarters in which to write and the excellence of a classical education with which to polish their offerings. Barnett speaks of their work as 'a highly selective, unbalanced and misleading version' of the war.

As far as the mass of people was concerned the poems of Brooke and Sorley had a bigger impact than those of Rosenberg or Sassoon, and the novels of Ruby M. Ayres and Ernest Raymond exceeded anti-war books in circulation. The building of memorials after the war indicated a desire to remember not forget, and the inscriptions are rarely pacifist. During the war Lord Northcliffe's *Daily Mail* and *The Times* were the leading opinion formers, and the most popular magazine was Horatio Bottomley's *John Bull* (1906) with its hate campaigns against the Germans. There is a considerable gap between reactions to the war and what some historians have led us to believe—and this must influence our view of the political and social possibilities raised by wartime conditions.

B. Liberals and the War, August 1914–May 1915

Asquith's government entered the war with several resignations, and a philosophy which ill equipped it for the sort of war that developed by 1916. Kitchener at the War Office and Churchill at the Admiralty conducted the war with little reference to Asquith, who believed it should be left to generals and admirals. No general discussion of the war occurred in the Commons until May 1915. To some extent Asquith was the prisoner of political circumstances, since he headed a minority government dependent on Irish and Labour and had just passed the Home Rule Act, which if it secured Redmond's backing, annoyed the Tories who remained critical. Even suffragettes continued their action policy until July 1915. Asquith thus acted cautiously by nature, political philosophy and expediency, and in the end this did not prove enough. His treatment of the war is shown by looking at three major issues:

1. *Raising an army*. The army was to be raised to 70 divisions to serve for three years or the duration. As well as 2½ million men for the army, 329,000 were raised for the navy and 60,000 for the new air force. But the method used was not wise. In Ireland the Ulster Regiment was formed, but the Catholics were spread through other divisions. The slaughter of Haldane's new officers was unwise, the loss of skilled labour in mines and engineering created difficulties, and industry was diluted with unskilled labour unable to match production targets.

2. *Financing the war*. After a short panic with the bank rate at 10 per cent the economy settled down to 'business as usual'. Lloyd George's war budgets were unimaginative. The first doubled income tax to 2s 6d and raised a £450m loan. The second, in May 1915, had no new taxation. But operating in a free market the government encouraged loans to our allies which eventually totalled £1,825m.

3. *Making munitions*. A Shells Committee existed from October 1914 to January 1915, but did not succeed in reorganising the army departments or shaking Kitchener's complacency. In April 1915 a new committee was set up, and Asquith said there was no truth in the rumours of shortage. French leaked information to Repington, military correspondent of *The Times*, who published it on 14 May together with a strong attack.

Government reaction was lethargic. In February they set up a Committee on Production, and from this emerged the Treasury Agreement (March) providing for dilution and the end of restrictive practices in return for worker participation, shop stewards and limits on profits. This was a new departure but it came too late. Every restriction was criticised by Liberal members as infringing their philosophy, and in Wilson's words 'from early in the conflict the Liberal government found itself in serious difficulties'.

During May 1915 the government's difficulties became insuperable. Two events are regarded as marking the end of the ministry: the resignation of Fisher after a conflict with Churchill, which Blake and Jenkins see as more important than the second, which was the shells scandal. This view has been challenged by Wilson who argues it underestimates the impact of the general decline in the government's fortunes, political pressure by Tories, and Asquith's calculation that a coalition was necessary to stay in office. Bonar Law, for instance, criticised Asquith's complacency and contrasted him with Lloyd George, and lent support to bitter attacks on Haldane as a pro-German. It is not clear yet if there was any contact between Lloyd George and the Tories prior to the formation of a new government although some Liberals suspected it. The government had 13 Liberals, eight Unionists and one Labour member, and Asquith argued that apart from sacrificing Haldane he had triumphed since Bonar Law was relegated to minor office as Colonial Secretary, McKenna whom the Tories disliked was the new Chancellor, and Lloyd George was given the nettle of the Ministry of Munitions. Grey remained as Foreign Secretary, and the only Tory in a position of any importance was Balfour at the Admiralty. The danger of the coalition was that it opened the way to further demands for inroads into Liberal policies on the war, the economy and Ireland and that it damaged Asquith's standing.

C. The Asquith Coalition, May 1915–December 1916

The main purpose of forming the coalition was not achieved since the war was no nearer to being won after its period of office, and the campaigns were marked by a series of disasters including Gallipoli, Salonika, Kut and the Somme, which Lloyd George frequently criticised.

Many Liberals and, at this stage, the Tories did not like Lloyd George, but it was clear his dynamism contrasted brutally with Asquith's lethargy, or as Haldane said, 'I only wish the Prime Minister would be strong.' The difficulty was that in introducing conscription and crushing the Irish Rebellion, which were both strong decisions, he alienated his party without winning over the Tories. Resignations bedevilled the government, and intrigue followed in their wake so that by December 1916 the *Manchester Guardian* could say, 'The House of Commons has reached the mood where it is ready to create another ministry.' Asquith lost Carson in October and Churchill in November 1915 and this seriously weakened the fighting spirit of the ministry. In November 1916 Carson led a Tory revolt on a minor matter, and Bonar Law realised which way the wind was blowing.

This gloomy view of Asquith's coalition is not held by all historians, and Medlicott stresses that although he lost ground with his colleagues because of his lack of plan or drive, 'all the basic British preparations for victory except the convoy system had been initiated before Asquith left office; during his administration the men, including Lloyd George, were appointed who made the preparations'. It is true that Asquith succeeded in bypassing Kitchener with the appointment of Sir William Robertson, and, soon after Kitchener was drowned, paving the way for Lloyd George as War Minister. But the appointment of a committee to investigate the Kut surrender (July 1916) could only bring discredit on themselves, and in various matters such as shipping the government seemed at a loss, and Runciman said in November 1916 that nothing could be done. The government launched war finance on a new footing in September 1915, and the Reading Mission went to America to raise a £100m loan. Labour relations improved, and measures of social reform were carried out, but Asquith remained distant from labour. Conscription was introduced but in a muddled way and at the expense of the Liberal party. The government had four main achievements to its credit:

1. *Conscription Act (May 1916).* In July 1915 a National Register was

compiled to find out who was employed in various industries, and it was clear that shortages had to be balanced against increasing demand from the war fronts. Asquith disliked conscription, and in January 1916 said he would never be a party to it. He tried to retain the voluntary system by the Derby Scheme for all between 18 and 42 to attest, bachelors being called up, and exceptions created for vital industries numbering no less than 160. In January 1916 Derby said 650,000 had not attested, and this forced the government's hand. Asquith was in great difficulties because Lloyd George had advocated conscription, and was forcing the pace, while many Liberals disliked the measure. The Conscription Act of 1916 merely enforced the Derby Scheme, thus letting Asquith off the hook and avoiding an election. But it annoyed Liberals because of the severe treatment of the early conscientious objectors. Simon resigned. In April 1916 Lloyd George pressed the issue again at a time when Liberals were annoyed by the Munitions Bill and the budget. Fear of losing office forced the Liberals to give in, and in May 1916 full conscription was passed.

2. *McKenna's budgets.* The budgets of September 1915 and April 1916 were the basis of financial victory, and helped to cement relations with labour. But they infuriated orthodox liberals. They raised income tax to 5s, and introduced a profits tax of 60 per cent on 1913 levels. They first introduced a 33 per cent duty on imported luxuries like motorcars, and the second the entertainment tax. A series of Treasury and overseas loans was raised, and the National Debt had risen from £654m in 1914 to £3,856m by early 1917.

3. *Ministry of Munitions.* Kitchener offered little resistance, and by December 1915 the War Office had lost its power over munitions supply to the new ministry. Two acts (1915, 1916) made it responsible for three million workers including 800,000 women. The ministry exploited economic planning for the first time in British history, and the results were spectacular. By the end of 1915 there were 73 emergency factories and the number grew to 218 by 1918. One example will indicate the extent of its success. From 6,103 machine guns in 1915 the number rose to 120,864 in 1918. The Ministry encouraged new ideas, including the tank. The workers did not always respond well—there were troubles on the Clyde—but economic measures and conscription won the cooperation of area committees over long hours, scrapping industrial practices, and highly dangerous work. In return they secured profit and rent control, and concessions like workers' canteens of which there were 867 by the end of the war. When Lloyd George passed to the War Office in July 1916 he showed the same skills, and secured the reorganisation of transport through Sir Eric Geddes.

4. *Cooperation with the workers.* Increasing government control and calls for the nation to act together against profiteers and shirkers led to a mood of 'War Socialism', and the Labour Party conference in 1916 made demands for nationalising banks, insurance and shipping—soon afterwards the Ministry of Blockade was joined by the Ministry of Shipping. The employers organised the FBI in 1916 to make cooperation with the TUC easier, and tripartite meetings became common. In November 1916 the Trade Card Agreement left the running of factories in the hands of shop stewards' committees who proved successful. There were serious strikes in South Wales coal in 1915 and Clydeside engineering, and in the latter

area Kirkwood, Wheatley and Gallacher were developing 'Red Clydeside'; the government deported the leaders. Two measures benefited workers— the Rent Restriction Act pegged rents at 1913 levels on houses under £35 a year in London, £30 in Scotland and £26 elsewhere. Also in 1915 a Pensions Act extended the existing act. Regulation of drinking hours was held to help safety in munitions and was introduced in June 1915, covering the whole country by March 1917. The Summer Time Act (May 1916) to provide longer hours also saved heating and lighting.

D. The Political Crisis of December 1916

The fall of the Asquith coalition was brought about by four main factors. The most important was failure of the war effort and disillusion arising from Lansdowne's peace memorandum in November 1916. This roused the Tories, and gave Aitken the opportunity to urge Bonar Law to come in with Lloyd George. Balfour supported this and deserted Asquith. The generals, led by Haig and Robertson, gave support and believed Lloyd George would be a dynamic leader. Closely allied to this was the failure of Asquith as Prime Minister, for which he must take much of the blame. Wilson indeed thinks that his great fault was not resigning earlier since he had held office for nine years. Lloyd George stood to gain from the situation. He did his best to embarrass Asquith, and started to interfere in matters not his concern. In July 1916 he put forward a plan for settling Ireland which involved implementing the Home Rule Act with the exclusion of Northern Ireland. Asquith ditched the plan when Lansdowne opposed it. Lloyd George interfered in foreign policy in an interview with an American journalist when he spoke of peace manoeuvres as pro-German and advocated a knock-out blow.

The fourth factor was the decision of the Tory party to support Lloyd George. This was taken under pressure from Northcliffe and Aitken, and from Carson's War Committee with about 150 supporters. Bonar Law, who had denounced Lloyd George as careerist in June, now saw him as the leader who could combine Tories, particularly Carson and the right, with the requisite number of Liberal MPs for a majority, since their War Committee also backed Lloyd George. The ensuing seven days' crisis was thus about power and policy, and not exclusively about one or the other. On one side Aitken (Beaverbrook), supported by Taylor, argues that Lloyd George and Bonar Law acted honourably, and that Asquith sought to destroy them and retain power. On the other, Jenkins and Wilson argue the two intriguers deliberately offered Asquith conditions, particularly Carson in the cabinet and the actual composition of the new War Council, which they knew he could not accept, and thus forced him out. Asquith's failure to serve under Lloyd George was partly pique, but it was also a product of the crisis itself. By the time it started, Lloyd George had the open support of some 49 Liberals and the tacit support of some 80 more, and there was little chance that Asquith would turn and fight, and none at all of his offering a genuine compromise to split Lloyd George and Bonar Law. The stages of the crisis were:

(*a*) 1 December. Lloyd George formally proposed to Asquith a War Council with himself in the chair without the Prime Minister. On 3 December Bonar Law met Chamberlain and Curzon and told them he was going to support Lloyd George's demand. They agreed to resign, and this threat led Asquith to reconsider the War Council proposal.

(*b*) 4 December. Asquith withdrew his consent to the War Council, because his followers argued he could do without Lloyd George and partly because he was offended by a leader in *The Times* giving details of the arrangement which he maintained had been planted by Lloyd George. Asquith did not quibble over this point, but attacked the substance of the proposal to make him an 'irresponsible spectator'.

(*c*) 5 December. Lloyd George and Bonar Law resigned, and Asquith himself resigned knowing that he had no majority in the House, but refusing Cecil's suggestion that he serve under Lloyd George since he believed the new coalition would not last. He felt that treachery and insults put a barrier between him and Lloyd George. Law said he was unable to form a government without Asquith, and advised the King to send for Lloyd George.

(*d*) 6 December. Lloyd George was asked to form a government. Henderson for Labour, Bonar Law for the Tories and Addison for the back-bench Liberals rallied to the new government. During the day Balfour accepted the Foreign Office and later Curzon agreed to serve, after insisting that Churchill should not be brought in. On 7 December Lloyd George took office.

These events were of great importance. They were not a 'people versus the establishment' issue as Taylor tries to make out, with the humble Lloyd George storming the citadels of Edwardian elitism. They were the result of ruthless intrigues justified by Asquith's inadequacies and Lloyd George's successes. In Seaman's words, the crisis 'ended Asquith's effective career immediately; limited that of Lloyd George to six more years; and destroyed the Liberal Party. Its only long-term beneficiary was the Conservative Party'.

E. Lloyd George's Wartime Coalition, December 1916–November 1918

E1. New Ministers

Lloyd George restructured the cabinet by dividing it into an inner War Cabinet of five, and by doubling the number of ministers to 88. Lloyd George, Curzon, Milner, Henderson and Bonar Law made up the inner cabinet and only Bonar Law as Chancellor had departmental responsibility. Other ministers were summoned when needed, but few apart from Balfour as Foreign Secretary had much freedom of action. It was essentially a dictatorship, as the treatment of Carson showed. He was put in the Admiralty, but when he annoyed Lloyd George, was elevated to the War Cabinet (July 1917–January 1918) to keep him quiet. Henderson left in August 1917 after being outmanoeuvred by Lloyd George (see Section E3), and was replaced by Barnes. When Derby failed at the War Office, Milner was brought out of the cabinet to take charge even though he was the Prime Minister's most loyal colleague. In Taylor's words, 'the war cabinet gave little direction. It was almost as distracted as its predecessor by being theoretically responsible for everything'.

The new Prime Minister's appointments received strong praise and much criticism. They were praised because they brought in new blood, balanced labour and capital, solved the pressing problems of 1917 and brought experts into contact with their particular field. Above all, they saved the day during the worst part of the war. Lloyd George added a galaxy of new ministries. These included Food under Lord Devonport, Shipping under Sir Joseph Maclay, Labour under Hodge, Pensions under Barnes and National Service under Neville Chamberlain. Later came a Ministry of Reconstruction under Addison and an Air Ministry. Churchill was kept out until July 1917 when he obtained Munitions. These appointments had an element of 'jobs for the boys' about them, and the indiscriminate scattering of peerages had started. Some proved highly successful but others did not.

Among Lloyd George's obvious failures were Carson and Derby at the Admiralty and War Office, where they sided against him with Jellicoe and Haig and made the existing situation worse. Devonport failed at Food, and was replaced by Lord Rhondda, who worked so hard that he died. Chamberlain failed at National Service and was replaced by Auckland Geddes. But these ministerial moves created bad blood, and Lloyd George showed scant concern for the courtesies of the governing class. When the Kut Report came out he allowed Chamberlain to shoulder the whole burden and resign. When Churchill grew restive out of office Lloyd George threw the whole blame for the Dardanelles on him. When he wanted Northcliffe's support, he offered him the Air Board behind Cowdray's back and the latter resigned. It is not surprising that attempts to get Asquith to take office in May 1917 failed, and that when invited to make a joint statement of war aims in January 1918 he gave Lloyd George a cool reception.

E2. New Machinery

The war cabinet was the main instrument of policy, and met 300 times, for example, during 1917. For the first time a secretariat was created under Sir Maurice Hankey to coordinate departments and even prepare policy statements. Cabinet minutes were to be kept. In addition, a private war cabinet staff (the garden suburb) was created, and its members such as Philip Kerr and Lionel Curtis came to have influence resented by ministers. The creation of new ministries developed bureaucracy, but it also solved many problems such as rationing and convoys. The strongest criticism of the new organisation was that it divorced the civilian and military heads of government, leading to confusion in strategy (Chapter 2, A3). On the other hand, Lloyd George had two bodies that showed he was directing strategy. In January 1917 a committee of Allied prime ministers met, and in March the same year an Imperial War Cabinet was constituted to which came Jan Christian Smuts, South African defence minister.

E3. Frocks Versus Brass Hats—Wartime Politics

Lloyd George's character as an 'outsider' combined with his ruthlessness to generate an atmosphere of dislike around him. Although Asquith tried to avoid trouble, other Liberals were furious and when Montague changed sides in July 1917 he was treated like a traitor. The Unionists contained a nucleus round Carson who opposed him with the special hatred of former friends, and were particularly virulent about the return of Churchill in July 1917. More than a hundred Unionists opposed the government's intention to proceed with the reform of the franchise, and this dislike soon included the generals with whom Lloyd George had feuded for years. In the end Asquith, after drawing back from direct criticism, decided to place his influence behind this 'diehard' opposition even though he only put up perfunctory resistance to anti-Liberal measures like the extension of conscription to Ireland.

The dispute between the 'frocks' and the 'brass hats' sprang from several sources. Lloyd George wanted civilian control whereas Haig wanted to run the show himself. Lloyd George was essentially an Easterner backing Salonika and Italy while the War Office were Westerners. Lloyd George thought he was the victim of a generals' plot to use the King against him, and the generals came to believe that Lloyd George did not have the root of the matter. This is true, for he 'was not a great leader in the field of grand strategy'. His astonishing reversal from criticising the generals for the Somme losses, saying 'we are going to lose this war', to advocating the 1917 offensive and then rounding on the generals again, convinced them he was incompetent. He created a Supreme War Council to take some of the direction of the war away from the War Staff, and then secured Foch's appointment as supreme commander in April 1918. He sent troops to remote areas and poured resources into the air force and navy so that there were shortages of troops on the Western Front, and during 1918, apart from sending troops to Russia, he advocated a massive Salonika offensive. He was certainly not 'the greatest prime minister of the century' when it came to military matters.

In February 1918 he proposed a joint reserve and when Robertson resisted he told the King he would go, thus forcing Robertson to resign. Lloyd George did not gain from this manoeuvre since the new CIGS was Sir Henry Wilson, a strong Tory and Westerner. In April the Western Front nearly cracked under German attack, and Sir Frederick Maurice, who had recently resigned as Director of Military Operations, published on 7 May a statement that Lloyd George had misled the House about the strength of the army in France on 9 April. It may have been true that Haig was short (Cruttwell says by 180,000) but Maurice had prepared the figures for Lloyd George himself, and Asquith's decision to press the demand for an enquiry to a division was thus unwise, particularly since he was backing the military against their civilian superiors. The vote on 9 May was 293 for the government, and against, 98 Liberals, six Labour, one Unionist and one Irish Nationalist. The main result was to quieten the generals, and the long-term effect was to divide the Liberals more deeply, with Asquith declining the Lord Chancellorship, saying the war cabinet was a 'crazy adventure'.

The Liberals hoped for reunification since Asquith played it calmly, and Lloyd George continually made conciliatory noises in order to keep the Tories in line. Since the party machine was in Asquith's hands Lloyd George set up his own organisation and fund. On the question of new MPs, both leaders left it to the local associations. In March 1917 a prominent Asquithian stood at South Aberdeen and a strong Lloyd Georgian decided to stand also. The Prime Minister intervened to stop him and, as Wilson says, 'for all its dissension, there was still a single Liberal party both in parliament and the country'. But full unity was a long way off and when the Liberal Federation met in September 1918 it ignored the issue.

Liberals were quick to point out that with nine Labour men in the government it was the Labour party that was gaining ground.

Labour had been given a crucial rôle in government, and this encouraged left-wing forces. Red Clydeside was the centre of action with strikes in May 1917, and the formation of the United Socialist Council from the ILP and the British Socialist Party. At Leeds in June 1917 there were demands for workers' soviets on Russian lines and a negotiated peace. Henderson was sent by Lloyd George to keep Kerensky's government in the war, but on the way he met French Socialists and was so impressed that he supported the idea of an international socialist peace conference at Stockholm backed by MacDonald and Snowden. The Labour party agreed, but the government refused to issue passports, and in August Henderson resigned to be replaced as leader by William Adamson. These developments led Lloyd George to put forward war aims to forestall the left in January 1918 (Section G2), and persuaded Labour to go it alone and produce a socialist constitution in February 1918. The Bolshevik Revolution and the Treaty of Brest Litovsk became the model for Red Clydeside, and Lloyd George was no longer concerned with waging 'implacable warfare against poverty and squalidness' as he was in 1909. Now he depended on the Unionists, and an election would follow the end of the war. Labour ended the by-election truce in June.

E4. Parliamentary Reform Act 1918

The war saw women resume their traditional occupations like nursing, and take on new rôles. Para-military organisations were formed, including the Women's Volunteer Reserve and a Women's Police Force. Women took on new rôles in old occupations, becoming ambulance drivers, or resumed a traditional rôle as farm workers with the 16,000 Women's Land Army. Above all, dilution and the relaxation of social convention enabled women to do work banned by Victorian factory laws as degrading. Some 2,971,000 were working in industry by the end of the war, although many were temporary, and domestic service remained the major occupier. Perhaps the most daring job was that of 'clippie', or bus conductress, first seen in February 1916, of which there were eventually 117,000. The rôle of women in clerical work expanded, and 934,000 were occupied in commerce.

Once the WSPU had faded into the background the NUWSS put forward the demand for voting rights, and won over Asquith. But the government decided on a wider measure because the lack of an election in 1916 meant there was time to prepare electoral reform. There was a demand that those who had fought should also vote, and Lloyd George's radicalism was favourable to this change. By January 1917 a Speaker's Conference had reported in favour of reform, and by the time the bill passed the Commons, only 55 opposed votes for women. In the Lords there was delay since proportional representation was in vogue for the first time, and after this had been added, the Act came into force in June 1918.

(*a*) The vote was given to all men over 21, and all over 19 who had been in combat with a six-month residence qualification. Conscientious objectors were disqualified for five years.

(*b*) The vote was given to all women over 30 who were local government electors or the wives of such, or possessed a degree or its equivalent.

(c) Provision was made for service voting for the first time.

(d) Plural voting was allowed to continue but limited to one additional vote.

(e) The university seats continued, but with the single transferable vote system.

(f) A deposit of £150 to deter frivolous candidates was started, and electoral procedure changed so that voting occurred on one day only.

(g) Apart from 10 two-member boroughs the rest of the country was divided into constituencies which were roughly equal in population.

Although there were still signs that property was given undue weight this was a major advance, and the electorate rose from 8¼ million to 21 million, of which 8½ million were now women. Some of its provisions were not enacted, in particular that on PR. As far as women were concerned the Act was followed by further reforming measures opening the professions, giving equal academic status, and strengthening legal rights. The long-term results were to provide Labour with a mass vote, and to provide the Tories with an inbuilt majority of women voters.

E5. Winning the War

Sir Maurice Hankey said, 'I wish to place on record my conviction that the man who won the war was David Lloyd George', but Taylor's view of Lloyd George as the greatest prime minister of the century cannot be sustained. In military matters he was noticeably deficient, and his personal character was neither moral nor impressive. The political scene, in Seaman's words, 'is one of the most distasteful features of the war', and on many grounds Churchill towers above him. But that does not detract from his achievements in social reform, and his capacity for organisation, change and getting things done, or as Spender put it, 'His successor had all the qualities in which Asquith was deficient. He knew how to arouse and excite, to manage crowds and newspapers, to keep at the highest pitch the grand high pressure of bustle and excitement which is proper in war-time.' He was a master politician and handled relations with all three parties so that he was retained in office at the end. His skills in five main areas illustrate these qualities:

(a) *Finance.* Bonar Law continued McKenna's policies. Income tax rose to 6s and profits tax to 80 per cent. Total revenue from taxes went up from £94m to £721m during the war, but by 1918 was only covering 36 per cent of expenditure. In particular purchases from abroad caused intermittent dollar crises. The government continued to borrow heavily and in February 1917 obtained a £1,000m loan. At home Bonar Law developed the issuing of War Bonds and introduced National Savings. Overseas investments equivalent in value to £300m were sold. In the end Britain lent £1,825m and borrowed £1,340m, the gap being made up by the sale of government securities. In Taylor's words: 'The war caused astonishingly little damage to her financial position in the world.' This was a major achievement.

(b) *Manpower.* The demands of battlefield and factory floor began to conflict. In March 1917 the Trade Card Agreement was replaced by more limited exemptions, and the Manpower Act of February 1918 swept away more. The final Conscription Act of April 1918 called up all between 18 and 50. With the need for greater production the shop stewards grew in strength and in December 1917 a national agreement recognised their position. The government appointed a Committee on Working Class Discontent in June 1917, which reported complaints about social problems, and Lloyd George's reforms and taxation policy reflected a need to conciliate. But the left gained ground, and by December 1917 the TUC and Labour demanded a negotiated peace. Lloyd George responded with a declaration of war aims and schemes for reconstruction, culminating in a speech on 12 November 1918, saying, 'Revolution I am not afraid of, Bolshevism I am not afraid of, it is reaction I am afraid of.' By the summer of 1918 there were widespread strikes. Lloyd George also started Whitley Councils (1917) for arbitration of wage disputes and discussion of working conditions.

(c) *Food*. The submarine campaign reached its height in 1917 and Lloyd George was determined to prevent starvation. In this he did not quite succeed since the average diet contained less than the minimum of calories. By the end of the war 85 per cent of foodstuffs were government controlled, the main exceptions being milk, fish and vegetables, and the government stemmed accusations of hoarding, black-market profiteering and favouritism. This was done by direct intervention in the market including bulk purchase, measures to control shipping and increase supplies and the introduction of rationing in February 1918, and measures, particularly the Corn Production Act (1917), to encourage a reversal of the pre-war trend away from arable, which doubled wheat acreage.

(d) *Industry*. Without any specific end in mind except winning the war, government increased its control over industry. By 1917 only 5 per cent of coal profits, for example, remained in the owners' hands. In 1918 the Committee on Commercial and Industrial Policy reviewed these changes, and suggested they should continue. Labour and a good many Liberals like Churchill and Lloyd George accepted nationalisation. Industry also profited from government aid in modernising and in 1916 the Department of Scientific and Industrial Research, with a budget of £200m, was established. Precision industries such as ball-bearings, magnetoes, pressure gauges and machine tools were swiftly developed. But it is important to realise that these changes were often initiated because of high profits, and that businessmen now played a far more important rôle in government. Directly war ended it was likely the trend would be reversed.

(e) *Reconstruction*. Under Addison the Ministry of Reconstruction began to provide blueprints advocating a national health scheme, new housing standards, local government reform, planning and changes in banking and industry. Some measures of social reform such as the Pensions Act (1916) and the Maternity Act (1918) were carried during the war, and the most important of these was Fisher's Education Act (1918), requiring all LEAs to draw up schemes covering all stages of education, and proposing a leaving age of 14.

F. The Irish Rebellion of 1916

The suspension of Home Rule and the treatment of Catholic Irish volunteers played into the hands of extremists, and in September 1914 the Irish Republican Brotherhood agreed to rebel against Britain. Support was sought in Germany and this policy coincided with German plans, so an agreement was signed in March 1916. The IRB was an American-based group founded in 1858 and financed by Clan na Gael, which had infiltrated the Irish Volunteers. Some 10,000 of these and, after January 1916, the Citizen Army provided a nucleus of military force, and £2m of American money provided the funds to buy arms. The O'Rahilly organised gunrunning, and arms were brought from Germany in April 1916. In Ireland emigration had largely ceased with the submarine campaign, and this left unemployed malcontents about. The coalition government included the supporters of Ulster like Bonar Law and Carson. Demonstrations started and priests prayed for German victory.

F1. Rebellion

The IRB was organised at two levels: on the surface MacNeill and Pearse, but behind the scenes a secret council with Pearse, Plunkett and Connolly. The plan was to seize Dublin while provincial risings held down troops. But the capture of Casement when he landed from a German submarine persuaded MacNeill that it was futile, and he countermanded Pearse's orders. As a result many did not act, and not more than 2,000 were involved in the rebellion (24–29 April). After sharp fighting the rebels were forced to surrender. The casualty figures were:

	Army	*Police*	*Rebels (and supporters)*
Killed	103	17	450 (only 52 IRB)
Wounded	357 + 9 missing	26	2,614

F2. Retribution

When the rebels marched to jail the people of Dublin booed them, for many had relatives fighting in the British forces, and rebellion in wartime was a serious crime. The government proclaimed martial law, and General Sir John Maxwell proceeded to punish the rebels. Between 3 and 12 May 15 were executed, including Pearse and Connolly, although under pressure from Redmond other sentences were commuted, including MacNeill and DeValera; 160 were convicted by courts-martial, and 1,862 were interned at Frongoch in Wales. On 25 May Asquith decided on a fresh attempt at settlement and Lloyd George was brought in as negotiator. After a conference with Carson and Redmond a settlement was in sight, since both Redmond and Carson saw the danger of being outbid by extremists, but Tory opposition killed the Heads of Agreement. When the detainees were released a fresh attempt was made—the Irish Convention (July 1917–April 1918)—but although there was some hope until Redmond died in March 1918, this also failed.

F3. Sinn Fein

The treatment of the rebels strengthened republicanism and this played into the hands of Sinn Fein who, in March 1917 proclaimed a National Assembly. In October they held their first convention, and the following month DeValera was elected joint president with Griffiths. A series of by election victories showed the extent of their support. The Irish Volunteers were reconstituted under Cathal Brugha with Michael Collins as Director of Organisation. When the Irish opposed the Conscription Act and a general strike was called, Lloyd George resorted to repression. Field Marshall Lord French became Viceroy, and in May 1918 the leaders of Sinn Fein were arrested although a few like Collins and Brugha escaped. The republican organisations were banned and some 1,100 political internees arrested. These moves did not deter Sinn Fein, and in the election of December 1918, 73 candidates, of which 34 were in prison, were returned. There were 26 Unionists divided between Ulstermen under Carson and Southern Loyalists under Lord Midleton. Only seven Home Rulers were returned and Dillon, their leader, lost his seat. Thus Lloyd George found himself, like Gladstone, faced with the choice of conciliation or coercion, and retaining power with a Tory majority he had little choice (Section 5E).

G. Foreign Policy During the Great War

G1. Allies and Secret Treaties

In August 1914 Britain, France and Russia were at war with Germany and Austria. Both sides tried to undermine their opponents and bring in fresh allies. Japan entered at once under the terms of the 1905 treaty, and in September the allies pledged themselves not to make a separate peace. The Central powers were not successful in their diplomacy although they managed to persuade Turkey (October 1914) and Bulgaria (October 1915) to join them. However, they benefited from Russia's change of government, since Britain's former ally published the details of the secret treaties made during the war and then accepted Brest Litovsk (March 1918). The Germans sought to provoke revolt in Ireland and made plans for undermining British influence in the Middle East.

The allies were joined by Italy (May 1915), then Portugal (March 1916), Rumania (August 1916) and Greece, which was dragged in against her will in June 1917. Provoked by submarine warfare and clumsy German diplomacy, America entered in April 1917, although she signed no treaty of alliance since this would have required ratification from Congress. During these changes Grey and Balfour committed Britain to contradictory promises which laid the basis for confusion at Versailles. The main treaties were:

(a) *Between the allies.* The Treaty of London (May 1915) promised Italy all Italia Irredenta, a mandate of Albania, an area of Asia Minor and colonial benefits. The Treaty of Chantilly (July 1916) promised Rumania so much territory that it would double in size. The Treaty of St Jean de Maurienne (April 1917) made further promises to Italy. Britain and France made a treaty with Japan in February 1917 promising her considerable territory in China. There was no common policy in these treaties, and the result was that 'the Conference of Versailles was guided by much the same considerations as the Congress of Vienna' as each party tried to interpret the conflicting claims.

(b) *About the Middle East.* In July 1914 the Kaiser said Germany 'must inflame the whole Moslem world to a savage uprising against this hateful, devious unscrupulous nation of shopkeepers.' The entry of Turkey on their side gave them an opportunity and Britain was thus involved in the Middle East. The Eastern Committee (March 1918) and a group including Cromer and Kitchener urged Britain to adopt a pro-Arab policy. McMahon negotiated an agreement with Hussein of the Hedjaz promising an Arab state in Syria. The British also made a promise of greater self-government to India (August 1917) to court favour with Moslems. But she had to consider her ally, France, who had interests in the area, and in May 1916 the Sykes–Picot Agreement partitioned the Middle East between the two. As a third complication reliance on Jewish international finance led to the Balfour Declaration (November 1917), which promised an unspecified homeland to the Jews.

(c) *With subject nationalities.* A group of academics urged the Foreign Office to back self-determination to break up Austria–Hungary and please expatriates in America who could influence elections. A conference of Oppressed Nationalities at Rome in June 1918 was one reflection of this policy, and a number were recognised, such as the Czechs and Poles. Unfortunately, while promising a greater Serbia Britain had promised a large part of it to Italy, and such conflicts cut across the principle of self-determination at the peace conference.

The secret treaties may have obtained Britain fresh allies (and fresh fighting commitments) but in the end proved to be millstones that dragged Versailles below the waters of success.

G2. Warmongers and Peace Merchants

At the start of the war the main aim was to prevent Germany from obtaining hegemony in Europe and to rescue Belgium. In November 1915 Asquith added the liberation of Serbia, and subordinate aims arose as the war changed its course. Traditional diplomacy was affected by the need to help civilian morale and meet the demands of labour, and by pressure groups advocating self-determination for smaller nations or a league of nations to prevent another war. Lansdowne's peace letters in 1916 and 1917 evoked a response on the left, and forced the government's hand so that by January 1918 Lloyd George had elaborated more detailed aims. These included the return of Alsace Lorraine, an independent Poland, recognition for the subject races of the Austrian Empire and a league of nations. Britain thus became closely involved in European diplomacy.

Surprisingly, the first proposals to be officially put forward came from Germany. They were put forward on 18 December and rejected on 30 December 1916 because they sounded more like the terms of a victor. Austria was more civilised, and under a new Emperor, Karl IV, opened peace discussions at Crillon in April 1917. These dragged on between Smuts and Mensdorff until December 1917 but were broken off because British promises to Italy and Serbia were too heavy a price for Austria to pay. The most persistent advocate of peace terms was President Wilson of America, who put forward proposals on 20 December 1916 which were rejected on 10 January by Lloyd George. When America entered the war, Wilson made a declaration of war aims stating they were fighting for democracy and world peace, and as the war went on Wilson's proposals for a settlement grew increasingly idealist. They included the Fourteen Points (8 January 1918), Four Principles, Four Ends, and Five Particulars. The Allies were annoyed by these, but the Germans accepted them on 23 October as a basis for negotiations. It was not until 4 November that the Supreme Allied Council considered the Fourteen Points and made modifications. Whatever Wilson might proclaim, he had feet of clay, and the European allies had suffered too much to be idealistic. As Seaman says, 'A peace which in large measure satisfied the wishes of the French and British governments was inevitable because their forces and not those of the United States had done the fighting in the war, and because they had not officially accepted the Fourteen Points and were determined not to.'

G3. Great Britain and the United States

Before 1914 relations between America and Britain had not been good after the failure of Chamberlain's proposals for alliance in 1898–99. America was a major economic competitor, and in the Far East her open-door policy in China conflicted with Britain's Japanese alliance and commercial interests. In South America the United States backed the Monroe Doctrine and sided against Britain in Venezuela and Panama. They were republican and anti-colonial except where they were concerned to build themselves an empire. American naval power was growing, with bases stretching across the Pacific. When America decided to enter the war it was not through altruistic motives as Wilson liked to pretend, since their knowledge of European affairs was sketchy and the country was isolationist. The loss of 500,000 tons of shipping and Germany's intention to violate the Monroe Doctrine by allowing Mexico to conquer California were too much to stomach. America joined no alliance and pursued her own diplomacy.

Lloyd George, panicking over disasters on the Western Front, stressed the massive power of America, and it is true that they had a million men in France by September 1918. However only nine divisions reached the front line and these had no aircraft, tanks or artillery. The American battle fleet of five ships was placed under British command, although it is true that destroyers contributed to submarine warfare and mine-laying. Barnett, in *The New Military Balance*, overstates the case—as yet Britain and France remained the world's chief military powers; what the United States gave was materials and loans, but Britain repaid the loans and the pound remained stronger than the dollar. America helped the allies to build their own war machine. In 1918 Britain was the most powerful allied nation, not the United States. By 1920 America had largely withdrawn from European commitments, finding she was overextended, but for a short time there was euphoria, and Wilson was received tumultuously. Barnett has argued this boded ill for Britain since America was not a natural ally, and forced her to choose between cordiality with Washington or a firm ally at Tokyo. In spite of this the period saw a false friendship—the special relationship—appear in diplomatic circles. This is accounted for by the false belief that the two countries were brother nations. In fact, two thirds of America were not British stock. The marriage of 130 Americans into the British peerage and gentry led the governing class to see the average American as part of the narrow Boston clique with which men like Balfour were acquainted.

G4. New Diplomacy

This was not the only false friendship to flower in this period, for under the stress of war the old diplomacy practised by diplomats pursuing individual countries' interests was seen as bankrupt, and according to Zeman 'the assault on traditional diplomacy was about to begin'. Under pressure of war concern for peace became so vital it prevailed over strategic thinking, imperial interests and even common sense. The new diplomacy believed in conferences with experts and interested parties instead of diplomatic notes and salon meetings, or, as Lloyd George put it, 'reconciling the irreconcilable'. It spoke much of the rights of subject peoples in the Empire, fashionably called a Commonwealth for the first time in 1916. It sought to avoid secret agreements or entangling alliances unless these 'kept the peace'. As Barnett has pointed out, keeping the peace without the means is a contradiction in terms. The new diplomacy was determined we should not reap the benefits of the war. Keynes opposed our financial gains. Smuts pressed for more concessions on dominion status, and by the time of the Irish War (1919–21) there was a strong current for conceding total independence, whereas Home Rule had been the furthest Liberal limit in 1914. The League of Nations Society (May 1915) advocated perpetual peace, and was supported by the 'ideas merchants' including Philip Kerr (later Lord Lothian), Lord Robert Cecil and Clifford Allen (later Lord Allen of Hurtwood). The traditionalists opposed the idea as inimical to our imperial interests. Hankey (May 1916) and Crowe (October 1916) submitted memoranda against the League, but Lloyd George relied on the garden suburb and Smuts and accepted it in January 1918. The Round Table, led by Lionel Curtis advocated major reforms in the Empire while a third group urged Britain to exchange an interest in her own dominions for one in the races of Eastern Europe. Versailles was to be a strange mixture of traditional diplomacy and new diplomacy.

Further Reading

Foot, D., *British Political Crises*, William Kimber, London, 1976.

Guinn, P., *British Strategy and Politics 1914–1918*, Oxford University Press, London, 1965.

Holt, E., *Protest in Arms (Ireland 1914–1922)*, Putnam, London, 1960.

Louis, W. R., *Great Britain and Germany's Lost Colonies 1914–1919*, Oxford University Press, Oxford, 1967.

Marwick, A., *The Deluge, British Society and the First World War*, Bodley Head. London, 1965, and available in paperback as Open University set text.

Medlicott, W. N., *Contemporary Britain 1914–1964*, Longmans, London, 1967.

Pollard, S., *The Development of the British Economy 1914–1970*, Edward Arnold, London, 1971.

Seaman, L. C. B., *Post Victorian Britain, 1902–1951*, Methuen, London, 1966.

Wilson, T., *The Downfall of the Liberal Party, 1914–1935*, Collins, London, 1966, available in Fontana Paperback, 1968.

Woodward, E. L., *Great Britain and the War of 1914–1918*, Methuen, London, 1967.

Questions

1. What do you understand by the phrase 'the impact of the war on British society' when applied to the First World War?
2. To what extent was Asquith's fall from office his own fault?
3. What difficulties did the First World War create for the Liberal party?
4. Was Lloyd George 'the man who won the war'?
5. Was there any justification for the Irish Rebellion in 1916?
6. Why did Great Britain constantly increase her commitments during the First World War?
7. What new factors influenced Britain's world position as a result of the First World War?

PEACEMAKING—GREAT BRITAIN AND WORLD POLITICS: 1918-22

At the end of the war, in spite of losses in men and materials, Great Britain looked more powerful than at its start. She owed money to the United States, but she was also a creditor nation with £1,825m to collect. The German Empire was hers. The German Navy had surrendered and the Admiralty was making plans to retain 30 battleships. British troops in Constantinople, Jerusalem and Baghdad controlled the Middle East. The Air Force was so large that she could give 200 planes to each dominion to start its own. Under these circumstances, Lloyd George was determined to play the rôle of world statesman, and after Versailles he went to 23 international conferences before he lost office. This globe-trotting added greatly to Britain's responsibilities. Mandates showered on her and the dominions. She became enmeshed in European politics with an army of occupation in Germany, and a large slice of reparations. British experts dominated disarmament and League of Nations affairs. Although he withdrew the army from Russia, Lloyd George contemplated using it in Poland and Turkey and British troops were to be found in Silesia in 1921.

Unfortunately, all these activities were too great for a tired nation after a period of intense activity. No attempt was made to rationalise Britain's commitments, and as a result efforts at imperial unity failed and the commitment to Europe became an embarrassment. In 1919 the ten-year rule laid down as policy the assumption of no major war for ten years. Trenchard and Churchill had to fight hard to keep the RAF, and it was only when the latter showed that a bombing war in Somaliland cost £70,000 instead of several million if the army had been used, that it was decided to retain it as a separate force. As for the Navy, in spite of warnings the Treaty of Washington (1922) brought to an end Britain's unfettered supremacy, and the ending of the alliance with Japan put Britain with extended commitments in a vulnerable position without a single ally. With a sixth of British forces defending the colonial empire commitment to Europe meant dependence on the French army and associating with France's extremist policies. Outwardly the Empire gained. By 1921 in a 'durbar' at Cairo the British stake in the Middle East was apportioned, but at the same time the Empire received three direct challenges in Ireland, Egypt and India and in each case Lloyd George's government oscillated between strong and weak policies.

In Ireland Lord French was Viceroy and a policy of repression was decided on in 1919. It had collapsed in ruins by 1921 (Section 5E). In India the firm action of General Dyer at Amritsar was condemned by the government, and constitutional reforms adopted on the urging of Curtis and Montague in spite of widespread disturbances. In Egypt Allenby was High Commissioner, but a report recommended scuttle and a treaty was accordingly signed in 1922. Lloyd George and Smuts had stressed imperial cooperation during the war, but it was short-lived. The dominions went their own way, and by 1923 the Imperial Conference could be described as 'an English defeat, worse, a surrender, which changed the course of the history of the Empire'. What happened was that the concessions made by Lloyd George in allowing the dominions representation at Versailles and in the League led them to assert a negative influence on British policy. Canada in particular veered to the American point of view, so to keep the Empire united Lloyd George and Balfour opted to jettison the Japanese alliance to please America and Canada. The Commonwealth idea spread rapidly and in Ireland, for example, Curtis and Smuts had rôles in the truce of 1921. It can be argued that failure to assess Britain's commitments, while extending them and reducing the means of defending them after the war, was the turning point that eventually led to the end of Empire and Great Power status, and that this was as much the fault of politicians as of circumstances.

A. The British Empire in War and Peace

A1. The Imperial Contribution

When war started the King declared it on behalf of the whole Empire, and in only one place was there outright opposition. De Wet raised revolt in South Africa only to be defeated.

(a) *The Imperial conquests.* In Africa Togoland fell in August 1914 and Kameroon surrendered in January 1916. German South West Africa was invaded from South Africa and surrendered in May 1915. In German East Africa, General Von Lettow Vorbeck defeated Brig. General Aitkin's attack at Tanga and Jassin. In February 1916 a new campaign was started under Smuts, and Dar-es-Salaam surrendered in September. There followed a guerilla war which cost £72m and the lives of 48,328 troops. Australia and New Zealand mopped up the German Pacific possessions, and Japan captured Kiao Chow.

(b) *The Imperial contribution.* Britain made little use of colonial troops apart from Maoris and Fijians as pioneers. India sent eight divisions to Europe and five to Mespot, but this was 0.3 per cent of India's population. The dominions raised 12 divisions and had plenty of war memories. The casualty figures were 209,000 killed out of 2,990,000 troops involved. In Canada, although the Military Service Law was passed in 1917, there was strong opposition. Hughes of Australia spent four months in Britain and returned pledged to conscription, but was unable to carry it. Only in New Zealand, where the service term was extended in 1916, was there no opposition.

A2. The Problem of Dominion Status

The dominions' contribution was impressive and demanded some reward. Lloyd George set up an Imperial Cabinet and invited selected colonial premiers to the War Cabinet, including an Indian although India was not a dominion. In March 1917 Smuts arrived from South Africa and stayed in Europe for $2\frac{1}{2}$ years urging the dominion solution, particularly in Ireland and India. Lloyd George was undoubtedly influenced by him, but Smuts would not have had an audience if the ground had not been prepared. Milner's Kindergarten included among its younger members Curtis and Kerr and in 1916 Curtis published *The Problem of the Commonwealth* —a phrase which Smuts was quick to adopt. Although Britain attended Versailles on behalf of the Empire, separate representatives from the dominions and India attended. When the mandates were distributed the dominions took their own and they joined the League separately. By the time Lausanne was signed in 1923 Britain no longer signed for the dominions, and they specifically did not join Locarno in 1925. By 1923 Canada had signed its first international treaty, and in 1924 Ireland appointed its own ambassador.

This development brought grave problems:

(a) The Colonial Laws Validity Act (1865) defined the constitutional relations between Britain and her colonies. Now a new legal status had to be worked out for the dominions, since 'dominion status' was something defined in the original acts of the Westminster Parliament.

(b) There was the international difficulty of knowing who Britain represented. Thus she signed Versailles on behalf of the dominions who were separately represented. At Washington she represented the whole Empire, but when in 1922 she sought to take action against Turkey in the old way, there was an outcry.

(c) The dominions resisted all attempts at federation and coordination of economic and defence policies, but they expected Britain to bear the defence burden, and their demands cut across the strategic demands of the Empire as a whole.

The post-war period saw a definite weakening of the bonds of empire:

(a) *The extension of internal self-government.* The Report on Indian Constitutional Reforms (1918) was the landmark. Produced under the influence of Curtis and Montague, it argued for change, although the demand came from a small minority. Curzon and Chamberlain pointed out how serious the move was, but in June 1918 the cabinet accepted the report. In Ceylon, after riots in 1915, a National Congress was set up in 1919, and by 1924 an elected majority. Malta obtained internal self-government in 1921 and Southern Rhodesia in 1923.

(b) *The doctrine of native paramountcy.* The acquisition of Tanganyika and colonial status for Kenya (1920) increased interest in white settlement. In January 1922 Churchill declared that Indians would not be allowed to purchase land in the White Highlands, and Montague objected. As a result, the policy was modified and a commission appointed. Its report in 1923 stated that 'the interests of the African nation must be paramount'. This policy operated elsewhere, and the overall effect was to leave the colonial empire as a defence burden and an economic liability.

(c) *Decline of economic cooperation.* In spite of the granting of a small measure of Imperial Preference (1921) and the Empire Settlement Act (1922), an Imperial Economic Conference in 1923 achieved nothing.

(d) *End of defence cooperation.* This finally disappeared in the 1923 Imperial Conference, when Mackenzie King successfully opposed standardising equipment or an imperial navy.

Since King also obtained assurances from the British government that no treaty affecting a dominion would be negotiated without their participation, and that the final word on treaties lay with the dominion parliaments, Britain's *rôle* was clearly substantially undermined, and this process continued in the 1920s (Chapter 11, C).

A3. Lloyd George and the Indian Empire

The viceroyalty of Lord Curzon had seen a policy of consolidation, and the reform of defence strategy, but the next few years saw the rise of opposition to the Raj by an unrepresentative and religiously divided minority. It was centred on two main groups: the Congress Party, led in 1920 by Mahatma Gandhi, which was Hindu, and the Moslem League, founded by Ali Jinnah.

Indian self-government had begun in 1892 when the governor's council was extended to include 10 to 16 nominated members who could be natives, and the provincial councils were likewise constituted. In 1909 the Morley-Minto Reforms secured one Indian member on the Viceroy's and provincial councils, and extended the functions of the legislative councils, giving non-official members a majority. Chamberlain, the Indian Secretary, felt no further moves should be made during the war, but a body of opinion in England differed. Using disturbances in the Punjab and Ferozpore in 1914 as examples, they maintained Indian opinion was ripe for further change. In 1917 Montague became Indian Secretary, who believed that 'we ought to have let the Indians run their own show from the beginning with all its inefficiency and imperfections'. A friend described him as having 'the trustfulness of a child' and, taking up his job, he said, 'I shrink with horror at being made responsible for punishment.' The Viceroys Lord Chelmsford and Lord Reading were not Indian experts, and Montague had things his own way until he resigned in 1922. His policy proceeded in three stages:

(a) *The Montague Declaration* (*August 1917*) stated that Indian policy was 'the gradual development of self-governing institutions with a view to the progressive realisation of responsible government in India'. Lloyd George accepted it.

(b) *The Report on Indian Constitutional Reforms* (*1918*). This spoke of Indian opinion, meaning 'those who have held or are capable of holding an opinion', and thus played into the hands of Congress and the League. It proposed a scheme by Curtis which came to be called 'dyarchy'.

(c) *The Government of India Act* (*1919*) announced there was to be a full implementation of the 1917 declaration and that this act was only a first step. In ten years a commission was to review its working. It provided a system of 'dyarchy', giving some power to elected provincial governments while retaining the chief Viceroy's powers.

The act was rejected by the extremists, who urged *swadeshi* (boycotting British goods) and *hartal* (non-cooperation). The new electorate covered some 5 million Indians limited on residence and tax grounds, and since only 6–8 per cent were literate this played into the hands of extremists. The government passed the Rowlatt Acts (1919) to control sedition, but there were serious disturbances:

(a) Hindus and Sikhs rioted at Lahore and Amritsar. In April 1919 Brig. Gen. Dyer shot at a crowd in the bazaar of the latter town, killing 379 and wounding 1,208. He was dismissed and censured in July 1920 by Churchill. In fact, the riots were suppressed quickly thereafter.

(b) In May, Afghanistan, affected by the Khalifate movement, declared war, and it was necessary to bomb Kabul on 24 May.

(c) Riots continued during the Prince of Wales' visit (December 1921) and in 1922, 21 police officers were burnt at Chauri Chaura. Gandhi was arrested and remained in prison until 1924.

In spite of this situation the new constitution was inaugurated in 1921 by the Duke of Connaught, who apologised for Amritsar and said, 'Today you are seeing the beginnings of *swaraj* ... and the widest scope and ample opportunity for progress to the liberty which other dominions enjoy.' However, Lord Reading was met with non-cooperation until 1923, when Das and Nehru agreed to elections. By 1924 the constitution was functioning, but many still believed with Heaslop in Forster's *A Passage to India* (1924): 'Here we are, and we're going to stop, and the country's got to put up with us, gods or no gods.' (Chapter 11, Section B).

A4. The Egyptian Question

When Britain annexed Egypt in November 1914, she granted the ruler the title of sultan, and the ruler after 1917 was Fuad. In November 1918 a political party called the Wafd, led by Zaghlul Pasha, demanded full independence, but the British refused and deported him to Malta; there followed savage riots in which the British were massacred on a train to Luxor. Lord Allenby was sent out, and the riots suppressed with planes and armoured cars.

(*a*) The Milner Mission. Milner, the Colonial Secretary, was now an advocate of the trusteeship line and his mission (November 1920–August 1921) supported the nationalist case with a number of conditions. No one except Curzon backed the report.

(*b*) Churchill tried negotiations in London but they broke down. In January 1922 Allenby declared that they must make up their mind or he would resign, and as a result a treaty was signed in February.

The protectorate was ended, and the sultan became a king. In 1924 Zaghlul returned and was swept to power, and by 1930 the constitution was based on one man, one vote. The British retained rights over communications, defence, foreign policy, minorities and the Sudan, but the Wafd claimed the Sudan. When this was refused in 1924 there were riots in Cairo and Sir Lee Stack, the Governor of the Sudan, was murdered. Britain compelled Egypt to pay a fine of £500,000 and evacuate all her troops from the Sudan but the issue remained stormy, with clashes in 1927 and 1928 and the breakdown of attempts to make a new treaty.

A5. Great Britain and the Arabs

The series of agreements that Britain made during the war complicated the Middle Eastern situation (Chapter 3, G1), and administratively the area was also confused with Foreign, Colonial, India and War Offices sharing responsibility. But Britain was determined to maintain her power in the area because:

(*a*) Oil discovered in 1908 was vital after the navy had completed its conversion.

(*b*) There was a Bolshevik threat, and British troops remained in Persia until July 1921.

(*c*) A strong pro-Arab group had developed round the Arab Bureau in Cairo (1916), including Storrs, Wingate, Lawrence, Gertrude Bell, and Percy Cox.

(*d*) The India Office was anxious to conciliate Moslems, and British recognition of Hussein as ruler of the Hejaz in November 1916 made him ruler of Mecca.

(*e*) Britain was aware of French designs, and their negotiations with the Arabs.

(*f*) The Balfour Declaration had to be honoured, and in January 1919 Feisal, Hussein's eldest son, had accepted it.

The Supreme Council awarded the Middle East mandates jointly to Britain and France and a new class of mandate—the 'A' class—was introduced to indicate that they were in a different category from more primitive places. In May 1920, at San Remo, the British and French partitioned the mandates with France obtaining Syria and Britain the rest. Feisal visited London but could obtain nothing, while his brother Abdullah arrived at Ma'an with an army in November 1920, having been driven there from Arabia by a new ruler. This was Ibn Saud of the Nejd, who Britain recognised and subsidised in December 1915, and who now attacked Hussein. When Churchill took over the Colonial Office with its newly formed Middle East Department a settlement was vital.

(a) *Palestine.* Sir Herbert Samuel became High Commissioner and Jewish immigration began. Between 1923 and 1933 numbers rose from 83,000 to 230,000. In June 1922 the Balfour Declaration was reaffirmed, but an attempt to introduce a constitution had to be suspended after a time because of communal disturbances in May 1923.

(b) *Iraq.* Churchill summoned a conference of the interested parties at Cairo. It was agreed to make Feisal king of Iraq, and hand the defence of the country over to the RAF, with Sir Percy Cox as High Commissioner.

(c) *Transjordania.* In order to deal with Abdullah, an emirate was carved out on the east bank of the Jordan, where Sir Henry Cox and Sir Alec Kirkbride acted as High Commissioners. Col. Peake organised an Arab Legion.

It was necessary to enforce the settlement:

(a) In Iraq there was a six month war that cost £40m and 10,000 casualties, and the rebel leader Sayid Talib was kidnapped. In April 1921 Feisal became king.

(b) Lawrence was sent to persuade Hussein to accept, but he refused and abdicated. His son fled, and Ibn Saud occupied the Hedjaz (1924–25). In November 1925 the Clayton Mission defined the frontiers of Iraq, Transjordan and Saudi Arabia.

(c) Transjordan was helped to prosperity by the British commissioners, and in 1928 signed a treaty with Britain.

Lawrence's *Seven Pillars of Wisdom* appeared for private circulation in 1925, but it must be admitted that the profits of the Iraq Petroleum Company were as important to the British as a desire to befriend the Arabs. Moreover, they had started something they could not stop, and by backing the desert Bedouins they stirred nationalism in the teeming cities. The twentieth-century pattern of the Middle East was imposed very largely by Britain in the period after the Great War, but it was an area where responsibilities soon began to outweigh benefits (Chapter 11, A3).

B. The Versailles Peace Settlement

The Versailles peace settlement stands as one of the great European peace settlements; together with the effects of the war itself it formed the perimeter of European affairs until it was torn up during the 1930s. Apart from Eastern Europe, it still forms the basis of Europe's political divisions, for the various treaties dealt with 4,000 miles of frontiers and created 10 new states. Apart from the treaty with Germany, the settlement included treaties with Austria, Hungary, Bulgaria and Turkey. Germany's opposition was limited by blockade and the threat of force, but Hungary held out for a year, and Turkey refused to sign. As a result a fresh treaty was drawn up in 1923 after Kemal Ataturk proved to be the first post-war dictator. The fact that the new treaty contained no territorial losses, reparations or disarmament was not lost on others. Russia was not included in the settlement and since Brest Litovsk had broken the treaty of September 1914 and been followed by the publication of wartime agreements and repudiation of debts, the allies refused to recognise it. Peace finally came to Eastern Europe at Riga in 1921.

Although Wilson's Fourteen Points denounced secret diplomacy, nearly all the treaties were negotiated in the usual way. The Supreme Council continued, and was given responsibility for enforcing the treaty. Early in 1920 it was replaced by the Council of Ambassadors, who tended to rival the newly formed League of Nations as a means of settling disputes. The whole question of war indemnity or reparations had already been aired in elections, and by December 1918 a British committee proposed £24,000m. Lloyd George would not accept this, and lower figures were sought, which included one from Keynes of £5,000m. It was decided to leave the determination of reparations to later discussions, which occurred in two stages. At Spa in July 1920 the amounts were allocated between countries, with France obtaining 52 per cent and Britain 22 per cent. France naturally got the largest share but it made her more sensitive than England about collecting them. The Reparations Commission then got to work and after a conference in London (February–April 1921) the total was fixed at £6,600m.

The treaties provided for disarmament, demilitarisation and occupation of Germany and the other powers, but much was left to be settled in the future. An Allied Control Commission was set up to deal with Germany, and in March 1923 it was announced that she had completed her obligations under the treaty. This was far from the truth. She scuttled her navy and burnt her zeppelins, but the allies were forced to allow troops to remain to contain Bolshevism and revolution. The disarmament clause stated that Germany's loss was 'in order to render possible the initiation of a general limitation of armaments of all nations' and accordingly in May 1920 the Permanent Mixed Commission, and in February 1921 the Temporary Mixed Commission, were set up to consider the problems of definition with military and civilian experts. The only disarmament that took place was unilaterally by Britain. An ominous pattern whereby Germany was slowly rearming while the allies were haphazardly disarming had started, and in 1922 the Treaty of Rapallo between two outcast nations, Germany and Russia, enabled this process to accelerate.

Proposals for a League came thick and fast and a commission was established in January 1919 to study them. In spite of the usual assumption that Wilson's views were decisive, this was not so. The British views with some American modification became the Hurst-Miller Draft of February 1919. Two mistakes were at once made. In order to placate American opinion, Wilson insisted on linking the League to the treaty, hence tarring the peace terms and the means of revising them with the same brush. It became a league of victors from the start. Secondly, the French proposed an international force for enforcing the treaties. Wilson threatened to leave, and when the matter was raised in 1922 it was again rejected. This made the French nervous, and they demanded additional guarantees. An Anglo-American-French treaty was put forward in June 1919 but America refused to ratify, and Lloyd George also declined. Since Lloyd George persistently tried to modify the treaties in Germany's favour, refusing French demands on the Rhine and in Poland, the key relationship on which the treaties depended was weakened. Britain would not back France in Poland, and France would not back Britain in Turkey, and the attempts of Lloyd George to save the situation in 1922 failed completely.

B1. The Conference of Versailles

The peace settlement has been much criticised for its contradictions, omissions and unnecessary severity; it has also been criticised for not being severe enough. But from the start the conference was not its own master for 'it was the war and not the treaty that was responsible for the major decisions'. Moreover, most critics have followed Nicolson in condemning the haste with which so much was done so soon after the war in an atmosphere of bitterness, the effects of wartime propaganda fresh in the delegates' minds. People with placards giving the figures of dead paraded before the ministers' houses, and each leader was under pressure from home to be more severe than in fact they were. It is important, therefore, to see the conditions under which peace was made:

(*a*) Thomson says the settlement 'was the confirmation and acceptance of a new order that was already taking shape around them'. The wartime agreements and promises, treaties like Brest Litovsk, the new nationalities and the statements of war aims all influenced the delegates.

(*b*) A number of immediate factors made for speed. The Comintern was set up, and Bolshevism spread in Germany and Hungary (1919). Economic dislocation on a widespread scale and the continuing blockade until July 1919 were affecting the European economy. A good many expert committees produced solutions to the various problems which harassed delegates accepted.

(*c*) In Thomson's words 'the time, place, composition, organisation and procedure' of the conference affected its outcome, and in a way unknown before, since newspaper publicity meant that the delegates worked like 'mere windlestraws in the storm of passion and egotism that raged about them'.

It is true, therefore, that 'the men in Paris never had a free hand' but a little too easy to say they could 'only trim the edges'. The delegates themselves must bear part of the blame for what followed. There were 1,037 of them and the British team numbered 200. They were divided into 58 committees and the main business of negotiation rested with the representatives of the powers. A Council of Ten became a Council of Three by late March, and even allies like Italy were treated with scant concern. Only six full sessions were held, and in spite of Wilson's 'open diplomacy', the conference resembled 'a study in fog' according to Nicolson. Nor were negotiations conducted in the normal way, since it was decided not to summon the defeated powers.

The Big Three were:

(*a*) Wilson, who had lost his Congress majority in 1918, ignored his Secretary of State, came to Europe, and brought no Republicans with him. He relied on Col. House for advice, and lacked understanding of Europe's problems. He relied on airy generalities, and assumed the Fourteen Points and other proposals would form the basis of the conference. However, he was unwilling to enforce the settlement, and unable to after 1920. He became 'increasingly a lonely and forlorn' figure attached to the League and forced to make concessions.

(*b*) Clemenceau of France had no illusions. He had witnessed 1871 and was determined to reap maximum benefit for France. Since the conference was in Paris and neither of the others spoke French, he had some advantage. After an anarchist tried to kill him in February 1919 he was up in a fortnight, although 78 years old, and received a large vote of confidence from the *Chambre*. He wanted massive reparations, a dismembered Germany, the Rhine boundary, and a guaranteeing alliance.

(*c*) Lloyd George, confirmed in power by the election of November 1918 and with all party support, accompanied by Balfour and Bonar Law, was in a powerful position. Britain's main aims outside Europe were secured and the ultimate Far Eastern settlement left aside. Thus, he was able to act as honest broker and although under pressure from home (at one point 370 MPs demanded harsher reparations), he was able to mitigate the settlement's severity.

The conference opened on 18 January 1919; by 7 May terms for Germany had been prepared, and she was given 22 days to agree under threat of war. At the time the delegates were referred to as the 'dawdlers of Paris'; later, it seemed too short a time. It was particularly unfortunate that the newly established Weimar government in Germany was made to bear the burden of the previous imperial government. The cabinet fell before another could be persuaded to accept and the treaty was signed on 28 June.

B2. Terms of the Settlement

(*a*) *Territorial changes.* These amounted to 11 per cent of German territory, and in only two cases (Alsace and Lorraine, Posen and West Prussia) involved direct session. Plebiscites gave North Schleswig to Denmark, Eupen and Malmedy to Belgium, and part of Upper Silesia to Poland. Danzig was made an international city.

This cannot be regarded as severe if compared with territorial gains made by Germany at Brest Litovosk. Moreover, Lloyd George intervened to keep East Prussia for her, thus creating the Polish Corridor, and sent British troops to supervise the Silesian plebiscite after Poles invaded the territory.

(*b*) *External relations.* The customs union with Luxemburg was dissolved, and Germany's property and concessions abroad confiscated. Her special rights in China, Morocco and Egypt were scrapped. All her colonies were handed over to the Supreme Council. Union with Austria was forbidden.

(*c*) *War guilt.* A clause was inserted (231) in order to provide a legal basis for reparations. Article 227 provided for the trial of the Kaiser. Articles provided for the trial of a list of war criminals, including Hindenburg.

In January 1920 Holland refused to give up the Kaiser, and a year later the League reported there was no adequate body for trying international crimes. In May 1921 Germany tried a dozen in her own Supreme Court, and six were convicted.

(*d*) *Economic penalties*. The 35 clauses of the armistice had already taken war equipment, together with many other materials. The Allied Supreme Economic Council demanded £52m to pay for food entering the country. Germany agreed to reparations, and to pay £1,000m on account. She was to surrender all merchant ships over 1,600 tons, and build quotas for the allies. Payment in kind including horses, cows and sheep were to be made to Belgium and France. Thirteen million tons of coal a year were also to be given, and the Saar placed under French control for 15 years.

The enforcing of the blockade had been harsh, and the Americans withdrew from the Economic Council in August 1919. It is true that by 1924 reparations had been scaled down and that the Saar was returned to Germany in 1935, but this does not acquit the proposals of some degree of vindictiveness. Smuts, on the other hand, argued for reparations on the humanitarian grounds of paying war pensions with them, and Germany had not been occupied.

(*e*) *Disarmament*. There was to be no conscription and an army of 100,000. The General Staff was to be scrapped. All existing munitions were to be surrendered, and all fortifications dismantled. There was to be no air force and no submarines. The navy was limited to six battleships of not more than 10,000 tons, six cruisers and 12 destroyers.

(*f*) *Enforcement*. The Allies were already in occupation of the Rhineland, and this was to continue with an army of occupation paid for by Germany which was to remain until 1935. There were to be no fortifications in the Rhineland. An Allied Commission was to supervise disarmament.

This was far less severe than in 1945 in terms of territorial loss, treatment of war criminals and occupation. Circumstances modified the losses, and the German armament industry and General Staff continued to exist. America left the occupying army in 1923, and it was completely withdrawn by 1930. The Allied Control Commission was removed in 1927.

B3. The Versailles Controversy

When Lloyd George returned, apart from scattered opposition for failing to fix reparations, only four voted against the treaty. Although the Union of Democratic Control and the MacDonald wing of Labour denounced it, Clynes and Adamson welcomed it. Yet almost at once it became the target for criticism by liberal opinion. Spender called it 'harsh, vindictive and unsparing' and Clifford Allen later 'that wicked treaty'. Reparations were singled out for attack by Keynes in *Economic Consequences of the Peace* (1919). Indeed, it is hard to distinguish right-wing German from left-wing British criticism of the treaty—with one fundamental difference: the English left wanted lasting peace and the League to ensure this and thought modifying Versailles was the means to that end; while the Germans wished to sweep away both the treaty and the League system. Thus, while the English criticised France for making strong demands and occupying the Ruhr in 1923, they supported German recovery as legitimate after their 'humiliation'. For this attitude there were a number of reasons:

(*a*) The growth of an alternative left-wing foreign policy which also influenced liberals. This centred on the Union of Democratic Control and its members like MacDonald.

(*b*) Lloyd George distrusted professional diplomats, and relied greatly on the aging Balfour. The unorthodox nature of the conference enabled him to ignore the balance of power and try to 'reconcile the irreconcilable', as he put it.

(*c*) There was strong dislike of France, dating from the slaughter and incompetence produced by the French army. Their demands were opposed, and attempts to enforce the treaty led to a complete split by 1923. Carr said 'the years of French supremacy were also the years of Germany's deepest humiliation', but the years after were the years of Hitler's successes.

(*d*) Many thought peace would be served by getting back on friendly terms with Germany, which they believed utterly prostrated. Curzon said in 1921, 'Our policy is frankly the re establishment of Germany as a stable state of Europe ... and any idea of obliterating Germany from the community of nations or treating her as an outcast is not only ridiculous but insane.'

In fact the treaty had not weakened Germany enough—indeed, with her economic recovery helped by American loans, she was in a more powerful position than in 1914, as Stresemann found when he turned Allied desire to be reasonable to Germany's benefit in his policy of fulfilment. This claimed that when Germany was fully restored as a nation and in the League all would be well, whereas the time was used secretly to rearm and secure the modification of the treaty.

In 1919 Balfour was aware of the problem, and Smuts drew attention to the settlement in eastern Europe which had still further strengthened Germany by surrounding her with small states and creating 'revisionist' sentiments in Austria and Hungary. But from the first, in Barnett's words, British policy was a compound of 'sentimentality, moral indignation, sense of guilt, and lack of strategic comprehension'. Britain worked to scale down reparations, to resist French enforcement and to ignore reports that Germany was defying the disarmament terms. Thus, in effect, the treaty 'was harsh where it might better have been lenient and weak where it might better have been strong'. After a brief enforcement period the treaty had been modified in all except its territorial settlement before Hitler came to power. Britain knew of French fears and ignored them, or as Balfour was to say in 1925, 'I do not think it is a good policy to do what the French always do—that is, to assume that there must be a great war ... I think that is absolute lunacy.' By the early 1930s much of the treaty had been dismantled without adequate safeguards.

C. Lloyd George's Diplomacy

C1. The Infernal Triangle

In January 1920 a period of treaty enforcement started which was successful. Among the steps taken were:

(*a*) First French occupation. The Germans sent troops into the Ruhr because of left-wing revolts in April 1920. The French occupied Frankfurt, Hanau and Darmstadt with Belgian support.

(*b*) The Spa Conference met to organise reparations. The Germans accepted the procedure and the distribution of reparations (July 1920).

(*c*) Proposals for reparations and sanctions were issued in January 1921, and when Germany resisted the French occupied Dusseldorf, Duisberg and Ruhrort in March. In May an ultimatum on reparations was accepted by Germany and the first payment made.

(*d*) The plebiscite on Upper Silesia proved indecisive in March 1921 so British troops returned in May, and a Silesian Commission of the League was established. In May 1922 a Polish–German convention accepted the final settlement.

(*e*) Germany asked for a moratorium on its second payment, but at the end of December 1922 was declared in default on timber deliveries.

These French successes were followed by Britain only with the greatest reluctance. France, on the other hand, still felt alarm at the prospect of German recovery and this was increased by the collapse of the Triple Treaty, the withdrawal of America from the Supreme Economic Council and her refusal to attend the Genoa Conference. These moves forced France to seek a League military force and a series of alliances to hold Germany down, but in doing so she stretched her resources too far and failed to carry Britain with her. Treaties were signed with Belgium and Poland and a series of military and economic agreements in eastern Europe called the Little Entente, such as the Czechoslovak treaty of 1924. When France decided to back Poland against the Bolsheviks in August 1920, Lloyd George refused to support the action, saying, 'the working classes were frankly hostile to intervention'. The French repaid Britain by signing a treaty with Turkey in October 1921, defining the border with French Syria, recognising Kemal Ataturk and withdrawing from the Straits.

Lloyd George was not unaware of this rift, and sought to heal it during 1922. He responded favourably to a request from Briand for a security pact.

(*a*) *The Cannes Conference* (January–April 1922). Hopes for the pact and a reparations settlement were dashed when Briand was persuaded to play golf by Lloyd George and made to look so foolish that he resigned, and his successor Poincaré repudiated the proposals.

(*b*) *The Bar le Duc Speech.* Poincaré made it clear that there could be no agreement with Russia without settlement of the debt question, and no security pact until reparations were settled.

(*c*) *The Genoa Conference* (April–May). In spite of much tact, the setting up of four commissions and a decision to continue talking at the Hague about the Russian question, nothing was achieved.

(*d*) *The Rapallo Treaty* (April). Although Lloyd George negotiated with the Russian Chicherin he neglected Rathenau, who was persuaded to sign a commercial treaty and a secret military pact. The British pretended this had no importance.

C2. The Bolshevik Threat

For a number of reasons, relations between Britain and Russia were at a low ebb by 1919:

(*a*) Russian withdrawal from the war, repudiation of debts, and signing of a treaty with Germany.

(*b*) The Comintern, founded in 1919, supported world revolution with a fund of 2m roubles.

(*c*) The government opposed Russia on ideological grounds: 200 MPs sent a telegram to Lloyd George in April 1919 urging non-recognition.

(*d*) Lloyd George himself exaggerated the Bolshevik threat in Britain, saying in April 1921, 'The country is facing a situation analogous to civil war.'

This view of Russia was shared by France, who feared that the new states of eastern Europe would prove a weak barrier either way to Russian or German aggression. An attempt was made to establish a *'cordon sanitaire'*, particularly by supporting Poland. The Curzon Line was drawn in December 1919 to mark their eastern boundary, but this failed to recognise the aggressiveness of the new Polish state. In April 1920 they invaded Russia, and had to be rescued by the French at the battle of the Vistula. When peace was signed at Riga in March 1921 the frontier was moved 150 miles east of the Curzon Line.

Intervention in Russia had been decided upon during the war (Chapter 2, C3). A contingent under Ironside numbered 30,000 and was at Murmansk. Contacts were opened with Kolchak in Siberia and Denikin in the south, and Churchill as War Minister urged large-scale intervention. However, this was not supported by Lloyd George. Some £150m of aid in gold and supplies such as surplus tanks were delivered, and in February 1919 Churchill drew up 'a definite war scheme' and got War Office support. Lloyd George used Kerr to warn Wilson that this was not government policy, thus ditching the scheme. Churchill then raised a force of 8,000 volunteers to help Ironside, but it was decided to evacuate Northern Russia and concentrate on Denikin in the south, where British planes raided Kronstadt in August 1919. After fighting a rearguard action, Ironside withdrew from the North by the end of September, and as soon as Denikin suffered his first reverses, Lloyd George urged a peace settlement in November 1919.

In February 1920 the Supreme Council changed its policy towards Russia and urged the making of peace. When Churchill criticised this policy Lloyd George attacked him. In March some of Denikin's troops were evacuated by the navy, but the Prime Minister insisted in November that only British refugees should be evacuated. Sebastopol fell to the Bolsheviks and Wrangel fled to Constantinople. In May 1920 a Russian trade delegation arrived, and in March 1921 an Anglo-Soviet Trade Treaty was signed. The treatment of Russia was one important reason for Tory disillusion with Lloyd George, and opinion since has been divided on the same issue. Taylor condemned 'futile intervention', but until the middle of 1919 there was still a good chance of White success.

C3. The Start of the League

During 1920 the League came into being. The Council met in Paris and London, and in November 1920 the Assembly met at Geneva. Lord Robert Cecil, the British delegate, asked for the admission of Austria and Bulgaria as members, and Hungary followed in 1922. The League had three main organisations: an Assembly, a Council and a Secretariat.

It spawned a new international bureaucracy of commissions to run the Saar, Danzig, Reparations, Disarmament, Minorities and Mandates. It was charged with a wide range of social functions. A Technical Organisation started in March 1921. Nansen was put in charge of refugees and POWs: 400,000 of the latter were dealt with, and aid sent to Russia. Transfers of Greek and Turkish populations were arranged. Associated with the League were an International Labour Organisation and the International Court of Justice.

Support for the League came from advocates of the new diplomacy, and never weakened. Wickham Steed could say the 'moral power of the League remains immense, and rightly exercised, probably decisive' even after it had failed in Memel and Corfu (1923), and as late as 1941 Lord Robert Cecil wrote *A Great Experiment*, justifying the course of League history. The League was technically efficient. During 1922 alone it organised a Danube treaty, provided loans for Austria and Hungary and secured a technical convention regulating inter-state rail travel and port regulations. But it was clear from the start that politically the League was dangerously impotent. It gave unmerited influence to small countries, and it encouraged colonial peoples to rebel by speaking of mandates as 'a sacred trust of civilisation'. The real crux was contained in covenant articles providing for action in the case of aggression or disputes, and limited sanctions if arbitration was not accepted. When France tried to strengthen these provisions, she was resisted and the League remained largely powerless unless France and Britain, its main members, could act together. In other words, it relied on old-fashioned diplomatic and military pressure and was an exponent of the very nationalism it sought to curb. It was a league of victors, ignored by America and shunned by Russia. The Geneva atmosphere, described by Wickham Steed as 'a reality, not a fiction', was, in fact, the reverse.

C4. The Far Eastern Settlement
In November 1921 the powers assembled at Washington for the Pacific settlement, but the British delegation came prepared to make large concessions. By May that year the cabinet decided that friendship with America was preferable to alliance with Japan. Japan had been noticeably aggressive in China and this provided a common bond between the two pro-China powers. At the Imperial Conference, Meighan of Canada had supported this argument although Hughes of Australia and Massey of New Zealand favoured renewal after Japan's aid during the war. Although Eliot, Britain's Tokyo Ambassador, warned that to cancel the alliance would lead to a loss of face, Britain decided to replace Japan with America, 'the people closest to our aims and ideals'. The British delegation was led by Balfour, a strong supporter of America, and Lord Lee of Fareham, who was married to an American. He was mainly interested in the fine arts, but had been made First Lord of the Admiralty.

Four agreements were reached at Washington in February 1922:

(*a*) *Two Power Treaty* (China, Japan). Japan surrendered Kiao Chow and the Shantung Peninsula.

(*b*) *Nine Power Treaty* (China, Japan, Britain, America, France, Italy, Holland, Belgium and Portugal). Chinese integrity was guaranteed.

(*c*) *Four Power Treaty* (Britain, America, France and Japan). Agreed not to build fortifications north of the equator.

(*d*) *Five Power Treaty* (America, Britain, Japan, France and Italy). Agreed to a battleship ratio of 5 : 5 : 3 : 1.75 : 1.75.

Balfour returned and received the Garter, but in fact it was a calamity of the first order, because:

(*a*) Britain had lost the Japanese alliance which terminated in 1922.

(*b*) By reducing Britain's strength and agreeing not to fortify 'the strategic position of Japan has been greatly strengthened'.

(*c*) It weakened the Empire, since Canada had imposed a veto, and the Pacific states duly took note of Britain's weakness.

(*d*) There had already been a naval holiday since 1919. The new ratio ended Britain's two-power status, and was based on no rational determinant of her naval requirements. As Balfour said, 'the British Empire came out worst'. Naval policy was placed in a straightjacket with a ten-year holiday, and a limit of 35,000 tons. The conference led directly to the naval weakness.

(*e*) In exchange Britain did not obtain the friendship of America. In February 1922 Coolidge demanded the settlement of all wartime debts not later than 1947 and at $4\frac{1}{2}$ per cent interest. In August 1922 the Balfour Note defined Britain's obligation to pay these debts, and in January 1923 she agreed to do so at a high rate of interest.

The Americans imposed strict immigration controls on the Japanese, thus making it clear that Japan now stood alone. The only decision of any sense taken was to build a new base at Singapore (1921), because oil-fired ships could not be fuelled so far east. But in March 1924, in spite of dominion protests, MacDonald stopped work on it. Truly, as Amery said in 1923, in war with Japan 'we should be in a position of extraordinary difficulty'. (Chapter 7, H2.)

C5. The Near Eastern Question

The defeat of Turkey and the lengthy series of allied wartime agreements necessitated a bold look at the Near East. For a time it looked as if Turkey would disappear altogether after the biggest Balkan share-out ever:

(*a*) The removal of the Turkish government. The allies had occupied the Straits under Gen. Harrington and in May 1919 they allowed Greece to occupy Smyrna. A nationalist movement in protest against this began and when the Turkish parliament returned a majority of nationalist deputies the allies objected in 1920, and occupied Constantinople. The Greeks were allowed to launch an offensive, and the British moved in more warships and occupied Mudania. The Turkish parliament was dissolved.

(*b*) In April the terms of the Treaty of Sèvres were issued. They involved the total dismemberment of Turkey with Armenian and Kurdish states in the east, the loss of mandated territory, a French enclave north of Syria, an Italian enclave north of Rhodes and Greek occupation of Western Anatolia. The Straits were to be demilitarised and internationalised. In July an ultimatum was sent, and the next month Sultan Mohammed VI gave way.

By then a Turkish national movement had appeared, led by Kemal Ataturk. The fleeing parliamentary deputies had gone to Angora where Ataturk had been sent to a non-existent military command by the Sultan. A Turkish state was proclaimed in April 1920, arms obtained from Russia and an army gathered. In November, Constantine returned to Greece and embarked on an extension of Greek influence in Asia Minor.

(*c*) *Division among the allies.* This first challenge to the treaties led to such difficulties that in May 1921 the allies declared themselves neutral in the Graeco-Turkish war. Two attempts were made to mediate, but after the failure of a London Conference in February, the pro-Greek element in the cabinet began to cool. In 1921 Italy withdrew, and in April 1922 signed a peace treaty because of domestic troubles. France was at war in Syria, and signed an agreement in October 1921.

(*d*) *The defeat of Greece.* The Greeks were routed and Smyrna sacked. The cabinet was divided, with Montague and Curzon favouring support for Turkey and Balfour, Birkenhead and Chamberlain for resolute action. Churchill switched to support Lloyd George at this moment. Nine warships were despatched to Constanza and on 11 September the Turks were warned not to enter the occupation zone.

This precipitated the Chanak Crisis, where Lloyd George, having scuttled in Egypt and Ireland, prepared at last to stand firm. The steps in the crisis were:

(*a*) 16 September. The cabinet agreed to despatch a further warning, and to ask for the backing of Britain's European allies, some Balkan states and the dominions.

(*b*) 17 September. A communiqué in war-like terms was issued before the cipher telegrams had reached the interested parties, giving them an excuse not to help. Curzon was furious as he had not read it.

(*c*) 21 September. In spite of Curzon's efforts, France and Italy withdrew their observers, and refused to help Britain. Canada refused and only New Zealand expressed much willingness to help.

(*d*) 23 September. Turks entered the zone and retired. A proposal of a conference was put with French cooperation.

(*e*) 27 September. A Greek revolution restored Venizelos, and the pro-Greeks rallied.

(*f*) 29 September. The Turks demanded the removal of British troops, and their cavalry entered the zone. An ultimatum was despatched in spite of Curzon's opposition.

Fortunately, Harrington delayed the ultimatum, and sought a meeting with the Turks at Mudania on 3 October. On 11 October an armistice was signed by which the neutral zone stayed, but the Greeks were to evacuate Thrace. The impact of the crisis was considerable:

(*a*) In Britain it drove the final wedge between Curzon and Lloyd George, and helped to bring about the Prime Minister's downfall (Chapter 5, F1).

(*b*) British coercion of the Sultan led to his deposition in November 1922, and he escaped on a British battleship. Kemal became *gazi*, or leader, of a republic in October 1923, and the first post-war dictator.

(*c*) The weakness of the Empire was revealed and made worse at the Imperial Conference of 1923.

(*d*) The League of Nations supervised the transfer of 1,377,000 Greeks and 410,000 Turks in the Aegean region.

(*e*) Negotiations for a peace settlement opened at Lausanne in November, although they were to run into serious difficulties (Chapter 1, A3).

Further Reading

Barnett, C., *The Collapse of British Power*, Eyre Methuen, London, 1972.
Cross, C., *The Fall of the British Empire*, Hodder and Stoughton, London, 1968.
Mansergh, N., *The Commonwealth Experience*, Weidenfeld and Nicolson, London, 1969.
Medlicott, W. N., *British Foreign Policy Since Versailles*, Methuen, London, 1968.
Monroe, E., *Britain's Moment in the Middle East*, Chatto and Windus, London, 1963.

Northedge, F. S., *The Troubled Giant: Britain among the Great Powers 1916–1939*, Bell, London and New York, 1966.

Thomson, D., *Europe Since Napoleon*, Penguin, London, 1966.

Thornton, A. P., *The Imperial Idea and Its Enemies*, Macmillan, London, 1959.

Williamson, J. A., *The British Empire and Commonwealth*, Vol. II, Macmillan, London, 1958.

Questions

1. What effects did the Great War have on the British Empire?
2. Why has Versailles been subjected to so much hostile criticism, and how much of it is justified?
3. To what extent does Versailles reflect the aims and actions of Lloyd George?
4. Account for the foundation of the League of Nations.
5. To what extent were Britain's difficulties in India after 1914 of her own making?
6. How effectively did Britain use her new power in the Middle East?
7. How was the Near Eastern Question solved during the peace settlement?
8. What was the 'problem of dominion status' after the First World War?
9. Was allied intervention in Russia after the Bolshevik Revolution justified?
10. Why was the Treaty of Washington (1922) both 'an outstanding success' and 'one of the major catastrophes of English history'?

5

LLOYD GEORGE—THE POST-WAR COALITION: 1918–22

The end of the war was not the beginning of peace. The electors had to wait until 1922 for the removal of Lloyd George, and until 1924 for the return of stability. The four years after Lloyd George's victory in 1918 have been described as a 'journey through chaos'.

There was much talk of social reform, prosperity and peace, but none of these was in sight in 1922. The atmosphere was one of heady excitement, foreign adventures, turbulent industrial relations and turgid political dealings. Politics, which had been at fever heat since 1909, continued to be so until 1922, and for this Lloyd George must take the major share of the blame, for it was his opportunist character that dominated these years. Gone were the pro-Boer sentiments or reforming budgets; instead there was a government of 'hard-faced men who looked as if they had done very well out of the war'. Lloyd George was a prisoner of the Tories from choice, not necessity, and he went much further to the right than he need have done. On matters like the 'Black and Tans' in Ireland and harping on the threat of revolution he displayed the characteristics of right-wing reaction. The growth of the newly organised left and the threat of Bolshevism were dealt with by a blend of reform and coercion. The industrial situation, in spite of honeyed words, was governed by 'return to normal' in which industries returned to private enterprise, taxes were cut, economies introduced and promises to coalminers and agricultural workers broken. Even social reforms were hacked to pieces by the Geddes' Axe in 1922. After post-war euphoria and a boom a down-swing with heavy unemployment occurred and policies of wage reduction were initiated, while strikes were broken with the use of troops. At a cabinet meeting on 9 August 1919 Lloyd George maintained that Bolsheviks had seized control of the unions, and that he was going to take a firm line for, if not, 'We should at once create an enemy within our own borders, and one which would be better provided with dangerous weapons than Germany'.

There were similarities in post-war Britain with post-war Europe, and it was true that Red Revolution had been tried there. In Britain there was a new Communist Party and, less well known, a proto-fascist party—the National Party—so there was a slight danger of revolution, but what happened in Glasgow in 1919 or over the *Jolly George* (Section 4C) in 1920 was a long way from it. The government can claim some credit for bringing the country through a traumatic convalescence, but they also share the blame for raising the temperature and restoring the violent political situation in Ireland and labour relations which they had encountered before the war.

The victory parade was held (July 1919) and soon the officers were in the Black and Tans and the ranks begging in the gutter. The Cenotaph was designed, the Unknown Soldier brought back, and Armistice Day commemorated with a two-minute silence (11 November 1920). The British Legion was formed, Poppy Day started and Haig became its president. The

Licensing Laws were retained (1921) and eventually summer time was made permanent (1925). For ordinary people these small things counted. The homeless, unemployed and wounded cared less, and Eliot's *The Wasteland* (1922) was a fitting epitaph on a period which began with Lloyd George proclaiming 'homes fit for heroes' and ended with unemployment demonstrations and dole queues over a million long. It was the era of Horatio Bottomley and Maunday Gregory, tanks in the streets of Glasgow, war in Ireland, the sale of honours and the Black and Tans. On Armistice Day 1922, 25,000 London unemployed stood by the mourners with a wreath 'From the living victims—the unemployed—to our dead comrades, who died in vain'.

A. Coalition Politics

A1. The Despotism of Lloyd George

Three men—Lloyd George, Baldwin and Wilson—may lay claim to be the most adroit Prime Ministers of the twentieth century. All have been attacked as betraying the interests of the country in return for political power, and for exercising power in order to retain office. Lloyd George's immense prestige after victory in 1918 left him in an unchallengeable position. Liberals and Labour were divided, and the Conservatives believed they depended on him. Although they fretted over Ireland and India, they accepted he was anti-Bolshevik. Some of the older Tories disliked him as an upstart, but there had been a swing in the kind of Tory MP in the counties from 65 per cent landed gentry in 1910 to 54 per cent outsiders in 1918. Larger government and dispersal of patronage by Lloyd George helped to oil the wheels. Thus, although the coalition lost 21 by-elections, Lloyd George was determined in September 1922 to appeal again to the country. If he had won, the Tories would probably have split like the Liberals, and virtual one-party government would have arrived in Britain the same year as it did in Italy.

This element of Caesarism in Lloyd George was reflected in moves for fusion during this period. After 1918 many Tories and Liberals were convinced he was a national saviour. It was Churchill in July 1919 who first mooted the idea. By March 1920 some 95 members were in favour of such a move, and Chamberlain was so in favour that he offered to stand down in favour of Lloyd George when he offered to go in February 1922. Tory insistence on the tariff and the advice of Sir George Younger, the party chairman, was in the end sufficient to prevent the idea getting off the ground, but when in March 1921 Bonar Law retired ill and Chamberlain took over pressure grew, an election in December was favoured, and only headed off by Younger under back-bench and constituency attack. In February 1922 Bonar Law resumed leadership and a motion attacking the coalition was defeated by 192 votes. Discussion of another election began.

Under Lloyd George government was very much by a Whitehall clique. It was the garden suburb and pressure groups that he liked to mix with, not the traditional governing classes. The King was shunned. The cabinet was rarely called together, and did not meet in full session until October 1919. The Prime Minister was often abroad for months, taking a direct hand in foreign affairs, to Curzon's annoyance. He was secretive by nature, confided in his mistress and retreated to country cottages. He set up a fund which reached £3m, and in January 1922 a separate Coalition Liberal organisation. The most notorious of Lloyd George's methods was the sale of peerages. Of 708 peers in 1923, 176 had been created since 1910 and although wartime was likely to yield a higher number, it was obvious that some were merely for contributions to party funds. Between 1917 and 1923 four marquesses, eight earls, 22 viscounts and 64 barons were created. In 1922 the Robinson Case caused an outcry.

Lloyd George's rule was also marked by an increasing trend to authoritarianism which has escaped his admirer, A. J. P. Taylor. One of the astonishing features of this was his support in 1918 for the National Party led by Brig. Gen. Page Croft and Sir Richard Cooper, who were elected and, in 1921, of two right-wing candidates. Much of the apparatus of control created during the war was retained, particularly the Special Branch and passports. In 1920 three Acts—Firearms, Aliens and Emergency Powers—created a new range of offences, and the last Act gave the government power to declare a state of emergency with three months' jail and £100 fines for disobedience. The government resorted to hiring gunmen and authorising reprisals in Ireland, and in Britain called for Defence Units and Citizen Guards: 70,000 were recruited in 1921, and during the coal strike that year the government called up the reserves, created military camps in prominent places, and held manoeuvres in coalmining areas. A Supply and Transport Committee was set up in 1919 to break any attempt at general strikes, and under Sir Hamar Greenwood it organised a system of local government. Mowat accurately summed up the mercurial Welsh wizard as 'a genius with a double dose of everything, good and bad'.

A2. The Coupon Election of 1918

The Reform Act of 1918 and victory were the essential conditions for electoral success, but Lloyd George was determined to capitalise on his record as a radical in order to defeat Labour. In a speech on 12 November he backed the Liberals as a progressive party. The election was a double stunt—a khaki one and a broken social promise one—and in the end it cost Lloyd George the hope of leading a united Liberal party or winning another election. Since Asquith had no intention of being the third leg of the government it was clear that something would need to be done to save the Liberals from the well-oiled Tory machine. The idea of a coupon endorsing candidates was hit on so that Lloyd George could send it to as many Liberals as possible to secure their return without Tory opposition. Although Mowat said it was not given to those who voted against him in the Maurice Debate, this was not so. Of the 106 who voted against only 71 were standing, and 17 got a coupon. Of the 159 coupons only 54 went to those who voted for him in that debate, and 4 who did were excluded.

Spender said the election campaign developed into 'an orgy of chauvinism', and 'for ten days this storm of anger and folly swept over the country'. Some have argued that Lloyd George himself was moderate, and others beat the drum. It was Asquith who insisted on reparations to the full and Barnes, leader of the NDP, who advocated the trial of the Kaiser. But Churchill at Dundee supported the latter demand. He spoke also of social reform, including the nationalisation of the railways. The results were:

	Coalition	*Non-Coalition*
Conservatives	338	48
Liberals	136	26
Labour	10	59
Irish Nationalists		7
Sinn Fein		73 (did not sit)

This was the first democratic election in British history, and has several interesting features:

(*a*) The Asquithite Liberals were annihilated, including Asquith, McKenna, Runciman, Simon and Samuel. Sir Donald Maclean took over as leader.

(*b*) Labour emerged still divided by the pacifist issue. MacDonald and Snowden were defeated, and the party was led by Adamson until 1921, when he was succeeded by Clynes. Only Barnes remained in office in the coalition. But Labour was now the second largest party for the first time.

(*c*) Only eight Unionists who stood were defeated so three fifths of the House were Tories. There were 260 new members, but the average age had risen to 51½. It was a parliament of 'men who had run the war on the home front', including 179 company directors. Only 68 members had served in uniform.

(*d*) Although a woman, Countess Marciewicz, was elected she was Sinn Fein and did not take her seat. It was Lady Astor, returned for Plymouth in 1919 after the Sex Disqualification Removal Act, who was the first woman MP.

(*e*) The Home Rule party was destroyed, and Sinn Fein refused to sit, so that views on Ireland were almost exclusively Tory.

A3. Coalition Cabinet

Medlicott described the cabinet as 'one of the ablest' in British history; it contained a galaxy of talent with Lloyd George at the height of his powers, but it was rarely able to exercise its genius. Until October 1919 a small inner cabinet of the Prime Minister, Bonar Law, Curzon, Chamberlain and Barnes handled matters. The 'garden suburb' handled League matters throughout the ministry. Law was left No. 11 to the annoyance of Chamberlain, the Chancellor, but apart from him Lloyd George treated the ministers with scant courtesy. Balfour was overshadowed at Versailles and Curzon ignored, while the Prime Minister chaired conferences galore. Lord Birkenhead, brilliant and bibulous, was made Lord Chancellor, Milner was Colonial Secretary, Montague was at the India Office. Churchill wanted the Admiralty but was given the War and Air Ministries. For Ireland, there was French as Viceroy and Greenwood as Secretary. Sir Robert Horne followed Chamberlain as Chancellor in 1921.

These men represented High Toryism, but there were several reformers in the government. Addison was at Health, Eric Geddes at Transport, Fisher at Education and Auckland Geddes at the Board of Trade for a short time. The resulting government was highly volatile, since the right-wing Tories and the left-wing Liberals were at loggerheads, and a number of moderate Liberals such as Addison and Montague were forced out. Barnes left in January 1920. In 1919 the Act requiring a minister to stand for re-election if he exchanged offices was repealed and this gave the Prime Minister power to shift men about. Thus, in February 1921 Churchill became Colonial Secretary, and War and Air were separated. Although the government has much to its credit, including further self-government for India, the Irish Treaty, the gains of Versailles and important reforms, it is hard to resist Seaman's claim that it was 'lurching from expedient to expedient, from ill-considered adventure to ill-considered adventure, until in the end it seemed to become an inextricable confusion of rival ambitions, rival corruptions, rival superficialities, and rival opportunities'.

A4. The New Government Machine

The Great War had increased the powers and functions of the state and, although this trend was partly reversed after 1918 by the abolition of ministries like Reconstruction or Shipping, the size of the government increased considerably. Health, Pensions and Labour reflected the growth of the collective state with its social function, and among other ministries were Transport and Air. Not only did this lead to a growth in the Civil Service, but also in the number of MPs beholden to the government. A vested interest by a greatly expanded middle class had been created so that there were more than 160 boards and commissions, like the Medical Research and Electricity Councils, and the Haldane Committee on government was ignored when it proposed to rationalise Whitehall. The number of civil servants rose from 57,706 in 1914 to 116,241 in 1923 and new posts of great influence were created, particularly the Permanent Head and the Chief Economic Adviser.

B. Government Economic Policies: Return to Normal

Although the war distorted the basic nineteenth-century pattern of the British economy, it had not been any more than a limited impact. The gold standard had been partly eroded, there had been piecemeal nationalisation, the government had involved itself in industrial organisation both in production and labour relations, taxation and debts had risen, overseas assets equivalent to two years' income from interest had gone and there had been a strictly limited increase in the fiduciary issue. A small tariff had appeared. Even this trend was likely to be reversed because a government of Liberals and Tories was unlikely to do anything else.

What is more, nearly all the experts were agreed that this should be the policy. The Balfour Committee on Industry, the Cunliffe Committee on Finance and the Treasury all agreed. In 1920 Montague Norman took charge of the Bank of England and added its weight to the traditional arguments. In spite of a depression in 1920–21, the average growth rate was 2.7 per cent a year, and by 1924 production was back to 1914 levels.

B1. The International Position

America remained isolated behind tariff barriers and made no attempt to regulate the world economy, although she was now an important creditor nation. Europe was devastated, and Britain's chief rival Germany temporarily in the dust. Over-production and inflation thus contributed to a boom which started to collapse in April 1920 and reached rock bottom by December 1921, but thereafter recovery started again. Britain was determined to use her influence to restore the pre-war European economy by preserving free trade, repaying wartime debts and returning to the Gold Standard.

B2. The Home Position

In the first post-war budget death duties rose to 40 per cent on incomes over £2m, and profits tax was raised again, but the main aim of the government was to balance and then reduce the budget. A deficit of £326m was turned into a surplus of £230m in 1920 and by 1922 tax cuts could start, and the estimates fell below £1,000m for the first time since 1915. Although the exemption limit for income tax was raised to £150 a year, the rise in incomes meant that the total number of payers had risen to 7¾ million. This enabled the government to lower the tax by 1s in the pound in 1922 without much loss of revenue. Profits tax was eliminated altogether by 1921. But these measures were not enough to satisfy the orthodox. A campaign was launched on 'squandermania', and in February 1922 the Geddes Reports advocated £85m cuts in expenditure, including defence, education and health. The government accepted £64m and combined this with £77m of internal economies, so that the total was near a tenth of government expenditure. The government also took measures to curb spending:

(a) Local Government Act (1921) gave powers to punish authorities that refused to levy poor law rates. This led to the imprisonment of 30 Poplar councillors led by Lansbury.

(b) Housing subsidies under the Addison Act were phased out, and when Addison objected he was removed.

(c) The Agricultural Wages Boards were scrapped, and the laws requiring eight-hour days on the railways and in the mines broken.

Reductions in direct taxation raised the issue of tariffs once more, particularly since the Tories were in favour of them, although they now talked about 'safeguarding' rather than imperial preference. The government responded with a number of small measures besides continuing the McKenna Duties. The Dye Stuffs Importation Act (1920) helped to protect the chemical industry, the Safeguarding of Industries Act (1921) imposed a 33⅓ per cent duty on certain specialist products, and the German Reparation Act (1921) imposed duties on German imports. These measures left Britain very much a free trade country since in 1929 only 3 per cent of her imports were affected by tariffs.

B3. Boom and Slump

The boom was stimulated by renewed confidence and government selling. Gratuities and war pensions were sunk in small businesses while on the land with government aid, 17,000 were settled on small holdings. The number of new companies started rose from 7,425 in 1913 to 11,000 in 1920, and there were considerable booms in cotton, shipping and engineering. One million acres of land changed hands by the end of 1919. There was strong pressure on companies to merge and grow, and in particular the banks were rationalised so that by 1920 the Big Five controlled 85 per cent of deposits. Then with the recovery of our competitors and the removal of surplus demand, prices began to fall and employers to cut wages as profits fell. Deflation led to a rise in unemployment as follows:

| December 1920 | 691,103 | June 1921 | 2,171,288 |
| December 1921 | 1,934,030 | December 1922 | 1,431,929 |

Thereafter it never fell below a million until 1940. In October 1920 the first unemployment demonstration occurred. In 1921 Wal Hannington founded the NUWM and there were disturbances in many towns.

B4. Period of Decontrol

Even during the election campaign, Bonar Law had persuaded Lloyd George to drop railway nationalisation, and after the FBI report of 1919 had come out in favour of private enterprise, it was only a question of time before the government withdrew, and the onset of depression made it certain that they would do so. There were a few isolated examples of continued government intervention, including the Forestry Commission and the Aerial Navigation Act (1919) giving powers to control air traffic. It was clear the government had departed from any socialist intentions. By 1926 Addison was in the Labour Party writing *Practical Socialism*. The four main areas of decontrol were:

(*a*) *Transport*. The original Ways and Communications Bill which would have given the new Transport Ministry considerable powers was watered down.

(*b*) *Railways*. In June 1920 a Railways Bill was introduced to reduce the 120 companies to seven, but after strong opposition, this was cut to four. The act of 1921 set up the GWR, LMSR, LNER and the SR and a railway rates tribunal.

(*c*) *Coalmines*. The Sankey Commission issued reports (1919) and came close to recommending nationalisation. In February and November 1920 Lloyd George accepted this, but instead the mines were decontrolled at an earlier date than promised.

(*d*) *Agriculture*. The Agriculture Act of 1920 guaranteed prices for four years and established wages boards. But the boom drove up average minimum wages from 30s to 46s a week by August 1920. Then the depression drove wheat prices down from 86s 4d to 40s a quarter. and faced with this the government repealed the law in 1921.

Lauterbach said the impact of these measures on the economy was not entirely clear but it can be argued that the return of industry and finance to methods developed in the middle of the nineteenth century was the root cause why industrial adjustment became industrial depression by the end of the 1920s. In Marwick's words, 'reconstruction turned to retrenchment, the land fit for heroes became the Wasteland'.

C. Labour in Vain: 1918–22

The war period served to advance the argument for socialism since the main political parties had nationalised, controlled and reformed on socialist lines, arguing it improved the economy. Many of all parties were convinced that this trend would continue and, had the reports initiated by the Reconstruction Ministry been applied, 1918 would have looked a lot more like 1945. Labour had increased its power with a rise in union membership, shop stewards and consultation and participation in government. The social problems of the war period such as housing gave added weight to the need for a radical solution, and the granting of one man one vote at last gave the worker some say in choosing the government. The war had, however, divided Labour as well. MacDonald, Snowden and Henderson differed

from Barnes, Adamson and Clynes on supporting the war, and this robbed
Labour of greater success in 1918. Thereafter, foolish fears that Labour
was Bolshevik added to their difficulties, and the existence of Syndicalism
and Red Clydeside kept many workers loyal to the Liberals as long as
Lloyd George parried Labour with reforms. Lloyd George's failure to
honour his pledges was the decisive factor in convincing many that Radicalism had shot its bolt, and although Lloyd George and Asquith later competed for the Radical crown they never succeeded in convincing the electorate. Lastly, the capitalist reaction and the onset of depression proved
grist to the Labour mill after 1920.

In post-war Britain the main forces on the left were:

1. *Labour Party.* With 72 seats by 1922 they were the main opposition party,
but neither Adamson nor Clynes was effective as leader. MacDonald returned as
an MP in 1922, but until then the party gave little evidence of political ability.
The constitution of February 1918, *Labour and the New Social Order*, largely
written by Sidney Webb, and the writings of men like Tawney provided a firm
intellectual basis for the left.

2. *Trade Unions.* In 1920 the TUC in its modern form and a National Joint
Council with Labour were created. The two moved into Transport House in
1928. From 1922 they financed the *Daily Herald*. Powerful unions continued to
emerge, including the AEU (1920), TGWU (1921) and GMWU (1924), although
the traditional big three—coal, railways and transport—held the field. By 1920,
60 per cent of adult male workers were in unions and total numbers had risen
enormously:

1918	6,533,000	1919	7,926,000
1920	8,348,000	1921	6,633,000
1922	5,625,000	1923	5,429,000

3. *Extreme Left.* This section was sharply divided on doctrinal issues. Red
Clydeside with the Clyde Workers Committee represented the most popular and
practical left-wing force. Wal Hannington's NUWM was a training ground for
Communists such as Painter and the Moffits, but had little influence with the
unemployed themselves. The British Communist Party was started in July 1920,
and organised at Leeds in January 1921. It had most influence on foreign policy
where it traded on war weariness to stop intervention in Russia.

Post-war Britain was a period of troubled industrial relations and fears
of revolution were expressed by the governing class. Apart from massive
strikes the period saw riots, direct action and pressure on government
foreign policy from the left, and these events have led some historians to
argue in favour of an aborted revolution. In one sense, by stressing this
the historians are using Lloyd George's argument for the mailed fist. Works
published on the shop stewards' movement (Pribicevic), Clydeside (Middle-
mas), syndicalism (Kendall) and the impact of the Russian Revolution
(Graubard) tend to study the left-wing movements as if they were the
mainstream rather than a tributary of political development. In fact, the
election of 1922 and the fate of the first Labour government showed how
marginal left-wing forces were in the political nation. Trouble in the armed
forces and police was contained. Labour efforts to intervene in foreign
policy had little impact on Anglo-Soviet relations. In Irish matters a Labour
report on British 'oppression' provided ammunition against the govern-

ment, but a TUC demand in July 1920 for a general strike to support the Irish rebels was not heeded. Widespread strikes were the most serious evidence of labour discontent, but by 1922 these had been contained, and wage cuts were in full swing. Thus, although the number of days lost in strikes was large, there is no evidence that they were a prelude to a general strike, since the Triple Alliance failed to work in 1921. The total numbers of work days lost were:

1918	5,880,000	1919	34,970,000
1920	26,570,000	1921	85,870,000
1922	19,850,000	1923	10,670,000

The main difficulties with the workers were:

1. *Demobilisation Riots*. The original plans for demobbing provided for selected categories to be returned rather than a first in, first out procedure. Moreover, the government extended conscription until April 1920 to meet its European commitments and many thought they would be cheated of their gratuities and offers of land. In January 1919 riots started at Folkestone and Dover, and spread elsewhere. Lorryloads of troops demonstrated in Whitehall. Army leaders pressed for stern measures and at Rhyl five rioters were killed. Churchill was put in charge and in under a year 2½ million men were dealt with successfully.

2. *Red Clydeside*. Led by Gallacher, Kirkwood and Shinwell, the workers demanded a 40-hour week and no wage cuts in order to hold on to wartime gains. On 27, 29 and 31 January 1919, mass demonstrations occurred in Glasgow with a brisk battle in George Square before the army moved in on 1 February. By 11 February the strike had failed, and a dozen leaders were in prison.

3. *Police Strikes*. After a strike in August 1918 a National Union of Policemen was started. Sir Nevil Macready was put in charge of the Metropolitan Police and banned it. This led to a second strike in August 1919 and from 1 to 3 August there was rioting at Liverpool. The police lost the right to have a union.

4. *Railway Strike*. Sir Auckland Geddes negotiated a wage settlement involving standardisation, i.e. reduction of some grades. On 26 September a strike began, and the government declared the railwaymen to be anarchists, used DORA to declare a state of emergency and appealed for citizen guards. J. H. Thomas was supported by Henderson and Clynes of the Transport Workers and on 5 October the government climbed down.

5. *Councils of Action*. In May 1920 dockers of Bevin's union refused to coal the *Jolly George*, said to be carrying munitions to Poland at war with Russia. After demonstrations a joint TUC-Labour Party decision to establish Councils of Action was followed by the setting up of some 350. In fact, the government had told the French they would not support intervention.

6. *Coal Strike*. Wages had risen in March, but in June the government refused a further demand, and there was talk of invoking the Triple Alliance with a meeting on 22 September. A strike began on 16 October and the NUR agreed to a sympathy strike. Although the government passed the Emergency Powers Act it resumed negotiations, and an interim settlement with some increases was secured.

7. *Black Friday*. The mines returned to private ownership on 31 March 1921, so the final settlement was left to the owners. Since prices were falling they decided on reductions. The government took firm measures, and the miners asked for the Triple Alliance's support. On 8 April they agreed. A general strike was to be called on 12 April, and this forced negotiations to start, but they

collapsed and a fresh date of 15 April was set. On 14 April MPs met Frank Hodge of the Miners, and a compromise emerged which J. H. Thomas urged them to accept. When they refused on 'Black Friday', the Triple Alliance called off its support. On 1 July the defeated miners returned, and although the government gave a £10m subsidy, wage cuts up to half were carried out.

D. A Measure of Reform

During the election campaign, there had been a demand for social reform, and Lloyd George had backed this. Although Mowat accused Lloyd George of 'socialism by the back door', it is generally agreed and most forcibly put by Abrams that social reform was limited and even reversed during 1922. Fisher's 1918 Act was severely mauled and Addison's Housing Act was run down, and Lloyd George seemed unwilling to defy Tory backbench opinion which called for low taxes and reductions in expenditure, and allowed many useful measures of his own to be stillborn. In only two respects—unemployment pay and council housing—could it be said that the Liberals continued the pre-war trend in any markedly novel manner. The chief reforms were:

1. *Old-fashioned Liberal reforms.* The disestablishment of the Church of England in Wales was carried. The Licensing Act was passed (1921).
2. *Consolidating pre-war measures.*
(a) In 1918 the Maternity and Child Welfare Act was passed, but it was curbed in 1922.
(b) In 1908 the Liberals had improved the Conciliation Act of 1896 by setting up panels, but these had been little used. In 1919 the Industrial Courts Act set up an arbitration court at the Ministry of Labour.
(c) In 1919 clauses in the Old Age Pensions Act restricting admission to the scheme were scrapped and benefits raised. Health insurance was extended to cover all those earning up to £250 per annum.
3. *Conciliating Labour.*
(a) In 1918 an act prevented wage reductions for six months, and this was renewed until September 1920.
(b) Out-of-work donations were given to ex-soldiers until March 1921.
(c) Rent control was continued by an Act in 1920, raising the limits to £105 (London), £90 (Scotland) and £78 elsewhere.
(d) The Sankey Commission was appointed to consider the mines. After the government failed to honour its pledges they passed the Coal Mines Act (1920), which provided a seven-hour day, a special Mines Department at the Home Office and a Miners Welfare Fund.
4. *Major reforms.*
(a) *Unemployment Insurance Acts.* In 1920 the insurance fund had a surplus of £22m, but the depression soon dissipated this, and the Unemployment Act of 1920, which extended the 1911 Act to all occupations except the Civil Service, agriculture and domestic service, was the cause. This led to the Unemployment Insurance Act of 1921 by which, after 26 weeks of benefit, people would receive 'transitional payment' or a dole instead of transferring directly to the Poor Law. The Unemployed Dependents Act gave benefits to families.
(b) *Housing Act.* With a deficiency of 600,000 dwellings, the government was not concerned about slum clearance but new houses. The Salisbury Committee proposals for subsidised houses were introduced in the Addison Act of 1919. Houses were to be built at the rate of 70,000 a year up to 1921. At first the rents would be low, but it was hoped that by 1928 an economic rent would be

paid. A capital subsidy of £260 a house was provided for private builders. By the time the Act was curtailed 213,000 houses had been built, but there was by then a shortage of 822,000.

Both these measures have been praised and criticised. Taylor maintains unemployment insurance prevented extremists using the unemployed as political fodder. Seaman regards the acts as starting 'twenty years of social and political controversy' about the unemployed rather than about the causes of unemployment. The nature of the acts set a pattern of legislative chaos, and by 1927 no less than 12 unemployment acts had been passed. When the limits were abolished in 1924 the costs proved counterproductive, with demands for dole cuts being added to Tory war cries. The Addison houses were built to the Tudor Walters standards, and these made new houses too expensive for those who really needed them. They started the vogue for estates with high rents and travel costs, which lowered the standard of living in hygienic surroundings. The economic rents were never paid, and the housing shortage grew worse until private enterprise took over in the 1930s.

E. The Irish Wars: 1919–22

The election of 1918 confirmed that the rebellion of 1916 (Chapter 3, Section F) had set in motion a demand for complete independence. The 73 Sinn Feiners refused to sit and on 21 January 1919 created an illegal government in Ireland. The government declared both Sinn Fein and the Dail illegal, and it was clear that a policy of repression had been decided on under the influence of the Tories, particularly Carson and Bonar Law. But, in Mowat's words, 'within three years the Irish had brought the British Empire, then at the peak of its power after victory, almost to its knees'. The result was the Liberals were forced to concede partition, which they had opposed, and the Tories to surrender the Southern Unionists, which they had refused to do in 1914. Lloyd George achieved the Irish settlement that lasted until 1969, and this is sometimes regarded as his highest achievement in view of the conflicting passions. But the settlement had a wider importance. In 1902 Britain had made war and annexed the Boers; now she conceded virtual independence to those who threatened the Empire. The government changed course under the influence of international opinion, opposition from former liberal imperialists like Grey and Asquith, pressure from Labour and criticism from the 'liberal' establishment. This too marked a precedent.

E1. The First Irish War: April 1920–July 1921

(a) Preparations. When DeValera had escaped from Lincoln Jail, he became president in March 1919, although he left almost immediately for America where he raised 5m dollars. Griffiths, president of the Dail, which met in April, was titular head with Brugha as Defence Minister and Collins, commander of the IRA, as Finance Minister. When the influenza epidemic led the government to release the MPs, the new government began to function by setting up alternative organisations to paralyse the authorities. Collins trained an army of about 15,000 but they wore no uniform, used guerilla tactics and rarely mustered full strength. Violence began to grow with 18 murders in 1919, and an attempt on Lord French's life.

(*b*) Government preparations. Recruiting for the RIC was extended to the mainland, with some 1,500 recruits, to swell the total to 15,000. The recruits were given a black beret and were known as the Black and Tans. A military division (Auxiliaries) of the RIC was established under Brig. Gen. Crozier. An intelligence service was organised by Col. Ormonde Winter. Hamar Greenwood, a tough-minded Canadian, became Secretary and the number of troops was raised to 60,000.

(*c*) It is difficult to fix casualties in a guerilla war, but the approximate figures for the first war were 399 police, 148 troops and 752 rebels killed. Since the IRA were not in uniform, the British argued they were not covered by the law of war. Each side used brutal methods. The IRA used flying columns who attacked soldiers at Fermoy and Kilmichael. They shot 73 informers, and resorted to hunger strikes, but after a death in October, gave these up. The British carried out reprisal raids, starting in July and culminating in the burning of Cork in December. Some 18 villages were attacked. Drum-head court-martials were begun, and 14 shot. The worst day was Bloody Sunday when 14 British officers were murdered, and reprisals at Croke Park football ground led to 12 deaths.

In August the Restoration of Order in Ireland Act was passed, followed in December by martial law, extended to eight counties by January 1921. It seemed that the government was determined to win.

E2. Creation of Northern Ireland

In December 1920 the Government of Ireland Act was passed which created two parliaments: one for a new province of Ulster, and the other at Dublin. The latter was a farce since only the four members for Trinity College sat and the other seats were held by Sinn Fein, who did not attend. The former, however, opened in June 1921 after elections had been held with proportional representation. In spite of this the results were a foregone conclusion. The Ulster Unionists, led by Sir James Craig, won 40 seats to 12 for Sinn Fein. Proportional representation was abolished in 1929, and Craig himself remained Prime Minister until his death in 1940. In addition, the new province continued to send 13 members to Westminster.

During the first two years of Ulster's existence, just over 400 were killed in disturbances of various kinds because the decision to partition Ireland was fraught with difficulties. These were:

(*a*) The new province contained only six of the eight historic counties, and one of them had a Catholic majority. The Act contained proposals for boundary revision and a council of all Ireland, which made the Protestants insecure. They also disliked giving up the Southern Unionists under Lord Midleton.

(*b*) The Orange Order was revived, and 25,000 Ulster Volunteers were transformed into the B Specials. By March 1922 they were 40,000 in number. Sir Henry Wilson gave up as CIGS to advise them on military matters.

(*c*) In the South fears were expressed for Northern Catholics, and the Dail saw it as an attempt to retain British power by taking away the industrial base of the country. They boycotted trade, and this combined with the onset of depression in shipping to cause an explosive situation in Belfast.

Rioting started during 1920 with clashes in Londonderry and Belfast. In the latter 4,000 were made homeless, 62 killed and 200 wounded, and riots continued throughout 1921 until severe measures were taken. In 1922 the Special Powers Act was passed (made permanent in 1933) which gave the government powers on arms, curfews, searches and imprisonment, and provided flogging and death penalties for breaches. When the treaty with Southern Ireland was signed, Northern Ireland was given the right to secede, which she did in December 1922.

E3. Pressure for a Truce

While the war went forward with some success and much suffering, pressure mounted for a peaceful settlement after Asquith had launched an attack on Lloyd George. He said the government was heading for 'political bankruptcy', and described its 'blind and indiscriminate vengeance' for which the Prime Minister could not escape responsibility. He was backed by Simon, Grey and other Liberals and from the Tory side by Lord Robert Cecil and circles favourable to the League. In January 1921 a Labour Report gave evidence of government complicity in outrages, and next month the Archbishop of Canterbury, Cosmo Lang, and bishops like Temple of Manchester condemned the government. In May George V complained to the Irish Secretary about reprisals, and his speech at the opening of the Northern Ireland parliament in June called for a peaceful settlement.

It is clear that by May the IRA were short of ammunition—hence their burning of the Dublin Customs House—but the pressure for a truce was too great and on 11 July one was agreed, although the rebels were allowed to retain their arms.

E4. Treaty of London, December 1921

(a) The negotiations fall into two periods. The first, from July to September, studied the British terms guaranteeing Northern Ireland dominion status, and British interests. This was necessary if the government was to carry outraged Tories with them, but DeValera did not approve and, using the rearrangement of the Dail cabinet as an excuse, he left for America again. Then followed a period of direct negotiations from October to December. The Irish delegation represented Sinn Fein rather than the IRA and consisted of Griffiths and Collins. They were opposed by an extremely powerful British delegation including Churchill, Greenwood, Lloyd George, Chamberlain and Birkenhead. The main problems encountered were defining dominion status and the possibility of eventual reunification. Pressure from outside made it look as if they would fail, and on 5 December Lloyd George tried brinkmanship. Griffiths gave in and on 6 December 1921 the articles were signed.

(b) The terms were:
(i) Southern Ireland was to become a Dominion called the Irish Free State.
(ii) It was to retain the monarchy and the oath of allegiance.
(iii) Clauses 11–15 incorporated the Government of Ireland Act of 1920, and gave Ulster the right to secede.
(iv) A Council of Ireland was to provide a common link.
(v) A boundary commission was to be established to rectify the border 'in accordance with the wishes of the inhabitants'.
(vi) Britain was to retain naval and air facilities. In war she could extend these in an unspecified manner.
(vii) The Irish would retain British citizenship in Britain, and there would be free trade. Dublin would accept its share of the national debt and provide compensation for the Southern Unionists.

Mowat described the Irish war as 'the greatest blot on the record of the coalition' and the treaty as a masterpiece—'the triumph of his dangerous dexterity as a negotiator'. The results of the treaty were:

(*a*) A split occurred in Southern Ireland. Griffiths and Cosgrave were opposed by DeValera and Brugha. When the Dail debated the treaty, the vote was carried by 64–57, and on 22 January 1922 Dublin Castle formally surrendered power.

(*b*) Since it was eventually accepted, the treaty is a decisive landmark. It brings to an end the struggle that had started in 1886. It remained the basis of relations until 1937. It secured peace for half a century.

(*c*) The Tories were furious. Midleton thought that to desert 300,000 Southern Protestants was 'deplorable', and the Tory Conference in November was seething with anger.

E5. The Second Irish War, March 1922–May 1923
The necessity to put the treaty into force, led to great difficulties:

(*a*) In England the Tories opposed it, but in the end only some 60 voted against Churchill's spirited defence. In June 1922 Wilson was murdered, and Bonar Law denounced the government's weakness. Churchill wanted to react by allowing Macready to support the new government and expel the IRA from the Law Courts in Dublin, but fortunately Macready delayed, and the order was stopped. However, Churchill had struck up a friendship with Collins during the negotiations so he lent him artillery, and the Irish Army cleared the courts themselves in July 1922.

(*b*) In Ireland elections were held in June to replace the illegal Dail, and the parliament of the 1920 act. The result was 58 Nationalists, 35 Republicans and 17 Irish Labour. The new Dail met to draw up a constitution which was passed in December. Healy became Governor General and Cosgrave Prime Minister. A two-chamber parliament included a senate with 16 Southern Unionists.

On 28 March 1922 the IRA split between the regulars who supported the government under O'Connell and then Collins, and the irregulars led by O'Connor, Lynch and O'Malley. DeValera formed the Republican Party to oppose the treaty, and was joined by Brugha. A war between brothers in arms began with no holds barred. Collins was murdered and succeeded by Mulcahy. Childers and O'Connor were executed. Lynch and Brugha were killed. The government increased the army to 60,000 and the war cost £17m, which the poor country could ill afford. The new government outdid the British in brutality by introducing martial law under which 77 people were executed, authorising reprisals in December 1922 after an MP was killed, placing 11,000 Irishmen in internment camps and permitting hunger strikers to starve to death. After this war the government was established. There were several loose ends left from the treaty, but these were settled by March 1926 (Chapter 11, D1).

F. The Political Crisis of October 1922

In October 1922 Lloyd George fell from power, and never regained it, although he remained an important political figure as late as the overthrow of Chamberlain in 1940. With him went the Liberal party created by Gladstone and Joe Chamberlain in the 1870s, and any hope of Asquith returning to office with a united party. Already some Liberals like Simon were moving right, others like Addison towards Labour, and the party was in such a weak condition that it had no decisive rôle to play in the election of 1922. There followed a period of virtually unbroken Tory rule until 1945, and naturally such a reversal of political fortunes has attracted much attention. Mowat said his departure was 'finally over personality and party rather than principle', while Wilson argues his fall was not due to the government's immediate difficulties like the Irish Settlement or Turkey, but to the collapse of the unnatural alliance of Tory and Liberal formed in 1915 to fight the war. But it surely owes something to the events he mentions for many leading Tories remained convinced that an anti-Socialist alliance was the best form of government. It was also true that Liberals were becoming disillusioned with the proportion of power wielded by increasingly right-wing Tories. Since an election was due in either 1922 or 1923 the issue became acute as Lloyd George wished to go on, and was strongly supported by Chamberlain and Balfour. Chamberlain undertook to rally the backbenchers and it was this miscalculation that led to the Carlton Club meeting which brought down Lloyd George.

F1. Reasons for Lloyd George's Fall

Lloyd George's personality had won the war, swept victoriously through the post-war settlement, surmounted industrial and Irish troubles and had been a prime factor in the successes of the coalition. He dazzled the Tory leaders, if not their followers. But his personality had its defects. It caused bitterness and cynicism by his abrupt dismissals of ministers and switches of policy so that, in Taylor's words, 'he aroused every feeling except trust'. His personal life, new residence at Chequers (1921), party fund and patronage aroused hostility, and there was a demand for 'clean government'. Lloyd George's foreign adventures were alarming. Wars in Russia, Iraq, Afghanistan, Somaliland, Egypt and Ireland, trouble in India and Turkey, and a hectic round of international conferences seemed to involve Britain ever more deeply. After failures at Cannes and Genoa these looked hollow. Curzon was infuriated by the Prime Minister's interventions, particularly over Chanak, and his desertion, which he had decided on by 15 October, gave an alternative government the next potential prime minister. There was a demand for tranquillity after so much activity, and Baldwin's view of dynamic forces' and 'clever men' stood the old praise of Lloyd George on its head as a criticism.

These dislikes would not have carried weight unless the Tories had come to realise their own party was at stake, and that his policy was not what they wished. The Anglo-Russian Trade Treaty, the Irish settlement, the criticism of General Dyer by Churchill, the shock of the Milner Report on Egypt and the declaration on Kenyan settlement policy disturbed Tory backbenchers. While men like Baldwin were concerned about moral issues, those like Joynson Hicks wanted right-wing policies. Younger, the chairman, made it clear in January 1922 that he did not favour an election on a united front, and in spite of criticism as a 'second-rate brewer' and 'cabin boy' he was not deterred from this point of view. He told Bonar Law that 184 constituencies would run anti-coalition candidates, although Chamberlain reported as late as October that a majority of Tories favoured coalition. From July backbenchers led by Baldwin had been meeting,

and they were hostile to the government going forw[...]
held together on Chanak and on 10 October, with [...]
Baldwin, they agreed to a coalition election. On 1[...]
brought his criticism into the open, and Bonar Law w[...]
act. Sensing perhaps that Chamberlain had taken a little [...]
Law listened, and on 18 October received Curzon, Younger and Baldwin.
By the end of the day he was largely convinced he must act, but still hesi-
tated next morning. Sale of peers

F2. The Carlton Club Meeting

On 19 October Chamberlain and Balfour spoke for the continuation of
the coalition. Baldwin then spoke, saying that if they did not give up Lloyd
George the disintegrating process in the party would 'go on inevitably until
the old Conservative party was smashed to atoms and lost in ruins'. Bonar
Law echoed this speech, and the vote was 187 to 87 for severance. Chamberlain and the leading ministers resigned, forcing Lloyd George to give up.
Bonar Law became Prime Minister, and then leader of the party after
Chamberlain had resigned. At the time no one thought that Lloyd George
was finished since he had taken all the talent with him, and the new ministry
was the weakest since 1892. During the coming election Lloyd George
played in low key, hoping for a revival of the coalition, but Bonar Law
won the election, and upset these calculations. Mowat says, 'Thus ended
the coalition. And thus ended the reign of the great ones, the giants of the
Edwardian era and of the war, and the rule of the pygmies, of the second-
class brains began, to continue until 1940.' In fact, this was not entirely
true. Baldwin proved to be a master politician, although at this time
Balfour described him as an idiot. As for the policies of appeasement and
the failure to adjust either the economy or the strategy of the country to
meet the post-war situation, some blame rested with the giants themselves.
Balfour's Treaty of Washington and Churchill's Ten Year Rule were not
without significance after 1930. Economic conservatism and dole queues
already shaped policies in the 1920s. Seaman makes another point:

'If the one indisputable achievement of the British in the period between the
wars is that they preserved their parliamentary institutions then the credit must
go first of all to the Carlton Club meeting of 1922.'

The setting up of the Tory 1922 Committee reflects this feeling, but it is
scarcely accurate. It was political tactics and the decisions of two ministers,
Baldwin and Bonar Law, that made the meeting possible, and the election
that secured its permanence. Moreover, although democracy was in a
sense preserved after 1931, it was very much in the form of a parliamentary
dictatorship made easier by the eclipse of the Liberal Party.

Further Reading

Foot, D., *British Political Crises* (for 1916 and 1922), William Kimber, London,
1976.
Holt, E., *Protest in Arms*, Putnam, London, 1960.
Kendall, W., *The Revolutionary Movement in Britain, 1900–1921*, Weidenfeld
and Nicolson, 1969.

.r, M., *The Fall of Lloyd George*, Macmillan, 1973.

wick, A., *Britain in the Century of Total War*, Bodley Head, London, 1968.

.iddlemass, K., *The Clydesiders*, Hutchinson, London, 1966.

owat, C. L., *Britain Between the Wars 1918–1940*, Methuen, London, 1955, and now available in paperback.

Owen, F., *Tempestuous Journey* (Biography of Lloyd George), Hutchinson, London, 1954.

Seaman, L. C. B., *Post Victorian Britain 1902–1951*, Methuen, London, 1966.

Taylor, A. J. P., *English History 1914–1945*, Oxford University Press, London and New York, 1965, available in paperback.

Questions

1. 'The Wizard Merlin'. How successful was Lloyd George as a politician?
2. 'Ireland ruined Lloyd George.' What difficulties did the Irish question present to Lloyd George, and how successfully did he overcome them?
3. Was the Coupon Election the first democratic British election?
4. Why was return to normal acceptable after such revolutionary changes during the war period?
5. Why was there so much labour discontent in the immediate post-war years?
6. Was Lloyd George more successful in foreign than home affairs?
7. How true is it to speak of a revolutionary movement in Britain in the period 1915–21?
8. Is there any evidence in the conduct of the post-war coalition to show that Lloyd George was a statesman of genius?
9. Why were two civil wars necessary to solve the Irish Question?
10. Account for the overthrow of Lloyd George in 1922.

6

THE AGE OF BALDWIN AND MACDONALD: 1922–29

The Great War cut like an axe at the tree of British power, and succeeded in lopping a few branches. It incised more deeply the fundamental concepts and structure of society, and although Mowat is right to stress that for most people the 1920s were a period of return to normal, it is also true that in the post-war atmosphere certain ideas, discernible prior to 1914, became widespread among thinking people. This was a prelude to the changes of the 1930s when what is recognisably 'modern' Britain appeared. The current of radical criticism was partly provoked by the war, and by the growth of socialist thought, but Bloomsbury was more than a brittle reaction to the Jazz Age. Conceptual changes in thinking about religion and philosophy opened the way for new sciences and social sciences increasingly to determine the way people thought about society and life.

In material life for ordinary people the 1920s also saw the fundamental move towards an industrial-urban society. Technology, mechanisation, mass production and urbanisation were all products of the nineteenth century, but it was only in the 1920s that their influence became pervasive. To take three examples: the horse was at last replaced by an alternative form of transport, the aeroplane brought to an end naval supremacy and radio created vast possibilities for politicians. Huxley's *Brave New World* appeared in 1932. In spite of much distress among the poor and unemployed, the 1920s saw the start of a mass market, catering for the tastes of those for the first time in history with time and money to spare for leisure. This trend was to accelerate in the 1930s amidst cries of horror, very often from the intellectual establishment. By 1926 MacDonald's Labour Party had moved away from socialist utopias and revolutions to more fabian tactics, while Baldwin was doing his best to move the Tories from entrenched capitalist and imperialist positions. Expenditure on the social services shows clearly that the collectivist or welfare state was now fairly launched on course.

These changes were least noticed and least effective among the ruling class. Morton's *In Search of England* (1927) contains no hint of that other England where most people were now living, and Stanley Baldwin's speeches give the same impression. The serious economic problems were hidden beneath return to normal, pre-war economics and trade recovery in the late 1920s. Although the persistence of a million out of work should have alerted people to serious economic dangers as well as exciting their compassion, neither party produced a solution in the 1920s. Baldwin's reply to the King's Speech in February 1928 was a paean of progress in the industrial field, whereas Britain was in serious difficulties in her main exporting industries and the state of torpor was such that British industry, while responding well to new consumer demand at home, had little answer to the nation's competitors.

This failure to grasp essential issues was marked in nearly all aspects of policy during the 1920s. In foreign affairs and defence it was a period of false hope following Locarno and misplaced confidence in the League, accompanied by a run-down in defence spending. In imperial matters the Conservatives yielded as far as a promise of dominion status for India, and Balfour papered over the cracks of dominion nationalism with his 1926 declaration. There was a serious failure to plan strategy, imperial and foreign policy with any regard to resources and interests during this period. Much sorry politics in the 1930s was conditioned by events in the twenties.

Seaman, however, says the 1920s saw the start of the drift to dictatorship in Europe with Mussolini (1922) and Primo de Rivera (1923), while tranquillity and moderation enabled Britain to retain democratic government and a relatively peaceful political scene. Neither Fascism nor Communism made any real impact on the British electorate. The mood of self-questioning and doubt in Europe, illustrated by Spengler's *Decline of the West* (1918), had no place on the grouse moors with MacDonald or Baldwin. This may have been a gain, but tranquillity turned to apathy and moderation to appeasement, and by 1931 Britain had a 'parliamentary dictatorship' dedicated to both. From 'return to normal', through 'safety first', to 'peace in our time' there is a connecting theme. It is either the preservation of democracy, or the failure to preserve Britain's power.

A. The 1920s—The Birth of Modern Britain

A1. Religion and Philosophy

The war may have strengthened individuals' religion, but the overall effect was to increase disillusion and to continue the decline in church attendance. In one London borough of 80,000 in 1902–03, 10,370 had attended at some place of worship on Sunday; in 1926 only 3,690 did so. This decline should not be exaggerated. Politicians were still themselves religious—the Baldwins prayed at their bedside each night—and continued to be conscious of religious influence on political issues. A poll in 1926 indicated that 71 per cent attended church at fairly regular intervals and 53 per cent accepted the Creed. There were a number of successful religious revivals and some notable defences of the faith, including Gore's *Reconstruction of Belief* (1926). William Temple, Bishop of Manchester (1921), was eager to show the Church had a social rôle, while Bishop Barnes of Birmingham (1924) argued religion and science were compatible. The Church Assembly Act (1919) brought the laity into the governing body of the Church of England, while in the free churches the Presbyterians reunited in 1929, and many of the Methodists in 1932.

The prevailing mood was one of doubt, and two important writers, Joad and Russell, led the attack on religion. The latter's lecture in 1927—'Why I am not a Christian'—became a best-seller. The attack on religion was threefold. Metaphysics were held to have been discredited by the new philosophy, psychology was said to have cast grave doubts on religious motivations, and humanists argued that 'the good life' could be attained without reference to either the sacraments or prohibitions of religion. Comparative sociology also suggested that Christians had no monopoly of spiritual truth. Wells in his *Outline of History* (1920) and *Science of Life* (1929) was the most effective popular writer in the new vein. Haldane in *Possible Worlds* (1927) and *Fact and Faith* (1934) argued the case against faith. There was a new freedom in discussion.

A2. New Intellectual and Scientific Ideas

Each of the changes in the 1920s was fundamental to the ideas which replaced nineteenth-century concepts by the 1950s. It was a seminal period in which Britain played a key rôle. The main changes were:

(a) *Philosophy*. Metaphysics and previous concepts of reality came under attack, first of all in Vienna, but later in Britain, where G. E. Moore (1873–1958), *Principia Ethica* (1903), and B. Russell (1872–1970), *Principia Mathematica* (1910–13), were the chief exponents.

(b) *Psychology*. Although Freud (1856–1939) had done much work earlier, it was not until after the war and use of his techniques for psychotherapy in military hospitals, that he became widely known. His work was taken up uncritically, ignoring Jung and Alder's later contributions. In 1921 psychology was discussed at the Conference of Educational Associations, and the National Institute of Industrial Psychology appeared.

(c) *Sociology*. It was Herbert Spencer who had laid the basis of British sociology. L. T. Hobhouse (1864–1929), author of *Social Development* and *Morals in Evolution*, became the first professor of sociology at London University.

(d) *Astronomy*. Major advances in this field included the discovery of Pluto, and the growth of telescopes encouraged new theories about the universe. Sir James Jeans, *The Mysterious Universe* (1930), and Sir Arthur Eddington, *The Expanding Universe* (1933), highlighted new developments.

(e) *Physics*. A new concept of matter as energy and particles developed. Max Planck's quantum theory (1900) was followed by the growth of atomic physics. Rutherford discovered the atom in 1910; it was split for the first time at the Cavendish in 1919, and by 1932 Cockcroft and Wilson had produced the accelerator. Newton's constant universe was replaced by Heisenberg's uncertainty principle (Nobel Prize, 1932). Above all, Einstein's relativity theory, put forward in 1916, was published in Britain in 1919.

(f) *Medicine*. Vitamins had been discovered by Funk in 1912, but it was Gowland Hopkins at Cambridge after 1914 who developed their study. Two important discoveries were insulin by Banting and Best in 1925, and penicillin by Fleming in 1928–29. Its isolation by Florey and Chain in 1939–40 paved the way for the massive increase of drug treatment in medicine.

A3. The People of England—The Rich and the Poor

The post-war population of Britain was one reason for its political decline. Emigration to the Empire fell, so that by the 1930s there was a net inflow. The total population grew slowly to 44 million in 1931, though Southern Ireland was lost. In spite of government aid, the flight from the land continued. By 1931, 80 per cent of Britain lived in towns, and rural population had fallen by 41,000 in a decade. At first the main topics of interest were the lost generation (Chapter 3, A1) and the excess of women over men, which reached a peak in 1921 and was, in fact, due to long-term trends. The expectation of life changed little and the most important trend was the falling birth rate, which reached 20 per 1,000 in 1923, and continued to drop so that predictions of declining population were in vogue by the 1930s. This fall was partly due to women's emancipation, although this was strictly limited, and more to contraceptives. A rise after 1916 in illegitimate births and also divorces (1910–12, 823; 1930–32, 4,249) was held to indicate decadence.

The heart of the great Victorian industrial cities began to beat less firmly as the population of more than 20 of them began to fall, while the chief population growth was to be found in the south and, above all, London, where numbers rose from 7¼ million in 1911 to 8¼ million in 1931. In 1924 the Maybury Committee first referred to traffic congestion in the capital. New population in the 1920s was found in four main areas:

(a) *The suburbs*. Cheap transport, low rates and chain stores helped to develop 'Metroland'. The extension in London of the Underground to Hendon (1923) and Morden (1926) indicated how suburbs were growing.

(b) *The estate*. Housing estates had begun in 1900 at Tooting, but it was the Housing Acts after 1919 that created this new phenomenon. The LCC estates at Beacontree or White Hart Lane were among the largest, but other cities like Birmingham (Kingstanding) and Manchester (Wythenshawe) followed.

(c) *Ribbon development*. Lack of planning and large numbers of small building companies combined with a decline in agriculture to provide a speculators' market, and private houses were built with little thought for the environment on the outskirts of towns.

(d) *Coastal growth*. This was particularly marked in southern England, and Osbert Lancaster satirised 'bungaloid growth'.

Besides housing with new council estates, the working class were better off in many other ways by the end of the 1920s, in spite of the dole queues. The working week fell on average from 55 to 48 hours, while real incomes, which had risen by 15 per cent in the war, did so again by 1929. Taxation still favoured the rich, but redistribution through social service payments increased during the decade as a result of several Acts.

With the expansion of the Civil Service and an industrial shift to service trades, a rise in the middle class was to be expected. The number of middle class rose from 1.7 million in 1911 to 2.7 million in 1925, and it was they who helped to determine much electoral policy in the period, putting in safe governments favouring low taxes and expanding services like education which they valued. The upper class remained intact, and was augmented by war profiteers. There were still 322 millionaires in the country in spite of death duties of 40 per cent on incomes over £2m. The sale of lands realised profits that were invested abroad, and expanding population provided a new source of land sales. In 1929 0.1 per cent owned one third of the National Income, and three quarters of the population owned less than £100 each. This marked a slight improvement on the pre-war position, but Bowley still found 16 per cent in primary poverty. Upper-class life flowed on as before and a large section of people returned to life as servants. In London's West End those with servants only fell from 57.4 to 41.3 per 100 compared with pre-war.

A4. The Silent Social Revolution

Apart from gains in housing and social services, the working class began to benefit from education during the 1920s. Although Pollard has claimed that 'higher education was still mainly for the rich', others like Medlicott have accepted a silent social revolution in educational opportunity. Perhaps the Battle of Britain was won in part in the science laboratories of the grammar schools and red-brick universities. The main emphasis was on improving academic education, and this led to a neglect of other spheres.

For example, nursery schools promised in 1918 numbered only 90 in 1937. The Geddes Axe and cutbacks in 1931 reduced the effectiveness of the Hadow Report as far as higher grade (i.e. secondary modern) schools were concerned. However, by then, one third of secondary children were in newly organised schools. The main changes were:

(a) *Grammar school education.* Under the 1902 Act, not only could LEAs build their own, but those which admitted 20 per cent to free places secured a grant. By 1931, 42.7 per cent of grammar places were free. The number of scholarships was increased to 300 in 1930. In 1926 the direct grant system began. Thus, although the school leaving age was not raised, Britain had more secondary pupils in relation to population than any other European country.

(b) *Universities.* The School Certificate, requiring passes in eight subjects in one sitting, was a strong inducement to high standards. As early as 1921, 39 per cent of university entrants came from state schools, and even at Oxbridge the ladder was not too steep. By 1938, 65.4 per cent of open awards were won from state schools. New university colleges were founded at Swansea (1920), Leicester (1921), Exeter (1922), Reading (1926) and Hull (1928), and by 1930 there were 30,000 undergraduates.

A5. The Long Revolution

Raymond Williams' *The Long Revolution* (1961) drew attention to the development of two cultures—one which might be called 'highbrow' and the other 'popular'. There had always been a people's culture and a wide difference between a Victorian drawing room and a music hall. Mass education and printing, the popular newspaper and magazine, and the possibilities of transmission and reproduction provided by electricity produced a new phenomenon during the 1920s, which was in full swing by the 1930s. Some older pastimes like country dancing became 'highbrow'; others like ballad singing or harvest homes died out. A long argument began on the question of falling standards, or whether there were any at all. Organised religion and family life suffered, but there was much gain. More people were reading classics in cheap series, watching or engaging in sport, learning from educational radio programmes, listening to or buying good music. The chief changes were:

(a) *Popular literature.* This specialised in four main types of book: ruritanian romance (Sabatini), upper-class social life (Elinor Glyn, Ethel M. Dell, Ruby M. Ayres), detective stories (Horler, Oppenheim, Christie) and thrillers (John Buchan's Hannay, Leslie Charteris' The Saint, Sapper's Bulldog Drummond, and Edgar Wallace).

(b) *Popular newspapers.* There was a bitter circulation war between the press barons, and by 1939 just over half the people read a daily. Rothermere's *Mail* and *Mirror* had been overtaken by Beaverbrook's *Express* and *Standard* when the war ended in 1932. By then the gift offer, the crossword (1924), horoscopes and gossip columns had appeared. After 1929 the *Daily Herald* became less left-wing, and except for the *Daily Worker* (1930) there was no left-wing press between the wars until the *Mirror* changed in 1934.

(c) *Radio.* In 1920 the Marconi Company transmitted the first broadcasts from Chelmsford. In 1922 the British Broadcasting Company was set up, but the Crawford Committee preferred a public corporation. J. C. W. Reith was made the first Director General under an Act passed in 1926. Regional services began in 1927, and by 1932 an overseas service.

(d) *The cinema.* During the war the bioscope had become 'the flicks', and during the 1920s film stars became national figures. For the first time Western Europe was influenced by American culture. A British industry started with Gainsborough Films (Michael Balcon, 1924), and two other companies. Studios appeared at Elstree and Boreham Wood and in 1927 an Act imposed a quota of British films starting at 5 per cent and rising to 20 per cent. In 1929 Hitchcock's 'Blackmail' and Grierson's 'Drifters' marked the beginning of a thriving era.

(e) *Gramophones.* Although known before the war, it was the production of the first jazz record ('Livery Stable Blues'), and the arrival of the Dixieland Band in 1919 that set things going. In 1925 the '78' started on its career.

(f) *Mass sport.* The opening of Wembley in 1923 marked football as a national sport as well as a working-class occupation. Gambling on race-courses was regulated by an Act in 1928, and some £230m was placed that year. Greyhound racing started at Belle Vue, Manchester, in 1926, and by 1932 there were 187 tracks with 8 million fans. It was regulated in 1934. Football pools cashed in on the new interest in 1923 when Littlewoods started.

A6. The Neo-Technocratic Age

Prior to 1914 science made little impact on ordinary life. British technical backwardness was well known and there were only 9,000 full-time scientists. The war developed technology in weapons, medical research, automated industry, synthetic products, faster transport and precision engineering. Products previously taken as a joke became part of everyday life, and in the home labour-saving devices helped to emancipate women and led to fewer servants. Moore's *Portrait of Elmbury* (1945) suggests this change was not a fast one, but life in a city full of gadgets attracted the attention of men like Lang in 'Metropolis' (1927) and King Vidor in 'The Crowd' (1928). Social chaos, human despair, dictatorship and world catastrophe were foretold by Wells in *The War of the Worlds*.

The most important changes were:

(a) *The electric tramcar.* Although the first tramway abandonment was in 1917, the tramcar was the main method of transport until 1927: 14,481 were owned by 160 authorities.

(b) *The motor bus.* Eastbourne first introduced a municipal service in 1903, and in London there was spectacular development. By 1925 there were 197 operators, bus races and crashes, and attempts by law to control the situation failed. The covered top was the main innovation. Wartime experience and the sale of derequisitioned vehicles helped to stimulate the country bus companies, and by the late 1920s there were 2,878 operators. Their impact on isolated villages was immense and the threat to the railways obvious. Cut-throat competition marked the period. Southdown started in 1915, for example, and took over 69 operators by 1939.

(c) *Motor cars.* The 1920s saw a rich man's luxury become a middle-class privilege. Motor cabs (1909) eliminated hansom cabs. Motor lorries challenged the railways. Above all, the Morris Oxford and the Ford Popular created a market for small, reliable, cheap family saloons. The figures were:

	Cars	Other motor vehicles	Horse-drawn
1922	314,769	975,783	232,865
1930	1,042,258	2,251,142	52,414

(d) *Railways.* Although good management, standardisation after the 1921 act and new locomotives such as the Gresley 'Pacifics' helped, the railways did not respond well to change. Steam power predominated and in 1938 the world steam record was achieved. By then 116 services travelled at over 60 mph, Electrification was slow, growing from 68 miles to 700 miles between 1914 and 1931. The main change was on the Southern Railway where the London to Brighton line was completed in 1933. Pullman trains and streamlining in the Silver Jubilee class gave an impression of modernisation, but lines were closing fast, and both passenger numbers and freight carried fell.

(*e*) *Underground*. There was considerable expansion in London, with lines reaching Upminster (1932) and Cockfosters (1933). From 1929 Charles Holden was responsible for a series of spectacular station designs.

(*f*) *Aeroplanes*. The first commercial service was started in 1919, and in 1924 Imperial Airways started with a government subsidy. The same year unified traffic control on the British system was adopted throughout Europe. Numbers of passengers rose from 870 in 1919 to 25,094 in 1930.

(*g*) *Telephones*. The kiosk was designed in 1922, and the total number of private telephones rose from 700,000 in 1912 to $2\frac{1}{2}$ million in 1930. The first automatic exchange was opened in 1927.

A7. Bloomsbury and Jazz

The modern 'twenties image' of jazz, emancipated women, cocktails and short skirts in London night clubs applied to a small, if influential section of the population. Ragtime appeared in 1912, and by the 1920s was said to be 'shaking suburbia'. It was followed by the Charleston and the Black Bottom. Young girls were freed from chaperones and drank cocktails, and a play in 1919—*The Emancipated Flapper*—highlighted this trend. But although women secured greater legal rights by Acts in 1920, 1923 and 1925, their freedom should not be exaggerated. Just as women's fashions changed from the twenties' short skirts and bobbed hair to thirties' elegance, so did other trends reverse. The 'fast set' became rather disreputable and the days when Mrs Meyrick ran three night clubs between stays in prison, and married three daughters into the peerage, came to an end. The 'Bloomsbury Set' is a phrase used to cover the literary society of the time. Intellectuals during the 1920s were influenced by pacifism, leftism (the word appeared in 1927), psychology and a more open attitude to sex and drugs.

(*a*) *The theatre*. The leading playwright was Shaw, whose *St. Joan* and *Back to Methuselah* appeared in 1924. Maugham's plays continued to be popular with *East of Suez* (1922) and *Our Betters* (1923), and in 1924 he was joined by Coward with *The Vortex*. The most controversial play, dealing with a love affair between a boy and his housemaster's wife – *Young Woodley* – was written by Van Druten in 1928. Coward turned to lighter stuff with *Hay Fever* in 1925 and the C. B. Cochrane reviews. Ivor Novello's *Glamorous Night* in 1925 was the start of the big musicals era, while for comedy B. Travers' *A Cuckoo in the Nest* (1925) and *Rookery Nook* (1926) were prominent.

(*b*) *Music*. Elgar's least great work, the Cello Concerto, came out in 1919, and during the decade he yielded to Vaughan Williams as the leading composer. His 'Pastoral Symphony' (1922) and 'Sir John in Love' (1929) were outstanding. Holst's 'The Planets' (1916) was followed by a wide variety of works, such as the 'Choral Symphony' (1924). There were many new composers of high quality —Bridges, Warlock, Ireland and Bax, for instance—but it was Walton's 'Façade' (1923) and 'Belshazzar's Feast' (1931) that marked him as the first important 'modern' composer. Covent Garden (1925), the BBC Symphony

Orchestra (1930) and Sadlers Wells (1931) reflected strong support for classical music by ever-widening numbers.

(c) *Architecture*. During the 1920s most main buildings were in 'Modern Classical', which attempted to unite mass, new materials, classical forms and Portland stone. Sir Edward Lutyens and Sir Giles Gilbert Scott were the chief architects. The former designed the Cenotaph and many private houses; the latter, Liverpool Cathedral and Cambridge University Library. Sir Charles Holden built monumentally for the University of London and London Transport Headquarters.

(d) *Art*. There was some movement towards 'Modern Art', but not much. Roger Fry's *Vision and Design* and Wilenski's *Modern Art* (1927) were seminal works. Some, like Eric Gill and Ben Nicholson, built on war artists like Lewis, Nash and Nevinson. Brangwyn, Augustus John and Munnings provided portraits.

The arts did not advance towards the main twentieth-century forms until the 1930s, mainly due to the conservatism of patrons. In literature there was more room for experiment, although Lawrence's exile was a warning about how far it could go. What influenced London did not necessarily affect the provinces. Conventions were flouted, standards challenged, new influences felt and basic ideas questioned, but the effects were not yet widespread. It became fashionable but not common to sneer at things once considered above criticism. The literary establishment was characterised by dubious morals, little patriotism, and less religion, but this has to be kept in proportion. In the 1920s Virginia Woolf went hand in hand with Bertie Wooster.

(a) *War literature*. The political impact of war literature has already been stressed (Chapter 3, A3). Earlier works like Ernest Raymond's *Tell England* (1922) and Ford Madox Ford's *Parade's End* (1924–28) gave way to anti-war works like Sherriff's *Journey's End*, Aldington's *Death of a Hero* and Manning's *Her Privates We*. War memories like Blunden's *Undertones of War* (1928) and Graves' *Goodbye to All That* (1929) culminated in Sassoon's three works—*The Memoirs of George Sherston*. A comparison of Edward Marsh's edition of Brooke (1918) with Edmund Blunden's Owen (1931) aptly points the change.

(b) *Literary Lions*. A group of writers, including Strachey, the Sitwells, Forster, Woolf and Joyce, seemed consciously to strive for cleverness. Strachey's *Eminent Victorians* (1918) was a good example of their biographical approach. Woolf's works like *The Waves* and *To the Lighthouse* (1927) were the most distinguished. Aldous Huxley's *Antic Hay* (1923), *Crome Yellow* and, above all, *Point Counter Point* (1928) reflected the West End mood as did Evelyn Waugh's *Decline and Fall* (1928) and *Vile Bodies* (1930). In poetry, T. S. Eliot's *The Wasteland* (1922) was seminal. Joyce's *Ulysses* (1922) and Lawrence's *Lady Chatterley's Lover* (1928) were published abroad.

(c) *The circulating library*. Baldwin preferred the rural novels of Mary Webb, and there were plenty of distinguished writers with wider appeal than Bloomsbury. Eden Philpotts, Michael Arlen (*The Greet Hat*, 1924), A. S. M. Hutchinson (*If Winter Comes*, 1921), Warwick Deeping (*Sorrell and Son*, 1925), W. J. Locke, Somerset Maugham, J. B. Priestley (*Angel Pavement*, 1930), John Galsworthy (*The Forsyte Saga*, 1922), Arnold Bennett, Compton Mackenzie, Hugh Walpole and P. G. Wodehouse were among the most important.

B. The Long Political Crisis: 1922–24

B1. Bonar Law and the Tory Second Eleven, October 1922–May 1923

When Law took office, he was the first Tory Prime Minister for 16 years (Chapter 5), and had been leader since 1911. He had played a key part in the government crises of 1916 and 1922 and had held important offices, but he was no more than a supreme handyman. By training a businessman, he had no sympathy with social reform or imperial change, and formed a cabinet of 16, seven of whom were peers, because the leading Tories stayed out believing the government would soon fall. It was a weak government, but the promise of 'tranquillity' was welcome and in November the election gave the Tories an overall majority of 88. The Liberals remained divided, and the real importance of the election was the rise of Labour to 142 seats, showing that a split between Liberals and Tories would benefit the left. The electors did not get tranquillity. The Ruhr Crisis, negotiations for a peace with Turkey, a row over a debt settlement arrived at with America and crises over Memel and Corfu kept the government busy. It was clear that Law's illness was a fatal one and in May he retired, dying five months later.

B2. Baldwin's First Ministry, May 1923–January 1924

Lord Curzon was the obvious successor to Bonar Law now that Austen Chamberlain was not leader. He had distinguished himself as Indian Viceroy, in the War Cabinet, and as Foreign Secretary. But there were snags. He was arrogant, partly because of a painful and secret illness, and partly from temperament. He had the reputation of a slippery customer in the crises of 1916 and 1922. Bonar Law said he did not wish to give advice as he was too ill. His private secretary gave the King's secretary, Stamfordham, a note prepared by Davidson which he said: 'expressed the views of Bonar Law'. However, Stamfordham advised the King to send for Curzon. George V sought advice from Balfour, who disliked Curzon and criticised a peer being prime minister—something which the King did not like either. Stamfordham was also told by Sir Stanley Jackson, the party chairman, that the constituencies favoured Baldwin, and fewer than 50 MPs backed Curzon.

Baldwin said he would form a cabinet 'of which Harrow should be proud', and there were seven Old Harrovians in it. Curzon loyally carried on as Foreign Secretary. After a short time of combining two offices, Baldwin gave Neville Chamberlain the Chancellorship of the Exchequer, thus building a bridge for the Tory First Eleven to return later. There were eight peers in a cabinet of 19. Sir Samuel Hoare began his long career by entering the cabinet as Air Minister, and Sir William Joynson Hicks arrived at the Ministry of Health.

It was not a very daring government. Abroad, tranquillity was assured by retreating from the Ruhr, signing the Turkish treaty, and paying Mussolini compensation for the Corfu Incident. At home the only measure of importance was a new Housing Act to improve that of 1919. This was the first of Chamberlain's reforming measures, and it provided a government subsidy of £6 a year for 20 years on council houses built to approved standards. Under it some 436,000 houses were built. The Act also started removing rent control on properties which changed tenants. The economic situation worsened and unemployment rose to 1,350,216 by the Autumn.

The Tory party had long been pledged to protection, and favoured some scheme of imperial preference. On 25 October Baldwin announced he favoured protection as a means of curbing unemployment. It was clear that the cabinet had discussed the matter; less certain that they had reached agreement to broach the topic. It meant an election would have to occur because Baldwin was bound by a previous statement of Bonar Law's that no major tariff change would be introduced without consulting the people. The suddenness of the announcement aroused much speculation about Baldwin's motives, and this has continued.

(a) Some argue Baldwin was not very able, and it was a mistake by an honest man. In his speech he said, 'I am not a clever man. I know nothing of political tactics.'

(b) Others cite Baldwin's own words later: 'The dissolution was deliberate and the result of long reflection.' It can be argued he thought that by reuniting Liberals under free trade he would force tariff Tories back into the party. Baldwin feared a Unionist Liberal Party forming under Lloyd George.

(c) Baldwin's explanation to Tom Jones many years later was that Lloyd George was going protectionist, and 'I had to get in quick.' This is unlikely.

The Liberals reunited, and Labour opposed protection as well. The election in December produced 258 Tories, 191 Labour and 158 Liberals. Demands were made to recreate the 1922 coalition, but this was something that Baldwin could hardly do. Liberals and Tories were opposed on the key issue of the election, while Labour and Liberals were not. Asquith argued Labour should take office, and that they could be controlled by the Liberals. He later claimed this as a farsighted decision to prevent the establishment ganging up against Labour. At the time he was strongly criticised for extracting no terms for his support. In January 1924 Baldwin was defeated on a vote of no confidence, and resigned. Although Asquith denounced 'hysteria' among those who feared a Labour government, 10 Liberals voted with the Tories, thus beginning the split that was to destroy the Liberals by 1931.

B3. James Ramsay MacDonald and the Labour Party

MacDonald was born at Lossiemouth in 1866. He came to London and lived on oatmeal sent by his mother, as he made his way up in labour politics, joining the ILP in 1894 and becoming secretary in 1900. He entered parliament in 1906, was elected leader in 1911 and resigned in 1914. Defeated in the 1918 election, he returned as member for Aberavon, and was re-elected leader in 1922. His early life was well to the left and in 1924 he still contributed to the ILP journal. He did not break with them until 1927. He was a pacifist and involved in the alternative labour foreign policy of the Union of Democratic Control. When he became Prime Minister in 1924 he seemed 'pre-eminently fitted' for the task. After two minority governments he lost his popularity in 1931.

MacDonald's early life was devoted to creating the Labour Party. His intellectual ability, deep integrity and magnificent public manner stood him in good stead. Above all, he made Labour respectable in an era when men such as himself had yet to taste political power. In spite of considerable sympathy for Bolshevism in the party and Tory 'red smears' from outside, MacDonald's first government was to show Labour fit to rule. There was fear then that Labour could not be trusted with foreign and defence matters, but MacDonald shone as an international statesman, resisted wholesale disarmament and acted firmly in imperial matters. This made him unpopular with 'Red Clydeside', but it gained him votes. It was a greater criticism that he pursued few socialist policies, but since he was dependent on the Liberals, this was unlikely. Moreover, the mood of the party was changing. Most saw Labour based on human brotherhood not class war, and after the failure of the General Strike this moderate stance was what was required as the 1929 election showed.

At the time there was criticism of MacDonald for accepting capitalist conventions and working within the system. Amusement was caused by the trouble Labour ministers had over court and evening dress. A critic yelled at Henderson and Thomas in their top hats going to the Palace, 'It's a bloody lum hat government like a' the rest.' But it would have been foolish to do otherwise. Labour had to scale the heights of the establishment if it was to take power. It is less easy to defend the lengths to which MacDonald went in London society. He was swept into country house and West End receptions with great ease, and the journey from his working-class constituency at Seaham Harbour to the Londonderry's country house was not far. In fact Labour was often to be perplexed by this problem, and a number of his critics like Kirkwood were to end in the Lords.

By 1924 the Labour Party was starting its long journey towards the consensus politics of the 1960s, and away from any socialist leanings it may have had. The SDF had left in 1901, and in 1911 had combined with the ILP to form the British Socialist Party. Then in 1920, with the founding of the Communist Party, they split again, and the ILP brigade returned to Labour. Their leaders were men like Allen and Brockway, and the most prominent group were the Clydesiders including Kirkwood, Shinwell, Weir (MacDonald's private secretary), Wheatley and Maxton. During 1923 this group had outraged the Tories by their parliamentary behaviour. There were numerous suspensions, and the Red Flag was sung for the first time in the House. These events were no more serious than Irish behaviour prior to 1914, but they provided grist to the Tory mill, and MacDonald was determined to curb them. The Labour Party had rejected the Third International in 1921. In 1924 no Communist was to be a candidate, and in 1925 none was to be a member. Communism and Socialism had parted company, and this was important. It prevented the right wing from going further right. MacDonald more than any single man created the Labour Party as a political force, but it was hard for workers and dedicated socialists to accept a man who said in July 1924, 'He could get on with the Tories. They differed at times openly, then forgot all about it and shook hands. They were gentlemen, but the Liberals were cads.'

B4. Labour Minority Government, January–November 1924

(*a*) *A Labour cabinet*. Mowat says the government was of 'curious construction'. MacDonald took the Foreign Secretaryship himself. Leading supporters were not well treated:

(i) Henderson was omitted altogether, then offered Chairman of Ways and Means, the War Office and finally the Home Office.

(ii) Thomas was proposed for Foreign Secretary, offered the Colonial Office which he rejected, and then accepted on hearing it had prestige.

(iii) Two previous leaders obtained lowly posts. Clynes was Lord Privy Seal and Adamson, Secretary for Scotland.

(iv) Snowden, a strong Free Trader, was offered the Exchequer in a scribbled note thrust across the table.

The radicals were Wheatley at Health and Jowett as Commissioner of Works. Liberal peers were included to give respectability and 'enable the King's government to be carried on'. Trevelyan at Education, Webb at the Board of Trade and Buxton at Agriculture represented the middle-class radicals. Among the Under-Secretaries was the first woman minister, Miss Margaret Bondfield. It was a moderate government and only contained five trade unionists in a cabinet of 20. MacDonald proclaimed they were at the start of 'a great adventure', and then said they 'must govern with prudence and sagacity'.

(*b*) *Labour policies.* Abroad (Chapter 7, F) the government was active. MacDonald went to Geneva and supported the Geneva Protocol. He sought to repair Anglo-French relations, and resettle reparations. He endeavoured to get good relations with Russia and Mexico. In imperial matters he stood firm in India and Egypt and increased expenditure on planes for Iraq. In defence matters a few small gestures were made: the Singapore base was halted, and the number of cruisers was cut from eight to five.

Snowden's finance was as expected. The McKenna duties were abolished, and duties on sugar and other imports reduced. The remaining profits tax was abolished. Thus, lacking money when it came to social policies, the government could do little more than try to remedy the cuts made by the Geddes Axe. Their achievements were:

(i) The Unemployment Insurance Act increased benefits, made uncovenanted benefit (the dole) a right, and abolished the time gap between insurance and dole payments.

(ii) Subsidies were extended to Imperial Airways.

(iii) The Agricultural Wages boards scrapped in 1921 were restored.

(iv) Education cuts were restored and Trevelyan appointed a committee under Sir Henry Hadow to reorganise secondary education. Its report in 1926 was the origin of the tripartite system.

(v) Wheatley's Housing Act increased the subsidy on council houses to £9 a year for 40 years, and under this act 521,000 houses were built.

(*c*) *Party politics.* For a minority government these were important. MacDonald set up a liaison committee with the TUC, and held meetings with the ILP. However, for five out of their 10 months there were serious strikes. Bevin's union started a tram strike, and widened it to include buses. At this point it emerged that the Minister of Transport was president of the TGWU. The Prime Minister used the Emergency Powers Act of 1920. Relations with the Liberals were bad. A Proportional Representation Bill was lost, and there was no regular consultation.

The Tories, on the other hand, had received a shock. At first there were murmurings against Baldwin, but the election brought about reunification. Austen returned first, Balfour and Birkenhead followed, and Churchill changed his mind once more. Baldwin reorganised Central Office, and created the first Shadow Cabinet, which greatly increased an opposition leader's authority. In June 1924 he made it clear they rejected tariffs. Baldwin was also determined they should support social reform, saying, 'Every government whatever party forms it, must be socialists in the sense that our grandfathers used that word.'

B5. Red Letter Day, October 1924

On 25 July 1924 the *Workers' Weekly* published a letter telling service men not to act during industrial disputes. The editor was prosecuted by the Attorney General under an Act of 1797. This led to criticism of prosecutions under outdated laws and an outcry among Labour. In August the prosecution was withdrawn. This produced a counter outcry from Tories and Liberals. Baldwin agreed to a censure motion while the Liberals wanted a select committee. MacDonald rejected the Liberal demand and decided to make it a matter of confidence. On 8 October the debate took place. At first Baldwin said he was not coming. It was not until late in the evening that he told the Tories to vote for the Liberal proposal instead of their own and defeated the government by 364 to 198.

The loss of the election by Labour was almost certain before the 'Red Letter' scare. Its record was poor, and relations with the Liberals were bad : 110 Liberals stood down to let Tories in. MacDonald tried to defend the Russian Treaty and a manifesto calling for 'a really Socialist Commonwealth'. Baldwin made the first effective election broadcast in which he said, 'We cannot afford the luxury of academic socialists or revolutionary agitation.' On 25 October a letter said to have been sent from Zinoviev to the British Communist Party was published by the Foreign Office with a covering letter to the Russian envoy complaining about it. The letter was dated 15 September, and it was suggested a cover up had been attempted. MacDonald kept quiet until 27 October, when he said he had learnt of the letter on 10 October, and had ordered delay until there was confirmation. It is likely that MacDonald realised the danger and intended to keep quiet, but the Foreign Office opposed him. They said the *Daily Mail* had a copy and intended to publish. It was not explained why the Foreign Office did not telephone MacDonald before publishing, nor how the *Mail* got a copy.

In Labour mythology, the Red Letter was held to be a Tory plot. In fact, Bolsheviks disliked MacDonald, and intended to use him as a front man for their own activities. The letter actually criticised him. A Committee of Enquiry set up by Baldwin said the letter was genuine. In 1928 the *Mail* editor admitted that a copy was given to him by a civil servant, but the government refused a further enquiry thus tarnishing Baldwin's clean government image. Even if the letter was not genuine, the Bolsheviks had aims similar to sentiments expressed in it, and other documents were found in raids in 1925 and 1927. There was a Communist threat, but it did not of course come from Labour. The results of the election were :

Conservatives	419	Independent	4
Labour	151	Communist	1
Liberal	40		

The importance of this election was that:

(i) It was the Tories' best election victory in a straight fight, and not under coalition colours. With a majority of 223, Baldwin was acclaimed as a great leader, and 1923 forgiven.
(ii) It reunited the Tories, and brought in Churchill. Neville Chamberlain beat Mosley at Birmingham to become the government's driving force.
(iii) Asquith was defeated and resigned, went to the Lords and died in 1928, leaving Lloyd George leader. It was the decisive election in the destruction of the Liberal party.

C. Stanley Baldwin's Government, November 1924–June 1929

C1. Baldwin and the Tory First Eleven

The Ministry saw the Tories reunited, and Baldwin at the height of his powers. Churchill described it as 'capable and sedate' but it was more than that. Indeed, 'it is something of a puzzle to answer quite why the party's fortune slumped so much' since their majority fell from 223 to 185 during the parliament. Yet the General Strike was defeated and followed by industrial peace, economic recovery occurred and Chamberlain carried out a programme of social reform, while abroad collective security advanced, the League grew in strength and imperial problems in Ireland, Egypt and India were soothed. In matters like the Balfour Declaration of 1926 or the granting of the vote to women between 21 and 30 in 1928, the government was progressive. But this picture has to be qualified. The return to the Gold Standard was ineptly handled. Unemployment remained high, and after a Safeguarding Act, Baldwin resolutely turned against tariffs. He appeared to yield in August 1928, but then firmly opposed protection for steel. Many younger Tories pressed for more social reform. In particular, Macmillan, Boothby and Stanley formed a group and in *Industry and the State* (1927) forecast the Tory move to collectivism.

Sir Robert Horne rejected the post he was offered. In 1925 Curzon died, and in 1928 Birkenhead was forced to retire. However, Balfour was brought in and the capable Lord Peel succeeded Birkenhead, so there is little evidence that the quality of the ministry declined. There was little political acrimony between ministers and only one resignation—that of Lord Cecil over disarmament in October 1927. Austen Chamberlain was rewarded at last with the Foreign Secretaryship and performed well (Chapter 7, D1). In spite of opposition from Birkenhead Baldwin was determined to press on with Indian reforms (Chapter 11, B). The Colonial Office was held by Leopold Amery, who was one of the few holders genuinely interested in colonial development. Churchill was Chancellor and worked well with the reforms of Chamberlain as Minister of Health. The latter proposed 25 bills and passed 21 of them. Unfortunately he lacked the public manner to make these popular, and infuriated Labour by 'economy' measures. Steel Maitland at Labour, Cunliffe Lister at Trade, and Lord Percy at Education were all sensible, reforming ministers. To say the government's policy was 'vindictive, silly or irrelevant' (Seaman) is unfair. Even its most contentious measure—the Trades Disputes Act of 1927—was accompanied by special mass meetings addressed by ministers, supported by trade union leaders like Spencer, and produced industrial peace for 15 years.

All governments have their fools. Joynson Hicks ('Jix'), the Home Secretary was cast in this role. He was closely involved with a fellow nonconformist, Sir Thomas Inskip (Attorney General, March 1928), in controversy over a proposal by the Church of England to introduce a new Prayer Book, which they claimed was too Catholic. After a series of weighty debates the measure was defeated (December 1928), and the bishops introduced it on their own authority. Jix's cravats and his authorship of *The Law of Heavy and Light Mechanic Traction* were enough to start the smiles. His determination to close down West End clubs caused trouble, which culminated in the Savige Case (1928) and an investigation into police methods. It was his indiscretion in debate while arguing with Lady Astor that forced the Tories to extend votes for women. Strangely enough, the government is rarely criticised for one of its major failings. Hoare at Air and Hailsham at War, aided by Churchill's determination to cut expenditure, brought about a serious decline in Britain's defences. (Chapter 7, A2.)

C2. Return to the Gold Standard

Nearly all financial opinion favoured a return to gold, including Bradbury, Montague Norman and the Treasury. Only Keynes opposed it. Churchill did his best to be fully informed, and during the debate Mond was the only leading parliamentary critic. What was wrong was not the return but the return at the pre-war parity. The aim was twofold: to restore Britain's international position as a lender, and to stimulate industry. The first worked. Other European currencies returned to gold, and together with German recovery, there was a boom culminating in 1928–29. The second did not because the government was unwilling to help the ailing giants of the export industries. Britain's highly priced exports suffered by a price rise of about 10 per cent. In 1926 Churchill restored the McKenna duties, and a few other gestures such as protection for the cinema industry were made, but a general tariff policy was ruled out. Britain's recovery was at a slower rate than her competitors, and too much money was used on overseas investment that would have better been employed on modernising industry. When the economic crash came, the limited nature of Baldwin's Boom became apparent.

C3. The General Strike, 3 May–12 May 1926

The period 1910–26 was the worst for industrial relations in the twentieth century until the 1966–1979, and the General Strike marked the end of an era because 'from then on the pendulum swung sharply to political action'. Syndicalists had long preached the effectiveness of general strikes, and in Europe they had met with varying degrees of success prior to the war. The Russian revolution in 1917 started with one, and although Red Clydeside in 1919 and an abortive attempt in Italy showed its fallibility, there had been two successful ones in Germany (1920, 1923). Tom Mann's *Power Through a General Strike* (1923) showed the idea was still current, and some of the 1926 leaders like Arthur Cook, the miners' leader, were syndicalists. But the strike came about primarily because of the coal dispute, and the revolutionary element was never more than minimal.

(*a*) *The state of the coal industry*. Mining, with nearly a million workers, was the country's chief industry. It had reached maximum production in 1913, but

was now in a state of serious decline. By 1925 over 100 owners had gone bankrupt, and their reaction was to cut wages three times, violate the seven-hour
day and force the price down. But the mines were inefficient, and this kept
costs high; 73 per cent of coal raised sold at a loss; 1,500 companies and 4,000
royalty owners hampered investment; and in 1925 just 14 per cent was cut
mechanically. Poland and Italy competed well and the Russian market was
closed. Demand for domestic and industrial use fell, and shipping was converting to oil. The Miners' Federation was determined to secure a national minimum, and had the worst strike record of any industry brought about by bad
conditions and isolated mining communities. Arthur Cook (Secretary, 1924–31)
built on a militant tradition started by Pickard and Smillie. Smillie, in *The
Miners' Next Step*, had proposed nationalisation in 1912, and after the failure
of the Sankey Commission (Chapter 5, B4) miners were bitter. Wages, standing
at 100 in 1920, had fallen to 59 by 1925. The Owners' Association, led by
Williams and Nimmo, was lacking in ability or humanity. In 1920, 1 in 50
entering mining was killed within 20 years, and half contracted serious illness
or injury in the same period.

(b) *Red Friday, 31 July, 1925.* The owners said they would terminate the
1924 agreement one month from 30 June, ending standard wages and increasing
hours. The miners refused arbitration and appealed to the TUC. At first Baldwin stood firm, saying 'all the workers of this country have got to take reductions in wages' but then gave way. A subsidy of £10m was given to
stabilise wages, while a fresh enquiry was held. Although Baldwin was attacked
for a sell-out, he told the Commons that if a serious threat was posed the
government was ready. Criticism from diehards in the cabinet, the FBI and the
National Council of Employers' Associations stiffened Baldwin's resolve.

(c) *Government preparations.* Sir John Anderson reorganised the Supply and
Transport Committee set up by Lloyd George. Civil servants were drawn from
the Health Ministry and liaison with the army set up. On 20 November, Circular
636 initiated the organisation. Only seven councils refused to cooperate, there
were more volunteers than were needed, and in Morris' words, 'every eventuality appears to have been covered'. A regional structure in 11 divisions
divided into 88 areas was created, special constables enrolled, plans for transport coordinated with the RAC, naval ratings prepared to run power stations
and protect docks, and alternative government communications by aircraft
prepared. Full military precautions were taken with naval forces in the main
Northern rivers, troops in London and 226,000 constables. In September the
Organisation for Maintenance of Supplies was set up to train people for vital
industrial jobs. Although the Communists had only 5,000 members, the Minority
Movement within the unions had more, and Cook was linked to it. Of the £2½m
raised for the strikers, £1m came from Russia. On 19 October 12 Communists
were arrested and sentenced to six months. These preparations show Baldwin to
have been determined and effective.

(d) *The Samuel Commission, March 1926.* Its main proposals were:

(i) Nationalising of coal royalties, reorganisation with amalgamations and research into modernisation.
(ii) Joint Production Committees and a number of fringe benefits, such as pit-
head baths, holidays with pay, improved housing and family allowances.
Profit sharing should be examined.
(iii) Subsidy to go, and wages cut in the short term, but there should be a
standard national wage and no increase in hours.
(iv) There should be no cuts until the long-term proposals had been agreed.

There followed a period of negotiations, but these were not direct wage
discussions. The miners delegated their rights to the TUC Industrial Com-

mittee and had no representatives on it. The owners rejected the proposals, and Baldwin was unwilling to bring government pressure to bear. When he did on 30 April, as Mowat says, 'he abandoned the role of arbitrator', and backed the owners. The subsidy expired on 30 April with no agreement, and the employers locked the miners out.

On 1 May the TUC agreed to back a general strike, but they had made little preparation. There were 11 workers' Defence Corps and 131 councils of action, but only in the north-east were they able to challenge the government's organisation. Two committees—government and TUC—met on 2 May separately. The TUC proposed withdrawal of strike notices in return for a fortnight to negotiate, but the government committee tabled its own proposals, saying they wanted to proceed within the framework of the Samuel Report. Baldwin interrupted to say there had been 'an incident'. This was unofficial action by a union at the *Daily Mail* which the TUC tried to stop. It was merely an excuse, since a tired cabinet had given way earlier in the evening to the strong line of Chamberlain and Birkenhead. When the TUC leaders returned, they found Downing Street in darkness. The strike began at midnight. Although Baldwin said in the Commons, 'Everything that I care for is being smashed to bits at the moment', there can be little doubt that, in Seaman's words, 'Baldwin's cessation of the talks was the most provocative action taken by a partipant'. Mowat says that 'in this sense' he was responsible for the strike, but this ignores the miners' determination not to yield, and the wish of some union leaders to make it a trial of strength. The alternative was higher wages which the employers would not give, or a subsidy which the Tories could not stomach.

(*e*) *The nine days of May*. Two biased pictures of the strike exist. On the right Churchill's *British Gazette*, with a circulation of $2\frac{1}{2}$ million said that it was ineffective and illegal. After the strike a number of left-wing accounts (Page, Arnot, Wilkinson and Postgate) argued it could have worked, but was betrayed. More recently, writers like Morris have argued that it was successful at grass roots level and betrayed by its leaders' leaving aside the issue of the consequence of a union victory. The fact was the majority opposed it, the workers were half-hearted and disorganised and the government determined, if not ruthless. TUC claims of 4 million workers in support are most likely to be $2\frac{1}{2}$ million. The first line of strikers came out almost to a man, and only one union voted against the strike. By the time the second line was to be called out the first line was wavering. The Southern Railway was carrying 19 per cent of normal passenger numbers, and 959 buses were running in London. The second line was not called out. Volunteers enjoyed themselves and did some damage, but the government organisation kept things smoothly running, and when picketing of food lorries in London grew severe, troops moved in. There was good cooperation between strikers and strike breakers, and at Lincoln the Trades Council supplied the special constables. No lives were lost. There were 1,760 prosecutions for violence with an average sentence of three months. Morris says a third of these were Communists. There were a number of other arrests, including the whole Birmingham strike committee.

(*f*) *The failure of the strike*. Once it became clear TUC action was ineffective, cabinet hard liners advocated conciliation. MacDonald for Labour declared, 'I respect the constitution as much as Sir Robert Horne.' Simon for the Liberals declared the strike illegal because it was not covered by the 1906 act. Reith refused the strikers access to the BBC and even a peace appeal by the Archbishop of Canterbury was banned. The *British Worker* failed to get good circulation, and the *British Gazette*, together with the radio, gave the government psychological control of the country. On 6 May Baldwin denounced the strike as an attack on constitutional government, to which Ellen Wilkinson replied, 'If the British Constitution makes a man work underground for less than £2 a week it is about time that constitution was changed.' When Samuel returned from Italy on 6 May, negotiations started in secret and reached agreement on 10 May. The drift back of workers like tramwaymen and printers belied the resolutions of strike committees to carry on. The miners would not agree, so on 12 May, the General Council called off the strike 'in order to resume negotiations', leaving the miners in the lurch.

C4. Labour Relations and the Act of 1927

There was a backlash among workers when this was realised, and by 15 May numbers on strike had actually risen. East End riots on 13 May were severe. Baldwin determined to calm matters. He stated, 'I am not out to smash trade unions, and I will not allow the strike to be made a pretext for the imposition of worse conditions'. The strike faded away. Employers practised wage reductions, loss of seniority, abolition of pension rights and the sack. They refused to let men return, unless they agreed to end closed shops. With loss of wages and existing unemployment the workers had no alternative.

The government made arrangements to buy foreign coal, and the miners' strike continued. Government and employers now made good offers but the miners resented attacks made on them by reduction of Poor Law benefits, and continued the strike. By December cold and hunger had caused the strike to collapse. District wages were restored, wages cut and hours lengthened. The Mining Industry Act (1926) facilitated amalgamations and imposed a levy on royalties for welfare, but the loss of production led the owners to even more reactionary attitudes, and the decline of the industry continued. Employers now wanted the government to curb trade union power for good, and some urged the 1906 act should be scrapped. Baldwin's Act (1927) provided that: all strikes except those 'in furtherance of a trade dispute' were illegal; intimidation of workers was defined and made illegal to prevent arbitrary picketing; civil servants were to belong to professional organisations, not to unions affiliated to the TUC; and contracting in replaced contracting out (Chapter 1, B3).

Labour opposed the Act, but outside the House workers showed little wish to oppose the measure. It damaged Labour by reducing their income by a quarter, but otherwise the Act had good results. It is strange that Mowat and Seaman criticise the Act for the consequences of political and sympathetic strikes, mass picketing and the interruption of essential services became increasingly apparent during the 1970s. Law was applied to industrial relations and worked. Numbers in trade unions fell back to the 1914 level and did not recover fully until 1945. The number of working days lost by strikes fell dramatically:

1926	162,000,000	1929	8,290,000
1927	1,170,000	1933	1,070,000
1928	1,390,000	1934	960,000

The 1930s were to be a period of good labour relations, low costs and rising real wages, none of which the unions had delivered in the previous period. The trade unions lost £4m by the General Strike, the total cost to the country in lost production was £150m, and the bill for social security was £9½m. It was an expensive way to conduct industrial affairs.

C5. Chamberlain's Reforms

The atmosphere of economic recovery and the need to conciliate labour underlay Tory reforming activities. Baldwin desired social reforms, and in Chamberlain and Churchill the government had two sons of radicals prepared to carry it out. The main measures were:

(a) *Industrial help*. The government did little to help industry, although it increased subsidies to Imperial Airways and extended public corporations. The Electricity Supply Act (1926) created a Council responsible for the national grid, which by 1933 had 4,000 miles. The main Tory measure was a Derating Act (1929), whereby agricultural land was exempted altogether, and industrial and railway property was relieved of three quarters of their rates.

(b) *Local government reorganisation*. In 1925 the Rating Valuation Act set up the basis of modern rate assessment, and Chamberlain transferred much of the burden from local rates to the tax payers by subsidies. Specific grants were replaced by block grants, giving local councils greater freedom. An act of 1929 increased powers given to county councils, and reformed the urban and rural district councils. The number of authorities fell from 1,435 to 1,047.

(c) *Reforming the Poor Law*. A major gap prior to 1914 was the failure to carry out the report of the 1909 Commission. Chamberlain was worried by the abuse of the Poor Law, particularly after the Poplar Case (1922) and the cost of the General Strike. Although he resisted demands to reduce relief rates, he demanded that the 1911 Circular be enforced, and in 1926 passed an act to punish Boards of Guardians in default. This was applied to three authorities. Many boards were heavily in debt, and 60 in mining districts in a bad way. An Act of 1929 replaced Boards of Guardians and transferred responsibility to Public Assistance Committees run by councils.

(d) *Extended insurance*. In 1925 the Widows, Orphans and Old Age Pensions Act built on the 1908 scheme a pension of 10s a week for widows and a children's allowance, 7s 6d a week for orphans, and 10s a week for insured workers and their wives at 65. Contributions were raised, but the Act covered all insured workers, and by 1937 with 20 million the pension scheme included about the same number as the health scheme.

D. The Election of May 1929—Safety First and Stanley Boy

D1. Party Changes

The late 1920s was a period of poor Tory organisation. The recruiting of an ex-MI5 officer, Joseph Ball, to spy on the Labour Party was no substitute for organisation, and by-elections show the Tories were complacent. Meanwhile the Liberals, united under Lloyd George, tried to recapture the political initiative. His fund and academic assistance enabled them to produce new proposals, including *Britain's Industrial Future* (1928) which argued for managed capitalism. Public ownership, planning, joint industrial councils, public works and flexible use of credit were advocated. In 1929 came *We Can Conquer Unemployment*, which included a national road system, telephone expansion, railway reform and a housing programme. The trouble was Lloyd George was too well known for broken promises, and workers blamed the Liberals for 1924 and remembered Asquith's attack on the General Strike.

In spite of Tory successes Labour had grounds for hope. Now that Bolshevik influence and industrial unrest had subsided, MacDonald was able to swing the party away from Socialism. He stopped writing for the ILP in 1927. A comparison of *Socialism in Our Time* (1925) with Tawney's *Labour and the Nation* (1928) illustrates the change. Socialism and nationalisation were not mentioned in 1929. Unemployment was to be solved by electrification, afforestation, assisted emigration and the same measures as Liberals proposed.

D2. The Campaign

The Tories made two errors. They used the slogan 'Safety First', which was timid. Colonel Waldron Smithers wrote (and the party produced 10,000 records) a song modelled on the hit 'Sonny Boy' and called 'Stanley Boy'. Labour fought a good campaign while the government was too complacent. It also held on too long with by-election losses. The results were: Labour 287, Conservatives 260, Liberals 59 and others 9. The ILP returned 37 candidates, but 17 were from Scotland. The Liberals had increased slightly, but had clearly not recovered from 1924. Baldwin ignored talk of a coalition with them, although Austen was soon advocating fusion. Baldwin advised the King to send for MacDonald, and without receiving specific Liberal commitment, he took office on 4 June.

E. The Career and Character of Stanley Baldwin

Apart from two short periods in 1924 and 1929–31, Baldwin controlled the majority party from 1923 to 1937 and was thus the predominant politician of the inter-war period. Such a position has inevitably led to extremes of praise and denigration. There can be little doubt that he stands with Lloyd George and Wilson among the most skilful politicians of the century. Traditional Tories had little respect for him. Curzon said he was 'a man of no experience, and of the utmost insignificance', while Austen Chamberlain held he was 'without a constructive idea in his head, and with an amazing ignorance of Indian and foreign affairs'. Sir Donald Somerville, Attorney General, however, said, 'they talk of honest, stupid Baldwin; believe me, he is the most ruthless and astute politician of the day', and this verdict has been confirmed by two of his strongest opponents. Harold Laski described him as 'a superb professional', and Churchill said 'he was the most formidable politician I have ever known in public life'. Apart from staying in office and winning three elections, his achievements were vast. He prevented fusion, and helped to bring down Lloyd George. Thereafter he kept him out of politics. He brought Churchill back to the Tories, but defeated his moves over India and rearmament. He defeated the General Strike. He brought about the National Government. He set the Tory party on the road to collectivism and managed capitalism. He forestalled the rise of Fascist extremism. He handled the Abdication Crisis. His failings in defence and foreign policy were great, but even here Churchill's criticisms are no longer accepted without qualification. He played a considerable part in creating the air force of 1940. Above all, he handled public opinion and the party with mastery equalled perhaps only by Macmillan.

(*a*) *Rise to power*. Born in 1867, the son of a Worcestershire iron master, Baldwin went to Harrow and obtained a third in history at Cambridge before joining the family business and acquiring some practical knowledge at Owen's College in Manchester. Through Austen Chamberlain and his father's influence, he entered parliament in 1908, and scarcely spoke half a dozen times before 1914. He became PPS to Bonar Law, a Junior Lord and, in June 1917, Financial Secretary to the Treasury. He was 'a regular glutton for work' and often deputised for Bonar Law. He soon mastered the House, and worked well with Austen. He was considered for Speaker in 1921. As President of the Board of Trade he carried the first major tariff measure in peacetime, and played a vital rôle in articulating backbench opinion on fusion and Lloyd George. As Chancellor he settled the American debt honestly if generously.

(*b*) *The image and the man*. Nicolson once described him as 'blinking. sniffing, neurotic', and he was a curious blend of sensitive and conservative in spirit. His marriage was happy. He loved family life and lived mostly at Chequers and Bewdley. He holidayed regularly at Aix-ler-Bains, never travelled by aeroplane and never aspired to cut a dramatic European rôle like MacDonald and Chamberlain. The latter carped at his vagueness, which increased with age, but this was never more than skin deep. He had an abiding interest in classical literature and the English language. His speeches were regarded by many as challenged only by MacDonald in his palmy days, and sold like wildfire. He wrote no memoirs, and destroyed incriminating documents before leaving office. Although he hated telephones, he mastered the radio. His life had started with a gesture in returning his firm's war profits to the Treasury and ended with a law to give a salary to the leader of the opposition. There can be little doubt that part of him was genuinely simplistic, conservative and honest. The man was more complex than the pipe-smoking image. A resolute fighter, a hard worker, he was close to a nervous breakdown by the end of 1936. He was devious and shrewd. Having broken Lloyd George by opposing coalitions, he supported one for six years. He harped on democracy, but in 1931 effectively deprived the electorate of a choice. He could act ruthlessly. In 1935 he removed Londonderry from Air on the grounds he was a peer, and appointed Swinton, another peer, in his place. In 1935 he told Hoare immediately after the Hoare-Laval Pact, 'We all stand together'; a week later he was sacked. He fought his party opponents, whether it was Beaverbrook or Churchill, with fire and skill.

E1. Social Conscience

Baldwin made it clear the Tories were interested in social reform. He was a radical in the Disraeli tradition, and his periods of office were as marked by social reform and the acceptance of the collective state as by dole queues and means tests. Like Macmillan, he reassured while he changed. Visiting Glasgow in 1925 to see slum conditions, he wrote afterwards, 'I near as two pins sat down and howled.' Throughout his life he resisted die-hard pressures and although some measures such as the Trades Disputes Act of 1927 or the Unemployment Act of 1934 were tough, the general tone of his governments was such that revolution was not even remotely possible in the decade when Spain, Italy and Germany fell to fascism. The claims made in the election campaign of 1929 to have cut unemployment, built nearly a million houses and for general prosperity have a modern ring as did those in 1935 (Chapter 9, A4).

E2. Foreign Affairs

Like Lloyd George and Wilson, Baldwin did not understand or succeed in foreign affairs. Unlike them he took no part, except to act as a brake. His periods of office are associated with a series of deplorable failures in defence and foreign policy (see Chapters 7 and 12), and with a series of contradictory and evasive speeches on these subjects. His support of dominion status for India and the Statute of Westminster changed the face of the Empire. His failure to insist on effective strategy in the 1920s laid the major planks of our political weakness in the 1930s. He excluded Amery, Chamberlain, Churchill and Lloyd George from these fields in order to keep the peace, and leant over backwards for years towards cooperation with Labour policies, supporting the League, disarmament and collective security, all of which collapsed by 1935 and in place of which he had nothing to put. His later unpopularity stemmed from this part of his career so that his actual contributions to rearmament were neglected. There can be no doubt that his greatest failings lay in these aspects of policy.

Further Reading

Brannigan, N., *Britain in the Twenties*, Weidenfeld and Nicolson, London, 1975.

Ford, B. (ed.), *History of English Literature: The Modern Age*, Penguin, Harmondsworth, 1961.

Graves, R and Hodge, A., *The Long Week End* (A social history of the period between the wars), Faber and Faber, 1950, and available in paperback.

Johnstone, J. K., *The Bloomsbury Group*, Secker and Warburg, London, 1954.

Lyman, R. W., *The First Labour Government*, Chapman and Hall, London, 1957.

Marquand, D., *Ramsay MacDonald*, Jonathan Cape, London, 1976.

Morris, M., *The General Strike*, Penguin Books, Harmondsworth, 1976.

Montgomery Hyde, H., *Stanley Baldwin*, Hart Davis, London, 1973.

Mowat, C. L., *Britain Between the Wars 1918–1940*, Methuen, London, 1955.

Raymond, J. (ed.), *The Baldwin Age*, Eyre and Spottiswoode, London, 1960.

Questions

1. What produced the important changes of attitude among British intellectuals during the 1920s?
2. What do you think particularly characterises the twenties?
3. How far was Stanley Baldwin typical of his time?
4. Why did the tranquillity promised in 1922 elude the country until 1926?
5. To what extent are MacDonald's achievements prior to 1929 underestimated?
6. Why did Labour lose the election of 1924?
7. What were the causes of the General Strike?
8. Does Baldwin's period of office from 1924 to 1929 justify the criticism that it was 'vindictive, silly or irrelevant'?
9. What were the consequences of the defeat of the General Strike?

THE RISE AND FALL OF COLLECTIVE SECURITY: 1922–33

The period between Lloyd George's involvement in conferences and potential wars and the appearance of Hitler as Chancellor in January 1933 is comparatively neglected by Mowat, Seaman and Taylor, but in recent years Barnett and Medlicott have drawn attention to its importance. At the time the twenties and early thirties were seen in hopeful terms by nearly everyone except the chiefs of staff and a few ambassadors. The years 1923–33 seemed to clear up most of the post-war problems. Europe seemed on the road to economic recovery, and even dictators like Mussolini were apparently peace-loving. The League of Nations was at its zenith, proposals for disarmament, the abolition of war and a united Europe showered on politicians. It was the age of Chamberlain, MacDonald and Henderson. Even more realistic statesmen pinned their hopes on 'collective security'— a revival of balancing alliances. People believed, as King Hall then wrote, 'if it was possible to have a world war it was equally possible to have a world peace'.

It has already been suggested that the roots of appeasement and the collapse of Britain's effective world power can be sought in the period of Lloyd George's supremacy (Chapter 3, G4, and Chapter 4, B and C), but the twenties were 'the real point of transition to the policy of appeasement'. By this is meant not just the policy adopted by Chamberlain after 1937, but the general tendency of Britain to disarm while allowing Germany to rearm and both Japan and Italy to increase their naval strength. In this respect Locarno, which had no military feasibility and deliberately exposed Eastern Europe to the dictators, was both the apogee of hopes in the twenties and the nadir of ineffective policy, as was to be proved in the 1930s. Churchill's account of the coming of the Second World War deliberately hurried over these years to put the blame squarely on post-1931 governments of which he was not a member, but it must be emphasised that the Tories pursued as eagerly as Labour worship of the League and horror of warlike planning, aided by Churchill's economies as Chancellor.

World economic crisis brought this period to an end in 1931 with the Japanese invasion of Manchuria. The crisis increased the number of European dictators, strengthened American and Russian isolation, made further inroads on Western defence budgets and increased the propensity for aggression in countries like Japan. The Manchurian Crisis revealed 'the paralysis of foreign policy' and 'the moment of truth', but it did not lead to significant changes in policy apart from a slow start to rearmament. The period from 1931 to 1933 was dominated by MacDonald and Simon, and saw a flourish of conference on reparations, disarmament and the economic crisis. The writing was on the wall, but it still had to be read by British statesmen.

A. Determinants of Foreign Policy in the 1920s

A1. Men

There can be little doubt that foreign policy during the period was influenced by the public mood. On the left the growth of the new foreign policy and, throughout the establishment, the influence of the new diplomacy were not isolated from but complementary to public opinion. Local councils banned the Officers Training Corps, and in 1928 it was proposed to change Armistice Day into World Fellowship Day. In 1933 the Oxford Union had its debate on 'King and Country' the month after Hitler took power. This public mood was strengthened by politicians' statements such as Baldwin's remark in 1932 that 'the bomber will always get through', by the considerable anti-war literature of the time (Chapter 6, A7), and by the 'army of the noble and the good'. Intellectuals like Russell, Murray, Forster and Keynes argued for disarmament. Allen, Dickinson and Noel Baker were pacifists.

Although they had public support, the statesmen bear the main blame. It was up to them to mould opinion, or take decisions knowing the extent of the real facts. The period opened with Curzon as Foreign Secretary. His 'intellectual mastery, eloquence, argumentative skill, fine drafts, his sense of his own importance and that of his country' seemed to date him in the new age. Lausanne was the last effective triumph of British diplomacy for many years (Chapter 7, D1). In the 10 years that followed, in Barnett's words, 'It was hard to tell the Commons' front benches from King Arthur's Round Table ... so knightly and Victorian was the tone.' Nearly all those concerned in foreign policy came from a narrow class, trained in the classics, not politics, brought up on *esprit de corps* and, in many cases, imbued with a nonconformist conscience that led to abhorrence of war, desire to sympathise with underdogs and a belief that everyone told the truth. At the Foreign Office there grew up a school of diplomats who disliked the French for their belligerence, sympathised with the Germans and determined to avoid entangling alliances. The politicians preached to Europe and were involved as never before, but resolutely failed to back words with arms. They placed their faith in the League and the Commonwealth of Nations, which were nebulous concepts and no substitute for a strong alliance and a powerful empire. They preached collective security, but failed to provide either a strengthened League or more powerful national armaments to make peace certain.

Baldwin knew little of foreign politics. MacDonald had ambitions to cut an international figure and a fond belief that all could be settled round a conference table. Their choice of Foreign Secretary therefore had a decisive impact on foreign policy. Austen Chamberlain was vain, sensitive and weak, although he had a deep interest in international affairs, and a fine brain. He was from a Liberal family and was a Unitarian. His contribution between 1925 and 1929 was directed at restoring Germany to the rank of respectable nations. In this he succeeded, while turning a blind eye to rearmament. Henderson, who succeeded in 1929, was a Methodist with 'the faith of a child in noble dreams'. There was friction between MacDonald and himself, but his policy led to the removal of allied armies from Germany (1930) and the scrapping of reparations (1932). His reaction to the Manchurian Crisis was non-existent and his main concern was the Disarmament Conference from 1932 to 1934. The first Foreign Secretary of the National Governments was Sir John Simon. A Liberal, pro-Boer in 1900 and Southern Ireland in 1920, he had resigned over the introduction of conscription during the war. He was unctuous and subtle, and even at the League was known as 'Uriah Heep'. His speech on Japanese aggression in Manchuria earned him the thanks of the Japanese delegate.

A2. Guns

The Ten Year Rule adopted in 1919 became accepted policy. After the folly of the Washington Conference (Chapter 4, C4), came the collapse of attempts to produce a coordinated Imperial naval policy. The whole emphasis was on reducing defence expenditure, which continued until 1933. Churchill said war with Japan was unthinkable and, in July 1926, spoke against 'alarmist policy and consequential armaments'. The French were criticised for their large army and for deciding to build the Maginot Line. The Ten Year Rule was made automatic in 1928, and only abandoned in March 1932. By that time the army was 'barely sufficient' to meet Britain's needs, and the 1932 Defence Review referred to one division ready for instant service. The army was seen in a defensive rôle, and one sixth was in India while European commitments mounted. Disarmament was more serious in the navy and air force, which needed a modern technical base. The army neglected mechanised warfare—an experimental force was only created at Tidworth in 1927—and the other services ran into technical backwaters. Aircraft design, in which Britain led in 1918, lagged, and only in 1931 was the Aeronautical Engineering College established.

(a) *The RAF*. Bonar Law wanted to scrap a separate RAF. Fortunately, Sir Samuel Hoare, the Air Minister, did not want his cabinet post abolished and fought for it, supported later by Baldwin when the Colwyn Committee reopened the issue in 1925. Air policy was chaotic. The vast forces of 1918 were whittled away, so Britain was the fifth air power by 1929, and much of that strength was dispersed in India and the Middle East. When the possibility of war with Japan came in 1931, it was found that Japan had 411 aircraft in the fleet air arm, while Britain had only 159. The country was defenceless against air attack.

(b) *The Navy*. Disarmament was pursued ruthlessly until 1930. Britain's lead in capital ships diminished. Churchill cut the cruiser programme in 1925, and by 1929 none was being built. In that year Britain had only 50 cruisers and 120 destroyers to defend a world-wide empire, and the Defence Review in April 1931 pointed out the Germans were building pocket battleships in spite of government economies. Singapore, decided on in 1922, had a completion date in 1937 and economies deprived it of landward defences. Japan and Italy refused to participate in later naval disarmament, thus obtaining an obvious advantage.

B. Anglo-Russian Relations

While Labour wished to appease the Bolshevik regime, the Tories were anxious for *realpolitik*. As a result, although Russia was moving closer to Germany, and after the appearance of Litvinov (1927) wanted to cooperate with the League, British policy fluctuated, and there were a series of diplomatic incidents reminiscent of the nineteenth century. To some extent this attitude was justified by the activities of the Comintern. In China,

Borodin stirred up opposition to British commercial interests until he was expelled in 1927. Nascent Communist parties threatened the empire and in 1929 the Meerut Conspiracy in India involved Communists. Bad relations laid the basis, according to some, for the failure to incorporate Russia in an anti-fascist front during the 1930s. The main developments were:

(a) *The Curzon deémarche*. Curzon adopted an anti-Russian line after the signing of Rapallo, and their backing for Kemal. In May 1923 he presented a deémarche demanding compensation for the death of two British agents and the seizure of two trawlers, and an end to Russian activity in Persia and Afghanistan. Three days later the Russians accepted the demands.

(b) *The first MacDonald treaty*. In February 1924 full diplomatic recognition was given to Russia. Between April and August a commercial treaty was negotiated which skated over the thin ice of British property seized in Russia. It was sweetened by a loan. Russia accepted responsibility for the confiscated assets and, in return for export credits to the Russians, Britain received most favoured nation status.

(c) *The Arcos raid*. Austen Chamberlain refused to ratify the treaty. Raids on Communist headquarters (October 1925) and Arcos, the trade mission at 49, Moorgate (May 1927), produced evidence of subversion. The government demanded an end to internal interference in February 1927, and ended relations with Russia by expelling their mission and scrapping the 1921 trade treaty. In July 1927 the Russians arrested 26 British 'agents' in Moscow.

(d) *The Second MacDonald treaty*. The Russians agreed to restrict their propaganda in September 1929, and relations were resumed somewhat hesitantly by Henderson. By April 1930 a new commercial treaty had been signed, but this was repudiated by the National Government in 1932. Thereupon the Russians arrested four Metropolitan Vickers men in Russia on spying charges. In return for renewing the treaty in February 1934 they were released.

C. The Ruhr Crisis and the Dawes Plan

The settlement of the interrelated questions of allied debts and the payment of German reparations was seen as first priority. Following Balfour's promise (Chapter 4, C4), Baldwin went to America in January 1923 to settle Britain's debts. To show distaste for French sharp practice, Britain negotiated alone, but the ensuing settlement by which she agreed to pay a higher rate of interest than other European countries on sums that were to reach £37m a year spread over 62 years, aroused criticism. However, it made Britain even more determined to restore the German economy and put German payments on a rational basis. Churchill completed the process by settling the repayment of debts to Britain by the Allies, particularly France and Italy by 1927. The French occupation of the Ruhr (Chapter 4, C1), therefore, brought Anglo-French relations to a new low. Curzon stormed, but Italy and Belgium backed the French and the occupation lasted to September 1923. The brutal French occupation with military rule provoked a general strike. Communist and Fascist riots disturbed Germany, and the mark fell so that it was worth 15 million to the pound by the autumn. However, Poincaré had overreached himself. The franc also tumbled from 67 to 90 to the pound and made negotiations inevitable.

(a) *Curzon and the French*. Mediation was started in April 1923, and it was

Curzon's last great triumph to get this going. Baldwin and Poincaré met and in November the French agreed to a new plan. They tried to wriggle out by supporting a separatist government in the Palatinate, but this collapsed when its leader was killed, and Curzon sent a stiff note condemning the French in January 1924.

(b) *The MacDonald negotiations.* In 1924 Stresemann, Herriot and Mac-Donald saw eye to eye on policy. A committee under an American, Charles G. Dawes, worked out a fresh arrangement and in April 1924 the plan was published. In August MacDonald skilfully chaired the London Conference, and agreement was reached.

(c) *The plan.* This time the total amount and the time limit for payment were left aside. Germany was to start paying at £50m a year, rising to £125m over five years. After 1928–29 a supplement based on total production and related to the exchange rate was to be added. A loan of £40m was given to Germany, and an organisation under an American Agent General, S. Parker Gilbert, was to organise repayment inside Germany on specific revenues and industrial debentures. For three years reparations went smoothly, with the allies receiving £400m.

D. The Locarno Pact and the End of German Disarmament

Britain, France and Germany now entered into negotiations to create a security pact, which was the missing item in the Versailles Settlement (Chapter 4, C1). Chamberlain was in the main concerned with reconciling France and Germany for Britain's benefit. The French wanted British support for their treaties with Poland and Czechoslovakia, but in February 1925 Chamberlain would not agree to this. Stresemann wanted to replace the enforcement of the treaties by a freely negotiated pact, but he was also following a policy of fulfilment. This meant that in order to secure German good behaviour the Western Powers would grant concessions. Versailles would be negotiated out of sight in return for general security and disarmament. The consequences of this policy were fatal. The agreement reached was inoperable, and collapsed in 1935–36. Germany rearmed while the Allies talked about disarmament and by 1932 Germany had secured the scrapping of disarmament, military occupation and reparations.

(a) *Treaty of Locarno, October 1925.* A treaty was signed between Germany, Belgium, and France to guarantee existing frontiers and demilitarisation of the Rhineland. Britain and Italy guaranteed the Pact. Almost at once, Stresemann demanded the return of Eupen and Malmedy. By 1928 he was declaring Germany's patience exhausted, and in 1930 Hindenburg demanded the immediate return of the Saar. It was clear Germany had not abandoned her intentions, and the French Maginot Line (1928) recognised this fact.

(b) *Germany enters the League.* In April 1926 the German-Russian Treaty was renewed, and the allies had to act. They allowed Germany to enter on her own conditions. Article 16 was specifically not to apply to Russia, and Germany was to have a place on the Council. Brazil and Spain withdrew because they had prior claim, and the matter was only settled in September by increasing the non-permanent seats to nine and allowing three of them to be re-elected.

(c) *End of the Allied Control Commission.* By February 1926 the French had agreed to withdraw some of their occupation troops early in return for the full maintenance of the ACC. Stresemann needed this out of the way. Although the cabinet objected, the French finally agreed, and in January the Commission left.

Its report in February 1925 had contained 160 pages, giving details of German rearmament.

The Locarno spirit continued to glimmer. There was a German-French commercial treaty. Emil Mayrich put forward plans for economic union, and a Pan-European Conference met at Vienna. In September 1929 Briand proposed European union, and in May 1930 a further system of Locarno guarantees covering Eastern Europe. He advocated a common market in capital, goods and peoples. Meanwhile, in Germany Seeckt organised the illegal *reichswehr*, so that an army on paper of seven divisions was in embryo one of 62 divisions. The General Staff was retained by working in other ministries. Aeroplanes, poison gas, tanks and submarines were made in Russia where training took place. A skeleton air-force was created in glider and civilian flying clubs. German war industries were reconstituted, and by 1928 they were being run by the ministries. In 1930 Bruening announced the pocket battleship programme. Locarno thus enabled diplomatic schizophrenia to develop on a large scale.

E. Half a League Onward

The years 1924 to 1930 were the period of the League's greatest prestige and authority. The members rose from the original 18 to 58 by 1934, and there were few withdrawals. On the other hand, neither America nor Russia was involved directly, although both sent observers and took part in the economic and disarmament activities of the League. After Germany joined, and Litvinov of Russia arrived in 1927, many believed that the League would guarantee peace. This was certainly the view of the Labour Party. Conservatives tended to be less enthusiastic, but it was always a useful substitute for action. In September 1924 MacDonald started a new trend for heads of government to visit Geneva, and during the rest of the twenties, six prime ministers made speeches. When the Palace of the Nations began to rise in 1929 hopes rose with it. This was due to the success of the League in non-political matters. Butler and Thomas developed the International Labour Organisation, Nansen cared for refugees, and in 1932 a Permanent Slavery Commission was set up. The International Court pronounced on over 50 cases, and just over 50 League members signed the Optional Clause, which required them to submit disputes with fellow members to the Court. The League Yearbook in 1934 contained 143 pages of activities. However, the enthusiasts should have pondered the failure to give the League teeth to deal with aggression, the frequent sidestepping of the League by the great powers, and the undue influence of small nations. The trouble was that the League was a posse of state police trying to behave like federal agents.

F. Disarmament and Outlawing War

During the period 1923–33 proposals and meetings proliferated on disarmament and the prevention of war. They were all futile, but this does not detract from the sincerity of the efforts; moreover, the time devoted to this aspect of international relations may explain why so little was done in other spheres. The main events were:

(*a*) *Draft Treaty of Mutual Assistance.* This was put forward by Lord Robert Cecil in 1923 for a universal agreement on arms limitation, and the resolution of disputes before the League within four days. Eighteen out of 29 governments consulted appeared favourable, but France got cold feet, and in 1924 Britain turned it down.

(*b*) *Geneva Protocol.* This was largely drafted by Henderson, and put forward in 1924. War was to be outlawed, there was to be compulsory arbitration of disputes followed by sanctions, the reference of legal disputes to the Court of Justice and clear definitions of aggression and sanctions. Britain, under a different government then, rejected it in 1925.

(*c*) *Preparatory Commission.* This replaced the bodies set up in 1920 to prepare for a conference on disarmament. It was set up in December 1925 with 10 Council members, America and Russia. The Commission had severe problems of definition, but in 1930, urged on by Henderson, it fixed the time for the conference as February 1932.

(*d*) *Kellogg Pact.* When Briand proposed to Coolidge of America in 1927 that they renounce war, the latter was put on the spot. In return the Americans suggested a general act renouncing war, and this was signed at Paris in August 1928. There was no machinery and no definition of terms, but eventually it was signed by 65 countries, including Russia.

Nor did better success attend unilateral attempts to disarm. The Americans were eager to follow up the Washington Treaties, and in February 1927 invited Britain to resume naval disarmament talks. A conference took place in June, but this time neither Italy nor France was willing to attend. The Americans proposed to extend the $5:5:3$ ratio to cruisers, destroyers and submarines, which was ludicrous, in view of Britain's different needs. The conference failed. When MacDonald returned to power he visited Rapidan in America (October 1929) and this was followed by the London Naval Conference of January 1930. This time France, Italy and Japan attended. France objected to low limits on cruisers and Italy demanded parity with France. Japan suggested parity with the Western powers. In April a treaty was signed by which the naval holiday was to continue until 1936, Britain accepted American parity in cruisers, destroyers and submarines, and Japan obtained parity in submarines, 60 per cent of Britain's tonnage in large cruisers, and 70 per cent in small ones and destroyers. The effect of the treaty was to enhance Japanese power, leave Germany untouched and, as Italy walked out, shackle only Britain's.

The Disarmament Conference met in 1932 and went on for years. Henderson was president. Simon put forward qualitative limitation by scrapping offensive weapons and only keeping those needed for self-defence. Apart from a renewal of an agreement not to use gas, nothing was achieved. In May Papen took over in Germany, and discussion became more acrimonious. At last in July further proposals to prohibit air attack, chemical warfare and large tanks and guns were voted on. Italy abstained. Germany and Russia voted against. Then the Germans demanded parity, and for a time withdrew. In January 1933 they resumed, and the 'MacDonald Plan' was outlined in March. The aim of this was numerical limitation to exact figures, but it would involve substantial French disarmament. The French put forward another plan, but Hitler was in power, and although Britain and Italy accepted the French plan, the Germans withdrew the same day (October 1933).

G. The End of Military Occupation and Reparations

By late 1928 the need to complete proposals on reparations in the Dawes Plan was apparent, and in September the Allies unwisely decided to link this to the withdrawal of occupation troops. The Young Committee published its proposals in June 1929. They were:

(i) A total of 37 annual payments of £100m followed by 22 smaller ones linked to the payment of war debts to be completed by 1988.
(ii) The 1924 control system to be replaced by a German one.
(iii) A Bank of International Settlements to organise loans.

In spite of doubts expressed by Chamberlain at Lugano and the German election results of 1930, the Allies pressed ahead.

(a) *Hague Conferences.* Agreed in August 1929, after haggling over an extra £4m demanded by Snowden, to bring forward evacuation to 1930 in return for German acceptance of the Young Plan. French demands for verification of German disarmament were met by a promise to drop agitation for the return of the Saar. A second conference in January 1930 accepted the Plan, and agreed to end occupation. The troops left in June.

(b) *Customs union.* When discussing Briand's plan for European union, it was suggested in January 1931 that Germany and Austria might form a customs union in view of the looming economic crisis. When the matter was put forward the Allies referred it to the Court at the Hague who decided it broke the Treaty of Versailles. British banks then gave loans to Austria and Germany as they were affected by the economic crisis.

(c) *Hoover Moratorium.* However, the economic crisis struck Austria, which German banks had to rescue, only themselves to suffer, and by recalling money from Holland and elsewhere, plunge Europe into economic chaos by July 1931. Part of the difficulty was that falling exchange rates increased the burden of reparations, and it was only in June 1931—too late—that Hoover issued a moratorium on Britain's debts, thus enabling a halt to reparations. But in January 1932 Bruening suspended payments.

(d) *Lausanne Conference.* In June 1932, with MacDonald presiding, this met to consider reparations. It was agreed to scrap them in return for a token payment of £150m. In fact, Germany had received more in loans (£1,500m) than she had paid in reparations (£1,000m), and had only paid a sixth of what had been decided.

In spite of appearances, British diplomacy did badly during the 1920s. Versailles had been rewritten in regard to reparations, inspections and occupation with Allied cooperation, and rearmament had taken place with their connivance. But more general schemes for strengthening the League, arbitration in international affairs and economic cooperation had failed. Indeed, the end of the 1920s boom brought with it an end of euphoria. Although Briand did not retire until 1932, France was heading for Stavisky, the Leagues and financial chaos. Stresemann died in October 1929, and Bruening and Papen pursued nationalist policies under pressure from Hitler. Chamberlain left office in June 1929, and was not restored in October 1931. Henderson and MacDonald were old and failing. A new world was dawning, but statesmen still slept with the dreams of the 1920s.

H. The Far Eastern Question

The first challenge to 1920s thinking revealed not only the folly of much proposed in the previous decade, and the inability of either the League or collective security to solve the problem of aggression, but exposed clearly the deficiencies in Britain's strategic policies. It came in the Far East while Britain was deep in economic crisis in 1931.

H1. Britain and China in the 1920s

Britain had considerable Far Eastern interests apart from Hong Kong, particularly the settlements at Shanghai and Tientsin which controlled British trade. In overall terms this was not great—it was only $1\frac{1}{2}$ per cent of total trade—but Britain was determined to maintain paramountcy. This was rendered difficult by three factors. The Treaty of Washington and the end of the Japanese alliance weakened Britain. The Chinese, whose government was confused and in the hands of war lords, were regarded as less civilised. However, the treaty had promised to respect China's territorial integrity, and this was awkward for Britain, who owned Wei-Hai-Wei. The activities of Borodin, a Russian agent, alarmed the British, but her resources were fully stretched to maintain a Far Eastern presence since Singapore was not built. If Japan chose to oppose Britain, there was little she could do.

(*a*) *The Canton incidents.* As early as 1923 marines were sent to Canton following threats, and in 1924 the Labour government did likewise. The Chinese objected to an upper limit of 5 per cent placed on their tariffs, extra-territorial rights and European power in their concessions.

(*b*) *The Shanghai incident.* Chiang Kai Shek proposed to levy an extra $2\frac{1}{2}$ per cent and later to raise tariffs to $12\frac{1}{2}$ per cent. Although Baldwin accepted this, and proposed negotiations, Borodin urged a direct attack on the concessions. He set up headquarters at Hankow, and in January 1927 the British depot there was attacked. The Shanghai Defence Force was despatched, but Baldwin also withdrew the concession. In July Borodin fled, and Sir Miles Lampson negotiated a settlement with Chiang by which Britain surrendered Wei Hai Wei in 1930.

Britain's treatment of China gave her little room to complain if others saw the country as fair game and in May 1927 the Japanese landed forces for the first time. Under a 1905 treaty they were allowed to keep 15,000 troops in Manchuria, and exploited this situation. In 1929, in response to the Japanese threat, the Russians attacked in Manchuria for the first time. The Far Eastern Question was thus triangular. The Russians cooperated with Chiang, handed Sinkiang to China (1933) and eventually in 1937 signed an alliance. Many in Japan saw Russia as the main enemy and favoured a 'strike north' policy, thus bringing Japanese ambition to bear on the rich industrial province of Manchuria.

(*c*) *The extra-territorial rights dispute.* In January 1930 Chiang, who was rapidly gaining control, denounced the existing European rights. Henderson invoked the Kellogg Pact and refused to act. In January 1932 Japanese forces attacked Chapei, a suburb of Shanghai, putting the concession at risk. Simon then acted, troops were sent and an armistice arranged. Under these circumstances, Simon had no desire to antagonise the Japanese as well as Chinese.

H2. The Manchurian Incident, September 1931

For a number of reasons, Japan was becoming increasingly warlike. The end of the 1902 treaty caused them to lose face. In 1924 America clamped down on Japanese immigrants at the very time the Japanese were suffering from the after-effects of the 1923 earthquake, which did £500m of damage. Japan's rapid growth led to serious population pressure, with two thirds of her farmers cultivating less than 2½ acres while tariff restrictions by over 40 nations seriously damaged her export trade. During the economic crisis (1929–32) Japan's trade fell by half. China added to her difficulties by imposing a boycott, and her friendship with Russia was seen as a menace.

(a) *The Conquest of Manchuria.* Chinese plans to build an alternative railway to the one the Japanese controlled combined with growing disorder to provide the Japanese with an excuse. They blew up part of the railway line, claimed it was an attack on them, and in four days had seized every town in a 200-mile radius. By 4 January the Japanese reached the Great Wall.

(b) *The Republic of Manchukuo.* China appealed to the League. This was the first time a major country had done so, and the powers' reaction was decisive in determining events in the 1930s. A resolution in September 1931 called on Japan to withdraw, but neither Britain nor America was willing to act. In December, Hoover said they would not act, thus leaving Britain alone at a time of economic crisis. Although the 1922 treaty had been broken, Simon was determined not to act.

(c) *The Lytton Commission.* The setting up of Manchukuo as a puppet state recognised only by Germany and Italy, forced the British to do something. Lytton, a former governor of Bombay, was appointed to head a commission, and when China renewed her appeal in January 1932 she was told to await its report.

(d) *The Lytton Report.* This appeared in September and was a masterly statement of the issues supporting the idea of an autonomous state recognised by China and Japan. Stimson and Simon refused to act and Simon's speech criticised the Chinese for failing to create a stable government. With one vote against, the League adopted the report (February 1933), but nothing further happened.

H3. Consequences

In the short term the Manchurian Incident demonstrated a number of important points. Japan left the League in March 1933, and was the first major power to do so. Support given by Germany was not forgotten, and in 1936 the Anti-Comintern Pact between Germany and Japan was signed. In 1933 Japan invaded Jehol, and in the next few years extended her control over Hopeh and Chahar. In December 1934 Japan renounced the Treaty of Washington, and relations between America and Japan progressively deteriorated. However, for a time this did not frighten the Japanese as the Neutrality Act (1935) effectively prevented any American military challenge. America recognised Russia (1933) and supported her admission to the League (1934) as some antidote to Japanese ambitions. British reaction was equivocal also. In February 1934 a subcommittee reported that support for Japan would prevent her being drawn into the German orbit, and break good relations with America. MacDonald and Simon argued for the American links which had brought Britain little gain, and the Orde Memorandum (1935) concluded that Japan was so aggressive Britain would only soil her hands by joining her. Chamberlain was worried, and pointed out in September 1934 that a belligerent Japan would menace India, while the Defence Review (1935) stressed war with both Germany and Japan should be avoided. A conference in London in December 1935 discussed the naval aspects of Washington, but no agreement could be reached, and they lapsed during 1936. Singapore was at last completed, but the dominions expressed grave doubts about Japan at the Imperial Conference in 1937 (Chapter 11, C4).

The Far Eastern question thus revealed as early as 1931 the inadequacy of Britain's forces for a world rôle and the nature of a British government's response to flagrant breaches of treaties. Their muddled response and America's wordy interventions were to be typical of each succeeding crisis during the 1930s, and while events in Europe attracted most attention, the consequences of 1931 worked themselves out. Angry with Britain and egged on by Germany, Japan turned from a northern strike to a southern one. Pearl Harbour and the fall of Singapore followed.

Further Reading

Adler, S., *The Uncertain Giant, American Foreign Policy 1921–1941*, Macmillan, London, and Collier-Macmillan, New York, 1965.

Barnett, C., *The Collapse of British Power*, Eyre Methuen, London, 1972.

Bassett, R., *Democracy and Foreign Policy* (a study of the Manchurian question), Longmans, London, 1952.

Carr, E. H., *International Relations between the Two World Wars*, Macmillan, London, 1965.

Friedman, I. S., *British Relations with China 1931–39*, Institute of Pacific Relations, New York, 1940.

Gathorne-Hardy, G. M., *A Short History of International Affairs 1920–1939*, Oxford UP, London, 1944.

Jordan, W. M., *Great Britain, France and the German Problem, 1918–1939*, Oxford UP, London, 1943.

Marks, S., *The Age of Illusion*, Macmillan, London, 1976.

Questions

1. What changes in the interpretation of foreign policy in the 1920s have taken place in recent years?
2. What influence did economic factors have on Britain's foreign policy in the 1920s?
3. Is there any evidence to suggest appeasement was as much a policy of the 1920s as of the 1930s?
4. What issues were raised by the Manchurian Crisis of 1931?
5. What accounts for the mood of wishful thinking in 1920s diplomacy?
6. What factors influenced Anglo-French relations in the 1920s?

8

DEPRESSION, UNEMPLOYMENT AND FINANCIAL CRISIS: 1929–31

A fortnight before the election of October 1931, Noel Coward's *Cavalcade* opened, and the author came on stage to say, 'After all, it is a pretty exciting thing in these days to be English.' In one sense historians share this view. Medlicott says 1931 was a 'turning point' and Taylor describes the crisis of 1931 as 'the watershed of English history between the wars'. But they would not agree with the patriotic message of *Cavalcade*. They might prefer another view point: 'It seemed in 1931 that the star of Great Britain had passed its zenith and that there but remained to chronicle the waning of that power upon whose empire the sun never sets.' Ahead lay recovery in the 1930s, and the Finest Hour in 1940, but in a long-term sense this statement is true. Whatever mistakes had occurred before 1929–31, the impact of the crisis made it almost certain they would not be rectified. The problems of decaying industries and unemployment rose to unprecedented heights. A crisis of great severity affected the capitalist world and this gave rise to suffering and poverty from which the mixed economy, welfare economics and many modern ideas were to come. The crisis would have affected Britain whatever government was in power, but the Labour government of the time proved unequal to the challenge. As Mowat says, 'Labour by desperate remedies might have saved the day. Instead it followed the half measures of its predecessors. When these failed, it forfeited the nation's confidence and opened the gate once more for the Conservatives. ... It fell a victim of its own shortcomings as much as of some strange political manoeuvres.'

A. The Declining British Economy of the 1920s and Early 1930s

In 1931 Siegfried's *England's Crisis* appeared. It was a critique of the British economy and opened with the argument that 'with the present decade passes the era of unrivalled British supremacy'. Trends long apparent (Chapter 1, D1) which had been delayed by the stimulus of war and post-war boom (Chapter 5, B3) now surfaced like rocks in the placid waters of Baldwin and MacDonald's Britain. The limited recovery of the late 1920s collapsed before the Great Crash, and all experts were agreed that Britain's economy was in serious trouble.

A1. The International Position

Britain was now second to the United States as the world's chief exporter, since between 1913 and 1929 the volume of imports rose by 20 per cent, and of exports fell by the same amount. While world export trade rose by 18 per cent, Britain's fell by 21 per cent. What Britain exported was too expensive and increasingly out of date. Her world trade was challenged by America and Japan; her European position was hurt by the closing of the Russian market, the rise of dictatorships aiming at self-sufficiency, and spreading industrialisation of countries like Poland and Czechoslovakia. The trade deficit rose from £134m in 1913 to £382m in 1929. Britain had scarcely any tariffs in spite of strong Tory demands for 'safeguarding'. In July 1930 the Manchester Chamber of Commerce at last voted for them, but by then the economic storm had burst. Britain tried to use her Empire markets instead of competing directly in the world's market place. Between 1913 and 1929 Empire trade rose 27 per cent in volume, but this was illusory. The white dominions were industrialising, and already had tariff systems. Any attempt to keep the Empire as a protected field for British products was doomed to failure.

In the same way overseas investment was illusory. A favourable balance of £103m in 1929 concealed that much investment was speculative and short-term, and that capital used up in the war had to be replaced. Since America was unwilling to adopt a world financial rôle, London remained the centre of world finance, with its overvalued pound putting a brake on exports. During the coming crisis, Britain continued to lend to Austria and Germany while borrowing from America and France. Thus, the economic development of the 1920s was based not on the reform of British industry or economic recovery, but on an expanding domestic market with real wages up and prices down. The new industries in Britain were mainly to cater for this market.

A2. Ailing Giants of British Industry

What had been bad before 1914 now became appalling. The million unemployed were heavily concentrated in the regions and industries that led the industrial world in the nineteenth century. Competition, tariffs and declining demand affected, with temporary booms, every major industry. Britain paid the penalty for being first. Industry was out of date, with high costs and low productivity. It did not use modern power or machines. Its management was stuffy; its workers hidebound. Siegfried particularly attacked management for being too willing to play the country gentleman, and the gifted amateur; a criticism which coincides with Barnett's assessment of the ruling class in political affairs.

It was not until the 1930s that a new generation of industrialists and the weakened position of organised labour enabled streamlining and modernisation to become key words, and the government scrapped the gold standard and started tariffs. The improvement was immense, and also a grave criticism of the enfeebled efforts of the 1920s. The share of the market held by new industries like cars, aircraft, rayon and electrical goods rose from 6.5 per cent in 1907 to 16.3 per cent in 1930, but as exporters they failed because they were undercapitalised, lacking in marketing techniques or good design, and manufacturers preferred to sell in the home market. In 1930 they accounted for 14.6 per cent of our exports. Again, it was the crisis that produced the sort of change needed. In 1930 Securities Management Trust was set up by the big banks to provide investment, and business efficiency became a major issue.

A glance at the major industries will indicate the position:

(*a*) *Coal.* Domestic demand fell as homes converted to other power sources and industry itself declined. Abroad coal exports fell by two thirds. There was a series of futile commissions and damaging strikes. Management were callous and inefficient. Output per man-shift in 1927 barely exceeded 1913 levels (Chapter 6, C3).

(*b*) *Iron and steel*. Iron suffered from over-capacity and total production fell from 10.3 million tons in 1913 to 6.3 million tons in 1925. Steel did better until 1930, when it fell sharply, and demands were made for a tariff to compete with steel cartels abroad.

(*c*) *Shipbuilding*. Over-capacity combined with post-war seizures and a decline in trade to lead to drastic decline. The navy ordered less. Thus, although Britain remained the largest merchant marine, her total share of world shipping fell from 60 per cent to 30 per cent in the 1920s.

(*d*) *Textiles*. Cotton was the largest export industry and also the most depressed. While world production rose by 20 per cent, Britain's fell by 6 per cent and her exports by 15 per cent. Home markets did not take an increasing share. Above all, India, with a tariff, took only 42 per cent of her pre-war figure. From providing 51.2 per cent of total exports in 1913, textiles fell to only 18.5 per cent in 1929. Outdated methods and poor organisation (700 spinning and 1,200 weaving mills in Lancashire) lost the market to Japan and America.

B. Unemployment—Myths and Realities

In Mowat's words, 'gradually it became clear that Britain had been in a state of depression ever since the war'. The main importance of this depression is to be measured in economic terms—and, stemming from that, in terms of political and imperial decline. But even under Lloyd George (Chapter 5, B3) unemployment had become the most talked-about consequence. This was unfortunate because discussion of the unemployed overshadowed discussion of industrial decline. Government attention was focused on dole queues to avoid electoral suicide, and a vast system of outdoor relief was created. Historians have been divided on the issue. One group harp on dole queues and hunger marchers. Some of them claim unemployment was directly the fault of the capitalist system, and blame the National Governments of the 1930s. But this is clearly a distortion. Liberals and Labour were also in office when there were a million unemployed. The worst rise in unemployed took place between 1929 and 1931, when Lloyd George and MacDonald both pledged themselves to do something about it. Under the National Governments, although the number remained high, it fell steadily. It is important to relate conditions among the unemployed to average working-class conditions, to compare dole money to the falling level of prices and to realise that for the overwhelming majority the period was one of rising prosperity after 1932. This is not to excuse the awful figures, but it is necessary to put an emotive subject in perspective.

B1. Unemployment Figures
The total figures for Great Britain, excluding Northern Ireland, were:

1929	1.2m	1930	1.9m	1931	2.7m
1932	2.8m	1933	2.5m	1934	2.1m
1935	2.0m	1936	1.7m	1937	1.4m
1938	1.9m	1939	1.3m		

The inter-war total of workless was concentrated in the areas of old export industries, and even within those into particular towns and branches of industry. This enabled an exaggerated picture to be formed by generalising from acutely hit areas, and at the time it enabled much of the electorate to ignore the problem. Three fifths could be found in six counties (Yorkshire, Lancashire, Staffordshire, Durham, Lanarkshire and Glamorgan). Thus, in 1937 the regional variation showed that London and the South East had a rate of 6.4 per cent, while the North had 13.8 per cent. Scotland and Wales had particularly high figures. In any given region there was a wide variety. In Manchester, which was able to attract new industries, the figure was 15.3 per cent, whereas a nearby town like Blackburn had 52.7 per cent. In towns dependent on one industry the figure was high. Jarrow had 67.8 per cent and Merthyr Tydfil, 61.9 per cent.

Other concentrations can be discerned. In a particular town there could be a discrepancy between ship and tram workers, or cotton and postal workers. Many jobs like policeman or teacher secured status and ample recruitment while others had a poor future. In particular, unskilled workers made up 30 per cent of the total compared with 14 per cent for skilled. Older people suffered more than the young, and those permanently out of work rose so that in 1939, 22.6 per cent of the working population had never had a job. As Orwell said, 'several million men in England will—unless another war breaks out—never have a real job this side of the grave'. He pointed out that percentages were more horrifying translated into ordinary figures. On this basis there were 89,000 workless in Glasgow and 84,000 in Liverpool in 1937. He said wives and children should be added to the figure to discover how many were dependent on the dole. On this basis, six million lived 'on the dole', and in a town like Wigan that amounted to one in three.

B2. Life on the Dole

During the 1930s for a number of reasons (Chapter 10, A5) there was a revival of social problem literature like that of the 1840s, and much left-wing work on social and economic life. Some of this dealt with the unemployed, and may be divided into three groups:

(a) *Novels*. The most famous of these was W. Greenwood's *Love on the Dole* (1934), based on Manchester and made into a play and film. P. Bentley's *A Modern Tragedy* (1934), A. J. Cronin's *The Stars Look Down* (1935), A. McArthur and H. K. Long's *No Mean City* (1935) and Cronin's *The Citadel* (1937) deal respectively with Yorkshire, Tyneside, Glasgow and South Wales.

(b) *Reporting*. The most famous of the accounts were Priestley's *English Journey* (1934) and Orwell's *Road to Wigan Pier* (1937).

(c) *Polemic*. There were plenty of left-wing works. Wilkinson's *The Town that was Murdered* (1936), about Jarrow, was perhaps the most well known. Another was Jennings' *Brynmawr* (1934), which was followed by a film *Proud Valley*.

Average working conditions in the 1930s were vastly different from those after the Second World War, and it is essential to compare those on the dole with those off it. *The Times* carried stories of those better off on the dole than off it, including a Southwark engineer whose income rose from 42*s* to 47*s*. After Labour abolished restrictions in 1930 this anomaly grew.

Mowat states that 'many people, particularly the younger married man, were better off on the dole', and Branson and Heinemann admit that even during the period of cuts (1931–35) falling prices and pressure on the government kept the dole at a level just short of the lower paid workers. These facts may not cover the psychological conseqences of living in a depressed area, but five million workers went into the armed services later, and did not prove notably demoralised.

It is important to realise that many of the commentators were sleeping comfortably on their royalties. Priestley wrote of Jarrow as a community of 'unrelieved shabbiness and deprivation outside the home as well as in it', and went on, 'My guide book devotes one short sentence to Jarrow: A busy town (35,000 inhabitants), has large iron works and shipbuilding yards. It is time this was amended into an idle and ruined town wondering what is to become of them.' He described the street corner dole queues and at Hebburn commented, 'It is not merely that two thirds of the town is living on the edge of destitution, tightening its belt another hole or two every month, but that its self-respect is vanishing—for these were working towns and nothing else—and it sees the sky for ever darkening over it.' In individual cases, life on the dole produced undesirable social effects. There was a trend to hopelessness, resort to inane occupations, wasteful spending of dole money to relieve monotony, immorality caused by poor living conditions and some class bitterness.

B3. Unemployment Pay

Unemployment pay has been seen as the means to stopping revolution and diverting attention from the real problem. When Sir John Simon in July 1935 spoke about tackling unemployment 'by every measure possible', it turned out later that the government's chief policy 'was simply to maintain the unemployed man and his family'. In 1927 a Committee investigated unemployment pay, and found it was 'hardly recognisable through the tangled mass of opportunist legislation'. The Acts of 1920–21 had been expanded and the insurance fund was in the red. Chamberlain introduced restrictions, but Labour removed them and passed the Unemployment Act (1930), which increased the number entitled to transitional benefit, provided new Treasury subsidies and abolished the 'genuinely seeking work' provisions. They set up the Gregory Commission to investigate the Acts, but its first report in July 1931 was overtaken by the crisis. It recommended cuts because by the summer the unemployment fund was overspending a million a week.

After the crisis (Section 8E) economies were introduced. The standard rate was cut by 10 per cent and stood by the end of 1931 at 23s 3d for a married couple and 27s 5d for a couple with two children. In addition, the National Government passed the Anomalies Act which limited benefit once again to 26 weeks, after which the PACs would carry out a means test before recipients went on the dole. Married women were disqualified unless they had been 'normally employed', cutting 134,000 off benefit. The means test was introduced in November 1931, and assessed the total income of a family so that relatives were included, and other assets such as post office savings. The test gave rise to accusations of snooping and favouritism, and helped to break up families. However, it led to a reduction of those on relief by substantial numbers. In Lancashire 33.3 per cent of applicants failed the test. Even those who passed found themselves on a lower rate than previously. The cuts in standard rate were restored by July 1934, and thereafter the rate rose slightly by 1939.

Once the Gregory Commission completed work in 1932 the government reformed the whole system with the Unemployment Act (1934). The motives behind this act, like much of Chamberlain's work, were mixed. In spite of the means test saving some £12m, some local PACs continued to give generous rates. The Act cut the number of authorities responsible from 200 to 28, strengthened Treasury control, and codified the law. It provided a new scale of benefits, set up the Unemployment Assistance Board with an independent chairman and local officers, brought all the unemployed under the new authorities whether they had been on PACs or the Poor Law and modified the existing means test. Unfortunately the first chairman turned out to be the previous Minister of Labour, Sir Henry Betterton. National scales meant that in some areas scales fell. Near Wolverhampton benefits were said to have fallen from 38s to 25s. In February 1935 Oliver Stanley, Minister of Labour, issued a standstill order, and it was announced the new scales would not come fully into effect until November 1936. When Ernest Brown brought the measure to completion in April 1937, it was agreed people would receive the PAC or UAB scale, whichever was the higher.

B4. Riots and Soup Kitchens

None of the political parties had a solution to unemployment, although a number of bold proposals such as Lloyd George's and Oswald Mosley's would have done much to help. The far left, apart from stressing that there was no unemployment in Stalin's Russia and calling for higher benefits, had no answer. Labour in 1929–31 proved this (Section C5), and some of their supporters like Orwell seemed to resign themselves to the situation. In 1936 John Strachey wrote that it was 'uncontrolled and uncontrollable'.

This does not excuse the failure of the Tories in the 1930s, but it does make clear the failure was universal, not just that of one party. Seaman has attacked the government for not yielding to Keynes' advice. His *General Theory* came out in 1936, and his views were not ignored by substantial numbers of people including Bevin and Macmillan. But Roosevelt's New Deal, based in part on Keynesian ideas, had more unemployed at the end than the beginning, and after 1974, high unemployment and high government spending were to coexist. Moreover, the logic of much that Mosley and others preached was the corporate state of the kind Italy experienced. In the end the Western countries all solved the problem the same way—with rearmament and conscription.

There was little revolutionary activity among the working class. Hannington's *Unemployed Struggles* (1937) puts the Communist view, but there was never any danger of either his or Mosley's views commanding much political support. The main troubles were:

(*a*) The 1932 Riots. Opposition to the means test culminated in the Birkenhead Riots, which lasted for four days and included police raids on tenement blocks. A hunger march was dispersed violently by the police in London's Hyde Park in October.

(b) In 1935 there were fresh disturbances. The unemployment offices at Merthyr were sacked, and there were riots at Glasgow, Maryport and Sheffield. A second hunger march to Hyde Park in November passed off without incident.

This was partly due to the limited nature of the problem; more to dole money, positive government economic policies (Section 9D) and a range of remedies including those of a voluntary character. It is easy to laugh at some of these, such as Rover Scouts training men as butlers and chauffeurs, but there was a whole range of schemes for helping. The government introduced Training Centres through which, on average, 14,000 a year were retrained, Domestic Training Centres for girls to train as servants, and Industrial Transference which arranged for workers to leave the depressed areas. Between 1930 and 1937, 90,000 moved. To these are added the voluntary work of the National Council of Social Services (1932). This founded clubs to help the out of work. By 1935 there were 400.

Orwell scoffed at 'YMCA cocoa drunkards' and, of course, these schemes only touched the surface, but added to the recovering economy they amount to substantial effort. To speak of 'stony indifference to human suffering' and 'industrial apartheid' as Seaman does is unfair. By 1935 unemployment had fallen by half from the total in 1931 and recovery was under way.

C. Labour Government, June 1929–August 1931

Although Labour was the largest party, it was still in a minority, and opposition from the Lords and harrying tactics by the Tories weakened it further. MacDonald failed to work out relations with the Liberals. At first Lloyd George stood aloof; then he worked for concessions in return for support, but MacDonald was unable to deliver an Electoral Reform Bill (Section C2). In foreign affairs, where MacDonald's interests lay, there was much activity (Chapter 7, F and G) and the Manchurian Crisis, but at home the government showed little intention of carrying out the bold programme announced in July 1929. MacDonald was starting to become vague and lose his faculties. The serious problems of industry and unemployment which should have concerned Labour were neglected even before the crisis of 1931.

C1. The Ministry

MacDonald agreed to have a Foreign Secretary. Thomas wanted the post, but Henderson secured it, leaving him as Lord Privy Seal and minister responsible for unemployment. He was assisted by Thomas Johnston and Sir Oswald Mosley. Thomas said he had 'the complete cure' and 'something up his sleeve'. It sounded promising. There were few new faces and hardly any radical ones. Lansbury was placated as Commissioner of Works. Clynes became Home Secretary. Sidney Webb entered the Lords as Lord Passfield and took Colonies. Thomas later obtained Dominions when they were separated in 1930, while India went to an ex-Liberal, Wedgwood Benn. Snowden, crippled with arthritis and orthodox finance, became Chancellor. The first woman cabinet minister, Miss Bondfield, went to Labour. Some new faces were Morrison at Transport, who carried out the government's major reforms, Alexander (Admiralty) and Greenwood (Health). In 1930 Attlee and Cripps entered the government.

C2. Politics

Lloyd George was disgruntled by the election, and in June 1930 refused to combine his fund with that of the party. Some Liberals, led by Simon, were increasingly convinced *laissez faire* had to go, and were moving towards the Tories; others had already shifted to Labour. Lloyd George succeeded in annoying everyone. By opposing the Coal Mines Bill he annoyed radicals; by supporting Agriculture and Electoral Reform Bills, his right wingers. In June 1931 Simon withdrew from the party whip and the Liberals were divided. Taylor puts this down to two factors: Lloyd George's new programme was too advanced for its time, and Lloyd George was 'a bad party man'. Neither he nor MacDonald was able to bring his party together.

Proposals for electoral reform were introduced in February 1931, but the government included the scrapping of plural voting and university seats as well as the single, transferable vote system. The Liberals refused to support the first, the Lords restored the second and limited the third to London and larger boroughs. MacDonald was considering the use of the Parliament Act when the crisis struck. Nor were relations with the Tories good. Actions like the seizure of the parliamentary Mace by John Beckitt in July 1930 annoyed them. MacDonald called them 'swine' and this made matters worse. By November 1930 relations were so bad that after one debate a Tory MP, Lord Winterton, was jostled and challenged to a fight.

C3. Tory Ructions

Baldwin had now lost two out of three elections, and his moderate policies were not popular. MPs with private incomes and substantial press backing could act in an independent manner, and in 1930–31 there was a move to shift the Tory Party to the right. Baldwin's defeat of this was one of his triumphs, and prepared the way for coalition. The main events were:

(a) *Empire Free Trade.* Beaverbrook devised this title for Imperial Preference, and launched a campaign in 1929. Baldwin met him half way; on 4 March 1930 declared himself in favour of a referendum on food taxes.

(b) *United Empire Party.* This was backed by Rothermere's *Mail*. They won two by-elections. In June 1930 Baldwin read out a letter from Rothermere demanding to know the composition of the next Tory cabinet, and won a vote of confidence.

(c) *The St George's By-Election.* Baldwin drifted closer to tariffs, but the UEP won two more by-elections. It was only when no Tory stood against the UEP candidate at St George's, Westminster, that Baldwin decided to act. Alfred Duff Cooper agreed to stand and Baldwin attacked the press lords. The Tories won.

(d) *Imperial issues.* Baldwin and MacDonald had a bipartisan policy on India. Churchill resigned from the Shadow Cabinet in January 1931 and gathered a party including Austen Chamberlain, Page Croft, Horne and Lord Lloyd. They attacked the Round Table Conferences and the Statute of Westminster. Like MacDonald, Baldwin was not unwilling to escape his extremists.

C4. The Government Programme

The measures passed were:

(a) *Coal Mines Act* (1930). This returned to the 7½-hour day, and allowed the owners to fix minimum prices and area quotas.

(*b*) *Housing Act* (1930). Greenwood's Act restored the Wheatley subsidies, and started subsidies for slum clearance.

(*c*) *Unemployment Insurance Act* (1930) (Chapter 8, B3).

(*d*) *Road Traffic Act* (1930). This dealt with conditions in the road haulage industry, limiting driving hours and creating the Traffic Commissioners to license vehicles. It reformed chaotic conditions among the many bus companies.

(*e*) *London Transport Bill* (1931). Morrison's act reformed London Transport by combining trams, buses and Underground in one public authority. It created the LPTB, and came into force in 1933.

(*f*) *Agricultural Marketing Act* (1931). Devised by Addison, this set up boards to grade and sell products, and to fix prices if a majority of producers agreed.

The government lost an Education Bill to raise the school leaving age to 15, which was rejected by the Lords in February 1931, A Land Utilisation Bill to set up a land corporation to buy farm lands was amended out of existence by the Lords. The Trades Disputes Bill (1930) to amend the 1927 Act, although it passed its second reading, was lost in committee due to Liberal opposition. Snowden's cautious budgets did not provide money for reforms; indeed, in April 1931 he scrapped the existing safeguarding duties. He made proposals to introduce a land value tax and deal with tax avoidance, but these were never brought forward.

C5. Failure to Cure Unemployment

When crisis struck in July 1931 Macdonald said, 'We are not on trial . . . it is the system under which we live.' If he believed this, he did little to alter it. The government set up a number of official bodies to investigate matters. The Macmillan Committee (under H. P. Macmillan) was set up in November 1929 to examine banking and finance to see if they handicapped employment. It included Keynes, McKenna, Bradbury and Bevin. The Gregory Commission on Unemployment Pay was set up. After Tory complaints in February 1931 Snowden agreed to a Committee on National Expenditure chaired by Sir George May (Chairman of the Prudential Assurance Company). In January 1930 an Economic Advisory Council appeared, including Keynes, Tawney, Citrine and Bevin. The trouble was that Macmillan, Gregory and May all reported in the summer of 1931 at a time of crisis, and suggested economies rather than expansion.

Unemployment rose sharply while the ministers laboured. Their proposals included :

(*a*) *Development Loan and Colonial Loan Acts* (1929). The government provided £42m for public works at home and abroad. Lansbury proposed retirement at 60 (he was 71), colonising Western Australia and land reclamation.

(*b*) *The Mosley Memorandum*, February 1930. Submitted behind Thomas's back, and without Snowden's support, it was doomed. It proposed tariffs, import quotas, bulk purchase agreements, state control of industry through a banking corporation, and raising public expenditure. On 6 July the team of three was disbanded, and MacDonald announced he was taking personal responsibility.

Mosley challenged MacDonald at the party conference, but was defeated by 202–29. In February 1931 he formed the New Party, determined to carry the logic of socialism towards a full Mussolini-type corporate state.

D. World Economic Crisis

By 1931 the government was in the middle of 'the deepest and most prolonged depression ever known'. In Britain there were four elements in the crisis. The existing economic situation was the underlying factor, and the failures of the Labour government were the immediate cause. By April 1931 the budget was in difficulties, and those out of work numbered 2,713,000. To this was added a world trade depression, made worse by the overvalued pound and free trade situation. Lastly, there was a financial crisis in which the complex reparations and allied debts question served as the long-term factor and the Great Crash in America as the immediate cause. Labour could not practise either economy or tariffs without splitting, and thus fell from office.

D1. Trade Depression

From 1929 to 1932 there was a sharp fall in world prices in primary products. This is indicated by the following prices indices:

Year	Foodstuffs	Materials	Commodities
1929	110	119	115
1930	96	97	97
1931	82	82	83
1932	79	81	80

The League of Nations estimated world trade contracted by a quarter, and its value fell from $68,641m to $26,611m in the same period. The impact of this fall was mixed. Since raw materials and food fell more sharply than manufactured goods, the terms of trade turned in Britain's favour, and falling prices meant that real wages actually increased during the depression. However, the poverty of primary producers meant they could not buy British manufactures. Trade competition increased and the result was a series of heavy tariff increases. An attempt to halt this process failed, and British manufacturers demanded tariffs. Industrial production fell by 16 per cent, and the trade figures reflected this decline:

Value in £m	1929	1931
Exports	838	453
Imports	1,200	861

Matters were not helped by the maldistribution of the world's gold supply, made worse by American and French hoarding, and determination not to devalue. Neither America nor the Bank of International Settlements acted effectively, and as prices fell the burden of international debt, particularly in Germany, soared to dangerous heights.

D2. Financial Collapse

During the 1920s there was a boom in America, stimulated by cheap credit. New capital issues rose from $6,789m in 1928 to $9,420m in 1929. Then on 24th October panic set in, and 12 million shares were sold. Financial collapse followed, with banks closing, and savings liquidated. The American response was to raise tariffs, hoard gold and recall its overseas debts. American capital exports of $1,126m in 1929 were only a small part of their total commitment. However, in Europe the money was more significant; in particular, the German economy was heavily dependent on loans. In 1927–29 there was a net inflow of $2,540m. American loans dried up by 1931 at the same time as falling prices doubled Germany's reparations. Germany was unable to pay, and President Hoover delayed until June 1931 before issuing a moratorium to take the pressure off Germany (Chapter 7, G).

Unfortunately, countries round Germany relied on her banking system, and a chain reaction developed which eventually engulfed Britain. In March 1931 the main bank in Austria collapsed, and had to be rescued by other banks and loans which included £4.3m from London. In June there was a run on German banks as confidence ebbed, and in one week £36m was withdrawn. Hoover's moratorium, and generous action by countries like Britain, who remitted £11m of debts owing from her allies, were followed by a credit of $100m from the BIS, and loans from France and London. The collapse of the Danat and Dresdner Banks led to a further run. A conference between Montague Norman and the Reichsbank president held on the Dover ferry produced the alarming news that Britain could lend no more. On 12 July the Bank of Geneva collapsed and in Germany banks closed for two days, and the bank rate rose to 15 per cent.

A conference in London on 20 July produced little except an agreement to halt movements of short-term funds, and on the day it dispersed the British bank rate rose to $3\frac{1}{2}$ per cent. Countries like the Netherlands, fearing a withdrawal of German money, decided to safeguard themselves by withdrawing money from London. Although on 27 July Britain agreed to participate in an Hungarian loan, the bank rate was up to $4\frac{1}{2}$ per cent, and £45m had been withdrawn. On 1 August the Bank of England was forced to obtain credits of £50m from America and France, since the reserves had fallen to £133m. When these were exhausted, foreign bankers demanded 'special conditions' before they would make a further loan. Britain needed £80m, and the bankers demanded cuts.

E. The Government Crisis of August 1931

E1. Bankers' Ramp
There can be no doubt that banking policy contributed to the crisis. The City helped to precipitate the crisis by lending long and borrowing short during the European crisis, which left Britain short of reserves. It is true the government acted on the Bank of England's advice, and that its representatives, Harvey and Peacock, argued 'the cause of the trouble was not financial but political, and lay in the complete want of confidence in HMG among foreigners'. Bevin called this a bankers' ramp or plot. This it was not; it was merely the working out of financial orthodoxy. Proposals for raising revenue rather than cutting expenditure were vetoed by Snowden, and his view was supported by the Treasury, Tories, Liberals, leading industrialists and Montague Norman.

E2. The May Committee
Government finance was already in difficulty by the budget of April

1931. When the May Committee reported, Snowden regarded it as a godsend. The publication of May coincided with the Gregory report advocating cuts in unemployment pay. It said there would be a deficit in the next budget of £120m unless action was taken. It proposed an increase in taxes of £24m, reduction in salaries of civil servants, and of service pay to a 1925 level. Since benefits had risen by 36 per cent and the cost of living had fallen 29 per cent, unemployment pay was to be cut by 20 per cent.

E3. Struggle for Economies

During August a crisis built up, which made it more difficult for the government to compromise, and was made worse by the sudden return of political leaders to London on 11 August. As early as 6 July MacDonald had mentioned the possibility of coalition, and his remark had been passed to Baldwin. On 13 August the first meetings occurred—unhappily MacDonald held them without stating terms, and indeed tended to base his case on what Baldwin and Samuel asked for. The stages in the struggle were:

(*a*) 19 August. Discussion of economics amounting to £56m. Snowden said that they could convert part of the National Debt to obviate massive cuts and that unemployment pay would fall by 10 and not 20 per cent.

(*b*) 20 August. MacDonald met opposition leaders, including Simon this time. They discussed another figure of £78m recommended by the Economy Committee, and Snowden alarmed everyone by quoting a possible deficit of £170m instead of £120m. The government agreed to proceed to further economies on this basis. The National Executive of Labour and the General Council of the TUC rejected them.

(*c*) 21 August. The cabinet agreed to £56m, but MacDonald pointed out that the opposition parties wanted more.

(*d*) 22 August. MacDonald demanded additional economies, and a split occurred. Snowden, dreading any assault on free trade, insisted that cuts must be the way out. The figure of proposed cuts was raised to £68½m.

(*e*) 23 August. MacDonald reported to the King, saying that the figure required was £78m, and that they could not secure agreement on the additional £10m. George interviewed Samuel and Baldwin, and the latter agreed to serve under MacDonald.

This offer by Baldwin needs explaining, since he had once resolutely opposed coalition. It was one way of excluding Lloyd George, Labour extremists and the Tory right wing. Since MacDonald, Simon and Baldwin were all prepared to accept tariffs, it seemed sensible to form a government that might carry a change of policy. Baldwin believed it would be more acceptable (or politically useful) if MacDonald led the government. At the time no one knew that the majority of Labour would desert MacDonald, or that the Liberals would split.

(*f*) 23 August. MacDonald returned to the cabinet, and a split occurred on the extra £10m needed. MacDonald was then supported by 7 ministers but opposed by the rest. They dispersed, expecting MacDonald would resign and a Conservative–Liberal coalition take over. That evening Baldwin, Samuel and Chamberlain sought to persuade MacDonald to form a national government. He did not reply, but obviously thought that loyalty to him would carry the day, and save Labour some power.

(*g*) 24 August. A meeting at Buckingham Palace opened by the King lasted one hour and fifty minutes. Samuel had told George the previous day that coalition under MacDonald was possible, and having secured Baldwin's assent now urged this course on the two leaders. The King supported him. That afternoon MacDonald resigned, and formed a new coalition government.

E4. The August Plot

Contemporaries praised MacDonald's decision. Winterton said he 'showed courage and patriotism of the highest order', and another writer said he 'showed courage and character in making a clean cut', but this view was bitterly attacked by the Labour Party which found itself leaderless, divided and out of office until 1940. Attlee described the move as 'the greatest betrayal in the political history of this country', and MacDonald's old colleagues in the ILP were deeply shocked. Other Labour men had a different view. Snowden supported him in 1931, and only turned bitter after free trade was sacrificed. Dalton later admitted that Labour fell because of their failure on the home front, and that this was 'largely justified'.

Some double talk was involved on both sides. MacDonald said, 'It is not a coalition government, I will take no part in that', and both Baldwin and he stressed it was formed only to deal with a national crisis. In fact, they appealed to the electorate three months later. MacDonald denied the bankers had laid down conditions when they had, and it is clear from the actions of the first National Government that the argument over the extra £10m was largely academic. But the government had been reduced to a majority of three on occasion, whereas the new one had a majority of 60. Thus, it was able to raid the Sinking Fund, go off gold and introduce tariffs. Clearly, if the alternative policies advocated by Bevin and others had been put into operation, they would have failed, and could not have been supported by either of the other parties. Equally, the Tories would have found it hard to carry strong measures with such a large Labour minority and would have followed right-wing policies into more extreme courses. MacDonald had to be persuaded at the end into the new government; that he became a prisoner as Lloyd George did after 1918 is no surprise, but it does not make him a traitor. The electorate supported his decision, as did a small section of Labour and a considerable section of Liberals. National unity of a kind was achieved, and the crisis overcome. That Labour was reduced to the position of the Asquithites in 1918 was partly their own fault. Only 15 MPs came with MacDonald.

There is, however, another issue. In 1932 Sidney Webb and subsequently others contended MacDonald all along favoured coalition. He had referred to a Council of State in 1929; there were meetings with Baldwin as early as November 1930. By July 1931 it was common political gossip. There was obviously a degree of sympathy between the two men, and both had extremists (or party loyalists) they did not like. It might have seemed like 'the government of the unburied dead' because it excluded so much talent, but a coalition with Mosley, Lloyd George, Churchill and Cripps would not have lasted long. It is clear that Samuel and Simon also played an important part in bringing the leaders together, and enlisting the King's support. On this last point controversy has raged, stirred by a remark of Cripps in 1934 that when Labour first took office 'there is no doubt we shall have to overcome opposition from Buckingham Palace'. In fact, George V was scrupulously constitutional, exercising his right to advise and warn. There was no palace plot.

F. The First National Government, August–October 1931

F1. Composition

MacDonald as Prime Minister and Baldwin as Lord President gathered an unusual cabinet round them. Snowden remained at the Treasury, and Thomas had Colonies and Dominions. Only three other Labour men were included, but the government did represent a coalition of Liberals and Tories. Samuel became Home Secretary, and Sir Rufus Isaacs (now Lord Reading) Foreign Secretary. Other Liberals included were Sinclair (Scotland) and Maclean (Education). The leading Tories were Hoare (India), Chamberlain (Health), Cunliffe Lister (Board of Trade), Gilmour and Betterton. Austen Chamberlain had the Admiralty but did not stay. What was remarkable and even suggestive of MacDonald's influence over Baldwin was that a number of able Tories were excluded. Horne, Amery, Steel Maitland, Hailsham and Churchill were omitted. The Liberals were pleased to be back at a time of internal strife. MacDonald was expelled from his party, and Henderson elected leader.

F2. Action

The government proceeded to carry out a policy to end the crisis:

(*a*) A credit of £80m was obtained, and the run on the pound ceased.

(*b*) Snowden's budget had a deficit of only £74m. Direct taxes rose by £51m, and indirect ones by £24m.

(*c*) The Anomalies Act, which had been introduced by MacDonald, was passed.

(*d*) An Economy Act was passed which cut unemployment pay by 10 per cent, reduced salaries and wages, as May had recommended, and effected £70m cuts in social services.

However, the cuts had an effect which the government did not expect. Service pay was badly handled and hit naval ratings hardest. Admirals lost 7 per cent, and able seamen 25 per cent. Large numbers of the *Daily Worker* were distributed in the fleet, and Communist agitators stirred up genuine grievances. On 15 September, 12,000 men refused to muster. Cuts were immediately all limited to 10 per cent. Later 36 ringleaders were dismissed. However, foreigners compared this with Kronstadt or Kiel, and a drain on gold began with the reserves falling to £130m.

(*e*) On 21 September a retrospective act abolished the gold standard, the Stock Exchange closed for two days and the bank rate rose to 6 per cent. It forced Norway, Sweden, Japan and other countries off gold, caused a financial crisis in France and led to anti-dumping laws being passed there and in Italy. The pound fell from 4.86 to 3.40 to the dollar. From 29 gold standard countries the number fell to four by early 1933.

F3. Party Strife

If the coalition brought harmony at the centre it produced widespread anger. Amery and Churchill denounced it for betraying Conservative principles. Labour howled at MacDonald as a 'low, dirty cur'. At first none of the leaders wanted an election since they were in bad cess with their parties. But many Tories urged an election to cash in since MacDonald (or National) Labour could hardly return to the fold, and on 5 October Simon said Liberal Nationals would support the government as well. Lloyd George urged Liberals not to join, but Samuel would not agree. Chamberlain pressed Baldwin for an election, and devised a programme called 'a doctor's mandate' to take whatever measures they thought necessary. Although MacDonald said 'there will be no coupons', the Tories cost National Labour 15 seats, and attacked Liberal free traders, defeating four government ministers.

G. The 'Doctor's Mandate' Election, October 1931

G1. Issues

There was bitterness on both sides, and one ex-Labour minister described the election as 'the most savage of modern times'. Only 68 per cent of the electorate turned out. National spokesmen were suitably confusing. On the major issue of tariffs, Snowden said there would be no mandate for them, Simon supported them, Samuel denounced them, Baldwin said they were desirable and Austen Chamberlain urged a big vote in their favour. On the other hand, Labour, according to Dalton, believed they would hold their existing strength and as National Labour had left them, the party swung to the left with 'Labour's Call to Action' which promised to reverse cuts, control banking and credit and bring into public ownership power, transport and steel. They, like Lloyd George, opposed any tariffs. This suggested that MacDonald had been sensible to leave Labour, and Taylor is incorrect to say their programme was 'not markedly different' from the moderate programme of 1929. Runciman started a scare that post office savings would be nationalised and Snowden backed him. The latter went on to describe the Labour programme as 'Bolshevism run mad'. MacDonald flourished a pound note and warned, 'My friends, d'ye want your menfolk to bring their wages home in a sack?'

G2. Results

Apart from two Irish Nationalists, three independents and two elected on a National label, the results were:

National			*Opposition*	
Conservative	471		Labour	52
Liberal National	35	(Simonites)	Lloyd George Liberals	4 = 56
National Liberal	33	(Samuelites)		
National Labour	13	= 552		

The immediate importance of these results was:

(*a*) It was the Conservatives' greatest ever election victory, and they stayed in power until 1945.

(*b*) For Labour it was traumatic. They lost all their ministers except Attlee, Cripps and Lansbury. The ILP under Maxton was reduced to five members.

(*c*) For the Liberals it was an illusory triumph. They increased their MPs by

13, and had an important share in the government, but they had only fielded 160 candidates, and of the 72 elected 62 had been unopposed by Tories. They were divided on tariffs and, in Mowat's words, were 'the real losers'.

The longer-term consequences were even more important:

(a) Baldwin was freed from dependence on his right wingers. He was able to fight off Churchill's challenges. By excluding able Tories he made the ensuing government, in one historian's view, 'one long diminuendo'. On the other hand, he prepared the way for consensus politics, the middle way, and a more modern Tory party.

(b) Through MacDonald Labour continued to influence foreign policy. The Disarmament Conference, ending reparations, backing the League and peace were presumably to their liking. In imperial affairs the Statute of Westminster and the Government of India Act marked fulfilment of Labour policies. But this was overshadowed by fury at MacDonald's following Tory home policies. In 1932 the ILP left the party, and Labour entered on a long period of disunity.

(c) The Liberals were finished. In 1932 the Samuelites left the government, and were cut to 17 in the 1935 election. Lloyd George retired to write his war memoirs. Liberals within the government became indistinguishable from Tories, and some like the ardent free trader Runciman, performed astonishing political changes. But again, it should be noted that a substantial strain of Liberalism pervaded the National government. In foreign policy and in social reform this bore considerable fruit, and in the first cabinet the Tories had only 11 out of 20 seats.

Thus, after a 'crisis of muddle' there was a general election of 'unrivalled confusion'. Some have seen the results as setting up a parliamentary dictatorship. 'It was a national triumph and a national disaster,' according to some. But Mosley's New Party and the Communists obtained no seats. Unlike Germany and France, where similar economic difficulties led to extreme governments of right and left, Britain preserved political sanity in 1931. Mowat says the ensuing government was not adventurous, and that Blum's France and Roosevelt's America were more stimulating—but their policies failed and, in France's case, disastrously. In 1939 there was no fascist or communist fifth column, and the National Government went on to fight and win the war. Their economic and social policies obtained considerable success. The left proposed popular front governments like those of Spain or France, or outright support for the planned economy of Soviet Russia, favoured by Cripps and Laski. At that time Stalin's full policy was not known. In 1935, 10 out of 11 Liverpool seats were held by Tories at a time when, according to Seaman, they displayed 'a stony indifference to human suffering'. The election of that year returned a large majority for the National Government, indicating people as a whole believed it had succeeded in the tasks it was elected for in 1931. The largest crowds to assemble in Britain during the 1930s were for the Jubilee and the Coronation, and this, in view of what happened in Europe, was something to be thankful for.

Further Reading

Bassett, R., *1931 Political Crisis*, Macmillan, London, 1958.
Booth, A. H., *British Hustings 1924–1950*, Muller, London, 1956.

Foot, D., *British Political Crises*, William Kimber, London, 1976.
Mowat, C. L., *Britain Between the Wars 1918–1940*, Methuen, London, 1955.
Pollard, S., *The Development of the British Economy 1914–1970*, Edward Arnold, 1971.
Skidelsky, R., *Politicians and the Slump: The Labour Government 1929–31*, Macmillan, London, 1967.

Questions

1. What were the main causes of Britain's industrial decline between the wars?
2. How extensive was unemployment in Britain between the wars?
3. Was 'life on the dole' as unpleasant as some make it out to be?
4. Why was MacDonald's second Labour government such a disaster?
5. Why was Britain seriously affected by the international financial crisis of 1929–31?
6. What happened in 1931?
7. Why does so much controversy surround the formation of the National Governments?

9

THE NATIONAL GOVERNMENTS OF THE 1930s

The unfavourable view of the 1930s taken until recently is undergoing considerable change. The National Governments have in the past been criticised on two main grounds. It has been argued that they were a period of middle-class and Tory hegemony during which domestic policy preserved inequalities in society, made little attempt to develop welfare and left the unemployed in the dole queues. With Richardson's work in 1967 on economic recovery, this view began to be less tenable. Taylor says, 'In 1933 Britain began a recovery which carried production and employment to an all-time peak by 1937'. Rising real wages, new industries catering for the consumer, government aid to agriculture and industry, and rising expenditure on social services were characteristics of the period just as much as dole queues, means tests and starvation wages. Secondly, the governments have been accused of 'calming the passions and rubbing the sharp edges off awkward questions'. Mowat speaks of the period as one in which the National Governments 'shambled' to Dunkirk. Seaman uses the words 'hotch potch', 'feeble action', 'restrictive' in describing slow recovery. It was consensus government. It excluded talent (or extremists). The massive victories of 1931 and 1935 indicated a degree of popular support for a free government unique in Europe.

The case for the National Governments is therefore twofold. They took Britain out of the depression, and secured greater productive growth than the 1970s dreamed possible. They preserved political sanity; indeed, Seaman earlier stresses this was the vital contribution of Baldwin and MacDonald. They were better than Mussolini and Hitler; preferable to Mosley and Maxton. To say, as Taylor does, 'hunger marchers filled the streets one day; demonstrators against Fascism followed on the next', is unfair. Mowat says Blum's government was more exciting than Chamberlain's, but in education, housing and welfare benefits British workers were far ahead of workers under the Popular Front. Moreover, coalition with Communism brought about Fascist reaction. France was savaged by violence and in 1940 fell to pieces, helped in part by Communist and Fascist defeatism. The National Governments rearmed, prepared a network of civilian defence, and went to war. Moreover, the left played its part in these years. It advocated a popular front which failed in Spain and France, and praised Stalin's Russia about which the truth was not known. It pressed for disarmament, opposed rearmament until 1937, and conscription in 1939. If there were defects in imperial strategy it was two Labour men, Thomas and MacDonald, who held office in this sphere most of the time. Liberals advocated Keynesian policies like the New Deal, but there were more out of work in America in 1939 than in 1933. Liberals such as Simon championed the government. What failures there were in the 1930s were not exclusively Tory, and they need to be balanced against the successes when democratic and capitalist society was undergoing its severest test.

A. The Second National Government, October 1931–November 1935

A1. The Ministry

MacDonald was Prime Minister until June 1935, when he exchanged offices with Baldwin and became Lord President of the Council. During this period he was ill and suffering from failing eyesight. He continued as a world statesman, and his ministry has three great achievements to its credit: it took Britain out of the slump and effected the major change to tariffs; it gave India virtual self-government; and it began rearmament in the teeth of Labour opposition. Snowden was also ill, was given a peerage, and became Lord Privy Seal. In his place as Chancellor was Neville Chamberlain, who dominated the cabinet by hard work and ability and followed his career as social reformer with an outstanding Chancellorship.

Mowat says of the other members of the government, 'little need be said'; in fact it contained men of ability. Simon was made Foreign Secretary, and Samuel became Home Secretary. Runciman at the Board of Trade and Betterton at Labour were competent as were Hilton Young (Health), Gilmour (Agriculture), Maclean (Education) and Sinclair (Scotland). Hailsham (War), Londonderry (Air) and Eyres Monsell (Admiralty) were perhaps the weakest of the cabinet, and defence spending reached its all time low in 1932–33.

A2. The Party Crisis of 1932

The reintroduction of a tariff was central to government policy. In January 1932, when it became clear this would conflict with free trade Labour and Liberal members, it was decided to have 'an agreement to differ'. This was to be done again over the Common Market referendum (1975), but was open to the criticism that it violated collective responsibility. The measures were passed, but the Liberal party in the country attacked the decision. Then came the Ottawa Treaty, and in September 1932 Snowden, Samuel and Sinclair resigned. The Liberals were fast losing their strength in the government since Maclean died in July 1932. At the end of 1933 Kingsley Wood, a close personal friend of Chamberlain, was admitted to the cabinet as Postmaster General so that by the beginning of 1934 only four of the cabinet were not Tories. In November 1933 Samuel accepted the logic of his position, and moved to the opposition benches. Labour was left with one member of the cabinet. Henderson was unable to find a seat until 1934, and Lansbury was leader of Labour. He was unable to prevent Maxton's ILP withdrawing in 1932 and was virtually an invalid after an accident, but remained until October 1935 when he was replaced by Attlee.

A3. Peace and Goodwill: East Fulham 1933

The economic crisis strengthened arguments for disarmament, and the period of the second National Government saw pacifist sentiment become an important issue at the polls. This had a serious effect on rearmament (Chapter 12, B3) and electoral policy. In 1932 an Anti-War Congress at the Hague was backed by Labour, who passed a motion against all wars at their conference. In February 1933 the Oxford Union voted it would not fight for King and Country. The League of Nations Union, the Peace

Pledge Union and a National Peace Council had a widespread following, ranging from Brig. General Crozier through Vera Brittain and Aldous Huxley to Canon 'Dick' Shepherd. In October 1933, at East Fulham, a National majority of 14,521 was turned into a Labour one of 4,840. It has been shown since that voters were less concerned about the Labour man's pacifist sentiments than his social policies, but the government yielded to the prevailing view.

Anti-war books continued to pour out. Philip Noel Baker contributed *Merchants of Death* (1934), accusing Tories of having vested interests in armament industries, and the government appointed a commission. Until July 1937 Labour wholeheartedly endorsed these policies. In June 1935 the results of the first national referendum were published, carried out in an amateur way by the Peace Pledge Union. Although 6 million voted for military sanctions against an aggressor, 10 million wanted arms cuts and control of arms manufacture, and 9 million the abolition of military aircraft. Baldwin placed himself behind these sentiments, and in October 1935 said, 'I give you my word that there will be no great armaments.'

A4. Baldwin's Great Election Victory

When MacDonald retired in June 1935, a number of government changes took place. Simon became Home Secretary, and Hoare became Foreign Secretary. Immediately after the election, Baldwin asked him to resign over the Hoare–Laval Pact (Chapter 12, D4), but he returned as First Lord of the Admiralty in June 1936. Hoare was succeeded by Anthony Eden, who had been Minister for the League of Nations. Malcolm MacDonald was the only new Labour man at Colonies, while Thomas had Dominions. After the election they exchanged office. Londonderry was removed from Air and made Leader of the Lords. The real reason was that he advocated using bombers in India. In his place was Cunliffe Lister, who was later given a peerage as Lord Swinton.

With this rearranged and competent team, Baldwin faced the election of 1935 which was a verdict on the first four years of National Government and the alternatives. There were two main issues:

(a) *Prosperity*. Led by Chamberlain, the government argued they had succeeded. The number of unemployed had fallen by half, the cuts in dole and other expenditure had been restored, a million houses had been built, the budget was balanced, real wages and profits were up, pensions had been increased, agriculture was healthy, and even in industry the output of some products like cars and steel had doubled since 1931.

(b) *Armaments*. Although Baldwin had said the League and collective security were 'hardly worth considering', he now pledged full support. Hoare and Eden backed the League in sanctions against Italy. Rearmament was hushed up, and in his election broadcast Baldwin spoke of 'repairing gaps'.

The opposition parties were in poor condition:

(a) In January 1935 Lloyd George had issued a 'New Deal'. No one believed him any more. Samuel, without the former's funds, could only put up 156 candidates.

(b) Labour was bitterly divided. In Glasgow ILP and Labour fought each other. The Labour Conference in October saw clashes over policy, and Cripps called for a 'workers' government in this country as they have in Russia'. The honours system was attacked, the Lords were to be abolished and the armament industry reduced. There was a clash on pacifism in which Bevin attacked Lansbury, and brought about his fall.

(c) The results were:

	National	Opposition
Conservatives	387	
Liberal	33	17 (+ 4 Lloyd George)
Labour	8	154

(d) *Importance*. The Conservatives were down a million votes. Labour recovered about a million votes, but only half as many seats as predicted. The Liberals were finished. Samuel was replaced by Sinclair. They now supported devolution for Scotland and Wales as well as proportional representation in order to restore themselves to power.

B. Economic Recovery

In 1934 Chamberlain said Britain could turn from Bleak House to Great Expectations. Although untrue for the unemployed, this was true as far as comparable standards in Europe and previous experience went. In spite of the National Governments' failure to embrace Keynes, or Socialism, there was recovery under what came to be known as 'managed capitalism'. Taylor, Mowat, Medlicott and Seaman agree there was an economic recovery, although they differ on the part played by government. It started slowly, gathered strength to 1937, faltered again, and then went forward under the impetus of rearmament. Contemporary works detailed a recovery, and Heaton's *British Way to Recovery* (1934) was impressive American testimony that much was being achieved. Since the volume of world trade showed little sign of recovery and totalitarian economies practised autarchy, recovery was impressive. Britain's industrial production rose by 20 per cent over that of 1929, while that of France and America remained static. By 1935 welfare cuts were restored, and spending was rising. In addition, government aid to industry and spending through rearmament made a substantial contribution. The way back was essentially *laissez faire*. Low taxes and low interest rates were to release money for spending and investment. Low prices meant wages could remain low but increase in real terms. Low costs allowed modernisation to occur and efficiency to rise (Chapter 10, D1 and 4).

B1. Return to Tariffs
It was a period of rising tariffs and tariff wars. After the collapse of a World Economic Conference in 1933, illiberal policies were pursued as each country tried to export its unemployment elsewhere. In Britain this meant reversing a policy pursued since 1846, and the achievement of Chamberlain's aim of tariffs. The steps by which Britain changed were:

(a) *Abnormal Importations Act* (1931) This ran for six months to prevent dumping: 50 per cent duties were imposed on pottery, cutlery, woollen and cotton goods.

(b) *Import Duties Act* (1932) put 10 per cent on almost all imports with the exception of Empire produce and certain foods and raw materials. A commission was appointed to plan further changes. It recommended 20 per cent increases, and even 30 per cent on some luxuries which was accepted. By 1930s standards it was a moderate tariff.

B2. Imperial Preference

Britain's main protected market was the Empire, and inevitably attention turned to its economic development. A Colonial Marketing Board was set up. Montague Norman encouraged dominion central banks (Australia, 1932, New Zealand, 1934) to cooperate in the sterling area and help investment. In 1932 an economic survey of the colonies was carried out and in 1933 colonial preference was started with a quota system. Since the dominions had discriminatory tariffs, a conference was called at Ottawa (July–August 1932) to attempt imperial preference. In the end some 12 agreements were signed, which provided for:

(*a*) Continuation and increase of colonial preference on British import duties so that about 80 per cent of Empire produce was duty free.

(*b*) British goods would receive preference since future tariff increases would not be applied. There were also a few reductions.

The effects were limited and the Imperial Conference of 1937 proposed reciprocity treaties instead. Britain increased her trade with the Empire more than with the rest of the world, but imports rose more sharply than exports. The figures (in percentages) were:

Imports		*1931*	*1935*	*1938*
	From Empire	24.5	35.1	37.9
	From elsewhere	71.3	62.4	59.6
Exports				
	To Empire	35.9	43.3	45.6
	To elsewhere	56.3	52.0	50.1

B3. The Sterling Area

After the fall of gold some alternative was necessary. A series of measures was taken to preserve Britain's position. Long-term loans were forbidden. This did not damage the balance of payments as shipping and insurance rose rapidly. The Exchange Equalisation Fund Act (1932) provided funds to control hot money movements. The fund reached £575m by 1938.

The sterling area came into existence as a region where countries agreed to relate the exchange rate to the pound, and in spite of strong American and French pressure this was established in most of Scandinavia and the Empire. By 1936 a Tripartite Agreement had been signed with France and America, and the rate was pegged at 3.37 dollars to the pound.

B4. Balanced Budget

Taylor and Mowat agree that Chamberlain's budgets were 'more modern than their critics supposed'. After 1937 Simon's budgets allowed for increased direct taxation for rearmament. Social expenditure continued to increase as a share of GNP. In a period of falling prices and slow growth of population, the total rose from £4,907m in 1919 to £5,963m in 1939. There was some economy; expenditure on roads fell by half under the second National Government but after 1936 capital expenditure also increased with radar stations, shelters and aircraft factories. Chamberlain's first budget had a deficit of £32m. By 1934 he had a surplus of £24m. During the same period he was able to reduce direct taxation, but this trend altered after 1936 and Simon proposed a capital levy to help with rearmament. When this failed in June 1937 income tax was raised and in 1939 surtax and death duties also rose. Those who lost most by the government's fiscal policies were bondholders affected by a Debt Conversion Scheme. In June 1932 Chamberlain converted war loan from 5 per cent to 3.5 per cent and urged stockholders to transfer. Ninety per cent did, and by 1936 the sum saved was running at £86m. The government repaid all loans obtained in 1931 by this method. In addition, of course, they had revenue from tariffs.

B5. Low Interest Rates

The government accepted a cheap money policy of low interest rates to reduce debt charges and stimulate investment. By June 1932 the bank rate had fallen to 2 per cent, and it stayed there until 1939. At the time it was held to be a significant policy but this view has been challenged. Increased investment was the product of recovery in the domestic market and the government's own reaction by its capital investment was not great. On the other hand, building societies were able to cut their rate to 4.5 per cent in 1935, and this provided much impetus for the housing boom and local authorities were able to embark on considerable expansion of social services.

B6. Rearmament Spending (See also Chapter 12, Section B)

From 1936 rearmament began to have an impact on economic recovery. The radar stations cost a £1m, for example, and there was plenty of construction work. The shipyards had new ships to build, and 15 old battleships to refit. There was an increasing aircraft building programme, but matters moved slowly and only in February 1939 was maximum production allowed. Moreover, as Barnett points out, Britain's technical deficiencies were considerable. The programme involved expensive imports like bren guns and bofors from Czechoslovakia and Sweden. In April 1938 the first purchase mission visited the USA, and after two years' stalling a Ministry of Supply was set up in April 1939. In 1936 a Director of Munitions Production, Sir Harold Browne, was appointed and he was responsible for stockpiling and defence factories. When the needs of civil defence are added, it is clear that industries like steel and construction gained from rearmament.

C. The Third National Government, November 1935–May 1937

C1. The Ministry

During his last ministry, Baldwin showed astonishing powers of survival. He overcame the Hoare-Laval Pact row and candidly admitted not rearming before producing the vital Defence White Paper of March 1936 (Chapter 12, B2). Critics within the party were outwitted by consultations and promises of a Minister for the Coordination of Defence. In March

1936 this was Sir Thomas Inskip. Churchill had been invited to sit on the Air Defence Research Committee in 1935 and remained there until July 1939. When Hoare returned to office in June 1936 he was authorised to give him confidential information. This effectively muzzled Churchill as it was involvement without power. After the election Baldwin made few changes. Halifax was Lord Privy Seal after Lord Londonderry was removed, and in his place at the War Office came Alfred Duff Cooper, victor of the St George's by-election. The budget of 1936 raised income tax by 3d and tea tax by 2d, and these facts were leaked by Thomas who was forced to resign. Towards the end of 1936 there were a few shifts in the cabinet, and Leslie Hore Belisha, who had been Transport Minister since 1934, was admitted, increasing Liberal representation. The abdication crisis effectively destroyed Churchill as a political threat. Baldwin's hand was sure on rearmament and the abdication, but it was slipping elsewhere. In foreign affairs the ministry marks the period in which Britain lost the initiative in European affairs—Chamberlain noticed this, and was determined to put it right when he came to power.

C2. The Tory Party of the 1930s

During this period the Tories acquired the image of being a middle-class businessman's party, 'the stupid party'. It was certainly a class party. Only one MP could claim to be working class in origin, and this was due in many cases to the freedom with which members could almost purchase seats by large contributions to party funds. Of the 415 National MPs in 1938, 125 went to Eton or Harrow, and 154 to other public schools; 272 had been to university and 188 of those were at Oxbridge. No fewer than 96 members had been regular army officers. Moreover, imperial and financial interests were strongly represented because members had previously seen service or made money in the Empire. They were authoritarian and out of touch. The party was an oligarchy for two reasons:

(*a*) Concentration of wealth: 181 MPs held no fewer than 775 directorships. An act passed in 1933 required disclosure of interest by those in local government, but this did not apply to parliament. The left particularly attacked the links between Tories and armament firms. Vickers, for example, had among its directors Anderson, Horne, and Gilmour.

(*b*) Relationship. There was a 'cousinhood' linking MPs to each other and with the House of Lords. It meant the party bore no relation to those who elected it. In 1938 the cabinet had seven peers and a baronet, nine members were related to peers, and among the 68 non-cabinet ministers and private secretaries five were peers, 20 related to peers, and 13 landed gentry. Among the MPs, 148 were related to the Lords. There were also 24 baronets and 64 knights, making a total of 240 titled MPs.

Baldwin and Chamberlain stand out as men who outclassed the majority of their followers, and their task in getting the ranks of shire knights, directors, peers' relatives and colonial diehards to follow, for example, rearmament policies against fascism or for social reforms, was not easy. It shows why moves towards a Russian alliance or greater social reform would not have worked. It was this kind of party that proved ~~~~~~~~ irrelevant during the 1940s, and was partly finished off in 194

C3. Drawing-Room Fascists

There was another unpleasant feature of the Tory Party at this time. The rage over India and Chamberlain's colonial appeasement which burst forth at every Tory conference was the tip of a right-wing iceberg. It was less obvious than that in France, but equally widespread. When Ribbentrop was appointed ambassador in October 1936 this was a shrewd move, as he was a friend of the Londonderrys, who were leading political hosts. There were plenty of advocates of a pro-fascist line, and it says much for Baldwin and Chamberlain that they held out against this just as they brought Mosley to an end as a political threat by the end of 1936. Among the chief pro-fascist organisations which attracted Tory support were the Anglo-German Fellowship (1935), which entertained Ribbentrop and was run by Londonderry and the link established by Sir Barry Domville. It was 'intellectual' and published the *Anglo-German Review*. Among its supporters were Page Croft, and Wardlaw Milne This situation explains the dislike of the left for the National Government, and their belief that it was betraying Britain to fascism. This was not true, but there was undoubtedly an element which wanted a right-wing government.

C4. The Abdication Crisis

One reason for the rise of dictatorship abroad had been the weakening of monarchy as a political force or, in some cases, its open sympathy with fascism. In Britain the peaceful solution of the abdication crisis showed no such change, but it brought rumours of a King's Party and sympathy between the new King, Edward VIII, and fascism. His German contact was Charles, Duke of Saxe Coburg, who had been a Brownshirt. In October 1937 the Prince unwisely visited Hitler, Göring and Ley. The attempt to form a King's Party came from both right and left. Churchill, Mosley and Beaverbrook led from one side and Communists demonstrated for him as an anti-establishment man. Although he sent money to the Miners' Distress Fund in 1926 and visited depressed towns, where he made remarks about something being done, he was also a socialite, impatient and selfish. 'I do hope he pulls his socks up,' commented Chamberlain when he became King in January 1936. He formed the King's Flight, walked about London in a bowler, scowled through the presentation of debutantes and only went to church two or three times. There were, therefore, defects of character before the Simpson affair started. In that sense the crisis was important. The main stages were:

(a) *Mrs Wallis Simpson*. Wallis was born in 1896. Her first huband was an alcoholic, and after a divorce she married Ernest Simpson in 1928. In 1930 the Prince of Wales bought Fort Belvedere to entertain. There in the autumn Lady Furness introduced them for the first time.

(b) *A London scandal*. By 1932 she was often with the Prince and during 1933 the liaison became obvious. In August 1934 they went for a cruise, and the Prince loaded her with jewels; it was obvious they were in love. In May 1936 Mrs Simpson started divorce proceedings, and during the summer they went for a cruise in the Mediterranean.

(c) *The divorce*. Evidence of adultery was given by Mr Warfield and Buttercup Kennedy, and the divorce obtained was absolute in six months. The King was clearly infatuated. When Baldwin at last raised the issue on 20 October the King replied, 'I am going to marry Mrs Simpson, and I am prepared to go.'

There is no evidence of an establishment plot. Baldwin was under pressure from the nonconformists in the cabinet led by Chamberlain and Wood, Dominion prime ministers, and awareness that outside London the Prince was fast losing popularity in areas like South Wales. Nor could newspaper silence be kept for ever.

(*d*) *The storm breaks.* On 1 December the Bishop of Bradford criticised the King's churchgoing. Taking this as a cue, the papers published the next day. Someone threw acid at Mrs Simpson, who left the country. Ten cabinet meetings followed. Morganatic marriage and other solutions were ruled out, and on 10 December Edward VIII abdicated.

(*e*) *The Abdication.* After making a speech, the King left for Schloss Enzesfeld. George VI made him a grant of £60,000 and a lump sum of £1m, but Mrs Simpson was not to bear the title of Royal Highness when Edward became Duke of Windsor. This bitterness was caused by his lack of consideration, particularly for his brother, who was quite unprepared to be King.

The *Daily Sketch* put the public's view in a pointed editorial: 'The Duke of York is a family man. ... He is happiest in their company. ... He, too, has a taste for religion. At maturity he accepted the obligations of his rank and position.' His sincerity, religion and humanity, combined with a determination to conquer a voice impediment and his beautiful wife to make him popular. He visited Paris in May 1938, Canada and America in 1939, and by then emerged with the stature necessary for the war years. It seems likely that the change of king was for the best, and Baldwin handled the matter superbly.

C5. Ministers of the Crown Act, 1937

In May 1937 MacDonald and Baldwin retired. The former died in November, but the latter, after taking a peerage, lived until 1947. His last important government measure was characteristic of his devotion to democracy. The Ministers of the Crown Act gave constitutional validity to developments which for long had been ignored in law. It made the Leader of the Opposition an official post at a time when Europe was littered with dictators, and it raised members' salaries because Baldwin thought Labour was treated unfairly. The office of Prime Minister was recognised and pensions and salaries for ministers increased. It may serve as his political swansong as well as the most important constitutional legislation between the wars.

D. Economic Reconstruction

The 1930s were a period of economic recovery. At the time many regarded government activity as playing an important part, and King Hall said, 'In the first three years of its life the National Government put across more socialism than had been thought of by the two Labour ministries.' He went on to say 'Socialism as such will cease to be a party issue. There will be less and less debate on the principles of socialism and more and more upon its technical aspects'. King Hall meant by socialism, not the

Labour party programme, but the involvement of the government in the economy. It was in this sense that Baldwin used the word, and in assessing recovery it is vital to bear in mind this element. Indeed, it has wider importance because the 1930s saw the development of a mixed economy. It was called planned capitalism, but it played into the hands of the left after 1945 (Chapter 10, A5). Clearly the British government did not pursue a New Deal or Corporate State, but it moved some way in that direction while the main impetus for recovery was the market mechanism.

D1. Agriculture

Two ministers, Elliot and Morrison, were responsible for measures which protected and reformed agriculture. They were:

(a) *Agricultural Marketing Act* (1933). This allowed boards to buy, sell, advertise, transport, grade or manufacture the product concerned, and organise statistics, research, education, cooperation and inspection in connection with it. Boards were set up for milk, hops, potatoes, pigs and bacon.

(b) *Milk Act* (1934). This introduced a subsidised scheme for milk in schools. By 1939 schools purchased 26 million gallons, and this helped to control the price.

(c) *Bacon Industry Reorganisation Act* (1938). The bacon board failed, so it was replaced by a subsidy system.

(d) *Cattle Industry Act* (1934) and *Livestock Act* (1937). These provided subsidies and regulated quality.

(e) *Wheat Act* (1932). This provided a guaranteed price of 45s a quarter up to a quota of 27 million hundredweight, and this was raised in the Agriculture Act (1937) to 36 million hundredweight. As arable was converting to pastoral this led to an undue rise in wheat at the expense of oats and barley. In 1937 they were subsidised.

(f) *Sugar Industry Act* (1936). This continued the subsidy in spite of an adverse report, and amalgamated the East Anglian factories into a corporation.

Tory interest in agriculture was traditional and selfish, but the period saw the creation of the basis of modern agricultural policy. The most traditional of industries became accustomed to government officials, and was accepting £100m by 1939, and a considerable amount of protection. Agricultural output rose by a sixth by 1937, and this helped the balance of payments. However, the long-term trend was not reversed. By 1938 farming accounted for 3.2 per cent of National Income, and between 1931–38 the industry lost 17 per cent of its workers. The reasons were low wages, technical backwardness and poor living conditions. Only 30,000 out of 366,000 farms had electricity in 1939; there were still 650,000 horses compared with 55,000 tractors.

D2. Transport

The government was involved in every aspect of transport development during the 1930s:

(a) *London Transport Act* (1933). Trams were converted to trolley buses, and subsidies given to electrify suburban lines. In London Green Line coaches were started, and new stations were designed.

(b) *Road Traffic Act* (1933). This completed the 1930 Act by licensing commercial vehicles and laying down working conditions.

(c) *National Shipping Act* (1934) provided a £9.5m subsidy to complete the *Queen Mary* and build the *Queen Elizabeth*.

(d) *Aircraft.* In 1935 a new company, British Airways, began to compete with Imperial Airways, which had a subsidy. Sir John Reith was put in charge of re-organisation, and in 1940 BOAC was created as a nationalised corporation.

By restricting bus services and encouraging railway omnibus pooling agreements, the government intended to help the railways. The late 1930s were a period of modernisation, and their profits were still good—if falling—in 1939.

D3. Rationalising the Old Industries

In this field the government's action was least successful, but there were improvements:

(a) *Coal.* Production rose from 207 million tons in 1933 to 241 million tons in 1937, and efficiency increased as the number of miners began to fall. The Coal Mines Act (1938) allowed for royalties to be nationalised. A Coal Commission appeared, and a new report—the Reid—was in preparation.

(b) *Shipbuilding.* Sir James Lithgow worked hard to make National Shipbuilders Security Limited work. Two fifths of capacity was scrapped since world demand was falling under a scheme (1921) which, for every two tons of old ship laid up, provided a subsidy on every one ton of new craft. Tonnage produced rose from 133,000 in 1933 to 920,800 in 1937.

(c) *Iron and steel.* A Research Council and an Exporters Association were set up to reorganise. In 1924 Sir Andrew Duncan took over the BISF. Old works were closed and new ones opened, including Corby (1932), Ebbw Vale (1938) and Shotton (1939). Demand from new industries and rearmament caused steel production to rise from 11 million tons in 1929 to 14 million tons in 1939.

(d) *Cotton.* A tariff system benefited the industry. The Lancashire Cotton Corporation set about reorganisation and scrapped 6 million spindles capacity. In 1936 came the Cotton Industry Reorganisation Act. However, bad industrial relations and failure to adopt a price scheme devised in 1934 until 1939 did not help, and cotton output fell from 8 million to 3 million square yards by 1939.

D4. Special Areas Policy

The government initiated a policy of helping industries in specific regions —Clydeside, South Wales, West Cumberland and Tyneside—under the Special Areas Act (1934). It provided a commissioner and four assistants to facilitate aid and encourage investment. The government gave £2m. The first commissioner, Sir Malcolm Stuart, resigned in disgust in 1936, but early next year an amending act increased government support to £5m to match a gift of £7m by Lord Nuffield. Rate, rent and income tax relief was given to employers starting factories in the areas. The main activities were:

(a) Grants were given to NCSS and industrial retraining schemes. All this was piecemeal and inadequate.

(b) 5,880 firms were approached to build, but there was little response apart from steel at Ebbw Vale.

(c) Trading estates were started at Treforest, Team Valley and Hillington in the worst areas, but they only employed 7,400.

The policy did not succeed, but it drew attention to regional planning

154   *Twentieth-Century British History Made Simple*

and industrial location for the first time. Marquand's *Wales Needs a Plan* (1936) and Holford and Eden's *The Future of Merseyside* (1937) were fruits of new thinking.

D5. Consumer-Led Boom

Two things, said Mowat, stand out in the 1930s' economy: 'increasing consumption leading to the development of the home market and the consumer and service industries'. Some new industries were important in exports. Britain was the world's largest motorcycle and second largest car producer in 1939, but the main thrust was towards providing new amenities and products at home. This further divided the areas of new from those of old industry, although the boom affected the larger towns in the depressed areas. With the increase in government activities and services the trend to non-productive occupations rose. The sources of the boom were:

(a) The fall in the cost of living, leading to rising real wages accompanied by a fall in working hours, and an increase in holidays with pay.

(b) Diversifying demand for goods and services, which was accelerated by women's wish for labour-saving devices and new household materials. The Hire Purchase Act (1938) enabled families to buy consumer goods.

(c) Low rates, cheap land, easy money, low taxes, easy transport and non-union labour enabled suburban industries to grow rapidly, diversify and advertise their products.

(d) The Resale Price Maintenance Act (1938) legalised, in spite of a government report opposing the trend, price fixing on some 3,000 branded products.

(e) New patterns in the retail trade were most marked by the growth of the chain store. The number of Marks and Spencer stores rose from 140 in 1927 to 230 in 1938.

The main effects were:

(a) Expanding service industries. Hotels, restaurants, entertainment, holidays and sport all expanded. A hundred holiday camps and 5,000 cinemas were built by 1938.

(b) A rise in electricity users from 750,000 in 1920 to 9 million in 1938. The industry employed 100,000 and 144 power stations were built. There followed an increase in domestic electric appliances. By 1938 there were 1 million electric cookers.

(c) Expansion in transport, distribution, public utilities, personal services, commerce and the Civil Service. For every two civil servants in 1931 there were three by 1939.

(d) A whole range of new industries like gramophones, radios, rayon, food processing, ice-cream, sweets and Bakelite. The number of private cars doubled in the 1930s.

D6. Housing Boom

The government brought to an end the policy of council house building. They sought to end rent control under the Rent Act (1933), which affected $5\frac{1}{2}$ million properties. Of the 2.7 million houses built, only 0.7 million were public authority ones, and these were mainly in areas where councils favoured them. Housing expansion proceeded at twice the rate of other industries and accounted for 30 per cent of the increase in employment. It stimulated other industries, and provided better living conditions, thus boosting consumer demand. New houses represented nearly a quarter of capital investment in the period, and by 1939 in absolute terms there was no housing problem as there were more houses than families. The sources of this boom were:

(*a*) Fall in the cost of materials and low wages for workers organised in small, non-union firms.

(*b*) Low interest rates led to cheap mortgages and encouraged companies to build flats.

(*c*) The change from rented to owner-occupier status began to influence the middle class. Cheap houses (one third cost less than £600) combined with public transport and outskirts shopping centres to encourage suburban development.

(*d*) Lack of planning control. Although this may be regarded as a mistake, it enabled building on agricultural land and desirable sites such as the coast to proceed without delay. The Town and Country Planning Act (1932) and the Ribbon Development Act (1935) were ineffective.

D7. Business Efficiency

The face of British industry, except in the depressed regions, began to change during the 1930s. Electricity provided a new power source away from coalfields. Motor transport widened distribution outlets, and allowed industry to move from the railways. Population shifts to the suburbs scattered industrial location to the outskirts of towns. New materials such as prestressed concrete and plastics enabled factories to improve, and the Factory Act (1937) by laying down new standards encouraged this change. It was the age of Slough, Luton and Watford which heralded a second industrial revolution when Britain changed from a heavy manufacturing exporter to a consumer-based importer. The workers in the new industries had undoubted gains. Consumption was back to 1929 levels by 1934 and wages had recovered by 1938. On the other hand, weak unionisation, small units of production and the threat of unemployment led to increasing industrial efficiency, but this was often at the risk of safety. Industrial accidents rose between 1931 and 1936.

In 1926 Charles Bedaux developed a business efficiency scheme with bonus payments and time and motion studies, and such schemes spread rapidly. By 1936, 240 large companies operated them including Lyons, where waitresses not surprisingly were called 'Nippies'. Between 1929 and 1937 there was an average increase of 17 per cent in per-man-hour output, and the results of this were largely seen in increased profits rather than wages. Management in the 1930s was ruthless. Amalgamations, price fixing, underselling and harsh employment tactics reaped financial reward but recovery, as Taylor rightly says, did nothing to reduce class barriers. A good example of 1930s progress was the aircraft industry, with its series of brilliant designs like Camm's Hurricane (1934), Mitchell's Spitfire (1935) and Short's Sunderland flying boat (1936). A good example of amalgamation, progressive price reduction and export performance would be the car industry, where the number of firms fell from 96 in 1922 to 20 in 1939.

E. The Fourth National Government, May 1937–September 1939

E1. The Ministry

Chamberlain's ministry lasted until September 1939, when it was reconstructed with a smaller War Cabinet. It shared with Lloyd George's post-war coalition, and Wilson's period of office, the record for ministerial resignations and changes. Although the ministry was to achieve substantial reforms, recovery and rearmament, and create the network of home defence, it has always suffered from its record of appeasement. It was fated to have the next three Tory leaders—Churchill, Eden and Macmillan—as critics. Although Labour opposed many of its policies like rearmament, they turned in books like *Guilty Men* on the Tory record.

The ministry contained four non-Tories. Simon became Chancellor, Malcolm MacDonald Dominions Secretary, Hore Belisha War Minister and Leslie Burgin took Transport. Hoare went to the Home Office and Eden remained Foreign Secretary. Duff Cooper obtained the Admiralty and Lord Swinton, Air. Lord Halifax was Lord President and formed with Hoare and Simon an inner cabinet closely working with Chamberlain. The usual group of effective ministers were there like Elliot (Scotland), Stanley (Trade) and Brown (Labour), and some less effective including Stanhope, Wood and Inskip. Some of the ministers such as Swinton, Hoare and Hore Belisha were substantial reformers, but others were to earn derision for their incompetence. While some like Halifax and Hore Belisha stood up to appeasement, and others like Duff Cooper and Eden were to resign, a substantial majority supported it throughout.

Ministerial changes were frequent:

(*a*) In February 1938 Eden and Lord Cranborne resigned (Chapter 12, E3). They were replaced by Halifax and Butler.

(*b*) In March Lord Winterton, Chancellor of the Duchy of Lancaster, was asked to join the cabinet to help Colonel Muirhead, Air Under-Secretary represent Swinton in the Commons. When the ministry was attacked, Chamberlain sacrificed all three ministers in May 1938. Kingsley Wood became Air Minister.

(*c*) After Munich, Duff Cooper resigned and was succeeded at the Admiralty by Stanhope. Sir John Anderson was brought in as Lord Privy Seal and Runciman became Lord President.

(*d*) During 1939 the tattered rug of the cabinet was shaken out twice. In January Inskip was succeeded by Lord Chatfield at Defence. In April 1939 Burgin became Minister without Portfolio. A commission had recommended a supply ministry, but Chamberlain rejected it twice. Then too late, and to avoid giving Churchill office, Burgin was given the job in July 1939.

E2. The Career and Character of Neville Chamberlain

Chamberlain shares with MacDonald a partially shattered reputation which has blinded critics to his achievements. He was half-brother to Austen Chamberlain, born in Birmingham in 1869. Apart from an effort at sisal planting in the Bahamas, his career lay in the Chamberlain empire. He joined a screw firm, and had an interest in Birmingham Small Arms. Lord Mayor (1911–16), he first took office as Director of National Service, where he failed. He entered the Commons in 1918 and was Postmaster General by 1922, Chancellor, and then at Health from 1924 to 1929. He was a principal advocate of Tory reunion after 1922, and an important reformer. After a period as party chairman he returned to office as Chancellor from 1931 to 1937—in itself a considerable achievement.

When he became Prime Minister he was 'a man of vast experience'. He pursued appeasement ruthlessly, and ran the party dictatorially. No rebellion against him succeeded, and ministers dropped like ninepins. Gilbert and Gott rightly say that in foreign policy 'Chamberlain and not Hitler was the far-sighted planner'. But he paid the penalty of pursuing the wrong plan.

(a) Character. Educated at Rugby and without university education, a strong nonconformist, there was a streak of stubbornness in him. He understood business better than politics, but he was not an ignorant man. He was shy and rarely spoke other than in clipped tones and terse speeches. Eloquence came rarely, but did so when introducing tariffs, and again at Munich. Unfortunately, he had a habit of coining phrases that would later rebound on him. Hitler could be 'relied upon when he had given his word'. Munich was 'peace in our time'. Described by Victor Raikes, MP, as 'the greatest European statesman of this or any other time', Chamberlain suffered a greater plunge in reputation than any other inter-war figure.

(b) Prime Ministerial power. Chamberlain was firm with opposition in his party, and could be so due to the large majority. Cpt. John Margesson was a forceful Chief Whip, and the number of rebels never exceeded 40. Offers of PPSs or attack through an MP's constituency association brought most to heel. Churchill was under pressure after Munich. The cabinet was often left in the dark and informed of *faits accomplis*. Parliament was misled, and treated firmly. When Labour opposed the motion for adjournment in August 1939 he turned it into a vote of confidence and, while appeasement over Poland was being tried, parliament was twice adjourned.

(c) Secret men. During the 1930s critics became vocal about secret government by faceless individuals in Whitehall (Chapter 10 A1). The establishment backed Chamberlain's policies, and that those who did not were dealt with. Sir Warren Fisher used his influence to purge the Foreign Office of pro-French officials, and secure pro-German ambassadors abroad. When it became clear that Sir Robert Vansittart, Under-Secretary to Fisher was anti-appeasement, he was shifted upstairs to be Chief Diplomatic Adviser (1938) and replaced by Sir Alexander Cadogan (1938–46). Sir Horace Wilson, son of a Bournemouth furniture dealer, became Chief Economic Adviser, but was given a room in Downing Street, and conducted foreign policy matters instead. He was Head of the Civil Service (1939–42).

Chamberlain enjoyed power and office, and overestimated his own abilities. He shut himself off from men in and outside his party, governed secretly using an inner cabinet, Civil Service expertise and the Whip system. Yet it should be remembered that in the end it was he who went to war, and Labour who refused to join him. Even in May 1940 the majority of Tories supported him, and Sir Henry Channon wrote, 'I am ... revolted by the ingratitude of my fellow men, nauseated by the House of Commons' when Chamberlain was attacked.

E3. The Munich Election?
Munich represented the high point of Chamberlain's influence. Backed by France, America and the dominions, the first reaction was of universal

support. Even Eden refused to join Churchill in sending a 'stand firm' telegram and made a careful speech in the October debate. There was only one resignation. When the Duchess of Atholl resigned as MP in protest and stood as an Independent, she was defeated. Attempts to extend the Popular Front to include Tory critics failed, and even Churchill never voted against the party. At Oxford, Quintin Hogg won a by-election supporting Munich. When Sir Sidney Herbert, MP for Abbey, made a speech about 'Tammany Hall' politics, this helped to scotch an election. But Chamberlain's supporters continued to back the idea. Wohltat, Göring's economic aide, was told by Sir Joseph Ball, director of the Conservative Research Department, that there would be an autumn election on the slogan 'Safeguarding World Peace with Chamberlain'. This was still under discussion in August.

E4. Conservative Opposition

Opposition to Chamberlain was considerable but disunited. Some came from younger, progressive Tories who wanted more social reform, and was typified by Macmillan's *The Middle Way* (1938). Most came from the right wing or ex-ministers, and this made it difficult to draw support from party loyalists or join forces with widespread opposition on the left. Three distinct strands may be seen to the opposition groupings:

(a) *Demand for a government of national unity.* Towards the end of 1936 the Arms and the Covenant movement managed to get Churchill, Citrine and Sinclair on the same platform, but this was killed by the Abdication crisis. In March 1938 Kingsley Martin advocated a coalition including Churchill, Liberals and Labour, but when urged to send a telegram before Munich to strengthen Chamberlain, Attlee, Sinclair and Eden declined. Churchill and Lloyd George cooperated in demanding an alliance with Russia in 1939, but Chamberlain rebuffed their demand for Eden to go to Moscow.

(b) *The Glamour Boys.* When Eden resigned some 25 Tories abstained, and there gathered round him a collection of opponents including Duff Cooper, Herbert, Nicholson and Cartland. But they did not constitute a formidable grouping and Eden was a lukewarm leader. He had been a strong supporter of appeasement, and saw himself as a future leader. Even at Munich he was careful not to be overcritical, and this paid off. In December that year he visited the United States where he was mobbed. An opinion poll in March 1939 showed 38 per cent for him as compared with 7 per cent for Churchill and Halifax.

(c) *The Churchill group.* Churchill's opposition had started over India, and it was associated with the pro-imperialist wing of the party. It was based on exaggerated figures, and at times commanded little support. He was howled down over the abdication and Munich, and there were no more than 30 abstentions after the latter. Moreover, his opposition was not consistent. Japan in Manchuria and Italy in Abyssinia did not arouse much anger. His group consisted of ex-ministers like Chamberlain, Amery, Horne; right wingers like Lloyd, Croft, Brabazon and Grigg; and members of the Lords like Trenchard and Salisbury. It also contained an element of 'young Turks' like Duncan Sandys, Brendan Bracken and Robert Boothby.

The group first sprang into prominence in July 1936 when a deputation waited on Baldwin. They were put off and returned in November, but were told their estimates were too gloomy. As Blake remarks, 'There was not much the anti appeasers could do.'

F. Labour in Torment and Opposition

F1. The Way Back

After 1931 the Labour party was in two minds. Some argued the radical programme of the election had done harm, and urged moderation. The election of Lansbury confirmed this point of view, and it was followed by Attlee, Morrison and Dalton, backed by Citrine and Bevin for the unions. It was opposed by Cripps, Strachey and Laski. Although they differed about home policy, all were agreed on disarmament, support for the League, collective security and opposition to the armament industry. It was when Fascist aggression after 1935 made this position untenable that foreign affairs became important in dividing the party. It is certainly true that one reason for failure in 1935 was lack of unity or policy.

(a) *Electoral recovery*. The period 1931 to 1935 was a good one for the party, who won 10 by-elections, and in 1934 won control of the LCC under Morrison. In the same year *For Socialism and Peace* defined their policy as progressive and moderate, and in 1935 they won 154 seats. With Attlee as leader, Dalton as chairman and Bevin as TUC chairman the party remained moderate.

(b) *Splinter groups*. Left-wing elements in the party resorted to splinter groups, or attempts by the National Executive to influence the party. In July 1932 Maxton's ILP left the party and was reduced to four members. The same year the Socialist League was established with Cripps and Laski as leading lights. In 1934 they demanded in *Forward to Socialism*, a five-year plan, total disarmament and 'the united struggle of the workers'.

(c) *The change on rearmament*. Henderson had committed the party to virtual pacifism, and the left disliked Tory armament barons. But union leaders wanted jobs, and increasingly felt sympathy for trade unionists suffering abroad. In 1935 the TUC were prepared to accept the logic that sanctions against Italy might mean war. When Lansbury the next month opposed this, Bevin said, 'It is placing the executive and the Movement in an absolutely wrong position to be taking your conscience round from body to body asking to be told what you ought to do with it.' In 1936 a resolution favouring collective security and opposing rearmament was carried, and at last in 1937 rearmament was accepted.

F2. Intellectuals Battle

The 1930s were a period of vigorous political debate and left-wing cultural achievement (Chapter 10, B). In this context, Labour discussed the issue of rapid or gradual socialism.

(a) *The gradualists*. In 1932 the New Fabian Research Bureau was founded by the Coles and attracted new moderates like Gaitskell. The programme required public ownership and welfare, including a health service. These policies were accepted by many and became the main Labour party theme. The chief writers were Dalton, *Practical Socialism for Britain* (1935), and Jay, *The Socialist Case* (1938).

(b) *The revolutionaries*. A series of books advocated an enabling act, or even dictatorship, seizure of factories by workers' control and a general strike. The main works were Laski's *The Crisis of the Constitution* (1932) and *Democracy in Crisis* (1933), Strachey's *The Coming Struggle for Power* (1932) and Cripps' *The Labour Party and the Constitution* (1932), *Can Socialism Come by Constitutional Methods* (1933), and *Why This Socialism?* (1934).

F3. The Popular Front

The usual practice of Communists was to attack socialists as lackeys of capitalism, but after this had helped Hitler to power by dividing the left, Moscow changed its line and advocated cooperation in a popular front. As a result, such governments were formed in France and Spain during 1936. Although both failed in a few months, the concept was strongly favoured. The matter was raised in 1933 and the party conference defeated the idea. The ILP thought differently, and in 1934 set up a joint anti-fascist committee. The outbreak of war in Spain brought renewed demands, but apart from reversing their support for non-intervention, the party would not budge.

In January 1937 a Unity Campaign was launched with Cripps for the League, Brockway and Maxton for the ILP, and Pollitt for the Communists. As a result the League was expelled from the party, and dissolved itself to leave individuals free to campaign within the party. Owing to changes in rules for electing constituency members to the executive, Cripps, Laski and Pritt were elected and demands for unity increased. The same year Cripps and Bevan founded *Tribune*. During 1938, with attempts to include Liberals and others, the United Front won control of 120 local parties. In January 1939 Cripps again asked for a Popular Front, and Strauss, Bevan and himself were expelled from the party. The Nazi–Soviet Pact put an end to these groupings until 1941.

F4. Trade Union Recovery

The 1930s were a period of recovery for the unions. Since many new industries were not unionised, and the 1927 Act was a powerful threat, if rarely used, strikes were low throughout the period. In 1938, for example, only 52,000 working days were lost in disputes involving more than 5,000 workers. Indeed, a number of years passed without any strikes in big industries. This situation was brought about by moderate union leaders, or as Bevin put it, 'we look upon ourselves as the labour side of management'. In particular, Sir Walter Citrine gave the unions a responsible image. In 1935 two circulars asked unions to exclude Communists from office, and trades councils to ban Communist delegates. The trades unions resisted attempts to make them take direct action on rearmament or Spain.

Arbitration was used frequently to settle strikes, and unions cooperated with management in allowing piece-work. Only where Communist influence was active, as in the Lucas (Birmingham) strike in 1938, was there any prolonged trouble. In 1939 the Bridlington Agreement provided for a settlement of one of the main causes of inter-union disputes—poaching of members.

Successful industrial relations also encouraged the government to discuss matters arising with unions. In 1931 the TUC was represented on one government committee; by 1938 it was on 12. Unions were consulted on bills to reorganise fishing and cotton, and when rearmament began, talks were held as early as the Spring of 1938. In 1939 the talks were renewed to include wages, dilution and to secure acceptance of conscription. When the Ministries of Supply and Food were created, the unions were ignored, complained, and were then consulted in October 1939.

F5. The International Brigade

In 1936 Gorer's *Nobody Talks Politics* appeared. This was a novel showing how the intellectuals of the 1920s who hardly ever mentioned politics had now become interested in them. It was the Spanish Civil War (Chapter 12, E) which, in Mowat's words, 'brought bitterness and class consciousness into foreign, and so into domestic policy, to an extent unknown before'. The left became obsessed with Spain, and this damaged them. By 1939 the popular front idea was finished, the ILP was a spent force, the Socialist League had disappeared, the unions and the Labour party were moderates. Similarly, uncritical support for Communism typified by the Webbs' *Soviet Communism: A New Civilisation* began to change in view of Spanish realities. Orwell's *Homage to Catalonia* (1937) revealed the attacks on Communists by other Communists in Barcelona.

The British sent a contingent of 3,000 to the International Brigades, fighting for the republic: 500 were killed; half of them Communists. The brigades achieved fame because they included writers like Bell and Cornford who were killed. They also contained ordinary working men of which one, Jack Jones, was to achieve fame after 1970 in a different context. In January 1937 the government banned recruiting, but as late as 1939 rallies in support of the republic were held. When the government recognised Franco in February 1939, Attlee divided the House. Britain itself was truly divided:

(a) Newspapers split, with the *Mail*, *Post*, *Sketch* and *Observer* on Franco's side; the *Chronicle*, *Herald*, *Express* and *Mirror* on the republic's. This in itself was a significant break in a usually solid Tory press front. Public opinion was largely on the republic's side, and Franco never got more than 14 per cent support.

(b) The right-wing Tories and many Catholics rallied to Franco. The Friends of Nationalist Spain represented British mining and farming interests. In the Commons Tory MPs cheered the sinking of republican ships.

(c) The opposition organised in many ways. Some £2m was raised for the republic by voluntary subscription. The miners in May 1938 decided to raise a 2s 6d levy. It brought in £83,000. The Basque Children's Committee brought 4,000 refugees to live near Southampton. The National Joint Committee for Spanish Relief raised supplies and despatched 29 food ships.

In the end, however, this energy and passion would have been better directed to conditions at home, which tended to be forgotten in the excitement of doing something for Spain.

Further Reading

Donaldson, F., *Edward VIII*, Weidenfeld and Nicolson, London, 1974.

Barnes, A. J. L., and Middlemass, R. K., *Stanley Baldwin*, Weidenfeld and Nicolson, London, 1969.

Feiling, K., *The Life of Neville Chamberlain*, Macmillan, London, 1946.

Mowat, C. L., *Britain Between the Wars 1918–1940*, Methuen, London, 1955.

Pelling, H., *Winston Churchill*, Macmillan, London, 1974, available in Pan Paperback, 1977.

Pollard, S., *The Development of the British Economy 1914–1970*, Edward Arnold, London, 1971.
Richardson, H. W., *Economic Recovery in Britain 1932–1939*, Weidenfeld and Nicolson, London, 1967.
Stevenson, J., and Cook, C., *The Slump: Society and Politics during the Depression*, Jonathan Cape, London, 1978.

Questions

1. What was national about the National Governments of the 1930s?
2. Assess *either* the overall contribution of MacDonald *or* that of Baldwin to political change between the wars.
3. What were Chamberlain's main assets and defects as a national leader?
4. Why did the National Government win the election of 1935 with so large a majority?
5. Why was the left wing so bitter and divided during the 1930s?
6. What were the main features of economic recovery in the 1930s?
7. How far did government policy aid recovery in the 1930s?
8. Was the Tory party of the 1930s complacent, flinty faced, and right wing in its sentiments and actions?
9. How did the National Governments deal with unemployment and the unemployed? (See also Chapter 8, B3 and 4.)

10

THE GLAMOROUS DECADE: BRITAIN IN THE 1930s

Appeasement and unemployment were important features of the 1930s, but they were not the most important. John Gunther, in *Inside Europe* (1938) commented that the government had produced 'not only complete stability but a striking measure of industrial recovery', and it was these features that are crucial to understanding the most controversial decade of the century. A society magazine commented that in the 1930s 'much of the pomp and luxury of the Late Victorian age was revived with a much greater feeling for elegance and style'. Three popular words of the period were 'glamorous', 'sophisticated' and 'streamlined'. It was the age of Ivor Novello, Noël Coward, Hollywood, Glenn Miller, long skirts, graceful sports cars and dancing at the Palais. The majority of the people had shorter hours, longer holidays, higher real wages, more welfare benefits, and a higher living standard. The benefits of technocracy and mass production became available to the majority. In 1936 a sociologist, Tom Harrisson, and a Marxist poet Charles Madge, started Mass Observation. For the first time the opinion of ordinary people was sought, and it was analysed for different reasons by politicians and businesses.

This state of affairs did not win universal approval from the cultural establishment. During the 1930s a strain of puritanism, particularly on the left, began to become apparent. People were urged to read Left Book Club choices instead of going to the cinema twice a week. In spite of widespread diffusion of classical music, cheap editions of classics and evidence that mass culture was useful, there was much criticism of England 'Blackpooling itself'. Since there was political stability and the left was politically impotent, the period saw a rise in political interest in the 'condition of England' question. Some of this came from the right, from Mosley's Fascists and Tories eager to cloth the scaffolding of the welfare state in more substantial materials. Much came from the left. Indeed, the period of Tory dominance saw a lurch to the left which was more than political. A whole group of ideas—the welfare state, planning and government intervention—which had previously been regarded as left wing became widespread. Appropriately enough, the war years strengthened the trend under a genuine coalition government. The shift to the left, and the rejection of old-style Socialism and right wing Toryism were to condition British change from the 1940s for 30 years. Issues about the powers of government, the need to intervene in the economy, the importance of welfare or the necessity of planning were still minority issues in the 1930s, but in debating them the old establishment was giving way to the new.

Just as the degree of Mass Culture can be exaggerated, so can the extent of left-wing influence at this time. Hoggart has pointed out 'the prevailing background in books, films and plays was middle class'. There was a wide gap between the left-wing author and what his parlourmaid read in the class-ridden society of the 1930s. However, there was a link between left-wing thought and much of what was known as 'Modern

Culture'. All periods have been modern in their time, but the use of the capital 'M' indicated a desire to break with the past. Trends of the 1920s now became self-evident, particularly in architecture, sculpture, and music. The stage and the novel tended to be more conservative; poetry was blatantly political. J. D. Bernal's *The Social Function of Science* (1936) was an important work, suggesting a link between scientific progress and social change. The new architecture used glass and concrete. It built health centres and housing schemes, not churches and country houses. Painters produced abstracts instead of portraits of the ruling classes. The interest in health, diet and the open air that characterised the 1930s was part of a striving for liberation from the dull world of the past. Mass culture received a strong injection from America. Minority culture received a strong injection from Europe, whose refugees (250,000) from dictatorships found freedom to practise their ideas. They were a mixed bag, but since they fled mainly from fascism, it was inevitable that they should give a leftward bias to the Modern movement.

There is a strong case for arguing that the 1930s was the decisive decade in the evolution of twentieth-century Britain. Trends that germinated round the turn of the century and had been seen but not heard in Edwardian times, surfaced by the 1920s, and found a measure of acceptability by the 1930s. In terms of economic decline, the change from Empire to Commonwealth and decline of great power status, this seems to be true. It is also true of the trend to a secular society based on a mass culture, a welfare state and a consumer economy; and the politics of consensus with bureaucracy seen as a threat, yet ever more necessary for a widening range of functions by a collective state. If liberty was the nineteenth-century watchword, equality was to become the twentieth. With capacity to spend and a new interest from above the working man emerges clearly in history during the 1930s. Speed and mass production made one England, while class and tradition still made several, but these were the birth days of modern British politics and society.

A. Politics of Liberty, Extremism and Moderation

By the 1930s the increasing powers of the state were apparent, while abroad totalitarian regimes were widespread. With the growth of the collective state, the number of laws affecting citizens increased in complexity, while delegated legislation and administrative action were arousing the interest of constitutional historians like Sir Ivor Jennings. In 1944 Hayek's *Road to Serfdom* exposed the trend of the previous decade. In *The Long Week End* Graves and Hodge argued that administrative action could lead to the corporate state, and that was fascism. It could also lead to the type of Soviet state then existing under Stalin. Both extremes had their supporters in the 1930s. The Communist party had 18,000 members, and the Fascists claimed 40,000. Neither presented a significant threat. But the desire to examine the rôle of the state and to combat extremism, combined with the seriousness of the economic crisis and the collapse of political norms in many countries, led to a wider questioning of the historical controversy between individualism and socialism.

A1. Defence of Liberty

Fear of encroaching government power came from two differer

(*a*) The Right. They objected to the extension of the state's functions, and the creation of administrative law as a challenge to common law. They feared the subordination of the individual to the state. Two important works were *The New Despotism* (1930), by Lord Hewart, and *Bureaucracy Triumphant* (1931), by C. K. Allen.

(*b*) The Left. They feared a right-wing corporate state emerging from Tory dominance of politics. They did not object to the state controlling the individual —only to a Tory state doing so and trespassing on left-wing causes. Greaves' *Reactionary England* (1936) and *The British Constitution* (1938) argued the nation was run by a right-wing establishment. Davies, in *National Capitalism* (1939), claimed there was a one-party state already.

The left opposed strengthening the powers of the state as far as political control was concerned. The reactionary measures of Lloyd George (Chapter 5, A1) were added to in this period by the Incitement to Disaffection Act (1934) to prevent attempts to suborn troops, and The Public Order Act (1936) which forbade political uniforms and gave police power to ban processions and meetings. The left criticised the prosecution of Mann and Llewelyn for calling an unemployed meeting, and the refusal of Hackney magistrates to use the Public Order Act against fascists. This discontent led to the formation of the National Council for Civil Liberties (1934), with Forster as president and supported by a wide range of people, including Wells, Attlee, Priestley and Herbert. They campaigned against the Acts and on behalf of minority groups.

A2. The British Union of Fascists

Gunther described British fascism as 'a watery English stew' compared with that on the Continent. There had been small semi-fascist groups since 1918, when a National Party had won two seats, and in the 1920s, when Mussolini was praised by many and *The Times* declared, 'The corporative state offers greater opportunities than the liberal state.' But Mosley's departure from Labour and the creation of the BUF in 1932 were the beginning of any political significance the movement was to achieve. Mosley was a left-wing politician who soon adopted right-wing views, thus combining reaction and populism—the source of fascist triumph abroad. In September 1932, in *The Greater Britain*, he outlined his policy.

Born in 1896, Mosley entered parliament as Tory MP for Harrow (1918), then became an Independent (1922) and finally Labour in 1924, returning to parliament as MP for Smethwick (1926). With a charming wife and plenty of money he had considerable influence and obtained office in 1929 to help deal with unemployment. He was only 33, but resigned the next year (Chapter 8, C5) and failed in an attempt to swing Labour behind him. Intelligent and magnetic, Gunther described him as 'the best orator in England', but he failed to keep his movement out of muddy waters. It became linked to anti-Semitism in an attempt to win votes in the East End, when only 0.8 per cent of the population was Jewish and the total of European refugees was no more than 50,000. The wearing of a uniform and the use of political violence by supporters destroyed links with some

Tories and Tory newspapers in June 1934 after the Olympia Rally. Thereafter he resorted to the streets, and in October 1936 and October 1937
sought to march through Jewish areas of London's East End, where he was
defeated by the East Enders and the police.

A3. The British Communist Party

At a time when, according to some, 'capitalism had broken down', the
Communist party was without political importance. In 1935 it returned an
MP, William Gallacher, leader of the Clyde Workers' Committee in 1915,
and member for East Fife. Harry Pollitt (Secretary in 1929) was the most
influential party figure and as a journalist was to develop the *Daily
Worker*. Apart from attempts to form a popular front after 1934 (Chapter
9, F3), the real difficulties of the party stemmed from backing the Moscow
line on foreign policy which required them to attack socialists like Maxton.
The Nazi–Soviet Pact and the Russian attack on Finland cut membership to
12,000 by the end of 1939.

A4. Separatist Parties

A number of factors stimulated the growth of separatist parties. Northern
Ireland had its own parliament, and inevitably other Celtic nations began
to consider their position. The economic depression hit South Wales and
the Clyde more severely than anywhere else. After 1935 the Liberals backed
devolution as one means of recovering power, and this stimulated nationalism.

(*a*) The Welsh Nationalist Party was founded in 1925 along the lines of the
Gaelic Movement in Ireland, calling for the revival of the Welsh language. They
secured the use of Welsh in schools and the broadcasting of Welsh.

(*b*) The Scottish Nationalist Party. There had been a literary revival. In 1936
the Saltaire Society was founded, but there were only 100,000 Gaelic speakers.
The real roots lay in economic discontent since in 1932 a quarter of Scotland
was unemployed. There was Irish immigration to the Clyde, and by 1939 one in
five births were Roman Catholic. This was resented when social conditions were
appalling, with 22 per cent of the country living in overcrowded tenements. The
Scottish National Party was founded in 1928.

A5. The Middle Way

Victorian England had a consensus of ideas—liberalism and democracy
for property owners, free trade, religious toleration, Christian morality,
laissez faire and self-help with occasional government intervention. These
had been sapped during the Great War, derided during the 1920s and,
although the upper classes retained the ideals of their boyhood through
much of the period, in intellectual circles and among younger MPs ideals
were changing. Consensus politics emerged from the need to find a new
basis for Western capitalist society after the old basis had been eroded. It
was not in essence socialism, but naturally the leftward trend gave it power
and took strength from it. It was all-party because it believed in a set of new
common denominators that would create a stable, prosperous society.

Dislike of the National Government and fascism abroad combined with
admiration for the Soviet planned economy and social awareness to create
a new creed. The advance of economics and sociology provided analytical

tools, and the development of the corporate state which had started in the 1870s (Chapter 1, E2), provided the means. The new consensus wished to avoid extremes in party and class conflict. In place of struggles between workers and management there was to be a modernised and rationalised economy in which government and private enterprise played parts. Moreover, the government was to see its rôle not divorced from economic laws, or bound by them, but able to manipulate them. A managed, mixed economy was to be the answer to the ills of the depression and Britain's still declining position. Planning was to extend to a wide field of human activities, including leisure, to utilise resources and create a civilised society, while social policy was to be based on a welfare state which was ever increasing its benefits and thereby raising living standards. The main developments were:

(a) The sociology of progress. There was a renewal of interest in social surveys like those at the turn of the century. There was a new 'Life and Labour of the People of London'. In *Human Labour* (1936) Rowntree worked out a new scale for minimum subsistence and carried out a survey of York (1935–36). Local studies were carried out among which Tout's of Bristol (1938) was the best.

(b) Science is not neutral. Science produced objective studies, but they were made use of for the purposes of reform. Falling population was causing concern (38 million by 1984 was predicted), and in February 1937 the first Commons debate occurred on the subject, stimulated by E. Charles' *Twilight of Parenthood*. R. Titmus, *Poverty of Population* (1938), drew attention to the link of planning, housing and population. Sir John Orr and Sir William Crawford did important work on food and nutrition, and works like Kirby's *Poverty and Public Health* (1936) drew attention to the need for social reform.

Some scientists, like Julian Huxley in *Scientific Research and Social Needs*, made no secret of their support for social reform, while social scientists provided information on society. In 1937 came Saunders' and Jones' *The Social Structure*, and Labour writers like Dalton drew on 'objective' figures to argue the case for change.

(c) Planning the future. In February 1931 *Weekend Review* published a National Plan advocating a Ministry of Economic Development, planning control and a national transport policy. Next month Political and Economic Planning started with a journal. There followed a PEP report *The Next Five Years* (1935) and *A Programme of Priorities* (1937). Among their proposals were nationalisation, financial planning, extended welfare, progressive taxation, an economic general staff, a development board and educational change.

Those involved in PEP came from a wide field of public life, and included Sir Josiah Stamp, Israel Sieff, Lord Allen, Lionel Curtis, J. A. Hobson, Gilbert Murray, H. G. Wells and Archbishop Temple. Inevitably both political parties began to take an interest in their work. The government responded by appointing Sir Montague Barlow (1937) to investigate population, and his report was one of the major blueprints for wartime planning of peacetime Britain. Keynes was already famous, but it was not until 1936, with *The General Theory of Employment, Interest and Money*, that his views became widely known. By focusing attention on national income, Keynes made possible what amounted to a new capitalism. Budget controls, including deficit financing and manipulation of interest rates and money supply, seemed to open a vista of governments' influencing economies like they did the policy of nation states. Since capitalism was to be saved by government spending, this also meant that wealth creation and government activity would go hand in hand. It was a model for consensus politics, as a book by a Tory backbencher, Harold Macmillan (*The Middle Way*, 1938), clearly showed.

B. Left-Wing Cultural Explosion

B1. New Gods for Old

'Quite suddenly,' said Orwell, 'in the years 1930–35, something happens. The literary climate changes.' In fact, the changes had been coming for some time, but in the 1930s the Bloomsbury gods were denounced as too intellectual, even fascist in tendency. Orwell's essay *Inside the Whale* analysed the new trend when 'the whole of the intelligentsia was at war'. A political viewpoint was regarded as essential, or, as Orwell said, 'somebody has chosen to drop the Geneva language of the ordinary novel and drag the *realpolitik* of the inner mind into the open'. Without political committal 'a novelist ... is generally either a footler or a plain idiot'. The 1930s were less concerned about literature than the expression of psychological and political views. There was plenty of moral uplift contemplating utopian futures, redressing the evils of war and capitalism and focusing attention on the crisis of left-wing conscience.

It was essentially a literature of protest and little of it, particularly the poetry, has stood the test of time. Orwell admitted that much written was merely 'a torrent of hate literature'. There was, in Mowat's view, 'a new sort of literature' which showed distrust 'of the government, parliament, the fundamental soundness of society and the constitution' or, as Orwell put it, 'all through the critical years many left wingers were chipping away at English morale, trying to spread an outlook that was sometimes squashily pacifist, sometimes violently pro-Russian, but always anti-British'. He commented that it was easy to attack patriotism, religion or the Empire, but less easy to see what was being put in their place. Orwell turned against the left after his Spanish experience, but others have seen the protest literature justified by poverty at home and fascism abroad.

B2. Spreading the Good News

While attacking the establishment, the left quickly formed one of its own. The movement got under way at Cambridge in 1932 with Cambridge Left and *Scrutiny*, in which F. R. Leavis was prominent. The same year came *New Signatures,* followed by *New Verse* (1933) and later *New Writing* (1936). Michael Roberts, the editor, brought together a number of poets and playwrights, who constituted the high priests of the movement including Auden, Day Lewis, Spender, Upwood, MacNeice, Isherwood and Lehmann. All public school, Oxbridge types, they were far removed from the realities they sought to portray. In 1934 *Left Review* appeared, edited by Wintringham and including the work of Jameson, Holtby, and Priestley. These works affected a small group, but many attempts were made to spread the good news:

(a) *Films.* There was little success, although films on working-class misery became popular, and included LOVE ON THE DOLE, and HOW GREEN WAS MY VALLEY.

(b) *Newspapers.* In 1930 the *Daily Worker* was founded with a subsidy from Russia. In 1934 the *Mirror* became a left-wing paper.

(c) *Theatre.* The Westminster produced some of Isherwood's works, such as *The Ascent of F6* (1936) and *On the Frontier* (1938).

(d) *Penguins.* In 1935 Allen Lane founded Penguin Books at 6d each. It was not a left-wing body, but Penguin Specials (1937) were left-inclined.

(e) *Picture Post.* This was founded by Stefan Lorent, a German refugee, and publicised in picture form both poverty and fascism (1938).

B3. The Left Book Club

In May 1936 Victor Gollancz founded the Left Book Club because so many publishers were in his opinion right-wing. It was followed by a Right Book Club and Socialist Book Club, but neither approached it in fame, with its peak of 40,000 readers. Even in 1943 it was still selling 20,000 and was not dissolved until 1947. By an arrangement with Lawrence and Wishart they produced Communist books at a cheap rate, and also published *Left News* (1937). Apart from works like *A Handbook of Marxism* and *A People's History of England*, the Club produced works on current topics. These included Hannington's *Problems of the Distressed Areas* and Wilkinson's *The Town that was Murdered*. It encouraged working men to write, including a taxi driver and a waiter. In 1940 it began a new series with *Guilty Men*, attacking the Tories, which went through 25 impressions in a year. Gollancz became disillusioned and edited *The Betrayal of the Left*, but there is no doubting the considerable influence of the organisation as 'a unique and irreversible process of socialist education'.

C. Modern Culture

The use of the term 'Modern' to identify style in the 1930s was deliberate. It was combination of rejecting old forms and identifying them with established ideas which a leftward-moving cultural milieu disliked. Among the new wave the Book Society and the Royal Academy were regarded as the final insult, not the first choice. There was an element of rebellion about art being something admired by people in evening dress with short sight. But it was more than that. Psychology and the decline of Christian morality opened a new range of human activities to public gaze. Relativism in standards replaced absolute canons of moral and aesthetic judgement. Nihilism and despair were certainly present. Christopher Wood, an artist, painted so much that he went off his head and flung himself under a train at Salisbury.

But there was also an awareness of new aspects of human life. Henry Miller's *Tropic of Cancer* (1931) took over where Lawrence left off. Moreover, technical change altered concepts of art. New materials enabled architecture to break from classical models. The camera seemed to have ousted representational art in favour of abstracts. Battle was joined between the society novel and existentialist works of men like Rex Warner; between Picasso and Munnings in painting; between Epstein's 'Rima' and Hardiman's 'Haig' in sculpture; between mock Tudor and flat-roofed concrete houses in architecture. This change was disturbing because it resented patronage and spurned public acclaim. Since the new artistic standards were often subjective, it was difficult to judge new works. Nor did the influence of Continental refugees endear it to many. Visiting a Surrealist exhibition in 1936, Priestley commented, 'They stand for violence and neurotic unreason.' In one sense at least they represented the coming decades accurately.

C1. Architecture

J. M. Richards' *Introduction to Modern Architecture* (1940) stressed the main features. He argued that functionalism was important because of cost and new environments, and that stockbroker Tudor and post office Georgian were the end of an era. Modern architecture was international and could draw on Frank Lloyd Wright or Le Corbusier. New materials such as concrete, tiles, plate glass, asbestos and aluminium could be put to use in different proportions in new buildings, and unity of style could be achieved by matching the interior fittings to the building. The founding of the MARS group in 1931, the same year as Le Corbusier was translated into English, might be taken as the real start of the movement which was greatly aided by foreign refugees including Lubetkin and Mendelsohn. However, a number of English architects took up the new style, including Coates, Tait, McGrath, Yorke and Fry. The 'Art in Industry' (1935) and 'New Architecture' (1938) exhibitions at the Burlington Gallery did much to publicise the trend, which was found in four main areas:

(a) *Domestic architecture.* When Yorke first published *The Modern House* he could only find a few examples. By 1938 he could fill a book as private clients experimented. There were also some examples of flats, including High Point and Lawn Road in London.

(b) *Public housing.* Elizabeth Denby's *Europe Rehoused* (1938) gave a good survey of European progress, and Kensal House, designed by herself and Maxwell Fry, was outstanding. Other authorities also experimented, including Quarry Hill at Leeds.

(c) *Industry and commerce.* Herbert Read's *Art and Industry* (1934) showed what could be done, and a number of modern factories were built at Letchworth and Welwyn.

(d) *Public Buildings.* Hugh Casson's *New Sights of London* (1938) was able to give a considerable list of modern buildings which ranged from the BBC to Finsbury Health Centre.

C2. Music

Encouraged by radio, music took on a new lease of life in the 1930s. After the BBC Symphony Orchestra, run by Boult and Bliss, came the London Philharmonia (1932). Sadlers Wells (1931) and Glyndebourne (1934) gave settings to two varieties of music which experienced a revival. Apart from popular writers like Eric Coates (1886–1957) there were many important composers:

(a) Vaughan Williams was at the height of his powers with a Fourth Symphony (1935), and went on to write nine.

(b) John Ireland, with his 'London Overture' (1936), became prominent, and his oratorio 'These Things Shall be' (1937) was strongly anti-war.

(c) Arnold Bax wrote four symphonies of considerable power by 1939, and added 'cello (1932) and violin (1937) concertos.

(*d*) Arthur Bliss was regarded as most avant guarde in his music for the film *The Shape of Things to Come*. He wrote an anti-war symphony—'Morning Heroes' (1930). In 1937 came music for the ballet 'Checkmate'.

(*e*) William Walton achieved real prominence with his First Symphony (1935) and Violin Concerto (1939). He also took over Elgar's rôle, writing the Coronation music for 1937.

(*f*) Benjamin Britten (1913–1976) collaborated with Auden in 'Ballad for Heroes' (1937), and was a pacifist and left-winger as well as a Christian. The 'Simple Symphony' and 'A Boy Was Born' (1934) established his reputation, followed by piano (1938) and violin (1939) concertos.

The 1930s were an exciting and experimental period in musical history, and a host of new names—Lambert, Moeran, Rubbra, Berkeley Tippett, Rawsthorne and Lutyens—demonstrated the continued strength of music as an art.

C3. Painting and Sculpture

In 1933 Unit One and Artists International were set up to encourage modern art, and 'artists who recognised the need to act as political men'. What happened was that ideas long current abroad established themselves in Britain, and supplemented the existing schools of portrait and water-colour painting. Augustus John (1878–1961) and Graham Sutherland (1903–1977) were important portrait painters, while the traditional school was maintained by Alfred Munnings and the landscapes of Philip Steer. Among new artists affected by surrealism and New Realism were Paul Nash (d. 1946) and a number of others including Wadsworth, Hiller, Gertler and Philpot. In sculpture Charles Wheeler (b. 1892) produced traditional work, while Barbara Hepworth and Henry Moore developed abstract art and the ideas of Epstein.

C4. Literature

The literary establishment remained conservative, and the law was strictly enforced on any attempts to introduce themes now often dwelt upon. Through the Book Club, Hugh Walpole in particular was an important influence, and his four-volume *Herries Chronicle* was completed in 1933. Some writers like Blunden and Eliot refused to be involved in the political uproar, and the majority of readers followed them. A good idea of the period may be obtained from Frank Swinnerton's *The Georgian Literary Scene* (1938). He saw the rising novelists as A. P. Herbert with *The Water Gypsies* and J. B. Priestley with *The Good Companions* (1929) and *Angel Pavement* (1930). The popular authors continued to be good story-tellers, more often than not writing about a small group of people in an upper-class setting. Dornford Yates and Warwick Deeping were well known, and close behind them came Denis Mackail, John Buchan, Somerset Maugham and Compton Mackenzie. The chief writers were:

(*a*) Virginia Woolf continued to write such works at *The Waves* (1931) and *The Years* (1937), but committed suicide in 1941.

(*b*) Aldous Huxley wrote *Eyeless in Gaza* (1936) and *Ends and Means* (1937). He became interested in yoga and mescalin, and went to California.

(*c*) Christopher Isherwood wrote *Mr Norris Changes Trains* (1935), *Sally Bowles* (1937), and *Goodbye to Berlin* (1939) before leaving for America.

...ner wrote *The Wild Goose Chase* (1937), *The Professor* (1938),
...e (1941) and *Why Was I Killed* (1943).

...Greene (b.1904) grew to prominence with *Stamboul Train* (1932),
...ale (1936), *Brighton Rock* (1938), and *The Power and the Glory*
(1940).

(f) Evelyn Waugh was well established with *Black Mischief* (1932), *A Handful of Dust* (1934) and *Scoop* (1938).

In poetry the chief figures were:

(a) T. S. Eliot (1888–1965) revealed in *Ash Wednesday* (1930) a change from his attitude in the twenties, which was followed by *The Four Quartets* (1935–42). In 1935 came his first verse play *Murder in the Cathedral.* As editor of *The Criterion* until 1939 he exercised considerable influence.

(b) W. B. Yeats (1865–1939) continued to write work of lyrical beauty, including *The Tower, The Winding Stair,* and *Last Poems.*

(c) Wystan Auden (1907–1973) published his first work in 1930, and by 1936 in *Look Stranger* had developed a clear style which also came out well in *The Quest* (1941). He collaborated with Isherwood, married Thomas Mann's daughter and went to America.

(d) C. Day Lewis (1904–1972) developed his style early in *A Hope for Poetry* (1934), *Collected Poems* (1935) and *Overture to Death* (1937).

(e) S. Spender (b. 1909) helped to found *Horizon* with Cyril Connolly, and was later editor of *Encounter.* His chief works were *Vienna, Still Centre* (1939) and *Ruins and Visions.*

D. Scaffolding of a Welfare State

D1. Two Nations

Marwick's chapter on the thirties is 'The Bitter Society'. There is much evidence that it was no such thing; Gunther commented, 'even the poorest are loyal. Visitors from abroad to Tyneside and Durham are incredulous that poverty of such miserable proportions does not produce revolutions'. Most contemporary observers like Orwell and Priestley commented the same way. The main economic reasons for this situation were that unemployment was contained and falling, real wages rose by 17 per cent between 1931 and 1937, labour relations were good, opportunities for overtime greater as hours fell and leisure time increased. In spite of social deprivation on a widespread scale there were $2\frac{1}{2}$ million new homes, and the range of articles inside them reflected the growth of a consumer society by no means confined to the lowly taxed middle class. In 1938, 60 per cent of furniture, for example, was bought on hire purchase. Cheap mortgages enabled one quarter of families to be owner-occupiers by 1939. After 1937 even the tax burden began to even out with the impact of rearmament, and throughout the period after the cuts had been reversed, the share of the National Income devoted to social services grew to 13 per cent in 1939. The pace of reform quickened in Chamberlain's ministry as it was likely to do with his previous record. However low standards of wages and living seem compared with the affluent sixties, the British worker in the 1930s was better off than any European contemporary. Gunther said that income per head was £87 in England, £46 in Germany and £43 in France.

In spite of widespread and increasing wealth Britain remained two nations, and this was not merely a question of accent, dress and education.

There was disparity between rich and poor in 'income and capital, nutrition, the death rate, infant mortality, and shelter. Three features clearly indicated differences between rich and poor.

Concentration of property ownership showed there had been only a slight fall since pre-war days. In 1911 the top 1 per cent owned 69 per cent; now it was down to 56 per cent. The period saw a rise in the middle-class salary earner. If one takes average income, only 1.2 per cent earned more than £10 a week, 73.5 per cent got under £4 and 35.7 per cent under £2 10s, or to put it another way, 18 million earned less than £250 a year in 1938. Regressive taxation meant that only 5.6 per cent of wealth was redistributed through tax at this time. Indirect taxes rose while income tax had its top rates frozen as exemption limits were lowered to include more.

D2. Extending Social Insurance

However much some Tories opposed the idea, a welfare state continued to grow. The range of unemployment benefits which kept in line with the cost of living was one example. The various forms of pensions were extended to increasing numbers, and were further widened by an Act in 1937. Limited health and accident insurance was available on a national basis, and the numbers involved in both schemes increased by more than two million during the period. But the situation could be criticised because it had parted from the insurance principle and it had not been made clear what new principle it was proceeding on. As a result 'the social services left many gaps where people crouched unprotected', and the greatest extremes of poverty were still found in old age. Above all, health insurance did not provide free treatment for dependants, and the hospital system was expensive and confused. Although £2m was raised in 1937 alone by voluntary donations, it was clear for years that a national hospital service was vital. The government ignored a BMA proposal for a General Medical Service, and the Cathcart Committee (1936), and appointed the Sankey Commission on voluntary hospitals instead (1937).

D3. National Government Reforms

Although practising economies and restricted by traditional economic doctrines, the National Governments achieved a wide range of reforms due to the influences of Liberals and 'middle way' ministers, and to Chamberlain's support. The main changes were:

(a) *Road traffic laws.* Road deaths were running at 6,000 a year, and economies prevented proper road building. Stanley and Hore Belisha were responsible for a range of measures carried in 1933–34. These included classification of roads, coordinated sets of road signs, traffic lanes, speed limits, pedestrian crossings, roundabouts, Belisha beacons, silent zones after 11.30 pm, rear lights, driving tests, 30 mph speed limits, one-way streets, compulsory windscreen wipers and dipping of headlights.

(b) *Education.* Capital expenditure cuts held up progress, but substantial moves were made to cut all-age schools and the size of classes. Between 1924 and 1939 the number of classes over 50 fell from 25,000 to 2,000. Reorganisation under Hadow proceeded so that by 1938, 63.5 per cent had been covered. In 1936 an Education Act raised the school leaving age to 15 in September 1939. One fifth of university entrants were from elementary schools—a narrow ladder up existed.

(c) *Young criminals.* In 1933 the Children's and Young Persons Act transferred remand homes to education authorities, and introduced approved schools. In 1938 the Cadogan Report advocated the scrapping of corporal punishment, particularly for young offenders. Hoare brought forward the Criminal Justice Bill, but it was suspended when war started.

(d) *Housing policy.* The Tories phased out council building, and were unwilling to accept much planning. However, a series of Acts paved the way for slum clearance, the most important being in 1933 and 1935. Some 266,851 slums were demolished, and overcrowding cut by a quarter by 1939. Authorities were required to draw up reports on overcrowding, and given grants for building high-density replacement flats. The country had 90,000 more cheap houses than families in 1939, but the slums and overcrowding remained.

(e) *Industrial legislation.* The Shops Act (1934) came into force in 1936, replacing the 1910 Act and introducing the 48-hour week. The Factory Act of 1937 replaced the 1901 Tory measure, scrapped the distinction of factory and workshop, introduced regulations on safety, fire, ventilation, heating, lighting, washing and cloakroom facilities. Women and young persons were limited to a 48-hour week. The Holidays with Pay Act (1938) encouraged trades boards to introduce them, and was to be compulsory after three years.

(f) *Social legislation.* The Divorce Act (1937) was the first since 1857 and allowed desertion and insanity as causes for divorce after three years. The Public Health Act (1936) and the Food and Drugs Act (1938) replaced Disraeli's legislation. The Physical Training Act (1937) empowered councils to acquire land for playing fields. The Hire Purchase (1938) and Building Societies (1939) Acts were partially to help the consumer.

D4. Standard of Living

What Marwick calls 'the sociology of progress' tried to provide statistical coverage of social problems, but as in all periods of history this proved difficult. Branson and Heinemann admit that 'statistics of wages and cost of living were quite inadequate'. Moreover, at times when classes were so disparate and extremes of poverty and wealth existed, average figures were not always of great value. As in most periods, some figures showed improvement and others reflected grave social problems.

(a) *Wages.* Productivity increased sharply in the thirties and much of this was reflected in increased profits. However, allowing for reductions in hours, there was a rise in real wages slowly to 1932, a pause until 1935, and then a steady rise to 1939.

(b) *The poverty line.* Rowntree's new standard was 53s a week for a man, wife and three children. This was a bare minimum. In York he found (1936) 31.1 per cent of the working class (17.8 per cent of the population) below that line. The three main causes were unemployment, old age and low wages.

(c) *Nutrition.* In 1936 Boyd Orr's survey divided the population into six groups. Only 30 per cent according to him had a balanced diet, while 10 per cent (4½ million) were deficient in all respects.

(d) *Health.* Overall figures indicated considerable improvements, with falls in death, infant and maternal mortality rates, and improvement in life expectancy. But the inadequacies of health provision, slum conditions and unemployment meant that in some classes matters were deplorable, and even getting worse. Thus, figures like death rates and infant mortality in depressed areas were twice as bad as those outside.

In all respects much remains to be done before an authoritative assessment of conditions in the thirties can be made.

E. The Changing Face of England

The 1930s produced good descriptive writing about the condition of England, which reflected two moods. One seemed unaware of change. It is brought out in Morton's works *The Call of England* and *I Saw Two Englands*, which are almost entirely set in an old-world atmosphere of country cottages and humble servants. Some who described the same scenes were able to impart a sharper edge. Macdonnell in *England their England* (1933) showed social consciousness, and Moore's *Portrait of Elmbury* (1945) commented on the late thirties as an Indian Summer when Tewkesbury 'seemed to grow old and slumbrous and apathetic'. Orwell took matters a stage further in his classic of descriptive journalism—*The Road to Wigan Pier*— describing a different country. Priestley's *English Journey* aimed to give a more realistic account of industrial England. He scoffed at 'Old England, the country and the cathedrals and minsters, and manor houses and inns, parson and squire, guide book, and quaint highways and byways', and wrote of 'a cynically devastated countryside, sooty dismal little towns, and still sootier grim fortress-like cities'.

This paradox was possible because the advance of the scientific agents that would end the old England—the motorcar, electricity and scientific farming—and the social conditions that would eliminate it—classlessness, welfare provisions and state intervention—were both in their growing stages. It was still possible to choose one England or the other. But the message of the thirties was that conditions unchanged since the Middle Ages were about to undergo a major upheaval.

E1. The Old Order

Gunther spoke of a 'fluid and impregnable ruling class' and outwardly at least Britain remained in the hands of a narrow, largely landed, upper class, whose background was public school and Oxbridge and who regarded the Houses of Parliament as one of their clubs (Chapter 9, C2). As Orwell said, 'A foreign observer sees only the huge inequalities of wealth, the unfair electoral system, the governing class control over press, radio and education, and concludes that democracy is simply a polite name for dictatorship.' Britain was a guided democracy where the politics of deference still held good; to succeed, as Gunther said, 'one must be to the country house born'. In Morton's *A London Year* in 1933 he spoke of a London season that 'revolves around the royal courts', and the thirties were the last time in British history when a rich governing class displayed wealth without concern. One quarter of the working women in the country were still servants. Political receptions in places like Londonderry House and weekends at Cliveden were still central to the political scene, as MacDonald found out. Literature catered for interest in the upper classes, and public school stories were read avidly in comics by starving urchins in the East End.

E2. Other Englands

Priestley saw four Englands: the old-world one, the people on the dole, the nineteenth-century one in industrial towns, and a new England which he did not like, saying it 'is simply a trumpery imitation of something not very good even in the original'. Orwell found himself faced with the same distinctions, and ended up not liking any of them. He denounced traditional England as 'the most class-ridden country under the sun ... ruled largely by the old and the silly'. He criticised the England of the dole and the industrial cities, where 'you lose yourself in labyrinths of little brick houses blackened by smoke, festering in planless chaos round miry alleys and little cindered yards where there are stinking dustbins and lines of grimy washing and half ruinous lavatories'. But he also took up the theme of a new England 'in the light industry areas along the arterial roads', and in *Coming up for Air* (1939) criticised life there as 'a civilisation in which children grow up with an intimate knowledge of magnetos and in complete ignorance of the Bible'. The people who lived there he described as an 'indeterminate stratum'; in other words, they were a new 'classless' class and still did not meet with his approval. He condemned the 'naked democracy of the swimming pool', and his criticism was an echo of Priestley's dislike of 'the England of arterial and by-pass roads, of filling stations, and factories that look like exhibition buildings, of giant cinemas and dance halls and cafés, bungalows with tiny garages, cocktail bars, Woolworths, motor coaches, wireless, hiking, factory girls that look like actresses, greyhound racing and dirt tracks, swimming pools, and everything given away for cigarette coupons'. In this list Priestley was attacking the synthetic mass-produced society in which everything and everybody was like the real thing, but at the same time he was descrying the rising standard of living and the products which were being used by a large number of people. Orwell and Priestley reflected the paradox of a theory that wished to give working men more, and yet provide a larger state to spend it for them; which wanted to liberate the working class and groaned when it resorted to cinemas. There was also an element of more traditional dislike for industrial society and therefore of technical progress. As the music hall was replaced by the gramophone, the argument went, things were not what they were, nor so genuine. It was an argument that twentieth-century technical change was constantly to renew, and it began in the 1930s.

E3. Skegness is so Bracing

This paradox is apparent when considering the use people make of the environment. During the 1930s car and motorcycle ownership combined with cheap coach trips to make the ordinary person more mobile than at any previous time. A Morris Minor cost £100. A Raleigh bicycle cost £5. As a result there was a new awareness of the countryside, and within a few years there were complaints that the countryside was fast disappearing under the rucksacks of new tourists. The interest in outdoors took two main forms:

(*a*) Attempts to revive village life. Its most remarkable expression was the Village Centres in Cambridgeshire, founded by Henry Morris in 1930, of which there were 11 by 1939. Women's Institutes, founded in 1915, grew in numbers. The Young Farmers' Clubs started in 1921. In 1926 came the Council for the Preservation of Rural England.

(*b*) Holidays in the open air. The caravan, invented by Hay Moulder in 1919, provided one sort of holiday. Following the German example, hiking became popular. In 1930 the Youth Hostels movement began and by 1939 there were

297 hostels. Holiday camps started, and in 1937 Skegness saw the first Butlin's camp. By 1939 there were more than 100.

This growth of interest in leisure produced a fresh impetus to planning. The Town and Country Planning Association, led by F. J. Osborn, began to relate planning of towns to use of land and provision of houses and factories to good open spaces and entertainment facilities. It was logical, and became typical of the twentieth century. One book emphasised the new mood by saying, 'We must plan for the leisure that is sheer fun ... as well as the leisure which is creative. We must plan for the people who want to be alone and for the people who want to meet in crowds.' The coming war would provide every opportunity for planners to conceive a new Britain.

Further Reading

Bruce, M., *The Coming of the Welfare State*, Batsford, London, 1965.

Branson, N., and Heinemann, M., *Britain in the Thirties*, Weidenfeld and Nicolson, London, 1971, available as Panther paperback, 1973.

Cross, C., *The Fascists in Britain*, Barrie and Rockcliff, London, 1961.

Gilbert, B. B., *British Social Policy 1914–1939*, Batsford, London, 1970.

Gilbert, B. B., *The Evolution of National Insurance in Britain*, Michael Joseph, London, 1966.

Graves, R., and Hodge, A., *The Long Week End; a social history of Britain between the wars*, Faber and Faber, London, 1950.

Harrison, J., *The Reactionaries*, Victor Gollancz, London, 1966.

Marwick, A., *Britain in the Century of Total War*, Bodley Head, London, 1968.

Mowat, C. L., *Britain Between the Wars 1918–1940*, Methuen, London, 1955.

Pelling, H., *The History of the British Communist Party*, Black, London, 1958.

Questions

1. Why can the 1930s be seen as 'the dawn of modern Britain'?
2. How left was politics and culture in the 1930s?
3. What is the evidence for poverty and prosperity in the 1930s?
4. What is meant by the term 'the middle way' in politics?
5. How do you explain the rise of mass or popular culture in the 1930s?
6. Why are the thirties the most controversial decade in modern history?

11

EMPIRE AND COMMONWEALTH: 1923–39

Between the wars the Empire seemed to be secure. Apart from the surrender of Wei-Hai-Wei (Chapter 7, H1) there were no territorial losses, although independence was conceded to Ireland, Iraq and Egypt with considerable safeguards. The Empire continued to grow, with extensions over the Gulf Arab states and Pacific Islands. The last annexation of the Phoenix Islands took place in 1937. With post-war mandates (Chapter 4, A1) treated like colonies, total land area clearly increased. Some colonies like Malta and Cyprus lost limited powers of self-government and even a dominion, Newfoundland, was demoted to a colony. According to Cross, 'British rule rested primarily on consent', and in view of the small number of troops and the muddled imperial defence policy, this was certainly true. In India in May 1940 there were only 39,000 troops. From a total colonial population of 62 million only 13,000 troops were raised to add to a small regular army. Apart from Palestine, Britain was faced with no widespread opposition in her colonial territories. Little wars continued like those in Iraq, Somaliland and Waziristan, and in 1939 'the colonial empire looked as if it were a permanent institution'. Churchill thought it might last a thousand years.

It was the calm before the storm. The critics of the Empire were gathering strength. In the Labour Party Laski and Brockway were starting to work with representatives of native opinion. In spite of claims that the Empire was an economic unit, it was also an economic burden. There was more investment by Britain in Argentina than in the whole colonial Empire. There was a net inflow of settlers to Britain. The colonies received only a quarter of their imports from Britain and sent only a third of their exports there in spite of colonial preference. Defence of the Empire involved Britain in major theatres of war throughout the globe, but the Empire itself was unwilling to work out a common policy or pay for a better one. In 1940 it was 'ill defended and immensely vulnerable' and Italy and Japan were able to seize territories during the war. India, where £438m was invested, was an economic asset, although its defence would cost a £1m a week during the war. However, in 1935 the Government of India Act made it clear for the first time that a non-white race was heading for full self-government. Trouble stirred in Burma.

The Empire did not attract large numbers of devoted workers. There were only 60,000 white men in the whole African empire, while in India the Civil Service was Indianised by 1939 and there was a short fall in English recruits. There is little evidence of exploitation; rather the reverse, of indulgent policies that brought little gain. Colonial policy favoured the natives (Chapter 4, A2) and it was only in dominions like Australia and South Africa that discrimination existed. The Colonial Office was never regarded as a key government post; nor was the newly created Dominions Office. Apart from Leopold Amery and Malcolm MacDonald no important political figure held the post.

Within the Tory party there was plenty of imperialist sentiment; 48 directors of Empire companies and 79 ex-soldiers and colonial administrators sat on the Tory benches. Lord Lloyd, Page Croft and Churchill could always rouse the constituencies on colonial matters, and when Baldwin listened to proposals for colonial appeasement of Germany, he ran into difficulty during 1936. Although Baldwin denied such talk in February, a motion put down in July obtained 118 signatures, and when Hoare tried to stifle opposition at the annual conference he was defeated. But proposals for colonial cession continued, and formed part of the Wilson Memorandum proposals in July 1939. It is not surprising that Ribbentrop once referred to 'your ramshackle Empire'. Moreover, it was the Tories in the Balfour Declaration (1926) and the Statute of Westminster (1931) who evolved dominion status, which amounted to independence, and when Ireland chose to carry her stand even further, signed a treaty in 1938 recognising the changes. Talk about imperial unity became 'a rubble of negative platitude' by the Imperial Conference of 1937. In an important colonial history published in 1929, Newton and Ewing said 'the prevailing impression left on our minds would be one of disintegration' unless more tangible factors were taken into account. But these did not amount to a policy for preserving the Empire. On the contrary, it was during this period that the stage was set for the loss of the Empire after 1945.

A. The Heyday of the Colonial Empire

A1. Imperial Façade

The British public, if they were aware of the Empire, were reassured that it was unchanging and successful. The most famous occasion was the British Empire Exhibition (1924–25), which cost £11m and covered 220 acres including Wembley Stadium. The monarchy was used to create an aura of imperial splendour as tribal chiefs made submissions and colonials struggled with top hats in the burning sun while the Prince of Wales was visiting. It was significant that when George VI wished to visit India for a durbar, the government would not agree and sent him to America instead. Royal occasions like the Coronation were used to give an impression of vast colonial contingents, whereas the reality of power was different. The BBC had an Empire programme (1932), and the Empire Marketing Board hired Grierson to make films like *Song of Ceylon*. The young had Empire Day at school, the Boy Scouts ($3\frac{1}{2}$ million by 1940), the *Boys' Own Paper* and the traditional novelists to read. Adults had the cinema, where a flood of imperialist films were shown.

A2. Imperial Reality

There was a powerful Empire well worth having, as both Mussolini and Hitler made plain. The navy was a world peace-keeping force. There was an all-red cable route and world communications were primarily British ones. There were a number of imperial air routes (India was reached in 1928) and world shipping, both passenger and merchant, was largely in British hands. The gold standard and subsequently the sterling area were important, and the network of insurance and banking, centred on London, yielded rich dividends. The Colonial Service contained many examples of officials who gave their lives to develop countries. Of the 34 governors in 1922, 19 were professionals rather than figureheads. A number of organisations had grown up to foster links. From 1924 to 1931 there was an Empire Marketing Board. In 1928 an Imperial Economic Committee was set up. A number of organisations continued to develop, like the Imperial Agricultural Research Council (1927), together with a range of humanitarian bodies like the London School of Tropical Medicine. There was also a range of societies like the Imperial Institute, and the British Empire Society that existed to stimulate interest, and chairs in imperial history existed in most universities. It would be wrong to deny some homogeneity to the Empire, but it was less than the propaganda claimed.

A3. The British in the Middle East

(a) *Treaty of Lausanne and Turkish relations.* By 1923 the distribution of mandates in the Middle East was settled (Chapter 4, A5), but events in Turkey (Chapter 4, C5) meant that Sèvres would have to be replaced by a new treaty which would not disturb the existing settlement. Lord Curzon was able to play the rôle of a latter-day Disraeli in achieving this at Lausanne. Although agreement was reached in January 1923 for the League to supervise the transfer of populations between Turkey and Greece, the conference came close to collapse because the Turkish delegate was influenced by the Russian delegate. Curzon proceeded by a mixture of threats and bluffs to secure agreement. The French were anxious to retain some capitulations and territory for Syria, but Curzon would not support them. By the time he left, the essentials were worked out, and the treaty was signed in July 1923. It was the first example of successful treaty revision, and its terms were favourable to Turkey. They included the return of Eastern Thrace to Turkey, including Adrianople, a demilitarised zone round the Straits, and the abolition of the capitulations, reparations and disarmament. The treaty ensured that although Turkey continued to be pro-Russian, it did not succumb to pressure for control of the Straits. Good relations with Turkey were maintained by a series of settlements:

(i) *Mosul.* After threats of war and League intervention, a settlement was reached in Britain's favour in 1926, and it was ceded to Iraq.

(ii) *The Straits.* In 1936 the Montreux Conference agreed to allow the Straits to be fortified.

Kemal was a nationalist and a dictator, and therefore found much to sympathise with in Russia and Germany. Although fear of Italian activity produced a Balkan Pact in 1934, Turkey was unwilling to be draw into an anti-German position. In 1938 there was a commercial treaty with Britain, followed by an Anglo-Turkish Agreement in May, 1937.

(b) *Relations with the independent states.*

(i) *Persia.* Britain was reluctant to surrender her powers under the 1907 agreement, particularly with a Bolshevik threat. In 1921 Persia signed a treaty with Russia, Reza Khan repudiated the 1907 treaty favouring Britain. In 1925 he deposed the Shah and took power. Following Kemal's example, he abolished all extra-territorial rights in May 1928. In November 1932 he withdrew the 1909 concession to the Anglo-Persian Oil Company and Britain went to the League, which produced a settlement in May 1933 by which the concession was to last to 1993, and Persia got £750,000 a year (Chapter 16, E2).

(ii) *Iraq.* In 1922 a treaty was signed between Feisal and Britain, but it was in constant process of revision. A new treaty in 1926 proved unsatisfactory and in 1930 Britain agreed to independence in return for a defence agreement. In 1932 she supported Iraq's entry to the League, but retained bases.

(iii) *Egypt.* After the troubles of 1924 (Chapter 4, A4) relations remained poor. King Faud and, after 1936, King Farouk were regarded as pro-British, while the Wafd stirred up trouble. Lord Lloyd used battleships on occasion, but was recalled in 1929. In 1930 Fuad tried one-man rule, but in 1934–35 was forced to restore the constitution. The Wafd demanded a new treaty and, worried by Italian policy, the British agreed in August 1936. It provided that: British military occupation was to end, but garrisons were to withdraw to a zone round the Suez Canal; Britain was to have the right to re-occupation in time of war; and the treaty was to last for 20 years.

In May 1937 all capitulations were abolished and Egypt entered the League. With all three countries Britain was still the paramount power, but her authority was weakened by 1939, and Mussolini and Hitler had schemes for occupying the Middle East.

(c) *The new colonies.*

(i) *Cyprus* was made a colony in 1925. In spite of rapid improvements, a demand for *enosis*, or union, with Greece developed. In 1931 there were riots and deportations. After a short interval the constitution was restored, and by 1941 political parties were permitted.

(ii) *Malta* had been granted responsible government in 1921. Two parties appeared: the Nationalists, who were strongly Catholic and pro-Mussolini, and the Constitutionalists. A row over the status of Italian occurred, and in 1930 the bishops condemned the government. After an attempt to murder the Constitutionalist leader the constitution was suspended. Agreement was reached in 1932 and the Nationalists took office. Furher riots occurred, and the constitution was suspended in 1933. In 1936 Malta again became a crown colony, and in 1938 a new constitution was drawn up.

(iii) *Aden.* Britain had occupied Aden in 1839, and won over the desert chieftains like Bahrein and Qatar. Between 1936 and 1939 Harold Ingrams signed a series of treaties that extended British rule over a wide area, and in 1937 Aden was separated from the protectorate and made a colony.

A4. The Palestine Question

Britain had no difficulty with the Transjordan part of her Palestine mandate. Coxe and Kirkbride developed the country. In 1928 independence under conditions was recognised and in 1939 responsible government was introduced. But in Palestine matters were unsatisfactory.

(a) *The Wailing Wall Riots.* Palestine prospered, supported by the pro-Zionist, Amery. Restrictions on Jews by USA and Poland caused a rise in immigrants, and in 1929 there were riots in Jerusalem. The League criticised Britain in June 1930 for failing in her mandatory duties. This encouraged the Arabs, led by Haj Amin, the Grand Mufti. When a round table conference was proposed in December 1930 the Arabs declined it.

(b) *The increase of immigration.* Trouble increased, particularly after Hitler seized power. In three years 134,500 Jews entered the country, which was still poor and depressed as a result of the fall of cereal prices. The Jews built Tel

Aviv, kibbutzim and 133 new factories, but the Arabs resented their presence. The British proposed responsible government, but the Arabs refused.

(c) *The Arab Rebellion.* In 1936 a general strike developed into an uprising. In July 1937 the Peel Commission proposed independence within 10 years, and partition. In the summer rebellion started again, martial law was introduced and the Grand Mufti deposed. Peace was restored in May 1939.

(d) *Restriction and partition.* The Jews reacted to the Arab threat by forming an illegal army (*Haganah*) organised by Jabotinsky and Orde Wingate. A fact-finding mission was sent out and in July 1938 the Evian Conference met to consider giving Jews homelands elsewhere. Only Dominica offered to increase numbers, so Britain was left with a problem. The Peel Report was condemned by the League (August 1937) so Britain tried again, but in 1939 a conference failed.

(e) *The MacDonald White Paper, May 1939.* This was moderate but it clearly went back on the 1922 Churchill White Paper. It proposed 25,000 at once and 10,000 a year for five years, and then no more. The Arabs were placated just in time, but the Jews were furious. In June 1939 the League rejected it. The action of the Mufti in forming an Arab SS Commando and touring concentration camps kept the Jews loyal to Britain in the early part of the war when a German victory would have been dangerous. After El Alamein their attitude changed (Chapter 18, B1).

A5. Trouble and Progress in the Colonies

The inter-war period saw two important developments in colonial policy:

(a) Conception of function. Lugard's *The Dual Mandate* (1922) stressed that the ownership of colonies implied support for native interests, and the Mandates Commission emphasised this trusteeship idea. The Ormsby Gore Reports on East and West Africa (1924, 1926) accepted this rôle for the colonial power. In 1925 a Colonial Conference to develop education policy was held, and the same year the first African university was founded at Achimota College.

(b) Economic development. This began with the Colonial Development Fund (1929) and led to the Colonial Development Act (1940). Money spent rose so that the African colonies received £4m by 1938.

Conditions varied from one part of the colonies to the other, but three important developments deserve attention. In Asia the rise of Japan and the activities of the Communists stimulated Asian nationalism. A Malayan Communist party began in 1930 and soon afterwards spread to Burma. As India advanced to self-government, this had an effect on surrounding areas. In Ceylon, fresh demands led to the Donoughmore Commission and a new constitution in 1931 providing internal dominion status. It was the first constitution to give an Asian people (male and female) the vote, and it worked well. In Burma a new constitution separated the country from India in 1937 with a system of dyarchy. Aung San formed a Freedom Bloc and in 1939 riots in Mandalay indicated a new trend.

The area which suffered most from British colonial policy was the West Indies which, although the colonies had representative government by 1936, did not progress economically. Indentures were not abolished until 1917, and in 1937–38 there were riots in Jamaica and Trinidad, caused by distress brought about by low sugar prices. The Moyne Commission (1938) was not published in full in 1940 because it might embarrass the government. It revealed half the population to be illiterate, stressed that diseases like hookworm were widespread and that housing conditions were 'indescribable'. It is not surprising that in this area Marcus Garvey's United Negro Association was able to link their discontent to that in the Southern states and start the growth of black nationalism.

By contrast, Africa was peaceful and could show many successful examples of colonial rule. In Tanganyika, for example, Sir Donald Cameron (1925) was able to develop the colony while in Kenya local native councils (1924) and native reserves (1926) ensured the white settlers would not have it all their own way. Only in Southern Rhodesia did policy veer towards a different line when in 1923, after a referendum on joining South Africa had been lost, the government conceded internal dominion status. In 1938 the Bledisloe Commission put forward the idea of a federation with Nyasaland and Northern Rhodesia, but the British government did not favour a settler policy. In West Africa the Gold Coast made most progress, and Hailey's *African Survey* (1938) charted improvements like combating soil erosion in Tanganyika, or sleeping sickness in Nigeria. But there were signs of discontent, including strikes in the Rhodesia copper mines and among the cocoa workers of the Gold Coast. Africa slumbered, but not for much longer.

B. British Raj in India

B1. General Conditions

India was the linchpin of the Empire—it contained 75 per cent of its population. Besides their own army there were 160,000 natives but there was no air force, and only a small navy. The India Office in London had only 432 civil servants, and the main burden of administration fell on the ICS. Education was poor, with only 2 per cent speaking English and 10 per cent literate. About 2,000 went to England for higher education, and it was from this tiny minority that the demand for a Hindu and then a Moslem India developed.

India prospered under British rule. Its population rose from 214 million in 1891 to 352 million in 1931 as a result of famine control; 30 million acres were irrigated, more than any other country except the USA; industrial development made India the seventh industrial power by 1939. Outwardly at least the British seemed to imagine they would stay. Missionaries worked on. There were 6 million Christians and a new Anglican cathedral rose at Delhi. Delhi's new imperial capital was opened in 1931. But with the British accounting for only 630 out of 5,500 civil servants and only 600 out of 187,000 police, the writing was on the wall. Government policy throughout the period was directed towards accepting this fact.

B2. The Simon Commission and the Irwin Declaration

Control of India lay with the Secretary of State. Birkenhead and Peel (1924–29) did not advocate change, but Wedgwood Benn (1929–31), with Sir Samuel Hoare (1931–35), pursued a bi-partisan policy. The Viceroys' policy varied from conciliation to repression in order to achieve the worst of both worlds. Lord Reading was followed by Lord Irwin (1926–31), later Lord Halifax, Lord Willingdon (1931–36), who had previous experience as Governor of Bombay and Madras and was a Liberal, and Lord Linlithgow

(1936–42). None of them exerted a decisive influence, and this illustrates Barnett's argument that the governing class had run out of steam.

After Gandhi was released (Chapter 4, A3), the Nationalists won the elections of 1926 and demands for *swaraj* developed from dominion status to complete independence in the Nehru Report (August 1928). The government appointed the Simon Commission earlier than it need have done to investigate the working of dyarchy. It arrived in February 1928 and was boycotted by Congress. Its members, according to Medlicott, were of little eminence although they included Attlee, and its report in June 1930 was brushed aside by MacDonald. But the decision to propose fully responsible provincial self-government had aroused new forces. In January 1929 Ali Jinnah had urged a federal India in order to protect Moslems from the Hinduism of Congress. Riots broke out in 1929. Then after a visit to London, Irwin returned and proclaimed in October 'that the natural issue of India's constitutional progress ... is the attainment of dominion status'. The government had advanced further than the Simon Commission, but not far enough for Congress. In April 1930 Gandhi launched a new civil disobedience campaign with a march to Dandi, where he picked up salt from the beach. Some 60,000 were interned and the leaders of Congress arrested.

B3. The Round Table Conferences and the Indian White Paper

MacDonald and Wedgwood Benn sought agreement by means of conferences:

(*a*) The first Round Table Conference (November 1930) discussed and agreed on an Indian federation, but Congress boycotted its meetings.

(*b*) Second Round Table Conference (September–December 1931). Gandhi attended and demanded a constitution that the Moslems, Untouchables and Princes rejected. On his return to India he resumed civil disobedience. Willingdon interned him.

(*c*) Third Round Table Conference (November–December 1932). Without Congress the government completed its proposals.

In March 1933 a White Paper gave details. Interest in Indian affairs had risen since the Simon Report and opposition had grown. Baldwin tried to head this off by a Joint Select Committee, but Churchill and Lloyd George unwisely refused to sit, saying it was packed. A motion condemning the committee was lost by 209–118, which was the lowest National Government majority. Rival organisations were set up to plead the case. Hoare's Under-Secretary, Butler, organised 'Union of Britain and India', and the opposition an 'Indian Defence Committee'. But in spite of spirited attacks at party conferences, Baldwin carried the day, and in December 1934 the White Paper was endorsed. By this time the Moslems were alarmed, and in 1934 Jinnah became their leader. The British were able to use Moslems and Princes to reduce Congress demands for independence under their exclusively Hindu regime.

B4. Government of India Act, July 1935

The main aim was to establish complete responsible government and autonomy in the 11 provinces; in other words, it carried out the Simon Report. The chief parts of the act were:

(*a*) The number of provinces was increased from eight to 11, each with a responsible legislature elected by a widened franchise.

(*b*) At national level the legislature was to be chosen by indirect election from the provincial assemblies, and to sit for five years. The Council of State was to be elected by a restricted electorate of 100,000.

(*c*) Each house was to include representatives of the Princes and they would choose their own electoral method.

(*d*) Dyarchy extended to central government with responsible ministers, except for certain reserved subjects and an ultimate viceregal vote.

Elections took place affecting some 30 million voters. Congress obtained a majority in six of the 11 provinces. Linlithgow urged Congress to co-operate, but after a confused period they opted out in 1939, forcing the governors to resume direct rule. In those provinces like the Punjab and Scinde, which carried out the act, it worked well. But it fell short of complete independence. India was quiet but restive in 1939.

C. Development of Dominion Status

Dominion status and the idea of the Commonwealth had developed just after the war (Chapter 4, A2) and the most important imperial development between the wars was the creation of a White Commonwealth. It was not intended to be exclusively for the colonies of settlement, although this affected the decision to give Southern Rhodesia a seat at imperial conferences while Ceylon, with similar internal status, did not receive one. The intention of the India Act was that when the Princes joined the central legislature, a responsible cabinet would be set up and the Viceroy replaced by a governor general. But since this did not take place, the Commonwealth was essentially a white man's club in the period to 1939.

This did not make for harmony, since the four dominions (Canada, Australia, New Zealand and South Africa) made imperial unity difficult. Indeed, only New Zealand showed unreserved support for the British government at times like the Abdication Crisis or Munich. South Africa embarked on internal racial policies in 1936 which conflicted with the idea of trusteeship elsewhere in Africa. Herzog's ultimate aim was a republic; held then to be incompatible with common allegiance. Canada's selfish regard prevented a common defence policy from being created. Ireland by 1937 had broken the conventions of dominion status and become the Republic of Eire. In economic policy the dominions resisted imperial preference except where it benefited them (Chapter 9, B3). The Ottawa Treaty was of limited use, and in 1937 Canada insisted on replacing it with a bilateral treaty.

Constitutionally, dominion status created large, but mainly academic problems. The dominions were to all intents and purposes independent nations by 1939. Because they were colonies of settlement, their characteristics and sympathies were still with the Mother Country, but these would weaken (Chapter 18, F1). When war was declared in 1939 these differences appeared for the first time. Australia, New Zealand and India went to war simultaneously. Canada waited a week. Ireland proclaimed neutrality. In South Africa war was declared only after a political crisis. During the war India rebelled, and Australia withdrew her troops from the North African theatre. In some ways the British Commonwealth resembled the old Holy Roman Empire; it was becoming a political mirage (Chapter 18, F1).

C1. The Dominions Secretary

The disputes of the 1923 Imperial Conference and the determination of the dominions to pursue separate foreign policies led to the creation of the Dominions Secretary in 1925, but the way in which the post was treated and the ministers who held it reveal the muddled thinking and low priority given by Britain to the most vital issue affecting the continuance of the Empire. It was often combined with the Colonial Office and the National Government left it in the hands of the Labour men Thomas and Mac-Donald or the incompetent Inskip.

C2. The Balfour Declaration, 1926

Division between the dominions occurred over the signing of Locarno (Chapter 7, D1). Australia and New Zealand wanted to sign, but Canada and South Africa did not. Ireland, under the 1921 treaty, had the option but supported Canada, who had already declared she was bound only 'legally and technically' by the Treaty of Lausanne. Balfour devised the Declaration for the Imperial Conference of 1926 to paper over the cracks. It said:

'They [Great Britain and the Dominions] are autonomous communities within the British Empire equal in status in no way subordinate one to another in any aspect of their domestic or external affairs, though united by a common allegiance to the Crown, and freely associated as members of the British Commonwealth of Nations.'

This declaration was astonishing. It ignored the need for a common imperial policy in defence and economic matters without which an Empire could not be said to exist. In several ways dominion rights to pass laws or conduct their judicial affairs were still limited. However, the declaration enabled Britain, in Cross's words 'to embark upon an era of self-deception and self-flattery'. In 1927 Britain decided that Labrador should go to Newfoundland and not to Canada, and in 1934 abrogated Newfoundland's status altogether. But with the four main dominions, such acts were not possible. There were rows over the status of the governor general. The dominions wanted them appointed by the dominion government, and not on the advice of the British government. In 1927 Hertzog got round this by 'making submission' of his choice which the British Prime Minister then advised the King to accept. In 1929 Australia chose Lord Reading. George V refused, but the Imperial Conference of 1930 resolved that the King should act 'on the advice of His Majesty's ministers in the dominion concerned'.

C3. Statute of Westminster, 1931

The continuance of difficulties led to a Constitutional Conference in 1929 and from this emerged the Statute of Westminster which, like Indian policy, was bi-partisan. Although Balfour had said the Empire 'is not founded upon negations', the reality was otherwise. The Act's main provisions were:

(*a*) No law passed in the British parliament would have validity in a dominion without the consent of its parliament.

(*b*) The Colonial Laws Validity Act (1865) was abolished as far as the dominions were concerned. They were given full extra-territorial law-making powers.

(*c*) Colonies was to be a term that specifically excluded dominions.

The Act was followed by sweeping changes in Ireland and South Africa. It did not settle matters and an unofficial conference at Toronto in 1933 on Imperial Cooperation got nowhere. When the Abdication Crisis came, the dominions were able to influence Baldwin by declaring against Edward VIII. As King Hall said, by 1939 'the Empire remained a deeper mystery than ever', since the King could now be at war with himself if the dominions took different sides. Yet statesmen took pride in the confusion as typically British.

C4. The Last Imperial Conference

Although constitutional issues remained unresolved, the focus of interest in imperial matters shifted slowly to defence. The dominions supported appeasement and their armed forces were derisory. Canada, for example, was left with a regular army of 3,600 and a navy of six destroyers, and Australia with 29,000 troops and a navy of eight ships. Britain continued to bear the burden of defence. MacDonald prepared defence reviews for the 1937 conference, and tried to stir the dominions to action. In this he succeeded. Canada voted $35m for rearmament, New Zealand set up three boards to modernise the services and, after an Australian election on the issue, rearmament started there. South Africa confirmed the Smuts-Churchill Agreement of 1922 in 1937, and started to rearm. However, it was too little too late when Munich came. The menace of Japan appeared more serious to the southern dominions and in April 1939 the Wellington Conference was held on Pacific defence. It achieved nothing important. In South Africa there was considerable sympathy for the Nazis in the *Broederbond*, and in statements by Herzog. Although Churchill argued imperial support was decisive in 1940, others have said it was a defence burden of little use. In real terms the Empire was much weaker in 1939 than it was in 1914, and this after a period dominated by Conservative governments.

D. Irish Questions: 1924–39

D1. Baldwin and the Irish Free State

A number of points were left by the 1921 Treaty for future decision, and in 1924 a Commission was appointed to consider the final border settlement (Chapter 5, E4). Although it rejected a plebiscite its proposals, published in November 1925, included limited adjustments which were rejected by Dublin. Baldwin and Churchill worked on agreement with the new dominion by which, in return for allowing the boundary commission and the Council of Ireland to lapse, a financial settlement would be possible. The Churchill-Blythe Agreement (March 1926) provided that Ireland was relieved of its share in the National Debt. In return the Free State agreed to meet liability for war damage and increase compensation to Southern Unionists by 10 per cent, and pay £5m a year towards settlement of land annuities under the Irish Land Acts (1870–1903).

These agreements finally secured Northern Ireland, where the abolition of proportional representation and the Special Powers Act consolidated Protestant ascendancy. But in the South they increased government unpopularity. In 1927 O'Higgins was murdered, and in the election De-Valera's Fianna Fail party nearly won. His policy was to repeal the 1921 treaty and secure a republic, and he attracted the Irish Labour Party by supporting old age pensions. Under the impact of depression DeValera came to power in 1932.

D2. Attack on the Treaty

The Statute of Westminster seemed to open the way for dominion status which was more radical than that in the 1921 treaty. DeValera proceeded to destroy the treaty.

(a) *Political changes.* The Governor General was forced to resign in 1932. In 1933 an Act removing the oath of allegiance and the text of the Treaty from the constitution was passed after opposition from the Senate. Thomas, Dominions Secretary, was furious but was unable to stop the Act or a bill introduced the same year, and upheld by the Privy Council in June 1935, abolishing appeals from Ireland. In 1934 a bill abolished the Senate where Southern Protestants had seats, and this became law in May 1936. In 1935 the Nationality and Citizenship Act and the Aliens Act deprived the Irish of British citizenship, and made the British aliens.

(b) *Economic warfare.* In July 1932 the land annuities were withheld, collected separately by the Free State, halved in March 1935 and then incorporated in general taxation. DeValera offered to go to the Hague Court but Thomas refused, and threatened to demand Ireland's share in the National Debt (£400m). Duties of 20 per cent were imposed on Irish imports to which the Irish responded with duties on coal, cement, iron and steel. Then the British raised the duties to 40 per cent. Although limited agreements were made in December 1934 and February 1936 this tariff war was a bitter one. The £4.8m withheld was recouped by the tariffs.

D3. Republic of Eire

Reaction to DeValera's policy was mixed. In Northern Ireland it produced a statement from Lord Craigavon that Irish unity was now impossible. In the south the IRA was revived, and during 1933 there was even a proto-fascist movement called the Blue Shirts. But DeValera pressed on and used the abdication of Edward VIII to carry matters further. The Constitutional Amendment Act removed mention of the King except for purposes of 'external association'. In May 1937 the new constitution made Ireland a republican Roman Catholic state, and demanded a united Ireland. There was to be a new senate representing sectional interests. In December the constitution came into effect, and in June 1938 DeValera obtained a majority. During 1939 the IRA mounted a new campaign on the English mainland which included attacks in London, seaside towns and arms centres like Coventry.

D4. Irish Appeasement Treaty, April 1938

As in other parts of the Empire, the National Governments pursued appeasement when faced with nationalist opposition, and in 1938 Chamberlain secured agreement on the outstanding issues with Ireland. The treaty was a defeat for Britain against which Churchill protested in vain. The terms were:

(*a*) The trade war ended with reciprocal free trade subject to certain quotas.

(*b*) Britain surrendered claims to money owing under the Irish Land Acts.

(*c*) An annual payment was to be made by Ireland for war damage.

(*d*) All claims on Ireland for her share of the National Debt were scrapped in return for a lump sum of £10m.

(*e*) All military rights under the 1921 treaty (Chapter 5, E4) were abolished.

Further Reading

Barnett, C., *The Collapse of British Power*, Eyre Methuen, London, 1972.

Cross, C., *The Fall of the British Empire*, Hodder and Stoughton, London, 1968.

McIntyre, W. D., *Colonies into Commonwealth*, Blandford, London, 1966.

MacInnes, C., *Introduction to the Economic History of the British Empire*, Colston Research Society, Bristol, 1935.

Williamson, J. A., *The British Empire and Commonwealth*, Vol II, Macmillan, London, 1958.

Questions

1. Was the British Empire a source of strength or weakness to Britain by 1939?
2. Why was no effective imperial defence policy worked out between the wars?
3. What evidence is there of growing nationalism in the colonies prior to 1939?
4. What do you understand by the concept of 'trusteeship' in the Empire between the wars?
5. How did dominion status evolve? What were the limitations left by 1939?
6. Was British rule in the Middle East a successful example of British imperial policy between the wars?
7. Why were Anglo-Irish relations unsatisfactory after the settlement of 1921?

12

TOWARDS WAR—APPEASEMENT AND REARMAMENT: 1933–39

The period between Hitler taking office in January 1933 and the outbreak of war in September 1939 remains one of the most controversial in British foreign policy. This is because the causes of the war are themselves a matter of dispute, which makes an assessment of Britain's part in events more difficult. Traditionally, the war was seen as a logical consequence of fascism, since war was seen by Hitler as a necessary and virtuous end of policy. Thomson says, 'Hitler's dictatorship was devised to wage war.' *Mein Kampf* made clear German demands for *lebensraum* and Nazi hatred for Communism, while Mussolini made no secret of his ambitions in the Mediterranean and Africa. What is less certain is whether the war was planned by the dictators or was caused more by default on the part of the Western powers like Britain and France. Stalin's pact with Hitler in August 1939 must also be taken into account. Whereas in Churchill's account of the coming of war the outbreak is seen as calculated and logically determined, this view has been challenged ever since Taylor's work on the 'Origins' of the war in 1961. Hitler is now seen more as a brilliant opportunist, taking advantage of fascist methods to outwit the Western powers and Russia. Thus, in Thorne's words, 'the timing and circumstances had been to a certain extent fortuitous, the responsibility was not'.

Causation of an event like the Second World War is inevitably long-term and complex. Many see the war stemming from Versailles, which created bitterness among revisionist states like Germany and Russia while failing to control future aggressors. The large number of small semi-democratic states created in 1919 failed to fulfil the hopes of statesmen, and except in Czechoslovakia fell victims to right-wing regimes which easily succumbed to fascism. Collective security bears some of the blame. Locarno in the West and the Little Entente in the East both failed, and France as Europe's most powerful nation did not fulfil her military obligations due to internal weakness. The League proved to be a failure. Disarmament became one-sided, and revision of the penal clauses of Versailles gave Hitler the opportunity to recreate German nationalism in the 1930s. Fascism owed much to internal conditions in the countries concerned—to wounded war pride, conservatives forces, economic disruption and ineffective parliaments. The economic crisis of 1929–31 tipped the scales towards dictatorship. This was a European trend, and the war sprang from it. Blame for Britain's involvement in war should therefore be sparingly apportioned. Gilbert and Gott state that 'Much of the blame for the outbreak of World War II has been attributed to the appeasers in the British government during the 1930s', but although there were guilty men in the National Governments blame must be cast on broader shoulders.

The new diplomacy (Chapter 3, G4) and Lloyd George's policies in the post-war period (Chapter 4, B and C) may be seen initiating appeasement in the general sense of preferring compromise to war. During the 1920s all parties advocated disarmament, collective security and support for the League, and it was during this period that fateful decisions were taken (Chapter 7, A1–2). Indeed, as the 1930s advanced, rearmament developed, strongly backed by Chamberlain, and the appeasement practised after May 1937 when he became Prime Minister was a coherent policy aimed at filling the vacuum left by Baldwin. The public, too, bear some blame for what happened in Britain, as in Germany. Revulsion from the war and the growth of pacifist sentiment that shrank from war (Chapter 6, A7) received confirmation from the electorate in the 1930s (Chapter 9, A3), and reached its climax in the welcome to Chamberlain when he returned from Munich. It is true the Conservatives were in some cases favourable to fascists (Chapter 9, C3), but they also had an honourable rôle of opponents (Chapter 9, E4) while Labour and the Liberals, who most fervently backed disarmament and the League, were in a less enviable position. The left-wing charge in *Guilty Men* that 'the genesis of our military misfortunes must be dated at 1929' was too narrow. The National Governments embarked upon rearmament (Chapter 9, B6), and although they failed in some respects, 1940 would not have been possible without the work done prior to 1939. Governments often accused of indifference to human suffering were deflected from war until the last moment by fears of that very thing, and the creation of civil defence with $1\frac{1}{2}$ million members by September 1939 is something for which ordinary people should praise Chamberlain.

Appeasement was two things: a policy adopted with Chamberlain's narrow logic, and the general drift of British policy throughout the inter-war years. Barnett has demonstrated the collapse of imperial strategy, the end of naval primacy and the incompetence of the governing classes, which contributed to the public mood and the political parameters. But Britain was not alone. The weakness of France, Britain's main ally in the same period, has been sufficiently exposed by Shirer in *The Fall of the Third French Republic*. The dominions backed appeasement (Chapter 11, C4). America pursued isolationist policies and as late as November 1940, 80 per cent of Americans were against entering the war. Countries like Poland were themselves dictatorships, ruthless aggressors and persecutors of Jews. Russia made grand gestures, but her military strength was either feared or derided, and in the end she made possible the elimination of France and the near defeat of Britain in return for security in Eastern Europe, and promises of world-wide gains at the expense of capitalist nations. The widespread nature of appeasement and the measure of rearmament need to be taken into account when assessing the policies of the National Governments in the 1930s. In the end they made a terrifying and right decision whatever their hesitations on the way to Armageddon.

A. The Nature of Appeasement

A1. Traditional Argument

Guilty Men and Churchill had one thing in common: they both argued the causes of war should be sought in the period 1929–39. It was not difficult for them to do this since the left felt betrayed by MacDonald, and

could criticise him as they had been out of office since 1931, while Churchill
had left the Shadow Cabinet and felt free to criticise Baldwin. Both sides
carried the argument to extremes. In *Guilty Men* the Conservatives alone
were held to be blameworthy. The Tories were seen as sympathetic to
fascism because they tried for agreement, and as negligent in failing to
provide particularly for Norway in 1940. As Seaman says, 'Educated
people in Britain ... were slow to understand Hitler and Mussolini. They
were ready to admire both of them.' Churchill, who had praised Mussolini,
had no wish to pursue that line of argument. Instead, he concentrated on
condemnation of Baldwin, and accused him of putting party before
country and deceiving the electorate. This was a convenient way of avoiding his own Ten Year Rule, which was largely responsible for the parlous
state of armaments, and his actions as Chancellor, which had cut spending.
With the elections of 1945 and 1950 in mind, both Labour and Churchill
sought an explanation for the war in terms that exonerated themselves.

A2. Objectives

The view that appeasement was a disastrous Tory policy alone has the
support of Mowat and Seaman, but it is open to numerous objections.
Medlicott stresses that the economic situation and strategic implications
of war with the dictators need to be taken into account. The Western
nations were seriously affected by the Great Slump, and just as Britain was
climbing to a successful recovery, France had a Popular Front government
and left the gold standard. The short-term advantages of reducing unemployment and stimulating growth had to be weighed against the need to
import expensive raw materials and reluctance to disturb the recovering
economy. It was easier for the dictators than Baldwin or Chamberlain to
put guns before butter. At the time the left bitterly opposed the limited
measures, and when rearmament began in March 1935, Attlee said, 'We
believe that the policy here outlined is disastrous.' Baldwin was right to
say that a Tory pledge to build up armaments in the election of 1935 would
have spelled disaster. The government, moreover, yielded to false counsels.
Baldwin said, 'the bomber will always get through', and Chamberlain tried
to frighten the French with a lurid picture of Paris being bombed. There
was a genuine fear of the next war. The Imperial General Staff added their
expertise to this fear. In 1937 they forecast a 60-day attack with $1\frac{1}{4}$ million
casualties, and figures based on the bombing of Barcelona were said to
show 70 casualties for every ton of bombs. Coffins would cost £300,000 a
month.

The decision to rearm was taken in spite of universal opposition—for
Churchill tended only to be backed by the more Blimpish elements in the
Tory party. When Mowat says 'Strong action against Italy in December
1935, or against Germany in March 1936, might have prevented the Second
World War', he is accepting Churchill's argument that the dictators could
have been deterred: but only with adequate armaments, and these Britain
did not have. Baldwin and Chamberlain would have been foolish if they
had ignored the Defence Staff and gone to war in 1935 or 1936. As for the
suggestion of Shirer that war in 1938 'might well have proved fatal' to
Hitler because of a generals' plot, this is hard to sustain in view of the
generals' later actions. Britain did not have dominion support. Her naval

strength was threatened by Japan, Italy and Germany. She had no effective anti-aircraft defences. War in 1940 was a close-run thing; war in 1938 would have been a risk. It was only after Munich, the swing of public opinion and the assurance of adequate armaments that Chamberlain began to adopt a firmer line. The arguments for appeasement were stronger at the time than those against. Chamberlain argued concessions to Germany should be made to preserve peace, and rearmament would deter more widespread war. This was a viable policy—except for one factor: the nature of the fascist dictators themselves. Although the government was well informed on what happened in Germany, it chose to ignore the evidence, but in this it was followed by many others. Lloyd George described Hitler as 'the greatest living German'. Neither Churchill nor Eden were white as driven snow since Eden called for the appeasement of the whole world and Churchill in October 1937 declared himself content with the measure of rearmament. There was less logic and consistency in the voices calling for action than in Chamberlain's quieter voice calling for peace. As Medlicott says, 'the critics asked too much'.

A3. Reassessment

The roots of appeasement lay in the attitudes and misconceptions of the governing class between the wars, and were supported by the misconceived ideas of the opposition parties. War hatred and war fear, Christian morality, the public school ideals that led to false trust in Hitler as a man who kept his word, liberal ideals of world brotherhood and rational solutions to the world's problems and ignorance of Europe helped to create an atmosphere in which appeasement flourished. Business interests and sympathy for certain fascist ideals, combined with dislike of Communism and contempt for the Slav peoples of Eastern Europe, served to provide a good seed bed in the National Governments for conciliation of dictators. Detente with fascism was popular in the 1930s.

But the Spanish Civil War made the left aware that it too had problems in facing the dictators (Chapter 9, F5). In July 1937, Labour agreed to abstain in defence votes, but by then the damage was done. The policies advocated by the Union of Democratic Control substantially contributed to the public mood against strong defences. It was only when the threat was from fascism that the left responded, and it was not easy, since demands for greater armaments meant reversing their attacks on Tory munitions barons. Chamberlain's policy was conditioned by events long before he came to power, and the pursuit of appeasement was congenial to a wide spectrum of political opinion for many years. Drift in the mid-1930s was replaced by a decisive policy. Rearmament, which had been slow under Macdonald and Baldwin, quickened under Chamberlain. Appeasement was shallow; the presence of fascism meant a war with men like Hitler and Mussolini in charge, but in seeking to avoid war Chamberlain made possible the winning of it when it came. Detente with the dictators was produced by an inward-looking decade more concerned with economic collapse and recovery than with the realities of power politics, and it was supported until a point where only Munich was possible.

B. The Rearmament of Great Britain

1. Beginnings: The White Paper of March 1935

Concern about rearmament began with the Manchurian Crisis (Chapter 7, H2 and 3). In March 1932 the Ten Year Rule was abandoned and a survey of defence needs was commissioned. Churchill's earliest references to rearmament in May and November 1932 were ill received, but the collapse of the Disarmament Conference in October 1933 combined with reports of German rearmament to influence the government. Defence estimates of £102m in 1932–33 were the nadir, and in 1934 they provided for only four new air squadrons. Churchill criticised Britain's position as fifth air power, and Baldwin said the government 'will see to it that in air strength and air power this country shall no longer be in a position inferior to any country within striking distance of our shores.'

In July 1934 the cabinet accepted the defence survey and it was agreed to revise the air estimates to increase the RAF from 42 to 75 squadrons. Baldwin was strongly criticised, and replied by stating that the Rhine was now our defensive frontier. By November, Churchill claimed this programme was being surpassed by Germany, and Baldwin replied, 'It is not the case that Germany is rapidly approaching equality with us ... our estimate is that we shall still have a margin in Europe alone of nearly 50 per cent.' Not until March 1935, with a 'Statement Relating to Defence', was rearmament stated to be necessary.

B2. Locust Years: The White Paper of March 1936

Rearmament began in a very muddled fashion. When Hitler announced his rearmament in March 1935 he told Simon and Eden that Germany had reached air parity. This was false, but gave rise to much alarm and reluctance to provoke Germany.

Churchill claimed he had been right about the German air threat, and Baldwin, ignoring Air Ministry figures which showed Churchill was incorrect, stated in May 1935, 'Where I was wrong was in my estimate of the future. There I was completely wrong. We were completely misled on that subject'. However, an election was likely that year, and Baldwin had no intention of losing it. He supported the League in taking sanctions against Italy, and said, 'I give you my word that there will be no great armaments.' However, the government increased the air estimates and specifications for the Hurricane and Spitfire were followed by prototypes in November 1935 and May 1936.

After the election, and failure to keep Italy out of the enemy camp, rearmament became more open. In March 1936 a White Paper and the appointment of Inskip as Minister for Coordination of Defence were announced, and in July Sir Hugh Dowding took over Fighter Command, and urged the government to lessen concentration on bombers. The White Paper owed much to Chamberlain. It provided for naval rearmament (including two battleships, one aircraft carrier and 19 new cruisers) and the increase of the RAF to a front-line strength of 1750 aeroplanes.

B3. The Loaded Pause

In November 1936, during a debate in which Churchill accused Baldwin of sloth in rearmament, Baldwin said, 'Supposing I had gone to the country and said that Germany was rearming and we must rearm? Does anyone think that this pacific democracy would have rallied to that cry at that moment? I cannot think of anything that would have made the loss of that election from my point of view more certain.' This was said in reference to East Fulham, but later twisted to imply that Baldwin had deceived the country in the election of 1935.

It cannot be denied that, in spite of rising expenditure (1935–36, £137m; 1936–37, £186m), the years 1936–38 were ones of wishful thinking, and slow rearmament. In the RAF, the Blenheim and Hampden bombers were developed, but only a few British planes could reach Germany. Development of new models was slow. The Hurricane and Spitfire did not enter service until January and August 1938 respectively. Although Sir Robert Watson Watt explained radar in 1935, it was only in 1937 that the decision to develop it was taken and 1939 before the chain was complete. In the autumn of 1937 Chamberlain said, 'I must frankly state that progress is not yet as fast as I should like.' Run-down defence industries responded slowly, so that two aircraft carriers had to have Czechoslovak armour while the Bofors gun was bought from Sweden. Expenditure on the air force and navy hamstrung the army, and in February 1938 Inskip was unable to persuade the cabinet to alter its low priority. He admitted the army had only two divisions, and that these were gravely deficient in tanks. Thus, although defence spending rose (1937, £198m; 1938, £253m) and Britain was spending a higher proportion of the National Income than France, she was behind Germany and falling further behind, in some respects, as the years passed. In March 1938 the Defence Staff declared war with Germany would lead to ultimate defeat, and this should be borne in mind when considering Munich.

B4. Almost Inexhaustible Resources

The crisis over Czechoslovakia brought defence matters to a head. In April 1938 a new programme of air development without financial restraints provided for 12,000, later 17,500, planes in two years. On 22 February 1939 production to the limit was allowed. Secret aeroplane works were developed and Arthur Purvis headed a purchasing mission to America which provided 400 planes. As Mowat says, 'It was in the strengthening of her air power that the breathing spell afforded by Munich was of supreme value to Great Britain.' The government began to borrow (£90m in 1938, £380m in 1939), in addition to increasing defence spending which reached £273m in 1939.

Duff Cooper had been ineffective at the War Office but his successor, Hore Belisha, began to get things changed. Re-equipping and stockpiling began, including the purchase of Brens from Czechoslovakia, and the limited rôle of the army was abandoned in January 1939. A BEF of 21 divisions was to be formed—10 were ready by January 1940. The Territorial Army was to double in size, and conscription was introduced in April 1939. Even the long-awaited Ministry of Supply appeared the same month. Hoare declared, 'I am convinced we could not be defeated in a short war by any knock-out blow, and that in a long war our almost inexhaustible resources will ensure final victory.'

B5. Civil Defence

In 1935 talks began at the Home Office, and in 1937 the Air Raid Precautions Act created Civil Defence. After Sir John Anderson was put in charge in October 1938 it expanded to include 1½ million people. Two million 'Anderson' shelters were provided. Provision for gas attack was made with the production of 38 million gas masks. Plans for evacuation and the hospital service were completed by Elliot at the Health Ministry. Provision was made to move 1¾ million children. Land girls, observer corps, auxiliary fire service and WVS personnel were recruited. The air-raid warden and rescue services were organised. A system of regional government was created. In January 1939 the *National Service Handbook* was distributed to every household, and in July 1939 the Civil Defence Act completed initial preparations. It was a meticulous programme, including every aspect of total war. At the time it excited jokes, and some of the preparations were unnecessary. But Britain was to be the first major industrial nation to face prolonged air attack.

C. The Overthrow of Versailles

C1. Response to Hitler

When Hitler took over, MacDonald and Simon were in control of foreign policy and did not alter course. This was because the British government was anxious to keep good relations with Germany and Italy, and traditional diplomacy was regarded as the best way to handle Hitler.

In May 1933 Hitler made the first of several 'peace' speeches, and it was curious how these were regarded as genuine, while his warlike outbursts were regarded as aberrations. In June a Four Power Pact between Britain, Germany, Italy and France agreed to settle disputes through the League. It was never ratified, and Germany left the League in October. In February 1934 Eden visited Germany to urge support for the League and the fading Disarmament Conference, but nothing came of the visit. The Disarmament Conference finished and although the British War Minister warned Germany any breach of Versailles would be followed by sanctions, the British government tacitly accepted the level of German rearmament.

The government also thought that Mussolini, resentful of Hitler's challenge to the leadership of the fascist world, would be prepared to support Britain. MacDonald visited Rome in March 1933. At this time Mussolini feared for Austria, where there were fascist disturbances. He accepted a British-Italian-French statement supporting Austrian independence in February 1934. Hitler was not yet strong enough to exercise a decisive influence in Europe, and in July 1934 his attempted coup in Austria failed and Mussolini showed his resentment by moving troops to the Brenner Pass.

The response to Hitler's appearance suggested no further action was needed. During 1934 the Balkan states drew together and this, combined with the Little Entente, was held to be sufficient in Eastern Europe. In January 1935 a Franco-Italian Colonial Agreement reflected their good relations. In May 1935 a Franco-Russian alliance was signed, providing for mutual aid against Germany, and the same month Russia signed a treaty with Czechoslovakia providing for aid if the French honoured their obligations under their treaty with Czechoslovakia. It seemed as if a common front between France, Britain and Italy, combined with the existing alliance systems, would keep Hitler in check.

C2. German Rearmament

Simon put proposals to Hitler about rearmament in March 1935. If Hitler would sign an Eastern Locarno, Britain was prepared to accept it and make an air pact. Then Hitler announced the existence of Germany's air force, compulsory military service and an army of 36 divisions in March 1935. The three powers acted, and in April issued a declaration from Stresa that they 'find themselves in complete agreement in opposing by all practicable means any unilateral repudiation of treaties which may endanger the peace of Europe, and will act in close and cordial collaboration for this purpose'. This was swiftly followed by a peace speech by Hitler in May stating that 'Germany needs peace and desires peace ... Germany neither intends nor wishes to interfere in the internal affairs of Austria.' The speech had proposals for disarmament, and *The Times* spoke of Hitler's sincerity. Although submarines were being built in defiance of Versailles, Britain signed the Anglo-German Naval Treaty in June without consulting Italy or France.

C3. Hitler Enters the Rhineland, March 1936

By now troubles between the powers over Abyssinia encouraged Hitler to see how far they could be pushed. In May 1935 he guaranteed Locarno and in the same month plans were initiated for reoccupation of the Rhineland. The Hoare-Laval Pact threw Britain and France into confusion while they were alienated from Italy, the other guarantor of Locarno, by sanctions. When the French ratified the Franco-Russian Treaty in February 1936, Hitler claimed this broke Locarno. Undeterred, Eden renewed proposals for an air pact. Although the German general staff doubted his wisdom, Hitler decided to enter the Rhineland, breaking Versailles and Locarno, with only two effective divisions. The West was so confused as to allow him total victory. As usual there was a speech proposing an air pact, German return to the League and a new treaty.

(*a*) On 9 March Eden denounced the German move and promised action if either France or Belgium were attacked.

(*b*) The Council of the League condemned the action. Staff conversations were held, and got nowhere. On 14 March Baldwin refused to move and it was decided to negotiate. On 7 May the Locarno powers addressed questions to Hitler who ignored them.

This Western failure has been strongly condemned. It is true that militarily Germany was weak, but Britain was in no position to send military aid, and the French high command stultified action. Its importance was tremendous, quite apart from the glow of success that seemed to attend Hitler's policy.

(*a*) Belgium decided to return to neutrality, and this was recognised in April 1937. Locarno was dead and the Maginot line turned in the north.

(*b*) Baldwin had said Britain's frontier was on the Rhine. The Germans could now start the West Wall and weaken France. Their bombers were within range of Britain.

(c) Mussolini, annoyed by sanctions and impressed by Hitler's coup, was willing to allow Hitler a freer hand in Austria. Although a German–Austrian Treaty in July 1936 guaranteed independence, secret clauses forced Austria to allow the Nazis to campaign.

D. The Fall of the League of Nations

D1. Response to Mussolini

British relations with Mussolini's Italy had been good. Italy guaranteed Locarno and took part in Stresa, and since Britain saw a triple naval threat developing, she wanted to keep Italy friendly. This was surprising since part of Mussolini's policy was to develop the Italian empire at the expense of the British. A radio station was opened at Bari to beam propaganda into British Middle Eastern territories, and Mussolini proclaimed himself the Protector of Arabs in March 1937. Libya was prepared for a war, and a coastal road stretched towards the border of Egypt. A treaty was made with the Yemen in 1937. This Italian threat was made clear by the Maffey Report (June 1935), but because of the stakes in Europe, Britain was willing to compromise over Abyssinia.

D2. War in Abyssinia

Both Britain (1867) and Italy (1896) had invaded Abyssinia before with mixed results, but in 1906 the two countries had signed a treaty to preserve the status quo. Italy received no colonial compensations in 1919 and part of Mussolini's policy was to reverse this situation. He also had false economic ideas about the value of Abyssinia for settlement and precious metals. Both Britain (1924) and France (1935) had given territory to Italy and, as they were colonial powers, Mussolini did not believe he would encounter much opposition. Although Italy had sponsored Abyssinia's admission to the League, preparations began in 1933. After a border incident in December 1934 Abyssinia appealed to the League in January and March 1935. From the first the government wished to compromise. Eden went to Rome and proposed partition in June, and in August a joint plan with France offered Italy a zone of economic penetration.

D3. League Sanctions

In 1935 there was to be an election in Britain. The government could not afford the resentment which would be caused by a deal with Italy, and Hoare, the Foreign Secretary, decided to take the wind out of the Opposition's sails with strong support for the League. On 1 August he spoke in favour of sanctions, and on 11 September said, 'The League stands, and my country stands with it, for the collective maintenance of the Covenant in its entirety, and particularly for steady and collective resistance to all sorts of unprovoked aggression.' After Manchuria this was welcome news, warmly backed by Morrison for Labour. But almost at once Hoare drew back, stressing that Britain could not act alone: it had to be collective action. Eden (Minister for the League) was in charge of appropriate measures. Although the Chiefs of Staff in August had told the government war with Italy was out of the question, a number of warlike moves were made, including reinforcing the Mediterranean fleet. Meanwhile, talks resumed between Britain and France to find a solution. Mussolini was provoked but not deterred and on 3 October invaded Abyssinia. With the election impending the British secured a resolution against Italy, and on 18 November sanctions were imposed.

(*a*) The aim of sanctions was to deny Italy war materials by freezing overseas assets, a trade embargo and an arms ban. It was believed that, like the wartime blockade, it would coerce Italy.

(*b*) They did not apply to non-members like the USA. Hungary, and other countries ignored them. Oil was not on the list of vital materials. The ban on arms came too late as they had been bought in Britain, and sailed through the Suez Canal. The League had no means of enforcing sanctions.

D4. The Hoare–Laval Pact, December 1935

On his way to Switzerland, Hoare stopped in Paris to find out from Laval how negotiations were proceeding. Laval, who wished to settle with Mussolini, leaked the discussions on 9 December. The plan to split up Abyssinia had been policy for months. But the shock, coming after an election fought on behalf of the League, was too much for the public. Although Baldwin defended Hoare, public reaction soon led him to change his mind. Hoare was sacked for six months, and the proposals dropped. Eden succeeded Hoare because he was a firm advocate of appeasement. His first action was to send proposals to Germany for a settlement in January 1936 and 'his appointment in December 1935 had no effect on the Abyssinian affair'. Gunther described him as 'the darling of the peace balloters', and it was only Churchill's later build-up of his successor that created a different image. In May Abyssinia was annexed. In June Chamberlain described sanctions as 'the very midsummer of madness' and they were abandoned.

E. Eden and the Spanish Civil War

In July 1936 a civil war began in Spain between a mixture of fascists and monarchists led by General Franco, and a coalition of left-wing groups including anarchists, communists and socialists. Both Hitler and Mussolini saw this as an opportunity to intervene on behalf of fascism, and provide training for their forces. The Comintern responded partly with direct Russian intervention and then through unofficial intervention.

(*a*) Russia had quarrelled with part of the Spanish Communist party. She insisted on payment, and gave £81m and 1,049 planes. The French Popular Front sent 260 planes, but the main left-wing intervention came from the International Brigades. These numbered about 40,000, of which a quarter were French. Britain sent 3,000.

(*b*) Portugal sent 20,000 troops, but the main aid was from Italy. Mussolini sent an army of 50,000, 765 planes, 950 tanks, 91 warships and £80m. Germany sent 10,000 troops and £43m, but took back raw materials. Her main contribution was the Condor Legion of aircraft and an anti-tank brigade.

Britain and France were divided on what action to take. Blum was for direct intervention. Strategically Franco would threaten Britain, but our economic interests in mining and agriculture favoured neutrality.

E1. Non-Intervention Agreement

Eden persuaded the French not to act, but set up a Non-Intervention Committee which would ban war supplies to both sides. The powers agreed in August, which denied the Spanish government belligerent rights while doing nothing to stop fascist intervention. It ignored the League. Labour backed the policy, but on 7 October Russia complained of violations, and they reversed engines. Whatever its intentions, the result was to aid Franco. The government passed the Foreign Enlistment Act to prevent people joining the International Brigade, but could do nothing to stop Italian troops pouring into Spain. When non-intervention was fully operative by April 1937 it was not working because there was no enforcement, and supplies entered from Portugal. Ships were boarded and sunk while engaged in lawful trade with Spain, but Eden denied he had information on the matter. In June 1937 the Germans and Italians left the Non-Intervention Committee.

E2. Nyon Agreement, September 1937

Eden believed that agreement with Italy was possible and in September 1937 the Nyon Agreement established a patrol of 80 destroyers to prevent further incidents. Churchill later praised this agreement, but by then Franco was well on the way to victory. The next month the British government sent an agent to Burgos, Franco's capital. In May and June 1938 attacks on British shipping were renewed. In Britain public opinion was roused on behalf of the Spanish government (Chapter 9, F5), but Conservatives continued to back Franco. On 27 February 1939 Franco was recognised by the British government before Barcelona had fallen.

E3. Resignation of Eden, February 1938

When Chamberlain replaced Baldwin a rift soon appeared with Eden, since the Prime Minister wished to intervene and Eden supported traditional Foreign Office methods of proceeding. The rift developed over a number of technical disputes which Eden's excitable and vain nature could not tolerate:

(*a*) When Japan invaded China in 1937 Eden called a conference at Brussels, and tried to persuade America to take action. Stimson was urged to freeze Japanese assets and discussion of joint naval action took place. Nothing happened, but Eden believed he could hook the Americans.

(*b*) When Roosevelt sent a personal message to Chamberlain in January 1938 advocating a conference of minor powers, Chamberlain snubbed him without consulting Eden. Eden demanded that he send a reply which agreed to the conference. By then Roosevelt had lost interest.

(*c*) In January 1938 Litvinov made a proposal for a conference which Chamberlain rejected as 'woolly rubbish'.

(*d*) When it came to negotiations with Italy, Chamberlain directly intervened, contradicted Eden in front of Count Grandi, and supplied him with the answers to Eden's questions.

On 20th February Eden and Cranborne resigned, not because they opposed appeasement or over a matter of principle, but over questions of procedure.

F. Axis signed and *Anschluss* Achieved

Britain's policy of keeping Mussolini out of Hitler's arms failed because her actions in signing the Naval Pact and supporting sanctions and non-intervention in Spain annoyed Mussolini, and Hitler took advantage of this situation to win him over and clear the way for the seizure of Austria.

(*a*) On 21 October 1936 the two countries signed the Axis. Italy joined the Anti-Comintern Pact with Germany and Japan in November 1937, which brought about the very combination that Britain hoped to avoid.

(*b*) Preparations made to seize Austria (Case 'Otto') appeared in a directive of June 1937, and on 5 November a special meeting heard Hitler's plans for future moves. The French told the British the same month they would not fight for Austria.

(*c*) Attempts were made to appease both dictators. During 1936 colonial concessions to Germany were discussed. In November 1937 Halifax visited Göring and proposals for a settlement were discussed. During 1938 proposals for an economic agreement were put forward.

(*d*) Attempts were made to placate Mussolini. In April 1938 an agreement was signed whereby Britain would recognise Italy in Abyssinia in return for the removal of volunteers from Spain and the end of hostile broadcasts from Bari. Although the agreement was not kept, Chamberlain and Halifax visited Rome in January 1939 and achieved nothing. When Mussolini grabbed Albania, Chamberlain refused to protest.

These diplomatic gestures to Hitler and Mussolini failed since the momentum of Hitler's success and the weakness of the West convinced Mussolini he was on the winning side. In May 1939 the Pact of Steel was signed, leaving Britain facing three enemies.

After Hitler had failed to bully the Austrians into surrender, they decided to hold a plebiscite on 13 March 1938. This forced him to act, although with only five effective divisions he was not in a strong military position. However, Mussolini agreed to stand aside. On 12 March German troops entered Austria, which had been softened up by the admission of Nazis to the government and riots in the main towns. Although many of the transports broke down, Hitler was able to enter Vienna on 14 March and tear up the Treaty of St Germain. The National Bank was seized and Britain handed over Austrian assets in London. Chamberlain had been told by the Defence Staff that without French support Britain could not act, nor did he have any intention of doing so in spite of warnings.

On 17 March Litvinov made a second proposal for a conference, since it was obvious what Hitler's next move would be. Indeed, on 20 March Chamberlain wrote to his sister, 'I have abandoned any ideas of giving guarantees to Czechoslovakia or to the French in connection with her obligations to that country.' On 24 March Litvinov's proposal was rejected, and Chamberlain stressed that giving guarantees to a country as far away as Czechoslovakia was foolish. But twice the French said they would abide by their 1924 treaty obligations, and this faced Chamberlain with the awkward problem that appeasement might fail.

G. The Munich Agreement, September 1938

Chamberlain's view was that Czechoslovakia was not worth fighting for and the borders of Versailles were not immutable, particularly if a deal would satisfy Hitler. Britain had a residual obligation to support France, and on a number of occasions (20 May and 27 August) appeared to accept that if France acted, Britain would follow. In fact, the French themselves weakened as the crisis approached and Chamberlain played on this weakness while telling the cabinet Britain could not act without them.

G1. The Czechoslovak Problem

Czechoslovakia consisted of a variety of territories, including the Sudeten area with 4 million Germans. Since 1933 Henlein had built up a Nazi party and claimed they were a persecuted minority. Versailles provided for boundary changes and protection of minorities. Many British officials were inclined to back the Germans rather than Slavs. Henderson called them 'an incorrigibly pig-headed people'. However, there was a strategic question. Czechoslovakia had a modern army of 20 divisions, a thriving munitions industry and good defences in the Sudeten area. If these were lost, the rest of Czechoslovakia would lie open to aggression. In July Chamberlain sent Lord Runciman to investigate against the Czechs' wishes. He reported, 'I have much sympathy with the Sudeten case ... I regard their turning for help towards their kinsmen and their eventual desire to join the Reich as a natural development in the circumstances.' His report to the cabinet exaggerated grievances, since his contacts had largely been with richer Germans. On 7 September *The Times* advocated cession, and this was an inspired leak.

G2. A Question of Intervention

The combined strength of France, Britain and Czechoslovakia could on paper defeat any German attack, and some German generals complained when Hitler decided on Case 'Green'. They were removed. Although there were only 12 German divisions in the West opposing 65 French divisions, the French insisted general mobilisation was necessary. The British general staff informed Chamberlain that war was not possible as Britain was defenceless against air attack. The Russians also had obligations, and Litvinov urged an appeal to the League under article 11, joint staff discussions and discussion with Poland and Rumania about the movement of Russian troops. Maisky (the Soviet ambassador) had a meeting with Lord De La Warr and Butler, and proposed a three-power conference. But although the Russians offered 30 divisions, the Western military attachés in Moscow had written off their army, and it was hard to see how it could come into action. The Western powers decided instead on a direct approach to Hitler, and Daladier appealed to Chamberlain.

G3. The Fatal Meetings

tt says the 'visits were a diplomatic blunder of the first magni-
e time the dramatic flight of a prime minister was regarded
ut Hitler saw in it only weakness. Chamberlain took with
nd Strang, and was not himself a skilful negotiator. He

appeared in the role of a spokesman for the Sudetens, and in the end was forced to do Hitler's work for him and coerce the Czechs.

(*a*) *Berchtesgaden, 15 September*. Hitler said the Sudetens must return to the *Reich* and Chamberlain accepted 'the principle of the detachment of Sudeten areas'. Hitler postponed military action so that Chamberlain could get agreement. On 17 September, armed with his findings and Runciman's report, Chamberlain persuaded the cabinet and, next day, Daladier and Bonnet. When the proposals were given to Benes on 19 September he declined, and suggested direct German–Czech discussions.

(*b*) *Godesberg, 22 September*, Chamberlain told Hitler 'he had got exactly what the Führer wanted'. In fact, by securing assent he had got ahead of Hitler, who wanted a military occupation, so the Führer now increased his demands and put a time limit (26 September) on his proposals. After argument, he postponed this to 28 September so that Chamberlain could secure agreement.

This proved difficult. On 25 September the Czechs and the French rejected the proposals and in the cabinet Halifax changed sides and supported the critics. The Czechs mobilised, the French ordered partial mobilisation and even Chamberlain was forced to act. On 27 September he agreed to a state of emergency, called up the auxiliary air force and mobilised the fleet. Trenches were dug, and gas masks given out. Halifax issued a statement that if a German attack was made upon Czechoslovakia, the result would be that France would come to her assistance, and Great Britain and Russia would stand by France. But this outwardly firm front hid the truth. The same day Chamberlain sent Wilson to Hitler to say, 'I feel certain that you can get all the essentials without war, and without delay', and his broadcast that evening was not that of a resolute man ready for war. When he said, 'I would not hesitate to pay even a third visit to Germany if I thought it would do any good', Daladier and Bonnet urged Mussolini to intervene, and Hitler agreed to a conference from which Czechoslovakia and Russia were excluded. After a dramatic announcement in the Commons and shouts of 'Thank God for the Prime Minister!', Attlee and Sinclair warmly supported Chamberlain.

(*c*) *Munich, 29 September*. Daladier, Chamberlain, Mussolini and Hitler soon reached agreement. The Germans drafted proposals which they gave to Mussolini to present as impartial. The Pact was signed on 30 September, accompanied by a joint declaration praising the Naval Treaty and Munich as 'symbolic of the desire of our two peoples never to go to war with one another again'. Cheered from Heston to Downing Street, he proclaimed 'this is peace in our time'. On 3 October Churchill was howled down for saying 'we have sustained a total and unmitigated defeat', and only Duff Cooper resigned.

Although a number of individuals were sickened by events, the overwhelming majority supported this decision. The people were not ready for war, as a panic migration of 150,000 from London showed. Chamberlain had not learnt his lesson. While he despised Hitler in some ways, describing him as 'the commonest little dog', he still believed 'that here was a man who could be relied upon when he had given his word'. The terms were that predominantly German territory was to be occupied by 7 October, allowing Hitler a peaceful military entry, whilst other territory was to be ceded after a boundary commission had sat. In areas disputed between the two sides, plebiscites were to take place under an international commission.

Hitler had already said, 'This is the last territorial claim I have to make in Europe', and he agreed to guarantee the new frontiers. Britain and France renewed their guarantee to the weakened country, and Britain provided a loan of £30m. Hitler got 11,000 square miles, including 800,000 Czechs. Poland seized 650 and Hungary 7,500 square miles, breaking the agreement before the ink was dry. On 9 October Hitler attacked British arrogance and said he would not tolerate 'the tutelage of governesses'. France and Britain had been shown as weak. Russia had been snubbed. Czechoslovakia was ripe for destruction. Hitler had again been proved right.

H. The British System of Guarantees

H1. A Golden Age

Although Chamberlain later claimed the Munich compromise was forced on him by lack of defence preparations and that the intervening period allowed him to prepare for the eventual struggle, the truth was that except in the air Britain was further behind Germany by 1939 than a year before, and Chamberlain's policy was determined thereafter by appeasement. Rearmament was progressing, but in January 1939 an Anglo-German Coal Agreement was followed by a series of meetings between industrialists and the Germans preparatory to a conference at Düsseldorf planned for 15 March. Even after this, economic appeasement continued with conversations in June and July 1939. In February, Henderson said there was a good chance of Hitler returning to 'normalcy', and on 10 March Hoare said Europe was settling down and a golden age was dawning.

H2. The Dictators' Intentions

The early part of 1939 was marked by a series of aggressive moves by the dictators and their supporters. Japan ignored a note from Britain and in March seized the Spratley Islands on the way to Singapore. In June the British concession at Tientsin was blockaded. Mussolini invaded and occupied Albania in April. Hitler intrigued with Slovak leaders, and detached Slovakia and Ruthenia from Czechoslovakia. On 15 March he occupied the rest of the country and on 23 March, Memel.

These moves should have convinced anyone that the dictators meant business. On 21 March Poland was asked to cede Danzig and amend the Corridor in exchange for a guarantee of frontiers. Poland rejected this demand on 26 March and asked Britain for help.

H3. The Birmingham Switch, 17 March 1939

When Hitler seized Czechoslovakia, Chamberlain said it had 'become disintegrated' and therefore the guarantee did not apply. He defended Hitler, saying he 'could not believe that anything of the kind was contemplated by any of the signatories'. Next day, Simon made similar noises. Then on 17 March Chamberlain switched his approach due to public opinion becoming hostile to surrenders and a stand by Halifax. Chamberlain felt that he personally had been insulted.

But although public opinion was changing, Chamberlain had not altered. He now determined to prevent war by threatening Hitler, and the age-old

British policy of combining the smaller nations together against an aggressor. He detailed Hitler's aggressions and asked, 'Is this the last attack upon a small state, or is it to be followed by others? Is it in fact a step in the direction of an attempt to dominate the world by force?' He added he was not prepared to make unspecified commitments to protect other countries.

H4. Firmness at Last

Poland was a militarist country which persecuted Jews and subject peoples, and had signed a non-aggression pact with Germany. But Beck, the Foreign Minister, was now worried by new German demands and, rather than court Russia, turned to Britain. Chamberlain had been asked by Litvinov to conclude a four-power pact with Russia, France and Poland but the Poles objected, and Chamberlain accepted this, saying, 'I must confess to the most profound distrust of Russia.' Poland chose Britain, and Britain accepted, thus excluding Russia. On 31 March it was announced that 'in the event of any action which clearly threatened Polish independence ... HM government would feel themselves bound at once to lend the Polish government all support in their power'. On 13 April guarantees were extended to Rumania and Greece.

(*a*) Mowat described these moves as 'incredible rashness'. Having said that Austria and Czechoslovakia could not be defended, he proposed to protect countries even further away.

(*b*) Hitler was not deterred. On 3 April Case 'White' was to be prepared, and on 23 May Hitler accepted that he might have to fight Britain and France as well. This worried Mussolini, but he was not in a position to halt Hitler.

I. The Struggle for the Russian Alliance

Although some historians represent the failure to get a Russian alliance as the last straw that led to war, this is difficult to sustain. Contacts between the two dictators had begun soon after Munich. Stalin did not think much of the Western forces and realised that in any war he would provide the bulk of the divisions. The West did not think much of Russia. Apart from dislike of a regime more brutal than Hitler's, Britain had little reason to suppose the Soviets would live up to treaty obligations. Stalin, however, was a realist. Isolated in Europe, he saw a pact as a means of recovering territory lost in 1919. Later he said, 'We secured peace for our country for one and a half years as well as an opportunity for preparing our forces for defence.' At the time he represented the alliance as common sense, as both sides disliked Poland and the Western democracies. It has been suggested that Stalin negotiated with the West as a blind to force Hitler to agree.

There was something to be said in favour of caution, but the British were excessively slow and Poland, having obtained a guarantee and opened staff discussions, had no intention of allowing Russian troops to enter the country. Although Churchill and Lloyd George urged acceptance of a treaty, Russian policy was changing as the negotiations proceeded. On 3 May Litvinov resigned and was replaced by Molotov, and this reflected a change in Kremlin policy. Discussions begun on 16 April were broken off on 15 May by Molotov. Chamberlain believed his guarantees and

Britain's rearmament would deter Hitler. He was fighting for peace, not to prepare for war. On 7 June a high-ranking official, Sir William Strang, took over the talks, but Halifax and Chamberlain declined to be involved. There was to be no flight to Moscow.

On 15 June negotiations reopened with each side demanding the other guarantee various lists of countries from aggression, but on 27 June Halifax agreed to the Russian list so that this point was cleared up. Molotov then switched and said any political agreement would have to wait on a military one, and pressed the British to secure Polish consent to Russian troops. But on 30 May the Germans had decided on direct negotiations, and it became a race against time as Hitler set 25 August as his Polish deadline. The British military mission was led by Admiral Sir Reginald Drax, who was not high ranking. He was not given specific instructions, and went to Russia by a slow boat. On 12 August military discussions started with Voroshilov, and on 15 August Russian negotiations with the Germans began. The Poles refused to allow Russian troops in and although the French offered to sign any terms, it was too late. On 23 August Ribbentrop and Molotov signed an agreement.

The treaty contained secret clauses for the partition of Poland. In spite of the Anti-Comintern Pact, Stalin believed he had a bargain. In fact, he nearly destroyed a second front in 1940, and brought his own country to defeat in 1941. But the strategic gains of the pact with Hitler remain today.

J. War for Poland

On 23 June the Reich's Defence Council met to prepare for war, and on 10 August SS plans for a frontier 'incident' were organised. In Danzig, Herr Forster was creating trouble and on 7 August visited Hitler to consolidate plans. The signing of the pact with Russia reassured doubters about a war on two fronts, and paved the way for invasion.

(a) British reaction was firm. General Ironside went to staff discussions at Warsaw. On 24 August Chamberlain said Britain's obligation remained, and next day signed a definitive treaty with Poland.

(b) Mussolini weakened in support for Hitler, declining to act and demanding a long list of war materials as the price of entry.

(c) Hitler postponed his attack and this gave time for the appeasers to work once more. On 26 August Halifax told Mussolini that Britain would try to persuade the Poles to make concessions. This policy was backed by Henderson in Berlin and opposed by Kennard in Warsaw. Secret negotiations were opened by Birger Dahlerus, a Swede, between Downing Street and Göring.

Hitler sent his proposals for Poland to Chamberlain, and a reply was drawn up by Wilson which was so 'fulsome, obsequious and deferential' that the cabinet would not accept it and it was redrafted. This reply was delivered on 28 August and on the same day a reply was given to the secret approaches, suggesting there was room for discussion. Henderson urged this strongly, and Kennard was told to persuade the Poles to come to a meeting. On 29 August Hitler replied, accepting negotiations, but insisting the Poles must send a qualified emissary to Berlin by midnight on 31 August. Although Henderson twice urged Chamberlain to accept, the cabinet would not agree. They said Germany should stop provocative frontier movements, and negotiate in the normal diplomatic manner.

When Henderson delivered this reply and demanded to know what proposals the Germans were making to Poland, Ribbentrop gabbled 16 articles at top speed and would not allow him a copy. One was obtained from Göring and taken by Dahlerus to London. While the generous terms were read on Berlin Radio next day, it was clear the cabinet would not agree to the Henderson-Dahlerus line. Halifax insisted on proper contacts. But on 31 August Hitler had decided for war. The Gleiwitz incident occurred in the early hours of 1 September, and Poland was invaded.

(*a*) Neither Britain nor France moved. Bonnet begged Mussolini to intervene, and proposals were sent to Berlin. Halifax spoke of a solution without war, although one was going on.

(*b*) An angry debate on 2 September nerved the cabinet to act. They told the French an ultimatum would have to be sent or the government would fall. It would have six hours' duration. The French wanted 48 hours.

(*c*) The ultimatum was sent, and expired at 11.00 on 3 September 1939. The reason Chamberlain gave in his broadcast was 'a situation in which no word given by Germany's ruler could be trusted and no people or country could feel itself safe, has become intolerable'.

Overtly war began over an issue of little importance for Britain. Essentially it was a war for a way of life threatened by dictatorship, military power and aggression.

Further Reading

Churchill, W. L. S., *The Second World War*, Cassell, London, 1948–1954 (6 vols).

Cowling, M., *The Impact of Hitler: British Politics and British Policy 1933–1939*, University Press, Cambridge, 1975.

Gilbert, M., *The Roots of Appeasement*, Weidenfeld and Nicolson, London, 1966.

Gilbert, M., and Gott, R., *The Appeasers*, Weidenfeld and Nicolson, London, 1963, available in paperback, 1967.

Mowat, C. L., *Britain Between the Wars 1918–1940*, Methuen, London and Chicago, 1955.

Rock, W. R., *British Appeasement in the 1930s*, Edward Arnold, London, 1977.

Seaman, L. C. B., *Post Victorian Britain 1902–1951*, Methuen, London, 1966.

Shay, R. P., *British Rearmament in the 1930s*, Princeton, New York, 1977.

Shirer, W., *The Rise and Fall of the Third Reich*, Secker and Warburg, London, 1959.

Taylor, A. J. P., *The Origins of the Second World War*, Hamilton, London, 1961, available as Penguin paperback, 1964.

Thompson, N., *The Anti-Appeasers: Conservative Opposition to Appeasement in the 1930s*, Oxford University Press, London, 1971.

Thorne, C., *The Approach of War 1938–1939*, Macmillan, London, 1967.

Questions

1. What do you understand by the word appeasement applied to British foreign policy in the 1930s?
2. How far was appeasement the policy of one party and one man?
3. What arguments can be advanced to justify the appeasement of the dictators?

4. Was appeasement the fruits of 'twenty wasted years'?
5. Were the men of Munich to blame for Munich?
6. Was England wrong in failing to create an alliance with the Soviet Union to counteract Hitler?
7. Was there an argument for appeasing Mussolini but not appeasing Hitler?
8. What was the relationship between appeasement and rearmament?
9. Why did Britain go to war in September 1939?

13

CHURCHILL AND THE WORLD WAR: 1939–45

The war that began in September 1939 lasted for exactly six years, and the British Empire was the only major power to fight Germany from start to finish. It was a world war and, although the destructive power of certain weapons increased and towards the end a new warfare of missiles and nuclear conflict was anticipated, it was the last of the old wars in which initiative by generals and by individuals could still count. The cause the allies fought for was one which all could agree implied a just war. The British contribution was a remarkable one, and it was not until June 1944 that the United States became the main military component of the Allied war effort. Her casualties in battle (412,240) were greater than those of the United States (322,000) and the mobilisation of her economy more intense, for 55 per cent of the labour force in Britain were engaged in the war effort compared with 40 per cent in America. In addition, Britain suffered 62,000 civilian casualties, while America suffered none.

The war has been veiled in 'a not unbecoming nostalgia' which it is important for the historian to control. Dunkirk, the Battles of Britain and the Atlantic, the Blitz and the onslaught of the V-weapons, the Desert and Burma wars, and the campaigns in Italy and the West made a decisive contribution to victory. Indeed, there is a strong case for arguing that the Battle of Britain was 'Hitler's first great failure, of far greater consequence than all his victories'. Churchill's leadership was decisive not only at home, but throughout the free world until the economic power of America began to give Roosevelt a greater say during 1944. Even then, Churchill's determination ensured that Britain was still in 1945 one of the Big Three. But the war brought that situation to an end. By 1945 'in name and in fact Britain remained a world power ... without the economic potential to sustain the rôle'.

The historian of the World War, therefore, needs to look at the events which led to this change as well as the more spectacular but less sustained gains from victory in the field. Britain had always intended to fight the war with allies, but by June 1940 was alone, faced with the Tripartite Pact of the three strongest naval powers and the active hostility of Soviet Russia, which provided economic aid for Germany. Although Britain was never alone because many European powers made small contributions and the Empire was, with a few lapses, loyal throughout, Britain sustained the only active war for a year until June 1941, when Hitler attacked Russia. But Russia was ill-prepared and became an additional drain on resources with convoys. The massive armies involved meant that Russia could make no contribution to the overall strategy of the war until she was ready to invade Eastern Europe. She gave no aid in the war against Japan, for example, and could hardly be expected to help Britain sustain her Middle East and African Empire. America gave material aid, although this did not flow effectively until after the crucial months of 1940, but remained opposed to entering the war. Pearl Harbour changed things, but once again by securing Australian resources and demanding landing craft, the American intervention weakened Britain's position in the Mediterranean.

With Russian, Pacific and European theatres, the allocation of resources and strategic issues became complex, and there developed the Grand Alliance. In fact, Britain and Russia were allies, but America signed no treaties. It was a strange misalliance of Communist Russia, Imperialist Britain and Capitalist America, formed to beat the Axis powers, and it did not last. Churchill soon found American economic interests and anti-imperialist sentiments provided links with the *realpolitik* of Stalin, who was determined to recapture Russian influence in the Far East and Eastern Europe. Thus, while the Big Three were able to chalk up a series of decisive victories, Hitler was able to increase his war base until late 1944, and the way to victory was through many a tortuous diplomatic lane culminating at Yalta. While Britain could claim to have played the decisive part in expelling Germany from Africa and defeating Italy, it was America that largely beat Japan and Americans and Russians who provided the greater part of victory in Europe. VE Day (8 June) and VJ Day (2 September) produced a new world which for Britain was rearranged in an unfriendly pattern. She had vast military forces and was about to embark on a period of conscription, military alliance and defence spending in peacetime never known at the height of the Empire. But the war produced two great powers, neither of which was friendly to Britain's world rôle, and both of which sympathised with the nationalist challenge to Empire which war had stimulated.

A. The European War, 1939–40

A1. Anglo-French Diplomacy

Neither Western power wanted war, or was able to do anything for Poland. A Supreme War Council was set up, and in March 1940 it was agreed 'they would neither negotiate nor conclude an armistice or treaty of peace except by mutual agreement', but below the surface lurked tensions and disagreements.

The French produced proposals for war that alarmed the British. These included an expedition to Salonika and proposals for the bombing and invasion of southern Russia, for which plans were drawn up in February 1940. The strategic consequences of this folly are obvious, and Chamberlain's caution was justified. However, both governments were under pressure to act. Churchill presented schemes including mining Norwegian territorial waters, invasion of Norway and Sweden, and naval action in the Baltic and White Seas. Since these were some distance from France, Daladier tended to support them and argued Germany could be defeated at long range by cutting off iron ore from Sweden and oil from the Caucasus.

(a) *British plans.* The BEF went to France, where 10 divisions were to be found by April 1940, but there was little action. The Germans constantly postponed their plans and the British, having appointed Wavell as Middle East C. in C., contemplated action there first if Italy should enter the war.

(b) *French government crisis.* Hostility to Russia was greater than to Germany and failure to act led to the fall of Daladier in March 1940. He stayed on in a new government under Reynaud.

Churchill pressed for action in Norwegian waters and Chamberlain decided against this at the end of February 1940. However, the *Altmark* Incident annoyed Hitler, and he yielded on 1 March to those who favoured a pre-emptive strike. Reynaud now urged action in Norway, and Churchill renewed pressure, arguing that troops prepared for Finland could be used. Anxious to persuade the French to accept the Rhine plan and to distract them from the Caucasus, Chamberlain agreed to Norway on 28 March. The Allies set 4 April for the Rhine operation and 5 April for Norway. The Germans planned invasion on the night of 8/9 April. Then it was decided to warn Norway first, and the British attack was postponed to 8 April. What was intended as a raid to lay mines turned into the first serious action of the war.

A2. Defeat in the East

Britain went to war to help Poland, but did nothing apart from rescuing a number of Polish nationals (one in 10 RAF pilots were Poles).

(*a*) *Partition of Poland.* The German invasion was almost uniformly successful, and on 16 September Russia invaded from the east. Warsaw fell and the last resistance was ended on 5 October. Poland was divided between Germany and Russia roughly along the Curzon Line.

Stalin was determined to seize every advantage from his German alliance and during October persuaded the Baltic states to accept Russian protection. The same demand was made to Finland, and when it was refused, Russia invaded and set up a puppet government.

(*b*) *Finnish intervention.* The Finns fought well, and the West reacted firmly. Russia was expelled from the League and the defeat of the Russians in January 1940 was seen as evidence of 'the military incapacity of the Red Army'. Aid to Finland would provide a good excuse for seizing Swedish iron ore. But as usual there was delay. Russia counterattacked and Allied plans were only agreed on 5 February for attack on 1 March. But negotiations started, and peace was made on 13 February by which Russia gained territory.

The discussions of Finnish intervention 'defy rational analysis', as Taylor has said, since invasion of southern Finland would not secure iron ore in northern Sweden, quite apart from the problems of forcing the Baltic or sending an army across the top of hostile Sweden.

A3. Disaster in Norway

Although preliminary warnings were received, heavy cloud prevented the RAF following them up. The fleet sailed to Norway and mined coastal waters. The sinking of a ship revealed the invasion moving on several points of the Norwegian coast after taking Denmark.

(*a*) *The Battle of the Norwegian Approaches.* The German plan was to disperse the invasion at five points with paratroops to spread alarm. Apart from Oslo, there was little resistance. In a series of encounters two German ships were sunk by the British and two more by the Norwegians. Ten German destroyers were sunk in two naval actions at Narvik. The British occupied the Faroes and Iceland to prevent German penetration.

Since intervention in Norway had been discussed for so long, it looked an excellent opportunity to strike at the Germans, but there was disagreement about what action to take. Some argued for direct attack on Trondheim and a march on Oslo, while others said this was too costly and advocated landings on each side of the town. In fact, there were only 1,700 Germans in Trondheim. Narvik was included as a third objective in order to secure the iron ore. The result was a ramshackle campaign.

(b) *The Battle of Norway*. In the north, Mackesey landed at Harstad, but quarrelled with Admiral Lord Cork, who urged a direct assault when the Germans fought back. Attempts to cut the German lines south were defeated, but Narvik fell on 28 May. Carton de Wiart landed at Namsos, where poor equipment and air attack halted him. He withdrew by 3 May. Morgan landed at Andalsnes. Heavy snow and German attack held him at Dombas and Lillehammer, and the vital supply ship was sunk. He withdrew on 1 May.

Even during the withdrawals naval losses continued to be heavy. With the invasion of France Narvik's fate was sealed, and it was evacuated on 8 June. Norway surrendered the next day.

(c) Importance. The campaign revealed Britain's lack of equipment and military muddle in planning and execution. This helped to overthrow Chamberlain (Chapter 14, A3). If the campaign had succeeded, it is difficult to see what it could have achieved, since war in Western Europe would have compelled withdrawal. The Norwegian government and shipping were saved. Most important, the naval battles had cost the Germans 12 large ships and their navy was unable to participate fully at Dunkirk or in invasion plans.

A4. Blitzkrieg in the West
The Allied plan to contain invasion involved a forward line on the Dyle in northern Belgium and assumed German repetition of the Schlieffen Plan. Since Belgium was neutral the plan was weak, particularly since the French retained troops in the Maginot Line and had no effective reserves. Weather, cautious generals and the capture of German war plans forced the Germans to rethink, and the new Manstein Plan aimed to break through further south towards Sedan, where the French were weak. Inaction had sapped French morale already, but in numbers the Allies were only slightly inferior to the Germans. They had more and better tanks, and were superior in artillery. On paper the French had air superiority although of their 3,289 planes, only 1,310 ever reached the front. When Hitler decided on invasion upon hearing rumours of British aid to Holland, the two sides were not unevenly matched.

(a) *The Fall of Holland*. On 10 May Holland was invaded. The government fled to England and, after a threat to bomb key towns, they surrendered on 14 May.

(b) *Battle of the Dyle*. The Belgians, the French and the BEF under Lord Gort faced the Germans in the north. Arguments about joint command with the Belgians caused delay before the Allies took up their position on the Dyle and checked the Germans. But French defeat further south compelled retreat, and the Allies began to withdraw by 20 May.

(c) *Battles of Sedan and the Meuse*. While the Allies believed this northern battle was the key, the Germans advanced through the difficult Ardennes in three days. On 13 May the Germans attacked at Sedan and the French broke. No proper counterattack was prepared and on 15 May the Germans started towards the coast. At the same time the second German punch came on the Meuse now the French flank was turned in the south. They were overwhelmed by a threefold crossing, and beaten.

These moves brought Churchill to France for the first time, when he promised additional air aid, but he was right to refuse more than four squadrons because the French had not committed their own forces. Reynaud thought he had strengthened his government by adding Pétain. Weygand replaced Gamelin on 19 May, but he was equally slow and for three days while the Germans had an exposed flank of 100 miles and an undefended rear, no action was taken.

(d) *Plans for counterattack.* Weygand planned to counterattack. The plan was for the British to strike south and the French north, cutting the long German lines. A British move led to a battle at Arras, which held the Germans for 48 hours. But although the gap between the Allies was only 30 miles at one point, Weygand delayed and then made a useless move forward.

(e) *Race to the sea.* While the Allies fumbled the Germans advanced to Abbéville on 20 May, reaching the Channel coast. They turned north and were held at Boulogne and Calais by gallant British actions.

(f) *Fall of Belgium.* Leopold sympathised with the Germans, and quarrelled with the Prime Minister. When the Germans resumed their advance in the north Leopold wavered, and on 28 May ordered a ceasefire, staying in Belgium while the government fled to Britain.

A5. Deliverance at Dunkirk

It seemed the Germans would envelop the Allied armies in the North, but on 24 May Hitler ordered the advance to halt. In this vital breathing space Churchill reversed his offensive spirit. Between 20 and 26 May, Operation Dynamo under Admiral Ramsey was prepared. What followed was not a miracle, but a military operation of great courage and resourcefulness.

(a) *The Battles of Dunkirk.* The Germans tried to prevent evacuation by attack on the salient. The Navy lost six destroyers and the RAF the equivalent of six squadrons, while on land the battle cost 68,000 casualties.

(b) *The evacuation.* This was carried out mainly by the Navy: 848 ships took part; 72 were sunk. The famous little boats in fact took off only 6,029 of the total evacuated. Between 27 May and 4 June 338,226 men were evacuated, of whom 123,095 were French.

Dunkirk was a defeat and completed a German campaign that had captured 1 million prisoners.

B. The British War, 1940

B1. The Fall of France

At first it seemed there was no imminent danger of French collapse. Gort was replaced by Alexander with four British divisions. Weygand had 60 divisions facing 120 German on the Somme.

(a) *The Battle of the Somme.* The French were defeated, the government left for Bordeaux and a retreat was ordered. British troops fought at Abbéville and

St Valery, but were cut off: 8,000 surrendered and the rest were withdrawn in a second evacuation involving 136,000 British. The Germans entered Paris.

(b) *Churchill's visits*. Reynaud asked him to send all Britain's fighter squadrons but Churchill refused. On his 11 June visit, Churchill was assured the French fleet would not be handed over. On his 13 June visit he urged Reynaud to appeal to America, asked for 400 captured Luftwaffe pilots to be turned over and said there could be no separate armistice without guarantees for the fleet. This British pressure stimulated the anti-British element led by Weygand and Pétain.

(c) *Italy enters the war*. Mussolini declared war on 10 June, but his attack on France was easily contained.

Immediately the government reached Bordeaux, conditions for an armistice were proposed and backed by Weygand.

(d) *End of the alliance*. Reynaud wanted a further meeting with Churchill, but his cabinet split on the armistice issue, and he resigned. Weygand complained that an offer of a union between the two countries was 'a state of vassalage' and told the cabinet, 'in three weeks England's neck will be rung like a chicken's'. Pétain took over the government, and De Gaulle fled to England.

Some French wanted to hold out in North Africa, and Churchill offered shipping, but Italy's involvement and the seizure of Tangier by Spain convinced Pétain that a North African redoubt was impossible. The armistice came into force on 2 June providing severe terms. A puppet government under Pétain was set up at Vichy.

(e) *The Vichy government*. The Germans seized northern France and the Atlantic coast. The French gave them the secrets of asdic, and the Germans now had U-boat bases on the Atlantic.

B2. The End of the French Fleet

Potential invasion and the Atlantic life-line dictated firm action, and the French had given proof of their untrustworthiness. Operation Catapult was prepared and executed on 3 July 1940. French ships in British ports were overpowered. Ships at Alexandria were persuaded to surrender, while those at Mers el Kebir were attacked with the loss of 1,297 French lives. On 8 July the *Richelieu* at Dakar was immobilised, and ships at Martinique agreed to be interned in America.

B3. Diplomatic Pause

The fall of France left Churchill and Hitler contemplating invasion. On 1 July the Channel Isles were occupied. The cabinet took no formal decision to fight on, but Hitler had to decide on an invasion. On 23 May he spoke of blockading Britain into submission. He was wary of war on two fronts, and when his Russian ally occupied the Baltic states he was reminded of this fact. Hitler believed England would sue for peace and wished to give her every opportunity. On 16 July he decided to prepare specific plans, and stated, 'As England, in spite of the hopelessness of her military position, has so far shown herself unwilling to come to any compromise, I have decided to begin to prepare for, and if necessary carry out, an invasion of England'. Churchill for his part was willing to play for time because although the military position was bad, each week saw an improvement. He had already tried to persuade Mussolini not to enter the war, using Roosevelt's good offices and even proposing colonial concessions. Hitler himself issued a peace appeal on 19 July, which was only rejected by Halifax on the 22nd.

B4. America Stands Aside

Churchill overestimated American support for Britain. With an election campaign coming, the Americans were in no mood for intervention, and there was much defeatism in high circles. On 26 June the Chiefs of Staff reported Britain would be defeated, and Kennedy in London supported this view. Thus, while America was willing to sell equipment when Churchill appealed for destroyers, Roosevelt dug his heels in and it was not until September that the deal was announced. Moreover, the British were to surrender a number of bases in the West Indies in exchange. Roosevelt feared that if the Germans won, the British fleet would be lost and on 24 May urged Britain not to hand over her fleet. Later he proposed it should be sailed to American waters. Churchill's speeches in the summer of 1940 harped on the need for American support. Apart from rifles for the Home Guard, none was forthcoming and even the destroyer deal was window-dressing, since only nine arrived early in 1941.

B. Operation Sealion

A German plan of invasion was drawn up on 16 July to take effect on 15 September.

(*a*) *The plan.* At first 20 divisions were involved, but this later fell to nine. The first plan was for a broad invasion from Ramsgate to the Isle of Wight, but this was modified to four divisions between Folkestone and Hastings, two between Bexhill and Eastbourne, and three between Beachy Head and Brighton, backed by airborne attacks at Dover and Brighton and a flank movement to Lyme Regis. A line would be secured through Canterbury-Tenterden-Lewes, and an advance made to Portsmouth-Guildford-Gravesend.

(*b*) *The difficulties.* To achieve success, the Germans would have to assemble and protect an invasion fleet, secure command of sea and air, and have the right weather and tide conditions, but Göring believed the Luftwaffe could provide the conditions.

There was initial panic with fear of airborne landings, but once Ironside was replaced by Brooke plans for defence were made. The German delay allowed the production battle to get under way, and total forces in Britain amounted to 25 divisions. For the Germans to have landed on exposed beaches in the face of mines, poison gas and fire would have been difficult and most writers agree if invasion in June might have worked, invasion by September was a dubious enterprise. The British counterattacked by bombing invasion craft and bombarding invasion ports. On 25 August raids on Germany began. On 3 September the first postponement came, followed by indefinite postponement on 12 October.

B6. The Battle of Britain

The Luftwaffe had not met modern aircraft combined with a system of radar, but were convinced they could obtain air mastery now bombers could be protected by fighters over the area of RAF bases. During July a preliminary encounter took place in the Channel area in which the RAF lost 150 aircraft and the Channel was closed to shipping, but by the time attack came, Dowding had 1,434 pilots ready in 55 squadrons. The battle lasted a month, and was divided into three phases:

(*a*) 12–18 August. A series of attacks on radar stations and aerodromes were a prelude to Eagle Day. But a flanking raid from Norway was heavily defeated and in the south Eagle Day was a disaster.

(*b*) 24 August–6 September. The aim was to destroy Fighter Command. German attacks were better directed—23 of 33 major attacks were on aerodromes. In both pilots and aircraft the margin narrowed so that there were no reserves.

(*c*) 7–30 September. As a result of the bombing of Berlin, Göring had been ordered to bomb civilians. He began on 7 September, and the alert was given to Home Forces as it was believed invasion was imminent. In fact, the switch gave the necessary breathing space and, after the heaviest battle on 15 September, it was clear the Germans could not obtain mastery, and the odds lengthened in Britain's favour.

The figures for the battle were:　　　　　　　　Aeroplanes

Phase	British Losses	German Losses
10 July–12 August	150	286
13–18 August	103	258
Pause	11	32
24 August–6 September	286	380
7–30 September	242	433
	792	1,389

At the time, exaggerated figures gave a greater margin of victory, but this did not detract from the decisive nature of the conflict. On 20 August Churchill observed, 'Never in the field of human conflict was so much owed by so many to so few.' Its importance was that:

(*a*) It halted Germany's onward march, and gave hope to the exiled governments in London.

(*b*) It provided a base for resistance in Europe, and for air attack on the Reich. Germany never had less than 40 divisions in the West and was forced to divert resources to building the West Wall.

(*c*) Hitler was left with war on two fronts, including the U-boat struggle in the Atlantic and, from February 1941, an African campaign as well.

(*d*) Britain was able to continue the war with Mussolini, and this helped to divert Hitler into the Balkans during 1941.

(*e*) Had Britain been defeated, there would have been no base for a European invasion and no point in American involvement in Europe.

C. The British War, 1941

Hitler's main intention was to invade Russia, but his flanks were menaced by Britain, and substantial armies were deployed there. Raeder urged a Mediterranean strategy based on Franco, Vichy and Mussolini, and then Mussolini's own activities in Africa and Greece forced Hitler to divert his attention to a region where his strategic understanding was weak. The British for their part did not have the means to defeat Hitler and embarked on a wide-ranging series of wars which 'denied Hitler the strategic victories that would have made him safe from the danger of war on two fronts'.

C1. The Coasts of Nazi Europe
The idea of highly trained specialist forces originated with Colonels Gubbins and Clarke. They would provide training and tie down German forces. Important raids were carried out on Spitzbergen in 1941 and Bruneval in 1942. The dry dock at St Nazaire was destroyed next month, and the most important raid was on Dieppe in 1942. Commandos and troops sustained losses of 4,340 out of 6,000, but it was an effective answer to those demanding a second front.

C2. The Special Operations Executive
The presence of nine Allied governments dictated that help should be given to their nationals who organised resistance movements. Rescue of Allied personnel, and valuable secret information would be also gleaned. Formed in July 1940, SOE was placed under the Ministry of Economic Warfare in August 1941. The numbers involved amounted to one division in strength. Aid was sent to the French and Polish resistance from the start, and in 1943 operations were extended to help partisans in the Balkans.

C3. The Strategic Air Offensive
In spite of evidence that the Blitz (Chapter 14, C2) had not produced the panic or destruction long predicted, Portal and Harris were convinced a bombing offensive could knock out Germany, and this view was supported by Cherwell and Churchill. It was the only way Britain could strike directly at Germany. Although it was argued military targets were the first priority, this strategy became confused with an attempt to destroy industrial potential, and with deliberate terror raids.

(a) *Opening moves.* Following the attack on Berlin came raids on Mannheim, Bremen and Kiel. The first offensive petered out in November 1941.

(b) *Bomber Harris.* When he took over in February 1942 he had only 378 aircraft. He fought for production priority. Successful attacks on Lubeck and Rostock raised morale, and in May 1942 came the thousand-bomber raid on Cologne. The improvement of location by the Pathfinder force and a number of ingenious scientific developments encouraged Harris to believe victory possible. The Lancaster entered service in December 1942.

The Americans agreed to participate in the offensive, and started with a period of daylight bombing until October 1943. Then they developed a long-range fighter and in March 1944 resumed operations at night.

(c) *Stroke at the heart.* In March 1943 the Ruhr was raided, and Essen severely hit. On the night of 16/17 May the Mohne and Eder dams were cut. In July Hamburg was raided to destroy U-boat yards. In August Peenemünde was successfully raided. Berlin was devastated in the winter of 1943–44. After June 1944 attention was turned to synthetic oil, which was cut from 170,000 to 52,000 tons. In April 1945 Dresden was raided to destroy communications on the Eastern front.

It remains a matter of dispute how effective the air war was. A 9 per cent loss was inflicted for 25 per cent cost in allied resources. Others argue particular raids were successes, and the cost to Germany should include elaborate civil defence services. Moreover, by late 1943 only 20 per cent of the Luftwaffe was at the front.

C4. The Naval Wars

The British Navy was superior to the German numerically, but most of the battleships were out of date and she had insufficient aircraft carriers for the air-sea conflicts that were to come. The navy had the jobs of block-ading Germany, destroying U-boats, protecting troop and supply convoys and destroying the surface fleet. To this were added a number of combined operations which gave new importance to landing craft. The navy did not appreciate the link of air and sea power quickly and suffered losses off Norway, Crete and Malaya. In the Atlantic, made doubly important by dependence on American supplies, Britain was deprived of Irish and French ports, and this shortened U-boat journeys while lengthening the voyage of naval protection vessels. Later an additional convoy to Russia took further heavy toll. By early 1942 Britain faced the three main naval powers. Fortunately, Italy was largely defeated, and America took on the main bulk of the Japanese fleet. As it was, Britain lost control of both Mediterranean and Far Eastern waters and came close to losing the battle of the Atlantic.

(a) Churchill at the Admiralty. The early period of naval warfare was marked by severe losses redeemed by a few successes:

(i) The Atlantic convoys lacked air protection, or enough destroyer escorts. Their listening device did not operate on the surface, whereas Dönitz favoured wolf-packs hunting there. Magnetic mines caused severe losses until one was found and techniques of degaussing were introduced.
(ii) Successes. *Deutschland* and *Graf Spee* were sent out as commerce raiders. The former returned after sinking only two ships. The latter sank nine before scuttling after an action off the River Plate in December.

(b) The Italian Navy. War in Africa and the need to route convoys through the Mediterranean instead of round the Cape required the defeat of the Italian navy. The Germans provided U-boat and air support from Sicily, and this produced serious losses. The main battles were: Calabria and Taranto in 1940 and Matapan in 1941. In spite of two further encoun-ters which accounted for eight destroyers, 1941 turned into a bad year in the Mediterranean with loss of the *Ark Royal* and *Barham*. Malta was besieged and supplies for North Africa made difficult.

(c) Hunting German raiders. Seven armed merchant ships were sent on cruises varying from four to 18 months, to disrupt shipping. Only three were sunk. The Germans also used battleships as raiders, and only one, the *Bismarck*, was successfully sunk at first.

When the raiders turned to the Russian convoys they were badly mauled in the battles of the Barents Sea (1942) and the North Cape (1943) where the *Scharnhorst* was sunk. Other actions put all German capital ships except one out of action by the end of the war.

(d) *The Battle of the Atlantic.* With so many campaigns, it was easy to forget the vital struggle for the Atlantic lifelines, but the losses were the most frightening wartime figures, and were very heavy on both sides. The British lost 36 per cent of their merchant fleet and the Germans all theirs. Of 1,333 U-boats, 782 were sunk with the loss of 32,000 personnel. The British Navy lost 51,578 men, and merchant fleet losses have been calculated as high as 50,525. In the end the U-boat was mastered, but not defeated. The entry of America and an agreement with Portugal in October 1943, together with long-range aircraft and centimetric radar helped to turn the tide during 1943, but Dönitz fought back with homing torpedoes and schnorkels. The U-boats were more successful than the surface navy and Hitler fought hard to keep the Baltic bases to the bitter end.

C5. Mediterranean Strategy

In September 1940 Germany, Italy and Japan formed a Tripartite Pact to deter America and persuade Russia to keep in line. It was clear Russia, although helping Germany in matters like ice-breaking ships, was out for diplomatic gains, and Hitler had to work with them as preparations for invasion started in December 1940 were not ready. Until then, he was anxious to secure his flanks by an initiative in the western Mediterranean. As Britain decided in August 1940 that Italy should be defeated first, and Mussolini was anxious to take advantage of Britain's weakness, the Mediterranean became the focus of events.

(*a*) *Failure of Axis diplomacy.* Hitler believed Franco could be brought in. In October 1940 Hitler met Franco at Hendaye. Franco demanded strategic goods and the initiative collapsed. A meeting of Hitler with Pétain secured no French moves.

(*b*) *Rift in the Axis.* Hitler was determined to secure control over the resources of Eastern Europe. Hungary and Rumania were incorporated into the Tripartite Pact, and pressure brought on Yugoslavia and Bulgaria. Mussolini was annoyed, and on 28 October told Hitler he had invaded Greece.

Mussolini had been successful so far against the British in Africa. He had conquered British Somaliland and Graziani had advanced 60 miles into Egypt. But the Greeks defeated the Italians and, after a winter lull, drove back their counter-offensive. On 8 February 1941 Greece appealed to Britain and on 7 March British troops arrived in Greece. This played a part in diverting Hitler as he had offered Mussolini aid in January 1941 and now felt called upon to help him in Greece.

(*c*) Defeat in Greece. On 6 April Hitler invaded Yugoslavia and Greece. By 29 April, 43,000 out of 57,660 British troops had been evacuated; 27,000 went to Crete. Airborne attack and lack of British air cover led to a disaster (28 May–1 June) and only 14,580 were evacuated.

The importance of these events was:

(*a*) The postponement of Russian invasion. Hitler raised the number of divisions in the Balkans from 18 to 28 and it took two months to effect the transfer. Even if he was delayed because of the weather, it would not have been as long without the Balkan war.

(*b*) Hitler had to retain 21 divisions in the Balkan region to enforce the partition of territory made with Italy and to resist partisans.

(*c*) Britain was able through SOE to aid partisans. In 1943 the British contacted Tito and in May 1944 transferred support to him.

(*d*) Hitler was drawn into the smaller African war between Italy and Britain, and this absorbed Luftwaffe and U-boat resources as well as the Afrika Corps.

D. The Coming of World War

D1. America Steps Forward

After his election victory Roosevelt was able to initiate policies more favourable to Britain, and he was helped by acts of sabotage by American Nazis and the sinking of American ships.

(*a*) *Lend Lease Act.* Passed in March 1941, this provided for British purchases of war equipment. It was not particularly generous, since it was followed by an agreement in February 1942 which sharpened the terms.

(*b*) *The war zone.* In April the American zone was extended east, and Greenland secured. In July America took over from Britain in Iceland.

The growing links were exemplified by the Atlantic Charter, signed in August 1941. This was a statement of aspirations common to democratic countries which also envisaged a new 'permanent system of general security'. By September 1941 the exiled governments endorsed it, and it formed the basis for the Declaration of the United Nations in January 1942, designed as a counterblast to Hitler's New Order.

D2. Russia enters the War

The alliance between Hitler and Stalin provided rich dividends but, whereas Hitler never wavered from his intention to invade Russia, it seems that Stalin was convinced no attack would come. In September 1940, after hard bargaining, a further treaty was signed. There is little evidence of military preparations, although Stalin expressed annoyance with German advance in eastern Europe. Until the last minute he preferred to believe Hitler to the Western democracies, and when eight warnings were received of attack they were ignored.

(*a*) *Hitler's Russian success.* A series of encirclements won the battle of the frontiers in a month. Hitler decided on a three-pronged advance to Leningrad, Moscow and the south with the main weight in the south. The German lines got wider apart, partisans sprang up when Germans started terror policies and the advance slowed until winter held it up. Russia lost a third of her industry and half her agricultural lands. But 25 divisions were moved from the Far East and on 5 December the Russians attacked before Moscow.

(*b*) *Western reaction.* Churchill had argued for a Russian alliance before the war. He responded by saying 'any man or state who fights against Nazism will have our aid'. An Anglo-Russian Agreement was signed on 12 July 1941 which provided for mutual aid and no separate peace.

D3. Anglo-Russian Relations

At any one moment Russia did not face more than half the Axis forces. She played no part in defeating Italy or Japan. The West might be forgiven for seeing Russia's promise of mutual aid as hollow, and grew to resent the demand for a second front launched in July 1941.

(*a*) *Second Front now.* When the British urged joint military planning, Stalin refused. He refused to cooperate with SOE or disclose military secrets. In

November Wavell and Paget were offered by Churchill and refused. Stalin demanded Britain should declare war on Finland, Hungary and Rumania. He saw the war in terms of territorial and strategic advantage for Russia. The demand for a second front was partly propoganda and partly wilful ignoring of five fronts already maintained, and the other half of German forces tied down in Europe.

(*b*) *The Russian convoys.* Through lend lease Russia received $11.3m of aid and from Britain £428m, including 22,000 aircraft and 13,000 tanks. Churchill offered supplies vital to Britain, and Beaverbrook went to Moscow to facilitate aid. With two interruptions owing to shipping shortages, convoys lasted from August 1941 to September 1943. Of 811 merchant ships, 92 were sunk.

The Americans disapproved of Britain's determination to secure close relations when Eden went to Moscow in December 1941. He was faced with a range of territorial proposals, and told that Britain could take bases in France and Scandinavia at the end of the war. After lengthy negotiation, an Anglo-Russian Treaty of mutual assistance to last for 20 years was signed in May 1942.

D4. Japan's Ambitions
Japan was the only major power not at war, and was courted by both sides:

(*a*) In June 1940 Britain concluded the Tientsin Agreement, and allowed the Japanese into Shanghai. They shut the Burma Road. In September, France allowed Japan to station troops in Indo-China.
(*b*) Matsuoka was sent to Europe. Germany urged Japan to make war on Britain, and to turn south. Nomura went to America to seek agreement, and discussions lasted from 8 March to 7 December. Roosevelt therefore brushed aside Churchill's warnings in August and refused his proposal of a Pacific summit at Juneau.

While these discussions went on two important changes occurred. In Japan the anti-Russian faction yielded to those who believed in the East Asian sphere. In America the Japanese war in China aroused bitterness, and a series of economic measures were taken. In July all Japanese assets were frozen, Churchill yielded to American pressure and the Burma road was reopened. It was clear America would not give Japan the free hand in China for which they asked.

D5. America Enters the War
In the spring of 1940 the American Pacific fleet had moved to Pearl Harbor, and in April 1941 stationed forward units at Manila. On 18 November an agreement was proposed in which America would lift the oil embargo and withdraw lend lease from China in return for Japanese withdrawal from Indo-China. Churchill complained and Roosevelt rejected it. On 1 December the Japanese resolved to fight, but the Americans knew this since they had broken their codes. On 3 December Japan asked her tripartite partners to help. They agreed, knowing nothing of a plan devised to attack Pearl Harbor.

(*a*) *Pearl Harbor.* The Japanese resolved to break off talks half an hour before the American fleet was attacked, but the message took so long to decode it was delivered late. On 7 December four battleships were sunk, four damaged and 10 other warships damaged or sunk. But the aircraft carriers were not there.

(b) *Reaction of the powers.* World war had come at last. Britain declared war on Japan next day. Hitler and Mussolini declared war on America on 11 December thus linking the two conflicts. Churchill commented, 'so we had won after all ... after seventeen months of lonely fighting ... united we could subdue everybody else in the world', but defeat, not victory was the first result of world war.

E. The War of the Grand Alliance, 1942–43

E1. The African War

Britain was in a weak position as regards resources and loss of naval control of the Mediterranean made supply problems worse. In addition, forces were diverted to Syria, Greece (Section C5), Iraq and Iran. The African campaigns were 'a tactician's paradise and a quartermaster's hell'.

(a) *East Africa.* The campaign lasted from March to May 1941 and East Africa passed into British hands.

(b) *North Africa.* Taking advantage of Mussolini's Greek adventure, Wavell and O'Connor launched a sweeping offensive (9 December–7 February) which captured 130,000 prisoners and 400 tanks.

This success led Hitler to aid Mussolini, sending Kesselring's air force to Sicily, and Rommel in February 1941. The British were reforming with new Australian troops, but O'Connor was captured.

(c) *First Axis offensive.* Rommel led a two-pronged attack to Tobruk which was besieged. In order to prevent aid to Crete, Rommel renewed the attack on 30 April, and the Axis reached Halfaya on 27 May.

(d) *Middle East diversions.* Although expressing annoyance at this setback, Churchill insisted on two diversions. When Rashid Ali rebelled in Iraq, a force was sent in May which defeated him. Fears of a German advance through the Caucasus (Section E2) led to a joint Russo-British Note in August. When it was rejected, Persia was occupied and a pro-Western shah installed.

Churchill concentrated attention on the Middle East, appointing a Minister of State at Cairo. He stung Wavell into a new offensive (Battleaxe), which failed in June. Wavell was replaced by Auchinleck, who annoyed Churchill by also delaying, but in November-December launched another offensive (Crusader). After a number of tank battles Rommel was forced to withdraw, but it was not decisive.

(e) *Second Axis Offensive.* Rommel's advance in early 1942 brought him to Benghazi. The 8th Army created defences around Knightsbridge, and on 25 May Rommel attacked. Severe armoured battles forced a British retreat, and on 21 June Tobruk fell, with 33,000 prisoners. In spite of a holding action at Mersa Matruh the British were forced to withdraw to a second defensive line at El Alamein.

(f) *First El Alamein.* Although there was panic the defensive positions could not to be turned. The RAF sank the fuel convoy, and the Germans had only 55 fit tanks. Rommel attacked and was held (July) and a second attempt was held at Alam Halfa (August). This was decisive, but Churchill showed little appreciation.

The American landings in North Africa were due, and Churchill was anxious to secure a victory. He went to Cairo, removed Auchinleck and brought Alexander from Burma. He intended to appoint Gott as field commander, but his plane crashed and Montgomery obtained the post. He built up a massive superiority in men and armour, while the RAF obtained air mastery. Rommel was ill and the Germans short of petrol.

(g) *Second El Alamein.* The battle (24 October–4 November) was decisive. The Axis were defeated and 30,000 prisoners taken. By November, after rapid pursuit the Allies were back to El Agheila. In January Tripoli fell, although the pursuit began to slow.

Church bells were rung for the first major victory of the war and Churchill made clear what the battle meant: 'I have not become the King's first minister in order to preside over the liquidation of the British Empire.' The African War had been an excellent example of Commonwealth unity and secured Britain's Middle East position.

E2. The Russian War
In 1942, determined to secure oil, and possibly to move into the Middle East, Hitler decided on a southern thrust.

(a) *Hitler's second Russian offensive.* Although successful in the initial stages, he again divided his forces. The advance to the Caucasus started in June, but halted by August. Attempts to advance further were prevented by hard terrain and lack of fuel. The oil wells were not reached.
(b) *Stalingrad.* Hitler's diversion of troops south prevented the capture of Stalingrad. On 19 November the Russians counterattacked and cut off the Germans, who were besieged until they surrendered in January 1943.
(c) *Russian offensive.* During 1943 a series of battles took place round Kharkov, but it fell to the Russians in July and they advanced in spite of desperate German efforts. The Russians won the great battle of Kursk, but Manstein's steady withdrawal deprived them of more than 98,000 prisoners.
(d) *Advance towards Europe.* In January 1944 the Russians entered Poland. To the north, Leningrad was relieved after an appalling siege. In the south, Odessa was captured and the Crimea cleared. By July the Russians were on the Vistula.

By this time the Russians had come 450 miles, and could go no further. Germany regrouped in southern Poland to face them. The Russians turned to their flanks. Finland made peace in September 1944. In the south a *coup d'état* overthrew the Axis government in Rumania, and an armistice was signed the same month. By October the Russians had cleared Bulgaria and joined hands with Tito. These enormous campaigns, largely ignored in the West, made a decisive contribution to the defeat of Hitler, but they created problems. Already relations between Russia and Poland had degenerated, causing friction between the Allies.

E3. The Pacific War
Following Pearl Harbor, the Japanese had four months' victories which stretched their defensive perimeter to the utmost.

(a) *China.* General Stilwell was placed in command. Although the Burma Road was again closed, the Americans continued to supply Chiang over the

Hump from July. American air bases were established at Chungking and raids carried out on Japan.

(b) *Hong Kong* surrendered on 25 December.

(c) *The Philippines*. The attack came on 22 December. Manila, an open city, was bombed. Bataan and Corregidor fell. MacArthur was forced to leave.

(d) *Malaya*. Wavell was placed in command, but there was confusion about the response. On 10 December *Prince of Wales* and *Repulse* were sunk. By 15 January the Japanese had turned Britain's Malayan position and advanced on Singapore by land. After a short siege Percival surrendered; 64,000 prisoners were taken. It was a major disaster, and a serious loss of face for the British in Asia.

(e) *The East Indies*. The British colonies there fell in quick succession and the Dutch East Indies were invaded. A fleet tried to stem the tide, but was defeated at the battles of the Java Sea. Java surrendered on 9 March with 20,000 prisoners, including 5,000 British.

(f) *Burma*. The Japanese advanced swiftly into Burma. Rangoon fell on 6 March and in April the British were driven out, and Wavell's command ceased to exist. After a naval defeat in the Indian Ocean, Colombo was bombed, but the Japanese had reached the limit of their penetration.

These startling events from the British point of view were accompanied by two other Japanese thrusts towards Australia and into the Pacific.

(a) Darwin was raided in February and Timor occupied. The Australians in New Britain (Rabaul) were overwhelmed and New Guinea invaded. In May Port Moresby was attacked and on 31 May–1 June, four Japanese submarines were sunk in Sydney Harbour.

(b) Wake Island fell and the Japanese pushed on, taking Tarawa in the Gilberts, and Bougainville in the Solomons. Not until the Battle of the Coral Sea (5–8 May) was their advance checked.

Inevitably this series of defeats led to confusion and argument. Roosevelt blamed the British for not being more aggressive in Burma, and Churchill blamed the Americans for diverting landing craft to the Pacific. Wavell was replaced by Mountbatten in August 1943, with Slim as field commander. In the Australian area MacArthur was in charge, with the Australian Blamey as army commander.

(a) *Midway Island*. The Japanese lost air supremacy in June 1942. When they decided to attack Guadalcanal the American counter-offensive began (7 August). A series of naval battles occurred as the Japanese sought to bring in reinforcements (the Solomon Islands, Guadalcanal). By stopping these, the Americans defeated the Japanese in February.

(b) *New Guinea*. The Japanese, defeated at sea, tried a land-based attack on Port Moresby (July 1942). They were defeated by January 1943. New Guinea was cleared during 1943 and, following American landings on the north coast in 1944, the Japanese were cut off by July.

(c) *Islands advance*. After a defeat at the Bismarck Sea (March 1943), the Japanese in Rabaul were isolated. By February 1944 The Admiralty Islands were regained, and 100,000 Japanese cut off. The Gilberts and the Marshalls fell. The Japanese fought hard at the Marianas, but were defeated at Saipan (June 1944). Guam was captured in July, and bombing of Japan from the islands started. The defensive perimeter was broken, and by mid-1944 the South Pacific was clear.

E4. Anglo-American Relations

Although Churchill spoke of a grand alliance, there was no treaty between Britain and America. Informal contacts were a disadvantage in such matters as the exchange of atomic secrets, and the relationship between the two leaders was never an easy one. The reasons for their difficulties were:

(*a*) *Relations with Russia.* Outwardly, Russia seemed to be cooperating. Roosevelt was sure he could handle the Russians, and told Churchill, 'I think I can handle Stalin better than either your Foreign Office or my State Department.' Roosevelt pledged a second front in 1942.

(*b*) *The Imperial Question.* Roosevelt disliked the British Empire as much as the Russians, and continually annoyed Churchill by proposals to give up Hong Kong or other territories. Roosevelt suspected Churchill of pursuing a Middle East strategy to benefit the Empire.

(*c*) *Other powers.* Roosevelt backed Chiang Kai-Shek since the Chinese held down half the Japanese army. Churchill backed De Gaulle while the Americans disliked him.

At first these political differences were obscured by the need to arrive at joint plans for world war. At the Arcadia Conference (December 1941–January 1942) it was decided to set up Combined Chiefs of Staff in Washington. Their 200 meetings were to determine the strategy of the war, and it was a remarkable example of cooperation. But within the organisation there was a considerable rift, since Admiral King wanted concentration on the Pacific while Marshall inclined to direct intervention in Europe. Few of the Americans favoured Churchill's wish for an African war, but since they were not the predominant partner, they were forced at first to accept British strategy.

(*a*) *Churchill and the second front.* The original plan (Gymnast) was replaced in April 1942 by Bolero and Round Up, but Churchill was unwilling to accept, and Dieppe proved him right.

(*b*) *Hyde Park* (June 1942). Churchill wanted priority given to North Africa and then to an attack on the soft underbelly of Europe. He criticised plans for a European operation (Sledgehammer) and insisted on an *aide memoire* stating Britain did not agree to a second front unconditionally. Rommel's successful offensive threatened Mediterranean communications and this in turn affected the Far East. Roosevelt therefore accepted North Africa first (Torch) in July.

Pressure in the Mediterranean had also caused convoys to be suspended, so Churchill flew to Moscow to tell Stalin there would be no Western second front. It is not clear if he promised one in 1943, although the Churchill line was that several fronts already existed. The North African landings produced further difficulties with the French, and the problem of the next move.

(*c*) *Casablanca Conference* (January 1943). Victories on all three main fronts meant that planning for the future could proceed. European invasion was to be in 1944. Russia was not to be given atom secrets. But there were two acrimonious disputes. Marshall wanted a direct build-up in Europe for 1943 but Roosevelt had to accept Sicily, as Britain had the larger share of the forces. However, in exchange he insisted on further Burmese offensives and an equal diversion of landing craft to the Far East after African victory. Unconditional surrender was announced.

The African campaign took longer than expected, but directly Sicily was invaded, the two Allies were at loggerheads again.

(*d*) *Trident* (May 1943). There were complaints from MacArthur that he was denied landing craft. Thus, although Roosevelt once again accepted the Churchill line and opted for Italian invasion, there was considerable delay which allowed the Germans to take control of the situation. It was agreed to give shipping priority to Overlord.

(*e*) *Quadrant* (August 1943). The defeat of Italy led to further rows since Roosevelt wanted a quick armistice, while Churchill wanted a full agreement with the royal government. Roosevelt insisted on diverting a proportion of troops to an additional offensive in southern France (Anvil) in return for agreeing to Churchill's insistence on reducing the odds before Overlord was attempted.

The Italian negotiations were not completed until 29 September, but although Britain got the fleet, Germany seized Italy.

(*f*) *The Moscow Foreign Ministers Meeting* (October 1943). Eden, Hull and Molotov tried to sort out the various issues. It was agreed Russians should be included on the Italian Advisory Committee and convoys restarted. The Russians were pleased at the decision for Overlord, and agreed that Austria should be treated as a defeated power. Hull insisted that the declaration in favour of a United Nations should be signed by China, and Stalin said Russia would enter the war against Japan. It was agreed to appoint a European Advisory Commission to consider the fate of Germany.

By the end of 1943 a rift was appearing in the Allies, brought about partly by the Anglo-American line-up, and more by a growing belief on the part of the Americans that they could deal with Russia directly. This coincided with growing fears on Churchill's part that Russia in matters like Poland was seeking to obtain advantage from the war. Roosevelt originally proposed a meeting with Stalin in Alaska, but it was then agreed to hold a meeting of the Big Three (Section F4).

F. The War of the Grand Alliance, 1943–44

F1. Victory in Africa

On 8 November 1942 Allied landings took place in North Africa, but the Americans had insisted on landings as far west as possible. This enabled the Germans to form a defensive salient round Tunis, and the offensive ground to a halt. In the south Montgomery had reached the Mareth Line (16 February).

(*a*) *Kasserine.* Rommel decided on a breakout between the two allied armies. The Americans were pushed back, but Alexander had taken over as commander and defeated the breakout at Kasserine (25 February).

(*b*) *Mareth Line.* Rommel was defeated in an assault at Medenine and, by a series of skilful manoeuvres, Montgomery turned the Mareth Line by 6 April. Rommel was recalled because of illness.

(*c*) *Fall of Tunis.* Although both British and Americans were held off by the Germans for a time, Tunis fell and the Italians surrendered on 13 May. The Allies took 250,415 prisoners.

The African campaign proved the Germans could be defeated. It provided useful experience for Anglo-American cooperation, and produced in Montgomery and Alexander two distinguished generals. It saved the British position in Africa, and opened the Mediterranean to convoys which were vital to the Far East. It paved the way for the fall of Mussolini. Above all, by costing the Axis a million dead or prisoner it provided an effective second front and made a decisive contribution to victory.

F2. The Burmese War

American concern with China and Roosevelt's insistence that he would only accept Churchill's Mediterranean strategy if he would make a larger contribution in the Far East led to pressure to start a Burma campaign.

(a) *The first offensives.* Wavell was pushed into an offensive down the Arakan coast to Akyab, but fear of the Japanese and disease weakened the effort, and it was driven back. In December 1943–March 1944 Slim renewed the offensive, but was halted by a need for reinforcements elsewhere.

(b) *The Chindits.* Wingate's brigade aimed at long-range penetration and boosting morale by showing Japanese could be defeated in the jungle. From February to May 1943 they sought to cut the railway lines, but casualties were high, and Wingate died in an air crash.

(c) *Allied failures.* To protect a new road to China (the Ledo Road) Stilwell attacked towards Myitkyina, but was held. It only fell in August 1944. To spoil an Allied offensive and prepare for invasion of India by cutting rail links to Stilwell's troops, the Japanese launched an attack on Kohima and Imphal where the garrisons were cut off.

(d) *The defeat of Japan.* Between April and June 1944 Kohima and Imphal were relieved after 80-day sieges and the Japanese defeated. In November the Chindwin was crossed, Stilwell's army met and the Irrawaddy crossed in January 1945. A surprise attack secured Miektila, and the Japanese were defeated, abandoning Mandalay. A rapid drive on Rangoon before the monsoon now followed and it was entered on 3 May.

The Burmese campaign was called 'the forgotten war', but it helped to wear down the Japanese. It was another British front that Stalin conveniently ignored.

F3. The Fall of Mussolini

The decisions at Casablanca and Mediterranean victory cleared the way for the invasion of Italy.

(a) *The conquest of Sicily.* Command passed to Alexander with Patton and Montgomery to command the landings. The landings of 9 July occurred in high seas and with an airborne attack failing. An attempt of the Axis to counter-attack from Gela was defeated by bombardment. The two forces linked up in Messina by August, but a German rearguard action enabled the Italians to evacuate 40,000.

In April 1943 Mussolini begged Hitler to make a truce in Russia and come to his aid. Hitler refused. The Chief of Italian Staff told Mussolini they could not resist, and Hitler could see his ally was cracking. Badoglio and the King removed Mussolini on 25 July in order to seek terms. Hitler was furious, since 700,000 Italians were in Russia and the Balkans, and he decided to save his ally and reinforce Kesselring. The same day Roosevelt said unconditional surrender must apply to Italy when Badoglio had opened negotiations. The armistice did not come into force until 8 September. The result was that the army was disarmed by the Germans and only 320 planes were secured. The government fled, but Hitler rescued Mussolini and set up a puppet republic in the north. Hitler moved 18 divisions into Italy, and the Allies were faced with a slogging campaign. An Italian partisan movement sprang up against the Germans and SOE sent in supplies. From Bari the Allies were able to aid Balkan partisans, and the defeat of Italy drew German and Italian forces from the Balkans to help their liberation.

(*b*) *Salerno.* Three landings occurred. One captured Bari and advanced up the east coast to Termoli. The diversionary attack by Montgomery came at Reggio and advanced through Calabria. The American attack came at Salerno and was nearly a disaster. By October the armies had linked, and drove on the line of the Volturno.

(*c*) *The Gustav Line.* After the capture of Naples, the Allies faced German defensive positions 10 miles wide. Although Montgomery crossed the Sangro (15 November) the Americans were held, and bad weather set in.

(*d*) *Anzio and Monte Cassino.* The aim was for a joint attack, but the American landing at Anzio in January 1944 failed, and the result was a hard slogging battle until Monte Cassino fell on 18 May. The Axis retreat then enabled the Allied forces to advance at last, and on 4 June Rome was entered.

Roosevelt insisted on 'Anvil,' and on diverting landing craft to the Pacific, and this caused delay. By January 1945, 13 divisions were diverted from Italy.

(*e*) *The Gothic Line.* The attack was started on 30 August and, after severe fighting, Rimini fell. The Americans also attacked, and by 25 September the Gothic line was turned, but an advance by the Americans towards Bologna failed and winter again halted advance.

(*f*) *The final advance* began on 9 April and Bologna fell. The 5th Army entered Milan and linked up with Americans from the north on 6 May while the 8th Army met the Yugoslavs. The Italians surrendered on 2 May, yielding 1 million prisoners. Italian partisans killed Mussolini on 28 April.

Because of failure to provide sufficient resources, the Italian campaign was lengthy and lacking in tactical surprises. The prize of Vienna, which could have been secured, was lost because of American reluctance to be drawn into Central Europe. But it held down 26 divisions which could have tipped the scales in the West or the East, and inflicted 556,000 casualties on the Germans for half as many losses.

F4. The Big Three Meet at Teheran

The two problems of wartime planning and post-war settlement were brought into vivid relief at the conferences of Cairo and Teheran. Wilmot says they 'not only determined the military strategy for 1944 but adjusted the political balance of post-war Europe in favour of the Soviet Union' with obvious consequences for Britain's world position.

(*a*) *The first Cairo meeting.* Churchill, Roosevelt and Chiang Kai-Shek met and Churchill wanted to face Stalin with an agreed plan. Roosevelt refused and insisted on pressing China's demand for a full-scale offensive in the Bay of Bengal which would reduce the margin of safety for Overlord even further. Churchill now urged further Mediterranean activity to divert German divisions from France. As they could not agree, the final decision was left until after meeting Stalin.

(b) *Teheran Summit* (28 November–1 December 1943), Roosevelt said, 'I have just a hunch that Stalin doesn't want anything but security for his country, and I think that if I give him everything I possibly can and ask nothing from him in return he ... will work for a world democracy and peace.' At Teheran he met Stalin separately three times and joked about Churchill behind his back. He called Stalin 'Uncle Joe' and believed he had made a conquest.

The main decisions taken at Teheran were:

(i) Stalin said the Balkans would be liberated by the Red Army and, although accepting Anvil, resisted Churchill's proposals for an advance on Vienna.
(ii) Stalin agreed to join the war against Japan which Roosevelt considered vital for American victory.
(iii) Stalin insisted on his 1940 gains staying Russian, and also said compensation would be taken from Germany and Poland. He objected to the Polish government in exile, and there was an argument over the borders.

Roosevelt and Churchill returned to Cairo, where the President was now willing to increase the allocation for Overlord. He told Churchill the original proposal that Overlord should be a British command was unsuitable, and that Eisenhower was to be appointed.

G. The Rise and Fall of Empires, 1944–45

The last 20 months of war had a double significance. At the time attention was concentrated on defeating Germany and Japan. Memories and fresh knowledge of their aggressions and crimes were uppermost in most people's minds including Roosevelt's. Churchill was less sanguine, and Stalin's thoughts remain an enigma. In the wish to defeat Fascism the West allowed Communism to make substantial gains. This was partly inevitable. The Red Army freed Eastern Europe, and many countries there had thrown in their lot with Hitler. The political and economic backwaters of Europe were ripe for a Communist new deal. But it was also partly a product of decisions—some taken by politicians, others by generals in the field—and it must remain an open question whether yielding Central Europe to Stalin's control was either inevitable or desirable. In Asia a similar pattern is discernible. Desire to destroy Japan led Roosevelt to support Chiang and urge greater British participation in that theatre of war. Directly this object was achieved, lend lease was cut off from Chiang, Russia was allowed to regain all the Czars had lost and become involved in China and Korea, while Britain was urged to surrender her imperial commitments.

G1. Planning a Brave New World

Planning for the world after the war was now progressing. As in 1918, America had idealist solutions which were against the interests of Britain, but in the interests of Allied unity and under the influence of utopian views a number of decision were made:

(a) *The trial of war criminals.* As early as October 1941 Roosevelt and

Churchill had condemned atrocities. The murder of Jews, prisoners of war and inhabitants of occupied countries, combined with systematic torturing and looting, were practised by Germans and Japanese. In November 1943 it was agreed to try German war criminals. A War Crimes Commission of 17 nations met in London and in August 1945 agreed on an international tribunal.

(b) *UNRRA.* In the White House Declaration of November 1943 an organisation for helping refugees and repatriation was established; 30 million had been displaced in one way or another, and work started in 1944 and went on until 1947.

(c) *Economic reorganisation.* In the Atlantic Charter, Britain agreed to the 'elimination of discrimination' in trade and in the Mutual Aid Agreement of 1942 repeated this pledge. The Bretton Woods Conference of July 1944 agreed to set up an International Monetary Fund, an International Bank for Reconstruction and proposed an International Trade Organisation which later (1947) became the General Agreement on Tariffs and Trade. These measures indicated the new American rôle as the world's financial master, and were counter to the interests of the sterling area and imperial preference.

(d) *A United Nations.* The Jebb Memorandum of 1942 proposed a world organisation controlled by the big powers and there were a number of proposals circulating. In 1944 the Dumbarton Oaks Conference discussed the formation of a United Nations. Russia opposed the west on three issues: the veto, the composition of the security council and the total membership.

G2. Planning D-Day

The invasion of Western Europe was the largest combined operation ever undertaken, and needed exceptional planning if it was to succeed. Hitler was preparing jet aircraft, flying bombs and long-range rockets, Albert Speer conducted a brilliant development of German defence industries and the Allies faced 60 divisions in Western Europe. It was essential surprise should be secured. A special operation (Fortitude) successfully persuaded the generals that invasion would be in the Pas de Calais. Command was shared between the Allies, but there was considerable friction. It was Eisenhower's particular skill to calm these service ruffles. Tedder was deputy supreme commander and Bedell Smith, Chief of Staff. The naval force was commanded by Admiral Ramsey, the air force by Leigh Mallory and the army by Montgomery until Eisenhower landed to take over. The American landings were under Bradley, and the British under Dempsey.

Although D-Day and the subsequent invasion involved $3\frac{1}{2}$ million men, 13,000 planes and 5,000 ships, there were still some moments when success hung by a thread. The Americans, believing in direct attack and underestimating the difficulties, disliked Churchill's constant interference and insistence on overwhelming strength.

G3. Liberating Western Europe

(a) *The assault.* Bradley landed on Utah and Omaha beaches, Dempsey on Gold, Juno and Sword (6 June). Apart from Omaha all went well. Bradley's army broke out and captured Cherbourg, then turned south and captured St Lo (24 July). But the advance from Omaha was delayed at Caumont.

(b) *Battle of Normandy.* The aim was for Montgomery to draw the German forces onto Caen to allow an American breakout. The first attack on Caen failed and the second (Operation Goodwood) succeeded. Caen fell on 20 July. The Americans broke out and seized Avranches by 30 July.

(c) *The breakout.* Patton advanced on 1 August into Britanny, and south to the Loire, reaching Nantes on 10 August. Hitler's insistence on counterattack trapped the Germans south of Falaise, where 50,000 were captured (20 August). The French were allowed to enter Paris first on 25 August.

This decisive victory severely mauled the Germans. But the Allies now dispersed their efforts and this began to slow the advance down.

(*d*) *Operation Anvil* started on 15 August with the French allowed to take the lead. Victories on the south coast were followed by advance up the Rhône and contact was made with Patton on 12 September. This produced an unnecessary concentration of forces in central France and helped to swing the balance to a broad advance.

(*e*) *Advance to Brussels*. Aiming to capture V1 and V2 sites and Antwerp, and enter the Ruhr, Montgomery advanced north, capturing Brussels and Antwerp (4 September), although the port was not usable. The American armies advanced to Luxemburg, the Moselle and towards Nancy, thus transferring a narrow into a broad front and creating transport problems due to petrol shortages.

G4. Arnhem and the Ardennes

Montgomery wanted an advance north to encircle the Ruhr and march on Berlin but Eisenhower condemned a 'pencil-like thrust' (which it was not) and opted for a broad front, yielding to pressure from Hodges and Patton and to domestic considerations that would not allow British forces to take the main credit for victory. The results of this decision were appalling: 48 divisions were spread over 600 miles, an attempt at advance was defeated and the Germans, who had massed their last reserves to form 40 divisions, were able to counterattack at the very moment Russia began her offensive in the east. The war was prolonged and the military balance shifted in Russia's favour just before Yalta.

(*a*) *The failure at Arnhem*. To secure a continuous advance, Montgomery decided on airborne attacks to clear the way for Horrocks' army. Landings at Eindhoven and Grave succeeded and Nijmegen was captured, but at Arnhem the drops were made too far from the objective, and unexpected German reinforcements were able to defeat the attack (26 September). Montgomery had to be content to clear the Scheldt estuary and open Antwerp in December.

(*b*) *Patton's advance* began again on 16 November. Metz, Belfort and Strasbourg fell by 23 November, but to the south the Germans in the Colmar pocket were able to tie down the Americans until February 1945. The Roer dams were captured to preserve a crossing point on the Rhine.

(*c*) *The Ardennes offensive*. Hitler aimed to capture Antwerp and split the Allies in their wide-open situation. The attack began on 16 December and was aided by bad weather, Allied intelligence failures and German deceptions. Reserves sent in were cut off at Bastogne. Eisenhower transferred command in the north to Montgomery and on 26 December the advance was held. Attack by Hodges from the north and Patton from the south eliminated the Bulge by 7 February 1945. The Germans lost 250,000 and their last Luftwaffe reserves.

G5. The Russians Enter Europe

During the second half of 1944 the Russian front remained stable in the centre as it was necessary to convert the gauge of the railway lines. Stalin's armies continued to advance into south-eastern Europe. Belgrade fell and, although the Germans annexed Hungary and fought for Budapest, the city fell after a long siege in February 1945. The Russians entered Vienna on 14 April 1945. The D-Day landings reduced the number of German divisions from 157 to 133, with a further 30 cut off on the Baltic coast. On 12 January advance into German territory was resumed. Warsaw fell on 17 January, and a sweep north to the Baltic cut off 500,000 Germans. The Russians advanced in the centre, and reached the line of the Oder. In Czechoslovakia partisans had risen, and a movement from north to south took the Russians to Prague on 9 May. Finally, on 16 April, the Russian advance on Berlin began, the city was cut off on 25 April, Hitler committed suicide; on 2 May Berlin surrendered.

But these victories were also defeats for the Western powers brought about by Roosevelt and Eisenhower, who did not approve of Churchill's increasing anti-Russian stance or the diversion of troops for political purposes. The Americans insisted on honouring Teheran decisions in spite of such events as the Warsaw Rising. A series of strategic decisions therefore yielded Central Europe to an ally who was at least suspect by the end of 1944. This situation caused Churchill great alarm, which he translated into action at two conferences:

(*a*) *Quebec* (September 1944). It was agreed to resume bombing of Germany, and to draw up plans for pastoralising the country at the end of the war. Zones of occupation for Germany were agreed between Britain and America. Britain agreed to enter the war against Japan with air and naval forces and Roosevelt raised no objection to the return of the British to Greece. Eisenhower's plan for a broad advance with the weight in the north was accepted.

(*b*) *Moscow* (October 1944). Churchill proposed agreement on spheres of influence as Eastern Europe was liberated. Eventually these were settled as 50–50 in Yugoslavia and Hungary, 90 per cent for Britain in Greece and for Russia in Rumania, and 75 per cent for Russia in Bulgaria. Churchill hoped that this would provide a background for agreement on Poland.

There was no proper government of Greece so, when the Germans withdrew, left-wing partisans were virtually in control. EDES supported the monarchy and as Greece, like Poland, had been guaranteed by Britain, Churchill acted. When a truce between the two sides broke down, British forces returned to Greece in December 1944. Churchill and Eden followed and a Regency was appointed with a new government (30 December). This action was criticised by Stettinius, the new Secretary of State, and in Britain was condemned by many on the left.

G6. The Yalta Conference, February 1945

The Yalta Conference was 'the most important of the wartime meetings' and lasted from 4 to 11 February. Whereas Taylor states 'Roosevelt was the only one who knew what he was doing', others have taken the view that he was ill, and under grave misapprehensions. Roosevelt was determined to bring Russia into the Pacific war to save American lives, and was prepared to make concessions. He did not believe there was a Russian threat in Eastern Europe, which was to be safeguarded by a Declaration on Liberated Europe. The decisions taken were:

(*a*) Eisenhower was to be allowed to communicate with the Russian general staff directly.

(*b*) Stalin agreed to Churchill's request that France should be included in the occupation forces.

(*c*) America announced her troops would be withdrawn from Europe within two years. Russia made no such announcement.

(*d*) Progress was made on setting up the United Nations when the Russians reduced their demands from 16 to three delegations from Soviet republics.

(*e*) A Reparations Commission was to be set up. Molotov demanded $20,000m, of which half was to go to Russia.

(*f*) Stalin was to enter the war in the East and was given territorial compensation at Chiang Kai-Shek's expense.

(*g*) The borders of Poland were to be drawn in Russia's favour, but a Polish Commission was to unite the government in exile with the Lublin government.

Wilmot called Yalta 'Stalin's greatest victory'. At the time it was regarded as a major success by nearly all. In the Commons only 17 voted against. At least it cannot be denied the West tried hard to obtain agreement with Russia and made a series of major concessions. Roosevelt praised Yalta, and even Churchill said he believed genuine agreement possible. But in the next three months the Russians became stubborn over the United Nations, refused to cooperate over Poland and took full advantage of the agreement to secure control in Eastern Europe. Instead of a 1919 *cordon sanitaire*, there was now a security zone protecting Russia. Poland was 150 miles inside it. In spite of Russian action, American troops halted on the Elbe and on 1 July withdrew sometimes up to 120 miles back, precipitating fresh droves of refugees. The middle months of 1945 were truly, in Seaman's words 'victory without peace'.

G7. The Defeat of Japan

In October 1944, with the Battles of Leyte Gulf and the end of Japanese sea power, the advance on Japanese Asia began. The main stages were:

(*a*) *Freeing the Philippines.* In January 1945 landings began. Manila was besieged, Corregidor was recaptured and by 4 July Luzon was secure.

(*b*) *Advance on the Japanese islands.* After bombardment, Iwojima was attacked, but it did not fall until 26 March. Okinawa was invaded on 1 April, but the Japanese did not collapse until 21 June with the loss of 107,000 in combat and 20,000 sealed in hideouts. The Japanese air force was destroyed with the loss of 4,000 planes.

Stiffening resistance was typified by the kamikaze pilots who sank 36 ships. Two operations for the invasion of Japan were prepared, and war into 1947 was visualised. Roosevelt overestimated the danger of last-minute resistance and Truman certainly neglected to respond clearly to Japanese peace feelers put out through Russia. But MacArthur urged Russian and British participation and the movement of substantial forces from Europe. From February to August, Japan was bombed severely, with 200,000 casualties in Tokyo alone. On 8 August Russia invaded Manchuria, and in 10 days advanced to the 38th parallel in Korea. Marshall thought this might be decisive, but Truman decided otherwise. There was now an Allied secret weapon that would win the war.

G8. The Fall of Germany

Although in the north and south the Allies had reached the Rhine, the

Ardennes offensive and the West Wall held them in the centre, and a triple advance was necessary to reach the river along its length during February and March 1945.

(a) *Crossing the Rhine.* In the north advance was made through Cleves to the Rhine by 1 March, in the south to Mainz by 22 March and in the centre to Remagen by 7 March. On 22–23 March the Rhine was crossed in force. By the first week in April it was cleared.

(b) *The Ruhr pocket.* Thirty generals surrendered with 323,000 prisoners in the Ruhr pocket. Eisenhower then turned south towards Leipzig, as had been agreed, and on 25 April reached the Elbe: Munich was entered on 30 April, and on 4 May contact made with the Allies in Italy.

(c) *The British northern advance.* Montgomery swept north. German troops in Holland surrendered after an agreement. Bremen was entered on 26 April, and Hamburg on 3 May.

Montgomery accepted unconditional surrender (4 May) and surrender to the three powers took place on 7 May. On 5 June the Allied Commanders (Montgomery, Eisenhower and Zhukov) signed the agreement for the Allied zones of occupation, and at the end of the month discussed the question of access to Berlin. Western requests were denied, and it was limited to one road, railway and air route. On 1 July Eisenhower withdrew his forces to the agreed zones.

G9. The Atom Bomb

Throughout the war scientists had responded to the demands made on them. This 'Wizard War' produced great advances in medicine, communications and aerodynamics. Computers, the jet engine, rockets and atomic power were brought to fruition by the necessity of war. Just as Hitler put faith in his secret weapons so did the West. Of these, the atom bomb was the most important.

During 1939 the scientific world was discussing the possibility of an atomic bomb. Einstein warned the American government of such a weapon. Since Bohr was in Copenhagen until 1943 and Germany had a vital supply of heavy water in Norway, it was essential to develop the bomb. During 1940 at Liverpool and Birmingham Universities a team led by Chadwick and three refugees, Rotblat, Frisch and Peierls, solved the basic problem of finding how much uranium was needed. Tizard empowered Sir George Thompson to set up the Maud Committee (April 1940). Oxford and Cambridge joined in, but it was still felt that little could be done. The Maud Report in July 1941 changed matters.

In August 1941 Churchill authorised work to proceed and in October Tube Alloys was set up under Sir John Anderson. Tizard gave the Americans details. Churchill failed to make a clear agreement when in June 1942 the Manhattan Project started, and British scientists went to America. By August 1943 the bomb was under complete American control. Britain destroyed the heavy water in Norway (February) and rescued Bohr (October), who arrived in Washington in November 1943.

On 16 July 1945 the test bomb was exploded. The Allies demanded unconditional surrender from Japan, but failed to mention the fate of the Emperor. The government declined to reply, and this was taken as final. The other two bombs were dropped. On 6 August Hiroshima suffered

129,000 and on 9 August Nagasaki 95,000 casualties. Next day the Japanese agreed to treat, although asking for special treatment for the Emperor. An armistice was agreed on 14-15 August and signed on 2 September.

G10. The Potsdam Conference, July 1945

Between Yalta and Potsdam the gap between Churchill and the Americans widened. Roosevelt remained convinced Russia could be appeased. His message to Churchill sent on the day of his death (12 April) said, 'I would minimise the general Soviet problem as much as possible.' Truman could not dissent from policies already laid down, and was a machine politician who had yet to find his feet. In June Stettinius was succeeded by Byrnes, who was even more determined to reach accord, and the Americans placed more emphasis on setting up the United Nations than in dealing with Europe. Attention was focused on the San Francisco Conference (25 April–26 June).

(a) *Soviet intransigence.* The Polish Commission found itself in difficulties from the start, and in April the Russians recognised the Lublin government. When Polish representatives were sent, 15 were arrested. They were tried to deter the London Poles from taking part in the new government.

(b) *Churchill's final bid.* With attention on the dramatic end in Germany and the discovery of the concentration camps it was difficult to argue for continued vigilance. Churchill tried. On 13 March he told Roosevelt, 'We are in the presence of a great failure and an utter breakdown of what was settled at Yalta.' Again, on 12 May he told Truman, 'I feel deep anxiety because of ... the combination of Russian power and territories under their control or occupied.'

America was not entirely pro-Russian. Roosevelt protested against Stalin's charge that the West wanted a separate peace, and Truman complained about Poland. America agreed to join in the military occupation zones, and denied knowledge of the atom bomb to the Russians. But on Eastern Europe, including the freedom of Poland, the rights of the Balkan states to democratic government, and the extent of Soviet military power, the Americans chose appeasement. Later they had to eat their words. But at the time the American line was conciliatory. Churchill wanted a fresh conference, but Truman said that he would prefer Stalin to call it. He then sent two missions to Europe:

(a) *The Davies Mission.* Davies came to Britain and in an interview with Churchill criticised him for being too friendly to Germany and hostile to Russia, and said they should rely on Russian good faith. He said Truman would meet Stalin alone.

(b) *The Hopkins–Harriman Mission.* This went to Moscow and the question of a meeting was raised. Stalin said Russia would not tolerate a *cordon sanitaire* including Poland, and it was agreed to have a three-power meeting about the two Polish governments, the informing of Chiang about Yalta and the veto question at San Francisco.

In June the London Poles at last arrived in Moscow, but the government set up had only six places for them out of 20. The new government arrived in Warsaw and was recognised by the West on 5 July.

(c) *Potsdam Meeting* (Terminal) (17 July–1 August). The background was the establishment of German occupation zones and the continuing war with

Japan. On 27 July Attlee and Bevin replaced Churchill and Eden. It was 'an untidy postscript' which clearly showed to the informed that the Grand Alliance was no more.

The main decisions were:

(*a*) A Council of Foreign Ministers of the Big Five to draft the peace treaties was accepted.

(*b*) Poland was discussed, but although Churchill objected to the shifting of the western border to the Oder–Neisse Line, there was little for the West to bargain with. All they got was a promise to hold democratic elections.

(*c*) Churchill wanted Germany treated as one ecomonic unit, but could not obtain this. The Russians obtained reparations including 15 per cent of capital equipment to be removed from the Western zones. Russia only dropped excessive demands in return for recognition of Poland's right 'to administer' land up to the Oder–Neisse Line.

(*d*) Stalin put forward demands for a trusteeship in Africa, involvement in Syria and a treaty with Turkey with territorial gains.

(*e*) There was agreement on the trial of German war criminals, and on the entry of Russia into the war on 8 August.

The war thus stands out in British history in two ways. On the surface it was the finest hour. Britain contributed so great a percentage of her resources that she was economically exhausted. She had fought for no territorial or economic gains as in 1914. The Empire had rallied, and those parts of it that had fallen to the Italians and Japanese were reconquered. The armed services stood at an all-time peak and British forces were found throughout the world. She had helped to destroy her rivals, Germany, Japan and Italy, but in depriving them of their empires in fact rendered them a service. By the 1960s all three had recovered and two were to be deadly competitors.

Russia had reversed her losses in 1919, obtained large gains and created a sphere of influence in Europe and Asia which preserved her territory from attack and gave her the basis for future advance. In territorial terms the victor was Russia. In addition, her military strength and her diplomatic involvement had ended her isolation, and made her a world power. She was opposed to British interests and eager to foster nationalism in the Middle and Far East.

America had lost fewer casualties and suffered less direct damage than any other major power. She had devoted a small percentage of her total wealth to the war, and emerged as the greatest world power with the 'almighty dollar', the atom bomb and new world-wide responsibilities. Although Britain still believed in a special relationship the Americans too had little sympathy for the British Empire. Its days were numbered.

Further Reading

Arnold–Foster, M., *The World at War*, Collins, London, 1973.

Churchill, W. L. S., *The Second World War*, Cassells, 1948–1954 (6 vols).

Collier, B., *A Short History of the Second World War*, Collins, London, 1967.

Collier, B., *The Battle of Britain*, Batsford, London, 1962.

Collier, B., *The Battle of the V-Weapons*, Hodder and Stoughton, London, 1964.

Feis, H., *Churchill, Roosevelt and Stalin*, Oxford UP, London, 1957.

Fleming, P., *Operation Sea Lion*, Hart Davis, London 1957, available as paperback, Pan Books, 1975.

Jones, R. V., *Most Secret War*, Hamish Hamilton, London, 1978.

Michel, H., *The Second World War*, André Deutsch, London, 1975.

Thorne, C., *The USA, Britain, and the War Against Japan*, Hamish Hamilton, London, 1978.

Wilmot, C., *The Struggle for Europe*, Collins, London, 1952, reprinted 1978.

Young, P. (ed.) *An Atlas of the Second World War*, Weidenfeld and Nicolson, London, 1973.

Questions

1. What is meant by saying that the strategy of the 1939–45 war was 'genuinely world wide'?
2. Why were the Western powers so easily defeated in the period to June 1940?
3. What is the significance of the year 1940 in military terms?
4. How effective was the Grand Alliance in fighting the war?
5. What was Churchill's overall contribution to world war politics and strategy?
6. Why can the war be seen as a victory and a defeat for Great Britain?
7. Were the British wars in Africa and Asia of any lasting value?
8. How effective was the strategy for reconquering Western Europe in 1944–45?
9. Was America or Russia the real victor at the end of the world war?

14

THE WORLD WAR—POLITICS, ECONOMICS AND SOCIETY: 1939–45

The parliament elected in November 1935 (Chapter 9, A4) was not dissolved until July 1945, and was the fourth longest in British history. Seaman and Medlicott almost completely ignore home politics after the crisis of May 1940 which brought Churchill to power and, apart from failing to do justice to the wartime achievements of the 'appeasers' parliament', this prevents understanding of the changes that politics underwent during the war. In spite of Churchill's personal popularity, 1945 proved very different from 1918, although the wartime coalition was politically comprehensive, reformist and successful in winning the war. The government did not win a single by-election and lost seats to reformists like the Commonwealth Party. Attlee refused to continue the coalition unless an election was postponed until October 1945, being determined to have no 'khaki stunt' as in 1918. Churchill therefore formed a Caretaker Government as a prelude to the election.

Three historians have done much to alter the state of neglect mentioned above. Marwick has drawn attention to the dynamic relationship between war and social change. Calder has given a good account of the more mundane but not unimportant aspects of the war, showing how in welfare, trade unions and class structure change was rapid, although he is inclined to doubt its depth. Addison's *The Road to 1945* covers the ground from a political angle for the first time, drawing attention to the way consensus was obtained over a wide area of policy. He shows how Bevin, Cripps and Beveridge emerged as the well-known names on the home front, and Labour, by running the home policy cabinet committees, came to have a dominant voice, while Churchill was more concerned with strategy and diplomacy. Labour acquired vital experience while it seemed the Conservatives were reluctant to change and guilt-ridden for events prior to 1940. Many appeasers like Halifax and Simon were in evidence still in 1945. Whatever Churchill might say about social reform, he was not believed.

This gave rise to the greatest paradox of all. In order to fight the fascist states, Britain adopted collectivist and socialist policies. The economy was mobilised to its highest point when there were no more labour or gold reserves left and Britain devoted a high proportion of her resources to fighting the war. Churchill, who constantly talked of liberty, was a dictator who mobilised women and children in the factories and mines. Whatever the outward forms of government, the Emergency Powers Act of May 1940 gave it absolute power. This was necessary, but it was not Conservative or Liberal policy, and the war effort thus brought a swing to ideas put forward during the 1930s in favour of a managed economy, planning, a welfare state and nationalisation (Chapter 10, A5). Circumstances converted many to ideas previously thought impossible, and the impact of total war compelled the government to pass measures which laid the basis for the acceptance of Labour plans in 1945. In Addison's words, 'the coalition proved to be the greatest reforming administration since the Liberal government of 1905–14'. But, although Churchill eventually backed the Beveridge Report and allowed Kingsley Wood to introduce a Keynesian budget, it seemed more logical to hand over the process to the left. The war which so changed Britain's world position brought about the only major economic and social change of the century by paving the way for the first effective Labour government. How this was accomplished is the inner story of wartime politics.

A. The Fifth National Government, September 1939–May 1940

A1. The 'Guilty Men' Ministry

It is said Chamberlain laid his head on the table for ten minutes after the decision for war; in political terms he had good reason. Labour and Liberals refused to join him and both parties continued to criticise the government in secret parliamentary sessions. The local government elections were suspended, and a system of regional government came into force side by side with the elected councils. No one seemed anxious to fight the war now it had come. There were plenty of 'peace Tories' including Halifax and Butler. Lloyd George urged talks with Hitler. Maxton, Cripps and Bevan condemned the war as capitalist, and the Communist Party adopted the same line. In November, 22 Labour MPs urged a peace conference. This spirit was evident in the government. Even Churchill agreed 'we should not take the initiative in bombing', and the dropping of leaflets was to be controlled in case a parcel killed someone. ARP was scaled down at the end of 1939, and Norway was to reveal shortages of equipment. Chamberlain concentrated on avoiding action, and was annoyed by Churchill's letters urging new policies.

(a) *Cabinet changes.* A war cabinet of nine was formed, but other ministers were so often called in that it was unwieldy. Chamberlain, Simon (Exchequer), Halifax (Foreign Secretary) and Hoare (Lord Privy Seal) constituted the inner circle. Hankey was brought in as Minister without Portfolio, while Anderson (Home Secretary) remained outside. The incompetents remained. Churchill (Admiralty) and Hore Belisha (War) were the only effective war ministers.

(b) *New ministries.* Unlike 1914 these sprang quickly into existence. Burgin at Supply claimed the Norway Expedition was the best equipped to leave these islands. Information failed, and in January 1940 Sir John Reith was brought in to reform it. Other ministries included Shipping, Economic Warfare (Blockade), Food, Home Security and National Service.

(c) *Ministerial changes.* Chamberlain relied on Wilson and Margesson and Tory musical chairs continued. When Chatfield was sacked in April Hoare went to Air and Kingsley Wood became Lord Privy Seal. One minister said 'the prime minister must be mad'. The most remarkable cabinet change was the resignation of Hore Belisha in January 1940 as a result of complaints from Gort, relayed by the Duke of Gloucester and supported by Ironside.

In spite of incompetents and its inbred nature, the ministry possessed considerable talent, and Churchill was to use much of it later. Organisationally the government was well prepared, but it lacked the will to carry out its policies. It displayed 'breathtaking indifference', and has been described by Taylor as a 'government of national pretence'. This may be illustrated by looking at its action in three important fields:

(*a*) *Military organisation*. Chamberlain set up a Military Coordination Committee with the Chiefs of Staff to liaise with the cabinet defence committee, but this was confusing, particularly when Churchill was asked to chair it. Hoare's Land Forces Committee agreed to create a 55-division army, but supplied no time limit.

(*b*) *Finance*. The government was responsible for two budgets. That in September raised income tax from 5*s* 6*d* to 7*s* 6*d* and imposed a 60 per cent excess profits tax. The budget of April 1940 did little more than raise postal charges and put 1*d* on beer. In December 1939 employers asked for a Minister of Economic Affairs, but all Chamberlain would do was create a Central Economic Service.

(*c*) *Manpower*. Unemployment continued to rise during 1939 to a peak of 1,400,000 in December. Even by May 1940 it had only fallen by 360,000. Meanwhile there were shortages of 21,000 engineers and 28,000 agricultural workers. Conscription was extended in September to all between 18 and 41, but not applied, and by May 1940 had only reached the age of 27.

A2. The Twilight War

The atmosphere of the Chamberlain war months seems incredible, realising what they faced. As usual, confident predictions of a short war were made, while songs like 'We're going to hang out the Washing on the Siegfried Line' were sung by Vera Lynn. One group held a Victory Ball in October and Christmas trade was up 10 per cent. Organisations like the BBC were dispersed, and plans were made for the government while art treasures and historic articles were hidden in quarries. The government took sweeping measures which proved unnecessary, although providing good practice for the ordeal to come. The chief government activities on the home front were:

(*a*) *Evacuation*. The scheme was implemented and 1½ million persons went under it, and possibly 2 million privately. As early as 14 September vermin, bedwetting and lack of shoes among the working class were the subject of discussion in the House—and one in five of Liverpool evacuees were lousy. Of Newcastle's 71,000 evacuees, an eighth had no shoes and a fifth were deficient in clothes. The *Evacuation Survey* by the Fabian Society revealed how important this move was in changing social attitudes and stiffening demands for reform. At the time it was largely wasted since nearly a half returned.

(*b*) *Blackout*. Anticipating air attack, probably with gas, the government had initiated stringent rules, and the ARP services tended to be overzealous in enforcing them. Until October 1940, 18 per cent of accidents were due to the blackout and only 3 per cent to raids.

(*c*) *Rationing*. At first Ministry of Shipping demands for a restriction of food imports were ignored, but sinkings were so great that rationing had to be introduced in January 1940. In addition, food subsidies of £72m were given, which were to rise to £250m by 1945. Together, these measures kept the cost of living stable about 25 per cent above 1939.

(*d*) *Identity cards*. A National Register was to be composed, and in January 1940 this led to the issuing of identity cards.

A3. The Political Crisis of May 1940

Chamberlain in 1940 was in a stronger position than Asquith in 1915. There was no threat to his large majority; nor is there much evidence to suggest a plot against him. Churchill behaved until the very end as a loyal member of the cabinet, defending Norway and covering up failure at sea by issuing exaggerated figures. But he made it clear he was in the running as a possible successor by letters to Chamberlain on general policies, correspondence with Roosevelt, skilful use of publicity, pressure on a wide range of new campaigns and his speeches. Chamberlain recognised his growing strength by putting him in charge of the Military Coordination Committee.

The government fell because it failed to wage war effectively. By May, 58 per cent of public opinion thought Chamberlain unsatisfactory, and this situation was brought about by the Norway campaign. On 3 April Chamberlain made a speech saying Hitler had 'missed the bus'. Next day Ironside said, 'Our army has at last turned the corner ... we are ready for anything they may start. As a matter of fact we'd welcome a go at them.' It was the return of the Norway troops that led to the outburst in the debate of 7–8 May.

Criticism of the government was varied. Attlee condemned the campaign and this, of course, included Churchill. Sinclair criticised the cabinet for having 'an almost uninterrupted career of failure'. Admiral Keyes and Leopold Amery made telling speeches. That evening Labour agreed to divide the house on the motion to adjourn—it was not a vote of censure—hoping to draw the Tories away from their leader. Chamberlain next day said, 'I call upon my friends to support us in the lobby tonight', and this called forth Lloyd George's stinging rebuke: 'It is not a question of who are the Prime Minister's friends. It is a far bigger issue....' The Eden group and the Boothby-Bracken-Macmillan group met together with Amery in the chair, and decided to vote against. The result was 281–200 for the government, reducing their nominal majority substantially. Apart from Labour, 33 Tories and eight others voted against, including Amery, Duff Cooper, Hore Belisha and Macmillan; 32 Tories were absent and only 15 of them were paired; 43 abstained. But Chamberlain was not yet out.

(*a*) 9 May. Chamberlain decided to fight on, and Lord Home was sent to canvass support. Labour was divided. Some wanted Attlee to join Chamberlain: others led by Dalton wanted Halifax as Prime Minister. There was no organised support for Churchill. Churchill lunched with Eden and Kingsley Wood, who urged him not to support Halifax. That afternoon Churchill, Halifax, Chamberlain and Margesson met. Halifax said it was unsuitable for a peer to be Prime Minister.

(*b*) 10 May. The invasion of the Low Countries led Chamberlain to consider going on, but Kingsley Wood urged him not to. Chamberlain got Home to telephone Butler to try to persuade Halifax to change his mind, but the Labour Executive Committee said they would only join under a new leader. That evening Churchill became Prime Minister.

This was regarded with alarm by many Tories, particularly establishment figures like Hankey. Orwell thought the end had come because in the previous ten years his record had been so unstable and right-wing. Halifax or even Lloyd George was considered preferable, and Eden still ranked as more popular. Above all, Churchill had to work with Labour and the appeasers' cabinet, both of which he had criticised for years. That he obtained a 381–0 vote of confidence is a remarkable tribute to the impact of Hitler's invasion of Western Europe had on members.

B. The Politics of Churchill's Coalition Government

Churchill had several advantages to offset his disadvantages. He was a party maverick who had been Liberal and Conservative, and had sat on platforms with Attlee. He had opposed the appeasers consistently after Munich. Perhaps most important of all, Chamberlain remained loyal to him. Churchill offered him the Lord Presidency and leadership of the House, but Attlee compelled the withdrawal of the latter. Chamberlain remained leader of the party, and it was due to him that Churchill received his first major ovation on 4 July; until then the Tory benches largely received him in silence. Even Attlee was compelled to recognise Chamberlain's administrative qualities before illness forced him to resign on 30 September. He died on 9 November. Churchill became party leader. In his own account of the war, Churchill pays little attention to home politics, and tends to underestimate party squabbles and parliamentary criticism.

B1. The War Cabinet and the Ministry

Churchill concentrated power in himself. Besides being Prime Minister, he was also Minister of Defence, and this post gave him control over strategy. As an ex-military man, he was in a better position than Lloyd George to deal with brass hats. He even resorted to military uniform himself on occasion. For the moment Attlee had to rest content with Lord Privy Seal and Deputy Leader of the House. He did not become Deputy Prime Minister until February 1942. Halifax remained as Foreign Secretary until November 1940, when he was succeeded by Eden. Already ill and a fervent admirer of Churchill, Eden enabled the Prime Minister to dominate foreign policy as well. After Chamberlain resigned, Sir John Anderson became Lord President and chaired the Home Policy Committee. He was succeeded as Home Secretary by Morrison. At this stage Churchill saw Anderson as the prime minister if he was killed. Eden only emerged later and Churchill did not consider Attlee as he was leader of the minority party.

Taylor has criticised Churchill for not sacking the appeasers, and says only Hoare was removed. In fact seven went and seven stayed. Churchill had to accommodate the majority of his own supporters and he had no wish to become a prisoner of Labour or provide the means for plots like that in 1916. Alone of the ministers apart from Simon, he had served in both war cabinets. Hoare became ambassador in Spain where he helped to keep Franco neutral. Halifax became Washington ambassador and did good work, particularly in starting the United Nations. Malcolm MacDonald went as Canadian High Commissioner after being driven out by Attlee, but Churchill firmly resisted any attempt to proscribe his own party. Simon became Lord Chancellor, and remained in office until 1945. Kingsley Wood received his reward and became Chancellor. He entered the war cabinet in October 1940 to balance out Ernest Bevin, Minister of Labour.

(a) *Labour's rôle.* Apart from Attlee and Greenwood, Labour obtained five other posts: Dalton (Economic Warfare), Morrison (Supply), Alexander (Admiralty), Bevin (Labour and National Security) and Jowitt (Solicitor General). In the whole ministry there were 52 Tories and 16 Labour. By April 1945 there were 27 Labour and, since Attlee, Morrison and Bevin largely dominated home affairs, they were in a strong position.

(b) *Liberal rôle.* Lloyd George was asked and declined, and a number of able Liberals like Johnston were left out. Simon was succeeded by Ernest Brown as Liberal National leader, and he was given Scotland. Sinclair, an old friend of Churchill's, was given Air.

(c) *Churchill's friends.* Like Lloyd George, Churchill surrounded himself with a band of devoted admirers. Bracken became his PPS, and minor posts were found for Macmillan, Nicolson and Boothby.

(d) *Broadening the base.* A number of able ministers were included whose contribution to winning the war was important. These included Sir Frederick Marquis (Lord Woolton) for Food, Beaverbrook for Aircraft Production, Reith for Transport and Hudson for Agriculture.

Although Bevan called for the impeachment of the appeasers, the ministry was the ablest since 1918. Many of its members were found peerages and, in Bevin's case, a safe seat. It was not an easy ministry to run. Bevin and Beaverbrook, Attlee and Morrison were often at loggerheads, and the combination of right-wing Tories and left-wing Labour was likely to cause friction. Whatever the charges against Churchill of bullying, interference and dismissals by letter, one of his greatest achievements was to make this cabinet work. Its record in social reform and labour relations stands well beside its fighting and production achievements.

B2. Military Organisation

One of Lloyd George's greatest faults had been his inability to stop the feud between frocks and brass hats (Chapter 3, E3). Churchill's relations with the generals were not always good. His treatment of Wavell and Auchinleck in the African campaign was harsh, and Montgomery was only his second choice for El Alamein. Harris at Bomber Command was allowed too much influence and independence, although in giving him this Churchill was influenced by Cherwell. The Defence Committee of the cabinet consisted of three service ministers, the chiefs of staff and two war cabinet members. It was superseded during the war, meeting only 10 times in 1944. The Chiefs of Staff Committee, with Churchill in the chair as Minister of Defence, was the main instrument of war policy, and met some 400 times a year. As a result, the departmental war ministers had little say. The Committee took over the military wing of the war cabinet secretariat under General Ismay. Ismay's career had been largely in the colonial army, but he had a first-rate brain and cooperated with Sir Edward Bridges, the Secretary of the War Cabinet. In spite of Barnett's attack on the governing class, Britain was able still to produce resourceful strategists who achieved victory with minimum losses apart from the strategic air offensive including Portal, Dill, Brooke and Pound.

B3. Cabinet Changes

Churchill relied on his small group of intimates. Beaverbrook was the most influential and his cabinet career was a hectic one. He began as

Minister of Aircraft Production, and achieved wonders in 1940. When this post was removed from the war cabinet (August 1940–May 1941), Beaverbrook became Minister of State and then in June 1941, Minister of Supply. In this post he clashed with Bevin and, in February 1942, Supply was removed from the war cabinet and Beaverbrook became Minister of War Production, strongly demanding a second front. On 19 February he resigned because of ill health and when he returned in September 1943 as Lord Privy Seal, he was not in the war cabinet. Bracken became Minister of Information and Cherwell, Paymaster General. All three were right-wing and opposed social reform.

The first changes occurred on Chamberlain's resignation. Anderson took his post and entered the war cabinet, and Morrison became the new Home Secretary. Eden replaced Halifax. Wood (Chancellor) and Bevin (Labour) entered the war cabinet. These appointments were not all satisfactory. Demands were made for an Economics Minister, but Churchill would not yield to this, fearing a rival. Instead, the Production Executive was set up in January 1941 and quarrels between Bevin and Beaverbrook developed over tanks and planes and the hours of work.

Several defeats combined with the ambition of Stafford Cripps led to the major changes in February 1942. Cripps was a brilliant intellectual, the youngest King's Counsel of his time and a left-wing polemicist. He had been ambassador in Moscow, and the involvement of Russia and demands for a second front gave him a new prestige. On his return in January 1942 he refused Supply and was given Lord Privy Seal and Leader of the House, thus compelling Churchill to elevate Attlee to Deputy Prime Minister, but in 11 volumes of cabinet proceedings Cripps scarcely made an appearance. By March 1942 the war cabinet consisted of Churchill, Attlee, Cripps, Anderson, Eden, Bevin and Lyttelton.

Cripps' mission to India did not succeed, and he was isolated on the home front. In October 1942 he resigned, but later returned as Minister of Aircraft Production outside the war cabinet. He was replaced as Leader of the House by Eden. Morrison, the Home Secretary, was admitted to the war cabinet. A coal production crisis led to the appointment of Gwilwym Lloyd George as Minister of Fuel and Power. Woolton became Minister of Reconstruction (November 1942) as thoughts turned to post-war planning, and in February 1943 Reith took over Town and Country Planning. Wood died and was replaced as Chancellor by Anderson in September 1943. Attlee was made Lord President. With this team Churchill went on throughout 1944. The changes themselves had given Labour experience but they had not noticeably diminished the old guard or given much hope of radical change.

B4. Parliamentary Opposition

Churchill's wartime career was remarkable for a man in his late sixties. He worked a 120-hour week and, apart from a few bouts of pneumonia and a slight heart attack, came through 'with a zest that rarely flagged'. This was done in spite of indulgence in whisky, cigars and good living, and against a background of 'Blitz' conditions in the War Room. He also travelled extensively over the world, visiting battle fronts and other states-men. Yet in the midst of this activity he remained devoted to the Commons and lavished on them some of his greatest speeches. These took eight hours to prepare and, as Bevan once said, he was losing battle after battle and winning debate after debate. It would be wrong either to exaggerate or ignore the opposition to Churchill. Maxton's ILP continued to oppose the war, but most of the opponents wanted to fight it differently from the government. Lees Smith was an ineffectual opposition leader, but he had the support of Bevan. On the Conservative side, appeasers like Winterton and reactionaries like Wardlaw Milne were ready to snipe.

(a) *Early troubles.* In July 1940 Winterton opposed more secret sessions, but was easily defeated. In May 1941 Churchill asked for a vote of confidence. Lloyd George launched a strong attack. In June the debate on Crete saw Churchill 'looking worried and wary' while casting blame on Hore Belisha for failure to equip the army prior to 1940.

(b) *The July 1942 debate.* After Singapore and Tobruk opposition mounted, and it seemed possible that Cripps might step in. But others were more concerned about running the war. A debate in May 1942 about the relations of Churchill with the Chiefs of Staff had not been attended by him. There was criticism from a wide range, including Hore Belisha, Davies, Winterton and Shinwell. The July debate was on a motion of no confidence 'in the central direction of the war', and it was led by Wardlaw Milne and Keyes. The idea was to put new men like Pile and Hobart in charge of strategy, but Wardlaw Milne ruined their case by proposing the Duke of Gloucester instead. The vote was 476–25 with 40 abstentions.

The government had to face Tory opposition to a number of reforms, and to the Beveridge Report. By 1945 its foreign policy was being brought into question by the left, who disliked Greece, and the right, who disliked Yalta. As early as October 1944 Attlee decided not to continue the coalition after the war. At first Churchill wished to go on until the defeat of Germany, then of Japan, but as this might take 18 months, Attlee insisted (21 May 1945) on an early election.

B5. Caretaker Government (23 May–26 July 1945)

For his last period in office, Churchill formed a government while he was at Potsdam. Addison unfairly describes it as 'a light-hearted review by Noël Coward'. In fact, it was a ministry revealing the talents and failings of parties in office ever since 1931. Churchill formed it in 48 hours without sufficient regard, seeing himself as inevitable victor and still having a Tory majority of 100 in the House. Anderson, Leathers, Duncan and Grigg remained at their posts. Woolton became Lord President and Beaverbrook, Lord Privy Seal. The Liberal National leader, Brown, was at Aircraft Production while Lord Rosebery led the party in the Lords and was Secretary for Scotland. Simon was Lord Chancellor, and Swinton and Hore Belisha returned. Apart from Bracken as First Lord there were plenty of new able ministers, including Macmillan, Butler, Sandys and Monckton (Section E2).

C. The People's War

Civilians had been involved indirectly in the consequences of previous wars, but for Britain the world war was the first time civilians were either subjected to direct attack or mobilised in such vast numbers. In addition, there was the possibility of direct invasion. Apart from three small groups, the whole population was united in its efforts to repel invasion, resist intimidation and deal with dislocation. The war years saw the last great triumph of voluntary effort, and the establishment of many of the principles of the welfare state. During the war there were 60 million changes of address; 5 million were in the armed services, most of them seeing parts of the world they had only seen in films; $1\frac{1}{2}$ million were in the Home Guard; another $1\frac{1}{2}$ million were in Civil Defence; $1\frac{3}{4}$ million women worked in industry, and 65,000 in agriculture. There were 61,000 deaths and 86,000 serious casualties on the 'home front'.

These changes brought about marvels of organisation, new welfare services, changed social attitudes, and at the same time regimented millions to accept planning and instruction from civil servants. Even the racial mix of population began to change. Imperial troops included West Indian pilots, there were $\frac{1}{2}$ million foreign minority groups like the Poles as well as the Americans. All brought new ideas and attitudes. At the time, the suffering imposed by war was unredeemed, but the blitzed cities had to be replanned and the shattered social life of the country restored. In order to secure civilian acceptance of their grim rôle, the government was pushed into social reform, and the position of the workers improved during the war. There was full employment at last. The number of trade unionists rose to its 1921 figure of 8 million by late 1944. As the cost of living was held at 30 per cent of 1938 prices, wages rose 80 per cent. Average weekly earnings rose from $53s/3d$ in October 1938 to $96s/1d$ in July 1945, and benefits available under the social services grew at the same time. Historians like Titmus, Addison and Bruce agree that 1940–41 saw a vital change taking place.

C1. Meeting Invasion

Norman Longmate has captured the atmosphere of the country during 1940 when there was every prospect of invasion, and, until late in the summer, of defeat (Chapter 13, B5). In recent years there has been a tendency to romanticise and even to scoff at the events of this year. Yet as Churchill said, 'If the British Empire and its Commonwealth last for a thousand years men will still say—this was their finest hour.' The Dunkirk spirit gave rise to a determination to win, exemplified by George VI's remark that he felt better now we were alone. The steps taken were superfluous, but they provided the necessary transition from the appeasers' cabinet to mobilisation for total war in 1941. The main steps were:

(*a*) *Military*. General Brooke was put in charge of military preparations. The main fear was parachutists—hence the construction of pillboxes, the removal of signposts and the sowing of obstacles at various points. On the beaches preparations were made to use burning oil and poison gas. An attempt to hold the Germans was to be made on a line running from south of Bristol to the Thames, south of London, through Chelmsford to the Wash, and north to York. The government was to be evacuated behind this line, and if defeated, withdraw to Canada with the fleet.

(*b*) *Resistance*. Leaflets were issued—'If the Invader Comes' and 'Beating the Invader'. Civilians were ordered to stand fast and parish and urban invasion committees were set up. In a 30-mile coastal strip Auxiliary Units, armed with new plastic explosives, were to emerge from hideouts to commit military sabotage. The Germans for their part issued 'Orders for Invasion' (September 1940), which included the looting of art works, the deporting of males to France and the seizure of industrial supplies. A Gestapo unit under Dr Franz Six, numbering 40, was to be established.

(c) *The Home Guard.* An appeal was launched by Eden. Called the LDV, they became the Home Guard in July 1940, and were given out-of-date American rifles and later, uniforms. There was an obsession with spies, a fifth column and parachutists, but the Home Guard did valuable duties that otherwise would have tied down regular troops.

By September it was clear invasion was not coming, but a threat of a different kind. During the Battle of Britain there had been raids on towns like Hull and Portsmouth. Attacks on aerodromes and aircraft factories involved civilian casualties, but towards the end of August a change occurred. German bombs fell on London on 24 August; the next night Berlin was raided. Göring believed that terror bombing would work, and to cover up the Luftwaffe's defeat accepted 'this stroke right into the enemy's heart'.

C2. The Blitz

The main air attack on Britain lasted from 7 September 1940 to 16 May 1941, although there were sporadic attacks before that, and later came the Baedeker raids, the Little Blitz and the V weapons. The main brunt of battle was borne by London, which was bombed on 76 nights and sustained nearly half the casualties. Daylight raids until 5 October were replaced by night attacks after the combined effect of fighters and guns had proved an adequate deterrent. On 14 November attacks developed on the arms towns, starting with a raid on Coventry which was the heaviest of the war, laying waste 100 acres. The raid proved the futility of such methods of destroying Britain's war base since factories had been dispersed, and production was back to normal within two months. Other towns raided included Birmingham, Bristol, Sheffield and Manchester. In 1941 came attack on the ports, designed to back the Battle of the Atlantic. The worst area to suffer outside London was Merseyside, where there were more than 4,000 casualties and one period of seven days' continuous raids.

Casualties were increased by the location of working-class overcrowded housing conditions in the areas concerned. The Communist Party tried to argue shelter policy was at fault and the *Daily Worker* was banned. But the bombing of Buckingham Palace and the House of Commons helped to break down class barriers. The King and Churchill were well received amid the ruins, and the slogan 'London can take it' was coined. At first Tories were worried about riots, but this fear was misplaced. The George Cross for civilian bravery marked a new recognition of the civilian part in war—there were few 'cushy billets' in the world war. The maligned ARP came into its own, aided by the AFS and WVS. Morrison and Wilkinson at the Home Office led the fight and 'chaos never became ungovernable'. By April 1941 four out of five people were provided with a shelter.

The impact was not what the Germans expected after the panic-stricken crowds of France in 1940. There were sudden panic flights, a rise in juvenile crime and some fall in education standards. But drunkenness and suicides declined and the birth rate, having fallen to its lowest ever in 1941, rose rapidly. A Hungarian doctor commented, 'I have not found one hysterical shouting patient', and there was no great increase in neurotic illness. War production was not damaged, and some towns like Leeds and Newcastle escaped relatively lightly. The populace was not cowed, and this made an important impact on neutral opinion in America. But the damage done was greater than anticipated—two out of every seven houses were damaged and 250,000 destroyed, recreating a housing problem.

C3. Churchill's New Deal

Churchill had an honourable reforming record, but it would be wrong to pretend he took a detailed interest in the social services. Morrison, Anderson, Greenwood and Bevin were the powerful directory at a time when expenditure on the war had reached £9m a day. But Churchill took some interest, and could have vetoed much with the excuse that there was a war on. He stands in relation to the changes like Disraeli to his social reforms—he approved, if he did not initiate. The main changes were:

(a) *Regional government*. A scheme was announced in April 1939 with a list of Civil Commissioners. The aim was to coordinate services on a regional basis as regards Civil Defence. In January 1940 Area Boards responsible for productivity were added, who later came under the Production Executive. They were wound up during 1945 instead of being used for reconstruction.

(b) *Post-Raid Services*. The old 'spikes' became Rest Centres, and Meal Service Centres were established. A Committee on the Homeless was set up to provide inspection and then grants. By the end of the Blitz the new services were functioning well and a million homes had been made habitable again.

(c) *National Assistance*. The UABs widened their function to provide benefits for the needy, starting with supplementary pensions and war benefits. In March 1941 the Determination of Needs Act abolished the old means test and replaced it with a simple test of personal income.

(d) *Hospital Service*. The Emergency Hospital Service scheme made inroads into the existing complex system of voluntary and public hospitals. By March 1941, 80 per cent of hospitals were involved, and by October mention was made of a national service. A Nursing and Midwives division of the Ministry of Health was created and a Nurses Act passed.

(e) *Fire Service*. By May 1941, 1,666 different fire-fighting forces were brought together in the National Fire Service.

(f) *Help for mothers and children*: 4.6 million children were born during the war years and, in spite of bombing, rationing and family disruption, proved the most healthy generation yet born. Diphtheria immunisation was added to smallpox, cutting deaths (3,000 in 1938 to 720 in 1945). A National Milk Scheme was started and in September 1941 free milk was extended to all schoolchildren. School meals were similarly extended and by 1945 half of children were receiving them. Due to lack of fresh food, cod-liver oil and orange juice under Lend Lease was distributed, and in December 1941, by providing special ration books, Woolton was able to discriminate in favour of mothers and children. The figures reflected improvement:

	1939	1945	
Maternal mortality	2.55	1.53	per 1,000 births
Infant mortality	51	45	

These changes undermined the selective nature of the existing services, some of which had been introduced before 1914, and were accompanied by increases in levels of benefit. In the Atlantic Charter, the British insisted on including 'improved labour standards, economic advancement and social security'. Arthur Greenwood, who had been Minister of Health (1929–31), appointed a committee in June 1941 after a delegation from the TUC had stressed the need 'for the linking up of all the social service schemes'. It was to take 'a number of practical steps' to implement change. Bevin lent him Beveridge to chair the committee.

C4. Labour and the Production Battle

Britain mobilised a higher proportion of her resources in manpower and money than any other ally, and had to take the consequences in 1945. But this mobilisation started slowly and was somewhat haphazard in 1940, when Beaverbrook insisted on long hours that were counterproductive and launched campaigns for bringing in saucepans and railings to build aircraft, which were little more than window-dressing. However, he produced 650 more planes than planned and raised £13m by means of public subscription. This showed there was plenty of slack and, under Bevin, the economy was fully mobilised in 1941–42. By 1943 it was approaching its peak, and in spite of Empire aid, Lend Lease became decisive. In 1941 only 10 per cent of Britain's munitions came from America, but by 1944 this had risen to 28 per cent. Britain was stretched to the limit. Workers were diverted from civilian industry, Civil Defence and the Home Guard were reduced in size, dilution was practised on a wide scale so the proportion of women employed rose from 9 to 34 per cent, and 200,000 prisoners put to work.

This battle for resources involved close cooperation with the unions, and Bevin was determined to use wartime conditions to improve the workers' position. Wages doubled as compared with prices and, although the standard of living fell 14 per cent compared with 1938, this mainly affected the middle classes. Taxation and social policy helped the workers; as did a range of canteen and entertainment facilities. There was less industrial trouble than in the Great War except in the mines. The unions, led by Sir Walter Citrine, continued to enhance their position. They sat on the National Joint Advisory Committee and the regional production boards. But by 1944 production was levelling off. The number of tanks produced actually fell in 1944. The aircraft programme never reached its monthly target by 300 after 1942. Only in agriculture did production rise continuously.

(a) *Organisation*. The Economic Policy Committee was reorganised in January 1941 as the Production Executive, with Bevin in charge. There were clashes with the Ministry of Supply and finally, in 1942, a Minister of Production emerged.

(b) *Transport*. The railways were in serious difficulties and Lord Leathers was brought in to reform matters. The railways were taken over in May 1942 as British Railways.

(c) *Coal*. It was here that the most serious difficulties were encountered. Production fell from 224 to 180 million tons during the war, and in 1944 two thirds of strikes were in the mines. In spite of prosecutions of Kent miners matters did not improve. Indeed, in 1944, the NUM was formed from the old federal union structure. Churchill's refusal to consider nationalisation and the conscription of the 'Bevin boys' did not help.

Bevin's work aimed at protecting trade unionists. His chief measures were:

(*a*) June 1940. Factory acts were transferred from the Home Office to the Ministry of Labour.

(*b*) March 1941. The Essential Works Order covered 6 million workers and insisted proper welfare services should be provided. Factory inspectors were given powers to enforce them.

(*c*) December 1941. The Juvenile Registration Order affected those between 15 and 18 whose conditions of employment had been poor.

(*d*) The Catering Wages Act (1942) dealt with this poorly paid section, and was forced through in spite of Tory opposition, followed by the Wages Councils Act of March 1945 to expand the old trades boards.

(*e*) Restrictive Practices Act (1942). All practices scrapped for wartime production were to be restored at the end.

C5. Uncle Joe and Uncle Sam

One interesting consequence of war was the impact on British life of her two major Allies. The Communist Party reached its maximum membership (56,000) during the war years, and there was a strange period when the Tories were enthusiastic for Russia. In 'Tanks for Russia Week' Mrs Churchill led an aid programme which raised £8m. American influence was more direct after their arrival in January 1942. By May 1944 there were 1,526,965 Americans in Britain, and they were not all withdrawn until October 1945. They took with them 70,000 'GI brides', and this helped to cement the special relationship at a new level. Britain had to bear the cost of 250 American bases and at first there was resentment, summed up in the slogan that Americans were 'overpaid, overfed, oversexed and over here'. Their poor performance in Africa and Italy did not help matters, and they were not really popular until after D-Day.

C6. Reconstruction—A Developing Argument

Churchill's New Deal was to help the war effort, and he had no intention of proceeding in a 'continual buzz of ardent discussion' towards more elaborate measures. The main impetus for reform came from Labour, and this naturally aroused Tory fears as reconstruction began to play an important part in thinking. Reform was based on three main ministries: Reconstruction under Woolton; Health under Willink; and Town and Country Planning under Reith. A fortnight after El Alamein the Beveridge Report was published: 635,000 copies were sold, and in a Gallup poll only 6 per cent were said to be opposed to it. Churchill spoke of 'false hopes and airy visions of Utopia', and although reforming measures continued there was also a considerable amount of opposition.

(*a*) *Churchill.* As early as October 1941 he had condemned the discussion of current affairs in the army, where the Army Bureau of Current Affairs was set up. By April 1942 Lord Croft, Under-Secretary of the War Office, was criticising it as left-wing, and in October Churchill wanted it closed. Churchill returned to the theme in August 1943, urging that resources should not be diverted. It is clear that Churchill was opposed to the spread of radicalism.

(*b*) *The Conservative Party*. Many opposed the trend to socialism by the back door. The opposition to coal nationalisation in 1942 and the Catering Wages Act in 1942 showed their strength, and in the debate on Beveridge 119 voted against. Aims of Industry was founded (1942) and the National League for Freedom (1943), under Waldron Smithers, backed by some 40 MPs. The Tory shire knights still carried great weight, and they did not like the new policies.

(*c*) *The Treasury*. Kingsley Wood led the objectors on the grounds of cost, and it became clear that Beveridge could only be carried out with a substantial reduction in defence expenditure as the country was poorer than in 1939. Anderson stressed defence must have first priority. Sir William Eady argued that proposals to end unemployment produced by Beveridge were unrealistic, and that exports were the main priority.

This opposition led to a slowing down in the pace of reform, and 'the House was in a critical mood in 1944 in regard alike to government measures and ministers'. Churchill accepted the outlines of Beveridge in September 1944 when it was too late, and Conservatives made it clear they opposed the more radical parts of such reports as Uthwatt on land development.

Other Conservatives wanted to abandon their pre-1939 'Poor Law and Dole' image and return to the Disraelian rôle of responsible reformers. They saw the rapid rise of left-wing views abroad and argued a Tory New Deal was the only way to prevent the rise of socialism.

(*a*) *Tory reformers*. As early as 1941 A Post-War Problems Committee under Butler started work, and this drew in a wide range of Tories. In March 1943 the Tory Reform Committee was set up. Among those involved were Maxwell Fyfe, Quintin Hogg and Thorneycroft.

(*b*) *Continuing reforms*. A Ministry of National Insurance was set up (1944) to prepare for reforms. A Town and Country Planning Act (1944) and a Location of Industry Act (1945) laid the basis for modern planning law. The Butler Education Act (1944) and the Family Allowances Act (1945) were both important measures. But the limited nature of government white papers suggested the will for change was absent.

The whole political argument was made more intense by the advent of a new party called 'Commonwealth'. Many of the reformers were Liberal-Christian rather than Socialist-Humanist in approach. There was a considerable amount of Christian idealism shown at the Malvern Conference in 1941, given strong support by Archbishop Temple in *Christianity and the Social Order* (1942). The founder of 'Commonwealth' was Sir Richard Acland. The party eventually obtained seven seats. Their existence showed reconstruction was not merely a socialist slogan, and it tended to emphasise how out of touch most Tories were with changing ideas.

D. Whitehall Knows Best—The Victory of Consensus

The war years with their upheavals and strains came after a period that many regarded as lacking in progress. But the same period had provided a wide range of new ideas (Chapter 10, A and B) and during the war these were turned into practical politics by distinguished reformers. New ideas accepted by the establishment were to form the basis of economic and social thinking until the mid-1970s. They were fundamentally to change the direction of government action and to prepare the way for a collectivist, egalitarian, welfare state.

D1. John Maynard Keynes and Managed Capitalism

(a) *Life.* Born in 1883, Keynes was educated at Cambridge, and entered the Treasury. He opposed large reparations in *The Economic Consequences of the Peace* (1919). In 1926 his *Economic Consequences of Mr Churchill* criticised the return to gold, and his unorthodoxy made him suspect. In 1936 came *The General Theory of Employment, Money and Interest*, which attracted attention in America. When the Central Economic Service was set up, Keynes returned to the Treasury, and his *How to Pay for the War* (1940) made plain the new theories. He was the main British delegate at Bretton Woods and in the 1945 loan negotiations, and was made a baron before he died in 1946.

(b) *Theories.* Keynes wished to make capitalism work by managing the National Income by direct government intervention. He believed this could defeat long-term unemployment and raise living standards. Since it seemed to offer the prospect of extending the nation's resources and involved planning and a 'social' element, it had consensus appeal. Roughly speaking, Keynes believed in stimulating economies out of depressions by government borrowing and deficit financing. If governments read the signs of the business cycle and used interest rates and other means they could prevent heavy downswings.

Now statistics of national income were available, the government could act and as only half the cost of the war was being met by taxes, it was an opportune moment. A White Paper—'The Sources of War Finance'—was followed in April 1941 by the first of the new budgets. 'We drank champagne that night and felt we had accomplished something,' Keynes wrote. The next budget in 1942 'contained few surprises', but the vital change had been made. Keynes made available the money for social reform.

D2. William Henry Beveridge—Welfare State and Full Employment

(a) *Life.* Born in 1879, Beveridge was a Liberal and concerned in social work at Toynbee Hall. He joined the Civil Service in 1908 and was involved in the Liberal reforms. He became Director of Labour Exchanges until 1916. He was then Director of the London School of Economics (1919–37) and Master of University College, Oxford (1937–44). He was called to chair the enquiry on coordinating social services, which produced the Beveridge Report (1942). He followed this with *Full Employment in a Free Society* (1944). He became MP for Berwick, but lost his seat in 1945. He was made a baron and died in 1963.

(b) *Theories.* Taking Rowntree's concept of a minimum standard of living, Beveridge argued that 'want' could be abolished by a universal contributory and free system of social benefit. It was scrutinised by the Government Actuary, and he stressed it was for benefits 'up to subsistence level'. As a Liberal, he saw the plan as cooperating between state and private sources of social benefits. It urged avoidance of mass unemployment, a comprehensive health scheme and family allowances. A Ministry of Social Security was to run the lot. In 1944 his Full Employment Report, influenced by Kaldor, stressed the need to accept Keynes to prevent a return to the 1930s. It is important to note that he regarded 8 per cent as full employment and thought unemployment could never be reduced below 3 per cent.

D3. Leslie Patrick Abercrombie—Regional and National Planning

(a) *Life.* Born in 1879 at Ashton-under-Lyme, Abercrombie was educated at Liverpool where he was Professor of Civil Design (1915–35) and then Professor of Town Planning at University College, London (1935–1946). His *Plan for Greater London* (1944) was the most dramatic expression of the new planning ideas, and he was involved in replanning Plymouth, Hull and the Clyde Valley. He was knighted in 1945 and died in 1957.

(*b*) *The Great Reports.* During the early 1940s a number of reports appeared which enabled the planners to get to work. The Barlow Report (1940) on the location of industry, population and housing was followed by the Uthwatt Committee (1942), which dealt with the financing of land transfers to public authorities and the Scott Report (1942), combined with Dudley Stamp's *Land Utilisation Survey* categorising land for various uses.

The reports included a range of proposals. Industry was to be controlled in its siting, development land was to be subject to compulsory purchase and rural amenities were to be improved. The government was less than happy with this invasion of private property, and the White Paper on Land Use (1944) was cool on many proposals. Planning ideas in vogue included green belts, industrial location, new towns for 'overspill', national parks, fuel conservation, smokeless zones, an integrated transport policy and motorways. It was stressed that a National School of Planning was needed.

D4. Richard Austen Butler—Education for All

(*a*) *Life.* Born in the Punjab in 1902, Butler entered parliament as a Conservative in 1929. In the 1930s he was Under-Secretary to Hoare and Halifax and strongly supported the Government of India Act and appeasement. He was among the Tory reformers, and helped to educate the Tory party to many of the new ideas, culminating in the *Industrial Charter* (1947). President of the Board of Education in 1941, he piloted the act of 1944 and became the first Minister of Education in 1945. He was Chancellor of the Exchequer (1951–55) and Lord Privy Seal (1955–59). He was then Home Secretary and in 1962, Deputy Prime Minister. He failed to get the Tory leadership in 1963, but became Foreign Secretary. In 1965 he became a life peer and Master of Trinity, Cambridge.

(*b*) *The Education Reports.* A number of reports on education came out during these years, including the Fleming Report (1944) advocating that a quarter of public school places should be for assisted state pupils, and the Percy Report (1945) on technical and further education. A White Paper, 'Educational Reconstruction' appeared in December 1943. A bill was passed in August 1944 and came into force in 1945.

The Education Act of 1944 was not Butler's unaided work. It relied on reports by Hadow, Spens and Norwood, and he was assisted by his Labour Under-Secretary, Chuter Ede, but the essential outline of policy was his, and it remains the major educational achievement of the twentieth century. Its main provisions were:

(*a*) Each area was to provide 'a varied and comprehensive educational service' and, with certain limitations, give parents freedom of choice.

(*b*) Education was divided into primary (age 5–11), secondary (11–15) and tertiary. The leaving age was to be raised to 15 by 1947 and 16 as soon as practicable, in view of the wartime bulge of births. Provision was made for day release to 'county colleges'.

(*c*) All fees were abolished in state schools, and the school meals, milk and medical services brought under the education authorities.

(*d*) There was to be a non-denominational religious assembly in all state schools, and religion was to be taught in each education division according to an agreed syllabus.

(e) There was to be a tripartite division of secondary education, although 'multilateral' schools were to be allowed. An exam at the age of 11 was necessary as the number of grammar school places was limited, although provision for transfer at 13 and 15 was included. The local authorities decided the form of the examination.

(f) 165 direct-grant schools continued to charge fees and fix their own entrance requirements.

The Act provided the framework for the education of the majority of children for 20 years. It was a period of rising educational standards, and an ever widening ladder of opportunity for the grammar schools who succeeded in competing with the public schools. It was a period when Britain's scientific, medical and technical progress was remarkable, considering her poor resources and weakened economy. But critics condemned the shortcomings due to lack of resources, and educational ideas became more egalitarian. By the time the major parties were led by grammar-school products the prototype was under attack. This came from the advocates of comprehensive schools, led by Sir Graham Savage, Education Officer for London. He had studied such schools in Canada and America in the late 1920s and was responsible for the first in London in 1949.

D5. White Paper Blueprints

The 1940s produced many white papers and reports which provided information for the incoming government in 1945. But the documents varied. Those by the Coalition Government were cautious; those by independent observers more radical. There was also fierce debate about the new ideas. Keynesian economics, planning, welfare economics and state education were not accepted without a murmur. But the overall impression of this period is that planning was accepted or, as Douglas Jay said, 'the man in Whitehall knows best'.

These blueprints were also made possible by the close cooperation of the consensus establishment that had been growing in the 1930s. Administrators, economists and university dons were joining the government at all levels. The word 'boffin', applying to a man possessed of specialist knowledge, was derisory, but it also marked a fear that the days of the traditional governing class were numbered and those of the meritocracy at hand. It was the transition from the world of Evelyn Waugh to that of C. P. Snow. One of the best examples of this was the '1941' Committee, to which Marwick draws attention. This included Acland, Priestley, Mary Stocks, Ritchie Calder, Francis Williams, Victor Gollancz, C. E. M. Joad, Thomas Balogh and Kingsley Martin. By 1945 a new establishment receptive to the ideas of the 1930s and war years was in being. This goes far to justify Bruce's remark that 'the decisive event in the evolution of the Welfare State was the World War'.

E. The General Election of July 1945

E1. Fall of the Coalition Tories

In 1942 the government began to lose by-elections. Symbolically, the first to go was Margesson's seat at Rugby when he gave up as Chief Whip. Later in the year a conscientious objector was elected for Malden. Thereafter the government was unable to win any by-elections; perhaps its most spectacular loss was Derbyshire West in 1944 when Lord Hartington was defeated by Charles White. Opinion polls in their infancy were little regarded but they constantly showed overwhelming support for Churchill and a steady swing against the government parties. Yet few Conservatives believed they would be defeated; and Labour had little confidence they would win. Bevin's comment on their victory was: 'The results are so good I am speechless.' Yet Labour had made the most efforts to recruit new members, starting in July 1943, while the Conservative organisation had run down. The main reasons for the Coalition defeat were:

(*a*) It was a government that had been in power since 1931. Some ministers had served for 14 years. There had been no election since 1935.

(*b*) The government was blamed for events before the war in *Guilty Men* and not forgiven for many of the earlier disasters. It was the government of Norway, Tobruk and Singapore as well as victory.

(*c*) Labour claimed credit for the social reforms, although, in fact, they had until early 1943 been all-party in content. But after that, Tories had seemed luke-warm on reform.

(*d*) The logic of consensus politics was that the best government to implement the new ideas was a left inclined one. Both Tories and National Liberals were associated with 'vested interests'.

(*e*) The war years had enhanced the pre-1939 leftward shift. This had occurred in army education and political writing. It had been further stimulated by the alliance with Russia. The left had acquired government experience and establishment support.

(*f*) War had changed much social thinking under the impact of evacuation, the Blitz, the American forces and the apparatus of control which had been broadly egalitarian.

E2. The Campaign

Labour's manifesto 'Let Us Face the Future' was clear, while Churchill's was pompous and vague even if making roughly the same promises. The main issue in Gallup polls was housing, and Labour policy of council and emergency houses was the most appealing. The Conservatives seemed to be summoning people to fresh foreign efforts at a time when people had been glutted with foreign news since 1938, while Labour put the material needs of the ordinary family first. The Labour party had produced more effective new ministers than the establishment parties, and their candidates were particularly good. Although the Liberals had Beveridge, they were also friends of the Tories, and still divided as they had been since 1931. Neither Sinclair nor Brown was an effective leader. The main issues in the election were:

(*a*) *Foreign policy*. Bevin's view that 'left could speak to left' was believed, and Tory scares about Russia ignored. The Greek Affair rankled with many, and the Tories were accused of backing foreign reaction.

(*b*) *Gestapo Speech*. On 4 June Churchill turned on Attlee, saying that in order to bring in full blooded socialism he would have 'to fall back on some kind of Gestapo, no doubt very humanely directed in the first instance'.

(*c*) *Harold Laski*. Churchill tried to raise a Red Scare by saying the Chairman of the National Executive, Laski, was claiming a veto over policy. Attlee sharply put down his pretensions in public letters.

During the election campaign the gap narrowed. The Labour lead was cut from 16 per cent to 6 per cent by polling day. But in the end the 'men of Munich' had to go.

E3. The Results

Labour	393	Conservatives	200
		National Liberals	12
		Liberal Nationals	13
		Independents	16
		Communists	2
		Commonwealth	1

The importance of this election was:

(a) It gave Labour its first majority government. By 1950 they had lost their lead, but had carried through the first part of their 1918 programme.

(b) Brown was defeated, and the Liberal Nationals became indistinguishable from Tories until in 1950 they signed a pact joining the Tories.

(c) Samuel in the Lords was ineffective, and Sinclair was defeated. The National Liberals' new Leader was Clement Davies.

(d) It established a two-party system which lasted until 1974 and ended a long period of multi-party politics and coalitions from which Conservatives had profited.

(e) Thirteen ministers were defeated, helping to clear out 'the old gang'. The Tory Party had a severe shock which it needed and deserved.

Further Reading

Addison, P., *The Road to 1945*, Jonathan Cape, London, 1975, available in paperback.

Calder, A., *The People's War 1939–1945*, Jonathan Cape, London, 1969, available as Panther paperback, 1971.

Cooke, C., *Stafford Cripps*, Hodder and Stoughton, London, 1957.

Cruikshank, C., *The German Occupation of the Channel Islands*, Oxford UP, London, 1975.

Gregg, P., *The Welfare State*. Harrap, London, 1967.

Harrod, R. F., *John Maynard Keynes*, Macmillan, London, 1951.

Longmate, N., *How We Lived Then, a history of everyday life during the Second World War*, Hutchinson, London, 1972, available as Arrow paperback, 1973.

Longmate, N., *Air Raid: The Bombing of Coventry*, Hutchinson, London, 1976.

Marwick, A., *Britain in the Century of Total War*, Bodley Head, London, 1968.

Young, K., *Churchill and Beaverbrook*, Eyre and Spottiswoode, London, 1966.

Questions

1. Compare the organisation of Britain at home in the First and Second World Wars.
2. Why was Churchill a more effective wartime leader than Lloyd George?
3. Was the wartime government a genuine coalition?
4. Why did the anti-establishment ideas of the 1930s become acceptable by 1945?

5. What is meant by saying that the war produc
6. What were the most important economic conseque
7. What was Labour's contribution to winning the war?
8. What social changes did the Second World War bring ab
9. Is there any connection between the military and diploma
   war years and home politics?

...t the post-war years were going to be
...tead of return to normal there was a
...ather than scrapping wartime controls
...vere seen as tools ready to the task. The
...s few wanted to see reversed, and many
wan... recent years there has been some criticism
of the ext... ...ist commitment, but the years of his first
government show... ...undoubted revolution in the life of Britain.
It took place in a little ... 15 months when the government passed 55
Acts. In spite of a slight decline at first in levels of taxation, there was no
return to pre-war inequalities. The Civil Service increased to 720,000. Some
20 per cent of industry, including the 'commanding heights', were nationalised. A welfare state which was compulsory, universal and free dispensed 14
benefits to the public by late 1948. Moreover, these changes and reforms
were achieved during a period of grave economic peril.

Britain was now a second-rate economic power. About a quarter of the
national wealth (£30,000m) had been used up. The country had less than
half her pre-war export trade, and merchant shipping had fallen from 17
million to 13 million tons. £1,118m of overseas investments had been sold,
and there was a balance of payments deficit of £1,250m. The gold reserves
had risen to £453m due to American spending but were still half the pre-war
level. With nowhere to export in a world of shattered or captured markets,
and no money to buy vital imports, Britain was in deep waters and would
need to raise her exports by 75 per cent to recover her pre-war position
in visible trade. Truman cut off lend lease in August 1945 and America had
secured British compliance with measures to curb the sterling area and
open her imperial markets to competition. The terms of world trade were
against her. At home industry was undercapitalised and much physical
damage had been done. The major industries like coal and cotton continued
to decline, and to them were added others like the railways. Five million
men were in the forces, and millions more in unproductive wartime
industries.

The Labour government fought back and, in Seaman's words, 'by 1950
it would be true to say that the battle had been won'. It was strange that the
first major Labour government should be so concerned to put capitalism
in working order, but with dependence on America and a vast social programme to finance at a time of extended world commitments they had no
alternative. They ate humble pie and signed the Treaty of Washington.
When the loans obtained then expired, they obtained the largest share of
Marshall Aid. They overcame a convertibility crisis in 1947, and a devaluation crisis in 1949. In 1950 exports were 77 per cent above the 1938 level,
and Britain's share of world markets had risen from 18.6 per cent to
25.6 per cent. £1,650m of new overseas investment had been created and a

major programme of colonial development was started. There was a favourable balance of trade of £297m. In doing this the government had an initial advantage. Wartime has accustomed people to hardship and shortage, and obeying government propaganda and officials. In 1945 three fifths of the national product was controlled by the government. A third of gross income went in tax and a third of expenditure was on items whose price was fixed by the government. By continuing controls, extending rationing and securing a wage freeze for nearly two years, controlling capital issues and dollar exports, and leaving the growth sector of the economy outside the scope of nationalisation, the Labour government secured a remarkable boom in productive industry. If 10 years' austerity made Britain a duller place in 1950, the benefits reaped by ordinary people made it acceptable. There was less than a twentieth of the strikes there were after 1918.

The Attlee government was an aging collection of Victorian socialists. Attlee and Morrison were ill. Bevin and Cripps killed themselves with hard work. But in addition to the enormous domestic programme, their interest was focused on the post-war diplomatic scene. In spite of Russian intransigence, the post-war settlement was more durable than in 1919. Bevin proved to be the best Foreign Secretary since Sir Edward Grey, and Attlee made no attempt to posture as a world statesman. The challenge of the Cold War was met successfully. If the government did not hasten towards a united Europe it started conscription, built the atom bomb, founded and played a key rôle in NATO, started a war against the Communists in Malaya and took Britain into the Korean War. Habits of patriotism and swift action on a world scene learnt in the war years were not forgotten. Against this, withdrawals from Greece and Palestine and defeats in Persia and Egypt did not yet look like a policy of scuttle. Above all the challenge of imperial change was met more successfully. India, Burma, Ceylon and Pakistan secured independence, and colonial constitutions were remodelled to provide legislatures and responsible ministries. Creech Jones proved one of the few enlightened colonial secretaries. As in 1918–22, the post-war period was a hectic time, but the Attlee government stands head and shoulders above Lloyd George's in nearly every aspect. Many of its policies become part of the political consensus accepted by the Tory governments of the 1950s, and many of its acts continue decisively to influence life today. It can scarcely be accused of not doing enough.

A. The Attlee Administration

A1. The Prime Minister and his Team

The Labour party under Attlee was the product of the moderate and middle-class element in its organisation. One third of the cabinet were public school and 229 MPs were members of the Fabian Society. Only 30 per cent were sponsored by trade unionists. Although there were some trade unionists like Bevin and radicals like Cripps and Bevan, few remained radical when confronted with the problems of government. This moderate stance was reflected in the way that the middle-class vote helped to secure their large majority. Cripps argued strongly for royal allowances, having formerly denounced the Palace; 100 peerages were given and accepted by men like Kirkwood. A new elite began to emerge, typified by men like George Gibson, former errand boy and asylum attendant, who became a director of the Bank of England and chairman of the North-West Regional Electricity Board.

This moderate stance was not to the liking of many in the party. Watt has shown how Labour was composed of about ten different radical strains from the noncomformist to the fellow traveller, and a number of members intended to keep up the class war. Mrs Bessie Braddock said of the Tories, 'I don't care if they starve', while Emmanuel Shinwell, Minister of Fuel and Power, said that workers outside trade unions 'do not matter a tinker's cuss'. The most famous remark was made by Bevan in July 1948 saying Tories were 'lower than vermin'. A 'Keep Left' Movement started led by Crossman, supported by Castle, Foot, Mikardo, Silverman and Zilliacus. It wanted more social reform, income redistribution, closer relations with Russia and opposed 'dollar imperialism' by America. In November 1946, 100 Labour MPs abstained in a debate on America, and the same year 73 voted against the National Service Bill. In 1950 the Cold War brought this division into the open, and Bevan assumed the leadership of the more radical element in the party.

(a) *Clement Attlee.* He was born in 1883 at Putney and after education at Haileybury and Oxford became a lawyer. Becoming involved in social work at Toynbee Hall, he joined the Fabians (1907) and the ILP (1908). He became a lecturer at LSE in 1913, and served in Gallipoli and 'Mespot', securing the rank of Major. He was Mayor of Stepney and MP for Limehouse (1922–50). He had held minor office in 1924 and 1929–31 and during the war had risen to be Deputy Prime Minister. He was leader of the Labour Party from 1935 until he retired in 1955, becoming an earl, and dying in 1967.

At the time some regarded him as 'a sheep in sheep's clothing', but he proved a remarkably successful prime minister. His incisive speeches punctured Churchill, his headmasterly manner kept a diverse cabinet running smoothly and he enforced the highest ministerial standards, removing ministers for inefficiency, or breaking constitutional conventions.

(b) *The Big Four.* Four eminent Victorians carried the main weight of power in this government, and apart from an abortive 'plot' in 1947, remained loyal to Attlee. Hugh Dalton, born in 1887, lawyer, lecturer and MP in 1924, had served in the war cabinet at Economic Warfare and Trade. He became Chancellor, but had to resign for revealing budget details in 1947. Herbert Morrison, born in 1888, had started life as a shop assistant, and became Secretary of the London Labour Party in 1915. Member for South Hackney and then East Lewisham, he was Minister of Transport (1929–31) and Home Secretary (1940–45). His great creations were London Transport and the National Fire Service. He became Lord President and Leader of the House, and in 1950 was unwisely made Foreign Secretary. His main dislike was for Ernest Bevin. Born in 1881, Bevin had started life as a bird scarer and drayman in Bristol, where he became a union official (1910). He built up the Transport Workers into the largest union, of which he was secretary (1921–40). He was a fervent anti-Communist who had broken the bus strike of 1937, and as Minister of Labour (1940–45) had been ruthless as well as reforming. MP for Wandsworth, he was made Foreign Secretary instead of Dalton, apparently on the King's advice, and proved himself a great statesman. Ill, he resigned and died in 1951. The fourth giant was Stafford Cripps. Born in 1889, son of Lord Parmoor, he was a barrister. In 1930 he was knighted, found a seat and became Solicitor General. He had been a left winger, but ended up saving capitalism. He had been Ambassador to Moscow (1940–42), head of a mission to India (1942), Leader of the House and Minister of Aircraft Production. Readmitted to the party in 1945, he became President of the Board of Trade and then, in 1947, Minister of Economic Affairs and Chancellor of the Exchequer. A vegetarian who worked 14 hours a day, he died in 1952.

The cabinet was not devoid of other talent. The welfare state was brought into being by two Welshmen—James Griffiths, the Minister of National Insurance, and Aneurin Bevan, the Minister of Health. Emmanuel Shinwell, born in 1884, was Minister for Fuel and Power but after the Winter Crisis of 1947 was transferred to the War Office. In 1947 Hugh Gaitskell and Harold Wilson became Ministers at Fuel and Power and the Board of Trade.

A2. The Conservative Opposition

Churchill was not an effective opposition leader, but there was no one else. He contented himself with memoirs and building an international reputation. The Tories had been in office almost continually since 1915, and had become the natural party of government. Their defeat brought about a series of major changes, which enabled the party to return after only six years and to take its place with the Christian Democratic parties forming in Europe as conservatism recovered with the revival of capitalism and the impact of the Cold War. The Tories had a number of important tasks to perform in opposition:

(*a*) To convince voters they were not hostile to the basics of the new state. Butler was appointed chairman of the Research Department, and in 1946 an Industrial Policy Committee was formed. It included Butler and Macmillan, and in May 1947 produced the Industrial Charter which accepted full employment, social security, Keynesian finance and nationalisation.

(*b*) To provide new policies. At the Research Department, Maudling, Macleod, Powell and Thorneycroft were at work, and in 1948 produced *The Right Road for Britain*.

(*c*) To reorganise. In 1946 Woolton took over. In the constituencies 527 paid agents were appointed. The Maxwell Fyfe Report urged that candidates should not contribute more than £25 to constituency expenses, although this had little effect until the mid-1950s. £1m was raised in 1947 and 1 million members found by 1948.

(*d*) To attract the young. In July 1946 Anthony Nutting became chairman of a reformed Young Conservatives which, by 1949, had 2,375 branches and was the largest political youth organisation.

These changes deserve attention since they prevented Britain evolving into a Swedish situation in which the conservative element in society becomes stagnant. They created a credible alternative to the Tory image of the 1930s. Nor did the impetus slacken. In 1950 came the 'One Nation' Group and in 1951 the 'Bow' Group. It was all very different from the days of Chamberlain.

A3. The Red Menace

From a Labour point of view the Cold War was a disaster, since it enabled the Conservatives to raise once more the 'Red' bogey, and the last years of the ministry coincided with the McCarthy Era in America.

Apart from events in Europe (Chapter 16, B1) and the Korean War, dislike of Communism was stimulated by spy cases which gave rise to security 'purges'. The chief case was that of Dr Klaus Fuchs, who had worked on the 'Manhattan' project and at Harwell. He was arrested in February 1950, sentenced to 14 years and deprived of British nationality. When released, he went to East Germany.

Although men like Fuchs claimed that as scientists they were anxious to stop the spread of nuclear weapons, their action speeded up the Soviet programme by 18 months and forced the West to adopt more powerful weapons. They also damaged Anglo-American relations, since the latter claimed British security was inadequate. This seemed to be confirmed in May 1951, when Burgess and Maclean fled on receiving a tip off from a 'third man'. This was Harold Philby, against whom nothing could be proved, who was asked to resign and later fled to Russia.

It was clear throughout the war the Russians had infiltrated the West while they were Allies and this shed fresh light on the origins of the Cold War, and helped to account for the bitterness between Bevin and Molotov. The Labour Party produced a banned list of over 50 'Communist' organisations. The Communist Party lost their wartime gains. In the 1950 election they lost both members, and all but three of their 100 deposits. In October 1948 the TUC issued *Defend Democracy*, condemning Communist tactics and in July 1949 banned all Communist officials. Between 1948 and 1955, 25 people were dismissed and 24 resigned from the Civil Service as a result of having Communist sympathies. In 1952 a Positive Vetting Procedure was established.

A4. The New Shape of Government

In order to carry out the new functions imposed on government, a considerable expansion of the Civil Service and associated bodies was required. This was not a new problem, since in 1932 a commission on ministerial powers had raised the matter. But it was not until after 1945 that many new ones were added, having judicial as well as administrative functions. It was not a change due only to Labour, since the Tories and Liberals had both created public corporations before 1939. But the rise of a bureaucracy was a development of major constitutional importance. By 1976 there were 2,000 tribunals, and the authority of ministers and Civil Service encroached on Parliament and the individual. The main developments were:

(a) *The growth of administrative law.* Delegated legislation allowing ministers to take action by Orders in Council or Statutory Instruments became more frequent. In spite of an act in 1946 and the Scrutiny Committee this gave ministers greater freedom to act.

(b) *Administrative tribunals.* These included such bodies as Rent Tribunals under an Act of 1946 and Land Tribunals under an Act of 1950. The latter had to decide on compulsory purchase and rating matters.

(c) *Public corporations.* In addition to the existing bodies each nationalised industry acquired a governing body like the National Coal Board and the Central Electricity Authority.

(d) *Regional organisations.* Under an Act of 1947 regional planning bodies were created and the National Health Act created the Regional Hospital Boards. Cripps created Regional Industrial Boards.

(e) *Government advisory bodies.* Some of the most important were the Production Advisory Council (with local Joint Production Councils), the Economic Planning Board (1947), the Central Economic Planning Staff under Sir Edwin Plowden, the Dollar Export Board (1949), the Capital Issues Committee, the Arts Council (1946), the Council of Industrial Design and the National Research Development Corporation (1949).

Many of these organisations were run by Tories and industrialists, but their number and influence began to raise doubts. In 1945 Orwell's *Animal Farm* anticipated the dangers of a new state where 'some animals are more equal than others' and where the friends so often became the enemies of the people, like Napoleon the prize pig. Nor was it surprising that on the farm there was an Egg Production Committee and numerous other organisations. In 1950 the Tory election cry was 'Set the People Free', but they were to prove willing to perpetuate this new kind of government. The people were to have their cake, but they were also to be told how to eat it.

B. Managed Capitalism

B1. The International Position

The United States was the world's chief economic power. The war years had been boom years as they were the only ally not to suffer directly and they devoted a smaller percentage of the economy under less stringent regulation to the war. As a result American investment overseas had reached $4,000m, and many countries were in her debt. America was determined to play her part as the world's economic power, and this conflicted with Britain as the relative fallen on hard times. In countries like Argentina, Britain was in retreat and America replacing her as the main source of capital and influence. The power of America was tremendous. Between 1943 and 1947 it gave $16,000m of aid and more than 22 million tons of supplies. Marshall Aid totalled $13,150m. But this was not mere generosity. The Americans were determined to build the world economy on lines which they approved. Through UNO and Bretton Woods they wished to create a *laissez faire* economy with free exchange of goods and money favourable to themselves.

As America paid she called the tune. GATT was organised in 1947, and tariff cuts followed. The IMF and the World Bank danced to America's bidding and countries obtaining loans did so with strings. In particular Marshall Aid to Europe was followed by an increased impetus towards freer trade. The Organisation for Economic Cooperation (OEEC) insisted on scrapping quotas in 1950. European recovery would only benefit Britain until her competitors recovered. Nor was America's treatment of Britain herself very generous. In December 1945 the Treaty of Washington provided for the cancellation of outstanding lend lease debts and a loan to Britain of £1,100m repayable over 50 years at 2 per cent, and the Commons were only given five days to accept. Boothby described it as 'our economic Munich', and in the vote 23 Labour and 22 Conservatives voted against, and 162 abstained. By the middle of 1947 this loan was nearly used up, but Britain had also agreed to restore full dollar convertibility. This lasted five weeks in the summer of 1947, and caused a massive run on the reserves.

The government had no alternative but to resort to Marshall Aid (Chapter 16, B4). Britain obtained 24 per cent of the total, which was more than any other country. By 1950 the favourable balance of payments enabled her to stop drawing but this was only achieved by devaluation. The terms of trade turned against Britain as the world economy picked up, and the dollar deficit rose from £82m in the first quarter of 1949 to £157m in the second, made worse by an American decision that drawing rights under Marshall Aid should be fully convertible into dollars. In September 1949 the pound was devalued from 4.03 to 2.80 to the dollar, a much larger fall than other countries. This enabled recovery to continue and by 1950 there was a favourable balance, soon to be wiped out by recession and rearmament.

B2. The Winter Crisis, 1947

The end of war did not see a consumer boom. On the contrary, to wartime shortage was added peacetime privation. Goods produced were primarily for export, while the government retained stringent import controls. Raw materials were restricted and utility furniture and clothes rationing continued. Petrol was rationed and building controlled by a licence system. Although in real terms workers were better off, rationing led to forced saving, and life was austere. One medical inspector said 'the housewife seeking food has to acquire some of the attributes of the primitive hunter', and a black market controlled by 'spivs' sprang up. This aspect of life was laid bare by the Lynskey Tribunal in 1948, which led to the resignation from the Board of Trade of John Belcher. There were two serious shortages:

(a) *Food.* The Ministers of Food found that world shortages combined with the feeding of the British zone in Germany to create a situation worse than wartime. In February 1946 rations of bacon, eggs and butter were cut, and a smaller loaf introduced. In July 1946 came bread rationing that lasted for two years and in November 1947 potatoes were rationed.

(b) *Fuel.* The run-down mines were not handled effectively and even before the bad winter of 1947 cuts were decided upon. Domestic consumers were urged to have 4 inches in the bath. Then came the worst winter since 1895 with three months' freeze-up.

The winter of 1947 took the edge off socialist reforms with 'something like complete industrial breakdown'. Unemployment soared to 1,800,500. Weekly magazines were suspended and daily papers reduced to four pages. Allocation of coal and electricity to industry fell, and transport virtually ground to a halt. Blame was placed on Shinwell, who was replaced by Gaitskell, and to some extent on Dalton, who had been in charge of a committee on transport. Cripps was called in as Economics Minister and Chancellor to save the economy.

B3. We Work or We Want

By 1950 Cripps, aided by Gaitskell and Wilson, was able to restore the domestic economy by setting agriculture and industry on their feet and starting to bring to an end the era of rationing and controls. Cripps' methods were a strange mixture of Biblical exhortation and economic rationality, but they suited the times and, if occasionally foolish (as in attempts to legislate against the New Look in fashion), achieved their end. The methods were:

(*a*) Putting people in the picture. 6*d* versions of white papers were issued, films and posters broadcast the message and Cripps himself tirelessly visited all areas.

(*b*) *Organisation.* The Distribution of Industry Act of 1945 was strengthened in 1947. An Economic Planning Board with regional offices was set up, and in October 1947 production targets were fixed.

(*c*) *Budgetary measures.* Apart from a single levy on capital (April 1948), Cripps relied on raising income tax and a 25 per cent profits tax. He shifted the burden from indirect to direct tax.

(*d*) *Rationing.* This was continued and extended together with a system of subsidies rising to £485m in 1949.

(*e*) *Wage control.* As a result of the welfare state and subsidies Cripps was able to persuade the TUC to a wage freeze lasting nearly two years. Workers were prosecuted for striking under wartime regulations in force until 1950, and troops were called out under the Emergency Powers Act in a dock strike (1949).

What is not often realised is that Cripps also began the relaxation of controls and rationing as the economy improved. Two 'bonfires' of controls were lit by the Board of Trade in November 1948 and March 1949. Clothes rationing had gone by 1950. The percentage of imports controlled fell from 96 per cent in 1946 to 73 per cent in 1950. By the time Churchill was talking about setting people free, Labour had advanced considerably in that direction.

B4. Moaning Middle Classes

Between 1938 and 1948 a considerable change in income structure took places for as wages rose by 35 per cent, salaries fell by 30 per cent in real terms. The papers were full of complaints from middle-class people about government interference (snoopers), the laziness of British workers (particularly servants) and increasing poverty. Taxation remained high, since the share of National Income in government hands had only fallen from 37 per cent in 1945 to 34 per cent in 1951, and taxation was more heavily weighted to income. The number of people earning over £6,000 a year fell from 7,000 in 1938 to 70 in 1948. Death duties, at an average of 20 per cent in 1938, had risen to 50 per cent by 1950, producing an impoverished aristocracy. By 1952 only half the 'landed gentry' owned land, and of the 500 peers claiming a country seat only 150 kept them up, some already assisted by the National Trust, and grants under the Historic Buildings Act. There was no radical redistribution of wealth in terms of capital holding, but the Labour government and the war together brought to an end the situation where the middle classes stood to gain from benefits and tax structure at the expense of working people.

From an electoral point of view, Labour made a mistake because the levelling brought about by taxes, rationing and welfare benefits eroded differentials among skilled workers. The economy was producing a larger middle class as the Civil Service expanded at all levels and service industries came to occupy a larger share of the labour market. 'White collar' workers increased by 50 per cent between 1938 and 1951. A range of new industries and 'professions' grew that did not see themselves as working class, and wanted incentives and differentials. The number of scientific workers had increased three times between 1931 and 1951 and aeronautics, atomic power or petrochemical industries needed such men. This was the start of the second industrial revolution and it brought not gratitude to socialism, but the meritocracy and 13 years of Tory rule.

C. Nationalisation

Prior to 1945 all parties had created public corporations and controlled private industry at some time or other. The Bank Charter Act (1844) and the Exchange Control Act (1932) had virtually nationalised the Bank of England. Railways for security reasons had always been subjected to stringent controls of operation and costs, and had been taken over in 1914 and 1942. The Liberals had taken over the telephones and set up the Port of London Authority and the Tories had created the BBC, the Electricity Board and a state airline. Wartime had produced nationalisation and industries like munitions run by the government.

Private industry was partly to blame for nationalisation. The mines and railways were in such decay that if they were not to collapse something needed to be done. Nor was the form of nationalisation adopted particularly sweeping. Morrison was convinced by his own experience that public corporations were best. Generous compensation was given, including £164m to the mine owners and more than £1,000m to those involved in transport. Although the boards were to be nominated by the minister the industry was to be run on a profit-making basis. They became government, not publicly, owned and in wage negotiation or in worker participation they were not in advance of private industry. At first they were almost unaccountable to Parliament until a select committee was set up in 1956. By 1950 Labour's faith in nationalisation seemed to have waned since the next list was shorter.

C1. The Commanding Heights

The following industries were nationalised:

(a) *The Bank of England* in March 1946.

(b) *Cable and Wireless* in January 1947.

(c) *Civil aviation* in August 1946, when BEA and BSAA were brought into a second public corporation alongside BOAC.

(d) *Atomic energy.* An Act in 1945 made the government responsible for its development at Harwell.

(e) *Coal.* Passed in 1946, the Act came into force in 1947 with eight regions and £150m for development.

(f) *Electricity.* Under the Act of 1947, 14 area boards took over 550 undertakings in April 1948.

(g) *Gas.* Passed in 1948, the Act came into force in May 1949.

(h) *Transport* (1947). The LPTB was replaced by London Transport Executive, docks and inland waterways were taken over, British Railways created, and 3,000 road haulage firms combined into 1,000 depots in January 1948.

This list contained some curious omissions like cotton and water supply, and did not make the government's task very easy. Gas and electricity were likely to compete with each other and with coal. The railways, mines and canals were loss makers. It was surprising that no effective plans for state control existed after so much talk, and matters were not helped by the 1947 crisis in fuel and power.

C2. Steel

Steel was an efficient industry that had been reorganised in the 1930s, and was producing 15 million tons a year at competitive prices. There had been a steady increase in productivity and there were good labour relations. The government itself was divided and as it was a base industry affecting Britain's export performance, unlike the other nationalised concerns, the Tories opposed nationalisation. The bill was introduced in October 1948 to take over 107 major companies. Although Lord Salisbury had wisely controlled the Tories in the Lords on this bill they decided to stand firm and in July 1949 turned it down. They agreed to pass the bill provided the government changed the vesting day to October 1950 (i.e. after an election), and in November 1949 the Act was passed.

C3. Agriculture

There was a curious silence on the Tory benches when it came to controlling and aiding agriculture, which may have something to do with the doubling of farmers' income between 1938 and 1949. The war put an end to agricultural depression, but it did so with the aid of subsidies for modernisation, guaranteed prices and a wages policy. The Agriculture Act (1947) provided a system of guaranteed prices in a February price review. The subsidy, which was £37m in 1940, rose to £300m by 1962. A National Agricultural Advisory Service, to operate through County Agriculture Committees, was to advise farmers on modernisation. By 1954 these were 400,000 tractors on farms compared with 55,000 in 1939. Productivity improved—the yield per cow was a third higher, for example—and by 1951 agricultural output was 50 per cent above 1938 levels. The government passed a Hill Farming Act (1946) to provide up to 50 per cent of the capital for improvement, and an Agricultural Holdings Act (1948) to provide security of tenure for tenant farmers. Hopkins refers to an 'agrarian revolution' and a 'scientific revolution' that gave farmers a 'secure place in the planned and managed economy'.

D. The Welfare State

The growth of a state providing an ever-widening number of services has been one of the main themes of this book. It was a continuous process dating from the 1870s, and all political parties contributed to its growth. the welfare state that was largely completed by 1950 was the culmination of this long process. Spending on the social services doubled on the figure for 1936, and noone was now outside the range of benefits provided. In 1946–47 central offices were established at Newcastle, and the number of civil servants involved rose from 5,600 to 40,000. When Rowntree did his last survey of York he found those living in primary poverty reduced from 31 per cent in 1936 to 2 per cent in 1950. The Poor Law officially ceased to exist in 1948, and it was proudly claimed that the ordinary man was provided for 'from the cradle to the grave'.

D1. Family Allowances Act (1945)
The aim was 'to encourage the birth and nourishment of extra children' at a time when large families were prone to poverty and the birth rate was low. Passed in 1945, the Act came into force in August 1946. It provided 5s for each child after the first, and by the end of the year 4 million children were receiving it. Money was provided from taxation, not from insurance, and after a free vote, it was to be paid to the mother.

D2. Help for Children
In 1945 the Curtis Committee was set up to examine the state provision for young children. The Childrens' Act (1948) placed responsibility on the Home Office and local authorities. It created a Central Training Council to provide child care officers. However, in this case the voluntary work of the churches and Dr Barnado's was continued alongside. The Employment and Training Act (1948) set up the Youth Employment Service.

D3. National Assistance Act (1948)
Created from the Assistance Board, National Assistance was designed to help all those not covered by ordinary benefits. Although a means test was imposed the benefits were of right, and the test was purely personal. The old rest shelters became Reception Centres for the homeless and needy, and many of the workhouses were turned into old peoples' homes run by the Welfare Committee of the local authority. Although it was intended the Act should be rarely used, failure to relate benefits to the cost of living meant that many came to depend on National Assistance.

D4. Industrial Injuries Act (1946)
This replaced the Workmens' Compensation Acts, and covered all workers and all accidents, injuries and disabilities 'arising out of and in the course of' employment. Equal contributions of 4d from the state, employer and employee were required and there was no limit to the benefits. Tribunals were set up to assess difficult cases, thus removing the onus from the worker to prove his case.

D5. National Insurance Act (1946)
This measure ran into opposition from the Tories, who claimed it was destroying the friendly societies and insurance companies, and from the Labour left led by Silverman and Castle, who wanted all limits on rights to benefits scrapped. Griffiths insisted on an actuarial basis and that benefits should be reviewed every five years, not related to the cost of living. The insured were divided into employed, self-employed or unemployed. Clause 12 listed the number of contributions necessary before benefits would be paid. Sickness benefit could only be claimed after 156 contributions, and unemployment benefit was fixed on a scale between 180 and 492 days. Benefits would be covered against interruption of earnings, but unemployment pay was not available to those on strike or who refused a reasonable job. There were numerous benefits, including burial and maternity grants, widows, orphans and old age pensions, sickness and unemployment. Pensions payable at 65 (men) and 60 (women) would be increased the

longer the recipient delayed drawing. The Act came into force in July 1948.

D6. National Health Act (1948)

Aneurin Bevan was chosen by Attlee to carry what became the most controversial legislation of the period. The Act introduced in 1946 was to come into operation on 5 July 1948, but in the interval there was a dispute with the doctors who had previously supported a national scheme. The BMA objected to turning doctors into civil servants and claimed damage to the doctor-patient relationship. It must also be accepted they were acting out of self-preservation and concern for their salaries. By making some concessions Bevan was able to win them over with the help of some members of the profession such as Lords Dawson and Moran. The Act provided :

(*a*) All treatment except injury and the school medical services was included in one service.

(*b*) Local authorities would administer midwives, health visitors, ambulances, vaccination and immunisation.

(*c*) Doctors would continue to practise privately, but a national network of doctors would be provided, so that everyone had a doctor. Some doctors would be moved to understaffed areas. All treatment would be free.

(*d*) All hospitals were to be state hospitals except for 36 teaching hospitals and a few private ones; 14 Regional Hospital Boards appointed by medical schools, local authorities and the medical profession would head the administration, and below them would be 388 Hospital Management Boards.

(*e*) A total of 6,000 pay beds were allowed out of 240,000, and doctors would now be paid for hospital consultancy previously done free.

(*f*) Local Medical Executive Councils composed of 50 per cent doctors and 50 per cent local authority and ministry representatives would draw up lists of approved doctors and chemists.

(*g*) Doctors were compensated for loss of the right to sell their practice and by an Amending Act in 1949 their income was to be a capitation fee and not a salary.

(*h*) To bridge the gap between doctors and hospitals, local health centres were to be set up for limited specialist treatment, thus reducing the hospital burden.

It was accepted there was some suppressed demand, but it was believed that once the nation was healthier expenditure would fall. Within 12 months 187 million prescriptions had been dispensed. The estimate for the first year was £140m; it cost £208m, and by 1950 had reached £358m and, although some charges were introduced (Section F2) costs continued to rise to £408m by the mid-1950s. The Health Service became the largest employer in the country and the second largest item in the budget and, although at this stage it was only taking 3½ per cent of the GNP, it was easy to criticise it for extravagance. There were complaints about wigs, and 400 patients using the Bath warm springs. On the other hand, its supporters argued that it was poorly financed. The first health centre (Woodberry Down) did not open until 1952, and the hospital building programme was cut by a third on pre-war.

Whatever the criticisms, the Health Service was a remarkable achievement unequalled then in any country except New Zealand. It brought to an end the chronic state of ill health which a high percentage of the working class had prior to 1939. It made medical treatment available to all and abolished the distinction between a 'panel' and a 'private doctor' or, as one doctor said, 'the local aristocracy have joined the NHS; they wait their turn in the surgery with the rest'. The results were plain. Height and weight differences between classes and illnesses resulting from malnutrition like rickets were eliminated. Tuberculosis and pneumonia ceased to be killer diseases for most, and other scourges like diphtheria were largely eradicated.. Between 1946 and 1956 maternal and infant mortality rates fell by half. In 1950 alone 165,000 patients visited specialists who would not have done so prior to 1939. By the early 1950s the NHS was the admiration of Europe.

E. Other Reforms

E1. Housing Policies

The government did not live up to its promises on housing. One reason was that the building licence system was geared to helping industry, and another was the Labour preference for council houses. In 1945 there was a shortage of 1¼ million houses and 22 per cent of existing tenants were overcrowded, but the building industry had contracted and its efficiency per man-hour had declined by a third. Under an Act of 1944, 157,000 'prefabs' were built, but this was not enough to meet immediate need, and in late 1945 there were invasions of West End properties and Nissen huts by squatters. The main measures were:

(a) Housing Acts in 1946 and 1948 encouraged council house building: 803,251 were built as compared with 176,558 private dwellings.

(b) Acts of 1946 and 1949 provided further protection for tenants and set up Rent Tribunals to hear complaints. Rent control was continued.

(c) The Town and Country Planning Act (1947) required planning to be undertaken by the larger local authorities, who were to draw up overall plans. The Act made provision for compulsory purchase and development charges.

(d) The New Towns Act (1946) created the New Towns Corporation to build new towns for London 'overspill'. The first was Stevenage (1946), followed by Crawley, Hemel Hempstead, Harlow (1947), Hatfield, Welwyn (1948), Basildon and Bracknell (1949).

E2. Trade Unions

Early in 1946 the government repealed the Trades Disputes Act of 1927. It was obvious they would do so, and it benefited the Labour party with a 50 per cent rise in income. When Citrine retired in 1946, he was succeeded by another moderate, Vincent Tewson, who maintained good relations with the government and helped to carry a wage freeze. The number of working days lost in strikes fell from 2,835,000 in 1945 to 1,389,000 in 1950.

E3. Extending Democracy

(a) *The House of Lords.* Although the Labour party had supported abolition, no move was made. The main reform proposals at this time were put forward by Lord Cecil for women peeresses and life peers. The Lords resisted a Parliament Act which cut their delaying power from three sessions to two, but it was passed in 1949.

(b) *The House of Commons.* In 1948 the Representation of the People Act was passed. It abolished plural voting by scrapping the business vote and 12 university seats. The six months' residence qualification was replaced by simple residence, and the register was to be compiled twice a year. Provision was made for postal voting. A redistribution of seats abolished the remaining two-member constituencies. A boundary commission to review seats was set up and equal electoral districts were established except in a few inner city areas. The number of members was cut from 640 to 625.

(c) *Local government.* In 1948 the local government vote was placed on the same basis as the national vote, abolishing the property qualification. An Equalisation Fund was set up to transfer rates to areas with below average rateable values.

F. The Fall of Labour, 1950–51

The 1940s and early 1950s were a period of public interest in politics caused by the universal nature of much of the legislation and the mass media, particularly newspapers, whose circulation rose to record heights. In 1945, 44 per cent of the radio audience listened to 26 electoral broadcasts, and party broadcasts became commonplace. Although the 1950 and 1951 elections were quiet, polls of 83.9 per cent and 82.5 per cent were records. In 1950 there was a record number of candidates (1,868) and the uncontested seats fell to 2. By 1955 there were none. This period of public interest also saw the creation of a two-party system which extended into local government, and at that time satisfied a majority of voters. In the election of 1951, 97 per cent of the voters favoured Tories or Labour. Thus, the period saw the end of other parties that had existed since the early years of the century.

F1. The Stalemate Election, 1950

Economic recovery was well under way, and Morrison was planning the Festival of Britain to open in May 1951. As Labour had lost no by-elections, Attlee had reason to suppose they would win. But the government was aging and there was little new blood, while the 1945 programme was largely exhausted. Above all the country reacted to 10 years of austerity, and when Labour pledged further nationalisation, including sugar, cement and water, the Tories were able to campaign under the slogan 'Set the People Free'. They intended to denationalise steel and road haulage. While Labour emphasised social justice through income redistribution and state action, the Tories argued for decontrol and taxation incentives. The result in February 1950 was Labour 315, Conservative 299 and Liberal 9. Although the Labour vote increased, the Tories had a million new voters, and those on the left of the party like Zilliacus were defeated.

F2. Labour in the Doldrums

Experience in 1964–66 and 1974–79 has shown that a government with a small majority can govern, although it is debatable whether this is desirable. Attlee saw his government as limited, and took no risks, since it was defeated seven times on minor matters. No important legislation was brought forward, and this led to recrimination in the party. In October 1950 Labour lost Cripps, and Bevan was annoyed when Gaitskell and not himself became Chancellor. Then in January 1951 Attlee moved Bevan from

Health to Labour which was, in fact, a demotion and when in March 1951 Bevin retired, Bevan's old enemy Morrison became the new Foreign Secretary. Labour was in increasing difficulties:

(a) *The Korean War*. Britain took part, and was also building a nuclear deterrent. With 1 million in the armed services and extended conscription it was decided to embark on massive rearmament. In September 1950 a programme of £4,700m over three years, absorbing 14 per cent of GNP, was announced.

(b) *Economic trouble*. The distortion of the world economy by American purchases led to a fall in the reserves, and plunged Britain back in the red. This suggested more austerity.

(c) *The Gaitskell budget*. The April 1951 budget proposed to raise income tax by 6d (the last rise until 1965) and put limits on public spending, subsidies and the Health Service, where charges would be made. Wilson, Bevan and Freeman resigned.

(d) *The Bevanite split*. Bevan's real objection was to rearmament, which he thought implied subservience to America. He also disliked Gaitskell and wanted a more prominent government rôle.

F3. Whose Finger on the Trigger?

The government became involved in misfortunes abroad which indicated that Britain's power was waning. Churchill wanted a summit meeting with Stalin, which Labour dismissed as a stunt. Labour retaliated by seeking to convince the electorate that Churchill was a warmonger with the slogan 'whose finger on the trigger'. But events in Egypt and Persia suggested that the victor of the World War might be more appropriate as a leader for the 1950s (Chapter 16, E2 and 3).

Attlee chose the wrong moment for an election, since Churchill's slogan 'Britain Strong and Free' had an immediate appeal. Churchill promised 300,000 houses and attacked Labour for 'Abadan, Sudan and Bevan'. The October 1951 election saw a uniform, but small, swing throughout the country so that although Labour had marginally more votes, the Conservatives obtained a working majority. The results were Conservatives 321, Labour 295 and Liberal 6. Like the 1906 Liberal government, Labour was exhausted before it left office, but both ministries stand out for their creative achievements. Labour secured economic recovery, social change and limited constitutional development in a period of grave financial difficulty. They faced up to Britain's changing economic and imperial position, and worked well with America. Their foreign and defence policy was a determined realisation of what Churchill had wanted, although conscription and the atom bomb could not hide the series of retreats.

Further Reading

Calvocoressi, P., *The British Experience, 1945–1975*, Bodley Head, London, 1978.

Cohen, R. K., *Nationalisation in Britain, 1945–1973*, Macmillan, London, 1973.

Gilbert, B. B., *The Evolution of National Insurance in Great Britain*, Michael Joseph, London, 1966.

Hopkins, H., *The New Look; a Social History of the Forties and Fifties*, Secker and Warburg, London, 1964.

Medlicott, W. N., *Contemporary Britain 1919–1964*, Longmans, London, 1967.

Monk, L. A., *Britain 1945–1970*, Bell, London, 1976.
Seasan, L. C. B., *Post Victorian Britain 1902–1951*, Methuen, London, 1966.
Sissons, M. and French, P. (eds.), *Age of Austerity*, Hodder and Stoughton, London, 1963.
Willcocks, A. J., *The Creation of the National Health Service*, Routledge and Kegan Paul, London, 1967.
Worswick, G. D. N., and Ady, P., *The British Economy 1945–1951*, Oxford UP, London, 1952.

Questions

1. Why did Labour win the 1945 election with so convincing a majority?
2. What evidence is there that Attlee is an under-rated prime minister?
3. What is meant by saying there was a 'social revolution' after 1945, and how far was this brought about by the government?
4. Was Labour's programme in the 1945–50 government more concerned with past pledges than future utopias?
5. How effectively did Labour handle Britain's new international economic position?
6. Was the creation of the Welfare State on Beveridge's lines the greatest achievement of the Attlee government?
7. 'In spite of their reorganisation, the Conservatives only secured a small majority of the seats, and a minority of the votes in 1951.' Why was this?

16

GREAT BRITAIN AND THE COLD WAR: 1945–57

In 1945 Churchill declared, 'The British Commonwealth and Empire stands more united and more effectively powerful than at any time in its long, romantic history', and as troops marched through London in the Victory Parade (June 1946) it was easy to imagine that, as in 1919, they had emerged more powerful than before. Barnett has pointed out with some exaggeration the country was 'completely exhausted and economically ruined'. She was 'the pensioner of the United States', as the abolition of Lend Lease and the signing of the Washington Treaty showed (Chapter 15, B1). During the war Britain's Asiatic empire had been conquered by Japan, and India had experienced grave unrest. In the Middle East, Britain had fought off the challenge, and in Africa quickly reconquered lost possessions. But the underlying impact of war was to weaken imperial bonds and encourage nationalism. In 1945 the Arab League was founded and a Pan-African Conference was held in Manchester.

But the habit of greatness dies hard, and there was much in 1945 that indicated Britain was still a great power. Although Empire faded in Asia, the late forties and early fifties saw a revival of interest in the colonies with economic development and federation schemes. Neither party thought yet in terms of liquidating imperial responsibilities. America denied Britain atomic secrets, so Labour decided in secret to build a British atom bomb (1948). But development was slow and expensive, and the first test did not take place until 1952. By then America had the hydrogen bomb. Britain followed, and her first hydrogen bomb was exploded in 1957. It was argued that possession of the bomb enhanced Britain's value to the United States and kept her as the third world power. In reality, it was Britain's Empire with its chain of bases and contacts that served America's purpose better.

In 1945 the army stood at 3 million and, although there was substantial demobilisation, the post-war period saw Britain take on new military commitments unique in her peacetime history. Under pressure from Montgomery, a National Service Act (1947) introduced conscription, and in 1950 it was extended. In 1952 the armed services totalled $1\frac{1}{2}$ million. The massive navy of 1945 was reduced, but in 1953 Britain had 150 capital ships. The RAF was at the height of its prestige and deployed 6,000 planes in 1952. During the 1950s it became clear Britain could no longer afford such military power, and in a White Paper in March 1957 the decision to go for a nuclear deterrent and end Britain's massive military presence was made. It was decisive, and a prelude to imperial decline. Apart from her imperial commitment in Europe, British troops formed part of occupation forces in Vienna (until 1955), Trieste (until 1954) and Berlin. In addition, the British occupied a zone of Germany, and the British army on the Rhine represented a reversal of previous policies. Ernest Bevin carried out a diplomatic revolution by making Britain the prime mover in the formation of NATO, and Anthony Eden completed the process by agreeing to place a strategic air force and four divisions permanently in Europe. Thus, at a time of declining resources, Britain undertook a greater military rôle in Europe.

A world view would enhance this deceptive picture of British power after 1945. The British were in occupation of the Italian empire. In the Far East, apart from reconquering Burma and receiving the Japanese surrender at Singapore, the British occupied Vietnam until April 1946 and Indonesia until November 1946. A British army was stationed in Greece, and even larger forces were deployed in Palestine and Egypt. Yet once again, reality and appearances differed. Britain was forced to withdraw from Greece (1947) and Palestine (1948). In the Far East, America was the major power, and the signing of the ANZUS Pact made this plain. America opposed Britain in Persia and in the oil crisis staked out a claim at Britain's expense. Above all in September 1947 the Indian army ceased to exist, and this reduced Britain's power in Asia. What appeared on the surface to be military might was undermined by economic reality and American policy.

During the war a 'special relationship' had grown up between Churchill and Roosevelt, but it was not the friendly affair so often portrayed in public. America took steps to assert her economic rôle at Britain's expense and, in political affairs, a combination of idealism and ignorance made the two nations less than harmonious. America disliked a Socialist government in Britain and was suspicious of European diplomatic methods. The Americans believed in the power of the dollar and in what they called democracy, although many of their Allies were right-wing dictators. They believed Britain to be luke-warm in her anti-Communism and, being more concerned with the Far East, saw British recognition of Communist China and the Geneva Settlement of Indo-China as appeasement. In the Middle East the large Jewish vote in the US helped to dictate a hostile attitude to Britain's Palestine position, and the increasing importance of oil determined America to oust Britain from the area.

What changed this picture was the threat posed by Soviet Russia. The advance of Russia into Eastern Europe had been accepted by Roosevelt, but as Stalinism took on an increasingly brutal face and showed no sign of halting its advance, American opinion changed. In 1945 she was prepared for isolation as far as Europe was concerned, but in September 1946 Byrnes declared, 'We are staying here.' An American military presence in Europe enhanced Britain's position as a vital base. In February 1947 Bevin declared Britain could not continue in the Balkans, and Truman responded. In the Middle East the Americans again moved slowly. They refused to join the Baghdad Pact and denounced British intervention in Suez, but soon after Eisenhower responded in January 1957 with an interventionist doctrine and Anglo-American policy agreement became feasible. In the Far East differences remained because Britain would not back strong action on Formosa or Vietnam, but the two powers came to cooperate in SEATO. Thus, by the mid-1950s mutual antagonisms had mellowed (Chapter 19, B2).

Russia's expansionism caused rearmament and British determination not to surrender empire bases, just as it was the cause of America leaving isolationism behind and embarking on a crusade directed against Communism. At the end of the war Russia was the main territorial beneficiary. She secured 20 million new subjects and shared in the occupation of Germany and Austria. The Russians controlled the states of Eastern Europe, and pressed claims on Turkey and Persia. Clearly these moves were designed for Russian security, but it was not easy to distinguish this justifiable aim from the forwarding of world Communism. Russia was weakened by the war but she did not disarm like Britain and America. Her foreign policy in the United Nations and the Foreign Ministers' Meetings was aggressive, and the blockade of Berlin showed her determination to press for every possible gain. In Asia the fall of Chiang Kai-Shek led the Americans to become almost paranoid over Communism, and the Korean War fulfilled their worst fears. Above all, the treatment of the states under Russian rule so soon after a war fought for liberty and democracy aroused the republican sentiments of Americans. To save other states, the almighty dollar and the marines went marching in, while in Europe America became the shield of Western defence.

In the post-war world, therefore, Britain faced three essential facts: the decline of her power, her dependence on a none too friendly United States, and the presence of anti-Imperialist Russia eager to exploit her decline. For 20 years, Britain strained under the triple obligations involved —the liquidation of Empire, the nuclear deterrent and massive defence expenditure. It was a period of almost continuous military operations and world tension. Instead of 20 years' peace as in 1919–39, Britain faced 20 years of world commitment. It is clear this contributed to economic decline and postponed integration with Europe because statesmen supported the world rôle, seeing Britain as part of three interlocking circles: the Commonwealth, the Special Relationship and Europe. Whether the American Alliance was wise or the Communist threat contained, it is too early to say, nor is it yet possible to say if the abandonment of Empire contributed to political freedom and prosperity for the Third World. As Barnett has said, 'The two decades that followed the World War constituted therefore a period of painful adjustment when all the power, wealth and empire won over two centuries after 1690 finally vanished.'

A. Making Peace

A1. The German Settlement and its Difficulties

Germany was in a worse condition than in 1919 and was treated more harshly. Territorially, East Prussia was partitioned between Russia and Poland, while the Saar passed into French hands. The partition of the country into four zones and of Berlin into four similar zones was carried out, and at first it seemed as if the Allies would persist in harsh treatment for Germany:

(*a*) *War criminals.* The Nuremburg Trials (1945–46) hanged 12 Nazi leaders and sent seven to prison.

(*b*) *Denazification.* A purge of the Nazi party was carried out. The Americans made a million arrests and tried 140,000. The British had little faith in the scheme which was difficult to enforce.

(*c*) *Reparations.* In September 1945 a committee to dismantle German industry was set up, and in March 1946 it was agreed to cut steel to 5.8 million tons a year.

During 1945–46 it became clear a four-power policy on Germany could not last. The British found the £130m cost of administering their zone too heavy. In May 1946 the British and Americans stopped deliveries of reparation goods. Byrnes proposed a union of their zones in economic terms and, by January 1947, Bizonia was created. The real problem, however, lay in deciding the political future of the country and singing a peace treaty. The Russians re-established political parties in their zone while in the Western zones political parties re-emerged by the end of 1945. The most important were the Christian Democrats under Konrad Adenauer.

(*a*) *A German Peace Treaty*. In 1945 Byrnes prepared a treaty, but it was rejected by Molotov in 1946. The problem was that Russia wanted a treaty with a united Germany under their control; so did the West. Both sides had strategic fears of Central Europe passing to the control of the other side.

(*b*) *The Stuttgart Speech*. In September 1946 Byrnes declared American troops would stay in Germany, Germany must be self-supporting and the boundaries of the 'New Germany' should be drawn. But five conferences of foreign ministers failed in 1946–47.

In June 1947 the Russians began to turn their zone into a one-party state, while in the Western zones it became clear a decision would have to be made on restoring full political life. The German Problem was back at the heart of European relations and seemed no nearer a solution.

A2. The Italian Settlement and Trieste

Italy had surrendered to the Allies and fought alongside them. Churchill had wanted to save the monarchy and treat the country leniently, but Stettinius had objected. The resistance movement had strengthened the Communist party so that it was the largest outside the Soviet Union, and the provisional government contained Communists. In 1946 a referendum abolished the monarchy, but it was not until 1948 that a new constitution was drafted. The Italian peace treaty was signed against this background in February 1947.

(*a*) *The Italian empire*. Britain occupied this and Russia laid claim to Tripoli. Tientsin was restored to China. Eritrea was ceded to Abyssinia. Somalia was eventually placed under Italian trusteeship. Libya became independent under King Idris in 1951, but signed a defence agreement with Britain in 1952.

(*b*) *European changes*. Russia agreed to cut her reparations demands to $100m in return for Italy paying reparations to Yugoslavia, Albania, Abyssinia and Greece. Allied troops were to leave Italy.

(*c*) *Trieste*. This town remained a serious problem, and it was proposed to make it a Free Territory. Zone A was occupied by British and American troops and Zone B by Yugoslavia. With the fall of the Iron Curtain, Western attitudes changed, and in March 1948 the West announced Trieste should be returned to Italy.

As a result, the city became a flashpoint in the Cold War. In 1950 Titoists won elections in Zone B while, during 1952, Italians rioted against British troops in occupation. As Yugoslavia became more friendly to the West, attitudes changed. Troops were withdrawn and a year later agreement was reached to cede the two zones respectively to Yugoslavia and Italy.

A3. The Treaty of San Francisco with Japan, September 1951
In August 1945 China accepted the Yalta proposals in a direct agree-ment with Russia, and the Soviet Union retained territory including South Sakhalin, Port Arthur and spheres of influence in Mongolia and Man-churia. By agreement in 1954 Port Arthur returned to China, but otherwise the settlement remained.

The other Far Eastern settlement lay between America and Japan, al-though the British were unhappy about this approach. America seized the former Japanese mandates. Korea was jointly occupied by America and Russia to the 38th Parallel, pending its reunification. In December 1945 an Eleven Power Commission for Japan was set up and an Allied Control Council in Tokyo, but both were subordinated to America, and MacArthur undertook the reconstruction of Japan. As China fell into Communist hands, Japan became America's new protégé. In 1948 the harsh occupation policy was reversed. On the day of San Francisco a Japanese–American Pact was signed. The territorial changes were confirmed and Japan was free to make alliances and resume full democratic government.

A4. The Start of the United Nations Organisation
The United Nations came into existence in October 1945. The intention was to make it more effective than the League, and to this end the rôle of the five great powers was made more decisive. The main parts of the organisation were:

(a) *General Assembly.* This was the forum for international debate. All mem-bers had one vote and decisions, except on certain reserved subjects, were by majority. It was to meet once a year, but could be called by a majority of the members or the Security Council at any time. It was to receive reports including one from the Secretary-General.

(b) *Security Council.* This was to consist of 11 members. Five (America, Britain, France, China and Russia) were to be permanent. The others would be elected by the General Assembly for two years. Decisions were to be on a majority vote of any seven for procedure, but all five permament members had to concur on other matters. If a member was involved, they must abstain.

(c) To deal with aggression, the Council could urge ceasefires and impose economic sanctions. Under article 43 they could utilise armed forces provided by members, and a Military Staff Committee was set up.

(d) *The Secretary-General.* Head of the secretariat, he acquired additional in-fluence because he could bring matters to the notice of the Security Council.

UNO spawned a range of other bodies as the permanent administrative organs. The Economic and Social Council was to supervise the agencies and call international conferences. The ILO was reconstituted and a large number of other bodies created, including FAO (agriculture), WHO (health), UNESCO (education, science, culture), the International Bank and Monetary Fund, refugee and disaster organisations. In 1948 they drew up the Universal Declaration of Human Rights.

At first the United Nations appeared to be as weak as its predecessor. It was unable to resolve great power disputes over Persia or Berlin. It failed to prevent a bloodbath in Palestine. Its deliberations were marred by rows between West and East, and the use of the Soviet veto. The defeated powers were not admitted and the Russians, angry at the packing of the Security Council by Western supporters, refused to allow new members. Up to 1950 only nine applications had been successful, and the organisation remained a white man's club. It was not until Korea that the United Nations was able to act, and not until 1955 that the log jam on membership was broken with the return of Germany and Japan. Above all, American insistence that Nationalist China and not Communist China should hold the fifth great power seat imported Cold War politics into the heart of the organisation.

B. Cold War in Europe

B1. Origins

Ever since 1917 there had been a great divide between Russia and the West; indeed, there had been with Czarist Russia before, since Russian policy was to expand outwards from her heartland and this now involved the spread of Communism. Wilson had sought *rapprochement* in 1919, but it had failed before Allied intervention and Communist-inspired revolution in Germany. Britain's rôle was equivocal. At first she supported intervention (Chapter 4, C2), later fitfully turned to trade relationships (Chapter 7, B), but at heart distrust of Russia remained uppermost, and after the Nazi–Soviet Pact (Chapter 12, I) this suspicion was seen as justified. Between the wars the Comintern trained future leaders of Communist regimes, and developed Communist parties in Asia and Africa, but had little success.

The war presented new opportunities for Russian gain, first with Hitler's connivance and then locked in combat with him. Anglo-Soviet relations were close (Chapter 13, D3) and Uncle Joe a popular figure (Chapter 14, C5), while abroad Roosevelt believed reconciliation was possible. At Teheran (Chapter 13, F4) the new world balance began to emerge, but throughout the Russians kept their eye on territorial gain. Churchill wavered in his support, and at Yalta and Potsdam (Chapter 13, G5, 6, 10) disagreement became clear on a range of issues. American secrecy over atomic weapons and Soviet wartime spying on her allies, Russian domination of Eastern and Central Europe, American interference in Europe and Asia, arguments over Germany, Poland Trieste, Vienna and reparations bedevilled post-war conferences and the UN. Since America and Russia were the two greatest powers it was inevitable they would collide on world issues, and since Britain had a large Empire vulnerable to Communist infiltration it was inevitable that she would choose America's side.

But this was not done in a hasty way. Bevin sought agreement. In December 1945 Russia was offered an extension of the 1942 treaty, and in June and December 1946 further approaches were made. Similarly, the Americans turned slowly away from isolationism, and it was not until Byrnes was replaced by Marshall that the switch in American policy became clear. This owed much to power politics and economic pressure, but it was also partly idealistic since the Stalin regime was seen to be a dictatorship as repulsive as that of Hitler. Anti-Jewish and East European persecution was reflected in the American electorate. A number of politicians convinced Truman a change was vital to America and the free world. The most important of these was Dean Acheson, who laid the basis for the Truman Doctrine and Marshall Aid. He was supported by Averill Harriman and George Marshall. George Kennan detailed a doctrine of containment to halt Soviet expansion. In the early 1950s J. F. Dulles, the Secretary of State, and his brother Allen, Chief of the CIA, operated a firm anti-Communist line which British governments did not always support.

What went on in Moscow is unknown, but the dissolution of the Comintern did not stop Russian penetration of the land mass surrounding her, and later Comintern (1947), Comecon (1949) and the Warsaw Pact (1955) systematised the Stalinist line. It was this more than anything else that angered the West. Throughout Europe the pattern was the same. The reactionary régime was eliminated. A people's republic was set up with a fatherland front, including all parties on an anti-fascist basis. Elections were rigged and the coalition dissolved. Gradually all other political parties were destroyed, and then nationally minded Communists were replaced by Moscow hardliners. Purges with state trials, executions and deportations were followed by state secret police, the presence of Russian troops and the KGB, censorship, religious persecution and economic reforms.

Speaking at Fulton, Missouri in March 1946, Churchill repeated a phrase he had used before. 'From Stettin in the Baltic to Trieste in the Adriatic an iron curtain has descended across the Continent.' At home there were complaints, and 105 Labour MPs signed a motion criticising the speech. Stalin attacked it, but within a year America was committed in Greece.

B2. Greece and Turkey—The Truman Doctrine

After Churchill's intervention, Stalin had for a time respected the agreement made on spheres of influence in the Balkans. But during early 1946 it was clear the Soviet thrust had not been contained. This was shown by the renewed civil war in Greece in May 1946 when ELAS received arms from Yugoslavia, Albania and Bulgaria.

At first the Americans were reluctant to alter the Roosevelt line. Britain was left to fight the Greek war, and eventually had 40,000 troops there costing £60m a year. In February 1947 Bevin told Truman that British aid to Greece and Turkey would cease on 31 March, and this precipitated action.

(a) *The Truman Doctrine.* On 12 March the President declared: 'I believe that it must be the policy of the United States to support free people who are resisting subjugation by armed minorities or by outside pressures.' This reversal of American policy meant they would replace Britain as the main power in the Near East, and it brought to an end isolation.

(b) *Aid to Turkey.* Turkey received £25m followed by Marshall Aid. The régime was hardly democratic and the economic structure was socialist. Turkey swung into the Western orbit, sending troops to Korea and joining NATO in 1952. The 1939 treaty with Britain was renewed (1948).

(c) *Aid to Greece.* Munitions, supplies and 340 'advisers' were sent to stiffen the Greek army and a right-wing government. The left admitted defeat in October 1949. Greece moved into the Western orbit, joining NATO in 1952.

B3. Communist Putsch in Czechoslovakia

The loss of Eastern Europe to Soviet influence was to some extent inevitable, but the West was sensitive about Poland and Czechoslovakia—countries which they had fought to liberate.

The Lublin régime in Poland (Chapter 13, G10) held elections in January 1947, which Britain and America denounced as undemocratic. During 1948 the Polish Communist Party was subordinated to Moscow. In June 1950 East Germany recognised the Oder-Neisse line as final, which marked the failure of Western policy for Poland.

The Allies let Russian troops enter Prague, and there was a purge in Czechoslovakia. The election of May 1946 was followed by a government which was all-party, but Interior, Information and Defence ministries went to Communists.

Trouble began in 1947 when Communist pressure forced the government to turn down Marshall Aid. In February 1948 the Interior Minister sacked eight non-Communist police chiefs. The right-wing ministers resigned, and Gottwald secured a Communist government. Zorin, the ex-Soviet ambassador, was in Prague at the time and, although there was no direct military intervention, the West reacted strongly to the suicide of Masaryk, the arrest of the ex-ministers and setting up of labour camps. It was the prelude Bevin needed for launching NATO.

B4. Marshall Aid

Although lend lease had been abolished, America had made extensive loans to Britain, France and the Low Countries. America's new policy was designed to render capitalism attractive, to help the governments of France and Italy to combat Communism and to ensure a continuing market for American goods. In June 1947 Marshall said, 'It is logical that the United States should do whatever it is able to do to assist in the return of normal economic health to the world, without which there can be no political stability and no assured peace.' Marshall said that requests would have to be made, but no one was excluded from the European Recovery Programme. Molotov denounced 'dollar imperialism' and turned it down. The Western powers were eager for aid and set up the Committee for European Economic Cooperation which presented a plan to America in September. Marshall Aid was passed in April 1948. Between then and June 1952, $13,150m poured into Europe, starting with aid for agriculture and later moving to industry; 69.7 per cent of the goods procured came from America, but European production rose above 1938 levels for the first time by 1950. Britain received most, followed by France, Italy and West Germany. The three European governments all swung to the right in the elections of 1948–50. Most important, the trend towards European cooperation (Section D1) was stimulated and in 1948 the Organisation for European Economic Cooperation (OEEC) was set up.

B5. The Berlin Airlift

It was now clear the Western zones of Germany were to be helped towards recovery, although there was considerable opposition to this in Britain. Meetings in London in February and June 1948 decided to create an effective West German economy. A constitution was to be drafted, and Germany admitted to the Marshall Plan. In order to facilitate this, the Reichmark was replaced by the Deutschmark (18 June 1948). Russian reaction to these moves was:

(*a*) March 1948. The Soviet delegation left the Allied Control Council ending the four-power administration of Germany.

(*b*) May 1948. Elections in the Eastern Zone were followed by a draft constitution.

(*c*) June 1948. Refusing the Western currency reform, the Russians introduced a new East German currency and tried to force it on the Western part of Berlin. The West then introduced the Deutschmark there also.

(*d*) April–June 1948. Harassing of Western movements into Berlin was followed by a complete blockade of all transport.

Swift action was taken to counteract the blockade. From June 1948 to May 1949 an airlift kept the 2 million inhabitants of Berlin supplied with food and fuel. Bevin said that Britain would stand firm even if it meant war. Within the city two administrations were created, bringing division, since East Berlin was incorporated into East Germany as the capital while West Berlin became a *land* of the new German state. The airlift cost £200m, and flew in 2 million tons of supplies. Britain supplied 23 per cent of the flights. Containment had worked in Western Europe, and Russian action had stimulated the West to support a return of normal government in their zones. But similarly the Russians now supported East Germany as a German Democratic Republic, thus making the chance of German reunification and a peace treaty more remote.

C. Communist Threat in Asia

C1. Nationalism, Neutralism and Communism

Japanese occupation had caused national movements to develop in European colonies in Asia, and in India the British government had conceded dominion status. The British surrendered India, Burma and Ceylon (Chapter 18, A), but resisted rebellion in Malaya. American reaction to this nationalist revolt was at first to support it, but their basic reaction was determined by events in China. A treaty with Chiang in 1946 was followed by continuing aid. The China lobby demanded the extension of the Truman Doctrine to China, but this was frustrated by the victory of Mao Tse-Tung in October 1949 and the flight to Formosa of Chiang. As America became hostile to Communism in Asia, she began to turn to the colonial powers to help resist it. Hence America disliked neutralism—the attempt of new Asian countries to stand aside in the great power conflict. America bore the brunt of Korea, and by 1954 was financing three quarters of French efforts in Indo-China. Above all, the American fleet protected Formosa, and there were mutterings about liberating the mainland.

Britain recognised a Communist threat, and in Malaya she was the only country to defeat a guerrilla movement. She recognised that 10 million Chinese outside China represented a potential threat, but was reluctant to alienate new Commonwealth members or damage trade by opposition to Communist China. In December 1949 India recognised Mao, and in January 1950 Attlee's government followed suit. Britain's moderating influence in Korea her persistence in achieving an Indo-China ceasefire in 1954 and her refusal to back America in crises over the islands between Formosa and China aggravated relations and led to Dulles' dislike of Eden. The British, however, saw the emerging force of neutralism as worth harnessing.

The West sought to meet this development by aid, starting with the Colombo Plan (1950). The leader of neutralism was Nehru of India, who announced the Five Principles in 1954 which aimed at non-interference and non-aggression. They were followed by the Bandung Conference (1955), where Asian and African states met together for the first time, and demanded 'respect for the sovereignty and territorial integrity of all nations, recognition of the equality of all races and of the equality of nations large and small'. This development favoured Chinese Communism and during 1956 Chou En-Lai visited many Asian countries. America therefore favoured military alliances and containment was secured with the creation of SEATO in 1954.

C2. The Korean War, 1950–53

In December 1945 America, Britain and Russia called for a provisional Korean government, but the Russians failed to implement this decision and in September 1947 Korea was referred to UNO. After a commission recommended elections and was refused admission to the north, South Korea was created. A month later North Korea was created. In June 1949 American forces left the South, but by this time the Chinese Communists had triumphed and could give aid to North Korea. North Korea invaded the South in June 1950. Truman appealed to the United Nations, and they took action:

(*a*) June. In the absence of the Russian delegate, the Security Council voted 9–0 for a resolution calling on members to assist South Korea.

(*b*) July. MacArthur was made commander, forces despatched to Korea and the Eleventh Fleet placed in the Formosa Strait.

(*c*) October. The United Nations called for a unified Korea, thus enabling the Americans to cross the 38th Parallel.

(*d*) November. The 'Uniting for Peace' Resolution was carried, whereby if the Security Council veto deadlocked discussion, an emergency session of the Assembly could be called.

(*e*) January 1951. The United Nations Truce Commission put forward a five-point peace programme, and when it was rejected America secured the condemnation of China as an aggressor.

Outwardly the Korean War was therefore a UNO action and the first indication that it was more powerful than the League. In fact, although 16 states were involved militarily, others saw it as American action under a UNO cloak. India in particular refused troops and would not condemn China. There were many in America who wished to see the war extended to rescue Chiang, or even invade China, and when in November 1950 the Chinese intervened on Korea's behalf there was a risk of world war. The main stages of the war were:

(*a*) *The North Korean advance.* Taken by surprise, the South Koreans lost Seoul and were driven back to the tip of the peninsula.

(*b*) *MacArthur's first advance.* After a bombardment by Commonwealth navies, a counteroffensive from Inchon was launched. Early in October the 38th Parallel was crossed and within three weeks he had nearly reached the Yalu River bordering on China.

(*c*) *The Chinese advance.* Following a North Korean counterattack early in November, 200,000 Chinese 'volunteers' crossed the border. The Allies were driven back to the 38th Parallel and on 4 January Seoul fell again.

(*d*) *MacArthur's second advance*. During March 1951 MacArthur advanced north again, and on 3 April once more crossed the 38th Parallel.

This was the first war since the 1670s in which Britain did not play a major rôle, although Britain undertook massive rearmament, rallied the Commonwealth, contributed a large naval force and sustained about 800 killed. The impact on America was greater:

(*a*) For America it was a large war with 50,000 dead, and the first evidence of their new world rôle. It was followed by massive rearmament to build up overseas bases and send four divisions to Europe.

(*b*) *The Attlee intervention*. When Truman said 'that there has always been consideration of its use', referring to the atom bomb, 100 Labour MPs condemned his words. Attlee flew to Washington in December 1950 and a counterstatement was issued.

(*c*) *Second Attlee intervention*. The condemnation of China was followed by a British statement opposing Chinese sanctions, and on 2 April by demands for a truce.

(*d*) *Fall of MacArthur*. Although in April 1951 Truman approved a programme of aid for Chiang, he was perturbed by MacArthur's proposals for attacking the Chinese mainland, and he was dismissed.

Russia was supplying China and found it expensive. Moreover, the war was building up American power in Europe. In June 1951 the Russians put forward a vague call for a ceasefire, and on 8 July negotiations opened. On 5 October they were reopened at Panmunjom. The armistice was hampered by charges of germ warfare, although when UNO asked the Red Cross to investigate, Russia used the veto. The Chinese said their prisoners had been brainwashed because only 6,000 out of 20,000 wanted to return, and the Americans would not agree forcibly to return them. Eisenhower had pledged to end the war and in January threatened China with a Manchurian offensive if they did not speed up the truce talks. Stalin's death enabled Russia to retire quietly to the wings, and Churchill declared peace was vital and there must be no extension of the war. In April the talks resumed and in July 1953 an armistice was signed. It provided for a Joint Armistice Commission and a United Nations Supervisory Commission to be set up with a demilitarised zone on the border, which was to be the 38th Parallel.

C3. Indo-China and the Geneva Conference, 1954

France conceded internal self-government to Laos, Cambodia and Vietnam. In Cambodia and Laos this worked well, but in Vietnam the refusal of Ho Chi Minh to accept the settlement led to a war which began in November 1946. It turned into a guerilla campaign and as China recognised Ho, American help was forthcoming. By 1954 Dulles wanted an Anglo-American air offensive to help the French.

(*a*) *Dien Bien Phu*. On 7 May 1954 badly positioned French forces were cut off and forced to surrender. On 24 March France appealed to America, but Eisenhower declined military aid—one reason being that Eden refused to participate, claiming it would alienate the neutralists.

(*b*) *Geneva Conference* (26 April–21 July). A new French government expressed willingness to negotiate, and Eden was keen on forming a general alliance to contain Communism. A Korean peace was awaited. The conference dead-locked on Korea and was hampered by American–French discussion of possible military intervention. Eden masterminded diplomatic efforts and worked well with Molotov.

(c) *The Settlement*. An armistice was secured, and Vietnam was divided along the 17th Parallel. There was to be demilitarisation and free elections by July 1956. A tripartite commission would supervise these points. Cambodia and Laos were neutralised, and all foreign troops were to leave.. America and Vietnam would not sign, but Russia, Britain and China became the guarantors.

The results were mixed. The seeds of dislike between Eden and Dulles began to sprout. In the north, Ho obtained Chinese aid and in 1960 formed a new guerrilla army called the Vietcong. In Laos the Pathet Lao caused trouble, and in 1959 the government appealed for help to UNO. A fact-finding mission accepted there was outside intervention and recommended neutralism. However, the Control Commission set up in 1954 had dis-solved in March 1958, and there was no means of making the policy effec-tive (Chapter 19, D4).

C4. Seato and Formosa

Because of American influence in the Far East, which Eden regarded as inexperienced, he was determined to establish an Asian equivalent of NATO. In September 1954 the Manila Pact created an alliance between Britain, USA, France, Australia, New Zealand, Pakistan, the Philippines and Thailand. If there was a threat there was provision for consultation, and the treaty covered the area up to 21° 30′ North, thus excluding For-mosa. It did, however, include all Indo-China. To avoid charges of neo-colonialism it was accompanied by a Pacific Charter with a number of wordy sentiments. The consequences were:

(a) It did not establish the Asian NATO hoped for, since its geographical distribution was confused. A permament organisation with a secretary general was established, but political consultation rarely took place.

(b) It led to increasing American involvement in Pakistan and Thailand. This, in turn, stimulated neutralism in other Asian countries particularly India. Con-tainment in South-East Asia was precarious by the late-1950s.

D. Atlantic Alliance and European Union

D1. Bonds of Unity

The weakness of Europe after the war necessitated economic coopera-tion, and the receipt of Marshall Aid provided the institutions. The Com-munist threat was common to the Western powers, and governments were anxious for political cooperation. There was a desire to prevent Franco-German discord, so long a cause of European conflict, and the British with a military presence in Germany were anxious to share their burden. American diplomacy supported European unity. The West Germans were anxious to re-establish their status as a power under the umbrella of co-operation. There were idealists and bureaucrats who saw Europe as a third force between America and Russia, or saw unity as a means of retain-ing power now European empires were dwindling. Others saw economic advantage in union. The search for unity took three forms: economic, political and military.

(a) *Economic.* The first stage had been a union of Belgium, the Netherlands and Luxemburg (Benelux), formed in 1944. Schumann proposed a plan to unite Benelux with other Western powers in coal and steel production. Britain produced half of Europe's coal and a third of her steel and did not join, although giving strong support. Established in April 1951, the Coal and Steel Community consisted of Benelux, France, West Germany and Italy.

(b) *Political.* Since Britain helped to liberate Europe and had been the centre of the exiled governments, she took the lead when Churchill at Zurich in September 1946 said: 'We must build a kind of United States of Europe'. A conference at The Hague in 1948 put forward a plan for a Council of Europe and a European Court. The Council was set up in May 1949 at Strasbourg, with a Consultative Assembly and a Council of Ministers. It included the Six, the Nordic countries and Ireland, together with Britain.

These impressive steps, however, were not wholeheartedly backed by Britain. Labour feared a capitalist Europe and a rearmed Germany. The Conservatives saw Britain as a great power with a large empire, in which her main economic and military interests still lay. They were alarmed by Monnet and Spaak speaking of a federal Europe. In November 1951 at Strasbourg Britain opted out of a federal Europe, and in January 1952 Eden confirmed this move. Britain drew back, and a fateful decision had been made to abandon a movement her statesmen had done much to stimulate.

(c) *Military.* Bevin was determined not to repeat the mistake of Grey and Chamberlain, leaving Britain outside the European military balances. He therefore reversed Britain's traditional policy. In November 1947 the Treaty of Dunkirk with France provided for mutual defence. Then in March 1948 they were joined by Benelux in the Treaty of Brussels. A common defence system was to be created and a committee under Montgomery was established.

The fall of Czechoslovakia and the Berlin Blockade showed Bevin's policy was right; it certainly encouraged America to abandon isolation since British resources were being added to Europe in a way unknown in her previous history.

D2. The Foundation of NATO

Only America could provide the defensive shield Europe needed and, with the passing of the Vandenburg Amendment, which allowed America to join regional pacts, a Washington meeting started negotiations which involved a reorientation of American policy. The treaty was signed in April 1949 by the two great powers, Canada, the other Brussels treaty countries, Norway, Denmark, Iceland, Portugal and Italy. Its terms were:

(a) The treaty was to last for twenty years, and was to cover the defence of the countries in the treaty, Algeria, the occupation forces including Berlin, and islands, vessels or aircraft north of the Tropic of Cancer.

(b) Article 5 declared: 'The parties agree that an armed attack against one or more of them ... shall be considered an attack against them all.'

(c) It set up a North Atlantic Council of ministers, a Defence Committee and a Military Committee consisting of Foreign and Defence ministers and Chiefs of

Staff. A standing group of Britain, America and France was to provide general guidance.

Critics argued the alliance prevented detente with Russia. Its supporters claimed the end of the Berlin Blockade and the Greek civil war revealed its effectiveness. Although there was some talk of liberating Eastern Europe, the purpose of the alliance was defensive and had to be because of the imbalance of forces. Over the next few years NATO was strengthened by:

(*a*) *New members.* In 1946 Britain and America had urged the overthrow of Franco in UNO, but America now reversed her position, giving Marshall Aid and urging Spain's association with NATO. The UNO resolution was revoked, but in February 1951 Attlee made it clear Britain did not support such a move. The result was the Treaty of Madrid (1953) between Spain and America providing for bases. The British attitude was inconsistent, since Portugal's Fascist ruler, Salazar, was accepted and in September 1951 the Azores were included in the NATO defence plan. Greece and Turkey were admitted in February 1952.

(*b*) *Military organisation.* In December 1950 Eisenhower became Supreme Commander. He set up SHAPE at Fontainebleau near Paris. After a row with Britain a Naval Supreme Commander was appointed in January 1952. The military committee remained in Washington and the Mutual Security Act (October 1951), combining American economic and military aid, provided equipment.

(*c*) *Political organisation.* After a conference at Lisbon (1952), it was agreed to make the Council a permament body and hold three ministerial meetings a year. There would be permanent representatives and a secretary general—the first being Lord Ismay—who would produce an annual review.

The original intention to produce an army of 50 divisions was never attained, and the Russians, with 180 divisions, kept conventional superiority. NATO became increasingly dependent on the nuclear deterrent, and therefore on America.

D3. Failure of Defence Community and Success for European Union

In the heady days of English cooperation with European union, Churchill had called in 1950 for a fully integrated European army with a Minister of European Defence. This call fell on willing ears among those in Britain opposed to German rearmament, and was particularly welcome in France. In October 1950 the Pleven Plan urged the creation of such a ministry together with a European army containing mixed units. The aim was clearly to prevent a separate German army being created.

The problem was made more difficult by the German situation. The creation of East Germany had led the Western powers to adopt a fresh approach to their zones. In September 1949 military occupation had been replaced by an Allied High Commission, and a year later the Western powers agreed to revise the occupation statute and relax economic controls. In January 1951 the Russians denounced this move, and this brought the European defence and German questions into alignment. By September 1951 a Foreign Ministers meeting agreed to incorporate German troops in the European Defence Community and, provided the Germans agreed to have no separate military rôle, occupation status would be terminated. During March and April 1952 Soviet pressure was directed against Western commitment to the EDC, but on 18 April Britain's adherence was announced, and the next month West Germany secured internal independence by the Bonn Agreement.

(*a*) *Signing the European Defence Community Treaty.* Russian pressure merely drew the West together. The treaty was signed in May 1952, supplemented by a direct treaty with Britain and an Anglo-American guarantee.

(*b*) *The French veto.* A tactless speech by Dulles in December 1953 promising 'an agonising reappraisal' of American commitment in Europe if the treaty was not ratified, annoyed the French. Although it was agreed to increase NATO strength and Britain made further concessions, the French rejected the treaty in August 1954.

(*c*) *Eden's Action.* Eden decided to widen the Brussels treaty to include Germany and Italy. Dulles cooperated after a visit to Europe, and a conference met in Paris (September 1954). In October the Treaty of Paris created Western European Union.

(*d*) *The terms.* West Germany and Italy joined. Limitations were placed on arms levels, and West Germany was not to have nuclear weapons of its own. But she was to join NATO and rearm. Britain agreed to maintain four divisions and a Tactical Air Force in Europe until 1998, to be withdrawn only for a national emergency but subject to reduction in 'the event of a heavy strain on the external finances of the United Kingdom'.

This treaty was of great importance since it committed Britain militarily to the Continent. It brought France and Germany together in alliance, paved the way for a new Germany and for the Messina Conference which ushered in the next stage of European unity. The great disadvantage was that German division had now occurred. In May 1955 West Germany became a sovereign state, and was admitted to NATO.

D4. Geneva Spirit and Fresh Conflict

Churchill was convinced that conferences like those during the war could solve the differences between West and East. When Stalin died in March 1953 he was quick to act and proposed a conference. Unfortunately Eisenhower was faced with strong anti-Communist feeling in America and demands for revocation of Yalta. Although friendly to Churchill, he chose Dulles as Secretary of State who did not get on with Eden. The proposal for a summit was therefore coolly received. A meeting at Bermuda in July 1953 was agreed, but owing to the illness of Churchill and Eden it was postponed. Salisbury and Dulles agreed to a foreign ministers' meeting early in 1954. The Russians showed willingness to talk, and offered sweeping proposals for disarmament, mindful of publicity.

After Stalin, collective leadership was tried with Malenkov as Prime Minister. After a Stalinist purge a power struggle began which led to his fall in February 1955. Khrushchev, the party secretary, was behind this move, but did not yet have full power. Bulganin succeeded, but by March 1958 Khrushchev had re-established dictatorship. The public attack on Stalinism, culminating in the February 1956 speech by Khrushchev, covered a shift in foreign policy, and enabled Russia to escape the consequence of Stalinist imperialism and atrocities. Concessions were made that rehabilitated Russia in the eyes of the new countries of Asia and the Middle East, but peaceful coexistence did not mean that a retreat from Stalinism had been followed by a retreat from Communism, and this explains the contrast between concessions and intransigence in the mid-1950s.

(*a*) *Signs of a thaw.* Settlements were achieved in Korea (1953), Vietnam (1954) and Trieste (1954). Austrian independence on neutral lines was conceded (1955).

(*b*) *Peaceful coexistence.* Greater independence was conceded to the Warsaw Pact countries. The Cominform was scrapped (April 1956). After a visit to India by Kruschev, Western colonialism was denounced, and the same month Russia lifted her veto on 16 new members of UNO (December 1955).

(*c*) *The Geneva Summit.* The Bermuda Meeting (Churchill, Eisenhower, Laniel) took place in December 1953. It did not achieve anything, but the Geneva Summit occurred in July 1955. The West demanded free elections and choice of alliances for a united Germany, while the Russians wanted a provisional government and neutrality for Germany. It was agreed to refer Germany to the foreign ministers and disarmament to the UN Commission. The foreign ministers' meeting late in 1955 did not make any progress. Eden continued his efforts and in April 1956 Khrushchev and Bulganin visited Britain.

These moves stimulated the satellite states to see how far they might go. In Poland Gomulka was restored to power after riots at Poznan. In Hungary an attempt to denounce the Warsaw Pact and appeal to the United Nations for help in November 1956 failed, and Russian forces destroyed the régime; 200,000 refugees fled to the West. A UNO Resolution was ignored, and lasting damage done to the Communist image in the West.

(*d*) *The Treaty of Rome.* A conference at Messina (June 1955) asked Spaak to draw up a report on further economic cooperation. Britain withdrew in November from these discussions, and thus when talks began in May 1956, was outside. In March 1957 the Treaty of Rome established a Common Market with free trade, a common external tariff, agriculture and transport policies, and free movement of people and capital. A European Atomic Community was created, followed by the European Court of Human Rights.

By the time Macmillan took over, Britain's position in Europe was a hybrid one. She played a leading part in military alliances, but she had opted out of greater union. Eden proposed a 'Grand Design' for merging all the consultative assemblies into one (December 1956) and in January 1957 a government report called for a European free trade area, covering all OEEC countries, but Britain was reluctant to surrender her world rôle and accept that Europe was ceasing to be the poor relation of the early fifties (Chapter 19, C).

E. Cold War in the Middle East—The Suez War

E1. Arab Nationalism

The British had encouraged Arab nationalism and felt in 1945 as powerful as ever in the Middle East. They had twice as many troops in Egypt as they were entitled to by treaty, and British forces also occupied Syria and Libya. It was the British who encouraged the formation of the Arab League in March 1945, consisting of Egypt and six other countries, and by 1947 this had established a secretariat in Cairo and was helping Arab nationalists. During the war those who defied British power—Reza Shah, the Mufti of Jerusalem, Rashid Ali and Farouk—had been sharply reduced to obedience. Her position was buttressed by pre-war treaties with Egypt, Transjordania and Iraq and by the mighty Canal Zone Base, which was as large as Wales.

The Middle East became more not less important after 1945 since the loss of India, if ending one reason for holding the region, increased the gap between Europe and the Far Eastern possessions. The Korean war strengthened this argument. Oil had grown in importance from 335,000 barrels a day in 1938 to 3,486,000 barrels a day by 1956. There was a Communist threat, made plain enough in Turkey and Persia in 1945, but for the time being Britain could not count on American support. Truman opposed the British in Palestine, and helped to ensure they surrendered the mandate (Chapter 18, B1) but when, after the Arab–Israeli war, the British, French and Americans issued a Tripartite Declaration (May 1950) to support the armistice, and thus leave the Palestinian Arabs as refugees, bitterness was caused among Britain's Arab supporters.

American interests were concentrated in Saudi Arabia, which depended on the American oil companies. Ibn Saud was an old enemy of Britain's protégés, the Hashemite kings, and in 1955 was involved in a dispute with Britain over Buraimi Oasis (Chapter 18, B3). America was drawn to Persia by lend lease and Russian vetos in the United Nations. In 1947 a military mission arrived and economic aid started in 1949. This secured the revocation of Persia's treaty of 1921 with Russia and oil concessions, and did not back Britain in her difficulties. As Egypt moved towards full independence and supported nationalist movements, America became involved. Only when Egypt turned to Czechoslovakia and Poland for arms and recognised Communist China, did Dulles turn and cut off aid, thus helping to precipitate the Suez Crisis. Britain thus mainly relied on the aristocratic Bedouin Arabs and reactionary rulers like the Sultans of the Gulf States.

E2. Persian Questions

Britain's dominant rôle in Persia since 1933 made it difficult for her to object to Russian troops in the North, which Stalin refused to move. In March 1946 Persia complained to the Security Council, and in May Russian troops left. Britain negotiated a fresh agreement in July 1949, but parliament opposed it led by Mohammed Mossadeq.

(a) *The nationalisation dispute.* In March 1951 the Persian Prime Minister, who supported the agreement, was murdered, and the new government hastened to nationalise the oil industry although the treaty secured Britain's position until 1993. Britain said the agreement contained provision for revision, and took the matter to the Security Council (September 1951). An ultimatum was sent to Britain, and Abadan was evacuated. The International Court said they could not intervene, and Mossadeq became dictator. In October 1952 diplomatic relations were severed.

(b) *The Persian Oil Agreement.* Mossadeq deposed the Shah, and was himself overthrown by the army in August 1953. This cleared the way for negotiations which once again Eden conducted with skill. The agreement in August 1954, to last for 25 years, allowed Anglo-Iranian (British Petroleum) £25m compensation and a 40 per cent holding in the international consortium that was to run the industry, paying to the National Iranian Oil Company 50 per cent of their profits.

E3. Britain and the Arab Rulers

Britain was faced with difficulties in each of the states with which she had treaty relations:

(*a*) *Iraq.* The regent and the Prime Minister, Nuri Al Said, were friendly to Britain, but oil altered the relationship. A treaty was signed at Portsmouth (1948), but it was not ratified. A new oil agreement was signed in 1951, Nuri won the first parliamentary elections and the new king, Faisal II, was loyal to Britain.

(*b*) *Transjordan.* Difficulties with the Jews and Ibn Saud induced Abdullah to continue the British connection. The country became the Kingdom of Jordan. In March 1948 a fresh treaty was signed providing a £60m subsidy. Abdullah was killed and the new king, Hussein (May 1953), was loyal to Britain. But pressure from Egypt and Saudi Arabia led to trouble. Hussein dismissed Glubb Pasha (March 1956) and disbanded the Arab Legion. Jordan drew closer to Iraq and in March 1957 the treaty was terminated.

(*c*) *Egypt.* In September 1945 the Egyptians asked for renegotiation and a treaty was completed by October 1946. However, Egypt laid claim to the Sudan, which was a model British colony. The new treaty was not ratified. In 1947 Egypt appealed to the Security Council over the Canal Zone and the Sudan, and from 1949 to 1951 abortive negotiations continued. The British continued to build the Canal Zone base.

When the Conservatives returned Eden found himself renegotiating his 1936 treaty, but the issues were complex. The Canal itself was a vital trade link. The base was less important, since fixed bases were being outdated by nuclear warfare. The Sudan remained, and the need to deny Egypt to an enemy. After an attempt to provide regional defence for the base had failed (Section E4), Egypt repudiated the 1899 and 1936 treaties.

(*d*) *The Suez Canal Zone.* Riots began, stimulated by Arab 'commandos'. HMS *Liverpool* fired on Port Said, and at Ismailia 40 were killed in a battle at Police HQ. In January there were riots in Cairo; 56 British soldiers lost their lives.

(*e*) *End of the Monarchy.* A series of confused governments led to a *coup d'état* in July 1952 which deposed Farouk. It was led by General Neguib. In November 1954 he was replaced by the extremist Gamal Nasser.

(*d*) *The Sudanese Treaty.* Eden concentrated on the Sudan issue, and in February 1953 a treaty was signed providing for independence and an international commission to supervise the change. Independence was secured in January 1956.

Eden now had to deal with the Canal Zone. At home the Suez Group opposed further surrender when talks resumed in April 1953. Agreement was reached in October 1954, whereby Britain was to surrender the zone and base within 20 months, but the base was to remain activated, and could be reoccupied by Britain in event of an attack on any Arab state. The Egyptians would continue to observe the 1888 convention on the running of the actual canal. Twenty-seven Tories voted against the Nutting Treaty, but Eden was determined to secure good relations, and the last British troops left in June 1956.

E4. Middle East Containment: The Baghdad Pact

Britain wished to safeguard her Middle East position and deter Communist aggression while the Americans wanted to do one without the other. Eden proposed a Middle East Defence Organisation with the Canal Zone as a base, but this was aborted by Egypt's actions. America evolved a 'northern tier' strategy to hold the ring by involving Turkey and Pakistan in a defence system. In April 1954 Turkey and Pakistan signed an agreement, and later the same month Iraq accepted military aid from America. Iraq, alarmed by Nasser's flirtation with Communism, broke off relations with Russia and in February 1955 signed a pact with Turkey open to other powers.

Eden saw the opportunity and in April 1955 Britain joined the Baghdad Pact, thus retaining her Iraqi bases, although terminating the 1930 treaty. It was joined by Pakistan and Persia. But the pact had three disadvantages. It linked Iraq to NATO and deepened the rift with Egypt. It encouraged the Arab states to turn the Arab League into a military body. Above all, it left America in an equivocal position since Dulles would not join, and discussions between Eden and Dulles in February 1956 got nowhere due to the Buraimi dispute.

E5. The Suez War, 31 October–6 November 1956

Although Britain's position in the Middle East was weaker, Eden had done well to secure settlements with Egypt and Iraq and to create the Baghdad Pact. The Suez War undermined his gains, and the reasons for it are likely, therefore, to be complex:

(*a*) Israel, which was democratic and pro-Western, was subjected to attacks by 'fedayeen', developed by Nasser in April 1955. These stimulated unrest among the Palestinians and Jordanian opposition.

(*b*) Jordan's reversal of her pro-British policy had been particularly insulting since it had been done while Selwyn Lloyd was in Cairo. Eden blamed Nasser, and by March 1956 was saying he had to be 'destroyed'.

(*c*) Egypt was the centre of anti-Western activity. In November 1954 the Algerian rebellion had started with Egyptian help. Nasser had done his best to scupper the Baghdad Pact and directed propaganda against Britain.

(*d*) A series of arms agreements with Communist countries led to the threat of a Russian base in Egypt. America placed an embargo on Middle East arms (February 1956) to stop the border troubles between Israel and the Arabs. The French broke this in May 1956. France and Israel drew together.

(e) In December 1955 the World Bank agreed to provide $20m if America gave $56m and Britain $14m towards building the Aswan Dam. But since Nasser had mortgaged the cotton crop for Soviet weapons the West hesitated. Nasser then claimed Russia would finance the project. Congress insisted on strings to their loan, and on 19 July Dulles cancelled American support, forcing Britain to do the same. Britain was not consulted.

(*f*) On 26 July 1956 Nasser responded by nationalising the Suez Canal. Eden heard while entertaining the King of Iraq, and was furious that Nasser had 'his thumb on our windpipe'. Article 8 of the 1954 treaty had been broken, together with the 1888 convention, although Nasser said the canal would remain open to all (except Israel) and compensation would be paid if assets were handed over. In international law he was exercising sovereign rights.

The reaction of the British to this was violent. Britain was the largest user with 28 per cent of its tonnage and the largest shareholder with 44 per cent. Egyptian assets were frozen, and precautionary moves taken, but it was not easy to see what the powers could do. Boycott would damage them and as the Cyprus base was not ready military force was not immediately available. More important was Eden's personal reaction. Signing the 1954 treaty, he had said Nasser could be trusted, and was proved wrong. He saw Nasser as a personal enemy and a pocket dictator. His finest hour had been 1938, and he reacted without consideration of the military power involved or the ultimate reaction of America. At first there seemed general agreement on firmness and in support of Eden's view.

(*a*) *Initial reaction.* Gaitskell on 2 August said the position 'is exactly the same that we encountered from Mussolini and Hitler in those years before the war', and that force might have to be used 'as part of some collective measures'. Eden on 6 August said, 'we all remember only too well what the cost can be of giving in to fascism'. Dulles said force could not be ruled out, and on 1 August in a meeting with Eden said 'a way had to be found to make Nasser disgorge what he was attempting to swallow'.

(*b*) *Diplomatic moves.* A conference of the 1888 powers was held in London (16–23 August) and proposed a Suez Canal Board including Egypt. A Five Power Mission led by Menzies went to Cairo, but this deadlocked on 9 September. On 4 September Dulles produced a plan for a Suez Canal Users' Association, but this was torpedoed by Nasser on 15 September. A second London Conference (19–21 September) worked out details of SCUA.

(*c*) *The United Nations.* From 23 to 26 September the Security Council received complaints from Britain, France and Egypt. On 5 October Britain asked for backing for SCUA, and Dulles agreed. Six Principles were agreed by the parties, but Russia vetoed the second part of the resolution.

Throughout this period, Eden was becoming increasingly frustrated. In particular the American attitude was hard to explain. Having admitted the risks they took a series of steps backwards. On 11 September Dulles said, 'the Suez Canal is not a primary concern of the United States', and Eisenhower added, 'we are committed to a peaceful settlement of this dispute, nothing else'. On 2 October Dulles denied there were any teeth in the SCUA proposals, and American ships continued to pay dues. There were three reasons why America pursued a different course. It was an election year. Only 4 per cent of America's oil came from the Middle East. America was playing the anti-colonial rôle. But it went deeper. Dulles resented Eden's Vietnam conduct and British failure to back America in Formosa. Nor did he yet accept that the Russian threat was serious, and he feared military preparations would lead to Russian intervention. Eden said to Eisenhower, 'we do hope you will take care of the Bear', but Eisenhower refused on 2 September. So, as one writer says, 'utterly disillusioned and exasperated by what he felt to be American indifference' Eden turned to France and Israel and, although this 'may have been defensible in theory' since it seemed the limits of negotiation had been reached, it was a decision which 'represented a fundamental departure of foreign policy'. What followed has been the subject of much controversy centred on two main points:

(*a*) *Collusion and secrecy.* Military plans were originally laid for an attack from Mers El Kebir on Alexandria and the despatch of armoured divisions to Cairo, while an air drop on the Nile covered landings at Suez and Port Said. But this ran into difficulties, and together with the diplomatic moves, they were sufficient to secure postponement (the attack was planned for mid-September). Contacts between the French and Israelis were close, and in late September the British were made aware of them. On 6 October a start was made on the second plan. On 16 October, at the Hotel Matignon, Eden agreed to react to an Israeli attack. The cabinet committee knew of this by 18 October, and on 24 October the Treaty of Sèvres formalised the arrangements. America was not informed, but this is easy to understand, after events since July.

(b) *Military incompetence.* Israeli forces attacked on 20 October, supported by a French airdrop and naval action, and swept towards the canal. The plan worked out with the French provided for an air strike followed by landings on the canal to 'separate' the combatants by paratroops, and then an invasion fleet from Malta. Cyprus was not ready and transport ships and aircraft were short. There were two chains of command. Landing craft were in short supply and of poor design. The government had to use civilian lorries and ships, working trade union hours. Swift surprise was essential, and seemed unlikely.

The ultimatum was sent on 30 October. The next day the bombing of Cairo and airfields began, and the fleet left Malta. Israel accepted, but could of course press on to the Canal. By 5 November they had seized Sinai. The bombing was successful. It destroyed the Egyptian air force and the Russians withdrew their bombers and technicians. On the same day landings were made at Port Said, although progress was slowed by cancellation of a bombardment. A ceasefire followed on 6 November with patrols 25 miles from Suez itself. British troops had left by 2 December, and Israel withdrew from all except Gaza and Aqaba by 22 January. The attack failed in its immediate purposes, since the canal was closed by block ships, and petrol rationing was introduced.

(c) *Reasons for withdrawal.* America and Russia cooperated in demanding an Arab–Israeli ceasefire, and criticised the British. A UN resolution was carried by 64 to 5. The Canadian government proposed a United Nations force (UNEF) and on 4 November UNO agreed to this unanimously. The first units arrived on 15 November. There was a run on sterling, and the need for an American loan compelled Britain to accept American policy. On 6 November Russia threatened Britain with nuclear attack and, although Eisenhower condemned this, there is some evidence that joint Russo-American action was contemplated.

(d) *The consequences.* There is much controversy. Northedge argues 'none of its after effects was as serious as was feared and prophesied by the critics'. Knapp argues 'the Suez invasion was a failure on almost every count'. To some extent the events made explicit trends already apparent, rather then creating a weakened position for Britain.

In favour, it may be argued that the United Nations, after failing to act, was stung to action. America was forced in the Eisenhower Doctrine to accept its responsibility in the Middle East and, in April 1957, move the Sixth Fleet to the Eastern Mediterranean. Eden's departure in January 1957 made it easy for Macmillan to repair the breach with America and, although British prestige suffered, Britain continued to intervene in the Middle East until 1971.

Against, it may be argued it enabled Russia to escape with her attack on Hungary, although this was planned before the British invasion. It strengthened Nasser and damaged Nuri Al Said. It destroyed the 1954 treaty, and Nasser was able to tear up the 1888 treaty when the canal reopened in Egyptian hands. Arab nationalism became stronger with a pact between Egypt, Arabia, Syria and Jordan in January 1957. Nasser was able to stir up trouble in Syria and Yemen. Israel and the Arabs were further embittered, and Nasser determined to seek revenge for loss of territory. The Baghdad Pact was weakened and Hussein revoked his treaty with Britain.

In international terms, Britain had defied the United Nations and used the veto, which damaged her standing and gave a useful handle to Russian propaganda. Her attack smacked of colonialism, and in January 1957 both Bulganin and Chou En-Lai announced their support for Middle East states. Russia financed the Aswan Dam in 1958. The Commonwealth was divided, with only Australia strong in support. To the world it revealed the weakness of the special relationship between Britain and America, and Britain's military power. In the Middle East it was the equivalent of the fall of Singapore. Britain went back, but it was never the same again. As Proudfoot says, 'to embark on a military adventure of this kind, and then not carry it through, was to make the worst of all worlds'.

Further Reading

Epstein, L., *Britain, Uneasy Ally; a study of Anglo-American Relations*, University of Chicago Press, Chicago, 1954.

Knapp, W., *A History of War and Peace 1939–1965*, Oxford UP, London, 1967.

Laquer, W., *The Soviet Union and the Middle East*, Routledge and Kegan Paul, London, 1959.

Nicholas, H. G., *Britain and the United States*, Chatto and Windus, London, 1963.

Northedge, F. S., *Descent from Power*, Allen and Unwin, London, 1974.

Nutting, A., *No End of a Lesson*, Constable, London, 1967.

Rees, D., *Korea, the Limited War*, Macmillan, London, 1964.

Thomas, H., *The Suez Affair*, Weidenfeld and Nicolson, London, 1967.

Questions

1. How had Britain's world position changed by 1945, and how effective was Britain in meeting the changed situation?
2. What were the main principles of British foreign policy in the Cold War period?
3. What were the causes of the Cold War?
4. How effective was the peace settlement after the Second World War?
5. Why was the special relationship between Britain and America very often an Atlantic misalliance?
6. Was Britain correct to see herself more as a world power than a European country in the period after the Second World War?
7. Why was Suez a disaster?
8. What part did Britain play in the early moves towards European unity?
9. What was meant by the 'policy of containment' of Communism, and what part did Britain play in this policy during the Cold War?
10. Why was NATO created?

17

THE AGE OF AFFLUENCE—THIRTEEN YEARS OF TORY RULE: 1951–64

The war years were followed by a period of austerity, and this was prolonged by the Korean War. People turned with relief to an expanding economy in which they could garner the fruits of Keynes and Beveridge and enjoy a better standard of living. By 1954, with the end of rationing, a new era started, 'the age of affluence'. It was an age of Conservative domination very different from that between 1931 and 1940, although the party was led by the last of the Edwardians, Churchill and Macmillan. But the reforms of the late 1940s held. Economic policy was characterised as 'Butskellism' to indicate the similarity of approach between Gaitskell and Butler. Cooperation with the unions was sought by the new Minister of Labour, Walter Monckton. Apart from steel and a section of road haulage, the Tories accepted nationalisation and thus a mixed economy. Indeed, the Atomic Energy Act (1954) added to the list, while Acts extended aid to agriculture. Plans for the various industries were produced and vigorous men like Beeching and Robens were introduced to implement them. After years of undercapitalisation, the early 1960s saw a determined effort to make nationalised industry work, culminating in the White Paper of April 1961 which required them to be profitable over five-year periods, and stated 'they are not and ought not to be regarded as social services'.

Conservative acceptance of socialist measures went further. Full employment was recognised as vital, particularly by Macmillan. When unemployment rose slightly in 1958 and Tories opposed Keynesian measures, they were sacked, and when in the winter of 1962–63 it reached 900,000, the government acted swiftly. A report, *The North East: A Programme for Growth*, was followed by development grants and an Industrial Training Act which laid the basis for regional policies. The Tories also accepted the welfare state and, during their 13 years, increased benefits five times. In April 1961 a graduated pension scheme was added. Education spending doubled and although for a time hospital spending fell, in January 1962 the Hospital Plan envisaged massive expenditure.

The early 1960s showed the Tories were anxious to continue along the same road. A series of reports foreshadowed major developments, including Robbins in education and Beeching in transport. Programmes of motorway building, atomic power stations and universities were well advanced. In September 1961 came a decisive change brought about by the failure of the government to secure sufficiently rapid growth without encountering inflation. A pay policy was introduced by Selwyn Lloyd. This was acceptance by Tories of the ideas put forward in the 1930s and was a further step towards a managed economy. In 1962 came *Incomes Policy: The Next Step,* the first of a long series of ill-fated documents, and the Cohen Report on 'Conditions Necessary for Economic Growth' highlighted technical backwardness. This departure, combined with the application to join the Common Market, created strains in the Tory party, and was followed by the cabinet purge of July 1962.

But the 1950s and early 1960s carried a distinctly Tory flavour as well as the taste of consensus politics. The accession of the Queen (1952) was followed by predictions of a new Elizabethan Age in which the marvels of science and the products of affluence would usher in a new era. The power of America meant the American Way of Life, with its emphasis on materialism and mass markets, would spread. The People's Capitalism that emerged was not easy for Labour to accept since it seemed to take people away from the ideals of equality into 'the Opportunity State'. The *Daily Mirror* produced a City page advising readers on the Stock Exchange. The workers' standard of living had improved out of all recognition by the mid-1960s, and by the election of 1959 it looked as if the Labour Party was on the way out. In a revisionist work, *The Future of Socialism* (1956), Crosland advocated coming to terms with the new capitalism, and by the early 1960s the Party constitution of 1918 was under attack. The Tories emphasised a property-owning democracy. By 1964 one in five lived in a new house. The Housing Programme (May 1963) envisaged every family in a new house by 1970 and this created a new working class, anxious to protect property rights and fill their houses with the products of affluence. In 1955 Independent Television began. In Hopkins' words, 'the day the television came forms a sort of post-war watershed' for many families as it brought the worker into contact with ways of life never dreamed of before.

In July 1957 Macmillan used the phrase 'You've never had it so good' and, far from regretting it, said in 1960, 'You've got it good; keep it good.' The campaign of 1959 was the first when advertisers dominated party propaganda. 'Life's better under the Conservatives', said the slogan, but there were many who were starting to disagree. Gambling on a widespread scale developed. Premium Bonds had been followed by betting shops and bingo. In the shops customers were wooed with gifts and stamps which had to be regulated. A boom in property values created a new kind of British businessman—the tycoon like Jack Cotton in Suite 120 of the Dorchester surrounded by Renoirs, and after the Rent Act (1957) tenants suffered from slum landlords. Crime rose sharply from 304,000 indictable offences in 1939 to 900,000 by 1961. In spite of the gains, affluence did not spread everywhere. Titmus, in *The Irresponsible Society* (1960), attacked the loopholes, and in 1962 Wedderburn published an article on 'Poverty in Britain Today'. In 1964, 1½ million people were still on National Assistance. In attacking the morality of affluence, the left, whose doctrines were determined by economic redistribution and who had demanded improved living conditions, found themselves in an obvious dilemma, but they were aided by attacks from the right on the kind of Britain that was emerging, typified by the film *I'm All Right, Jack* (1959). The image of 'Swinging Britain' in the early 1960s with Carnaby Street, the James Bond films and the Beatles was not approved of by many outside the left. There was a rising tide of opposition to the permissive society and its assault on traditional values (Chapter 20, A2). Hailsham said, 'Our nation is being destroyed before our eyes by a conspiracy of intellectuals without faith, delinquents without honour and muck rakers without charity or compassion.'

In intellectual terms this revolt against the Tory fifties was represented by Angry Young Men, Kitchen Sink Theatre and the Pop Movement. In 1962 'That Was the Week That Was' on television began to satirise society and during the next two years the Tories, afflicted by spy scandals, the

Profumo Affair and the 1963 Conference at Blackpool lost their hold, particularly on intellectual opinion and the young. The 'condition of England' questions was revived in articles like those in the July 1963 *Encounter* entitled 'Suicide of a Nation'. The governing class were seen as outdated and narrow, ill fitted to manage the second industrial revolution. Seven of 19 cabinet ministers were relatives of the Prime Minister; one third were Old Etonians. Memoirs of the ruling classes had titles like *The Inner Circle* and *The Ruling Few*. Reinforced by Oxbridge and public school domination, the old school tie and class distinction were rampant. Macmillan himself, seen plodding in plus fours across the grouse moors, seemed to personify this kind of society. 'All through this book,' commented Sampson in his *Anatomy of Britain* (1962), 'I have felt haunted by the Victorians.'

Conservatives replied by stressing their achievements in raising living standards, widening property ownership, expanding the welfare state and carrying out major reforms. For example, the Mental Health Act (1959), the Shops and Offices Act (1960) and the Factory Act (1961) were all worth a place in history books alongside Disraeli's reforms. Benefits had risen by 125 per cent and wages had only risen by 110 per cent, while prices had only risen 50 per cent. But British economic development was starting to lag behind its competitors and 'stop-go' policy based on fiscal and monetary controls was not working. In 1961 Shanks' *The Stagnant Society* voiced this criticism. In September 1966 *Time* magazine had an article 'How the Tea Break Could Ruin England' which attacked restrictive practices and outdated methods. It also condemned the class-ridden society and argued that economic malaise was the result of 'psychological factors and cultural attitudes'. By 1957 strikes had reached their worst year since 1926 and in Frank Cousins, the first of a new kind of union leader had emerged. The Tories failed to tackle this problem and the Minister of Labour, Mr Hare, said in 1963, 'The most satisfactory way of dealing with all this is for the unions to put their house in order.' Among other major issues ignored by the Tories was immigration, and by 1964 race had appeared at Smethwick as an election issue. If writers as varied as Medlicott and Gregg could still write in 1964 about the amount of progress made, there were many more who saw the preceding era as 'thirteen years of Tory misrule' and in 1964 Labour returned with a small majority to deal with a nation they claimed was on the way to bankruptcy and decline. The Tories left them with a £748m unfavourable balance of payments as if to emphasise the nature of their spendthrift prodigality.

A. The 1950s—The Age of Consumer Democracy

A1. The Shape of Twentieth-Century Britain

When the Barlow Report was issued, a falling population was the concern of many and this continued until 1941. There was a rapid rise culminating in the 'bulge' year of 1947. This continued until 1955 and thereafter at a slower rate through the sixties. The Royal Commission on Population (1949) thus reported in a different atmosphere, and the postwar period saw a rise in emigration to the Commonwealth. By 1961 the population had risen to 53 million in the United Kingdom. This rise is mainly accounted for by younger and therefore more fertile marriages, reduced infant and maternal mortality, which fell to half that in 1939, and the atmosphere of prosperity and emphasis on the home that characterised the 1950s. The main points to note about this expanding population are:

(a) *Concentration.* Britain now had a density of 790 people per square mile, which was the second highest in Europe; 80 per cent lived in towns and 40 per cent in the Inner London region and six conurbations, the most important being the West Midlands.

(b) *Town life.* The novels of the era dealt with urban life. The word 'commuter' was introduced to describe a phenomenon found in all large towns, caused by the decline of inner city populations and changing transport patterns.

(c) *Transport problems.* Harlow New Town was planned with one garage for every 10 people, and this proved inadequate. The number of private cars trebled in 10 years, creating problems of congestion, pollution and accidents. Environmental questions began to develop.

(d) *Shifts in population.* The decline of rural population was arrested by the influx of town dwellers and retired people, although the agricultural population fell from 900,000 in 1945 to 396,000 by 1968. Scotland lost most people, with 254,000 leaving between 1951 and 1961, and there was a continuing drift from the North except Tyneside. Wales continued to decline until the early 1960s. Regional development was designed to arrest the decay of these areas.

(e) *The South-East problem.* In spite of new towns, the area continued to be saturated and in 1964 a report proposed 'overspill towns'.

(f) *The age pyramid.* The population was living longer. Expectation of life rose from 56 to 67 for a man and from 60 to 74 for a woman between 1920 and 1960. There were also more young people. Consequently there was a greater strain on the social services and the working population made up a smaller proportion of the whole. Within the working population the number engaged in manufacturing fell to 28 per cent by the 1970s.

Some important features of British society in the period were:

(a) *Growth of the middle class.* They registered a 30 per cent growth in the period as white collar replaced blue collar jobs, the Civil Service grew and a new group of professions emerged. This was the 'endless middle' with advertising agents and television producers and people in service and distribution industries. The rising standard of living also dictated a rise in the number in older professions like teaching and nursing.

(b) *Preservation of the upper class.* In spite of taxation policies, 1 per cent of the people still owned 43 per cent of the capital and 16 million had less than a £100 of it in 1962. The number of servants actually rose to 300,000 in 1960. Although certain features of upper-class life like being presented at court went, others remained. Guttsman and Sampson pointed to the influence of the aristocracy in government and the public school—Oxbridge stranglehold on the City, diplomacy, the Civil Service and the Church remained.

(c) *The survival of the hereditary principle.* After 1964 no more hereditary peerages were created, but the Lords remained unreformed, mainly hereditary and unique. Life peers strengthened its importance as a political forum. After a period of adulation following the Coronation, the monarchy was criticised for its cost, stuffiness and soap opera characteristics, but lived down the criticisms. By 1969 Cawston's film 'The Royal Family' reflected a new informality and the 1977 Jubilee proved the monarchy as popular as ever.

(d) *Teenagers.* With the falling age of maturity and rising incomes, young people began to create a generation gap and provide a subculture of their own.

The Teddy Boy was followed by rock and roll and pop. A mass market in clothes and records was created. Grave disquiet developed about crime and changes in sexual attitudes. But CND and Voluntary Service Overseas indicated all was not lost.

(e) *Immigration.* This was to prove one of the most important changes, but it took place largely unheeded until the 1964 election. By 1968 there were 1,113,000 immigrants, amounting to a fifth of the population in some cities. At first they had been mainly West Indian, but by the 1960s the shift was towards Asian and West African. There were disturbances in Nottingham and London's Notting Hill in 1958, and in 1962 the Tories imposed the first restrictions. By then major social problems were looming and racial prejudice was inflamed.

A2. The Miracles of Science: Second Industrial Revolution

The 1950s saw the end of the line for the major exporting industries left over from the nineteenth century which had been in decay for so long. Coal, for example, rose to a post-war peak of 218 million tons, but thereafter fell, and by 1965 government plans were in terms of 170 million tons a year. Apart from the use of alternative fuel, the Clean Air Act (1956) reduced its use as a domestic fuel. Cotton production peaked in 1951, and thereafter fell in competition with synthetic fibres from 2,202 million yards to 718 million yards by 1970.

Britain moved into a second industrial revolution which had gestated between the wars. It relied on products, many of which were science-based and consumer-orientated. Industrial production until the early 1950s concentrated on traditional products for export, but thereafter production for the home market became easier, and Britain's export position began to suffer as Western Europe recovered. Her position in 1951 as Europe's chief car manufacturer, for example, was bound to be undermined. What was needed was concentration on advanced technology and more sophisticated products. In some respects the 1950s showed Britain well able to do this. The aircraft and car industries were modernised, the steel industry was consistently profitable and in some developments such as hovercraft and atomic power Britain had a substantial lead. But by the early 1960s the old criticism of Britain as out of date was heard again. In spite of nine colleges of advanced technology and nine new universities, provision for higher education was insufficient, and the Robbins Report emphasised the need for more scientists. The percentage spent on research (2.35 per cent of the National Income) was too small, and half of it was in defence. The setting up of a Science Ministry in 1963 was a small step but Labour made much of the need for technical innovation in the election of 1964. By 1960 more worked in service and distribution than in manufacturing industry and the need for change to keep up exports was ever more pressing as rising consumer-based industries and higher standard of living brought pressure on imports. Among the chief industrial and technical developments of the period were:

(a) *Atomic power.* The opening of Calder Hall (1956), followed by a £300m programme, took Britain into the nuclear age. By 1966 nine stations had been completed. By the late sixties 11 per cent of electricity came from this source.

(b) *The jet engine.* In 1957 more people crossed the Atlantic by air than sea for the first time. Britain took the lead in aviation with the De Havilland Comet, which started regular jet flights in 1952. Design defects spoilt its record, but the Vickers Viscount gave Britain a lead in turbo-prop development.

(c) *Automation.* The automated factory line was known in the 1930s, but its adoption by Austin Morris in 1951 was a breakthrough. The process of automation spread into many spheres of life, including the telephone system and office equipment. In 1965 Bevercotes, the first fully automatic pit, was opened.

(d) *Computers.* The science of cybernetics enabled computers to reproduce human effort. IBM arrived in 1951, and a wide variety developed. The largest was at Newcastle, operating the National Health Service.

(e) *Transistors.* The first was invented in 1948. By replacing the valve they enabled radio and electronics industries to become highly sophisticated. Portable radios, stereophonic record players and tape recorders were household examples.

(f) *Television.* The BBC returned to the screen in 1946, and in 1955 was joined by ITV. Processes became more complicated, starting with Eurovision in 1953. In 1964 a new system of lines was adopted, and in 1967 colour was introduced. Satellites enabled world-wide coverage after Telstar began in 1962.

Although British industry and education were lukewarm or even hostile to science, the period was one in which the miracles of science became a talking point and life became increasingly mechanised. This was seen in the home and on the farm, where 'factory' methods became controversial. Britain often lacked the resources to follow up her own developments, and tended to engage in prestige projects she could ill afford. However, given the relative size of Britain to the two main powers, her contribution was sometimes impressive. The DSIR had a budget of £14m by 1962, affecting 5,000 projects, and it ran 14 research stations. Others were worried by a brain drain of distinguished men lured abroad. Among the important scientific developments of the period were:

(a) *Theories of the universe.* The development of radio-astronomy at Jodrell Bank (1957) under Sir Bernard Lovell maintained interest in this field. The theory of Hoyle (1949) concerning the nature of the universe was contradicted and scientists were divided between the steady state and expanding views.

(b) *Space exploration.* The launching of a sputnik by Russia in 1957 began a new era of satellites, including the first for weather in 1963. Man entered space in 1961 and landed on the moon in 1969.

(c) *Medicine.* With 500 new drugs a year, a new industry and new treatment methods became possible. Diphtheria and smallpox were largely eliminated. Polio was treated by the Melrose Heart-Lung Machine and vaccination with the Salk vaccine. By 1963 there were only 55 cases. Mass radiography helped virtually to wipe out tuberculosis. Artificial body parts like kidney machines were developed and surgery reached out towards heart transplants.

(d) *Biology.* The electron microscope enabled detailed investigations to be made, and interest centred on genetics and the cell. In 1962 Crick and Watson discovered DNA, which they claimed to be the fundamental substance of cell development.

(e) *Physics.* The concepts of matter remained central to development in this field, and several fundamental particles were discovered culminating in omega minus in 1964.

A3. The Affluent Society

At the turn of the century two books appeared which anticipated what happened to British society at this time. In 1899 Veblen's *Theory of the Leisured Classes* drew attention to capitalism's creation of a surplus devoted to conspicuous consumption. Luxuries became necessities, and people's expectations rose to dizzy heights. In 1901 Stead wrote *The Americanisation of the World*, predicting America's overwhelming economic power in the future. What happened during the 1950s was not simply the creation of a higher standard of living; it was a change in the way of life of the country as significant as that brought about by the Industrial Revolution. The growth of material prosperity was not immoral in itself; that it had certain consequences like an increase in crime was another matter. Similarly, the possession of washing machines or central heating did not indicate decadence, but electricity pylons created an environment problem.

The consequences of affluence were often a change in life style—teenage values, casual clothes, informal table manners, new kinds of packaged food or impersonal service—that offended the middle class, while working people worried about the break-up of old communities by planners and widening horizons. Affluence was subject to as much argument as pre-war poverty, and in each case there was a tendency among critics to exaggerate the moral consequences of material changes. In 1958 Galbraith's work on affluence came out, and thereafter there were other critiques like Peacock's *The Welfare Society* (1960). Some looked at the impact of a more egalitarian society because of mass production, while others saw the rise of a meritocracy creating a new division in society between those with a degree and those without. Differentials for skilled workers were soon a burning issue for socialists. The chief characteristics of the new society were:

(a) *Rise in incomes.* In spite of inflation this was the most impressive advance for ordinary people. The average working wage was £6 2s 8d in 1946. By 1959 it was £13 16s 6d, and by 1964 it was £18 8s 10d. Added to this were increases in overtime and welfare benefits, and a rise in the number of working women. Young people's wages rose also in a demanding labour market, and the average family succeeded in more than doubling its real income in 10 years. This was greater than in the rest of the century.

(b) *Rise in the standard of living.* In 1962 a new method of computing living standards was introduced since consumer expenditure had undergone such changes as the purchasing power of real incomes rose by 42 per cent between 1951 and 1963. Although Labour made much of Tory emphasis on consumer goods, this rise was reflected in nearly 4 million new houses and 8,000 new schools. Hospital spending doubled and the number of patients treated rose from 3 million in 1949 to 4.7 million in 1964. There was a rise in hire purchase debts from £90m in 1951 to £1,115m in 1964. £450m were invested in premium bonds by 1965, however, and total saving rose from £107m in 1951 to £1,953m in 1963, so accusations of a spendthrift society needed modifying.

(c) *The spread of consumer durables.* The two most important purchases for the average family were the television and the car, both of which supported big industries. The number of cars rose from 2¾ million in 1951 to 7½ million in 1964, while over the same period the number of television licences rose from 343,000 to 12,885,000. The washing machine (1947) was found in 6 million houses by 1964.

(d) *The growth of service industries.* There was a large growth in the retail trade, including 11,000 supermarkets, and in professional services such as catering, hotels, dry-cleaning, hairdressing and recreation. By 1964, of 25 million employed, 9 million were in manufacturing, 1 million in building, 1 million in transport, 3 millon in distribution and 5 million in service industries. The reduction of the working week from 48 to 42 hours by 1961, higher wages and increased mobility led to broadened horizons for many. While cinema attendances fell from 1,255 million in 1953 to 471 million in 1961, bowling and bingo replaced them. Dance halls catered for 5 million people a week by 1963; 85½ million LPs were sold in 1963.

(e) *Consumer interests.* Fanned by the massive circulation of women's magazines, a critical awareness of shopping developed. In 1957 the Consumers' Association and *Which?* were started and by 1963 the government had started a Consumers' Council. In 1961 the Consumers' Protection Act was passed. There was concern about the massive advertising industry, and an Act on advertising in 1957 was followed by the Trades Descriptions Act (1968).

The new society produced new problems. The motorcar was responsible for many of them, including the decline of public transport. Television was held responsible for a decline in reading, an increase in violence and vicarious occupations replacing hobbies and outdoor activities. Others argued cookery and gardening were stimulated by television, and 8 million watching *Panorama* was good for democracy. Factory farming produced cries about cruelty to animals by a population now addicted to the frozen chicken. Drink, tobacco and excessive eating produced serious health hazards. Clearly, all was not gain, but it would be difficult to argue the changes of this period were not the most spectacular and beneficial so far obtained in any decade of the present century (see Chapter 20, Section A).

A4. Kitchen Sink and Angry Young Men: The Culture of Humanism

Reaction to the war was different from 1914–18 for the cause was more congenial to many intellectuals in spite of the flight to America by some and pacifism among others like Britten and Tippett. The extension of democracy at home, and the mood of idealism for building a socialist new world also had its appeal. The war years deepened the trends of the 1930s, as Richard Hillary's *The Last Enemy* (1942), the poems of Alun Lewis and Sidney Keyes or the *Shelter Sketchbook* of Henry Moore indicated. At the same time it brought new influences, particularly from abroad. In 1940 Connolly took over *Horizon*, and through this introduced the works of Camus, Sartre, Moravia and Pasternak. Similarly, Seiber and Boulez introduced twelve-note music to the composers' world, and made the names of Schoenberg, Webern and Berg familiar. The war deepened cultural appreciation. The work of CEMA, later the Arts Council, in taking Shakespeare to the provinces or providing lunchtime concerts with Myra Hess and Kathleen Ferrier was valuable and even the film industry grew up a little under directors like Michael Balcon, and by 1947 'English films were receiving fine reception with American audiences'. The Brains Trust on the radio promoted a high level of discussion, while in 1946 the Third Programme was started to cater for new cultural interests. In music there was a major revival of English opera, and Britten's Aldborough Festival (1948) provided a fine setting. The Blitz and the activities of the planners provided scope for modern architecture to come into its own. Functionalism triumphed in new towns like Harlow or Peterlee. The movement in architecture culminated in the Festival of Britain, and this in its turn combined with the ending of austerity to create new standards in interior design.

But to many writers the 1950s were becoming commercialised and stereotyped. It might almost be true to speak of an upper-class reaction against years of left-wing and proletarian-dominated culture. Eliot's plays like *The Cocktail Party* (1949) and the novels of Angela Thirkell were some indications of the trend. Against this the Angry Young Men revolted, and British culture experienced a tropical heatwave of change. It had many roots. Overt sexuality in literature and art became commonplace while on the stage the end of censorship allowed cruelty and the absurd to emerge. The X Certificate in 1951 was the start of a process by which the cinema became experimental in ways unheard of in pre-war Hollywood. The visual arts became so subjective it was not easy to judge them. Architecture took the principles of Le Corbusier and Gropius to their logical conclusion, and the defeat in 1956 of the Neo-Classicists who wanted to rebuild the area around St Pauls with colonnades may be seen as decisive. In painting, surrealist and abstract art was followed by pop art and constructions. Music developed even more abstruse forms like musique concrète and electronic composition. Literature rediscovered the working class for the second time in the century.

It was on the stage that the greatest changes were to be found. Joan Littlewood's Theatre Workshop (1953–61), which produced *Oh What a Lovely War!*, did much to popularise the Brechtian style. The Royal Court (1956) and the Round House put on the latest works and the Mermaid (1959) experimented with new stage settings. After Peter Hall took over the Royal Shakespeare Company in 1960 this underwent rapid change, with Shakespeare in modern dress. John Osborne's *Look Back in Anger* (1956) was the play which focused attention on the new wave, but there were many vital dramatists at work in the period. The television companies needed 400 plays a year, and this provided a new field for experimentation, starting with the famous production of *1984* in 1953. Two dangers were that new concepts were incomprehensible in a way Dickens or Barrie were not, creating a cultural divide with the mass market, and they tended to be sensational and subjective, aiming for instant impact rather than lasting values. The chief cultural developments of the period were :

(*a*) *Architecture.* In new towns and estates, tower blocks, open planning and new materials were used. Aslin and Henderson's Hertfordshire schools set a trend. Robert Matthews' Royal Festival Hall was the first noteworthy post-war building. Sir Hugh Casson (b. 1910) masterminded the Festival design. Sir Frederick Gibberd (b. 1908) worked on Harlow and designed the new Roman Catholic cathedral in Liverpool. Sir William Holford as a professor at London University (1948–70) influenced the new generation. Sir Basil Spence (1907–76) designed Coventry Cathedral and new buildings for Sussex and other universities of the plate-glass era.

(*b*) *Sculpture.* There were two outstanding artists. Henry Moore (b. 1898) utilised outdoor life forms and primitive art. Barbara Hepworth (1903–75) used stone, but popularised other media including concrete and aluminium.

(*c*) *Painting.* The works of L. Lowry (1887–1976) achieved recognition in the 1940s. Paul Nash (1889–1946) and John Piper (b. 1903) were the outstanding war artists. Piper turned to stained glass for Coventry, where the great tapestry was the work of Graham Sutherland (b. 1903), a distinguished portrait painter. Abstract art was produced by Ben Nicolson (b. 1894), Ivor Hutchins and Victor Passmore.

(*d*) *Poetry.* T. S. Eliot (1888–1965) received the Nobel Prize in 1948, and was the pre-eminent poet. C. Day Lewis in *The Stand To*, S. Spender (b. 1909) in

Ruins and Visions and Edith Sitwell (1887–1965) in *The Raids* represented the pre-war generation. The four main war poets were Alun Lewis, Sidney Keyes, Keith Douglas and John Pudney. After the war a Scot, Hugh Macdiarmid, and a Welshman, Dylan Thomas (1914–63), attracted attention. In 1956 *New Lines*, edited by Robert Conquest, was designed to restore form to poetry. The three main poets were Thomas Gunn, Ted Hughes and Philip Larkin.

(*e*) *Music.* Benjamin Britten (1913–76) was pre-eminent with operas like 'Peter Grimes' (1945) and 'Billy Budd' (1951), and 'War Requiem' (1962). Bax, Rubbra and Walton continued to provide new works. Tippett (b. 1905) with his Piano Concerto (1956) and Concerto for Orchestra (1962) was outstanding, as were Williamson (b. 1931), Rawsthorne (1905–71), Bennet (b. 1936), Lutyens (b. 1906), Arnold (b. 1921) and Davies (b. 1934).

Although these achievements were impressive, it was in plays and novels that the period was most prolific. At the beginning Coward, in brilliant productions including *This Happy Breed* and *Brief Encounter*, continued to hold his own with Priestley (*The Linden Tree*, 1947), Eliot (*The Confidential Clerk*, 1953) and (*The Elder Statesman*, 1955) and Rattigan (*Separate Tables*, 1954). Then followed the renaissance of which the main writers were:

(*a*) John Osborne (b. 1929). After his first success came *The Entertainer* (1957), *Luther* (1961) and *Inadmissable Evidence* (1964).

(*b*) John Arden (b. 1930), who wrote *Live Like Pigs* (1958) and *Sergeant Musgrave's Dance* (1959).

(*c*) Samuel Becket (b. 1906), whose *Waiting for Godot* (1955) confused audiences and is often regarded as the first 'modern' play of the time.

(*d*) Harold Pinter (b. 1930), who wrote *The Birthday Party* (1958), *The Caretaker* (1960) and *A Night Out* (1961).

(*e*) A. Wesker (b. 1932), who wrote *Chicken Soup with Barley* (1958), *The Kitchen* (1959) and *Chips with Everything* (1962).

(*f*) P. Shaffer (b. 1926), whose chief works were *Five Finger Exercise* (1958) and *Royal Hunt of the Sun* (1964).

A classification of novelists can be made into classical, popular and the Angry Young Men groups:

(*a*) *Classical novelists.* Greene dominated this field with *The Heart of the Matter* (1948), *The Quiet American* (1955) and *Our Man in Havana* (1958). Waugh completed his wartime trilogy, and *Brideshead Revisited* (1948). Orwell wrote *Animal Farm* (1945) and *1984* (1949). Among new novelists the chief were C. P. Snow (b. 1905) with his 'Strangers and Brothers' series (1940–70) including *Corridors of Power* (1964), J. Cary (1888–1957) with *The Horse's Mouth* (1944) and *A Fearful Joy* (1949), L. P. Hartley (1895–1972) with *Eustace and Hilda* (1947), *The Go Between* (1963) and *The Hireling* (1957), L. Durrell (b. 1912) with his *Alexandrine Quartet* (completed in 1960), A. Powell (b. 1905) with his *Music of Time* series (1951–75), I. Compton Burnett (1892–1969) with *Mother and Son* (1955) and *A Father and His Fate* (1957), and Iris Murdoch in *Under the Net* (1954), *The Sandcastle* (1957) and *A Severed Head* (1961).

(*b*) *Popular novelists.* These were mainly characterised by crisp dialogue and clear if long-winded description and included N. Shute (1899–1960) with *No Highway* (1948) and *A Town Like Alice* (1949), Howard Spring (1889–1965) with *Fame is the Spur* (1940) and *The Houses in Between* (1951), R. F. Delderfield with *The Dreaming Suburb* (1958), *A Horseman Riding By* (1966) and *God is an Englishman* (1970), and Nicholas Montsarrat with *The Cruel Sea* (1951).

(c) *Angry Young Men*. The chief were Angus Wilson (b. 1913) in *Anglo-Saxon Attitudes* (1956), W. Golding in *Lord of the Flies* (1954), J. Wyndham in *Day of the Triffids* (1951), John Braine (b. 1922) with *Room at the Top* (1957), A. Sillitoe (b. 1928) with *Saturday Night and Sunday Morning* (1958), K. Amis (b. 1922) with *Lucky Jim* (1954), D. Storey (b. 1933) with *This Sporting Life* (1960), M. Spark with *The Prime of Miss Jean Brodie* (1961) and S. Barstow in *A Kind of Loving* (1960).

B. Winston Churchill's Peacetime Administration, 1951–55

B1. The Return of the Tories to Office

Medlicott described it as 'the most successful peacetime ministry that the country had seen since 1918'. Eden as Foreign Secretary had a series of successes, defence and security were improved and Commonwealth affairs went well with success against the Mau Mau and in Malaya. The new reign, with talk about an Elizabethan Age, contributed to the mood of euphoria. World economic recovery helped and with the end of rationing in July 1954 the first of the fifties' consumer booms was under way. Although the ministry contained more peers than any government since 1923 and was recruited from a narrow social circle and Churchill's wartime cronies, it was a strong team. The government possessed three advantages which enabled it to become more popular.

(a) *Churchill*. Although he had already had two strokes and suffered two more he remained firmly at the helm and immensely popular until his resignation.

(b) *The cabinet*. Eden wanted office at home, but Churchill would not agree. The Chancellorship went to Butler, the Home Secretary was Maxwell Fyfe, Labour was handled by Monckton and Housing by Macmillan. Lyttelton at Colonies, Macleod at Health and Thorneycroft at Trade represented the younger element.

(c) *Divided opposition*. Attlee decided to stay on until 1955, thus depriving Morrison of the chance of leading the party. Meanwhile, Labour was divided by the formation of a common front between the Bevanites and the Keep Left Group. Bevan left the shadow cabinet.

Some appointments gave rise to criticism. Woolton as Lord President of the Council had responsibility for Food and Agriculture, but retired in November 1952. Lord Leathers was responsible for Transport. Lord Cherwell became Paymaster General. Churchill operated a system of 'overlords' using these men, but their presence in the Lords proved unworkable. Cherwell and Leathers retired and the system was abandoned. Alexander gave up Defence in October 1954, which went to Macmillan. The only resignation was that of Sir Thomas Dugdale, who chose to interpret the doctrine of ministerial responsibility to include himself as responsible for the Crichel Down Affair (1954) when it was revealed that the government had sold a farm to a tenant, brushing aside the original owner who had been promised its return.

B2. Butskellism—Consensus in Economic and Social Policy

By 1951 the two parties had worked in harness for 10 years and, since the Conservatives accepted the mixed economy, welfare state and full employment there was little to distinguish their basic response; only later did Tories place more emphasis on reducing taxes and home ownership. The main developments in the economy were:

(*a*) *Opening crisis, 1951–52*. Trade disruption caused by the Korean War and the armament programme had to be dealt with, and Butler began with restrictive measures in November 1951 and March 1952. He initiated a period using the bank rate as an economic regulator by raising it to 4 per cent. Food subsidies were cut, and hire purchase restricted. A favourable balance was obtained by the end of 1952.

(*b*) *Boom time, 1953–54*. The working through of devaluation, an improvement in the terms of trade and the removal of restrictions encouraged a boom, and output rose 4 per cent in a year.

(*c*) *Renewed difficulty*. Falling reserves and a renewed deficit were ignored by Butler in the April 1955 budget which cut taxes by £150m. But the bank rate had already risen to 4½ per cent, home demand had boosted imports and a series of strikes in the summer following the election made matters worse. In July and October restrictionist measures were taken including a reduction in nationalised industry programmes and the raising of purchase tax and hire purchase deposits.

This initiated the policy of 'stop-go' in which successive chancellors wrestled with the problem of securing expansion without inflation and a favourable balance of payments. The main achievements of the ministry were:

(*a*) *A successful housing programme*. With the removal of controls in 1953 and the abolition of the Ministry of Materials, Macmillan was able to pass the election target by building 327,000 houses in 1953 and 354,000 in 1954.

(*b*) *Denationalisation*. Two measures were produced: the Iron and Steel and the Road Transport Acts. Apart from one firm, iron and steel was returned to private hands subject to an Iron and Steel Board, but in 1956 a further Act left intact a nationalised road haulage business, consisting of half the vehicles.

(*c*) *Education*. There was a rise in expenditure, and by 1956 there were 89,000 students. New universities came into existence—Southampton (1952), Hull (1954), Exeter (1955) and Leicester (1957). In 1956 colleges of advanced technology were started.

(*d*) *The Health Service*. Benefits were raised in 1953, and the Guillebrand Report (1954) rejected accusations of waste and inefficiency. However, a prescription charge of 2*s* was added to Gaitskell's measures.

(*e*) *Town planning*. Town and Country Planning Acts in 1953 and 1954 modified some aspects of the 1947 Act, including abolishing the development charge.

Continuity had been secured due to work of civil servants like Sir Robert Hall, Economic Adviser from 1947 to 1961, and to the wish of ministers like Butler and Macmillan to carry out reforms in the Tory democrat tradition. Churchill had no wish to oppose them as the government did not lose a single by-election, and the smooth transfer to Eden was followed by an election victory (Section D1).

C. The Career and Character of Sir Winston Churchill, 1874–1965

C1. Early Years
Churchill was born in 1874 at Blenheim Palace, the son of Lord Randolph who died in 1895 after ruining his political career, and Jennie Jerome, his American wife who survived until 1921. He went to Harrow in

1888 and did well at some subjects like history, and in sports like fencing. Entering Sandhurst, he was commissioned 20th out of 130 and joined the 4th Hussars in 1895. He volunteered for service in Cuba and saw action with the Malakand Field Force, in the Sudan with Kitchener and in South Africa. He wrote for newspapers, and turned his experiences into books designed to attract political attention. After losing a by-election he won Oldham for the Tories in 1900.

(a) *Liberal reformer.* His father had been a Tory Democrat, and in Churchill's biography of him sympathy for his views is clear. In addition, he had been in-fluenced by works like Seebohm Rowntree's. Chamberlain's tariff policy led him to leave the Tories in 1904, and he returned as Liberal MP for North-West Manchester in 1906. He held office as Under-Secretary for the Colonies and President of the Board of Trade before becoming Home Secretary (1910–1911) and First Lord of the Admiralty (1911–15). He attacked the sweated industries, backed Lloyd George against the peers and criticised defence spending. There was criticism of him for his actions at Tonypandy and Sidney Street, but he carried several reforms including labour exchanges and a Mines Act. As First Lord he improved pay and reduced the severity of discipline, created a Naval Staff, brought in new men like Beatty and started the conversion from coal to oil (Chapter 1, C and E).

(b) *The Great War.* He ordered naval mobilisation at the start of war without cabinet authority and pursued an active policy at sea. He was involved in the unwise sending of troops to Antwerp, and then caught up in the Dardanelles Controversy (Chapter 2, D1). Although the report in 1917 cleared him, the Tories excluded him from office in the 1915–16 coalitions. He served with the Royal Scots in France, but Lloyd George was impressed with his ability in parliamentary secret sessions, and in July 1917 gave him Munitions. He set up the Munitions Council, and by spending a fifth of his time in France won the confidence of the officers.

(c) *The fusion period.* Churchill strongly backed Lloyd George and was a prominent advocate of fusion. He was made Minister of War in 1919 to clear up the demobilisation muddle, but he used the opportunity to advocate inter-vention against the Bolsheviks. He also held the Air Ministry and strongly backed Trenchard, but initiated the Ten Year Rule in defence matters (1919). In 1921 he became Colonial Secretary, much to Tory anger since he was now in-volved in the Irish Treaty. He put out statements on policy in Palestine and the African colonies which were liberal, presided at the Cairo Meeting which partitioned the Middle East and was a close supporter of Lloyd George over Chanak (Chapter 4, A and C, Chapter 5, A).

From 1922 to 1924 he was out of parliament, but gradually moved towards the Conservatives, influenced by his dislike of Labour and Asquith's decision to support them in 1924. When Baldwin disowned tariffs, Churchill returned as Constitutional candidate for Epping in 1924.

C2. Study in Failure

Rhodes James argues that between the wars was a period of failure for Churchill culminating in 10 years (1929–39) out of office.

(a) *Chancellor.* Churchill has been criticised for his return to the gold stan-dard in 1925, but his policy was carefully considered and generally accepted at the time (Chapter 6, C2). His other budgets were well presented and successful, and gave strong backing to Chamberlain's reforms in the late 1920s. He has also been criticised for his conduct during the General Strike in editing the *British Gazette*, but it is also true he was an advocate of conciliating the miners (Chapter 6, C3). Between 1927 and 1931 Churchill's first major literary work— *The World Crisis*—was published, to be followed by *Marlborough* (1933–38). By 1929 he had held office for 20 years and many regarded his career as drawing to a close.

(*b*) *The wilderness*. Churchill fell out with his party and seemed destined for obscurity. In 1931 he left the shadow cabinet over India (Chapter 8, C3) and pursued the government for four years in his most sustained parliamentary activity (Chapter 11, B3). His advocacy of rearmament had much to do with the more right-wing element in which he moved in the party during these years, and Baldwin was able to outwit and finally muzzle him by letting him onto the Air Defence Research Committee (Chapter 12, B). His opposition to appeasement was less consistent than he later argued, since he did not oppose Japan or Italy in the period prior to 1938. Even at Munich he did not vote against the party. Moreover, his advocacy of a King's Party during the Abdication Crisis led to his humiliation.

Recalled by Chamberlain in 1939 as First Lord, Churchill was hamstrung by previous inefficiency and there were a number of grim disasters, unlike 1914. He bears part of the blame for Norway, and Chamberlain was able to contain his criticisms. His rise to power was due as much to others as to himself (Chapter 14, A3).

C3. The Finest Hour (see Chapters 13 and 14 for details)

Churchill served in three service ministries and had seen active service. He took the Ministry of Defence so that he could play the main part in deciding strategy. In this sense he was closest since Cromwell to a military dictator. Since the war revelations about the operations of SOE and the secret use of broken German Enigma codes have shown how little his wartime speeches revealed, and that he was a ruthless leader. He surrounded himself with a kitchen cabinet like Bracken and Beaverbrook, and relied too closely on men like Cherwell. Ministers were informed by letter of their dismissal, opponents were browbeaten, ministers and generals pressed to action when it was impossible. But unlike Lloyd George, Churchill's manner and his speed of forgiveness left little rancour. There was no feuding with the generals and little political intrigue. Churchill was careful for citizens' lives at home and still more careful of service lives, delaying D-Day until it was certain there would be no bloodbath. His phenomenal energy, frequent visits to the front, long journeys in dangerous conditions to conferences, ceaseless memoranda and direct interventions made him the most effective war leader of the century. His rôle as world statesman meant that in 1943 he was absent for 20 weeks of the year and missed 80 out of 176 cabinet meetings, but he was on hand to deliver orations to the Commons. Entrusted with powers of a dictator, he never ceased to be a democrat at heart, and humane in spirit. His conduct of home affairs underwent a change. At first social reforms occurred (Chapter 14, C3), but as the war continued, he let the initiative pass to Labour. Surrounded by sycophants, he failed to see his popularity would not guarantee success at the end of the war. His foreign policy was forced to yield to the growing power of America, and resented the increasing strength of Russia. His efforts to sustain a world rôle and preserve a world empire sapped Britain's resources.

C4. 'The Greatest Living Englishman'

Churchill was an ineffective leader of the Opposition after 1945, and his duels with Morrison were known as 'Children's Hour'. He was willing to allow the party to be reshaped in favour of Tory Democracy, but he remained attached to the old guard and was primarily concerned with foreign affairs.

(a) *World statesman.* Since 1944 Churchill had been concerned about the Russian threat, but at Yalta and Potsdam Roosevelt had been against him and Britain's declining share in the war prevented him from saving Central Europe. After the war his Fulton Speech crystallised the Cold War situation and thereafter he advocated European union on political grounds at Zurich (1946) and the Hague (1948). On taking office, Churchill again sought to restore summit diplomacy which was attained only after his resignation. At the same time, in the Global Strategy Paper and in the decision to make the hydrogen bomb, Churchill determined Britain's defence rôle for a decade.

(b) *Peacetime prime minister* (Chapter 17, B). In spite of defects in his health and choice of ministers, Churchill's last ministry saw the acceptance by the Tories of the major advances of the previous administration and the start of the long economic boom of the fifties. Abroad, it was characterised by a vigorous world rôle.

(c) *Achievement.* Apart from Gladstone and Palmerston, Churchill was the only prime minister in office at so great an age. He remained in the Commons until 1964 and died in 1965. By then he had been more honoured than any other figure in twentieth-century British history. Apart from 20 honorary degrees and 50 freedoms of cities, Churchill received the OM in 1946 and the Garter in 1957. He was awarded the Nobel Prize for Literature (1953). He was a Fellow of the Royal Society (1941) and of the Royal Academy (1948). His interest in scientific developments from tanks to mulberry harbours was far more than superficial, and his painting was being exhibited by the late 1940s. In 1963 he became an Honorary Citizen of the United States. When 19 volumes of his speeches are added to this list of achievements, it is clear that Churchill stood above all other political leaders.

Although the Conservatives claimed him as their own after 1945, this was not the whole picture. He had been a Liberal from 1904 to 1924, and served in coalition governments for 10 of his 29 years of office. He was kept out of office by Bonar Law, Baldwin and Chamberlain, and in 1940 was strongly disliked by the majority of Conservatives. This explains his success. He was an eccentric and a *bon viveur*, a man of the world with an artistic temperament, but he was not a snob or an habitué of aristocratic society. His friends of the twenties like Birkenhead and Beaverbrook were individualists. Churchill was concerned more about character than party, and this had national appeal. Labour may have detested his record as Home Secretary and Chancellor, but they had to admire it as President of the Board of Trade. Tories disliked his record as Colonial Secretary, but admired him as First Sea Lord and War Minister. Liberals applauded his work as a reformer. Conservatives admired his stand during the General Strike. Churchill was able to combine parties in a common cause, and as early as 1936 had brought all the three parties together in 'Arms and the Covenant'.

C5. Achievements

Churchill's place in history is a varied one. He was a major reformer in 1906–11 and 1940–41. He was a service minister making decisions vital to British strategy in 1911–15, 1919–21 and 1939–40. He was the first Minister of Defence. He was the greatest wartime prime minister, apart from Pitt, in British history. He was an important Colonial Secretary and a competent Chancellor of the Exchequer and although never Foreign Secretary, his influence as a critic in the 1930s and as a statesman in the 1940s was decisive. He was a fine House of Commons man, although subject to grave lapses, and his budgetary and wartime speeches are masterpieces. He was a poor party man, having the rare distinction of being defeated at the polls by Joynson Hicks and a Prohibitionist, and he won only one election and that by a small majority. His scientific interest has been discussed by R. V. Jones and his backing for science was a vital contribution to victory only now becoming clearer. His historical skills have been discussed by Ashley and, while his works suffered from being dictated, there can be no doubt his two accounts of the wars are minor masterpieces, and his *Marlborough* a definitive biography. Yet, as Rowse has remarked, 'Transcendant as were the services yet to come from Churchill, 1940 must rank as his finest hour, along with the nation's, for in that year his contribution made the difference between defeat and survival.'

D. The Eden Interlude, April 1955–January 1957

D1. The New Ministry

Churchill's resignation occurred in April 1955, and polling was fixed for 25 May. An 'election budget' and the success of the previous ministry augured well, and a rash of strikes including the newspapers did not help Labour. Eden was billed at 58 as 'this new young Prime Minister', contrasted with Attlee. The Tories offered the workers more than Labour seemed to promise, and they were still associated with austerity. Their party had been sharply divided. The result was Conservatives 344, Labour 277 and Liberals 6. The latter reached their lowest point in the period with only 722,000 voters. It was a quiet election with a low turnout.

(a) *The Prime Minister.* Born in 1897, Anthony Eden went to Eton. He volunteered for service in 1915 and won the MC in 1917. The deaths of two relations and what he saw in France made him a life-long advocate of negotiation rather than war; Suez in that sense was tragic irony. He went to Oxford and obtained a First in Persian and Arabic. He was fluent in French, and seemed made for diplomacy with his suave manner. In 1923 he became MP for Warwick and Leamington, where he remained for life, and by July 1926 was PPS to Austen Chamberlain. Although lacking in parliamentary skills, he worked his way up to Under-Secretary (1931), Minister for the League (1934) and Foreign Secretary (1935). Described by Mussolini as 'the best-dressed fool in Europe', he backed appeasement until his personal ego was offended by Chamberlain, and he resigned in February 1938 (Chapter 12, E3). Thereafter his supporters, 'the Glamour Boys', did little to hurt Chamberlain. Foreign Secretary during the war, he undertook a major reform of the Foreign Office, uniting the service with the diplomatic and consular, and securing competitive examinations, but his policy successes were overshadowed by Churchill. Several bouts of illness (1945,

1949, 1953) indicated his weakness, and he told a colleague 'I'm afraid I'm the prima donna they say I am'. But as Foreign Secretary from 1951 to 1955 he was outstanding, and after his second marriage in 1952 he seemed to recover. He did not like elections or parliament and lacked experience of high office.

(*b*) *The ministry*. Few changes followed. Macmillan went to the Foreign Office, Selwyn Lloyd to Defence and Home to Commonwealth Relations. In December 1955 came changes. Macmillan succeeded Butler at the Exchequer and Lloyd became Foreign Secretary where he remained until 1960. Butler became Leader of the House and Lord Privy Seal. An inner group of Salisbury, Butler, Macmillan and Eden dominated policy making.

Things soon went wrong. Economic boom was replaced by a sustained period of 'Stop' and labour relations deteriorated. Eden's popular support fell from 70 to 40 per cent, and after a press campaign he took the unwise step in January 1956 of denying he might resign. Abroad, foreign affairs did not go well. Macmillan was not a wise choice for Foreign Secretary as he clashed with Eden, and events in the Middle East encouraged the Suez Group to harry the government. Heath was appointed as Chief Whip to ensure discipline in the ranks.

(*a*) *Economic policy*. In July 1955, restraint measures were taken, including hire purchase restrictions, and an October budget raised purchase tax. The rising price of imports and the failure to export enough brought pressure on the pound, and in September Butler had to deny devaluation. Macmillan inherited this policy, raised hire purchase restrictions again, and bank rate to $5\frac{1}{2}$ per cent. In February food subsidies and investment in nationalised industries were cut; the budget brought further cuts and the start of Premium Bonds to encourage saving. The economy started to come right with a 6 per cent rise in exports, and by the end of 1956 there was a favourable balance of £209m. Although the Suez war had a limited effect speculation against the pound and American refusal of a loan without strings indicated the fundamental weakness of the economy.

(*b*) *Government measures*. The Eden ministry did not pass any major legislation, but it had a number of limited measures to its credit. They were the Clean Air Act (1956), which reduced smoke pollution by 30 per cent over 10 years, the Food and Drugs Act (1955), which consolidated pre-war laws, the Housing Subsidy Act (1956), which selectively began to restore subsidies to council building, the Road Traffic Act (1956), introducing vehicle tests above a certain age limit, and the Restrictive Practices Act (1956), which extended the powers of the Restrictive Trade Practices Court.

D2. The Politics of Suez (Chapter 16, E5)

Eden gained popularity during the crisis, and his resignation in January 1957 was genuinely on the grounds of illness for his colleagues did not wish him to resign, and he was not affected by unpopularity in certain quarters or by a sense of failure. The Suez War had important effects on domestic politics:

(*a*) *The question of cabinet responsibility*. The government's policy was dictated by a small group of ministers and the committee responsible consisted of Butler, Macmillan, Selwyn Lloyd, Head, Lennox Boyd and Salisbury. Procedure was similar to Chamberlain's high-handed conduct at Munich, but it seems clear the leading figures backed him throughout.

(*b*) *Tory opposition*. It is wrong to speak of a split. Two minor ministers—

Boyle and Nutting—resigned. Eight MPs abstained in the vote of 8 November. Heath enforced discipline. There were also 25 in the Suez Group who wanted harsher action and resigned the Whip in May 1957 to protest against Macmillan's leniency.

(c) *Labour policy*. Gaitskell had just become Leader and was determined to make a showing. Having given tacit support to firm action in August, he then attacked Eden and in a broadcast called on Tories to disown him. The scenes in the Commons were the worst since 1911, but the Tories secured votes above their nominal majority. Gaitskell's action paved the way for the Bevanites to return to the fold during 1957.

(d) *Public opinion*. Much work has been done on the vexed question of public reaction. There was a decided swing to the Tories from 48½ per cent (30 October) to 60½ per cent (21 November) and the Chester by-election was much improved on the earlier disastrous one at Tonbridge.

D3. Choosing a New Prime Minister

The sudden removal of Eden left the Tories with the possibility of Butler or Macmillan. In terms of domestic policies there was little to choose between them, although Butler was held to be the weaker of the two. The Queen consulted Churchill and Salisbury, and the latter polled the cabinet. The Chief Whip, Heath, and the Party Chairman, Lord Poole, were also consulted, but it is unclear if Eden followed Bonar Law's precedent of not giving advice. There was criticism of involving the Queen in politics, although she was merely performing a constitutional duty, and of 'a magic circle' determining the leadership. In fact, they chose rightly as 1959 was to prove.

E. The Macmillan Era, 1957–64

E1. The Last of the Edwardians

More than any other politician, Macmillan is associated with the affluent period of the fifties and sixties in the way Baldwin epitomises Tory leadership of pre-war days.

(a) *Career*. Born in 1894 and educated at Eton and Oxford, he served with the Grenadier Guards and, while acting as *aide de camp* to the Duke of Devonshire, married his daughter, thus linking his publishing business to the aristocracy. As MP for Stockton (1924–29, 1931–45), he was a reformer in the Tory party and resigned the party Whip for two years over unemployment. He strongly backed reformist trends in the 1930s and wrote *The Middle Way*. An opponent of appeasement, he obtained office in 1940 as Minister of Supply, but then acted as a diplomatic adviser in North Africa, Italy and Greece. Defeated in 1945, he returned for Bromley in a by-election and strongly supported the Butler reforms. In 1951 he was Minister of Housing. Then, in swift succession, he was Minister of Defence, Foreign Secretary and Chancellor. After his resignation in 1963 he wrote distinguished memoirs and was awarded the OM in 1976.

(b) *Attitudes*. Sampson's biography of Macmillan is called *A Study in Ambiguity*, and this reflects the man. Outwardly Macmillan represented the past. He was the last prime minister to wear top hat or white tie as to the manner born. His manner was haughty and flippant, but he mastered the Commons and was brilliant on television. He was member of five clubs and was frequently to be seen in them or on the grouse moors. His party and the cabinet remained a bevy of dull, solid men with country estates and his social circle was inbred and aristocratic. Christened 'SuperMac', he had flair and was able to win the 1959 election, which remains a unique political achievement. The image had the defect of making England look quaint in the modern world and, as security matters were to show, the image sometimes corresponded to reality.

Macmillan had astute political sense, genuine concern for the welfare of ordinary people and the quality of world statesmanship. His period of office was one of affluence, but it also saw a decisive shift in 1961–62 into the managed economy. Although Britain's economic performance lagged by the early 1960s, he grasped the nettle of the Common Market and converted most of the Tories. In foreign affairs his achievements were on a massive scale. He restored Britain's position in the Middle East after Suez and presided over the essential stage in the transference of colonial power. He reformed defence policy and defence organisation, lived with the nuclear threat and ensured that Britain played her part as a great power, even to the point of overstretching her resources. Macmillan became detached from home affairs and as the economy went sour in the winter of 1962–63, this was unfortunate. Like Chamberlain's government after 1937, Macmillan's after 1959 was reformist but hamstrung by its image.

E2. Restoration Work, 1957–59

Macmillan's government was not a reshuffle of the old pack of Tory cards. Only five ministers were left from Churchill's time. Selwyn Lloyd remained as Foreign Secretary, Butler was rewarded with the Home Secretaryship, while Thorneycroft became Chancellor. Apart from the resignation of Lord Salisbury in March 1957, the transition was smooth. Macmillan believed in delegating responsibility and allowing the cabinet to debate issues. Consequently, apart from a Treasury Crisis in 1958, it was a successful and proven team that approached the 1959 election.

(a) *Master Boom and Miss Slump.* The government was unable to halt the 'stop-go' situation and underestimated its effect on growth. Although the Cohen Report drew attention to the inflationary trend, this too remained relatively unchecked. Indeed, Macmillan was clear there was to be no return to deflationary pre-war policies. The aftermath of Suez led to petrol rationing and to rises in school meals and health charges, but by the time of the budget Thorneycroft felt able to relax. Taxes were cut by £100m. Dividend control and overseas credit restrictions were removed and concessions made to companies operating in the export market. A short boom followed, but by September pressure on the reserves led to a bank rate of 7 per cent.

(b) *The Treasury Crisis.* There was disagreement about what weakened sterling. Some argued it was caused by speculation. Others argued inflation at home was the cause, following strikes in shipping, engineering and power during 1957. Thorneycroft, backed by his Treasury Ministers, Powell and Birch, and by the Bank of England insisted there must be a credit squeeze to cut public investment, and estimates for expenditure should be kept 'within the level attained' in 1957. Several in the cabinet, led by Butler and Macmillan, would not agree, and in January 1958 the three ministers resigned.

(c) *Heathcoat Amory and expansion.* During 1958 the economy recovered as a fall in world commodity prices helped the balance of payments and investment in industry reached the highest level since the war. By December 1958 sterling was fully convertible. Strikes were contained on the railways and buses and inflation was held in check. Restrictions were removed starting with relief for small businesses in the budget, and by the end of the year the bank rate was down to 4 per cent.

(*d*) *The Electionist Budget.* In April 1959 Heathcoat Amory took 9*d* off income tax, cut purchase tax, removed 2*d* from the price of beer and restored investment allowances for industry. Welfare benefits were increased in June. There followed a boom, with an 11 per cent rise in production.

Outwardly there was plenty of evidence for affluence, but the Tories had not dealt with the major issues facing the economy. In September 1957, led by Frank Cousins, the TUC rejected wage restraint 'whoever wraps it up', and the year saw the loss of 8½ million working days. Incomes were still rising at 7 per cent a year. 'Stop-go' interrupted investment programmes and in industries like the railways the effect was serious. As the Common Market prospered, Britain's industrial efficiency fell behind and there was inadequate investment in private industry. Some argued too much capital was flowing overseas and the Radcliffe Report on the Monetary System (1959) was evidence of such concern. Although the government had set up a Council on Prices, Productivity and Incomes, it was advisory and at this stage the Tories ignored the Common Market. The prevalence of unemployment, which rose to 2.8 per cent by January 1960, indicated all was not well, and industry lacked the will to expand. Macmillan was increasingly drawn to his older faith in planning. It was clear the economy needed major surgery.

In legislation the period marked a continuation of a light load of laws and measures acceptable to the political consensus. The main measures were:

(*a*) *Constitutional Reform.* The Conservatives rehabilitated the Lords. In 1957 expenses of three guineas a day were started and in 1958 the televising of the opening of Parliament brought them in nineteenth-century splendour before the public. In 1958 the Life Peerages Act created life peerages; in July, 14 were made including three women, the hope being they would liberalise the House.

(*b*) *The Death Penalty.* The executions of Bentley and Evans brought to a head disputes about the value of capital punishment. A Report in 1953 cast doubts on execution and a pressure group led by Gollancz and Koestler was formed. In 1955 Sidney Silverman introduced a bill to suspend executions. After trying to coerce the Tories, a free vote was allowed and Silverman's bill passed in July 1956, but was rejected by the Lords. Butler therefore introduced the Homicide Act, which reduced the categories of murder and allowed the defence of diminished responsibility.

(*c*) *The Rent Act, 1957.* This sought to reverse the effects of the acts passed since 1915 by removing restrictions on rents on 810,000 houses with a rateable value of more than £30 (£40 in London and Scotland) and allowing some increase in rents on 4.3 million others. Brooke's Act was attacked by Labour as a landlords' charter. In fact, the number immediately decontrolled proved to be only 317,000 and there was little increase in rents. But later, property owners were to exploit tenants in inner city areas and particularly the coloured immigrants.

(*d*) *Other measures.* The most important social reform was the Mental Health Act (1959), which codified and reformed the Lunacy Acts and provided that mental cases should be regarded in the same way as physical illnesses. Admissions were to be voluntary in all except extreme cases and an appeals procedure for compulsory detainees was created. The Agriculture Act (1959) extended safety, health and welfare provisions from factories to farms.

E3. The Television Election, October 1959

The Tory election victory in October 1959 was the first time a party in power increased its majority three times. It was an interesting election because in three ways it marked a transition from the quiet affairs of 1951 and 1955. For the first time opinion polls were given publicity in the papers, advertising was used by the Tories over two years, and with Macmillan's rather 'presidential' style, television interviews became important. Macmillan first appeared in May 1958 and was successful. Just before the election a talk with Eisenhower helped him considerably. But the reasons for Tory victory were not simply tactics. The Tory record was a good one and issues like the Rent Act or nuclear disarmament raised by the opposition attracted little attention. Neither Labour nor Liberals were effective as opposition parties.

(a) *The Labour party.* At the end of 1955 Hugh Gaitskell (1906–63) had been elected leader by 157 to 70 for Bevan. He had come out as a determined leader at the time of Suez and by persuading Bevan to oppose unilateral disarmament in 1957 hoped to unite the party. But the CND wing gained in strength and at their conference in 1959 a motion on the subject was put forward. Labour was also divided over economic policy. Revisionists like Crosland argued for the replacement of the 1918 constitution and a dispute developed over public ownership.

(c) *The Liberals.* From 1956 to 1967 the Liberals were led by Jo Grimond. Married to Laura Bonham Carter and tucked away in a Highland constituency, he was not the most likely of dynamic leaders. An increase in the Liberal vote at Rochdale for Ludovic Kennedy and a victory for Laura's brother, Mark, at Torrington in 1958 were heralded as a revival. But the issues of devolution, proportional representation and the Common Market were not of public concern in 1959.

During the election, Gaitskell unwisely pledged himself to no increase in income tax and to a reduction in purchase tax, while at the same time promising subsidies for recreation, the arts and depressed areas, and higher pensions. The result was:

> Conservatives 365
> Labour   258
> Liberal   6
> Speaker   1

There was a 78 per cent poll and the two major parties still commanded the support of 87 per cent of the voters.

E4. The Golden Age

From 1959 to 1964, in spite of underlying problems and failure to enter the Common Market, the Conservatives were able to increase the momentum of economic growth. While the proportion of the National Income from tax fell from 32 per cent to 26 per cent and welfare benefits rose three times as fast as prices, real wages increased. Although some of this growth was simply crude capitalism, some of it was the product of the second industrial revolution. Proudfoot comments that 'the foundation of Mr Wilson's much vaunted technological age was well and truly laid by this Conservative government'. Although they wilted under the successive blows of a pay pause (July 1961), a cabinet purge (July 1962) and failure to enter the Common Market (January 1963), the momentum was kept up. A new school a day was opened and educational expenditure rose by 10 per cent. One million new houses were built and 253,000 slums cleared. Expenditure on roads rose from £60m in 1959 to £120m in 1963 and 260 miles of motorways were built. A range of vital projects, including the Victoria underground line and bridges over the Severn and Tay was started. Expenditure on scientific research doubled and programmes for university and hospital expansion were announced. If one considers the introduction of planning and incomes policies and the seminal reports, including Robbins which was the most vital social reform document since Beveridge, it is, in Proudfoot's words 'impossible not to be impressed'.

(*a*) *The economy*. The period saw no change at first in the basic 'stop-go' policy. Although the 1960 budget abolished entertainment tax, it introduced the idea of special deposits and tightened hire purchase. By June the bank rate was up to 6 per cent and special deposits were doubled. The Chancellor introduced the regulator (adjusting indirect taxes between budgets) in April 1961. But by July a serious crisis had developed, blamed on inflationary wage claims. The bank rate rose to 7 per cent, an IMF loan was obtained, special deposits increased, 10 per cent put on purchase tax and import duties raised. A pay pause was introduced. The budget of 1962 was designed to encourage exports against the background of Common Market entry and included a levy on speculative gains for cosmetic purposes. In July 1962 Maudling succeeded Selwyn Lloyd and, in his 1963 and 1964 budgets, went for growth, injecting £330m into the economy. Once again the Tories laid themselves open to the charge of an electioneering budget and the balance of payments situation worsened rapidly.

(*b*) *Pay policy*. Selwyn Lloyd proved an imaginative Chancellor willing to accept arguments for planning. Since the growth rate was 3 per cent and incomes rose by 6½ per cent in the last part of 1960, he argued for a period of pay restraint. The pause introduced in July 1961 applied to government employees, and hit groups like nurses and teachers. Trouble with postal and railway workers soured the measure, but when it ended in March 1962 Selwyn Lloyd replaced it with a guiding light of 3–4 per cent, based on a White Paper 'Incomes Policy—The Next Step'. By late 1962 this had been broken 77 times and the first attempt at an incomes policy had failed.

(*c*) *Indicative planning*. A number of economists backed the 1930s concept of planning. Macmillan was an old supporter and the government introduced policies which were 'considerably more radical than Labour had been in the 1940s'. At the Treasury forecasting techniques and forward planning were developed in a special department. In September 1961 the NEDC was formed under Sir Robert Shone and in January 1962 the TUC joined. A report in May 1962 advocated a 4 per cent growth rate. Then in 1962 a National Incomes Commission to discuss wages was started, but in September 1963 the TUC refused to support it.

(*d*) *Regional planning*. A sharp rise in unemployment in the winter of 1962–63 gave added impetus to the government's support for regional development. In 1960 the Local Employment Act (added to in 1963) provided for government aid in certain areas and £81m in grants provided 90,000 jobs. In January 1963 Lord Hailsham was made responsible for Tyneside and expenditure in the area rose from £55m to £90m by 1964. A new town at Washington was started. Regional surveys followed, including one of the Clyde, where a new town at Livingstone was started. In 1964 a South-East Survey advocated new developments at places like Newbury and further out at Ashford or Stansted.

(e) *Agriculture*. This remained a top Tory priority. From 1957 to 1963, 200,000 farm improvement schemes costing £200m were carried out with government aid. The Small Farmers Act (1959), added to in 1962, led to improvements on 50,000 farms costing £34m. Acts in 1960 and 1964 provided grants for market gardeners. More than 6,000 were helped under the first act.

This was a satisfactory record and places the Macmillan Ministry with other reforming ministries, but the early 1960s saw no slackening of effort. A number of Acts reformed the management of the nationalised industries, including the Transport Act (1962). Following the Beeching Report (1963), the government intended to modernise the railways by closing half the stations, widespread electrification and a new system of freight liners based on a hundred container depots. In January 1962 Powell announced a building programme for hospitals and in April 1963 a further large programme for the Health Service. In education the government seemed to be aware of the challenge of a scientific age. The Crowther Report (1959) led to the adoption of a higher leaving age. The Albemarle and Newsom Reports concentrated attention on the needs of 'deprived areas', remedial and outward bound work and an expanded Youth Service. Above all, a major programme of tertiary expansion was under way with the founding of seven new universities between 1961 and 1965. The Robbins Report envisaged an increase of students from 216,000 in 1963 to 390,000 in 1973, an increase of 10 per cent in the number doing postgraduate research, heavy investment in science teaching and the upgrading of CATs to universities, which began with Bath in 1966. Other reports included the Buchanan Report (1963) on traffic and the government intended to appoint a commission on the prison service which would be the first since 1895.

The government was weak on institutional reform, apart from the Greater London Council Act (1963) which abolished the LCC. The only important constitutional change affected the Lords in 1963 as the result of a campaign by Anthony Wedgwood Benn. The Peerage Act allowed hereditary peers to renounce their titles for their life-time. Benn ceased to be Lord Stansgate, but only half a dozen followed suit. In 1963, however, the renunciations by Lords Hailsham and Home were to be of major importance. Lady peeresses in their own right were admitted to the Lords. Otherwise the government had an impressive legislative record. The main measures were:

(a) *Commonwealth Immigrants Act* (1962). The rise in numbers coming each year from 21,600 in 1959 to 136,400 in 1961 required action. The Act provided immigrants could only come if they had a job, possessed skills or qualifications valuable to the country or came within quotas to be laid down by the Minister. Labour opposed the act, but numbers were cut to 49,626 in 1964.

(b) *Law and order*. Although Butler resisted efforts to reintroduce corporal punishment, he secured laws increasing penalties. The Criminal Justice Act (1961) developed detention centres and raised fines and sentences. In 1964 the Compensation for Injury Act introduced a new idea. The Legal Aid Act (1960) made this facility widely available. In April 1964 the Home Office issued *The Sentence of the Court* to help magistrates arrive at common verdicts.

(c) *Moral legislation.* The government seemed to favour the permissive society that was developing. The Betting and Lotteries Act (1959) led to the introduction of bingo and betting shops. The Licensing Act (1961) made the obtaining of liquor in restaurants and hotels easier. The Obscene Publications Act (1964) relaxed the existing law.

(d) *Social reforms.* The Factories Act (1961) and the Shops and Offices Act (1963) were major reform measures. The Payment of Wages Act (1960) allowed cheque payments and the Condition of Employment Act (1963) laid down statutory notice periods. The Industrial Retraining Act (1964) provided for 18 new training centres.

There was also legislation to help consumers (Chapter 17, A3) and this produced the repeal of resale price maintenance in 1964. The aim was to stop agreements with wholesalers not to sell below a minimum price and, although passed, it split the Tory party (Chapter 17, F).

E5. The Night of the Long Knives and the Profumo Affair

Ministerial changes under Macmillan were frequent and he was willing from the start to bring in new men. In 1959 Heath, Marples and Maudling represented the younger non-landed element in the party. In July 1960 Heathcoat Amory resigned as Chancellor to be succeeded by Selwyn Lloyd, and in his place Macmillan made Lord Home Foreign Secretary. This was criticised at the time, but he soon mastered the department and proved firm over Berlin and Cuba. Then, on 13 July 1962, came the most dramatic cabinet purge of the century and Macmillan, often accused of overmuch consideration for relatives and old school friends, acted savagely. For this purge several reasons were given:

(a) The pay pause was unpopular and the guiding light had been breached. By-elections were going badly. At Orpington (March 1962), in an 80 per cent poll, a Liberal won. At Stockton, after a visit by Macmillan, the Labour majority rose and at Middlesbrough Labour won the seat from Tories. A sacrifice to the polls was necessary.

(b) Macmillan was impressed by the Kennedy Image in America and was anxious for younger men to take over—Boyle was 38 and Joseph 44. Reports on a wide range of issues would require fresh action.

(c) There was discontent in the party with Macleod's Chairmanship and Macmillan acted to stifle discontent by fear and promotions at the same time.

(d) As a prelude to entering Europe, he wanted pro-Europeans in the key posts.

The result was that Selwyn Lloyd and six other ministers resigned. Butler became Deputy Prime Minister, Home remained as Foreign Secretary and Maudling was the new Chancellor. Among the newer names were Joseph (Housing) and Boyle (Education). Thorneycroft at Defence and Powell at Health were restored to favour. The team was 'one of the strongest of this century' and major reforms were planned in a wide field. But it did not work. The popularity of the government continued to fall and when the winter of 1962–63 raised unemployment, Labour had their biggest lead for 17 years. The government was defeated in two by-elections and in April 1963 Lord Poole was recalled to help Macleod stop the rot. The local elections in May were disastrous. For this slide there were a variety of reasons:

(a) Opposition inside the party to Macmillan. Led by right wingers, it had little following but suggested disunity. The Common Market aroused fresh opposition led by Lord Sandwich and Walker Smith and fuelled by Beaverbrook in his last political crusade.

(b) The pay pause, followed by the rise in unemployment and the continuation of restraint in the 1962 budget, took the gilt off the affluent society. *The Times* commented in July 1962, 'The you've never had it so good philosophy has been rejected. It cannot be replaced merely by new ways to having it better.'

(c) The collapse of the Summit Conference and then of the Common Market negotiations suggested a failing in foreign policy to which Macmillan had directed attention. (Chapter 19, B3, C3.)

(d) A series of spy scandals engulfed the government and attracted attention because of the nuclear issue (Chapter 19, B1). They led to the resignation of Galbraith, following a press witch hunt. He was cleared and two journalists imprisoned for refusing to declare their sources. This led the papers to attack the government and search for scandal.

On 18 March 1963 *The Times* published an editorial which was a criticism of society under the Tories. It said, 'The truth is that in a quiet way very much is going seriously wrong.' It was against this background that the biggest political scandal of the century burst in the summer of 1963.

(a) *Roots.* John Profumo was a successful minister. He had taken office in 1952 and become War Minister in 1960. In 1961 he had a brief affair with a model called Christine Keeler. She and another girl, Mandy Rice Davies, both lived with Stephen Ward, a society osteopath who also ran a call-girl ring. Miss Keeler attracted attention because she was attacked by two West Indians. They were tried in 1963 and given seven and three years respectively. Miss Keeler fled to Spain before the first trial and became 'the missing witness'. Mandy Rice Davies was kept by a Polish property dealer, Peter Rachman, who was exploiting the 1957 act in premises for call-girls. Miss Keeler also had an affair with Captain Ivanov, a military attaché at the Russian Embassy, and claimed that he asked her to get military secrets from the War Minister. This later proved quite untrue, but there was a security risk involved. Ivanov fled in January 1963. Ward knew Ivanov and the Security Services, aware of a link as early as 1961, warned Profumo to end his association with Ward, which he did.

(b) *Exposure.* George Wigg, a Labour MP, had been angered by Profumo's suppression of a report on medical deficiencies in the army. Approached by John Lewis, MP, with a story about Keeler, he was alerted to the security risk and took the matter to Wilson. Profumo made two firm denials early in 1963. In March four MPs raised the matter in the Commons. Profumo, after a meeting with five ministers (excluding the Home Secretary responsible for security), issued a denial. Macmillan, angry about Galbraith, was disposed to accept the denial and the sloth of the Security Services enabled him to do so with ease. Profumo said 'there was no impropriety whatsoever in my acquaintanceship with Miss Keeler'. Wigg met Ward a few days later. On 13 May Wilson demanded action from Macmillan and on 19 May Ward made his accusations. The result was that, on 5 June, Profumo resigned.

The atmosphere of high society and low life, the spy element and the melodramas of trials and secret meetings aroused public attention to fever pitch and gave the Opposition their chance to discredit the government. Wilson had taken over as leader in February 1963 and used his opportunity to the full. *The Times* said, 'Eleven years of Conservative rule have brought the nation psychologically and spiritually to a low ebb.' On 17 June the matter was debated and Macmillan was criticised by Fell, who quoted Browning's poem *The Lost Leader*, saying there could not be 'glad confident morning again' if Macmillan remained.

The government survived, but its majority fell from 98 to 69 with 27 Tory abstentions. Labour looked united and the Tories divided. Although the Denning Report in September dispelled the rumours and showed there was no security leak, the damage was done.

Macmillan fought back. Hailsham said 'a great party is not to be brought down because of a scandal by a woman of easy virtue and a proven liar'. Moral indignation among ordinary people was tinged with amusement and their attention was soon diverted by the Great Train Robbery. Macmillan produced the Test Ban Treaty and in September felt able to declare, 'All being well, if I keep my health and strength, I hope to lead the party into the election.' It was made clear this would occur in 1964 when the air had cleared, but speculation about a new leader remained.

E6. The Blackpool Intrigue, 1963

When the Tories assembled at Blackpool in October 1963 they were in high hopes that Macmillan would rally them. Before the Conference Macmillan intended to win the next election and then hand over to Hailsham who, educated at Eton and Oxford, was the kind of politician that appealed to him. He had a brilliant mind and was the darling of the constituencies. The Peerage Act of 1963 would enable him to renounce his title. Suddenly, crisis struck. The main stages were:

(*a*) 8 October. Macmillan was taken ill during a cabinet meeting. Prostate trouble was diagnosed and an operation followed.

(*b*) 9 October. Butler arrived in Blackpool and, as Deputy Prime Minister, said he would make the wind-up speech. A Gallup poll showed that Butler, Hailsham and Maudling were the main contenders for the leadership.

(*c*) 10 October. After assurances from Amery and Maurice Macmillan, Hailsham announced he would give up his peerage.

(*d*) 11 October. It became clear there was hostility to Hailsham and that a compromise candidate might be useful. Home's name was mentioned.

The intrigues at Blackpool had created an unfavourable impression. When Macmillan recovered he was determined to act. The steps taken were:

(*a*) 15 October. Dilhorne was to poll the cabinet, the Chief Whip, Redmayne, the MPs, Lord St Aldwyn, the Lords and Lords Poole and Chelmer, the constituency chairmen. This would enable Macmillan to advise the Queen if asked. It would also eliminate Butler and Hailsham, who both had strong enemies. It was, in fact, the most democratic sounding of Tory opinion ever held.

(*b*) 17 October. The soundings showed Home was preferred as the compromise candidate. Hailsham and Maudling agreed to serve under Butler. Powell, Macleod and Maudling met to head off Home, although they had all agreed to the poll process.

(*c*) 18 October. Macmillan resigned. The Queen, in an unprecedented gesture, went to his nursing home and received a copy of Macmillan's soundings. That day Home was asked to form a ministry.

It is still not clear precisely what happened, but the cabals collapsed. It seems likely this was due to Butler's refusal to carry matters further. Hailsham and Maudling then switched to Home. Only Macleod and Powell were left out. On 19 October, Lord Home became Prime Minister.

F. The Home Ministry and the Election of October 1964

Born in 1903, educated at Eton and Oxford where he got a third, Lord Home had been Parliamentary Secretary to Chamberlain (1937–40) and MP for South Lanark from 1931 to 1945. After a brave fight with illness, he had returned to politics as Minister of State at the Scottish Office (1951–55). He entered the Lords in 1951 and returned to the Commons as MP for Kinross and West Perth in November 1963. He had been Tory Leader in the Lords (1957–60) and held office as Secretary for Commonwealth Relations (1955–60) and then Foreign Secretary. Reputed to be a reactionary he was, in fact, a strong supporter of Macmillan's policy in Africa. He was experienced; certainly more so than his successor, Heath, was in 1965. But the image was wrong. Wilson lashed the 14th Earl, the whole process of appointment was distasteful and the Prime Minister was ill equipped to argue with Wilson on economics. Wilson emphasised the need for technological revolution and the end of 'grouse moor leadership'. Following disastrous local elections, Sir Alec announced in April there would be no dissolution until the Autumn. During the intervening period a number of factors further weakened the Tories:

(*a*) *The Resale Price Maintenance Repeal Act of 1964.* Heath annoyed the Tories and 21 voted against his bill, 12 abstained and 23 were away. This was the most serious defection of the 13 years and confirmed an impression of disunity.

(*b*) *Rachmanism.* Property prices in the overcrowded South-East rose and revelations of extortionate rents made by Ben Parkin, Labour member for North Paddington, damaged the Tories and led to a censure motion.

(*c*) *Wages.* The failure of the guiding light was followed by a wage explosion defying the NEDC norm. Several groups received high awards, including 6½ per cent to the postmen given by the government. This fuelled fears of inflation which the budget did nothing to contain.

(*d*) *Rookes versus Barnard.* A number of cases culminating in this one in 1964 restricted union rights to organise a closed shop. The TUC claimed this deprived them of immunities under the 1906 Act, but the government said they would not act.

(*e*) *Balance of payments.* Failure to enter Europe combined with relative industrial decline and inefficiency to damage the export picture. During the summer an unfavourable balance of £200m was announced, and the final total was £748m. It was argued the Tories allowed this to happen for a pre-election boom.

The ministry was dominated by electioneering, and in this Harold Wilson proved a master. His abrasive modern image contrasted with the puckish appearances of Home. He attacked the 13 years of Tory misrule, promised a way out of 'stop–go' policies and in his manifesto—*The New Britain*—struck the right note and made promises on all sides. But by the time the election was announced for October the Tories had recovered, and cut

Labour's lead to 5 per cent. Home was convinced that concentration on the nuclear deterrent and Britain's world rôle would pay off and the Tory manifesto—*Prosperity with a Purpose*—emphasised this viewpoint. While Labour promised new ministries, an Ombudsman, regional planning boards and comprehensive schools, the Tories had little to offer besides a commission on the trade unions and 400,000 houses a year. During the election Home declined a meeting on television, was badly heckled and referred to welfare benefits as the 'dole' in an interview. Although Maudling accused Labour of producing 'a menu without prices' and costed their programme at £1,200m, he did this too late. When the result came it was close in spite of two years' misery for the Tories, and Labour returned with the smallest majority since 1847. The result was:

Labour	317
Conservatives	304
Liberal	9

The importance of the election was:

(*a*) It ended 13 years of Tory rule. On a 77 per cent poll, Labour's popular vote actually fell and their majority was to fall to one in the next few months. Had the Tories not suffered a series of misfortunes, their victory would have been likely—the advent of Home could be said to have helped or hindered.

(*b*) At Smethwick the Tory candidate, Peter Griffiths, won on an anti-coloured platform defeating Gordon Walker, the Shadow Foreign Secretary. This was followed by two failures on Walker's part to return to office and an attack by Wilson on Griffiths as a 'parliamentary leper'. He lost his seat in 1966.

(*c*) The Liberal vote increased by 2 million to 3,093,316, their largest total since 1929, but they still only had nine seats. Clearly, many of the missing 1¼ million Tories turned to the Liberals following the Orpington pattern.

(*d*) Disappointment, distaste and unease contributed to the Tory defeat. It was good for democracy that there should be a change, and since a spirit not unlike 1945 prevailed and as Wilson was clearly a first-rate politician who could unite left and right in his party, all seemed set fair for 'the smack of firm government'.

Further Reading

Boyd, F., *British Politics in Transition, 1945–1963*, Pall Mall Press, London, 1964.

Churchill, R., *The Fight for the Tory Leadership, 1963*, Heinemann, London, 1964.

Dow, J. C. R., *The Management of the British Economy 1945–1960*, Cambridge UP, Cambridge and London, 1968.

Gregg, P., *The Welfare State*, Harrap, London, 1967.

Irving, C., *Scandal 1963*, Heinemann, London, 1963.

Macmillan, H., *Memoirs*, Macmillan, London, 1966–72 (6 vols).

Medlicott, W. N., *Contemporary Britain 1914–1964*, Longmans, London, 1967.

Proudfoot, M., *British Politics and Government 1951–1970*, Faber and Faber, London, 1974.

Sampson, A., *Macmillan, a Study in Ambiguity*, Allen Lane, London, 1967.

Worswick, G. D. N., and Ady, P., *The British Economy in the 1950s*, Oxford UP, London, 1962.

Questions

1. What is meant by the phrase 'affluent society' applied to Britain in the 1950s?
2. How effective was the response of Britain and its government to the challenges of the second industrial revolution?
3. Why was the 1950s an 'angry decade' in the world of the arts?
4. What is meant by describing economic policy in the fifties and early sixties as 'stop-go'?
5. Why was the successful raising of living standards criticised as 'Coca Cola democracy' by some?
6. Why were the Tories able to maintain themselves in office for 13 years?
7. How effective a prime minister was Harold Macmillan?
8. How was the welfare state developed during the period 1951–64?
9. Why may the years 1961–64 be seen as a watershed between post-war and modern history?
10. Why did the Tories lose the election of 1964?

18

THE END OF THE BRITISH EMPIRE AND THE FORMATION OF THE COMMONWEALTH

The Second World War was an imperial war, in which, apart from Eire, the dominions gave Britain support even if on their own terms. Britain's declaration of war was followed immediately by India, Australia and New Zealand and within a few days by Canada and South Africa. In spite of Barnett's argument that the Empire was ill prepared and a defence liability, Britain gained much from its involvement. Five million troops were raised, including a volunteer army of 2 million from India. In the Middle East the Eighth Army and in Burma the Fourteenth were imperial forces. In 1940 Dominion forces provided half Britain's front-line defence and 256 of the Battle of Britain pilots. Commonwealth generals like Blamey, imperial statesmen like Mackenzie King and Smuts and lesser known figures like the Canadian, Sir William Stephenson, who masterminded British Security Coordination, played vital rôles. British resident ministers were appointed for the Far East, the Middle East and North Africa. There were imperial heroes like Orde Wingate or Spencer Chapman. If Singapore fell, Malta did not, and if parts of the Empire were lost, they were regained. Singapore was described as 'temporarily in hostile Japanese occupation' and in September 1945 prisoners emerged from Changi Jail to see the surrender of Yamashita, while in Hong Kong rule was restored as the executive emerged from Stanley Prison.

Imperial losses were considerable. The colonies lost 21,085 and India 36,092. For each white dominion the losses were: South Africa (8,681), Australia (29,395), New Zealand (12,262) and Canada (39,319). Japanese and American intervention made the conflict world-wide, drawing in the dominions more directly than in 1914. Yet this time they did not fight for mandates or to seize (apart from Italy) another nation's empire, but to preserve Britain's. Canadians at Dieppe or on D-Day, Australians in the Pacific or Greece, New Zealanders at Crete, South Africans in Tobruk or Indians at Mersa Matruh played a vital rôle in securing for Britain her restoration in 1945. But this was a false impression. In the Empire this involvement had not gone unchallenged. Curtin had withdrawn Australians from the Middle East to defend the homeland in spite of Churchill's complaints. There was opposition in Canada to conscription for, whereas 62 per cent of all Canadians supported it, only 28 per cent did so in French-speaking Quebec. In India there was rebellion, and an army to fight for the Japanese (the Jiffs) had been formed in 1943. In Burma the independence movement had sided with the Japanese. Canada signed a defence treaty with America in 1940 and by 1951 Australia and New Zealand were linked to the United States, with Australia's Prime Minister saying they looked to America 'free of any pangs as to our traditional link or kinship with the United Kingdom'. The Empire had sustained defeats and revealed its weakness and victory only temporarily obscured these tendencies.

The post-war period saw a momentous change which altered Britain's rôle. If the Empire was casually obtained, its liquidation was equally discreet. In a 1947 poll only half those asked could even name a British colony. From 85 territories and 600 million subjects in 1945, it had been reduced to 30 territories with 20 million inhabitants by 1965. For this there were four main causes. Britain was economically and politically unable or unwilling to continue her imperial rôle, and it was argued her future in Europe and the weakening domestic economy necessitated the end of world-wide commitments. The British had exported their own political competition. The white dominions were already independent, and white settlers in Rhodesia and Kenya demanded the same treatment. India had been promised dominion status, and Ceylon nearly had it. Even in the tropical colonies the eventual intention was self-government. Once European nationalism spread to the Empire, accelerated demand for change became inevitable. The choice was to suppress it or lead it down favourable channels.

America adopted an equivocal position. She opposed Britain in India and the Middle East. Her economic power undermined Britain throughout the world. But in America's fight against Communism, Britain's bases and contacts became important to her global strategy. In CENTO and SEATO Britain played a key rôle, and bases like Singapore and Simonstown were keys to containment. For a time the contest with Soviet Russia held up British decline. On the other hand, Communism proved an enemy of imperialism. When the African Congress met at Manchester in 1945 its leaders had all been Moscow trained. Non-aligned nations were willing to listen to Russian charges of Western imperialism. They were anxious to receive experts and cash from other than their former colonial masters; a theme well illustrated in Padmore's *Pan-Africanism or Communism* (1956). At first in Asia, then in the Middle East, the Soviet Union became a new colonial power with economic aid, technicians, bases and finally an army. China with her appeal to 10 million Chinese outside her borders, her sufferings under imperialism and her toiling peasant masses affected the same regions.

These changes were reflected in the UN, which grew from 51 nations dominated by the West in 1945 to 120 nations in 1967, with ex-colonial states making the greatest number of members. In November 1961 a resolution calling for the end of colonialism was carried by 97–0 with Britain, France, Portugal, South Africa and Spain abstaining. In September 1963 Britain used her veto for the third time against a similar resolution and, although Lord Home pointed to double standards that left untouched Soviet and Chinese imperialism, the mood of the UN was anti-Western. When South Africa left the Commonwealth in 1961 this change in the balance of power was clear. Britain's shift to supporting developing nations meant a shift in her political stance. The UN continued to condemn colonialism and in 1967 described it as 'a crime against humanity'. Britain as a world trading nation was compelled to accept that the new states would organise politically. In 1958 the first Pan-African Congress met. At Cairo in October 1964, 47 nations called for an end to colonialism and foreign bases.

These mighty changes took place when British governments were run by the last of the Edwardians, like Eden and Macmillan, who saw Britain as a continuing world power. Eden was the last prime minister to refer to the

Empire and Macmillan was as firmly dedicated to the Commonwealth. Although he sometimes spoke imperially, saying Britain 'had not lost the will or even the power to rule', Macmillan also accepted 'our real need was to cut down expenditure for defence and overseas aid' and heed the wind of change. Attlee's measure in 1946–48 were complemented by Macmillan's in 1959–63. Reality came slowly, but it dawned in time to prevent the ugly end of empire achieved by other Western powers. The India Office was abolished. The Dominions Office became the Commonwealth Relations Office (1947) and this merged with the Colonial Office into the Commonwealth Office (1966). In 1968 the Foreign Secretary became Commonwealth Secretary as well. A similar contradiction in defence took place. In 1963 the Chief of the Imperial General Staff disappeared and the three service ministries—War, Admiralty and Air—began a process of amalgamation within the Ministry of Defence which was completed in 1967.

The methods and consequences of this change are still a matter of debate, but what is perhaps most remarkable is that they were achieved relatively smoothly and, in large part, by the Conservatives. Like the Holy Roman Empire, the British Empire refused to die; it experienced resurrection in a Commonwealth. Macmillan was the first British Prime Minister to tour the Empire in 1958 and 1960, and held that Common Market membership would strengthen Britain's world rôle. He tried hard to keep the Commonwealth intact and to secure associate membership for the colonies. The Commonwealth was to some extent a smokescreen erected to hide the retreat from power. Britain continued as a world capital, although the organisation itself seemed to have little cohesion or power. Moreover, the Commonwealth changed from a white man's club to a multiracial world organisation. It was illogical, but it enabled Britain to remain the focus for world events. For a time atlases even coloured the Commonwealth red like the old Empire. Since the organisation gave a world platform to new, small, impoverished nations, they preserved it also.

Although the period was marked by colonial wars more extensive than any since the 1890s, Britain seemed able to retain goodwill. Supporters of terrorism like Kenyatta and Makarios emerged as prime ministers. Nehru, Nkrumah, Banda and others emerged from jail to lead new countries. Apart from the Middle East they all joined the Commonwealth. But when Acheson made a speech in 1962 about Britain's world rôle, he said:

'Great Britain has lost an empire and not yet found a new rôle. The attempt to play a separate power rôle—that is, a rôle apart from Europe, a rôle based on a special relationship with the United States, a rôle based on being head of a commonwealth that has no political structure, or unity or strength, and enjoys a fragile and precarious economic relationship by means of the sterling area and preferences in the British market—this rôle is about played out.'

Macmillan replied attacking it, but as membership of Europe became a central political theme and the contradictions of Commonwealth structure more apparent, this more sceptical view began to prevail. The Commonwealth was viewed by optimists who spoke of 94 constitutions, the rule of law, multiracial harmony and economic assistance, and by pessimists who saw it much as pessimists had seen the Empire by the end of the 1930s as a lost cause.

A The End of the British Raj and British Rule in Asia

A1. The Impact of World War

Although the majority of Indians remained loyal and had much to fear from a Japanese invasion, the war period saw important developments:

(*a*) *Pakistan*. A Moslem League meeting in May 1940 announced a separate state of Pakistan for Moslems.

(*b*) *Congress and 'Quit India'*. During 1941 renewed strife led to 13,000 being imprisoned. In July 1942 Congress renewed civil war with the 'Quit India' resolution. Gandhi and Nehru were arrested. Over 100,000 were imprisoned and 1,000 killed.

(*c*) *British promises*. In August 1940 Indians were admitted to the Executive Council, and the Viceroy announced Britain would hand over to a responsible government of all India. The Cripps Mission (March 1942) promised the right to independence at the end of the war.

Meanwhile, the British continued with the 1935 Act and by 1943 six out of 11 provinces had elected governments. But Jinnah's Moslem League had captured Bengal and the North-West Frontier Province and this led to friction with Congress. A Meeting of Jinnah and Gandhi in May 1944 got nowhere. The Sikhs of the Punjab were restive and the Indian Princes discontented.

A2. Lord Wavell, Viceroy, 1943–47

After considering Eden, Churchill appointed Wavell as Viceroy in June 1943. He was a shrewd diplomat, but tainted by defeat in North Africa and Burma. He continued Indianisation and his executive council was all Indian by June 1945. Unfortunately his viceroyalty coincided with a famine brought on by cyclones and floods that destroyed a million tons of grain; 11,000 perished in the cyclones and $1\frac{1}{2}$ million in the famine, adding to discontent. In March 1945 Wavell came to Britain and, while he was away, the Executive Council split because Congress would not accept equal representation for the Moslem League, who would accept nothing less.

(*a*) *The 'Three Wise Men' Mission*. In January 1946 Attlee appointed Cripps, Alexander and Pethick Lawrence to find a new settlement. The Mission was not bipartisan as in pre-war days and it was shunned by Congress, the League and the Princes.

(*b*) *The British Plan, May 1946*. This proposed a complicated system of three federations and an Interim Government which Congress and the League rejected. Elections were boycotted and there was rioting in Calcutta with 4,000 killed.

(*c*) *The Interim Government*. This led Congress to change its mind and accept places in the Interim Government, followed by the League who launched a campaign for Pakistan. Violence spread with hideous massacres and about 6,000 deaths.

(*d*) *The Constituent Assembly*. This met in December to draft a constitution boycotted by the League and the Princes. Wavell and Nehru were ill and Jinnah was dying. A new start was needed.

A3. Lord Mountbatten, Last of the Viceroys, 1947

Wavell was replaced by Lord Mountbatten, second cousin of the Emperor and a distinguished general. He was only 46, lively, sociable and able.

By the time he arrived in India in March 1947 matters were serious: 20,000 troops were needed to secure temporary order.

(*a*) *The Transfer Statement.* In February Attlee announced India would be independent not later than June 1948 in order to force the factions' hands. In two months Mountbatten had 133 meetings with the leaders and Congress conceded the need for Pakistan.

(*b*) *The Second Transfer Statement.* In June Mountbatten announced that independence would now come by August of the same year. This forced Congress and the League to accept and work towards settlement.

(*c*) *The Radcliffe partition.* In 72 days Lord Radcliffe drew the boundaries of Pakistan, and on 15 August the Dominions of India and Pakistan were created.

Mountbatten remained as Governor General until June 1948 when he was replaced by an Indian. India became a republic. Jinnah became Governor General of Pakistan but died in September 1948. Pakistan became a republic in 1956. The immediate consequences of independence fulfilled Churchill's warnings in the 1930s:

(*a*) *Transference of population.* To effect partition, some 12 million refugees were created, and their movement brought chaos.

(*b*) *The independence massacres.* About 500,000 perished in violence worse than any during the British raj. Auchinleck, the Commander in Chief, set up a Boundary Force, but it could do little. The Indian Army was disbanded in September and the last British troops left Bombay in February 1948. Gandhi was murdered in January 1948.

(*c*) *The Princes.* Although they had treaties with Britain, these were broken and all were required to sign an Instrument of Accession. The Princes kept titles, property and personal privileges.

A4. The Dominion of Ceylon

Ceylon had self-government (Chapter 11, A5) and a new constitution in May 1946 extended this. In September 1947 Senanayake became Prime Minister and the country became a dominion in February 1948. Britain retained two bases, which were abandoned in 1957. Lord Soulbury became Governor General and in 1954 a Sinhalese obtained the post.

A5. Independence for Burma

The Constitution of 1937 had separated Burma from India and given internal self-government, but the advance of the Japanese gave a new twist to the Nationalist movement led by Aung San. He formed an army to help the Japanese. The Japanese proclaimed Burmese independence in August 1943. After the British reconquest, Aung San offered his services to the British (August 1944). The Governor wanted Aung San tried for murder and treason. However, Mountbatten allowed him to receive arms, and in March he attacked the Japanese. A new governor was appointed and, after a London Conference (December 1946–January 1947), independence promised. Elections were held and Aung San became Prime Minister. He demanded republican status, but on 19 July 1947, with six cabinet ministers, he was murdered. A new government was formed and in October 1947 a treaty signed. Burma became independent in January 1948.

A6. The Malayan War, 1948–61

In 1946 a Malayan Union, including federated and unfederated states and two of the three Straits Settlements, was formed, but the rulers opposed it and in February 1948 a more federal structure of nine states each with a Malayan Executive and a British Resident was formed.

(*a*) *Communist Rebellion*. The 2½ million Chinese were discontented with what they claimed was domination by 3 million Malays and in April 1948, led by Chin Peng, revolt began. Jungle, swamps and mountains made ideal guerrilla conditions and the war lasted officially until July 1961.

(*b*) *The campaign*. Sir Gerald Templar (January 1952–May 1954) successfully organised a campaign against the terrorists. New controlled villages with good facilities were established, protected by 250,000 'Home Guards', and in this way the people were won over and supplies denied to the rebels: 11,000 were detained and many rehabilitated. The rebels were largely defeated by 1956.

The government continued to promote political change and this was largely due to the British High Commissioner for South-East Asia, Malcolm MacDonald (1946–1955). In July 1955 Malayan elections were held and the party led by Tunku Abdul Rahman won all but one of the seats. In August 1957 Malaya became independent with a monarchy of its own, rotating among the rulers on a five-yearly basis. In October Malaya joined the Colombo Plan and signed a defence treaty with Britain. In June 1959 Singapore became self-governing with a responsible ministry led by Lee Kwan Yeu.

A7. The Malaysian Federation, 1963–65

Britain wished to retain her military position in Singapore and believed that if the Chinese and Malay elements could be balanced in a federation this would make for stability. Negotiations were undertaken by Duncan Sandys and in September 1963 the federation came into being consisting of Malaya, Singapore, Sarawak and North Borneo (Sabah). An integrated command was formed in November 1962. But it soon ran into difficulties:

(*a*) Brunei was unwilling to join, and this upset the racial mix in favour of the Chinese. A rising against the Sultan occurred which was suppressed by Britain (December 1962–May 1963).

(*b*) There was racial discontent between Chinese and Malays in Singapore and riots in 1964. In 1965 Singapore seceded, became a Commonwealth member and a republic.

(*c*) Indonesia and the Philippines objected and demanded a UN Fact-Finding Mission. The Americans interfered and a conference was held at Tokyo (June 1964) without result. Indonesia supported guerrilla attacks.

(*d*) The Borneo Campaign (April 1963–August 1966). A Commonwealth army was involved in a campaign along 970 miles of jungle frontier. Particular use was made of helicopters for jungle warfare and it was described 'as one of the most efficient uses of military force in the history of the world'.

The success of this campaign combined with trouble in Indonesia to bring about the Treaty of Djakarta in August 1966. British forces withdrew from Singapore in December 1968 and, in spite of protests from Australia, and New Zealand, Britain refused even contingency forces for SEATO.

B. The End of British Rule in the Middle East: The Palestine and Aden Wars

B1. Failure of the Palestine Mandate

Although the British proposals of 1939 (Chapter 11, A4) were unacceptable to the Jews, the Nazi threat secured *havlagah*, or restraint. The Jews, trained by Wingate in Hagannah, were not allowed to form a regiment until August 1942, but by September 1944 there was a Jewish brigade in Italy. This gave considerable military advantage to the Jews, who also seized arms. In January 1944 a breakaway group led by Stern, and called Irgun, started trouble and in November murdered Lord Moyne. Churchill spoke of 'a new set of gangsters worthy of Nazi Germany', and Britain determined to create an independent Palestine and restrict Jewish immigration. A blockade was enforced and only five out of 63 ships got through.

America began to agitate for a change in policy under the influence of the Biltmore Programme (1942) which urged a Jewish state of Israel. Roosevelt accepted this policy in 1944. He urged Britain to admit 100,000 Jews, and the discovery of the concentration camps made this an emotional issue. The World Zionist Conference called for the admission of a million Jews and the Arab League said this would lead to war. In October 1945 Attlee rejected the Biltmore Programme, but dependence on American aid forced him into a compromise.

(a) *The Anglo-American Mission.* For the first time Britain allowed a foreign state to directly intervene in imperial policy. A joint mission (December 1945–April 1946) recommended an independent state with local autonomy. Both sides rejected the proposals.

(b) *The London Conference* (1946) was boycotted by the Jews and the Arabs demanded their own state. Bevin conducted secret negotiations with Ben Gurion, but got nowhere.

(c) *Britain's abdication.* In 1947 fresh proposals for partition into Arab and Jewish zones under British trusteeship were rejected by both sides, and Bevin announced Britain would submit the mandate to UNO. This was done on 2 April.

These delays, combined with the racial conflict between Jews and Arabs and the distress caused by the blockade, particularly in returning the Exodus to Germany, led to a bitter civil war. General Cunningham, the High Commissioner, eventually had 80,000 troops in the country, but both Jews and Arabs were armed and he fought a losing battle.

(a) *The Palestine atrocities.* The war was marked by brutality against what the Jews called 'The Nazi British regime'. In July 1946 British HQ in the King David Hotel was blown up with the loss of 91 lives. When Britain reimposed the death penalty in January 1947, the Jews seized hostages and in July executed two British sergeants.

(b) *The British position.* Britain could not afford the military effort or offend Arabs and Americans. Anti-Semitic feeling grew in Britain.

(c) *The United Nations solution.* In September Britain said she would surrender the mandate in May 1948. In November UNO voted for partition, which Jews accepted and Arabs rejected. Britain did not approve and America urged delay, but it was too late with rising violence and British troops withdrawing towards Jerusalem and the coastal strip. On 14 May 1948 Britain left Palestine. The policy formulated in 1917 had failed.

B2. The Failure of the South Arabian Federation

Britain seemed uncertain where to locate her Middle East base after leaving the Suez Canal Zone. It was moved to Cyprus, Aden and Kenya.

(a) *Federation of South Arabia.* Britain controlled the sultans of South Arabia. In 1958 the Jifri brothers stirred up trouble in Lahej where Britain deposed the Sultan. These events led Britain to federate six of the states in February 1959, and by early 1963 the number of states had risen to 14.

(b) *The Yemen threat.* In September 1962 a coup removed the Imam of the Yemen and installed a pro-Nasser ruler. His rival organised the royalist tribes from neighbouring territory and Nasser brought in 28,000 troops, aircraft and even poison gas. The tribes of the Radfan grew restive and there was trouble in Aden Colony itself.

(c) *South Arabia Federation.* After a conference it was decided to merge the federated states and Aden and this took place in January 1963. In July 1964 Britain promised independence in 1968, with retention of the base. Disturbances in Aden led to the resumption of colonial rule in September 1965, when 760 were arrested and a third deported. In February 1966 Britain announced she would abandon the base as well.

(d) *The Radfan War* (January 1964–November 1967). Britain fought against Yemeni infiltrators and the National Liberation Front. In June 1967 the South Arabia Army mutinied and killed 22. Britain withdrew from the tribal areas and in September the federation was dissolved.

B3. Britain Leaves the Persian Gulf

Along the Persian Gulf, Britain had a protectorate over the seven sheik-doms of the Trucial States, Muscat and Oman and Bahrein. In 1951 Britain established the Trucial Oman Levies to protect the states from Saudi Arabia and Persia. The discovery of oil and the growing wealth of the area made it valuable to Britain.

(a) *The Buraimi Oasis.* In 1952 Saudi Arabia seized Buraimi, which Abu Dhabi claimed. In 1955 the Trucial Levies ejected the Saudis.

(b) *The Trucial Oman War* (July 1957–January 1959). The Sultan was threatened by the Imam, backed by Cairo. After a mission by Amery, it was agreed to give aid as the rebels were armed with Russian weapons. With the aid of the Levies and the Special Air Service the rebels were defeated.

(c) *The Kuwait Expedition* (July–October 1961). Kuwait became independent and was threatened by Iraq; 6,000 troops were sent. The War Office was criticised for inadequate protection and water supply in a temperature of 125°F. The British forces withdrew, to be replaced by Arab League ones.

The Arabian and Persian threats seemed to secure Britain's position, but the rising oil revenues led to discontent with the rulers. In August 1966 a military agreement with Persia relieved some of the burden, but this necessitated British support later for Persian claims to islands in the Gulf. In July 1967 Wilson reaffirmed Britain's intention of remaining and observing the treaties. Two events weakened this resolve: devaluation required further cuts and in the Middle East War (June 1967) the Gulf presence did not safeguard oil supplies.

(e) *The Federation of Arab Emirates.* In January 1968 the government said it would withdraw from the area by 1971. The decision was criticised, as it broke treaties and because Abu Dhabi offered to pay Britain to remain. In May Britain cancelled the 1961 treaty with Kuwait. A Federation of nine Gulf States was formed, backed by Arabia and opposed by Iran.

(*f*) *Heath's failure.* Heath promised to renegotiate Britain's position, but on returning to office backed Iran against Qatar and in August 1971 gave Bahrein independence. In November 1971 Britain withdrew her military presence.

C. The British Retreat from the Mediterranean

C1. Gibraltar

Spain renewed her claim to Gibraltar and in 1964 placed the matter before the UN. Spain rejected a British proposal to refer the matter to the International Court (December 1966). By 1964 Britain had created a government with a Chief Minister who asked for integration with Britain (July 1965). A plebiscite recorded 44 votes for union with Spain out of 12,762 voters (September 1967). In May 1969 Gibraltar was given limited integration and the Integration Party won the elections.

C2. Malta

Malta returned to self-government in 1947 (Chapter 11, A3). Her population rose rapidly to 320,000, and the Maltese Labour Party led by Mintoff favoured integration with Britain. The Nationalists wanted dominion status. A conference in 1955 was followed by a referendum that voted (February 1956) for integration. Fearing it would set a precedent and impose a heavy financial burden, Britain would not agree.

(*a*) *Struggle for dominion status.* Mintoff demanded more aid and when refused, declined to cooperate (April 1958). Britain resumed full colonial government. It was announced the naval dockyard would be converted to civil purposes, the budget deficit made good and £29m of aid given. In March 1961 Britain announced new proposals and a new constitution was introduced in 1962.

(*b*) *Problems of independence.* In September 1964 Malta became independent, but signed a 10-year military pact with Britain in return for £50m aid. The decision to run down the British military presence led to a crisis (January–March 1967). Britain agreed to slow down withdrawal and increase aid.

C3. The Eoka War in Cyprus, April 1955–December 1959

Britain restored political life in Cyprus in 1941 and in 1948 a new constitution was proposed. In 1951 Greece raised her demand for *enosis* and this time it received support from the Greeks on the island, who made up 80 per cent of the population. Their leader was Archbishop Makarios III, son of a shepherd who had trained at the Methodist College at Boston and had risen to archbishop by 1950. In 1951 he met George Grivas, an officer of the Greek army. In November 1954 Grivas arrived on the island to organise guerrillas who numbered about 300. In June 1954 Middle East HQ moved to the island and the government declared it 'can never expect to be fully independent'.

(*a*) *The Eoka Campaign.* This began in April 1955; Sir John Harding became governor and a state of emergency was declared. In March 1956 an attempt to assassinate the governor failed and was followed by the first big operation in the Trodos Mountains. In 1957, Drakos, the second in command, was captured, but Grivas remained hidden in a cellar in Limassol. In October Sir Hugh Foot came from Jamaica and secured a Christmas truce, but in March 1958 trouble began again and in July 7,200 Greeks were interned. Following the murder of Mrs Cutliffe, British attacked Greeks at Famagusta and six weeks of rioting forced civilians to go armed. A second Christmas truce commuted eight death sentences and, after a final sweep in the Trodos, the emergency ended.

(b) *Deportation of Makarios.* When ammunition was found in his palace, Makarios was deported to the Seychelles (March 1956). Grivas' diary showed the archbishop's involvement. By February 1957, 57 priests were detained. When Makarios offered to denounce terrorism, Macmillan had him released to Athens.

(c) *Turkish opposition.* The Turkish government wanted the status quo or partition, while Makarios insisted on self-determination. Led by Dr Kutchuk, the Turks cooperated with Britain and their resistance movement—Vulcan—was directed against the Greeks. In June 1958 Greeks and Turks were killed in communal riots, adding a new dimension to the problem. The dispute between Greece and Turkey threatened NATO.

The British tried to secure peace, starting with a conference in 1955. In June 1958 the Macmillan Plan for three-power supervision of a responsible government was put forward, but Makarios destroyed it. A proposal for NATO intervention in October 1958 was rejected. But the riots convinced all of the need for settlement and in February 1959 the Zurich Conference between all parties produced a solution. The terms were:

(a) Cyprus to be an independent republic with no *enosis* or partition.

(b) The constitution was to guarantee Turkish minority rights with a Turkish vice president, 30 per cent of the parliamentary seats and three members of the cabinet.

(c) Britain, Greece and Turkey agreed to defend the settlement and intervene if it was broken.

(d) British bases at Dhekelia and Akrotiri were to be continued.

A constitution was worked out and Makarios was elected president. Independence was delayed by a dispute over the bases, but Britain obtained 99 out of the 120 square miles she wanted. In March 1961 Cyprus entered the Commonwealth. Middle East HQ shifted to Aden the same year. But trouble soon began between Greeks and Turks and, when Makarios proposed constitutional changes, riots in December 1963 killed 200. Sandys went out and arranged a truce along the Green Line, but trouble was renewed at Limassol.

(a) *The first Cyprus intervention.* Makarios repudiated the three-power treaty and Turkey made war-like preparations. Britain and America referred matters to UNO and in March 1964 a mixed force of 5,000, including 1,000 British troops, was sent.

(b) *The second Cyprus intervention.* In November 1967 Greek police started to patrol Turkish areas and there were riots. The Turks demanded withdrawal of Grivas and an end to the build up of Greek forces. U Thant and President Johnson secured Greek agreement to this in December. Britain did nothing.

(c) *The third Cyprus intervention.* In 1974 Grivas died and Makarios was overthrown by a pro-*enosis* coup. On 14 August Turkey invaded and occupied the area north of the Attila Line for the Turks. In 1975 a federal state was proclaimed by the Turks. Britain did not intervene.

C4. Libya

Britain had installed the monarchy in Libya in 1951 and concluded a favourable treaty. In 1964 parliament demanded the removal of bases and Britain withdrew from Benghazi in 1966. In 1969 King Idris was deposed. In March 1970 British troops left Tobruk.

D. The End of Britain's African Empire

D1. African Nationalism

Four main sources of African Nationalism can be traced. There was the growth of interest in negritude which led to Pan-African Conferences and a determination to restore the culture and history of Africa to its rightful place. There was left-wing influence by men like Brockway, Laski and Padmore. Thirdly, Africans went abroad to be educated, particularly to America. Banda of Nyasaland was educated at Chicago and Nashville, for example. Lastly, the Asquith Report (1943) advocated the extension of university education in Africa and colleges like Makerere, where Nyerere of Tanganyika was educated, were started.

The educated class of Africans was bound to demand political change in spite of the backward nature of much of the continent and the Second World War, fought in parts of Africa, aroused political concern. In 1943 Azikiwe of Nigeria wrote *The Atlantic Charter and British West Africa* and next year founded a political party. Danquah founded the Gold Coast Convention in 1947, taken over by Nkrumah in 1949. In Nigeria, where Azikiwe represented the Ibos of the East, Tafawa Balewa founded a northern political party and in 1951 Awolowo one for the Western region. In Kenya, Tom Mboya founded the Kenya African Union (KANU) in 1947 of which Kenyatta became leader. In Uganda, Obote founded the Uganda People's Congress and in neighbouring Tanganyika, Nyerere set up the African National Union (1954). In Southern Africa, Kaunda formed the Zambian African Congress in Northern Rhodesia (1958) and the same year Banda returned to Nyasaland to control the Malawi Congress he had formed in West Africa in 1955.

D2. West Africa

(a) *Ghana.* In 1946 a constitution provided the first elected legislature in Africa and political action developed, followed by riots in 1949. Danquah and Nkrumah were imprisoned, but in 1950 a new constitution made a majority of the Executive Council elective. Nkrumah won the election and became Prime Minister in 1952. A further constitution in 1954 led to independence in 1957.

(b) *Nigeria.* A new constitution in 1946 was federal with three regional councils, round which political parties developed. In 1951 a central legislature indirectly elected was formed and in 1954 the regional governments acquired prime ministers. East and West became self-governing in 1957, and North in 1959. Nigeria became independent in October 1960.

(c) *Sierra Leone.* Dr Margai became chief minister in 1954 and the country progressed steadily to independence in 1961.

(d) *Gambia.* Smaller than Yorkshire and with only 320,000 people, it refused to join Senegal and in 1965 became independent.

Each West African country tended to follow a similar pattern. Ghana became a republic in 1960, and was followed by Nigeria (1963), Gambia (1970) and Sierra Leone (1971). Nkrumah, who took a lead in the Pan-African Congress, became a dictator (1960–66) and was overthrown by a military coup. Civilian government was not restored until 1969. In Nigeria a military coup in 1966 led to rule by Generals Ironsi and Gowan, while Sierra Leone experienced two military coups. The most serious post-imperial difficulty arose in Nigeria where, in 1966 after the massacre of 30,000 Ibos, the Eastern Region led by General Ojukwu seceded and a civil war was started. Wilson gave support to the Federal government providing a fifth of their arms, while France backed the Ibos. Britain feared Russian aid and the loss of Eastern Region oil. Some Commonwealth countries like Tanzania recognised the rebels, but by September 1969 Biafra was largely subdued and in January 1970 Ojukwu fled (Chapter 19, E4).

D3. East Africa

(a) *Somaliland*. An elected assembly appeared in 1956 and in 1960 Italian and British Somaliland were united in Somalia as a republic.

(b) *Uganda*. Mutesa II, Kabaka of Buganda, had treaty relations with Britain and, although his tribe made up only 17 per cent of the population, wanted concessions. But Uganda was well developed and Obote resisted this move. A federal constitution was created when the country became independent in 1962 and the Kabaka became president in 1963.

But difficulties developed; Obote deposed the Kabaka and, after an uprising, fled to Britain. In 1967 Uganda became a republic and the African kingships were abolished. In 1970 British property was nationalised, but next year during the Commonwealth Conference Obote was deposed by General Amin. A reign of terror followed, with the expulsion of the Asian population (1972) and spectacular murders including the Chief Justice, the Vice Principal of Makerere and the Archbishop of Uganda.

(c) *Tanganyika*. This colony was a model example of the road to independence from the day the first African took office (1951) to 1961.

(d) *Zanzibar and Pemba*. Following self-government in June, Zanzibar became independent in December 1963 under its Arab Sultan. In 1964 he was overthrown and in October Zanzibar merged with Tanganyika to form Tanzania. Contacts with China were opened and a one-party state introduced. The Marxist régime nationalised foreign property in 1967.

D4. Kenya and the Mau Mau Emergency

With 70,000 Europeans, 170,000 Indians and 6½ million Africans, Kenya presented a more difficult problem. Settlement in the White Highlands had been encouraged after the war and there was a colour bar. However, slow progress was made and in 1952 the first African entered the Executive Council. Provision was made to increase native representation in the legislative council. In 1954 Lyttelton announced a new constitution with elected ministers and in 1956 elected legislature members. Under pressure from Mboya, African representation was twice increased and Michael Blundell worked with KANU for a settlement.

(a) *The Mau Mau campaign*. Kenyatta's return in 1946 led to unrest among the Kikuyu. In 1953 he was imprisoned for 10 years for complicity in Mau Mau and not released until 1961. The movement was essentially ancient superstition with oaths and ceremonies, but it used modern gangster methods and possibly secured a million sworn supporters, although the hard core was about 15,000.

(b) *The Emergency*. It began in September 1952 and continued until January 1960. The governor, Sir Evelyn Baring, and the commander, General Sir George Erskine, were resolute and took advantage of experience from Malaya. A total of 11,503 Mau Mau were killed, 1,817 loyal Africans murdered, 32 Europeans killed and 590 of the forces killed; 22,000 were placed in camps.

(c) *White opposition*. Macleod ended the emergency, released Kenyatta and held a conference for further advance. In April 1962 Kenyatta entered the government, a second conference was held and Maudling, the Colonial Secretary, set aside 1 million acres for African settlement.

Elections were held in May 1963 and Kenyatta became Prime Minister. In December independence was secure and in 1964 Kenya became a republic.

D5. The Failure of the Central African Federation

As early as 1938 the idea of federating Northern and Southern Rhodesia and Nyasaland had been in the air. The Labour Colonial Secretary, Griffiths, and Sir Andrew Cohen backed the idea in 1950 because it envisaged a multiracial society free from the taint of South Africa, utilising vast resources and eventually ending the privileges of the white community in Southern Rhodesia. But the white settlers, numbering 210,000, a third of whom were South African born, had different ideas, seeing federation as a means of preserving their power over 3 million Africans. Accordingly, as early as April 1952, African political leaders opposed the move and Labour changed its position when Lyttelton decided to proceed.

(a) *Formation and growth*. Huggins in Southern and Welensky in Northern Rhodesia welcomed federation and in September 1953 it was inaugurated. For a time it prospered. An African Affairs Board was to refer to Britain any bill against African well-being, but it did little, and in Southern Rhodesia pass laws and land apportionment continued.

(b) *Lack of constitutional progress*. In Nyasaland the new constitution of 1955 only allowed indirect election and there were disturbances. When Banda returned in 1958, the governor declared an emergency. The National Congress was outlawed and Africans were killed in riots.

(c) *Conservative policy*. It seemed clear the intention was to strengthen the federation. In 1957 the London Agreement promised dominion status and the British government surrendered their veto. In 1958 the voting system for federal elections was modified in favour of the whites, and the blacks boycotted the elections. The Devlin Report criticised the severity of the state of emergency and the government appointed the Monckton Commission to review the constitution. It reported that a majority of Africans opposed the federation and therefore the right of secession should be allowed. It urged a bill of rights, a wider franchise and restrictions on federal power. Macleod released Banda in April 1960 and agreed to negotiate new constitutions.

(d) *White opinion*. This backtracking on 1957 produced a violent reaction led by Welensky, the Federal Prime Minister, Whitehead (until 1962) and Field, Prime Ministers of Southern Rhodesia. Field and his successor, Ian Smith (April 1964), were leaders of the Rhodesian Front Party, determined to preserve the white position.

Macleod from October 1959 to March 1962 and Butler thereafter pushed through a liberal policy in the face of strong opposition in the Tory party and Southern Rhodesia.

(a) *Northern Rhodesia.* Under Kaunda, Northern Rhodesia was allowed to secede in March 1963 and became independent as Zambia in October 1964.

(b) *Nyasaland.* In December 1962 its right to secede was acknowledged and in July 1964 it became independent as Malawi. It became a republic in 1966.

(c) *Southern Rhodesia.* A new constitution providing for an African majority soon after 1980 was introduced, but in April 1963 Britain rejected a demand for early independence unless five principles were met. They were a modified constitution for swift progress to black rule, no retrogressive amendments, better political status at once for blacks, the ending of racial discrimination and acceptance by the people as a whole of any new constitution. The Victoria Falls Conference failed and in December 1963 the Federation was dissolved amidst bitter recrimination.

D6. The Rhodesian Question

The closeness of South Africa and the prevalence of white rule made Rhodesia an awkward problem for Britain. In April 1964 Nkomo was imprisoned and a little later African parties were banned. An *indaba* of 600 chiefs and a white referendum were claimed by Smith as evidence of his popular support and in May 1965 he won an election on the restricted franchise.

(a) *The break with Rhodesia.* In July 1964, 18 Commonwealth members pledged not to recognise Rhodesia and a special UNO Committee was set up. Two visits to London by Smith achieved nothing in negotiations with Bottomley, the Commonwealth Secretary. In November 1965 Smith declared independence but claimed loyalty to the Crown.

(b) *Rhodesian sanctions.* This move aroused bitterness in the Commonwealth. Ghana and Tanzania broke off diplomatic relations. Since Britain had sent troops to Swaziland in 1963, it was thought at first that military intervention would follow. Thorpe of the Liberals called for bombing, and aircraft were flown to Zambia. The OAU demanded action and Wilson resorted to sanctions completed by January 1966. He then called for an oil embargo, saying it would be weeks rather than months before the régime fell, but oil continued to enter through South Africa and Mozambique, and the government had to impose a costly blockade off Beira. Pressure from a Commonwealth Conference at Lagos (September 1966) was followed by mandatory United Nations sanctions in December 1966. In April 1968 Wilson said force would not be used and asked for further sanctions.

(c) *Smith in power.* The governor remained in office until relieved by the Queen in June 1969. The High Court ruled in favour of *de jure* independence (1968) in spite of the Privy Council overruling this decision. Guerrilla attacks from Zambia were beaten off and five rebels executed in violation of a royal pardon in March 1968. In June 1969 a Land Apportionment Act divided the country equally between white and black, and a new constitution was devised. Britain broke all relations and in March 1970 Rhodesia became a republic.

The Wilson government made repeated diplomatic moves designed to placate international opinion, but insisted on the Six Principles, while Smith insisted on a slower pace. Great distrust and bitterness grew. Two meetings were held between Smith and Wilson in December 1966 (HMS *Tiger*) and

October 1968 (HMS *Fearless*), but they were further apart at the second meeting. Heath promised a further initiative by Lord Home which also failed.

E. Winding up the Colonial Empire

Black Nationalism and American influence combined with considerable poverty to unsettle the West Indies and Britain sought an answer in federation. There was a common court of appeal and development organisation and it was hoped poorer would be helped by wealthier islands. A conference at Montego Bay in 1947 set up a committee and in April 1953 discussions started. By 1956 agreement was reached and the Federation came into existence in January 1958.

E1. Failure of the West Indies Federation

On paper it looked impressive as it included most of the islands: 77,000 square miles and a population of 3 million. The federal government dealt with foreign affairs and defence. But a number of factors led to its failure:

(a) British immigration policies aroused resentment and helped to weaken traditional West Indian loyalty.

(b) Williams in Trinidad, Bustamente and Manley in Jamaica and Adams in Barbados wanted power for themselves and were unwilling to help the poorer islands.

(c) Jamaica had evolved into a politically sophisticated country. In September 1960 it voted to withdraw.

The British government fought the trend, but a referendum in 1961 went against and when Trinidad and Tobago withdrew, the federation was terminated in February 1962. An attempt was made to form a smaller federation, but Barbados insisted on independence, achieved in November 1966, and this became impossible. Anthony Greenwood was responsible for devising 'associated status' for the other islands in December 1965, to be completed in June 1967. The Bahamas chose independence in 1973 and Grenada in 1974.

E2. South American Territories

(a) *British Guiana.* A new constitution in 1951 led to riots. In 1953 British troops were sent, and the constitution suspended. In 1957 it was restored, but trouble continued with riots in 1962 and 1963. In May 1964 more serious riots led to suspension again. British troops remained until independence as Guyana in 1966. In 1970 it became a republic.

(b) *British Honduras.* This colony was claimed by Guatemala and had a permanent garrison from 1948. In 1963 limited self-government was introduced and Guatemala broke off relations. Renamed Belize, the colony remained British and troops were sent again in 1972.

E3. The British Indian Ocean Territory

Withdrawal from Aden, Singapore and Simonstown left a serious gap in Western defences. The build-up of the Soviet Fleet, which penetrated the Mediterranean and Indian Oceans by 1968, persuaded the government to use the Indian Ocean islands for defence.

(a) *Seychelles.* Given responsible government in 1970, the islands became independent in 1976.

(b) *Maldive Islands.* Separated from Ceylon in 1948, they became independent in 1965 and a republic in 1968. The Air Base at Gan, started in 1956, was abandoned in 1976.

(c) *Mauritius* became independent in March 1968 and in 1978 a Marxist republic.

(d) *British Indian Ocean Territory.* This was formed in 1965 and the most important islands were the Chagos group, where the American base of Diego Garcia was sited.

E4. The Pacific Islands

Independence was slowly extended to the most underdeveloped part of the Empire. Fiji became independent in 1970. The Gilbert and Ellice Islands were separated in 1975. The former became self-governing in 1977, while the latter became independent as Tuvalu in 1978. Nauru joined the Commonwealth in 1968, and Tonga in 1970. The same year Samoa, independent since 1962, also joined. In January 1944 Australia and New Zealand formed a joint policy for their possessions. The Cook Islands became self-governing in 1964. Papua–New Guinea, including New Britain and the Admiralty Islands, became independent and a member of the Commonwealth in 1975.

F. The Formation of the New Commonwealth

By 1975 the British Empire no longer existed. Only scattered territories remained, including Hong Kong, where riots in 1967 led to the despatch of troops. The UN complained, but withdrew the complaint on China's request. Spain claimed Gibraltar, Guatemala Belize, and Argentina the Falkland Islands, but their peoples wished to stay with Britain. Rhodesia remained a rebel colony. A number of West Indian islands retained associated status, and islands in the main oceans were British. A new Commonwealth consisting in 1978 of Britain and 35 other countries had come into existence.

F1. End of the White Man's Club

Until 1947 the Commonwealth consisted of self governing 'white' dominions, but independence for India produced need for change. This was coming about already, as older members were less influenced by the 'kith and kin' argument, determined to secure full political independence and aware that Britain's economic and defence role for them was a diminishing one.

(a) *Canada.* When Field Marshal Alexander retired as Governor General in 1952 the oldest dominion appointed a Canadian for the first time. By 1951 half Canada's population was non-British in descent, and American investment was four times greater than Britain's. Canada pursued an independent defence policy with the United States in agreements of 1947 and 1958.

(b) *New Zealand.* Not until 1947 did New Zealand accept the Statute of Westminster, as the $2\frac{1}{2}$ million inhabitants remained largely of British descent. After 1949 a long period of Conservative rule under Holland and Holyoake, broken only in 1957–60, tended to make New Zealand traditional in its loyalties.

(c) *Australia.* After Labour ministries who resented the British link, Sir Robert Menzies, 'the last of the Queen's men', was Prime Minister from 1949 to 1966 and strongly backed Britain. Australia was vigorous in her foreign policy, sending troops to Korea, Malaya and Vietnam. But the population ceased to be largely British descended by 1960 and trade with Japan soon outstripped that with Britain. Australia felt let down by the Common Market negotiations and Britain's refusal to back SEATO.

(*d*) *South Africa*. A complicated racial pattern existed with 12 million blacks, 1½ million coloureds, 1½ million Afrikaaners, 1½ million British and ½ million Indians. In 1948 the Nationalist party was returned to power with a policy of separate development or *apartheid*. There were rows with the UN over South-West Africa, incorporated into the Union in 1949, and over a report on racialism in 1954. By November 1956 legal opposition had been overcome, full *apartheid* policies were enforced and the laws consolidated and expanded in 1964.

This presented Britain with a grave difficulty. South Africa was important to Western defence with the Simonstown Agreement. A third of their trade was with Britain. On the other hand, in UNO and among the new Commonwealth resentment gathered strength. The change to a republic in March 1961 indicated that South Africa was moving away from traditional loyalties. Macmillan was anxious to retain South Africa in the Commonwealth and went there to make a speech, warning them: 'The wind of change is blowing through this continent and whether we like it or not this growth of national consciousness is a political fact.' But he failed. At the Commonwealth Conference of 1961 Canada and Malaya led the attack and South Africa left in May, although the defence agreement and the sterling area remained. Labour failed to supply arms (1964–70), but Heath restored them in spite of Commonwealth fury in 1971. Labour cancelled them again and terminated Simonstown in 1975.

F2. Constitutional Change

In order to respond to the older members' demands for full independence and reconcile new members considerable changes occurred in the constitution of the Commonwealth worked out in 1931. These were included in Acts in 1949 and 1953 and provided:

(*a*) 'Dominion' was dropped and replaced by 'realm'. Thus, the monarch became the individual king or queen of each country.

(*b*) 'British' was dropped from Commonwealth and the sovereign became 'Head of the Commonwealth', which was a symbol of the free association of the states involved.

(*c*) It thus became possible for the Queen to remain 'Head of State' in countries that became republics and to rule territories of other monarchs.

When Ireland left the Commonwealth in 1949 she retained privileges including the right to vote in British elections and the absence of passports. The British Nationality Act (1949) allowed Commonwealth citizens to choose British or their own nationality. A series of Acts starting in 1962 restricted the rights of Commonwealth citizens to enter Britain. These moves divided the Crown against itself and put an end to the proud boast of a common imperial citizenship. By 1970 it was hard to see what constitutional status the word Commonwealth possessed.

F3. Commonwealth Relations

Periodic meetings of Commonwealth heads of government occurred in

London and on a few occasions elsewhere, but from 1961, when disputes over South Africa and joining the Common Market occurred, these meetings became more acrimonious.

(a) *Political divisions.* Differing views on defence and the wish to be non-aligned were followed by more serious divisions. Commonwealth countries seized British property and broke off diplomatic relations and one-party states were established. Britain was powerless to prevent Marxist states being set up.

(b) *Military weakness.* Britain lacked the military capacity to suppress Rhodesia. Britain was unable to prevent bitter civil wars in Nigeria (1966–69) or Pakistan (1970–71). Britain let down rulers with whom she had made treaties and made defence cuts that were opposed by Commonwealth members. SEATO became a dead letter when Heath's proposals for a regional defence pact ended in a £6m mouse. CENTO never operated. In 1965 India and Pakistan went to war. It was the Russians who arranged peace at Tashkent in 1966.

(c) *Economic decline.* Although in 1950 a fifth of Britain's trade was with the Commonwealth, the trend was reversed in the next 20 years. Commonwealth countries made their own regional agreements for trade and aid and traditional markets vanished. In 1961 Macmillan argued membership of the Common Market and the Commonwealth were compatible, but the 1960s did not reveal such a trend. The figures were:

	EEC (£000m)		*Commonwealth (£000m)*	
	Imports	*Exports*	*Imports*	*Exports*
1958	538 (14%)	448 (14%)	1,336 (35%)	1,239 (38%)
1968	1,551 (20%)	1,196 (19%)	1,867 (24%)	1,408 (23%)

F4. Aid to Commonwealth Countries

The post-war period saw an expansion of British aid for colonial development under Acts like those of 1945 and 1955. A Colonial Development Corporation was set up in 1947, while the Colonial Office trebled its staff and quadrupled its expenditure on a declining Empire. The Commonwealth Development Corporation (1962) had 134 projects on hand in 1965. In 1958 aid was made available to independent Commonwealth nations and the amount doubled by 1962. In 1964 a Ministry of Overseas Development was formed (scrapped 1970–74) and in 1965 the interest-free loan was introduced. By 1970, 90 per cent of aid was on this basis and in 1978 the government wrote off outstanding Commonwealth debts. Although such aid represented only 20 per cent of development capital in the countries concerned and about 0.83 per cent of Britain's GNP, it was substantial in view of Britain's deteriorating economic position. Aid rose from £80m in 1957 to £400m in 1970. Between 1945 and 1969 Britain spent £1,697m in aid and a roughly equal amount was invested by private enterprise.

(a) Those opposed to aid argued it was 'an attempt to preserve the capitalist system in the third world' which neglected basics like agriculture for prestige projects, went into the hands of the elite or the military, did not win friends, diverted resources from Europe and was tied to purchases in Britain to help the sterling area.

(b) Those in favour argued it was a moral duty, Communist countries and UNO did the same, the smaller countries could not exist without it, Britain got £3 of exports for every £2 of aid and that the most serious problem in the world was that of 2,000 million on the verge of starvation. The Commonwealth, with established organisations, was fitted to help.

F5. Pessimists and Optimists

Those opposed to the Commonwealth wanted Britain to concentrate on Europe and join the Common Market. They argued it was post-imperial *folie de grandeur*. Political strife and incoherence combined with widely differing forms of government to render it politically impotent. The demands of the new nations and their treatment of Britain ran contrary to her interests. Wars between members and membership of rival political systems made it almost 'a farce'. Those in favour said the monarchy remained a valid link, as the Jubilee Commonwealth Tour indicated, and meetings were of value because the Commonwealth was multiracial. They pointed to the Singapore Declaration of 1971 as evidence. Even if states were not democratic, they were linked to those that were, and hostile power blocs awaited them outside the Commonwealth. Common language or legal systems provided bonds and in education, culture and medicine there was a considerable exchange of personnel. Voluntary Service Overseas started in 1958. The Commonwealth Office and Secretariat (1965) provided a framework for action and bodies like the Parliamentary Union (1911) and the Commonwealth Foundation (1965) were valuable world services. Commonwealth countries were given unrivalled contacts and a world platform, however small. The number of states continued to grow and no one showed any desire to abolish it. But Britain's involvement in Europe during the 1970s would clearly produce a fresh challenge.

Further Reading

Blaxland, G., *The Regiments Depart*, William Kimber, London, 1971.

Harper, S., *What Happened in Aden*, Collins, London, 1978.

Hutson, H. P. W., *Rhodesia, Ending an Era*, Springwood, London, 1978.

Kirkman, W., *Unscrambling an Empire; British Colonial Policy 1956–1966*, Chatto and Windus, London, 1966.

McIntyre, W. D., *Colonies into Commonwealth*, Blandford, London, 1966.

Majdalany, F., *State of Emergency—The Mau Mau in Kenya*, Longmans, London, 1962.

Miller, J. D. B., *Britain and the Old Dominions*, Chatto and Windus, London, 1966.

Morris, J., *Farewell the Trumpets*, Faber and Faber, London, 1978.

Watts, R. L., *New Federations*, Oxford University Press, London, 1966.

Questions

1. At what point would you say the decline of the British Empire became inevitable?
2. Why was the decline of Empire more rapid in Asia than in Africa?
3. What part was played by the Cold War and the struggle with Communism in either preserving or destroying the Empire?
4. In what respects was the 'special relationship' with America a disadvantage in relation to Britain's world position?
5. What particular difficulties faced decolonisation efforts in Africa after 1957?
6. Why did Britain fail to establish larger federal units in the Empire during the 1950s and 1960s?

7. What similarities and differences are there in the relations between Britain and the underdeveloped nations before and after independence?
8. Of what practical benefit were the efforts to create a Commonwealth?
9. What are the arguments for and against Commonwealth aid?
10. Why does the Commonwealth contain no Middle Eastern members except Cyprus?

19

MACMILLAN AND FOREIGN POLICY IN THE NUCLEAR AGE—THE END OF GREAT POWER STATUS: 1957–70

When Macmillan became Prime Minister in 1957 he had to face the aftermath of the Suez Crisis (Chapter 17, E5). He saw his priorities as dealing with the practical effects such as the closed canal and Britain's weakened position in the Middle East, restoring good relations with America and the Commonwealth and reforming British defences to meet the needs of the nuclear world. The effects of Suez were surprisingly small and within a short time Macmillan was acting the rôle of world statesman. He was the last of the Edwardians, most of the time convinced 'this is a great country and do not let us be ashamed to say so'. His memoirs show his precoccupation with a bewildering number of Commonwealth (see Chapter 18) and foreign policy issues. He was the last important British world statesman and there were ominous signs that the strains of defence, Commonwealth change and great power status were proving too much for a nation which was becoming weaker economically. It was for this reason that the Tories placed such emphasis on the nuclear deterrent.

After the Defence White Paper of 1957 the run-down of military strength necessary to maintain an Empire was progressive. Tory attacks on Wilson came ill from a party that abandoned several bases and left the country with forces so small that the Rhodesian rebellion could not be crushed. What Wilson did was to accelerate under party and economic pressures the defence changes started by the Tories. Macmillan was a superb showman who covered up the realities of declining power, but by Wilson's time the nakedness of Britain's position was too obvious to hide any more. Macmillan travelled extensively abroad, and made two Commonwealth tours. He was also the first Prime Minister to visit Moscow since 1944 and the first to address the United Nations in 1960. His colonial policy was enlightened and moved to the left steadily during his period of office. Quite apart from the Wind of Change Speech in 1960, the importance of Commonwealth aid was given fresh impetus from 1958.

After a long period of Tory dallying, Macmillan took the plunge into Europe against hostile reaction from his party and the Commonwealth and, although personally defeated, lived to see that aim achieved. Friend of the aristocracy and patron of the grouse moor, he wrestled with nuclear strategy and international spying, not always successfully, and claimed to have kept for Britain an independent nuclear deterrent. For this boastful claims were made. It was 'by itself enough to make potential aggressors fear that our retaliation would inflict destruction beyond any level which they would be prepared to tolerate'. As Wilson pointed out, this implied Britain could fight a nuclear war with some other power—an unlikely concept. But Macmillan checkmated failure to enter the Common Market with the Nassau Agreement (December 1962). The deterrent also 'continues to give us an effective voice in world councils on peace and disarmament'. Although those opposed to the nuclear deterrent harped on the threat of nuclear war, the Macmillan era was marked by the Geneva Talks and the Test Ban Treaty (August 1963). In the Wilson era Britain played no important rôle in the next stage which led to the Non-Proliferation Treaty (November 1968).

Macmillan was helped by his personal friendship with Eisenhower, who was happy with the 'special relationship'. When Kennedy became President in 1960 Macmillan assumed the role of political uncle, helped by the fact that the President's sister was married to a brother of the Duke of Devonshire, and by the marriage of his daughter to David Ormsby Gore, Britain's Washington ambassador and a friend of Kennedy. At the opening of the Cuba Crisis, Kennedy told Macmillan, 'we shall have to act most closely together'. Relations between Wilson and Johnson were less amicable. Macmillan got on well with Adenauer, but less well with De Gaulle, whose period of office (1958–69) was marked by anti-British actions which broke Macmillan's and Wilson's attempts to enter the Common Market (1963, 1967). Thus, outwardly in the Berlin Crisis or in continuing military interventions in the Middle East, Britain continued to play a great power rôle and in 1963 embarked on her longest war since Korea with Indonesia, which lasted until 1966.

But Macmillan was an enigma. In his memoirs at one point he speaks of Britain as 'still a great and dominating nation ... throughout the world', but elsewhere he said the country could 'no longer exert a decisive influence on these world events'. Suez had already shown the limits, but it was the Congo Crisis (1960–61) in which Britain, a paramount African power, played no significant rôle and allowed the interests of the West to be sacrificed, which revealed the gap between pomp and power in Tory foreign policy. This became much clearer when Rhodesia revolted; no armed action was taken and a costly naval blockade off Beira was unable to halt the supply of oil. Yet at first Wilson spoke in terms not unlike those of Macmillan. In 1964 he said, 'we are a world power and a world influence or we are nothing', and Britain would 'maintain and use' her African position. In 1965 he said, 'Our frontiers are on the Himalayas' and he did not abolish the nuclear deterrent. But as defence cuts showered on the country and bases were abandoned amidst protests from rulers and Commonwealth partners, it became clear Britain was naked in the conference chamber. Claims by Heath that he would halt this process proved unfounded, since by 1971 he had completed withdrawal from the Far East and the Gulf States.

It was an age of abdication. Acheson's speech in 1962 proved to be no more than the truth: 'Great Britain in attempting to work alone and to be a broker between the United States and Russia has seemed to conduct policy as weak as its military power'. The era of the three interlocking circles was at an end. The Commonwealth was changing, as the Lagos Meeting (1966) showed most acutely, and the attempt to enter the Common Market did not help matters. Nor did failure to support Britain's SEATO partners, Australia and New Zealand, in Vietnam. The special relationship came to an end with Johnson, who wanted British support in Vietnam and scuppered Wilson when he thought he might have got a ceasefire. Neither in Washington nor in Moscow was Wilson able to play an important rôle, and communiqués even ceased to be issued. In Europe De Gaulle exercised his veto, Germany and France drew together after the treaty of 1963, the German problem remained unsolved and when Russia invaded Czechoslovakia in August 1968 parliament was, in Wilson's words, 'quiet, shocked, determined—and impotent'.

By 1967 this impotence was becoming painfully obvious. A bitter civil war in Nigeria (1967–69) was out of Britain's control and the rebel leader refused even to meet Wilson. When the Middle East War erupted in 1967, Britain was unable to do anything in an area traditionally hers, while Eden's predictions about the threat to her livelihood if Britain did not have the canal came true. The canal was closed, costing £20m on the balance of payments and oil supplies were denied by half a dozen countries. Wilson claimed the war was the principal reason for devaluation later that year. British embassies were burnt and no retaliation occurred. Commonwealth countries including Tanzania, Zambia and Uganda seized British property. In 1970 Libya and the Sudan did likewise. At the UN Britain was criticised for Rhodesia and Gibraltar and when Wilson went to speak, African delegates walked out. Commonwealth members broke off diplomatic relations over Rhodesia. By 1969 the Duncan Report on Overseas Representation described Britain as 'a major power of the second order'. During the 1960s, acording to Northedge, 'Britain may be described as the Austria or Spain of the late twentieth century'. By 1970 he says that America, Russia and China 'now interacted on a plane of status and power far beyond those of their European allies'. During the 1960s both parties tried to pretend otherwise and both were brought face to face with reality.

A. Nuclear Deterrent or Nuclear Holocaust: Defence Policy, 1957–64

A1. The Sandys White Paper, April 1957

Defence proved to be one of the most difficult posts in the cabinet; there were nine ministers in 13 years. Conventional rearmament had occurred during the Korean War and Britain still had military commitments to NATO, CENTO and SEATO. She had surrendered some bases like Suez (1954) and stopped using others like Hong Kong (1959), but was still a world power. At the same time the decision to have the hydrogen bomb and intercontinental ballistic missiles (ICBMs) meant Britain also had a nuclear force. It involved expensive research on an ever increasing scale and the pace of technology brought about a situation where a choice had to be made between higher defence spending and less social expenditure, since the national product was not rising fast enough to provide both. The Sandys White Paper was the first attempt to rationalise this situation. It provided:

(*a*) Conventional forces were to be scaled down. National Service was to be phased out with the last call-up in 1960. This was unique among European nations.

(*b*) The Strategic Nuclear Force of V-Bombers were to provide the backbone of defence.

(*c*) Battleships would be abandoned (the last went in 1959), but new aircraft carriers would be built.

(*d*) There was to be a reorganisation of regiments, grouping them into brigades, and thus starting to break down the county system developed in 1870. The process was completed in April 1964. The Territorial Army was to be strengthened.

The decision to base Britain's defences and world rôle on nuclear force was not to result in a reduction in defence spending as was claimed. In 1963 defence accounted for a quarter of the budget and 8 per cent of GNP. Britain was second only to America with 11.2 per cent of her GNP in this respect. Defence involved 5.6 per cent of the labour force, 20 per cent of all research personnel and 40 per cent of all research expenditure.

A2. The Independent Nuclear Deterrent

From the first it was not clear what 'independent' meant, since a close relationship with America existed. In March 1957 it was agreed to supply Britain with ICBMs and this agreement was announced in February 1958. In October 1957 Eisenhower agreed to amend the Macmahon Act and this was carried into effect in July 1958, allowing Britain to receive American nuclear knowledge. But in return Macmillan kept up the closest relations with the Americans. They were allowed as observers at the British hydrogen bomb tests and each new missile meant a new concession. In November 1959 it was agreed to let America have a base in Holy Loch for their nuclear submarines. In November 1960 it was agreed to establish part of the American early warning system at Fylingdales in Yorkshire. In return, the Americans helped Macmillan out of difficulties arising from the decision in April 1960 to abandon Blue Streak. In June the Camp David Agreement gave Britain Skybolt air-to-ground missiles for the V-Bombers. Then in December 1962 the Americans decided to abandon Skybolt and Macmillan went to Nassau to get Polaris. There he found 'the arguments more violently contested', as the Americans insisted Polaris missiles should be part of a multilateral NATO force and Macmillan agreed with the proviso that Britain could withdraw them in a national emergency whose nature was not made clear. It was true that De Gaulle had exploded a French bomb in 1960, rejected an offer of Polaris and created a small *force de frappe* by 1964, so that Macmillan was not acting in a way inconsistent with other powers. It was also true that many missiles like Bloodhound and Blue Steel were effective in spite of the failures. Work on one missile helped with the development of others, but two criticisms of the whole concept were clear by 1964. It was too costly and it was not independent.

A3. Ministry of Defence

The switching of the deterrent from the air force to the navy produced inter-service rivalry and it was obvious the three services meshed together in nuclear defence policy. In July 1958 Macmillan proposed to strengthen the Ministry of Defence by subordinating the three service departments to it. An outcry led to postponement, but in 1962 he returned to the matter when Thorneycroft was appointed Defence Minister. With Mountbatten as Chief of the Combined Services Committee, reorganisation was carried through. The aim was to create an English Pentagon and the scheme was put into force in April 1964. Healey carried through complete integration by 1967.

A4. The Treaty of Moscow, August 1963

When Macmillan and Kennedy met in December 1961, the President said the Americans were going ahead with anti-missile missiles and would resume nuclear tests now Russia had done so. Macmillan urged restraint, but after Khrushchev refused a test ban treaty, tests were resumed in April 1962. The long-standing Geneva Conference was deadlocked on the question of inspection and in March 1963 broke down. The Cuba Crisis was a solemn warning of how close nuclear war could come and a number of distinguished voices were raised in favour of stopping the ever mounting cost and risk involved. On 16 March (ignoring a rebuff he had received in February), Macmillan again opened the question of a test ban treaty and persuaded Kennedy to send a joint letter on 15 April 1963. After a delay, Khrushchev gave way and a conference was held and a test ban treaty signed in August 1963. It was a triumph for Macmillan and for the argument that possession of the bomb enabled progress on disarmament to be made.

B. Khrushchev's Cold War, 1958–64

B. The James Bond Era

In the early 1950s British Intelligence was reorganised, but few were aware of the results. As the Cold War was concentrated on the nuclear race spying became a matter of national importance, as the popular literature and films like *The Spy Who Came in From the Cold* illustrate. On the left there was concern about the invasion of civil liberties, not unmixed with a desire to embarrass the Tories, which gave rise to the 'Spies for Peace' Affair in 1963, when details of regional security centres for use in the event of nuclear attack were revealed. It was, as Macmillan said, 'another security failure' and of these there were a considerable number in the early 1960s, including the Portland spy ring, the Blake case and the Vassall Affair.

Macmillan was responsible for security, although at the time many believed it was solely the Home Secretary's responsibility. The atmosphere of spy mania was distasteful to him. This was unfortunate, since a further case involving security got less than it deserved of the Prime Minister's attention. This was the Profumo Affair (Chapter 17, F) and once again an enquiry was necessary. By this time 'a kind of Titus Oates atmosphere prevailed'.

B2. The Special Relationship

Macmillan's period of office saw more reality than before in the 'special relationship'. Eisenhower was an old friend of Macmillan's and Kennedy was closely linked to him. Moreover, he found Macmillan a valuable friend and a direct telephone line was set up reminiscent of the Roosevelt–Churchill relationship. Khrushchev's renewal of Cold War attitudes over Berlin, the bomb and Cuba drew the two countries together. Cooperation had replaced mutual distrust in the Middle East and, as yet, Vietnam had not started to divide them once more over Far Eastern issues. The main meetings were:

(*a*) March 1957. Bermuda. To re-establish good relations after Suez and to discuss the giving of ICBMs to Britain. America agreed to support the military organisation of CENTO.

(b) October 1957. Washington. Held at the same time as the first royal tour of America since 1939. A Declaration of Common Purpose was issued stating they would cooperate together against Communism. It was agreed to modify the Macmahon Act.

(c) March 1959. Camp David. To discuss the results of Macmillan's Moscow visit and urge the case for a summit conference. For a year Macmillan urged this course and returned in March 1960 to add the finishing touches to persuasion.

There were signs that America and Russia might start to settle matters directly between themselves. In September 1959 Khrushchev paid the first Soviet visit to America and when Kennedy became President he began by a personal meeting with Khrushchev at Vienna in June 1961. But this proved abortive whereas an informal visit to London the same month cemented friendship with Macmillan. But the existence of this relationship, beneficial to Britain's world position and defences, was less congenial to De Gaulle who recalled his wartime experiences with the Anglo-Saxons. He resented Anglo-American domination of NATO, the British deterrent and the international rôle of sterling. The Macmahon Act was not modified in favour of France and all Macmillan's visits to Rambouillet could not placate De Gaulle. During 1962 MacNamara, the American Defence Secretary, criticised the French deterrent and brought forward proposals for a multilateral NATO deterrent which would give West Germany a share in nuclear weapons. This seemed to De Gaulle to be unwarranted interference and was a factor in his hostile attitude to Britain (Section C3).

B3. The Paris Summit, May 1960

After a foreign ministers' meeting (May–August 1959) failed to settle Berlin, Macmillan was convinced a summit meeting could settle matters. In February and March 1959 he visited Moscow. The first few days were frosty with Khrushchev complaining of toothache. Macmillan felt it necessary to converse in the open air due to bugging. Gradually the atmosphere changed and the visit ended with a remarkable television broadcast by Macmillan. The idea of a summit was floated and the ice broken. Trade (May) and Cultural (December) Agreements with Russia followed. Eisenhower became more receptive to a summit and it was agreed he should visit Moscow later.

(a) *The U2 spy plane.* It was well known that each side in the Cold War spied on the other's military installations. On 5 May 1960 Khrushchev announced a U2 plane had been shot down. Eisenhower denied it and Khrushchev then produced the pilot, who had not killed himself as instructed. Eisenhower disowned responsibility, then accepted it. Although it was only 'a minor incident of espionage', it suggested American insincerity.

(b) *Failure.* Khrushchev said it would not destroy the conference, but when he arrived in Paris he demanded an apology, punishment and no further overflying. For two days Macmillan tried to save the conference, but it collapsed on 18 May. It seems likely that Khrushchev was facing internal opposition to his conciliatory line and changed his policy, using the U2 incident as an excuse.

B4. The Berlin Question

Since the Geneva Conference the German question remained unchanged, except that West Germany and Berlin prospered as part of NATO, while the East remained poor. Between 1945 and 1961, 4 million Germans left the Eastern zone and many were leaving through Berlin. Berlin was a standing reproach to Communism.

(*a*) *The first crisis*. In November 1958 Khrushchev announced a peace treaty would be signed with East Germany in six months and Russian occupation rights in East Berlin would be handed over to the new régime. The Four Power Agreement of 1945 was unilaterally denounced. In December these moves were rejected by the West.

(*b*) *The second crisis*. In June 1961 Khrushchev told Kennedy, 'West Berlin is a bone that must come out of the Soviet threat' and renewed his intention of signing a separate treaty.

(*c*) *The Berlin Wall*. On 13 August 1961 East Germany erected a wall between the zones, violating the 1945 agreement. De Gaulle and Adenauer wanted war and America offered six more divisions. Macmillan tried to reduce the tension, saying it was 'all got up by the press' and apart from a protest no action was taken.

The issue now became a sore on the body politic of Europe. Escapers were shot and ministers stood grim-faced at the wall. When Kennedy visited the city in June 1963 he declared, '*Ich bin ein Berliner.*' Lord Home said 'one false step over Berlin could easily plunge the continent of Europe into war'. France and West Germany drew together in a treaty in January 1963. Macmillan's efforts as a broker were sharply reduced, and stalemate was reached.

B5. The Cuban Crisis, October 1962

Khrushchev devised a clever way of breaking the stalemate in Russia's favour. In 1959 Castro established a Communist state in Cuba. In February 1960 a treaty with Russia provided massive credits and the purchase of the sugar crop. American property was seized and diplomatic relations broken off. In the summer of 1962, while Kennedy was rallying the Organisation of American States to repel Communism, Che Guevara and Raoul Castro visited Moscow and agreed to missiles and Ilyushin bombers being stationed on the island. Khrushchev had refused discussion of Berlin until the Autumn, when he intended to trade his position in Cuba for that of the Americans in Berlin. An ultimatum was ready for 6 November. The stages of the crisis were:

(*a*) 18 October. Revelation of six missile sites. Acheson wanted war on Cuba, but was opposed by MacNamara and, eventually, by President Kennedy himself.

(*b*) 23 October. The issue was taken to UNO; Adlai Stevenson had large-scale photographs to show the delegates.

(*c*) 24 October. Decision to impose a blockade. Of the 25 Russian ships approaching the island, 12 turned back.

(*d*) 27 October. Khrushchev proposed the removal of sites in return for the removal of NATO bases in Turkey. But by then his nerve was cracking.

(*e*) 28 October. Khrushchev climbed down. Eventually 42 missiles and 10,000 Russian personnel left the island by December.

It was 'one of the classics of a skilfully played diplomatic hand' and throughout Kennedy and Macmillan conversed each day, with Macmillan in favour of moderate councils at every stage. The world had been brought face to face with nuclear war and the Cuban Crisis marked the last conflict of the Cold War period directly affecting Europe.

C. Macmillan and De Gaulle: Failure to Enter the Common Market

C1. Anglo-French Attitudes

When De Gaulle became Prime Minister in 1958, France had suffered a series of defeats in war and her government was a byword for confusion. France stood to gain most from the Common Market, which had come into being in January 1958, and De Gaulle saw Europe as a third force standing up to Russia and America, developing its wealth and world contacts. France retained a closer union with its colonial territories and gave a higher proportion of income to overseas aid than Britain. Differences between the two countries stemmed from the special relationship with America which De Gaulle resented. In January 1961 the French approved of Britain's trying to enter the Market, but by November the atmosphere was chillier and by December 1962, with the British rocket deals, matters reached breaking point. It was also true America had a special relationship with Germany and there was a danger of France taking second place to the other two powers. De Gaulle secured a direct treaty with Germany in January 1963 to cement their joint hegemony in Europe. His anti-British line was clearly shown in violating Rhodesia sanctions, supporting Biafra and backing Quebec separatists during 1967.

C2. Crusade for Europe

(*a*) *Setting up EFTA*. The government first sent Maudling to secure a loose association with the Common Market by expanding OEEC, but after a year negotiations collapsed in November 1958 with opposition from France and Germany. Britain then organised EFTA (Britain, Sweden, Norway, Denmark, Austria, Switzerland and Portugal), which was established by the Treaty of Stockholm (November 1959).

(*b*) *Changing attitudes*. This was obviously second best and America through GATT was urging wider tariff cuts rather than regional organisations of this kind. The Common Market was highly successful. Between 1953 and 1961 production in France (75 per cent) and Germany (89 per cent) increased far more than in Britain (30 per cent) and the standard of living rose faster. Between 1955 and 1960 real wages in Britain rose 11 per cent compared with 15 per cent in Italy and 27 per cent in Germany. It was argued that a big market of 167 million would stimulate industry. Much was made of the changing pattern of world trade, since the relative amounts going to the Commonwealth and Europe indicated Britain's vulnerability.

But to many, including Macmillan, these economic realities were not the most important reason for change. When announcing the application, he said that in an age of larger groups Britain stood to gain politically by joining the Market. This roused doubts about sovereignty if it implied closer political union. Moreover, Britain had relations with America and the Commonwealth and since joining would undoubtedly harm Commonwealth trade, there was another danger. Some industries and possibly agriculture might suffer and special arrangements would have to be made. Macmillan stressed a more properous Britain would trade more with the Commonwealth and argued there was no conflict of interest. The movement gathered strength in the establishment and was seen as a panacea for all ills. A European Movement (1961) was set up to support entry. Tories recalled their earlier enthusiasm for Europe and as early as February 1960 Macmillan regretted not entering sooner. In July 1961 it was announced Britain was to apply.

C3. The French Veto

Macmillan masterminded a complicated series of negotiations necessary to secure political support:

(a) *The government team.* Pro-Europeans moved into the key ministries—Soames to Agriculture and Sandys to Commonwealth Relations. Heath was put in charge of the negotiating team.

(b) *Preliminary consultations.* Meetings with EFTA showed Denmark was going to apply and only Sweden and Switzerland expressed much opposition. Five ministers were sent to Commonwealth countries. Macmillan himself pressed Adenauer and De Gaulle to give support.

(c) *The Conservative party.* Although there were anti-Common Market candidates, Macmillan secured support by stressing the power, leadership and anti-Communist aspects of the Market.

These were substantial achievements and made the way easier for Heath. Detailed negotiations began in October 1961, the government stressing that it entered with three prior conditions: the interests of Britain, the Commonwealth and EFTA. The main issues that arose were:

(a) *Commonwealth trade.* A trade agreement for India, Pakistan and Ceylon was secured. Associated status was offered to African and West Indian colonies and it was agreed that bilateral arrangements could also be made. The real difficulty lay with the Ottawa Treaty countries where Britain would have to abandon preferential tariffs. In particular, cheap food from Australia and New Zealand seemed likely to suffer and deadlock ensued.

(b) *Agriculture.* The community protected its farmers with a tariff and had higher prices than Britain, where farmers were protected by a subsidy which kept prices down while guaranteeing output. France opposed this situation and deadlock ensued.

In both cases France with her inefficient, small farms was the main reason for deadlock, but De Gaulle after his Algerian surrender could not risk offending the mass of his voters. On 14 January 1963 he delivered his veto, saying Britain was 'widely different' from European countries and unwilling to surrender her privileged position. But he gave his real reason later, saying that enlarging the Market would produce 'a colossal Atlantic grouping under American dependence and control'.

D. Third World Diplomacy

D1. Last Moves in the Middle East

Throughout the period Britain's Middle East power was declining (Chapter 18, B), but this was not yet followed by an abdication of res-

ponsibility, since CENTO and American intervention under the Eisenhower Doctrine secured continuing involvement.

(a) *Repairing the damage of Suez.* The canal was opened by April 1957 and
Macmillan encountered Tory opposition in paying dues to the Company. But
the government had ended petrol rationing and the cost of the Cape route was
too great. In May shippers were advised to use the canal. In February 1959 dues
were paid and in December diplomatic relations were restored.

(b) *Nasser's new position.* In 1958 came Nasser's challenge which Eden had
failed to halt. In February the United Arab Republic was formed with Syria
(which lasted until 1961) and in March Yemen joined. Later 40,000 Egyptian
troops entered Yemen to support the left-wing republican régime and stir up
trouble in Aden.

Russian and Egyptian ambition alarmed other Middle Eastern states,
thus providing a basis for continued intervention. In March 1957 the
British treaty with Jordan ended and there were disturbances when Hussein purged pro-Nasser elements. The US Sixth Fleet moved into the
Eastern Mediterranean. In February 1958 Jordan and Iraq formed a
Federation to protect themselves. But the main crisis centre shifted north-
wards:

(c) *The Syrian crisis.* Diplomatic rows between Syria and America were
followed by a Syrian–Russian Treaty (August 1957) and aggressive acts against
Turkey. America announced an airlift of arms to Jordan and when Turkey
appealed to the UN, America said that any attack on Turkey would be met by
force and on 31 October Syria gave way. As Macmillan said, 'You've done a
Suez on us.'

(d) *The Lebanon crisis.* The union of Syria and Egypt created a threat to
pro-Western Lebanon. In May 1958 there were riots and in June the UN voted
to send observers.

(e) *The Iraq crisis.* In July 1958 a *coup d'état* by General Kassem led to alarm
in Lebanon and Jordan. American military intervention occurred in Lebanon
and British in Jordan (17 July–2 November) to stabilise the region.

Russia sought to intervene and demanded a five-power conference on
the Middle East which the West rejected. Instead the headquarters of the
Baghdad Pact were moved to Ankara pending the final removal of British
forces in March 1959 from Iraq. In August 1959 CENTO was announced
and American aid was strengthened. Thereafter the Middle East was quiet
and when Kassem threatened Kuwait in 1961 Britain intervened.

D2. The Rôle of the United Nations

After Suez the authority of the UN was enhanced. New nations found
it a ready-made forum and the great powers continued to use it for Cold
War battles. Under Macmillan British attitudes to the UN were determined
by its strong attacks on British colonial policy and its double standards
which increasingly emerged after 1960–61 when it intervened in the Congo.
In May 1963 a dispute broke out because some powers like Russia were
in arrears in paying for international forces and Britain and France took
the lead in criticising them. But in September 1960 Macmillan went to
UNO to speak when Khrushchev had gone to win third-world attention.
Britain agreed to a UN peace-keeping force in Cyprus. The United Nations
was able to secure a number of important international agreements which

sought to bridge the gap between the great powers and the underdeveloped countries. These included treaties on Antarctica (1959) and Outer Space (1967), forbidding territorial claims, the setting up of the International Atomic Energy Commission (1958) and of OECD to replace OEEC by including America and Japan (1960).

D3. The Congo Crisis, 1960–64

The new problem of dealing with emerging nations, and the UN's first, became apparent in the civil war that followed the granting of independence to the Congo in June 1960. The government of Lumumba was faced with troop mutinies and separatist movements and in July appealed to the UN. Tshombe proclaimed the province of Katanga independent and, as this was between British and Portuguese territories and rich in minerals, the Katanga Lobby urged Macmillan to support the secession. The main stages were:

(a) September 1960. Lumumba was removed and replaced by Ileo and soon after civil war started. Hammarskjold sent in troops and tried to be neutral, but by the end of the year a number of countries had withdrawn from the force because Russia backed the Lumumba group.

(b) July 1961. A period of confusion between the rival leaders was followed by the secession of Katanga under Tshombe. A new prime minister, Adoula, was appointed. UNO recognised him as the only legitimate government.

(c) September 1961. UN forces attacked Katanga and Hammarskjold was killed in a plane crash. His successor, U Thant, strongly backed the attack on Katanga and Macmillan supported the UN, sending arms and the Lansdowne Mission to make Britain's position plain. Atrocities by UN troops occurred.

(d) August 1962. Britain, Belgium and America joined in a plan proposed by U Thant to bring pressure on Tshombe. In January the secession ended and in June 1963 he fled.

The result of the Congo Crisis was to establish a Marxist state in Africa and it clearly revealed the limitation of Western powers in former colonial territories.

D4. The Laotian Settlement

After the end of the Control Commission set up in 1954 (Chapter 16, C3), a new crisis emerged in Laos. The main stages were:

(a) 1960–61. Civil war broke out between the Pathet Lao, the right wing, and the neutralists. In April 1961 America began military aid and Macmillan feared a situation like that in Vietnam in 1954. Britain and Russia called for a cease-fire, which came into force in May. The Geneva Conference of 14 nations was reconvened to secure a government acceptable to all factions.

(b) 1962. A joint appeal by Home and Gromyko was followed by the formation of a government in January, but in May this broke down. Kennedy demanded the reactivation of the Control Commission. American and British forces went to Thailand as a precaution. In July agreement was reached and the forces had left by September. Peace had been secured, but only just as Pathet Lao remained active.

D5. The Coming of the Vietnam War

After the Geneva settlement, Vietnam had not remained peaceful. After fighting in 1955, South Vietnam became a republic. Meanwhile, North

Vietnam came increasingly under Chinese influence following a treaty in 1955, and as the ideological war between Russia and China developed, the area seemed a suitable one for China to show her dedication to spreading Communism, particularly since Russia, like Britain, was a co-chairman to the Geneva Conference. In 1960 the Vietcong was organised and in March 1962 South Vietnam began operations to remove guerillas who had violated the 17th Parallel. America slowly became involved:

(*a*) In June 1961 technical aid started, to be followed by $40m. Unfortunately the government was overthrown and a series of military coups gave little evidence of stable, democratic government in the South. In February 1964 Russia warned America not to be involved. MacNamara replied in March that aid would be given until the Vietcong were defeated. He rejected neutralism. Britain backed the American stand in April and December.

(*b*) In August 1964 attacks on American ships were followed by the Gulf of Tonkin Resolution allowing the President to take all military steps necessary to support any member state of SEATO. Aid to South Vietnam in December was followed in February 1965 by bombing raids on North Vietnam. In March the first American combat troops arrived.

Britain, as a member of SEATO and an ally of America, was bound to support attempts to resist aggression. But the Cold War had abated in Europe and the British always adopted a less hostile line to Chinese Communism. Thus, the British wished to act as mediators.

E. Age of Abdication

E1. The Healey Defence Cuts

The election of 1964 (Chapter 17, F) involved argument over Britain's defences. Home stressed the deterrent and its independence, while Labour denied it was independent and said they would renegotiate Nassau. Dislike of dependence on America and abhorrence of nuclear war were both strong in the Labour Party. Cost and a desire to reorientate foreign policy were more practical reasons for a change. Although Wilson spoke of Britain's need to be technologically in the lead, one of the first acts of the government was to follow the advice of the Plowden Committee that 'the development of an expensive and untried major aircraft was beyond the capacity of the British economy'. This meant more dependence on America and, in the long run, it meant decline in research and resources that would prevent Britain having a credible deterrent. A bitter debate occurred in December 1964, when Wilson said 'the fact is there is no independent deterrent because we are dependent on the Americans', claiming to have ended a 'long chapter of sterile argument'. The following decisions were made:

(*a*) In December 1964 Wilson visited Washington and told Johnson he would not support the MLF. Instead he proposed to put the British deterrent at the disposal of NATO as part of an ANF.

(*b*) Although four were built, a fifth nuclear submarine was cancelled in 1965.

(*c*) The TSR2 bomber was cancelled in April 1965 with an assurance that it would be replaced by the American F–111. By March 1967, 50 had been ordered. Then in January 1968 the order was cancelled.

The government claimed in the 1966 Defence Review to be reshaping in order to prove less of a strain on the economy by withdrawing from world-wide military capacity back to a 1914 situation. But successive economic crises and pressure from the Labour party led to cuts not only overseas but in Europe and withdrawals from abroad, which broke agreements and recent pledges. The main cuts were:

(*a*) In the RAF the P–1154 vertical take-off aircraft and HS–681 tactical transport were scrapped in February 1965.

(*b*) In the navy further aircraft carriers were cancelled and the Navy Minister, Mayhew, resigned in protest.

(*c*) In the Army the completion of brigade integration enabled further cuts to be made, culminating in reductions announced in January 1968.

(*d*) In February 1966 the Territorial Army was wound up, although replaced by a small Army Volunteer Reserve. In February 1967 Civil Defence and the Auxiliary Fire Service were scrapped.

Conservatives had, of course, cancelled projects, but now protested that these cuts prevented Britain playing a flexible rôle or even protecting her interests. They involved a series of decisions (July 1967, January 1968) to withdraw from all bases east of Suez by 1971. This was done by Wilson and Heath with unfortunate results in the areas concerned (Chapter 18, A7, B3). It reduced Britain's usefulness to America and opened the way for Soviet penetration of the Mediterranean and Indian Oceans during 1968. Although the cuts did not achieve major savings until 1967, they were sufficient to prevent Britain intervening in Rhodesia, Nigeria or the Middle East. Healey was in office throughout the period and proved a capable minister. He was not merely concerned with cuts. He completed the integration of the services by 1967, and brigade reorganisation. He set up a Defence Sales Organisation which was selling £250m of goods by 1970. He carried out a reform of service pay which was announced in February 1970.

E2. Vietnam and the End of the Special Relationship

The Conservatives had supported American policies in Vietnam, while Wilson wanted to act as a mediator. With strong opposition to America inside the party and student violence culminating in the Grosvenor Square Riot in 1968, Wilson had no alternative but to disassociate himself from the American war. Unfortunately he was ill served by Foreign Secretaries. Gordon Walker and Michael Stewart made little impact, and George Brown's term was not that of an international statesman. Wilson himself did not carry the weight of his predecessors because of the contraction of Empire and armed forces. America was already drifting away from the Special Relationship after the murder of Kennedy in 1963, and Johnson's period of office until 1968 marked an increasing coldness to Britain's pretensions. The Vietnam War led to rioting and division at home more severe than anything since the slavery issue and British 'lukewarmness' was therefore particularly objectionable.

(*a*) *Stages of the war.* In March 1965 the American war started in earnest and in July Australian, New Zealand and South Korean forces arrived. After a Christmas truce, bombing resumed in January 1966. Marshal Ky demanded the invasion of North Vietnam, but America would not go this far, although bombing became more intensive. In February 1967 a bombing pause occurred again and in March Thailand agreed to the use of her bases for the war. In January 1968 the Tet Offensive, reaching to Saigon, showed how weak America's position was, in spite of massive aid programmes. This was partly due to the incompetent and cruel régime of Ky and Thieu. In March bombing of 90 per cent of the North ceased and in May the first direct peace talks were held. They failed, although a complete cessation of bombing was ordered in October. Troops reached 541,000 and 72,000 Allies, but Nixon began to withdraw troops and in June 1970 the Tonkin Resolution was repealed.

(*b*) *Wilson's moves.* His first attempts to intervene were met sharply by John-son, who told him, 'If you want to help us some in Vietnam, send us some men and send us some folks to deal with these guerrillas', and Johnson did not bother to issue communiqués after talks with the Prime Minister. In February and July 1966 Wilson tried to persuade Kosygin to move and achieved nothing. In February 1967 he tried again when Kosygin visited London, and later de-scribed his failure as due to American diplomatic incompetence. Nixon would not accept a visit by Wilson to America and insisted on seeing him as only one among Europe's leaders. In August 1969 Wilson had to trail after the President to an American airbase at Mildenhall for a talk.

Wilson's attempts to intervene in Vietnam were not limited to direct approaches to Moscow and Washington. A mission of Gordon Walker was banned from Hanoi and Peking in early 1965 and a Commonwealth Peace Mission failed in June the same year. Stopping the war rather than ending it on satisfactory terms became an end in itself and an end no British minister could accomplish for obvious reasons.

E3. Failure to Enter the Common Market

Labour opposed the Common Market in the early 1960s and Wilson had been helped to the leadership by his lukewarm attitude to Europe. In 1964 he believed in a world rôle for Britain. But by early 1966 successive economic crises and, above all, slow growth and the need for technological change convinced him Britain should apply. George Brown at the Depart-ment of Economic Affairs, who wanted growth, was delighted in January 1966 when Wilson told him, 'we're going in'. An import surcharge imposed in 1964 had annoyed Britain's EFTA partners and trade with the EEC was growing faster than with them, while Commonwealth trade continued to decline. The full operation of GATT from 1967 precluded colonial prefer-ences and doomed the Ottawa agreements. In Proudfoot's words, 'a strong European rôle might be preferable to a weak global rôle.' In November 1966 the announcement was made and Wilson stressed foreign policy was a thing apart and Britain would retain her special relationship with America. In the vote for opening negotiations (488–62) the government secured the largest majority on a contested issue in the twentieth century.

But there were snags. Although Wilson stressed Britain's NATO rôle, De Gaulle was feuding with NATO and even this rôle had its difficulties, since a stiff agreement had to be made with Germany for them to purchase supplies in return for Britain remaining on the Rhine. Moreover, De Gaulle sought good relations with Russia and resented the attempts of Wilson to secure détente, particularly Kosygin's visit to Britain. The existence of divisions in the cabinet and Labour's previous record on Europe were not in favour, and continued economic weakness led De Gaulle to imagine

Britain wanted to join Europe with a begging bowl for new regional policies. He feared an influx of other EFTA members, in spite of the Rey Commission which reported in September 1967 that they would do no harm.

Nor was Britain's attitude to Europe as friendly as it might have been. There were examples of cooperation, including the July 1966 agreement to cooperate with France on Concorde and the Channel Tunnel. But at other times Wilson stressed the folly of prestige projects and Britain cancelled an agreement for joint production of military aircraft and left ELDO. However, negotiations began. By April 1967 discussions with EFTA had reached a satisfactory end. Wilson and Brown toured Europe in January-March to sound out the EEC countries. They found five strongly in favour and were particularly pleased with the German response. Unfortunately, too much emphasis was placed on this support, annoying De Gaulle still further, although it is difficult to see what Labour could have done not to offend him. This time it was not Commonwealth issues, but the position of sterling and the CAP that were the main attacking points. In May a formal application was made, and within four days De Gaulle cast doubts on it. Wilson pressed on and Lord Chalfont took charge of negotiations. By September the Commission reported in favour, but devaluation was the last straw for De Gaulle, who brought matters to an end in November.

This produced a change in Labour. Douglas Jay emerged at the head of an anti-European section. Wilson refused to be deterred and once De Gaulle stepped down discussions resumed under George Thomson, and it had been decided to reopen negotiations in the summer of 1970. Terms for entry were drawn up, which Brown and Thomson subsequently asserted were the same as those Heath later put forward. But while pursuing this line, Wilson also yielded to the anti-marketeers. Greater emphasis was laid on the 'terms' by the end of 1969, suggesting the Conservatives would enter without any; in fact, they had set terms out from the start. An argument with Heath was followed in February 1970 by a report on the cost of entry, saying it would lead to an 18-26 per cent rise in food prices and add 5 per cent to the cost of living, besides having adverse effects on the balance of payments. Heath accused Wilson of adopting an anti-Market stance and in the debate Wilson said, 'We can rely on our own strength outside the Community.' By the end of 1970 anti-Market motions were only narrowly lost at the TUC and Labour conferences and many Labour ex-ministers changed sides, including Callahan and Healey. The latter was for it in May and against it in July. In the end Heath had to fight for entry in a divided country—a task which neither Macmillan nor Wilson had faced to the same extent.

E4. Political Impotence in Africa, the Middle East and Asia (See also Chapter 18, C3 and F3)

In spite of the effective end of Empire, persistent economic crisis and strong opposition within his party, Wilson continued to assert a world rôle for Britain, but specific events in world diplomacy moved away from London. In Europe, Kissinger and Brandt advanced the *Ostpolitik* concept, leading to treaties between Germany, Russia and Poland accepting the borders of Eastern Europe (1970). China, after securing a nuclear force

(1964), proceeded to expand her influence in Asia and Africa and to secure admittance to UNO in 1970, and her bitter relations with Russia were the key to a major shift in American policy under Nixon. Vietnam was settled in 1973 without British participation and the Geneva Settlement was a dead letter. In the UN bitter resolutions were passed against Britain as a colonial power and Wilson's visit was met by an African walk out. In disarmament talks, the Americans did not bother about the British who were not invited to Glassboro' (August 1967), which led to the Non-Proliferation Treaty in 1968.

Unfortunately, the Labour government was infected with the idea that moral leadership might be a substitute for real power. After securing the rejection of a Spanish order for frigates, a long-standing row developed over Gibraltar. Arms for South Africa were banned and, after a supposed cabinet row about resuming them in 1967, the ban was reaffirmed. When Greece was seized by a military junta, Britain took the lead in securing her removal from the Council of Europe by backing an offensive censure motion (December 1969). Wilson disassociated Britain from American bombing of North Vietnam in June 1966. This mood of high moralising, rarely directed to Russia or China, took no account of Western needs. The government argued it helped Britain retain her position in the third world, but reaction suggested this was not so:

(a) *The Middle East.* After the withdrawal of the UN forces Israel, provoked by the Palestine Liberation Organisation (1964), went to war and in six days in 1967 defeated the Arabs, seizing territories from Egypt, Syria and Jordan. It is claimed Wilson wanted to intervene militarily and rumours to this effect led to riots that smashed British embassies, closed pipelines and the Canal and affected sterling balances.

(b) *Nigeria.* The outbreak of civil war was followed by Wilson's correct decision to back the Federal government and supply arms. But a great outcry against General Gowan claiming atrocities and genocide (which were never substantiated) led to Labour party dissension and Wilson therefore gave way and became a mediator. Two missions by Lord Hunt studied relief problems and he organised relief when the war ended. Wilson's visit to Lagos (March 1969), with HMS *Fearless* anchored offshore for a meeting with the rebel leader, failed.

Constant debates were held on Rhodesia, Biafra and Vietnam, like those in December 1969, revealing Britain's inability to do anything decisive. Descriptions of Britain as a 'toothless Bulldog' and 'the sick man of Europe' became more commonplace and by 1970, in Proudfoot's words, 'she was excluded from the mainstream of European development. She was becoming ever less credible as an ally for the United States and her Commonwealth rôle was fast becoming a thing of the past'.

Further Reading

Bartlett, C. J., *The Long Retreat, British Defence Policy 1945–1970*, Macmillan, London, 1972.
Beloff, N., *The General Says No*, Penguin, Harmondsworth, 1963.
Camps, M., *Britain and the European Community 1955–1963*, Oxford UP, London, 1964.
Crankshaw, E., *The New Cold War*, Penguin, Harmondsworth, 1963.

Cunningham, G. (ed.), *Britain and the World in the Seventies*, Weidenfeld and Nicolson, London, 1970.

Driver, C., *The Disarmers*; *a study in protest*, Hodder and Stoughton, London, 1964.

Kitzinger, U., *The Second Try: Labour and the EEC*, Pergamon Press, London, 1968.

Northedge, F. S., *Descent from Power*, Allen and Unwin, London, 1974.

Windsor, P., *City on Leave*; *A History of Berlin 1945–1962*, Chatto and Windus, London, 1963.

Questions

1. Was the 'long retreat' in defence and foreign policy in the 1960s inevitable?
2. What were the restraints at home and abroad on British freedom of action in foreign affairs by the mid 1960s?
3. Why may Macmillan be regarded as the last British statesman of world stature?
4. Which was the greater threat to British interests between 1957 and 1967—the Special Relationship with America or the policies of General De Gaulle?
5. What effect on foreign policy did the decline and disappearance of the Empire have?
6. Why did Britain fail in 1963 and 1967 to enter the Common Market?
7. How far can Khrushchev's period of office be seen as a continuation of the Cold War?
8. Why did Macmillan and Wilson cling so long to a world rôle for Britain?
9. To what extent was Britain's adjustment of her world rôle accomplished smoothly rather than painfully in the decade prior to 1970?

20

THE WILSON YEARS AND THE HEATH ADMINISTRATION—ENTERING THE COMMON MARKET: 1964–74

During the sixties and early seventies Britain came to terms with her changed world status with all that implied in national life. In some ways it was the most important change since the onset of the Industrial Revolution and the growth of Empire, and the differences encountered were, to some extent, inevitable and of long-standing growth. It was the end of an era or, as Delderfield wrote of Churchill's coffin entering St Paul's in 1965, 'the very passage of the cortège up the steps towards the slowly opening doors was the finale of an epoch ... it was as though in that moment of time a century of human experience peculiar to these islands was being taken away out of the stream of history'. It was not surprising the affluent society turned sour and by the end of the period there was talk of Britain as an ungovernable country. What happened was a common historical process in which a world power has to accept existence as a second-class state. Wilson and Heath therefore held office at the most crucial period since 1940. Both glimpsed the need for a new direction and spoke in terms of revolution. Wilson concentrated on technological change and Heath on entry into the Common Market, while both governments grappled with major constitutional and administrative changes.

But their solutions were tried against an increasingly grim background. It was inevitable the country would have to undergo a measure of humiliation abroad, but the continued attempts of Wilson to play a world rôle made this process more painful. Far too much time was devoted to issues where Britain's defence and financial resources made her of little account. Wilson says in his record of the Labour government, that Rhodesia was the 'most urgent problem' and the 'greatest moral issue' facing the country in the sixties, which was far from reality. Heath pretended he could reverse the process of world decline, but in fact exchanged the world rôle for Europe in 1972. This involved some surrender of sovereignty by Parliament, and elsewhere the unity of the United Kingdom came under attack. During the 1960s attempts to implement reforms in Northern Ireland brought about a crisis in 1968–69 and for the next 10 years there was civil war. Dissatisfaction with Westminster brought about a revival of Welsh and Scottish Nationalism and in 1966–68 MPs for both parties were returned. The Kilbrandon Report (1973) advocated devolution or home rule for Scotland and Wales, and both political parties accepted their findings.

Within England particularly, race became the focus of political passions. Starting with Wilson branding an MP for Smethwick as a 'parliamentary leper', each successive Race Relations or Immigration Act led to bitterness in both parties. This culminated with a speech by Enoch Powell in April 1968 in which he spoke of the nation building its own funeral pyre and compared the racial issue to the infiltration of the Roman Empire by barbarians. A further element in this issue was the revival of fascism in Britain under the guise of the National Front. However, violence and extremism were not confined to the extreme right. The activities of the IRA and the Angry Brigade created a new climate of political violence. The Angry Brigade was responsible for 27 bombings. On the left in politics a number of splinter groups like the Workers' Revolutionary Party or the Socialist Workers' Party demanded direct action on syndicalist lines. Student violence, fanned by the Paris Riots of 1968, was followed by industrial violence. Between 1971 and 1974 there were 100 factory occupations. Pickets became violent with the Shrewsbury building workers (1972–73) and the miners at Saltley (1972) being the most notorious. The Heath government proclaimed five states of emergency and there was a whiff of Weimar in the air.

Economic issues became increasingly dominant. In 1964 Wilson made much of the balance of payments as a political issue. The ensuing government, in his own words, 'was dominated by an inherited balance of payments problem' in all but one year. The country faced successive crises in 1964, 1966 and 1967, culminating in devaluation. From 1966 to 1971 it experienced a period of stagnation with steadily rising unemployment and when the Barber Boom occurred in 1972–73 it proved a disaster, followed by strife with the miners in 1973–74, the three-day week and the onset of a period of sustained unemployment not seen since the 1930s, combined with rising inflation which again produced comparison with Weimar. Neither major party dealt with the fundamental failing of the British economy, which was its uncompetitive production. The sixties saw a revival of faith in planning, culminating in the Regional Planning Boards and the Industrial Reorganisation Corporation. But the Brown Plan (September 1965) proved a dead letter. Heath's government started with a dash to free enterprise, but sharply reversed engines in 1972. Its resort to Keynesianism under Barber helped produce massive inflation. Government took an increasingly large share in economic life. It took more in taxes, passed more laws, created more organisations, interfered in more industries and even sought through a series of prices and incomes policies to control the mechanism of demand and supply. Apart from the questionable value of the growth of the collective state the policies were themselves a failure.

This failure on the part of government was most marked with the trade unions. Labour's Trade Union Act (1965) strengthened the unions. In spite of condemning restrictice practices and Communist influence, Wilson dodged the issue with the Donovan Commission. A Declaration of Intent in December 1964 was all that was obtained. In 1969, with Labour proposals *In Place of Strife* and the Tory *Fair Deal at Work*, the nettle had to be grasped. But the bill which Wilson and Castle planned was defeated by Labour party diehards, and all that was left was a Solemn and Binding Agreement (August 1969) which was where they came in. Heath fared no better. His Trade Union Act (1971) strengthened some rights of unions but its penal clauses aroused violence and opposition. It was said law could not be brought into union relations, although the unions themselves lived by the rule book and sheltered behind the 1906 Act. Heath was inadequately prepared to meet the miners and was defeated, in sharp contrast to Baldwin in 1926. The new government's Trade Union Act (1975) strengthened their power.

Issues like Rhodesia or Northern Ireland began to drag on interminably.

Governments seemed to lose the will or fail to find the men to deal with the issues and the electorate, by resorting to smaller parties or abstaining, increasingly showed a dangerous apathy to democratic processes, which talk of participation and worker directors did little to halt. Those voting in the general election fell from 82.6 per cent in 1951 to 72.8 per cent in October 1974. The percentage of those supporting the two major parties fell from 97 per cent to 65 per cent. This gave rise to criticism of parliament and the government machine and to demands for proportional representation—a method of voting that in Weimar had proved damaging in the inter-war period. Public apathy extended to local government in spite of a major reform and even to interest in current affairs. Television audiences for *Panorama* fell from 8 million to under a million. This lack of confidence in traditional politics was again typical of a declining power, but it was accompanied by governments which seemed ill equipped to restore public confidence. This was surprising. One of the main criticisms of the fifties had been the existence of the old, narrow governing class. Wilson and Heath represented a new governing class from the grammar schools, and both deliberately sought to break with the past. But neither seemed in command of events. Wilson said incomes policies were wrong and adopted them. Heath did the same. Wilson said the Common Market was vital to our survival; then that it was not. He said trade union reform was vital, and caved in. Heath refused to help 'lame ducks' in industry, and then did so. The public could be forgiven for a degree of cynicism with regard to politicians.

Between Wilson and Lloyd George there is a close comparison. Both were politicians determined to retain office. Both presided over coalitions—for Wilson's Labour party was increasingly divided between Tribunites and Social Democrats. Both delighted in political manoeuvres. Government changes reflected friction and confusion within and it has emerged that Wilson, like Lloyd George, relied on a kitchen cabinet and was locked in bad relations with outstanding ministers, like Brown. The government revealed in the Crossman Diaries and in Marsh's autobiography clearly bears part of the blame for the sorry state of Britain by the early 1970s. Heath's determination to ease out right wingers and purge candidate lists produced a different sort of Tory party, but one uncertain it was the natural party of government. Many members of his cabinet had little experience, including Barber and Davies, while he suffered from the loss of Macleod and Maudling. Neither party was free from an undercurrent of scandal of various kinds, which again bore resemblance to the days of Lloyd George. The Poulson Affair was the most spectacular of several *causes célèbres* in these years. As the seventies developed it was clear the previous decade had contributed little to solving the deep-set economic difficulties, and that these stemmed from a lack of statesmanship or national purpose. 'The trouble is,' said a cabinet minister quoted in Sampson's *Anatomy of Britain*, 'we don't believe in anything.'

A. Great Britain or Little England?

A1. The Condition of England Question Again

In the 1960s the question of the general direction the country should take began to affect intellectuals, media and, finally, public discussion. In 1964 writers were still commenting in optimistic terms about the progress of the country. Medlicott said that in 1964 there was no problem except the financial one facing the country and that the area of consensus in politics was as great as ever including planning, incomes policy, increased productivity, the mixed economy, full employment, technological and educational growth. Gregg said 'although there were dangers not far below the surface at the end of 1964 no one would compare the economy with twenty or even ten years earlier without satisfaction ... few of the citizens of the United Kingdom would contemplate their own material conditions with anything but pleasure ...' But both writers had a subordinate theme. Medlicott referred to discussion of the state of England question 'with remarkable thoroughness and gloom', while Gregg had a chapter which expressed concern about illegitimate births, rising crime, the 'alarming' rise of drug taking, the battles of Mods and Rockers and the decline of religion. Both writers were standing at a crossroads. The previous decade had seen more progress than any other of the century, but there were clearly rising doubts as well.

These doubts were first aired in *The Times*. As early as July 1961 it said, 'If Britain goes on as she is, there will come the economic crisis which she cannot survive' and, during 1962–63, in several editorials, it developed the case that something was seriously wrong with the country. In July 1962 came the comment that 'it is not enough for a society to be affluent for it to be healthy' and in March 1963 it claimed 'very much is going seriously wrong'. The themes were to some extent contradictory. Some argued it was economic decay that needed to be put right; others the moral consequences of affluence which would presumably increase if economic growth increased; both in fact were sensing Britain was changing fast in a way that could be interpreted as decline. Some writers were:

(*a*) A. Sampson. His *Anatomy of Britain* (1962) was the first major investigation of the affluent society to capture the public imagination. He was strongly critical of the Victorian attitudes of the 'public school proletarast' who ran British business, the cult of the amateur and the 'apparent lack of dynamism and stimulus'.

(*b*) E. Powell. In *Freedom and Reality* (1969) he warned against introspection and sought a way out by criticising the mixed economy, planning, the Commonwealth and other 'myths' of the time.

(*c*) G. M. Carstairs, *This Island Now* (1962), A. Hartley, *A State of Britain* (1963), and J. Mander, *Great Britain or Little England* (1963) were among many others.

The left criticised class structure, private squalor behind the public affluence and crass materialism in the new society. The right bemoaned the decline of traditional values, the loss of quality in production and services, the decline of religion and lack of national purpose. By 1964 all agreed something should be done and many believed Wilson was the man to achieve another 1945. 'It is difficult to recapture,' says Proudfoot, 'even a short time later, the excitement and hope which swept the country after the 1964 election.'

A2. The Permissive Society

The background to doubts about the political future, economic efficiency and the integrity of government was a malaise called the permissive society. The change was partly a reaction against long years of restriction and regimentation since 1940. It was a product of the affluent society, particularly among younger people. The Ingleby Report (1960) stressed the link between affluence, crime and the decline of the family amidst many new pressures. It spoke of 'a complete change' in relationships between classes, sexes and individuals and also in the 'basic assumptions which regulate behaviour'. Tynan gave the National Theatre 'a progressive, adventurous look' and Carlton Greene referred to the satirical television programme *That Was the Week That Was* as 'positive and exhilarating'. Joan Littlewood declared, 'The theatre is the soul and identity of the people. It is the opposite of religion and the Cross.' But the change was, above all, produced by the change in Britain's world position. The virtues of a great power became the jokes of a lesser nation. There was a strong wish to throw off British conventions and beliefs typified by admiration for Sweden with its permissive, affluent society or even by a return to the life of hermits (known as hippies or dropouts) reflected in the poetry of Bob Dylan. It was the age of the anti-hero in literature. None of this was particularly new in historical terms. It happened to Imperial Germany after 1918, but it was a shock to those who had grown up since the turn of the century. The *Yorkshire Post* referred to 'a picture of widespread decadence'. But the movement had come to stay. In *Towards a Quaker View of Sex* (1963), the writers said they 'felt compelled to question the whole basis of judgement as to what is right and what is wrong ... [and] reject almost completely the traditional approach of the organised Christian Church to morality'. The main changes that took place were:

(*a*) *Breakdown of censorship.* The X-certificate in 1951 started a process by which the cinema became more uninhibited. Television, although bound by the BBC Charter and the IBA, seemed to exercise little restraint, and the *BBC Handbook* for 1964 stressed they would continue to screen plays with sex and violence. After the acquittal of the publishers of *Lady Chatterley's Lover* in 1960, publication became freer. In 1963 Miller's *Tropic of Cancer* was published and in 1966, *Last Exit to Brooklyn*. In the theatre the Edinburgh Festival fringe events of September 1963 marked a decisive breakthrough and the Lord Chamberlain's powers of censorship were abolished in 1968.

(*b*) *Growth of sexology.* The two Kinsey Reports (1948 and 1953) opened an era when sexual matters were more openly discussed. The Family Planning and Marriage Guidance Councils encouraged this move and sex education in schools became controversial. The Wolfenden Report (1957) on Homosexuality and Prostitution renewed discussion of these vices and the Street Offences Act (1959) and the Sexual Offences Act (1968) followed. Dr Alec Comfort's *Sex in Society* (1963) was an important work in popularising the new views.

(*c*) *Decline of Christian morality.* Although church decline had been a feature of the twentieth century, it was not until the 1960s that large numbers rejected the traditional teachings on moral matters as well. Divorces increased from 24,505 in 1958 to 50,670 in 1968. An Abortion Act (1968) led to 54,000 in 1969. Illegitimate births rose from 4.9 per cent to 8.2 per cent of all births by 1970; 41,000 were born to unmarried mothers under 20. Between 1953 and 1963, VD cases increased by 73.5 per cent. Carstairs in 1963 said, 'chastity is no more a virtue than malnutrition'.

(d) *The New Morality*. This seemed to many a combination of old heresies and old immorality, but it gained ground, particularly in the Church of England, while stricter Catholics and fundamentalists rejected the change. In *Honest to God* (1963), by Bishop Robinson, battle was joined. Williams edited *Objections to Christian Belief* by the members of the Cambridge Divinity faculty. The Church was attacked for its narrow morality, exclusiveness and lack of social conscience. The Authorised Version of the Bible, the Prayer Book and the English Hymnal were revised or abolished out of existence. Robinson said there were no absolute or eternal moral principles. Instead there was either situation ethics or existentialism. Provided 'love' was involved, it seemed anything went. The Beatles said on television, 'Christianity will go. We are more popular than Jesus now.'

(e) *The crime wave*. Permissive treatment of crime became Home Office policy backed by the Institute of Criminology at Cambridge (1959). In particular, Acts in 1963 and 1969 made treatment of 'young offenders' more lenient. Crimes of violence rose from 5,869 in 1955 to 21,046 in 1968. Murders rose from 129 in 1958 to 185 in 1968. Drug offences rose from 588 convictions in 1962 to 3,071 in 1968. Half the crime was by those under 21. The total of offences rose to 1,489,000 by 1969. Gang violence by mods and rockers, skinheads and Hell's Angels increased.

(f) *Educational decline*. In the early sixties the British education system was admired by foreign nations, but the picture began to change. Disquiet simmered until March 1969 when the first 'Black Paper' broke the surface of complacency. Illiteracy, violence and indiscipline, truancy, poor teaching standards, riots and low standards in universities, falling examination standards, inadequate progressive teaching methods and failure to equip either with basic skills or adequate general knowledge were among the topics raised.

These developments took the carefreeness away from the affluent society. There was talk of ghetto areas in towns, blackboard jungles, problem families, alienation from society and the generation gap. Greater freedom and better information did not lead to a more sensible and rational organisation of the family or of personal lives. More illegitimate births accompanied by more contraceptives and more sexual crimes accompanied by more outlets for frustrations seemed to contradict each other. The remorseless rise in the prison population by 43 per cent during 1956–64 did not suggest crime was responding to the soft touch except by increasing. The removal of formality and the preaching of a more generous gospel in personal relations merely emptied the churches faster. Families surrounded by social workers and government aid and with a high standard of living were increasingly prone to division and crime. Ingleby commented, 'Is it that in the upheaval of social change, the mechanism by which one generation communicates its beliefs and values to the next has broken down, or is it that we have been a generation without beliefs and values which we thought worth communicating?' The questions remained unanswered.

A3. The State of the Economy

Britain entered the 1960s with a managed mixed economy in the throes of the second industrial revolution. The government accepted Keynesian economics and it was held as the central tenet of economic policy that full employment should be secured. Whenever it looked as if unemployment figures were rising, corrective measures were taken. Between 1954 and 1964 the annual average unemployed rate was 1.6 per cent. 'Stop-go' fiscal management had been used to control downswings, but it had been more successful pumping in money than controlling the inflation that followed. Three important issues dominated economic policy:

(a) *Maintaining full employment.* During the sixties, with the restructuring of industry, running down mines, railways and older occupations and increasing automation in others, unemployment steadily increased. The government sought to cushion the blow by redundancy pay and retraining schemes, but by the mid-seventies the return of unemployment to pre-war levels indicated the weakness of the economy was greater than any Keynesian injection of money would solve. The figures were:

Year	Number	Percentage of work force
1964	393,000	1.7
1966	353,000	1.5
1968	564,000	2.5
1970	602,000	2.6
1972	855,000	3.7
1974	600,000	2.6
1976	1,270,000	5.3

(b) *Preserving a favourable balance of payments.* Rising living standards renewed pressure on imports so that whenever cash was injected into the economy, there was inflationary pressure making exports uncompetitive. Governments therefore had to curb demand by fiscal means and by 1968 the fiercest peacetime budget ever was reached, followed by temporary success. But the Wilson régime did not break out of the 'stop-go' spiral and was faced with successive crises. The freeing of international trade, the end of imperial preference and the impact of the Common Market weakened the trading position. Trade was thrown off course by the Middle East War (1967) and the Arab Oil Price War (1973), but it was too easy to blame international factors. The reality was that, as a trading nation, Britain was becoming increasingly less competitive, and failure to enter the Common Market until 1973 further weakened her. Only in 1971 did the balance of trade show a favourable figure and only in 1966 and 1969–72 was there a surplus on the current balance of payments. Government determination to preserve the pound as an international currency with sterling balances and fixed convertibility acted as a straightjacket until the mid-seventies. The government was forced to contract the domestic economy to preserve the pound and the balance of payments—or, put another way, accept strings from the IMF and international bankers for the loans it obtained. The figures were:

Year	Visible Trade Balance (£000m)	Current Balance (£m)
1964	−498	−353
1965	−223	−27
1966	−64	+103
1967	−554	−298
1968	−667	−272
1969	−156	+460
1970	−25	+695
1971	+280	+1,058
1972	−702	+105
1973	−2,353	−922
1974	−5,194	−3,565

(c) *Controlling the rate of inflation.* Between 1955 and 1965 the money value of the National Income rose by 82 per cent, while real output went up by 33 per cent. Britain did not produce enough to pay for her high social expenditure or her imports, and her standard of living was based on borrowed or printed money. Some argued inflation was fuelled by costs—above all, wages—which did not match productivity. Some claimed state expenditure raised the money supply, causing prices to rise and thus fuelling wage demands. Others argued a rising tax burden fuelled non-productive expenditure and further wage demands, while reducing incentives to invest or work harder. The total raised in tax went from £6,648.6m in 1963/64 to £12,887.8m in 1968/69 alone. Clearly the government share of the National Income was rising and therefore less was available for investment. But union pressure and electoral considerations reinforced an ever expanding govenment rôle. It was not until the early seventies that 'monetarists' began to challenge Keynes and urge that monetary control was necessary to curb inflation. Since this implied lower wages and state expenditure it was not heeded until after the serious crisis of 1974–76.

The figures illustrating inflation were (1963 = 100):

Year	Retail Prices	Money Wages	Real Wages
1964	103.3	107.1	103.7
1966	112.5	122.5	108.9
1968	120.7	136.8	113.3
1970	135.3	164.4	121.5
1972	158.6	205.7	129.7
1974	201.1	275.2	126.9
1976	288.9	403.2	139.6
1977	335.2	443.9	132.4

Although governments struggled with these three objectives, none was achieved and by 1975 heavy unemployment, a trade deficit and soaring inflation combined in the worst crisis since 1929, revealing the bankruptcy of policies over the previous 20 years. But the 'dreary and debilitating cycle' of the economy had its roots in the deepest problem of all—production. If rising production could be achieved, there would be little unemployment, higher real wages and a favourable balance of trade. But, as Gregg said, 'British productivity fails by every test'. The figures were:

	Annual Percentage Increase in GNP			
Year	USA	UK	W. Germany	Japan
1960	2.4	4.9	8.8	15.0
1962	6.4	1.3	4.2	7.6
1964	5.4	5.7	6.6	14.0
1966	6.4	1.9	2.3	10.4
1968	5.0	3.7	7.0	14.4

In 1960 those employed in non-productive industry passed those employed in manufacturing industry, thus making the industrial base on which export success depended narrow and vulnerable to such actions as the seamen's strike (1966). Britain's growth rate fell steadily and by 1974 disinvestment was taking place. The figures were:

Gross Domestic Product
Percentage Increase Annually

Year	at constant prices	Industrial production
1964	5.7	7.7
1966	1.9	1.1
1968	3.7	6.0
1970	1.7	0.1
1972	2.9	2.2
1974	−0.7	−2.7
1976	1.1	0.5

Since the figure for growth in the National Plan was 4 per cent a year and this was not met, it was clear that industry was not producing enough to maintain Britain as a major economic power or preserve her standard of living. By 1974 she was the poor man of Europe, both in real wages and in social benefits. Each party to the problem blamed the other. Unions argued lack of investment was the key and called for government grants. Management blamed unions for restrictive practices and high wage demands. The government accused management of being out of date, and the unions of inability to control their members. Some argued government spending and the investment and wages policies in the nationalised industries were a serious threat to prosperity. Gregg summarised the issue as follows:

'British prices are too high, Britain sells less abroad than her competitors. The reasons are that her investment rate is low, her incomes growth is not related to her productive growth, she devotes too much of her resources to immediate consumption and to the social services, she is insufficiently automated, she does not make full use, or the best use, of her equipment, she has not mastered the art of redistributing her labour, she has failed to train it for some of the most urgent of today's requirements ... with income increases being pressed on every side—and this includes dividends and profits as well as wages and salaries, with trade unions claiming shorter hours, resisting dismissals or transfers, with labour of all kinds and grades slacking in various ways, with the social services inviolable, there is no easy way out.'

B. The First Wilson Administration, October 1964–March 1966

B1. The New Ministry

Wilson said a small majority would not prevent Labour from governing even if it delayed measures like steel nationalisation to left-wing annoyance. Wilson survived on a majority that fell to one and carried a major programme of 76 Acts. It was to be good practice for 1974–76. In June 1965 Grimond offered to join a coalition, but as the Liberals voted against the government twice as often as they voted for it, Wilson rejected the idea. The Tories fell to recrimination and reorganisation and proved less of a menace to a slim majority than they had in 1950–51. Home was blamed for the election defeat and lack of dynamic opposition, while Heath's able leadership during attack on the 1965 budget proved a focus for these discontent. Although Wilson's government contained only three experienced ministers and took office under the shadow of a serious payments deficit, he was able to sustain a successful period of office and deserved his electoral triumph in 1966.

(a) *The Prime Minister.* Born in 1916 at Huddersfield, Wilson was educated at Wirral Grammar School and Jesus College, Oxford, where he obtained a first in PPE. Wilson was thus the first prime minister from the grammar schools, and the first equipped with specific economic training and interest in technology. During the war he served in the Ministry of Fuel and Power and subsequently became the President of the Board of Trade during the Cripps era. In 1950 he resigned in support of Bevan, but returned to the shadow front bench following Bevan's resignation from it in 1954. He beat George Brown for the leadership in 1963 by 144–103 and established his parliamentary reputation during the Profumo Affair. He was an able debater, skilful politician and good publicist. His pipe, Gannex raincoat and holidays in the Scilly Isles provided an alternative image to that of Macmillan.

(b) *The shape of government.* Although the cabinet stayed at 23, the total of ministers rose to 111 because Wilson believed in creating departments and official bodies as each eventuality arose. Some like the Sports Council worked, while others like the Land Commission were failures. Intending to create a framework to solve problems neglected by the Tories, Wilson also increased friction by frequent transfers and personal interventions.

(c) *The ministers.* Gordon Walker was made Foreign Secretary, but after losing a by-election in January 1965, he was replaced by Michael Stewart. Soskice became Home Secretary and James Callaghan the Chancellor. A Department of Economic Affairs was led by George Brown, while the Ministry of Technology went to Frank Cousins. A Welsh Office was established under the veteran James Griffiths. Crossman at Housing, Gunther at Labour, Healey at Defence and Bowden as Leader of the House were other important ministers. Barbara Castle went to the new Ministry of Overseas Development, while in the Foreign Office ministers for the United Nations (Lord Caradon) and Disarmament (Lord Chalfont) reflected the new trend.

The team worked well under the shadow of a small majority and there were no resignations. By 1966 Labour fielded a large experienced team of able ministers, while the Tories had begun to look like an out-of-tune one-man band, splitting three ways on Rhodesian sanctions while the front bench abstained.

B2. Continuation of 'Stop-go' Policies
Wilson's claim to end 'stop-go' policies, thus creating dynamic growth, was not fulfilled, although not for lack of trying, since in his first ministry a large amount of planning to this end was initiated under the forceful direction of Brown. The main measures were:

(a) *Wages policy.* A Joint Statement of Intent on Productivity, Prices and Incomes in December 1964 started the move towards an incomes policy. In February 1965 a White Paper announced details and in March a Prices and Incomes Board under the ex-Tory MP, Aubrey Jones, was created in an advisory capacity. In September the TUC refused to cooperate and Wilson moved towards a compulsory policy.

(b) *The Brown Plan.* In September 1965 a National Plan was produced, setting out objectives of policy which were so reasonable that there was no division on it in the House. It argued for a 25 per cent rise in output by 1970 or an annual growth rate of 3.8 per cent. To achieve this, wages would have to rise at 3.2 per cent and exports at 5.5 per cent. Since wages were already rising at 9 per cent and economic crises destroyed the estimates, the Plan became a 'great wastepaper pyramid' by the middle of 1966.

(c) *Government spending.* It was recognised that some control was needed to curb inflation. A White Paper in February 1966 said it would be held at 4.25 per cent per annum until 1969–70 and defence cuts came the same month. Once again the target was broken and then had to be met by even more savage cuts in 1967–68.

(d) *Regional planning.* By September 1965 there were 13 regional NEDCs and the number later rose to 23, covering nearly all aspects of industry, aiming to provide services for modernisation. The Ministry of Technology made efforts to support computers and machine tools through NRDC.

But planning made little difference to basic economic facts. The balance of payments and wage inflation needed correcting, but unhappily by concessions to the unions and generous fiscal policies the government created doubts about its economic sense. Starting with an import surcharge of 15 per cent which annoyed Britain's EFTA partners, in October 1964, the government followed the next month with a statement raising social benefits and abolishing prescription charges. This blunted the impact of tax increases and more sensible policies such as the creation of a Commonwealth Council to stimulate trade.

There followed the first sterling crisis caused, according to Wilson, by speculators, although he admitted British law gave little leeway to her own. More likely as a cause was foreign lack of confidence in socialist policies. The bank rate rose to 7 per cent and the government borrowed £1,071m from the IMF, the Club of Ten and Swiss bankers. This annoyed the left wing and started a straightjacket for Labour policies, but was soon used up so that during 1965 a credit squeeze twice as hard as any previous Tory one was introduced in two stages in March and July. The budget of 1965 raised £267m in extra taxes, including a rise of 6d in income tax. As a sop to the left, expense accounts were to be taxed while the major change was the introduction of capital gains and corporation taxes during the next fiscal year. However, further loans were needed in May and further measures had to be taken. Although the balance of payments improved a breakthrough had not occurred and heavy debts provided a new burden for an already weak economy.

B3. Legislative Achievement

The main achievements of Wilson's first government were:

(a) *Labour relations.* A Trade Union Act rescinded Rookes versus Barnard and restored rights under the 1906 Act. The Redundancy Payments Act (1965) provided for 1½ weeks pay for each year of employment and was designed to help labour mobility. By 1969, £171m had been paid to 785,000 workers.

(b) *Education.* Circular 10/65 asked local authorities to prepare plans for comprehensive education, but there was no compulsion. The proportion of children in comprehensive secondary schools rose from 8.5 per cent in 1964 to 20.9 per cent in 1969.

(c) *Rent Act* (1965), This was designed to replace Brooke's Act. It restored control on properties of £400 rateable value in London and £200 elsewhere, and applied to furnished and unfurnished property alike. Its main effect was to deter landlords from letting.

(d) *Death penalty.* The government supported a private member's bill to abolish the death penalty for a trial period of five years (1965). The House rejected a limited renewal in November 1966 and the death penalty lapsed in 1969.

(d) *Race Relations Act* (1965). Although seen by some as a restriction of freedom of speech, the Act provided penalties for incitement to racial hatred and discrimination in public places. A Race Relations Board under Mark Bonham Carter was established.

B4. The Election of March 1966

In February 1965 the Tory Party accepted a scheme to elect their leader. It left the election to MPs and thus was less wide than the previous consultation procedure. It ran the risk of providing a leader out of touch with the local organs of the party and, by drawing him from outside the governing elite, it cast doubts on the Tories as the natural party of government. In future they would have to compete with Labour on more equal terms if the politics of deference were finally eliminated. In July 1965 the first election was held and the result was Heath 150, Maudling 133 and Powell 15. Heath's policy statement, *Putting Britain Right Ahead*, seemed little more than a tacit acceptance of many Labour policies. Heath had little talent for debate and was easily beaten by Wilson in the House.

With the Tories in disarray, an early election seemed the best plan. Wilson says he took the decision even before the Hull North by-election in January 1966 showed a 4 per cent swing to Labour on the grounds that a Spring poll would provide a favourable atmosphere at a time when the new electoral register favoured Labour. Perhaps looming rows over the impending incomes policy also played a part in his decision to break with precedent and go for a March election. There was a quiet campaign and the electorate seemed disposed to remember 1962–64 and to accept that the government needed a fair chance after a competent performance. The results showed a uniform swing to Labour and the figures were Labour 363, Conservative 253 and Liberals 12. With a majority of 97 Wilson felt he could act confidently, while the Tories, who had seen Thorneycroft, Soames and Brooke defeated, retired to reform. Apart from the retirement of Griffiths and Soskice, few cabinet changes occurred and all seemed set fair for radical change at last.

C. The Second Wilson Administration, March 1966–June 1970

However, it was not to be. Until early 1970 economic crisis dogged the government, including devaluation (1967) and the most stringent peacetime budget (1968). The balance of payments came right, but at the cost of much of Labour's programme, rising unemployment and falling living standards. Matters reached a crisis when the government failed to carry union reform in 1969. Wilson claimed that the government had not neglected social reform. In 1967, he said, 'We have ended the slide to social inequality and public neglect' and later he claimed, 'we carried through an expansion in the social services ... unparalleled in our history.' Unfortunately, this was done by doubling the load of taxation, which bore heavily on industry trying to expand and by increasing the money supply. Inflation soon ate into benefits or wage increases and no more was heard of the affluent society.

For the government's failure, Wilson must take the heaviest share of the blame because he sought to govern in a 'presidential' manner and his

methods were at fault. Like Lloyd George, he lived for the moment, welcomed crisis almost in personal terms but lacked any coherent strategy or
firm principles. He had scant regard for cabinet government. Ministers
like Brown resigned because of the influence of a Downing Street cabal
and later other ministers as diverse as Crossman and Marsh wrote in
scathing terms about rows and muddle at cabinet level. Although a master
of debate, Wilson had great difficulty in keeping up his majority in the
House. Nominally 97, it fell on one occasion to 28. Strains inside the party
were severe even if Wilson could dispose of Heath's stereotyped opposition.
Wilson was accused of government by gimmick and foolishly intervened
in matters best left to departments. He claimed to have been involved directly in only five industrial disputes, but hasty meetings at Downing
Street and impromptu statements heightened an atmosphere of crisis and
sometimes added to speculative fever. He had a passion for secrecy like
Lloyd George and an almost pathological distaste of the media, but
demands for open government, the lack of a tightly knit governing class
and investigative journalism meant much did not remain hidden and there
were several cabinet and party leaks. In Proudfoot's words, 'the years
from 1966 to 1970 were distinctly stormy, and it took Mr Wilson all his
time to remain on top'. As a result, consistent policies went by the board.

It is true that Wilson shared a taste for gimmickry with Churchill and
Baldwin as well as Lloyd George, but it could not last. With a large
majority and an able cabinet, Wilson's government should have achieved
more in $4\frac{1}{2}$ years than it did. After he left office, Wilson was ill served by
publicity. Marcia Williams' (Lady Falkender) *Inside No. 10* (1972), though
by an admirer, was quite as critical as the Crossman Diaries or the Marsh
Memoirs. In 1978 the Bingham Report, with Thomson, Stewart and Brown
all contradicting Wilson's version of Rhodesian sanctions, revealed extreme
incompetence on a matter Wilson himself constantly said was the most
important problem facing him.

C1. The 'All Fools' Ministry

Wilson's second government took office on 1 April, and there followed a
bewildering number of changes in ministers and organisations which encouraged talk of government muddle and provided an endless source of
gossip and recrimination. The changes reflected Wilson's inability to
secure a loyal and united cabinet and by 1970 claims about efficient government had worn a little thin, to Heath's advantage.

(a) New ministry. A few changes occurred at once, including the appointment of Jenkins as Home Secretary, Castle to Transport and Marsh to Power.
A new Ministry of Social Security combined all the social services.

(b) Cousins' resignation. Even before the election Cousins seemed to violate
the doctrine of collective responsibility by opposing a wages policy. He resigned
in July 1966 and was succeeded by Benn.

(c) August 1966. Following severe economic restraint in July, Brown threatened to resign. Wilson felt the time had come to move him. He unwisely made
him Foreign Secretary and Stewart transferred to the DEA. In August 1967
Wilson announced he was taking direct responsibility for economic affairs.

(d) August 1967. Seven PPSs were sacked for opposing the vote to open
negotiations with Europe. Wilson felt the time had come to reconstruct. Stewart

was followed at DEA by Shore, but left in the cabinet as First Secretary to oversee social policies. Gordon Walker returned to Education and Prentice got Overseas Development.

(*e*) November 1967. Callaghan, the Chancellor, said in July that devaluation 'is not the way out of Britain's difficulties'. After devaluation he exchanged posts with Roy Jenkins, who proved the government's most consistently able minister.

(*f*) Brown's resignation. When Brown resigned in March 1968, he said it was because 'decisions were being taken over the heads and without the knowledge of ministers.' Stewart shuffled back to the Foreign Office.

(*g*) April 1968. Gordon Walker again departed and was succeeded by Edward Short. Barbara Castle, after considerable success at Transport, transferred to the new Department of Employment and Productivity. She was the first successful woman minister in British history. Crossman replaced Stewart, coordinating the social services. Marsh went to Transport and was succeeded at Power by Ray Gunther who had criticised the unions when he was Minister of Labour. In June he resigned.

(*h*) October 1969. The DEA and Power were abolished. The latter and the Board of Trade were swallowed up by the Technology Ministry under Benn. Marsh was dropped. Local Government and Regional Planning was formed under Crosland and Public Buildings and Works abolished. Further reforms were planned and put into force by Heath.

C2. Party Matters

While Heath's Tory party was seeking to expunge its aristocratic and public school past, many in the Labour party wanted to break with the 1918 constitution, last revised in 1937. Led by Crosland and Jenkins, they were increasingly European minded and saw workers there with higher living standards and welfare services, less taxation and weaker trade unions. Wilson, who had been a Bevanite, seemed to accept the revisionist pattern in the 1966 manifesto and to be more concerned with office than socialism. This was not entirely true, since the government nationalised steel (1967), turned the Post Office into a public corporation, controlled North Sea Gas and set up the Shipping Industry Board. However, Wilson's acceptance under bankers' pressure of cuts and an incomes policy had echoes of 1931, while in foreign affairs a range of issues roused left-wing anger, including limited support for America in Vietnam, failure to use force in Rhodesia and support for Nigeria instead of Biafra. The Tribune Group in the House doubled in numbers to about 60 and caused the government much trouble, while in the constituencies a trend towards ousting Social Democrat or moderate men set in to culminate in the departure from the party of Marsh, Taverne and Prentice. In September 1973 the proscribed list of 1949 was lifted and links with Communists abroad and at home were fostered. Even in the cabinet itself Benn and Foot pressed the left-wing line.

Since the electorate was hostile even to Wilson's pragmatic socialism, had the policies of the Tribune Group been tested at the polls, disaster would have followed. It was therefore with elastic consciences that they opposed but did not overthrow their master. In March 1967 Wilson hit back, warning MPs 'every dog is allowed one bite' and that they might not be readopted, but attempts to curb the rebels failed. Shinwell resigned as party chairman because he thought Crossman too indulgent, and when the Chief Whip, Silkin, tried to discipline persistent rebels, he was dropped in

1969 and replaced by Mellish, who immediately gave way. Peace was preserved at a price while in the country Labour remained unpopular in the extreme. The Tory lead reached 25 per cent and critics of Heath were silent as Labour lost all but two of the 12 major cities (1967) and all but five of the London boroughs (1968) in local government elections. In by-elections the government lost all 16 contests. Welsh (1966) and Scottish (1968) Nationalist MPs reflected growing disenchantment with Whitehall government and there were frequent press scares about Wilson's fall.

C3. Four Years' Hard Slog

For a time Wilson continued as before the election, restricting demand less severely than Tories would have liked, while relying on investment and incomes policies to put things right eventually. The budget of 1966, strongly influenced by Kaldor, introduced SET instead of the expected increases. The tax was levied on employers for each employee at 25s a week (12s 6d for women) and collected through raising National Insurance contributions. It was to be refunded to manufacturers with a bonus and to nationalised industries and agriculture without it, thus hopefully accelerating the policy in the Redundancy Act of shifting labour into export industries. The government scrapped refunds except to development areas (November 1967) and increased rates by 50 per cent in March 1969.

(a) *Dock Strike and July measures*. On 16 May 1966 a 47-day dock strike began due to the harsh conditions of work in the docks. A meeting at Downing Street failed and on 23 May a state of emergency was proclaimed. The dockers rejected the limited Pearson Report and Wilson agreed to a wide-ranging enquiry. On 20 June he attacked 'the tightly knit group of politically motivated men' involved in the strike and named eight of them saying 'no strike occurs anywhere in this country' without Communist influence. The strike affected exports and sterling slumped, forcing the government to the July measures. The regulator raised indirect taxes by 10 per cent and there was a 10 per cent surcharge on surtax. A £50 travel allowance was started which lasted until January 1970. There were cuts in public spending, overseas aid, defence, local authority cash and nationalised industries. The bank rate soared to 7 per cent. There was to be a six-month stand-still on wages and then six months of severe restraint and a 12-month freeze on prices and dividends. As a result, foreign bankers lent $1,000m and the position of sterling was saved.

(b) *Incomes policy*. In early 1966 Wilson said, 'I do not think you can ever legislate for wage increases', but after voluntary restraint failed, he had little alternative. The Prices and Incomes Act (1966) said it was voluntary but there were penal clauses. The TUC accepted a voluntary policy. The Act for 1967 gave the government power to hold increases for 12 months. Wage claims were not to exceed $3\frac{1}{2}$ per cent and compulsory powers were used. The policy just passed the TUC. The 1968 Act renewed the measure, in spite of promises to the contrary, until December 1969 and the TUC came out in opposition.

These policies ushered in a period of deflation which lasted until 1971, and unemployment in July 1967 was the highest figure for that month since 1939. The government was soon under pressure to reflate. The bank rate fell to 6 per cent by March and a series of optimistic statements were made by Callaghan, saying 'the measures are doing what the government expected of them', and the balance of payments was 'in a position of basic balance and growing strength'. A standstill budget was accompanied by

£600m of new spending by government. But by the summer it was clear things were not going well. The reserves fell by £36m and a trade gap of £39m appeared. After a denial of devaluation, Wilson took command of the economy and was faced with a deficit of £162m for October, brought about by a Middle East War and another dock strike. De Gaulle vetoed Common Market entry and the Kennedy Round of GATT tariff reductions damaged Britain.

(c) *Devaluation and the Letter of Intent.* Since further deflation was ruled out by opposition within the party, devaluation seemed the only possibility. It occurred on 18 November and involved a cut from $2.80 to $2.40 to the pound. The bank rate was raised to 8 per cent. Callaghan resigned, but Jenkins published his Letter of Intent to the bankers so that all could see the constraints. There were two packages of measures, the immediate ones including restoring hire purchase restrictions, raising corporation tax, abolishing SET refunds and restricting bank lending. Heath said the government had 'reduced Britain from a prosperous nation to an international pauper', but Wilson sought to present devaluation as a challenge 'to break out from the straightjacket of these past years'). He even said 'this does not mean that the pound here in Britain in your pocket or purse or in your bank has been devalued', when Callaghan had previously said devaluation was an attack on the living standard of every working man.

(d) *Jenkins' régime.* Early in 1968 cuts totalling £750m were introduced. Defence, the school leaving age, the housing programme, free school milk, prescription and dental charges were among these, contradicting claims for social growth. Such cuts were long term in effect and public spending would still be higher in real terms during 1968, so further measures were needed. Incomes policy was toughened and to avoid a spending spree, the budget was advanced to March. According to Wilson this was 'the most punishing budget in Britain's peacetime history', taking £923m in taxes by raising petrol, vehicle, wines, spirits, beer and cigarette taxes, reducing tax allowances, raising SET and corporation tax and imposing a once for all levy on incomes over £3,000 a year. The aim was to produce a surplus of £500m before starting on growth again, thus eliminating 'stop-go'.

Unhappily, severe though the measures were, they did not seem to work. Further borrowings were needed in June and September and there were flurries of crisis in the City in May and December. The latter was the more serious when the reserves fell by £82m in a month and rumours of a government collapse followed doing further damage. In fact this was caused by foreign currency fluctuations as much as anything. Wage drift meant consumer spending did not fall as anticipated and imports remained high. Jenkins began the procedure of introducing supplementary budgets when in November taxes were raised by a further £250m.

Jenkins bravely persisted in the policy, although it may have cost him any hopes of a future in the party. The combined effects of world recovery, devaluation and the cuts would work through in 1969 and all he had to do was hang on. Thus, the April 1969 budget was the third harshest since the war, raising purchase tax, SET and corporation tax yet again. But this time there were a few concessions, including higher pensions, raising of the tax threshold to benefit a million and limited spending programmes including £105m for education. Jenkins firmly backed incomes policy and announced impending trade union reform. Although its majority fell to 28, the government battled on and began to hint at better things to come, including an earnings-related pension scheme on which Crossman was working and equal pay for women.

(*e*) *Favourable balance of payments.* In September 1969 a favourable balance was announced for which the government deserved great credit, since it lasted until 1972. As the wages policy ended, a Commission for Industry and Manpower was to take over with emphasis on rationalisation. A further Industrial Relations Bill acceptable to the TUC was in the pipeline. The bank rate fell to 7 per cent and the March 1970 budget was able to inject £220m of tax relief and take a further 2 million people off tax. However, wages started to spiral and so did public spending as the election approached. There was a deficit of £31m for July. But the overall picture was a good one with the reserves at £1,130m and a surplus of £460m for the year. A start was made on repaying the £1,650m of debts.

Although Labour got the payments situation right in 1966 and after 1969, this was achieved at considerable cost in terms of devaluation and debts. They had tried to stimulate manufacturing industry, but planning, grants and advice had not done the trick. Productivity remained low and costs high because, in spite of four years of incomes policy, trade union power remained uncurbed and each period of restraint was followed by a catching-up process. Frequent changes in government policy reduced confidence abroad and brought about an investment freeze at home. Although attempts were made to curb spending, the government slit its own throat by lavish policies which demanded high tax. In turn, this stimulated further wage demands. As Proudfoot said: 'some things looked good, but the continual and unchecked increases in wages and prices led many to dark foreboding'.

C4. Legislation and Reforms

The government had a respectable record of law making including, for example, the Divorce Reform and Children and Young Persons Acts, the Transport Act that started the breathalyser and the Decimal Coinage Act (1969) which came into force under Heath. The main preoccupation was with institutional reform and with forming new government bodies. The Civil Service grew by 80,000 and among new bodies were the Shipping Industry Board, the Countryside Commission and the Open University (1969). Disillusion with institutions is common to declining powers when discontent with events or failures by politicians can be blamed on organisations. To some extent the Wilson government, by increasing legislative pressure on Parliament and multiplying government bodies, added to the growing criticism of institutions while at the same time trying to reform them. Apart from the modernisation aspect, there was growing concern about apathy to the democratic process and some of the new ideas such as worker participation or local government reforms were designed to check this. The Liberals pressed for devolution for the regions, proportional representation and regional government and their ideas were taken up by non-political bodies and achieved widespread popularity. Both Wilson and Heath were concerned in the process of constitutional change which reached its peak with the Kilbrandon Commission on the Constitution in February 1969. The main reforms were:

(*a*) *Administrative law.* Disquiet continued about the power of the executive to control individuals through delegated laws and tribunals. The left attacked secrecy and the right concentrated on faceless bureaucracy. After the Franks Report an Act (1958) tried to reform procedures at tribunals and provide for appeals in certain cases. After the Chalk Pit Case a new set of rules was implemented between 1962 and 1965 and the Tribunals and Enquiries Act (1971) consolidated the law. In 1967 the Ombudsman was created by the Parliamentary Commissioner Act.

(*b*) *The Lords.* In June 1968 the Lords rejected by 193–184 a statutory instrument imposing a trade ban on Rhodesia, and Wilson promised reform of the House. In fact, the proposals were inter-party. The aim was to abolish the rights of hereditary peers and the veto and replace the Lords with a nominated chamber with a delaying power of six months. The Lords accepted this by 251–56, but in the Commons Foot and Powell led opposition and the measure was dropped in April 1969.

(*c*) *Local government.* In 1965 the 1963 act setting up the GLC instead of the LCC came into force. It abolished the county of Middlesex and extended London's boundaries. It cut the number of authorities in this area from 95 to 32— 12 inner and 20 outer London councils. ILEA ran education only in the inner group, but otherwise services were common to all authorities. In 1966 the Local Government and Rating Acts established rate support grants and rate rebates. In 1969 the Redcliffe Maud Report on Local Government was published proposing sweeping changes.

(*d*) *Law reform.* The Law Commission Act (1965) set up a body to weed out obsolete laws and streamline modern ones. The Administration of Justice Act (1970) reformed the 1873 Act by moving Admiralty to the QBD and creating from Probate and Divorce the new Family Division.

(*e*) *Age of majority.* The Representation of the People Act (1969) lowered the voting age to 18 as well as increasing permissible expenses for candidates and allowing political parties to be named on ballot papers. The same year the Family Law Reform Act made 18 the age of majority for marrying and making contracts.

(*f*) *The Fulton Committee.* This report in 1968 on the Civil Service was the first since 1854. It proposed, and the government accepted, a Civil Service Department for recruiting, training and career structure separate from the Treasury, the amalgamation of the administrative, executive and clerical grades, the creation of a Civil Service College to train in management techniques, secondment to industry, interchange within departments, more specialists and specialist entrance examinations. The aim was to end the cult of the gifted amateur and move to modern specialisation.

Because of the economic situation these changes were often overlooked. But in one area violent controversy was aroused and this was on racial matters. Although numbers of immigrants entering under the 1962 voucher system had fallen from 30,000 to 4,000 a year, the number of dependents rose from 24,000 to 50,000, meaning there was no effective drop in numbers entering. Since they went to ghetto areas where the social services had massive problems and since total numbers and projected numbers were a matter of dispute, racial fears developed which both political parties tried to push under the carpet. In April 1968 Powell, the Tory defence spokesman, made a speech at Birmingham, followed by others at Walsall and Eastbourne in which he brought the issue into the open. Heath dismissed him from the shadow cabinet with unfortunate consequences for the Tories, since Powell advised people to vote against Heath in 1974 and then led the

Ulster Unionists in opposing the Tories in the minority situation that followed the electoral débacle that year. Labour had accepted the Mountbatten Report (1965) advocating continued restrictions and had no intention of repealing the 1962 Act, as they said they would prior to 1964. Their two main measures were:

(a) *Commonwealth Immigrants Act* (1968). Fears that Kenyatta's racial policies would lead to a flood of 120,000 Asian immigrants led Callaghan to pass a bill in one week imposing severe controls at the rate of 1,500 extra vouchers a week. Macleod and 14 Tories voted against the bill and so did 35 Labour MPs.

(b) *Race Relations Act* (1968). This strengthened the 1965 Act by banning discrimination in housing, employment and other services. The RRB was to conciliate first and then seek legal redress while a new Community Relations Commission was set up. The Tories were divided with Boyle and 24 abstaining and Berkeley leaving the party.

C5. 'In Place of Strife' and the Election of June 1970

As early as September 1966 Wilson said 'the restrictive practices that are still too prevalent today amount simply to a means of laying claim to a full day's pay for less than a full day's work', and Gunther, the Minister of Labour, had been equally forceful. The number of days lost through strikes rose towards the 1957 record figure by 1969 and the seamen's strikes particularly damaged the economy. When the Donovan Commission reported in 1968, Wilson decided to reform the unions as he had other institutions, particularly since Heath's *Fair Deal at Work* made much of reforms.

(a) *The Donovan Commission.* The main proposals were localised agreements which were to be registered, civil action against unoffical strikers who broke agreements, an industrial relations commission, union internal reforms and protection against unfair dismissal. In January 1969 Wilson and Castle published *In Place of Strife*, proposing a conciliation pause of 28 days for unofficial strikes, a ballot for official ones and penalties for those breaking collective agreements as well as accepting moves for strengthening workers' rights.

(b) *Attack on 'In Place of Strife'.* Feather, the TUC President, was not a very forceful leader, but Jones of the Transport Workers and Scanlon of the Engineers were, and were determined to oppose the policy. The Labour Party rejected it in March, and the TUC in May. Callaghan voted against in the NEC and was removed from the inner cabinet until October. Wilson said, 'I have to tell you the passage of this bill is essential to the government's continuance in office'. But Labour MPs would not back the policy while ministers, including Short, Owen, Shore and Mason, changed sides. On 19 June the bill was dropped. It was replaced by an undertaking of the TUC to vet disputes, but as Wilson said, 'strikes did not diminish in number, scale or duration'.

This was a bitter blow, playing into Heath's hands and revealing the growing rift in the Labour party between moderate reformers and hardline left-wingers. It marked the decline of Jenkins' influence and the rise of Callaghan's. Then in the Autumn the government suffered another defeat and this time Callaghan was to blame. In April 1969 the Boundary Commission published its report on the size of parliamentary constituencies, scrapping some seats and dividing large inner city constituencies, raising the number of MPs to 635. In June Callaghan announced the number would be cut to 626 and no decision taken until after the Redcliffe Maud

Report (or until after the election, according to one's point of view). The Lords amended the Redistribution of Seats Bill to require him to lay orders before the Commons by March 1970. The government rejected this amendment and the bill was defeated in the Lords by 270–96. Since Callaghan had to place orders before the House in the original version, he got members to vote them down so the changes were not implemented until after the election, when the number of MPs rose to 635.

The government's position early in 1970 was therefore precarious. Lords reform, trade union reform and local government changes had been defeated and, although the balance of payments was good, inflation was rising. Relations within the party and with the unions had been soured and controversy over the publication of the costs of entering the Common Market had stirred fresh hostility from the Left. Jenkins' budget was his most favourable so far, and an upswing in the local elections finally decided Wilson to go for a June election, opposed though this was at the time by Transport House. Throughout the campaign the polls seemed to vindicate Wilson's choice. By the time a mood of disillusion had gripped many people. Student demonstrations, civil war in Northern Ireland and an unpleasant campaign to stop this South African cricket tour added fuel to public disquiet. Meeting at Selsdon Park, the Tories seemed to propose a significant change in society which would involve dealing with the law and order issue, restoring Britain's prestige abroad and cutting down government intervention. This had immediate appeal.

Heath's campaign was based on the need for 'a vigorous competitive policy' and 'a new style of government'. It was stressed there would be an end to incomes policies. Common Market entry would be sought and trade union reform carried. But in the main it was a vote against the previous four years rather than for anything. The government had produced £750 of debt for every person in the country, a worsening strike record and £3,000m extra taxation. There were few who had not suffered and since the Liberals under Thorpe made little impact, Heath was the alternative. During the campaign there were signs that all was not well. Lord Shawcross, an ex-Labour minister, said there might be another devaluation. Crossman, resisting a doctors' pay claim, said they faced 'extreme economic peril' from inflation. The doctors then got 30 per cent. There was a national press strike which, did not help Labour and on 15 June came a trade gap of £31m. For once Heath did well in the final television broadcast and a few polls detected a last-minute swing. The results were Conservatives 330, Labour 287 and Liberals only 6. The other parties returned six including the Rev. Ian Paisley. On a low poll of 72 per cent there was a uniform swing of 4.5 per cent and Labour lost through abstentions and holidays.

D. The Ministry of Edward Heath

D1. Heath and the Heathmen

(a) *Career and character.* Heath was born at Broadstairs in 1916 and went to Chatham House School and Balliol College, Oxford. He served in the Royal Artillery and then worked for the *Church Times* and as a trainee banker before becoming MP for Bexley in 1950. He was a supporter of the One Nation Group and in 1955 became Chief Whip. After a stint as Minister of Labour, he achieved prominence as Lord Privy Seal when he was negotiating entry into the Common Market in 1962. He was Secretary for Industry and Regional Development and carried the bill to repeal RPM. He led the attack on the budget of 1965 and in the first election of a Tory leader beat Maudling. As Opposition Leader he was poor and seemed more concerned with behind the scenes policy making. The shadow cabinet often abstained on votes and the party divided over Rhodesia and immigration. Aided by Boyle and Walker, Heath was determined to end the Macmillan era. Sandys, Amery, Thorneycroft, Lloyd and Powell left and by 1970 there were few old faces. After Barber took control of the party machine in September 1967 local candidates' lists were purged. However, by 1970 Heath had asserted full control over the party and was regarded as 'the toughest operator since Neville Chamberlain'. Heath had little personal following. His interests—music and yachting—contrasted with the machine politicians, Wilson and Callaghan. His manner was unfortunate on television, where his performances were likened to those of a 'glove puppet'. As a politician, he was outclassed by Wilson.

(*b*) *Policies.* As a statesman he had greater depth. He was concerned to produce an updated Conservatism. This was to be based on competitive free enterprise and management techniques applied to a streamlined and reformed government machine. Controls were to go and as Britain entered the Common Market, the keen wind of competition would set things going. 'There has been too much government; there will be less', he said in 1970, and cut the number of ministers from 111 to 84. Major reforms were to be carried through in central and local government. Above all, in economic policy, 'we utterly reject the philosophy of compulsory wage control'.

The new departure was made with a relatively new team, apart from Home (Foreign Secretary), Hailsham (Lord Chancellor) and Maudling (Home Secretary). Tragically, Macleod, who was made Chancellor, died soon afterwards and was replaced by Barber. Later Maudling chose to resign while the police were investigating the Poulson Scandal and was replaced by Robert Carr. Previously he had been Secretary for Employment and was succeeded in that post (1972) by Maurice Macmillan. William Whitelaw led the Commons and then transferred to Northern Ireland, where he (1972–73) and Francis Pym (1973–74) handled direct rule. Whitelaw became Employment Secretary. James Prior was leader in the Commons (1972) after a period as Agriculture Minister. John Davies was Secretary for Industry, but after the policy shift of 1972 was succeeded by Sir Geoffrey Howe. In the social service ministries the chief names were Margaret Thatcher at Education, Peter Walker at Environment and Sir Keith Joseph at Social Services. It was a competent and somewhat inexperienced team, but at least the country was spared the rancour of the previous ministry.

D2. The Northern Ireland Question

Ever since 1921 Northern Ireland had been ruled by the Ulster Unionist party which had strong ties with the Tories. Although immensely loyal to the Crown as their voluntary effort during the war showed, the Unionists were out of date and the province faced a number of difficulties. It was economically backward with 6.1 per cent out of work in 1965. There were sectarian differences between Protestants and Catholics and these spread into social policy where there was discrimination in housing and employment. The Ulster government feared the Republic, which stood for a united Ireland and gave shelter to the IRA.

(*a*) *The O'Neill reforms.* With strong support from Wilson, O'Neill had embarked on reform, but it led to the formation of a Civil Rights Movement, a revival of the IRA in Ulster and the growth of left-wing opposition led by people like Miss Devlin and Mr Fitt. Disturbances developed into riots in August 1969 and in return for a Downing Street Declaration that reforms would go on and the B Specials go, Wilson sent in troops.

(*b*) *Civil war.* Between 1969 and 1977, 1,600 were killed and 20,000 wounded in the worst Irish troubles since the 1920s. The Protestants, feeling isolated after the B Specials and the Special Powers Act had gone, formed the Ulster Defence Volunteers. Meanwhile, 16,000 troops and the Ulster Defence Regiment seemed unable to curb the war.

(*c*) *Direct rule.* Heath had said there would be no change in Ulster without a vote of the Stormont Parliament, but inept handling of the situation led him to a different course. At first, internment and the clearing of 'no-go' areas suggested a firm policy, but during 1971 when Faulkner replaced Chichester Clark, tripartite meetings with the Irish Prime Minister began which infuriated the Protestants. In March 1972 direct rule was imposed at the moment devolution was being considered elsewhere in the Kingdom. The Ulster Unionists severed their connection with the Tories.

(*d*) *General strike.* Whitelaw's policies, including abolishing the death penalty and meeting the IRA, roused a backlash and in 1973 a general strike paralysed the province as James Craig and Ian Paisley took the lead among Unionists. A referendum showed 591,820 for union with Britain and 6,463 for a united Ireland.

Heath was unable to deal with Northern Ireland. He set up a new assembly in June 1973 elected by proportional representation. It was to have a mixed Executive which came into being in January 1974, but this collapsed in May and direct rule was resumed.

D3. Entering the Common Market

Negotiations started immediately, led by Geoffrey Rippon, and in January 1972 the Treaty of Brussels was signed. Eire and Denmark also joined, thus breaking up EFTA, and the treaty came into force a year later. The go-ahead for a Channel Tunnel was given. Entry was fiercely fought in the House and there were a 100 divisions on the ratification. It passed by 365–244 with 89 Labour and 31 Tories against and with Labour committed to renegotiate. The terms obtained were essentially those in the brief prepared for Labour prior to the election and were:

(*a*) Britain entered the market with the same representation as France, West Germany and Italy, i.e. two Commissioners and 36 seats in the European Parliament.

(*b*) Over $4\frac{1}{2}$ years Britain was to accept the common tariff.

(*c*) Britain accepted the CAP for farming over a period of years with special provision for New Zealand dairy produce and West Indian sugar.

(*d*) Britain was to retain her 12-mile fishing limits pending agreement.

(*e*) Britain was to pay 20 per cent of the budget, but her full contribution was only to be reached in 1978.

(*f*) Britain was to participate fully in ECSC, Euratom and the Investment Bank.

These were favourable terms, considering the state of the British economy, and the surprising feature of the period is the reversal by Labour in October 1971, when they came out against the market, led by Jay, Benn,

Foot and Shore. Wilson, who had previously said he was opposed to a referendum—'I shall not change my attitude on that'—now came out for it. When Labour returned to office, Callaghan was in charge and renegotiated terms were passed by 396–170 with 144 Labour MPs opposed. This suggested that Wilson's ploys of renegotiation and a referendum were designed to keep Labour dissidents in line rather than achieve any clear advantage. The cabinet was allowed to differ as they had not done since the tariff dispute of 1931–32, since seven ministers opposed him. In June 1975 a referendum on a 64 per cent turnout gave 67.2 per cent for and 32.8 per cent against. But it was Heath not Wilson who had the imagination and ability to take Britain into Europe; it was his greatest achievement.

D4. Radical Toryism and the Barber Boom

Heath set out to carry forward the radical changes in British institutions which Wilson had started. The main changes were:

(a) *Central Government.* The reorganisation of government departments was completed with the setting up of Environment and Trade and Industry. The Central Policy Review Staff was set up.

(b) *Devolution.* The Kilbrandon Report in 1973 was followed by Heath's Perth speech accepting devolution. This trend towards accepting nationalism at the same time as reaching out to the larger unit of the Common Market seemed inconsistent.

(c) *Local government.* The Act of 1972 was the first important measure since 1899. It scrapped aldermen and all councils were to consist of salaried councillors, elected on a four-term basis at staggered annual periods. The 1,400 local authorities were cut to 400 outside Greater London. There were to be six metropolitan areas with 36 municipal districts and 333 county districts. The number of counties was cut from 58 to 52, with eight new ones for Wales and six in England, combined with boundary changes. The Act created expensive and impersonal authorities, damaged civic pride and interfered with historic counties. There was no evidence that it increased democratic interest in local affairs.

(d) *The Courts Act* (1971) abolished assize courts and quarter sessions and replaced them with crown courts. It was difficult to reconcile the abolition of ancient ceremonies of assize and borough with Tory respect for tradition.

(e) In 1973 the National Health Act altered the structure of the 1948 Act by creating 14 Regional Health Authorities and 90 Area Health Authorities. There was again an increase in bureaucracy which contradicted the Heath line that he was cutting government size. In 1974 an Act created Regional Water Authorities controlling sewage, water supply and rivers, and water rates rose sharply.

These measures show the Heath government was radical in outlook, but the area where people most expected change was in the economic sphere. At first they were not disappointed. The Land Commission, the Consumer's Council and the Industrial Reorganisation Corporation were scrapped. British Transport Hotels and Cooks were to be sold off and the nationalised breweries denationalised. Social benefits were to be selective and charges for prescriptions were increased, while charges for museums and art galleries were introduced. The move to comprehensive schools was slowed down and free school milk curbed. Davies spoke of 'lame ducks' in industry which would not be supported. Then in 1972 the government reversed engines as the Barber Boom got out of control. Faced with sit-ins and the impending collapse of Rolls Royce, which supplied 81 airforces, Heath restored investment grants to depressed regions and by an Industry Act provided £650m, or four times the amount spent by the defunct IRC. A Director of Fair Trading performed the function of the aborted Consumer's Council. An incomes policy was introduced in clear defiance of the manifesto with a Pay Board and a Price Commission. Following the Poulson and Lonhro Affairs Heath attacked the 'unacceptable face of capitalism' which his previous policy of competitive free enterprise had helped to stimulate.

(a) *The Barber boom.* Throughout 1970–72 the favourable balance of payments achieved by Labour was maintained and the problem was to stimulate the economy. A budget in October 1970 began tax cutting. That of April 1971 cut more taxes and injected £550m. Restrictions on hire purchase and credit were removed. The Bank of England repaid its special deposits and abolished the lending ceiling. In March 1972 the budget injected £1,900m—the largest ever Keynesian handout, together with further tax cuts of £960m. Free depreciation on investment was allowed and the money supply increased. At the same time Barber carried through several important changes. SET was scrapped and replaced by VAT, the bank rate was replaced by the minimum lending rate and a floating pound was introduced. Thus, after delaying reflation, the government expanded too rapidly and by mid-1972 were in trouble.

(b) *Economy off course again.* In spite of the government's measures investment rose little while inflation was generated. After talks on voluntary restraint failed in November 1972, Heath introduced a 90-day standstill which lasted until April 1973 and was replaced by Stage 2. This controlled pay increases to £1 a week plus 4 per cent with an overall maximum of £250 a year. This was followed in November by Stage 3, which was either a 7 per cent increase with a maximum of £350 a year or £2.25 a week, together with concessions for anomalies and unsocial hours and a new bank holiday on New Year's Day. But unemployment continued to rise to 700,000, indicating undercapacity, while inflation suggested overheating. This produced a standstill budget in March 1973 and a further budget in December, reducing public spending and reintroducing credit controls. The balance of payments was £922m in the red for 1973 and by the end of the year the government was failing in all four main economic aims: controlling inflation, preserving the balance of payments, increasing production and reducing unemployment.

D5. The Union Question and the Miners' Election, February 1974

Heath was determined to secure trade union reform, which both parties had agreed in 1969 was essential, but with the swing to the left in the Labour party reflected in opposition to the Common Market and the failure of *In Place of Strife*, Wilson opposed Heath's attempts to carry out reremarkably similar proposals.

In 1971 the Industrial Relations Act was passed. A National Industrial Relations Court was set up. Provision was made for a cooling-off period and ballots for strikes. Fines were to be imposed for breach of collective agreements and unfair industrial practices like 'blacking'. Pre-entry closed shops were declared illegal and post-entry ones were to be adopted by ballot. The right to belong to a union was guaranteed and compensation for unfair dismissal introduced. Union rule books were to be submitted to the Ministry when they registered, as all were required to do. Since most of the provisions were already in force in Britain's competitors and the unions constantly harped on their legal rights and rule books, there seemed no reason why they should not accept the measure.

But within a few months violent opposition to the measure developed and the left became more influential in politics than they had been since the late 1930s. Consensus was broken since Wilson chose to ride the union tiger for political advantage. The opposition was led by Jack Jones and Hugh Scanlon and backed at local level by Communists like James Reid of Upper Clyde Shipbuilders and Arthur Scargill of the Yorkshire Miners. The year 1972 proved the worst for strikes since 1957 and, during the miners' strike, 'flying pickets' were responsible for violence at places like Saltley. For its part the government reacted by using the 1875 conspiracy law to jail Shrewsbury building workers guilty of intimidation. A series of disputes occurred including the miners, engineers and transport workers.

Then came war in the Middle East in 1973 which cut oil supplies by 15 per cent. The Arabs decided to raise the price of oil by 70 per cent and this imposed severe strains on the balance of payments and fuelled inflation. Coal suddenly became more attractive as a fuel and the miners, led by Mr Gormley put in another claim. In fact, 12 million workers settled under Stage 3 and the real confrontation in 1973 was the miners against government policy as it had been in 1926. But this time the government's economic policies and the struggle over the Act confused matters.

(a) *The miners' strike.* Gormley later maintained that during September compromise would have been possible by using the unsocial hours aspect of Stage 3 and that a meeting took place in secret with Heath. However, it failed and on 12 November an overtime ban started. In January a strike ballot was held (188,000 for, 44,000 against) and the strike began on 9 February, this time with no flying pickets. They were unnecessary as coal stocks at power stations were low and ASLEF refused to deliver any more. On 9 and 21 January Mr Murray for the TUC offered to hold off other claims if the miners' was met, but Heath argued the miners' claim was bound up with comparability and other claims would inevitably follow.

(b) *The Black Winter.* The government set up a National Security Committee and declared a state of emergency, but it was ill prepared compared with 1926. Fuel economies were introduced, including a 50 mph speed limit, prohibiting of lighting for display purposes and the closing of television at 10.30 pm, but over Christmas this only annoyed people. Then on 31 December a three-day week was started to curb fuel supplies and massive short-time working began.

On 7 February Heath announced an election on this specific issue for 28 February, which was a grave tactical error. Like Balfour in 1906, he threw away his majority. To hold a winter election after months of deprivation and to expect people to grasp the issue in three weeks was naïve. Moreover, Wilson emphasised other aspects of government policy including poor labour relations and the grim economic situation. His slogan was 'Back to Work with Labour'. Since January 1972 he had worked out a Social Contract with the TUC, promising them repeal of the Act, an end to wages policies, stricter control of prices and rents, increases in benefits and tax concessions to the lower paid. Although 78 per cent voted, more than 38 per cent showed indecision by not supporting the major parties. The result was Conservative 296, Labour 301, Liberal 14 and Nationalists (Welsh, Scottish and Ulster) 24. This produced a minority situation but after four days Heath failed to persuade Thorpe to support him and Wilson took office with the first minority government since 1929 at a time of grave division and economic peril. A further election in October yielded Labour a majority of three (Labour 319, Conservative 276, Liberal 13, others 27) and clearly confirmed the end of two-party politics and consensus prevalent since 1945. The new government, with Foot at Employment and Callaghan at the Foreign Office, was further to the left than in 1966.

The three-day week ended and the miners' claim was conceded in full. Stage 3 and the Pay Board were scrapped in July and massive wage increases followed. Three budgets in March, July and November by Healey, the new Chancellor, imposed massive tax increases, but also large-scale social expenditure to meet the Social Contract. The public sector deficit rose to £5.5m. A grave economic situation (stagflation) developed with payments £3,565m in the red by the end of 1974, inflation at 4 per cent by early 1975 and unemployment at 1.3 million by early 1976. Less was produced than during the three-day week and production fell by 5 per cent. The problems posed since 1964 seemed no nearer a solution.

Further Reading

Beckerman,W., (ed.), *The Labour Government's Economic Record 1964–1970*, Duckworth, London, 1972.

Brittan, S., *Capitalism and the Permissive Society*, Macmillan, London, 1973.

Calvocoressi, P., *The British Experience 1945–1975*, Bodley Head, London, 1978.

James, R. R., *Ambitions and Realities; British Politics 1964–1970*, Weidenfeld and Nicolson, London, 1972.

Jenkins, P., *The Battle of Downing Street*, Knight, London, 1978.

Lapping, B., *The Labour Government*, Penguin, Harmondsworth, 1970.

Lloyd, T. O., *Empire to Welfare State 1906–1967*, Oxford UP, London, 1967.

Pelling, H., *A History of British Trade Unionism*, Macmillan, London, 1977.

Proudfoot, M., *British Politics and Government 1951–1970*, Faber and Faber, London, 1974.

Winkler, H. R. (ed.), *Twentieth-Century Britain*, Franklin Watts, New York, 1976.

Questions

1. Why was the 'condition of England' question revived in the sixties? Were many new or valid solutions offered to the long-term problems being discussed?
2. What were the arguments for and against joining the Common Market by 1970?
3. Why was Harold Wilson so successful a politician?
4. 'Government by gimmick.' How far is a comparison between the style and methods of Lloyd George and Wilson tenable?
5. Why did Britain enter a period of sustained economic crisis in 1966, and remain there until early 1970?
6. What issues were involved in the outbreak and continuation of civil war in Northern Ireland after 1969?
7. Why did two-party politics become increasingly unattractive to the electors in the period 1964–1974?
8. What were the chief factors involved in the trade union problem by the early 1970s?
9. How effective were either Harold Wilson *or* Edward Heath in fundamentally reforming British institutions?
10. What was at stake in the Miners' election of February 1974?

Index